A DICTIONARY OF
OPERA
and
SONG THEMES

A DICTIONARY OF
OPERA
and
SONG THEMES

Revised Edition

INCLUDING CANTATAS, ORATORIOS
LIEDER, AND ART SONGS

Originally Published as
A Dictionary of Vocal Themes

Compiled by

HAROLD BARLOW
and
SAM MORGENSTERN

Crown Publishers, Inc.

NEW YORK

Library of Congress Cataloging in Publication Data

Barlow, Harold.
    A dictionary of opera and song themes.

    In the 1950 ed. Barlow's name appeared first
on t. p.
    1. Vocal music—Thematic catalogs. I. Morgen-
stern, Sam, joint author. II. Title.
ML128.V7M793 1975   016.784   75-30751
ISBN 0-517-525038

Second Printing of Revised Edition in February 1978.

Introduction

WITH THE completion of our *Dictionary of Musical Themes*, we started on a book which would do for vocal music what *Musical Themes* did for instrumental works. It took several years of research to compile this *Dictionary of Vocal Themes*, which includes the salient and rememberable themes from operas, cantatas, oratorios, *Lieder* and art songs, as well as many miscellaneous vocal pieces not belonging to any of the above categories.

Since, in addition to the notation of the themes, this book contains the words of the music quoted, we have indexed first lines as well as titles. The reader can thereby identify a piece through its composer, title, or first line, as well as its notation.

Man has sung from the beginning of his existence, and one lifetime would not suffice to extract the themes from only those melodies which he has noted down. We were, consequently, forced to limit ourselves in some fashion or other, and decided to confine the contents of this book for the most part to those works which have been recorded here and in Europe.

The problems confronting the compiler of such a volume as this are legion. Should he include folk music? To what degree should he include popular songs? What about those works, ultra-modern ones in particular, in which a clearly defined theme is hardly discernible? Should he use original or English translations?

Having no precedent, we tried to solve these questions in what seemed to us the most practical and satisfactory manner. Folk themes and their endless variants could easily fill a book the size of this one. We therefore chose those which have been edited and arranged by composers steeped in their own national folk idiom—Bartók, Kodaly, Vaughan Williams, Warlock, Weckerlin, to name a handful—and which through recordings have become an international heritage. If a popular tune has been recorded several times by concert artists of repute, achieving thereby a kind of classical status, we have tried to include it in our book.

Operas such as *Pélleas and Mélisande, Electra* and *Salome* we omitted. Here, every vocal line is thematic or not, as you choose, and quoting them would have meant literally copying the whole score. What the general reader might remember from *Salome*—the themes from the "Dance of the Seven Veils"—is included in our first book. Most of the leitmotifs in the later Wagnerian operas appear in the orchestra rather than in the vocal line. Since these are plentifully quoted in our *Dictionary of Musical Themes*, we have used opening phrases from scenes as they are recorded. Otherwise, we would have been obliged again to quote line for line.

In such early church works as, for instance, Palestrina's *Missa Brevis* and the *Marcellus Mass* there is a constant melodic flow, any part of which could be thematic. We have quoted the opening phrases from the various sections of these Masses and the ecclesiastical motives which form their bases.

Wherever possible, we have gone to original sources for our material. All the Bach and Handel quotations were culled from the *Gesellschaft* editions. To have quoted the entire vocal output of Bach and Handel we would have had to compile two separate volumes. Here, too, our yardstick was the recorded works plus whatever we felt might be of use to the amateur, layman and professional musician. If there are any gross omissions we hope our readers will call them to our attention so that they may be included in subsequent editions.

An examination of scores of recital programs as well as record catalogues governed our choice of the songs of Schubert, who wrote close to six hundred *Lieder*. We handled Brahms, Wolf, Strauss and other great *Lieder* composers in the same manner.

Though we chose the arias and concerted numbers from operas, we did include a certain number of recitatives which are as well known as the arias which follow them.

In a limited number of songs where we felt the accompaniment theme was as important as the vocal line, if not more so, we quoted both. Thus, the eighty repetitions of the same note in the solo part of Peter Cornelius' *Ein Ton* are supplemented by their accompanying motive in the piano part. The accompaniment to Debussy's *Spleen* and the violin obbligato to Braga's *Angel's Serenade* follow immediately on their vocal themes.

Some composers, who in their lifetime may have been very prolific, are here represented by perhaps one or two songs. Time and neglect have made these composers practically obsolete, and their scores for the most part unavailable. We have, therefore, chosen a few pieces representative of their style and still occasionally heard, on the chance that some reader might recall their themes.

A few of the songs quoted here may seem unimportant to the American student. The international distribution of our *Dictionary of Musical Themes* was the basis for the inclusion of these pieces, unknown here but of interest to musicians and laymen in other lands.

Wherever possible we used original texts, though in many cases only translations were available. Of these we chose the best we could find. Because of script difficulties and the possibility of error in phonetic spelling, we used only translations of Russian texts. Here, the choice of French,

German or English was governed by the quality of the text and its adherence to the musical line.

The variety of interval combination in vocal literature is perhaps not so great as in instrumental works (what is playable is not always singable), and the reader will find a greater similarity in vocal than in instrumental themes. We came across a good deal of unconscious as well as conscious plagiarism. Though *La Paloma* is Yradier's best-known, almost only known, song, we also included his *El Areglito* because of its quasi note-for-note similarity to the "Habañera" from *Carmen*. When this obvious fact was called to Bizet's attention he frankly admitted the plagiarism, saying that he could not have invented a better theme for his "Habañera" than Yradier's.

Our own *Marines' Hymn* is, consciously or not, almost a photograph of the "Couplets des deux hommes d'armes" from Offenbach's *Geneviève de Brabant*. Though rhythmically dissimilar, the "S'io S'io dir potessi" from Handel's *Ottone* parallels the first subject of Bach's *G minor fugue* in the first book of the *Well Tempered Clavichord* and is in the same key. This is without doubt unconscious plagiarism, if plagiarism it can be called.

Of interest to readers will be the many and varied settings of the same lyrics, especially those of Heine, Goethe and Verlaine.

For the most part, we have catalogued the themes alphabetically according to categories (cantatas, *Lieder*, operas, oratorios, songs, etc.). However, in the case of some composers, we have catalogued them according to opus numbers. Mozart themes are numbered in the order of their Köchel listings.

We have proofed and re-proofed this book, yet we can only identify ourselves with the Chinese author who always included an error or two so that the reader would be flattered by recognizing it. No matter how minutely such a book is proofed some errors are bound to creep in. We shall be grateful to our readers if they call our attention to any.

A book such as this cannot be created without the help of many kind friends. First and foremost, we wish to thank Mr. Philip Miller of the Music Reference Division of the New York Public Library whose advice and aid were invaluable and constant. Mr. Miller examined our entire card index, adding a great number of works which he felt indispensable to such a book. We also wish to thank Edward Bauer, Louis Kabasakalian and Elma Alexander of his staff.

Miss Gladys Chamberlain, Director of the Music Library Branch on 58th Street, and her co-workers, Miss Mary Lee Daniels and Miss Lilly Goldberg, gave us unreservedly of their time and advice and turned over to us all the resources of their splendid collection. Misses Mildred Lorres, Heather Moon, Melva Peterson, Florence O'Neill and Margaret Quinn were also very cooperative.

We want to thank Mr. Herbert Weinstock and Mr. Ben Meiselman for the use of their scores. Dr. Hans Heinsheimer of G. Schirmer, Inc., put his entire vocal department at our disposal and Mrs. Verona Clifford, Willard Lanzillo, William Kulkman and William Terranova were more than helpful in suggesting works and supplying us with practically everything we needed in the Schirmer catalogue.

We are especially grateful to the music publishers who gave us full cooperation and assistance. However, one publisher refused to let us show the themes from certain compositions published by him. The law on the matter is not clear at this writing, and therefore there are certain entries without notation. We trust the reader will understand that these regrettable omissions were unavoidable.

Lastly, we want to thank Mr. Robert Simon of Crown Publishers for his constant advice and encouragement.

Sam Morgenstern

New York, N. Y.
September, 1950

A DICTIONARY OF
OPERA
and
SONG THEMES

In a very few instances, copyright difficulties forced the use of blank staves. The reasons are given in the Introduction.

ABT, Franz (1819-1885)

Am Neckar, am Rhein, Op. 89 — O wär'___ ich am Ne-ckar, O wär'___ ich am Rhein___ — B

Gute Nacht, du mein herziges Kind — All' A-bend be-vor-ch zur Ru-he geh' blick' ich hin-aus_ in die Nacht — C

Über den Sternen ist Ruh, Op. 128, No. 1 — Ü-ber den Ster-nen ist Ruh,___ ü-ber den Ster-nen ist Ruh___ — D

Wenn die Schwalben heimwärts ziehn (Agathe) — Wenn die Schwal-ben heim-wärts ziehn, wenn die Ro-sen_ nicht mehr blühn — E

ACQUA, Eva dell' (1856- ?)

Chanson provençale — Par les nuits sans ri-va-les, Les bel-les nuits d'é-té — G

Villanelle
Copyright 1923, G. Schirmer, Inc. — J'ai vu pas-ser l'hi-ron-del-le_ Dans le ciel pur du ma-tin:___ — H

ADAM, Adolphe Charles (1803-1856)

Cantique pour Noël (Christmas Song) — Minuit,___ Chré-tiens, c'est l'heure so-len-nel-le — J

Vallons de la Helvétie, from Le Chalet — Val-lons de l'Hel-vé-ti-e ob-jet de mon a-mour — K

Mes amis, écoutez l'histoire, from Le Postillon de Longjumeau Act I (opera) — Mes a-mis, é-cou-tez l'his-toi-re d'un jeune et ga-lant pos-til-lon — L

Si J'Etais Roi (opera) Act I — Dans le som-meil l'a-mour, je ga-ge vous fit voir — M

J'i-gno-re son nom, sa nais-san-ce, lors_ qu'é-per-du — N

Un re-gard de ses yeux vien-drait fi-nir ma pei-ne — O

Zé-pho-ris est bon ca-ma-ra-de, mais c'est un pê-cheur fort_ mau-vais: — P

Act II (Nemea's Aria) (A) — Des___ sou-ve-rains du ri-va-ge d'A-si-e — Q

(B) — Dis un seul mot sou-dain ta cour va de-ve-nir le doux se-jour — R

Vous m'ai-mez dites - vous Ah! vot-re ma-jes-té veut se jou-er i-ci — S

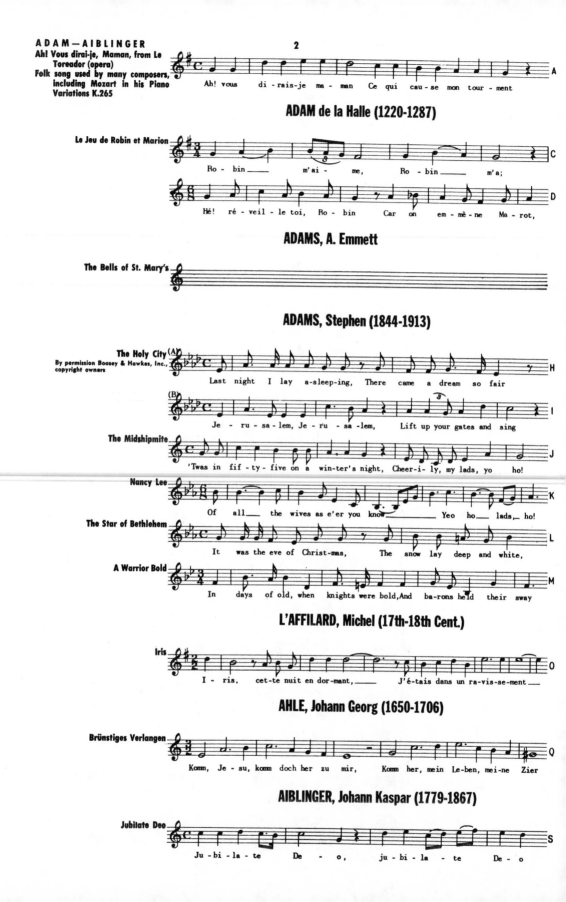

Ah! Vous dirai-je, Maman, from Le
Toreador (opera)
Folk song used by many composers,
including Mozart in his Piano
Variations K.265

Ah! vous di-rais-je ma-man Ce qui cau-se mon tour-ment

ADAM de la Halle (1220-1287)

Le Jeu de Robin et Marion

Ro - bin ____ m'ai - me, Ro - bin ____ m'a;

Hé! ré - veil - le toi, Ro - bin Car on em - mè - ne Ma - rot,

ADAMS, A. Emmett

The Bells of St. Mary's

ADAMS, Stephen (1844-1913)

The Holy City (A)
By permission Boosey & Hawkes, Inc.,
copyright owners

Last night I lay a-sleep-ing, There came a dream so fair

(B)

Je - ru - sa - lem, Je - ru - sa - lem, Lift up your gates and sing

The Midshipmite

'Twas in fif-ty-five on a win-ter's night, Cheer-i-ly, my lads, yo ho!

Nancy Lee

Of all ____ the wives as e'er you know ____ Yeo ho ____ lads, ho!

The Star of Bethlehem

It was the eve of Christ-mas, The snow lay deep and white,

A Warrior Bold

In days of old, when knights were bold, And ba-rons held their sway

L'AFFILARD, Michel (17th-18th Cent.)

Iris

I - ris, cet-te nuit en dor-mant, ____ J'é-tais dans un ra-vis-se-ment ____

AHLE, Johann Georg (1650-1706)

Brünstiges Verlangen

Komm, Je - su, komm doch her zu mir, Komm her, mein Le-ben, mei-ne Zier

AIBLINGER, Johann Kaspar (1779-1867)

Jubilate Deo

Ju - bi - la - te De - o, ju - bi - la - te De - o

AICHINGER, Gregor (1564-1628)

Factus est — Fa - ctus est re-pen - te de coe-lo so — — — — — — nus   B

Regina Coeli — Re-gi-na coe - li loe-ta——— re, loe-ta——— re, al - le-lu - ja   C

Salve, Regina — Sal - ve, Re - gi - na, Ma-ter,—— mi-se-ri-cor-di-ae, Vi - ta,dul-ce-do,   D

Ubi est Abel — U - bi est A - bel fra - — — — — — ter tu - us   E

ALABIEV, Alexander Nikolaevich (1787-1851)

The Nightingale — Nach - ti - gall, O   Nach - ti - gall, san - ges - rei - che—   G

ALAIN, Albert (15th Century)

Le Paradis — Beau ciel, tu m'ap - pa - rais—— Comme un lieu clair et frais——   I

ALBÉNIZ, Isaac Manuel Francisco (1860-1909)

Amor, Summa Injuria
Copyright by Salabert, Paris, N. Y.
— Par - don-ne:— Quand tu m'as ai-mé — Je fus cou-pa-ble—   K

Le Paradis Retrouvé
Copyright by Salabert, Paris, N. Y.
— Dans un jar-din, je ne sais où,—— Sont mille oi-seaux chan-teurs—   L

Quand je te vois souffrir
Copyright by Salabert, Paris, N. Y.
— Quand je te vois souf-frir,— J'ou-blie les verts jar-dins,— le bleu du ciel   M

Le Refuge
Copyright by Salabert, Paris, N. Y.
— J'ai re-non-cé à ce mon-de vain:Pour moi la coupe est vi-de,   N

ALBERT, Eugen d' (1864-1932)

Möchte wohl gerne ein Schmetterling sein, Op. 27, No. 2
By permission Associated Music Publishers, Inc.
— Sag-te ein gol-de-ner Schmet-ter-ling zu sei-ner sil-ber-nen Frau——   P

Tiefland (opera) Prologue
By permission Associated Music Publishers, Inc.
— Ich grüss' noch ein - - - mal mei - ne Ber - ge.   Q

Act 1 Traumerzählung — Zwei Va-ter-un-ser bet' ich vor dem Schlaf-en geh'n, das er-ste bet' ich   R

Wolfserzählung — Mein Le - ben wagt ich drum,— ja, ja, mein— Le - ben!   S

ALFANO, Franco (1876-1954)

ALFVEN, Hugo (1872-1960)

ALNAES, Eyvind (1872-1932)

ALVAREZ, F. M. (-1898)

AMBROSE, R. S.

ANONYMOUS

Act 2

Hüll in die Man - til - le dich fes - ter ein,

Psyche wandelt durch Säulenhallen, from Die Toten Augen (opera)
By permission Associated Music Publishers, Inc.

Psy - che wan - delt durch Säu - len - hal - len Sü - sse Klän - ge

Dieu de Grâce (Dio Pietosa), from Resurrection (opera)
Copyright by G. Ricordi & Co., Inc.

Dieu de grâ - ce, fais qu'il vien - ne, en - fin!

Skogen sover
Copyright by Lundquist, Stockholm

Sko - gen so - ver.__ Strim-man- på fä - stet fläm-tar matt.__

Lykken mellem to mennesker

Lyk - ken mel - lem to men - ne - sker er hver-ken-hu! el - ler

Nu brister i alle de Klofter, Op. 26, No. 2
Copyright by Hansen, Copenhagen

Nu bri - ster i al - le de klof-ter, som spraeng-te og fu - red mit sind__

Los Ojos Negros

Pa - ra jar - di - nes Gra - na - da__ Pa - ra mu - je - res Ma - drid

La Partida

De__ la Pa - tria los ul - ti - mos e - cos los ul - ti - mos e - cos

One Sweetly Solemn Thought

One sweet-ly sol - emn thought Comes to me o'er and o'er

Hymn of St. Adalbert 10th century

Mo - ther and mai - - - - - den, Mo - ther of God, Bless - ed __

Alleluia—Angelus Domini 11th century

Al - le - - - - lu - ia Al - le - - - lu - ia

Alleluia Psallat 13th century

Al - le - lu - ia psal - lat haec fa - mi - li - a__

O Miranda Dei Caritas (from Aubry's Cent Motets) 13th century

O mi - ran - da De - i ca - ri - tas

Puellare Gremium (End of 13th century—14th century?)
Pu - el - la - re gre - mi - um mun - do fu - dit

The Descent of the Holy Ghost (Spanish) 14th century
All bless-ings that our God hath giv'n, In to - ken of his dear son's love,

German Flagellants' Hymn Year of the Plague 1349
O Ma-ry Moth-er Vir-gin mild, For - get not Christ-en-dom thy child

Greensleeves
A - las! my love you do me wrong to cast me off dis-court-eous-ly

L'Amour de Moi 15th century
L'a - mour de moi s'y est en - clo

Drink to me only with thine eyes
Drink to me on - ly with thine eyes And I will pledge with mine

Have you seen but a whyte lillie grow
Have you seen but a whyte Lil - lie grow

Londonderry Air (Air from County Derry)
Would God I were the ten - der ap - ple blos - som

Oh! Dear! What Can the Matter Be?
Oh! dear! What can the mat - ter be? Dear! dear! What can the mat - ter be?

Ralph's Ramble to London
I am a poor in-no-cent clown, And late-ly I ram-bled to town

The Slighted Swain
Chlo - e proves false, but still she is charm - ing

When Love is Kind
When love is kind, cheer - ful and free

ARCADELT, Jacob (1514-1570)
(attributed to Arcadelt)

Ave Maria
A - ve Ma - ri - a! gra - ti - a ple - na

Il bianco e dolce cigno
Il bian - co e dol - ce cig - no Can - tan - do mo - re

ARCHANGELSKY, Alexander (1846-1924)

Hear My Prayer
Hear my prayer, O God O God, hear, O hear my prayer

ARDITI, Luigi (1822-1903)

Il Bacio (The Kiss)
Sul - le, Sul - le lab - bra, sul - le lab - bra se - po - tes - si

Leggiero invisibile — Lag-ge — — ro, invi-si — bi — le Qual au — — ra sui fio — — re,

Parla! — Più nel dub-bio non far-mi pe — na — re,

ARENSKY, Anton (1861-1906)

But lately in dance I embraced her — But late — ly in dance I em-brac'd her

The Little Fish's Song, Op. 27, No. 1
Copyright 1944, G. Schirmer, Inc. — Ah, stay____ with me, My love-ly boy, oh,___ stay!

ARNE, Michael (1741-1786)

The Lass with a Delicate Air — Young Mol — ly, who____ lived at the foot___ of___ the___ hill,

ARNE, Thomas A. (1710-1778)

Blow, blow thou Winter Wind — Blow, blow,___ thou___ win-ter wind,____ Thou art___ not___ so un — kind

Come Away, Death — Come, come, come a-way death, And in___ sad cy -press let me be laid

Preach not me your Musty Rules
(from Comus: a Masque) — Preach not me ___ your mus — ty rules, Ye drones that mould in i — dle cell,___

Now Phoebus sinketh in the West — Now Phoe-bus sink-eth in___the West, Wel — come song and wel — come jest,

Rig-our now is gone to bed And ad-vice with___ scrup-'lous head

Orpheus with his Lute — Or-pheus with his lute, Or-pheus with his lute, with his lute____ made___ trees.

Rule Britannia — When Brit — ain first_____ at Heav'ns com — mand

This was the char — ter, the Char — ter of the land

Rule Brit — tan-nia, Brit- — tan — nia rule the waves

Tell me where is fancy bred — Tell me where is___ fan-cy___ bred,___ Or in the___ heart or in the head?

Under the Greenwood Tree — Un — der the green — wood tree, Who loves___ to lie___ with me

Water Parted from the Sea

Wa- ter part- ed from the sea___ May in-crease_the riv- er's tide___

When Icicles Hang by the Wall (from Love's Labour Lost)

When i- ci- cles hang by the wall,__ and Dick the Shep-herd blows_ his hail

When Daisies Pied

When dai- sies pied and vio- lets blue, and la- dy smocks all sil- ver white,

Where the Bee Sucks

Where the bee sucks there suck I, In a cow- slip bell_ I lie,

ARNOLD, Dr. Samuel (1740-1802)

Amo, Amas, I Love a Lass

A- mo, A- mas, I love_ a_ lass, as a ce- dar tall_ and_ slen- der

ATTEY, John (d. c. 1640)

Sweet Was the Song

Sweet was the song the vir- gin sang When_ She to Beth-le-hem_ was come

AUBER, Daniel François Esprit (1782-1871)

Le Domino Noir: (opera) Flamme Vengeresse

Flam- me ven- ge- res- se, tour-ment qui m'op- pres- se

Act II La Belle Inès Fait Florès

La belle I- nès__ fait flo-rès__ elle a des at-traits_ des ver-tus

Fra Diavolo: (opera) Act I Voyez Sur Cette Roche

Vo- yez sur cet- te ro- che ce brave à l'air fier et_ har- di

Act II Barcarolle

A- gnes la jou-ven-cel- le aus- si jeune que bel- le

Quel__ bon-heur_ je res-pi- re,_ je suis_ seule i- ci

Pour tou-jours,_tou- jours, di-sait el- le, je suis__ à_ toi

L'Eclat de Rire (Laughing Song) from Manon Lescaut

C'est l'his-toire a- mou- reuse Au-tant que fa- bu- leuse

La Muette de Portici: Act II Barcarolle

A- mis,_ la ma-ti-née_est bel-le sur le ri-va- ge as-sem-blez

Duet

A-mour sa- cré__ de la pa-tri- e, rend nous l'au-dace__

Act IV

Du pauvre seul a- mi fi- dè- le, de- scends_ à ma voix__

AURIC, Georges (1899-   )

Le Gloxinia
By permission Associated Music Publishers, Inc.

Je vou-drais qu' à ma fe- nê- tre Fleurisse un ten-dre glo- xi- nia;

Printemps
By permission Durand & Cie, Paris; Elkan-Vogel Co., Inc., Phila., copyright owners

Quand ce beau prin-temps je voy, J'ap-per-çoy Ra- jeu-nir la terre

BACH, Carl Philipp Emanuel (1714-1788)

(See also BACH, Philipp Emanuel)

Die Himmel rühmen des ewigen Ehre

Die Him- mel rüh- men des E- wi- gen Eh- re

Jesus in Gethsemane

Schau'hin Dort in Geth-se- ma- ne klagt, trau-ert

Der Phoenix

Der Mann, der nach den Flit- ter-wo- chen aus Lie-be küsst

BACH, Johann Christian (1735-1782)

Non è ver, from Carattaco (opera)

Non è ver, che as-si- se in tro- no bel-le an-cor le col- pe so- no

BACH, Johann Michael (1648-1694)

Ich weiss dass mein Erlöser lebt

Ich weiss, dass mein Er- lo-ser lebt, ich weiss dass mein Er-lo-ser lebt

BACH, Johann Sebastian (1685-1750)

CANTATAS, Church, No. 4: Christ lag in Todesbunden (Easter Cantata) No. 1

Christ lag in To- des- ban- den

No. 3

Den Tod, Den Tod, Den Tod, Den Tod, Den Tod Nie- mand zwin- gen kunnt

No. 5

Hier ist das rech- te O- ster-lamm, das rech - - - - te O-ster-lamm

No. 5: Wo soll ich fliehen hin No. 5

Ver- stum- me ver-stum-me, ver- stum- me, Höl - - - len- heer,

No. 6: Bleib' bei uns No. 1

Bleib' bei uns, bleib' bei uns, den es will A - - - bend

No. 2

Hoch- ge- lob- ter Got- tes Sohn

No. 7: Christ unser Herr zum Jordan kam No. 6

Men- schen glaubt doch die- ser Gna- de

CANTATAS, Church, No. 8: Liebster Gott, wann werd' ich sterben? No. 4

Doch wei- chet ihr tol- len ver-geb—li-chen sor- gen   A

No. 10: Mein Seel' erhebt den Herren   No. 2

Herr, Herr, Herr, der du stark und mäch-tig bist,der du stark und mäch-tig bist   B

No. 3

Ge-wal— ti-ge, Ge-wal— ti-ge stösst Gott von   C

No. 6

Sein Sa- me muss-te sich so sehr wie Sand am Meer   D

No.12: Weinen, Klagen, Sorgen, Zagen   No. 4

Kreuz und Kro-ne sind ver-bun-den, Kampf und Kleinod sind ver-eint.   E

No. 13: Meine Seufzer, meine Thränen   No. 1

Mei- ne Seufzer,mei- ne Thrä- nen kön-nen nicht zu zäh- len sein   F

No. 2

Äch- zen und er- bärm- lich wei- nen, Äch- zen,   G

No. 17: Wer Dank opfert, der preiset mich   No. 3

Herr, dei- ne Gü- te reicht,so weit der Him- mel ist,   H

No. 5

Welch Ü- ber-mass der Gü- te schenkst du mir!   I

No. 18: Gleich wie der Regen und Schnee von Himmel   No. 4

Mein See-len-schatz ist Got-tes Wort, Mein See-len-schatz ist Got-tes Wort   J

No. 20: O Ewigkeit, du Donnerwort   No. 3

E— wig-keit du machst mir ban— ge   K

No. 6

O Mensch er-ret- te dei- ne See- le, ent-flie— he   L

Part II, No. 1

Wacht auf, wacht auf, wacht auf, wacht auf wacht auf,wacht auf,   M

No. 21: Ich hatte viel Beküm-merniss   No. 2

Ich Ich, Ich, Ich hat-te viel Be-küm-mer-niss,Ich hat-te viel Be-küm-mer-niss   N

No. 3

Seuf-zer,Thrän-en,Kum- mer, Noth,— Seuf- zer, Thrän- en, ängst-lich's   O

No. 5

Bä- che von ge-sal- zen- nen Zäh- ren—   P

Part II, No. 4

Er-freu- e dich See- le, er- freu- e dich, Her- ze   Q

No. 22: Jesus nahm zu sich die Zwölfe   No. 2

Mein Je- su, zie— he mich nach dir,   R

CANTATAS, Church, No. 22: Jesus nahm zu sich die Zwölfe, No. 4 — A

Choral — B

No. 26: Ach wie flüchtig, ach wie nichtig   No. 4 — C

No. 27: Wer weiss wie nahe mir mein Ende   No. 5 — D

No. 28: Gottlob, nun geht das Jahr zu Ende   No. 1 — E

No. 29: Wir danken dir, Gott, wir danken dir (Rathswahlkantate)   No. 3 — F

No. 5 — G

No. 30: Freue dich, erlöste Schaar   No. 5 — H

No. 31: Der Himmel lacht, die Erde jubiliert   No. 4 — I

No. 6 — J

No. 32: Liebster Jesu, mein Verlangen   No. 3 — K

No. 33: Allein zu dir, Herr Jesu Christ   No. 3 — L

No. 34: O ewiges Feuer, O Ursprung der Liebe   No. 3 — M

No. 35: Geist und Seele wird verwirret   No. 2 — N

Part II, No. 3 — O

Part I, No. 3 — P

No. 36: Schwingt freudig euch empor   No. 7 — Q

No. 39: Brich dem Hungrigen dein Brod   No. 5 — R

No. 40: Dazu ist erschienen der Sohn Gottes   No. 3 — S

A. Mein Al-les in Al-lem, mein e——wi-ges Gut

B. Er-tödt' uns durch dein' Gü-te   Er-weck' uns durch dein'Gnad'

C. An ir-di-sche Schä-tze das Her-ze zu hän-gen ist ei-ne Ver-füh-rung

D. Gu- - -te Nacht, gu- - -te Nacht,— gu- -te Nacht,du Welt-ge-tüm-mel,

E. Gott- lob! nun geht das Jahr zu En- de,

F. Hal - - - - - - - - - - le-lu-jah, Stark'— und Macht—

G. Ge-denk——— an— uns— mit dei - - - - -ner Lie - -be

H. Kommt, ihr——— an- ge-focht'-nen Sün-der,

I. Fürst des Le-bens,star-ker Streiter, Fürst des Le - - - - - - - - -bens,

J. A-dam muss in uns ver-we-sen, Soll der neu-e Mensch ge-ne-sen,

K. Hier, in mei-nes Va-ters Stät-te,

L. Wie furcht-sam' wank - - -ten mei - - - -ne Schrit-te

M. Wohl euch, ihr aus- er-wähl-ten See-len,

N. Geist——— und See- - - -le wird ver- -wir- -ret,

O. Ich wün-sche mir bei Gott zu— le-ben ach,— wä-re doch— die Zeit—schon— da,

P. Gott hat Al - - - - - - - - -les wohl ge-macht,

Q. Auch mit ge-dämpf-ten schwa-chen Stim-men

R. Höch-ster, was ich ha-be, ist nur dei-ne Ga-be,

S. Höl-li-sche Schlan-ge, wird dir nicht ban- ge?

11   **BACH**

CANTATAS, Church, No. 41: Jesu, nun sei gepreiset   **No. 2**   A

Lass uns,__ O höch-ster Gott,__ das Jahr__ voll-brin-gen,

No. 42: Am Abend aber desselbigen Sabbaths   **No. 3**   B

Wo zwei und drei ver-samm-let sind in Je-su theu-rem Na----men,

No. 6   C

Je-su ist ein Schild__ der Sei---nen,

No. 43: Gott fähret auf mit Jauchzen   **No. 3**   D

Ja tau-send mal Tau-send be-glei-ten den__ Wa-gen, dem__ Kö-nig der Kön'-ge

No. 8   E

Ich se------he schon im__ Geist,

No. 44: Sie werden euch in den Bann thun   **No. 5**   F

Es ist und bleibt der Chri-sten Trost, dass Gott für sei---ne Kir-che__ wacht,

No. 45: Es ist dir gesagt, Mensch, was Gut ist   **Part II, No. 2**   G

Wer Gott be---kennt aus wah-rem Her---zens__ grund,

No. 46: Schauet doch und sehet, ob irgend ein Schmerz sei   **No. 3**   H

Dein Wet-ter zog sich auf__ von__ Wei-tem,

No. 5   I

Doch Je-sus__ will auch bei der Stra-fe der From-men Schild__ und Bei-stand__ sein

No. 48: Ich elender Mensch, wer wird mich erlösen   **No. 4**   J

Ach, le-ge das So-dom der__ sünd-li-chen__ Glie-der, wo-fern es dein Wil-le,

No. 50: Nun ist die Heil und die Kraft   K

Nun ist die Heil, und die Kraft, und das Reich, und die Macht un-sers__ Got-tes

No. 51: Jauchzet Gott in allen Landen   **No. 1**   L

Jauch - - - - - - - - zet, Jauch - - zet Gott in al--len Lan-den

No. 2   M

Wir be--ten zu den Tem-pel an, da Got-tes Eh-re woh-net,

No. 3   N

Höch-ster, Höch-ster, ma-che dei-ne Gü-te fer-ner al-le Mor--gen__ neu,

No. 4   O

Sei Lob und Preis mit Eh - - - ren Gott Va-ter, Sohn, hei-li-gem Geist!

No. 53: Schlage doch, gewünschte Stunde   **No. 1**   P

Schla-ge doch ge-wünsch-te Stun-de, brich doch an, du schön-er Tag

No. 54: Widerstehe doch die Sünde   **No. 1**   Q

Wi-der-ste-he doch die Sün-de, Wi-der-ste-he doch die Sün-de

No. 3   R

Wer Sün-de thut, der ist vom Teu - - - - - - - fel,

No. 55: Ich armer Mensch, ich Sündenknecht   **No. 3**   S

Er-bar--me dich, er----bar--me dich

CANTATAS, Church, No. 56: Ich will
den Kreuzstab gerne tragen
No. 1

A

Ich will den Kreuz-stab ger-ne tra - - - - - - - - - - gen,

No. 3

B

End- lich,____ end - - - - lich wird____ mein Joch____

No. 57: Selig ist der Mann
No. 1

C

Se - - - - - - lig,-se - - - - - - lig, se - - - lig,se-lig ist der Mann

No. 3

D

Ich wünschte____ mir den____ Tod,____ ich wünschte mir den Tod____

No. 4

E

Ja, ja, ich kann die Fein-de____ schla - - - - - - - - - - gen,

No. 61: Nun komm, der Heiden
Heiland   No. 3

F

Komm, Je- - su, Komm - - - - - zu dei- - ner Kir - - - che,

No. 4

G

Öff- ne dich, mein gan- zes____ Her - - - ze

No. 62: Nun komm, der Heiden
Heiland   No. 2

H

Be- wun- dert, O Men- schen dies gro- - sse Ge- heim-niss,

No. 64: Sehet, welch' eine Liebe
hat uns der Vater erzeiget
No. 5

I

Was die____ Welt in____ sich____ hält,

No. 7

J

Von der____ Welt ver- lang' ich nichts,nichts, nichts,nichts,

No. 65: Sie werden aus Saba
No. 1

K

Sie wer- den aus Sa- - ba Al- - - le kom - - - - - men

No. 2

L

Die Kön' ge aus Sa- ba ka- - men dar, ka - - - men dar,

No. 6

M

Nimm____ mich dir____ zu ei- - - - gen hin

No. 7

N

Ei nun,mein Gott, So fall ich dir ge- trost in dei- - - - - ne Hän- de

No. 66: Erfreut euch, ihr Herzen
No. 3

O

Las- set____ dem____ Höch- sten ein Dank-lied er- schal- len

No. 5

P

Ich fürch- te zwar des Gra- - bes Fin- ster-nis- - sen,

Q

Ich fürch- - te nicht,ich fürch- - te nicht des Gra- - bes Fin- - ster-nis- sen

No. 67: Halt' im Gedächtniss
Jesum Christ   No. 2

R

Mein Je- sus ist er- stan - - - den, al- lein, was schreckt mich noch?

No. 68: Also hat Gott die Welt
geliebt   No. 2

S

Mein gläu- bi- - - ges Her- - ze, froh- lo- cke,____ sing',scher- ze

CANTATAS, Church, No. 69: Lobe den Herrn, meine Seele No. 5

Mein Er- lö- ser und Er- hal-ter, nimm mich stets in Hut und Wacht,

No. 70: Wachet, wachet, seid bereit allezeit　Part I, No. 3

Wenn kommt der Tag aus dem wir zie- hen aus dem E- gyp-ten die- - - ser Welt

Part I, No. 5

Lass' der Spöt- ter Zun- - - gen schmähen, es wird doch, und muss ge- sche-hen

Part II, No. 1

Hebt eu- er Haupt em- - - por und seid ge-trost, ihr From- men,

Part II, No. 3

Se- - - - lig- - - - ster Er- qui- - ckungs- tag

No. 71: Gott ist mein König　No. 4

Tag und Nacht, Tag und Nacht ist dein, Tag und Nacht, Tag und Nacht,

No. 72: Alles nur nach Gottes Willen　No. 2 (Arioso)

Herr, so du willt, so muss sich Al- les fü- - gen!

Mit Al- lem, was ich hab' und bin Mit Al- lem was ich hab' und bin

No. 5

Mein Je- sus will es thun, Er will dein Kreuz ver- sü- ssen.

No. 73: Herr, wie du willt, so schick's mit mir　No. 4

Herr, so du willt, Herr, so du willt, Herr, so du willt, Herr, so du willt,

No. 74: Wer mich liebet, der wird mein Wort halten　No. 4

Kommt! Kommt! ei - - - - - - - - - - - - - let!

No. 6

Nichts kann mich er- ret- ten von höl- li- schen Ket - - - - - - - ten,

No. 75: Die Elenden sollen essen　No. 3

Mein Je- - - sus soll- - - - - mein Al- les sein

No. 5

Ich neh- - - me mein Lei- - - - den mit Freu- den auf mich!

No. 76: Die Himmel erzählen die Ehre Gottes　Part I, No. 3

Hört, ihr Völ- ker, Got- tes Stim- me, hört, ihr Völ- ker, Got- tes Stim- me

Part II, No. 3

Has- - - - - - se nur, has- se mich recht, has- se nur, has- se mich recht,

Part II, No. 5

Liebt, ihr Chri- - - sten in der That, liebt ihr Chri- - sten in der That

No. 78: Jesu, der du meine Seele　No. 1

Je- su, der du mei- - - ne See- - - - - - - le,

No. 2

Wir ei- - - - - - - - - - len mit schwa- chen, doch em- si-gen Schrit-ten

CANTATAS, Church, No. 104: Du Hirte
Israel, höre   No. 1

Du Hir - - - te I - srael du Hir - - - te I - srael.

No. 5

Be - glück - te Heer - de, Je - su Scha - fe, be - glück - te lleer - de Je - su Scha - fe,

No. 105: Herr, gehe nich in's
Gericht   No. 3

Wie zit - tern und wan - ken der Sün - der Ge - dan - ken,

No. 5

Kann ich nur Je - sum__ mir zum Freun - de ma - chen,

No. 106: Gottes Zeit ist die allerbeste Zeit   No. 1

Got - tes Zeit, Got - tes Zeit ist die al - ler - be - - - - ste,

In ihm le - ben we - - - - - - - - - ben

Es ist der al - te Bund: Mensch, du musst ster - - - ben, du musst

No. 2

In dei - ne__ Hän - de, In dei - ne__ Hän - de be - fehl'__ ich__ mei - nen Geist

Mit Fried und Freud ich fahr da - hin in Got - tes Wil - - len,

No. 3

Glo - rie, Lob, Ehr' - - - - - und Herr - - - lich-keit

No. 110: Unser Mund, sei voll
Lachens   No. 4

Ach Herr! was ist ein Men-schen-kind, dass du sein Heil so schmerzlich su-chest?

No. 6

Wacht auf, wacht auf! __ wacht auf, wacht auf! __ wacht auf, ihr A - dern

No. 112: Der Herr ist mein getreuer Hirt   No. 2

Zum rei - nen Was - ser er__ mich weist, das mich er - quick - en

No. 114: Ach, lieben Christen,
seid getrost   No. 5

Du machst, O Tod,__ mir__ nun nicht fer - ner__ ban - ge

No. 115: Mache dich, mein Geist,
bereit   No. 2

Ach, schläfri - ge See - le, wie? Wie? Ach, schläfri - ge See - le, wie? ru - hest du

No. 117: Sei Lob und Ehr' dem
höchsten Gut   No. 7

Ich will dich all mein Le - ben lang, O Gott, von nun an eh - - - ren,

No. 120: Gott, man lobet dich in
der Stille   No. 1

Gott, man lo - - - - - - - - - - - bet dich in der Stil - le

No. 4

Heil__ und Se - gen Heil__ und__ Se - - gen soll und muss zu al - ler Zeit,

No. 121: Christum wir sollen
loben schon   No. 3

Jo - han - - - nis freu - - - den - vol - les Sprin - - - gen,

CANTATAS, Church,

No. 147: Herz und Mund und Tat und Leben No. 10 (Jesu, joy of man's desiring)

No. 148: Bringet dem Herrn Ehre seines Namens No. 4

No. 149: Man singet mit Freuden vom Sieg No. 4

No. 151: Süsser Trost, mein Jesus kömmt No. 1

No. 3

No. 152: Tritt auf die Glaubens- bahn No. 4

No. 153: Schau', lieber Gott, wie meine Feind! No. 6

No. 154: Mein liebster Jesus ist verloren No. 1

No. 3

No. 155: Mein Gott, wie lang No. 4

No. 156: Ich stehe mit einem Fuss im Grabe No. 4

No. 159: Sehet, wir geh'n hinauf gen Jerusalem No. 4

No. 160: Ich weiss dass mein Erlöser lebt No. 1

No. 161: Komm, du süsse Todes- stunde No. 3

No. 167: Ihr Menschen rühmet Gottes Liebe No. 1

No. 170: Vergnügte Ruh, beliebte Seelenlust No. 1

No. 172: Erschallet, ihr Lieder No. 3

No. 4

No. 175: Er rufet seinen Schafen mit Namen No. 2

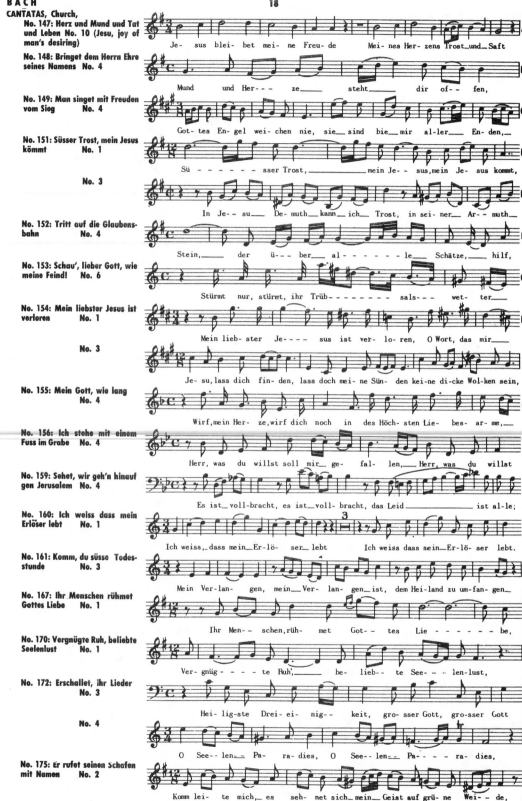

CANTATAS, Church, No. 182: Himmelskönig, sei willkommen No. 3

A — Star- kes Lie- ben, star — — — — — kes Lie- ben,

No. 4

B — Le- — get ___ euch dem Hei- land ___ un- — ter,

No. 5

C — Je- su, lass ___ durch ___ Wohl ___ und ___ Weh,

No. 183: Sie werden euch in den
Bann thun No. 4

D — Höch — — — — ster Trö- ster heil' — — — — ger ___ Geist,

No. 186: Ärge dich, o Seele,
nicht No. 8

E — Die Ar- men ___ will der Herr ___ um- — ar- men,

No. 187: Es wartet Alles auf
dich No. 3

F — Du Herr, du krönst ___ al- lein das Jahr mit dei- nem ___ Gut,

No. 4

G — Da- rum sollt ihr nicht sor- gen noch sa- gen: was wer- den wir es- sen

No. 5

H — Gott ver- sor- get, Gott ___ ver- sor- get al — — — — — les Le- ben, ___

No. 189: Meine Seele rühmt und
preist No. 1

I — Mei- ne ___ See- le, mei- ne See- le rühmt und preist ___

No. 2

J — Denn seh' ich mich und auch mein Le- ben an, so muss mein Mund

No. 3

K — Gott hat sich hoch ge- se — — — — — tzet, hoch ge- setzet und sieht auf Das

No. 5

L — Die- ne Gü- te, dein Er- bar- men, Dein Er- bar- men wäh- ret, Gott, zu- al- ler Zeit,

No. 197: Gott ist unsere
Zuversicht No. 3

M — Schlä — — — — fert al- — — — — ler Sor- — gen ___ Kum- mer

No. 210: O holder Tag (Wedding
Cantata) No. 3

N — Ru- — — het hie, mat — — — — — — — te Tö- — — ne,

CANTATAS, Secular
No. 158: Der Friede sei mit dir
No. 1 Recitative

P — Der Frie- — de ___ sei mit ___ dir, du ängstli- ches Ge- wis- sen!

No. 2

Q — Welt, a- — — de! ich bin ___ dein ___ mü- — de,

No. 3 Arioso

R — Da ___ bleib ich, da ___ hab' ___ ich Ver- gnü- gen zu woh- — — nen,

No. 4 Choral

S — Hier ist das ___ rech- te O- ster- lamm, da- von hat Gott ge- bo- ten

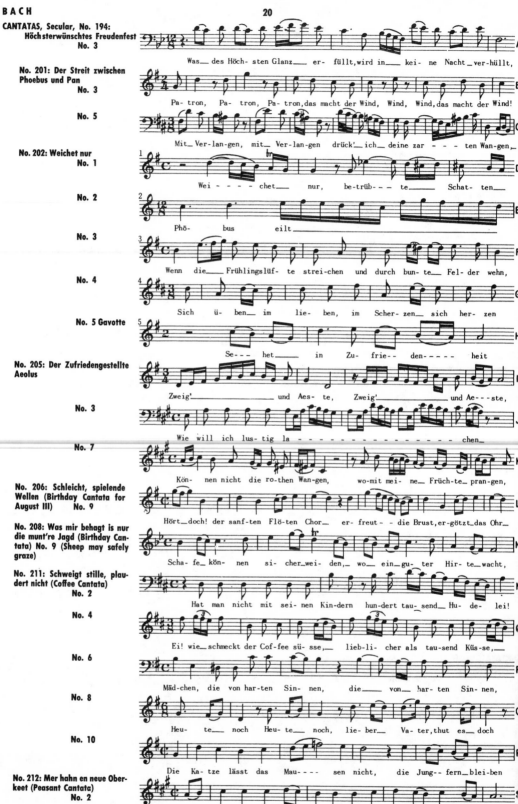

CANTATAS, Secular, No. 194:
Höchsterwünschtes Freudenfest
No. 3

Was des Höchsten Glanz erfüllt, wird in keine Nacht verhüllt,

No. 201: Der Streit zwischen
Phoebus und Pan
No. 3

Pa- tron, Pa- tron, Pa- tron, das macht der Wind, Wind, Wind, das macht der Wind!

No. 5

Mit Verlangen, mit Verlangen drück' ich deine zar - - - ten Wangen,

No. 202: Weichet nur
No. 1

Wei - - - chet nur, betrüb - - te Schat- ten

No. 2

Phö- bus eilt

No. 3

Wenn die Frühlingslüf- te streichen und durch bunte Fel- der wehn,

No. 4

Sich ü- ben im lie- ben, im Scher- zen sich her- zen

No. 5 Gavotte

Se- - - het in Zu- frie- den- - - - heit

No. 205: Der Zufriedengestellte
Aeolus
No. 3

Zweig' und Aes- te, Zweig' und Ae- - -ste,

No. 7

Wie will ich lus- tig la - - - - - - - - - - - - - chen

No. 206: Schleicht, spielende
Wellen (Birthday Cantata for
August III) No. 9

Kön- nen nicht die ro-then Wan- gen, wo-mit mei- ne Früch-te pran-gen,

No. 208: Was mir behagt is nur
die munt're Jagd (Birthday Cantata) No. 9 (Sheep may safely
graze)

Hört doch! der sanf-ten Flö-ten Chor er- freut- - die Brust, er-götzt das Ohr,

No. 211: Schweigt stille, plau-
dert nicht (Coffee Cantata)
No. 2

Scha- fe kön- nen si- cher-wei- den, wo ein-gu- ter Hir- te wacht,

No. 4

Hat man nicht mit sei- nen Kin-dern hun-dert tau- send Hu- de- lei!

No. 6

Ei! wie schmeckt der Cof-fee süs- se, lieb-li- cher als tau-send Küs-se,

No. 8

Mäd-chen, die von har-ten Sin- nen, die von har- ten Sin- nen,

No. 10

Heu- te noch Heu- te noch, lie- ber Va- ter, thut es doch

No. 212: Mer hahn en neue Ober-
keet (Peasant Cantata)
No. 2

Die Ka- tze lässt das Mau- - - sen nicht, die Jung-- fern blei-ben

Mer habn en neu- e O-ber-keet an un-sern Kam-mer-herrn.

CANTATAS, Secular, No. 212: No. 4 Mer hahn en neue Oberkeet (Peasant Cantata)

Ach es schmeckt doch gar zu gut, gar zu gut, wenn ein Paar recht freund-lich tut; A

No. 6

Ach Herr Schösser, geht nicht gar zu schlimm mit uns ar-men Bau-ers-leu-ten um, B

No. 8

Un- ser treff-- lich- er lie- ber Kam-- mer-herr C

No. 10

Das ist ga-lant, es spricht niemand von den ca-du-cken Scho-cken D

No. 12

Fünf- zig Tha-ler baares Geld trock'-ner Wei se zu ver-schmau-sen, E

No. 14

Klein-zschocher mü-sse so zart und sü-sse wie lau-ter Man-del-ker-ne sein F

No. 16

Es neh- me zehn-tau-send Du-ca-ten der Kam-mer-herr al- le Tag' ein, G

No. 18

Gieb, Schö-ne, viel Söh-ne von art'-ger Ge-stalt, H

No. 20

Dein Wach- stum sei fe- ste und la- che vor Lust I

No. 22

Und dass ihr's al- le wisst, es ist nun-mehr die Frist zu trin-ken, J

No. 24

Wir gehn nun wo der Tu-del-sack, der Tu-del-Tu-del-Tu-del- Tu-del- K

CHORALES: Eine feste Burg

Ein fe-ste Burg ist un-ser Gott, ein' gu-te Wehr und Waf-- fen L

In dulci jubilo

In dul- ci ju- bi- lo sin-get und seid froh, M

Lobet den Herrn

Lo-bet den Her- ren, lo-bet den Her-ren, denn er ist sehr freund-lich, N

Die Sonn' hat sich mit ihrem Glanz

Die Sonn' hat sich mit ih-rem Glanz ge- wen- det, und, was sie soll O

Vater unser in Himmelreich

Va- ter un- ser im Him-mel-reich, der du uns al- le heissest gleich P

Wer den lieben Gott lässt walten

Wer nur den lie-ben Gott lässt wal- ten, und hof-fet auf ihn al-- le-zeit Q

Magnificat in D 1. Chorus

Ma - - - - - - - gni-fi-cat, ma-gni-fi-cat, ma-gni-fi-cat, R

II. Aria

Et ex- ul- ta-- vit spi- ri- tus me- us S

Magnificat in D
III. Aria
Qui - - - a___ re- spe- - - xit hu- mi- li- ta- - tem

IV. Chorus
O-mnes, o-mnes ge- ra- ti- o- - - - - - - - - - - - nes,

V. Aria
Qui- a fe- cit_mi-hi ma-gna, qui po - - - - - - - - - - ten

VI. Duet
Et mi-se- - - ri- cor- di- a,___ mi- se- ri- cor- di- a

VII. Chorus A
Fe- cit po- ten- - ti- am, fe- cit po- ten- - ti- am

B
Fe- cit_po-ten - - - - - - - - - - - - - - - - - ti- am

VIII. Aria
De po - - - - - su-it, de- po - - - - - - - su- it

IX.
E- - - su- - ri- en- - - tes im- ple - - - - - vit bo- nis

X. Trio
Su- sce- pit___ Is- ra- el pu- e- rum su- um

XI. Chorus
Si- cut lo- - - cu- - - - - tus est ad pat- res no- - - stros

XII. Chorus
Glo- ri-a glo- - glo-(Tenor) glo-(Alto)glo-(2Sop) glo-(I Sop)- - - ri-a Pa-tri,

Glo- ri-a glo - - - - - - - - - - ri- a Pa- tri,

Mass in B minor I. Kyrie
Ky- ri- e e- le- - - - - - - - - i- son Ky- ri- e e- le- - - i- son

II. Christe Eleison
Chri - - - ste, Chri-ste e- lei - - - - - son, e- lei - - - son

III. Kyrie
Ky- ri- e e- lei - - - - - son, e- le- i- son,

IV. Gloria
Glo - - - - - - ri- a in ex-cel - - - - - - sis De- o,

et___ in ter- ra pax ho- mi-ni-bus bo-nae vo- lun- ta- - tis

V. Laudamus Te
Lau- da - - - - - - - - - - - - - - - - - mus te

VI. Gratias agimus tibi
Gra - - - - - - ti-as a - - - - - - gi-mus ti- bi

Mass in B minor
VII. A. Domine Deus

Do- mi-ne De- us,rex coe — — — — — — stis,

B. Qui tollis peccata mundi

Qui tol-lis pec-ca — — — ta mun- di, mi-se-re-re no-bis,

VIII. Qui sedes ad dextram Patris

Qui se — — — — — — — — — des ad dex-tram Pat-ris,

IX. Quoniam tu solus sanctus

Quo — — ni- am tu so — — — lus san- ctus

X. Cum sancto Spiritu

Cum sanc-to Spi — ri- tu in glo-ri-a De — i Pat-ris,

XI. Credo No. 1

Cre- do in un-um De- um, in un-um De- um, in u-num De-um

XII. Credo No. 2

A Cre-do in un-um De- um, cre- do in u-num De- um,

B Pa- trem o- mnipo- ten- tem, fac- to- rem coe-li et ter- rae,

XIII. Et in unum Dominum

Et in u-num,in u-num Do — — — — — — — — — mi-num

XIV. Et incarnatus est

Et in-car-na- tus est, in-car-na — — tus est, in-car-na- tus est

XV. Crucifixus

Sop. Ten. Alt.

Cru-ci-fi- xus,(Cru-ci- fi — — xus)Cru-ci-fi — — xus,

XVI. Et resurrexit

Et re-sur-re — — — — — — — xit, re-sur- re- xit

XVII. Et in spiritum sanctum

Et in spi- ri-tum san-ctum Do — mi-num et vi- vi- fi-can — — tem

XVIII. Confiteor

Con- fi- te- or,con-fi — te- or, u — num ba- pti- sma,

XIX. Sanctus A

San- ctus, san — — — — — ctus, san — — — — — ctus

Sanctus B

Ple- ni sunt coe-li et ter-ra glo — — — — ri- a e- jus,

XX. Osana

O- sa- na, O- sa- na O- sa — — — — na,O- sa-na

XXI. Benedictus

Be — ne- di- ctus, be — ne- di- ctus qui ve — nit,

XXII. Agnus dei

Ag- nus De — i qui tol — lis pec-ca — ta mun — di,

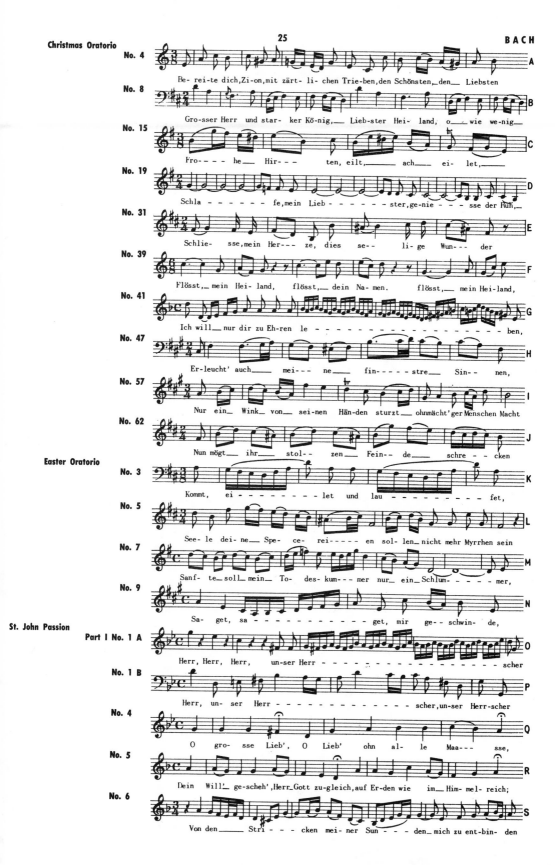

St. Matthew Passion
Part I No. 12

BACH

No. 16

No. 17

No. 19

(Chorale) No. 21

No. 26

No. 29

(Chorale) No. 31

No. 33 A

No. 33 B

No. 35

Part II No. 36

(Chorale) No. 38

No. 41

(Chorale) No. 46

No. 48

(Chorale) No. 49

No. 51

(Chorale) No. 55

St. Matthew Passion
Part II No. 58

Aus Lie - - - - - - - - - - - - - - - - - - be, aus Lie-- be,   A

No. 61

Kön-nen Thrä - - - nen mei ner Wan - - - gen nichts er-lan - - - - gen   B

No. 66

Komm, sü- - - sses Kreuz, komm, sü - - - - - - - sses Kreuz   C

No. 67

Der du den Tem-pel Got-tes zer-brichst, und bau - - est ihn in dreien Ta-gen   D

No. 70

Seh - - - - - - - - - - - - - - - - - - - et   E

No. 74

Am A-bend da es küh - le war, ward A-dams Fal-len of-fen-bar   F

No. 75

Ma-che dich, mein Her-ze, rein - - - ma-che dich, mein Her- ze rein, -   G

No. 78

Wir - - - se - tzen uns mit Thrä- - nen nie - - - der   H

SONGS

Bist du bei mir (Anna Magdalena Bach Notebook)

Bist du bei mir, geh' ich mit Freu-den zum Ster-ben und zu mei-ner Ruh'   I

Brich entzwei, mein armes Herze
(Schemelli Gesangbuch No. 6)

Brich ent-zwei, mein ar-mes Her- ze, mein ar-mes Her- ze, brich ent-zwei;   J

Dir, dir, Jehovah, will ich singen
(Schemelli No. 14)

Dir, dir, - - - Je- - ho-vah, will - - - ich sin- - - gen   K

Es ist vollbracht (Schemelli
No. 20)

Es - ist voll- bracht! Ver-giss ja nicht! Dies Wort, mein Herz, das Je-sus spricht   L

Gedenke doch, mein Geist,
zurücke (Anna Magdalena Bach
Notebook)

Ge - den - - - ke doch, mein - Geist, - zu- - - rü- cke an's Grab -   M

Gieb dich zufrieden (Anna Magdalena Bach Notebook)

Gieb dich zu-frie-den und sei stil- le in dem Got- te dei-nes Le- bens,   N

Ich halte treulich still (Schemelli
No. 30)

Ich hal-te - treu-lich still und lie-be - mei- nen - Gott,   O

Jesus, unser Trost und Leben
(Schemelli No. 39)

Je - - - sus, un- ser Trost - - - und Le- ben   P

Komm, süsser Tod (Schemelli
No. 42)

Komm, sü-sser Tod, Komm, sel'-ge Ruh! Komm und füh-re mich in Frie-de   Q

Kommt, Seelen, dieser Tag
(Schemelli No. 43)

Kommt, See- - - len, die-ser Tag - muss hei-lig sein be-sun- - - gen,   R

Liebster Herr Jesu, wo bleibst du
so lange (Schemelli No. 48)

Lieb- ster Herr Je- su, wo bleibst du so - lan- ge?   S

SONGS

Mein Jesu, was für Seelenweh
(Schemelli No. 51)

Mein___ Je-su,was für See-len-weh be-fällt dich in Get-se-ma——ne   A

O Jesulein süss, o Jesulein mild
(Schemelli No. 58)

O Je-su-lein süss, O Je-su-lein mild,dein's Va-ters Will'n hast du er-füllt   B

Qui Tollis, from Mass in A major

Qui tollis pec-ca-ta, qui tol-lis pec-ca-ta, pec-ca-ta mun-di   C

So oft ich meine Tabakspfeife
(Anna Magdalena Bach Note-book)

So oft ich mei——ne Ta——baks-pfei——fe mit gu-tem Kna——ster an-ge-füllt,   D

Willst du dein Herz mir schenken
(Aria di Giovanni) (Anna Magda-lena Bach Notebook)

Willst du dein Herz mir schen-ken, so fang' es___ heim-lich an,   E

BACH, Philipp Emanuel   (see also Bach, Carl Philipp Emanuel)

Bitten

Gott, dei——ne Gü——te reicht___ so weit   G

Lied

Ich___ ging un-ter Er-len am küh-li-gen Bach   H

Passionslied

Er-for——sche mich,___ er-fahr___ mein___ Herz,   I

BACH, Wilhelm Friedemann (1710-1784)

Kein Hälmlein wächst auf Erden

Kein Hälm-lein wächst auf Er-den, der Him-mel hat's be-taut   K

BACHELET, Alfred Georges (1864-1943)

Chère Nuit

Chè——re nuit___ aux clar-tés___ se-rei——nes,   M

BACKER-GRONDAHL, Agathe (1847-1907)

Mot Kveld, Op. 42, No. 7

Al-le de dugg-vaa-te blom-ster har sennt, So-len det siss-te God-nat   O

BALAKIREV, Mily Alexeivich (1837-1910)

Oh come to me!
Copyright 1911, G. Schirmer, Inc.

Oh come to me when breez-es stir the si-lent trees with lan-guid sigh-ing   Q

BALFE, Michael William (1808-1870)

Bohemian Girl (opera)

In the gyp-sy's life you read___ the life that all would like to lead___   S

Bohemian Girl (opera)

I dreamt that I dwelt__ in mar- ble halls, with vas-sals and serfs at my side,__ A

The heart bow'd down by weight of woe, to weak-est hopes__ will__ cling B

Then You'll Remember Me

When o- ther lips and o- ther__ hearts their tales of love shall tell C

Trav'llers All of Ev'ry Station, from The Siege of La Rochelle (opera)

Trav'l-lers all of ev'- ry sta- tion, Trav'l-lers all of ev'ry sta-tion draw long D

Come into the Garden, Maud

Come in- to the gar- den, Maud, For the black bat, Night has flown; E

Excelsior

The shades of night were fall-ing fast As thro' an Al- pine vil-lage passed__ F

Killarney

By Kil-lar- ney's__ lakes and fells, Em'- rald isles and__ wind- ing bays G

BANTOCK, Sir Granville (1868-1946)

A Feast of Lanterns
By permission of Galaxy Music Corporation, N. Y., Copyright by Elkin & Co., Ltd.

In spring for sheer de-light I set the lan-terns swing-ing through the trees I

The Parting
(Words by Ross)
Copyright by G. Ricordi & Co., Inc.

Oh he cam' whist-lin' up the glen,__ And, smi-lin' I gaed doon to meet him;__ J

BARBER, Samuel (1910-   )

The Daisies, Op. 2, No. 1
Copyright 1936, G. Schirmer, Inc.

In the scent- ed bud of the morn- ing O, when the wind- y grass L

I hear an army, Op. 10, No. 3
Copyright 1939, G. Schirmer, Inc.

I__ hear__ an__ ar- my charg-ing up- on the land M

A Nun Takes the Veil, Op. 13, No. 1
Copyright 1941, G. Schirmer, Inc.

I have de-sired to go where springs not fail N

Sleep now, Op. 10, No. 2
Copyright 1939, G. Schirmer, Inc.

Sleep now, O sleep now O you un- qui- et heart! O

Sure on this shining night, Op. 13, No. 3
Copyright 1941, G. Schirmer, Inc.

Sure on this shin- ing night of star-made shad- ows round, P

With rue my heart is laden, Op. 2, No. 2
Copyright 1936, G. Schirmer, Inc.

With rue my heart is lad- en for gol-den friends I had Q

BARLOW, S. M. L. (1892-   )

The Cherry
Copyright by G. Ricordi & Co., Inc.

Jo- seph was an old man, an__ old man__ was he; S

BARNABY, Sir Joseph (1838-1892)

Sweet and low

Sweet and low, sweet and low, wind of the wes- tern sea

BARTLET, John (17th cent.)

Of all the birds that I do know

Of all the birds that I do know, Phil- ip my spar- row hath no peer

BARTLETT, James Carroll (1850-1929)

A Dream
Copyright by Oliver Ditson Co.
Used by permission.

Last night I was dream- ing of thee, love, was dream- ing,

BARTÓK, Béla (1881-1945)

Hungarian Folksong Settings
A gyulai kert alatt
By permission Boosey & Hawkes, Inc.,
copyright owners

A gyu- la- i kert a-latt, kert a- latt Bar-na le-gény roz-ma-rin- got a- rat

Által mennék én a Tiszán

Ál-tal-men-nék én a Ti-szán la- di-kon, la- di-kon, de la- di- kon,

Aszszonyok, Aszszonyok

Asz- szo-nyok, asz- szo- nyok, had' le- gyek tár- sa- tok,

Elindultam szép hazámbul

El- in-dul-tam szép ha- zám- bul, Hi- res kis ma-gyar- or- szág- bul.

Feketeföd
one theme

Fe- ke- te föd, fe- hér az én zseb- ken - - - - döm

El- ha- gyott a leg- ked- ve- sebb sze- re- töm

Ha kimegyek arr' a magas tetőre

Ha- ki- me-gyek arr' a ma-gas te- tő- re Ta-lá-lok én sze-re-tő-re ket-tő-re.

Istenem, Istenem
one theme

Is- te-nem, Is- te- nem á-raszd meg a vi- zet Had' vi-gyen el en- gem

a pám- ka- pu já- ra;

Nem meszsze van ide kis Margitta

Nem mesz- sze van i- de kis Mar- git-ta, Hor-to-bágy-nak vi-ze kö-rül foly-ja.

Töltek a nagy erdő útját

Töl-tik a nagy er-dő út- - - - - ját, Vi-szik a szé- kely ka- to- - - - - nát

Vévig mentem a tárkányi sej, haj

Vé- vig men- tem a tár- ká- nyi sej, haj, nagy uc- cán;

32
BATESON, Thomas (1570-1630)

Cupid in a bed of roses

Cu- pid in a bed of Ro- ses in a bed of Ro- ses

Have I found her

Have I found her? have I found her O rich find- ing

BAX, Sir Arnold (1883-1953)

A Christmas Carol
By permission J. & W. Chester, Ltd.,
London, copyright owners

There is no rose of such vir- tue As__ is the rose_____ that bore

Cradle Song

I heard a Piper Piping
By permission Oxford Univ. Press,
London, copyright owners

I heard a pi-per pi- ping the blue__ hills a- mong_____

Mater ora filium (unacc. double choir)

The White Peace
By permission J. & W. Chester, Ltd.,
London, copyright owners

It lies not on the sun- lit hill__ Nor__ on the sun-lit plain:

BAYLY, Anselm (1719-1794)

Long, long ago

Tell me the tales that to me were so dear, Long, long a- go, Long, long a-go

BEACH, Mrs. H. H. A. (1867-1944)

Ah, Love, But a Day
Copyright by Arthur P. Schmidt Co., Boston
Used by permission.

Ah, Love but a day____ And the world has changed! __

The Year's at the Spring, Op. 44, No. 1
Copyright by Arthur P. Schmidt Co., Boston
Used by permission.

The year's__at the spring,__ And day's__at the morn;__ Morn-ing's__at sev-en,

BECKER, Reinhold (1842-1924)

Frühlingszeit

Wenn der Früh- ling auf die Ber-- ge steigt

BEETHOVEN, Ludwig van (1770-1827)

**Fidelio, Op. 72 (Opera)
Act I, No. 2**

O wär' ich schon mit dir, vereint, und dürf- te mann, dich nen-nen!

No. 3 (Quartet)

Mir ist so wun- der-bar, es engt das Herz mir ein;

BEETHOVEN
Missa Solemnis, Op. 123
III Credo

B

Con sub-stan-ti- a- lem pa-tri per quem om-ni-a fac-ta sunt,

C

Et in-car-na- tus est de spi-ri-tu sanc-to ex Ma-ri-a vir-gi-ne,

D

Et vi- tam ven-tu- ri sae - - - - cu-li, a - - - - men, a - -men,

IV Sanctus

A

Sanc- - tus__ Do-mi-nus, Do-mi-nus De-us Sa- - ba-oth,

B

Ple- ni sunt coe- li et ter-ra glo - - - - - - - - - ri-a tu- a

O- sa-na, O- sa-na in ex-cel - - - - -sis, O- sa-na, O- sa-na

V Benedictus

Be- ne-dic - - - -tus, qui__ ve- - nit, qui ve-nit in no-mi-ne Do-mi-ni,

VI Agnus Dei

A

Ag - - -nus, ag-nus De-i qui tol-lis pec-ca-ta, pec-ca-ta, pec-ca-ta mun-di,

B

Do- - - - - na no- bis pa - - - - - - -cem,

C

pa- - cem, pa - - - - - - - - - - - - - - - - - - - cem,

D

Do - - - - na no- - -bis pa - - - - - - - - - - - -cem

Mount of Olives, Op. 85 (oratorio)
I

Mei-ne See- le ist er- schüt-tert von den Qua-len, von den Qua-len, die_ mir_

II

A

Preist, preist des Er-lö-sers__ Gü- te, preist, Men-schen,_ sei-ne_ Huld

B

O Heil euch, heil euch, ihr_____ Er- lö-sten!

III

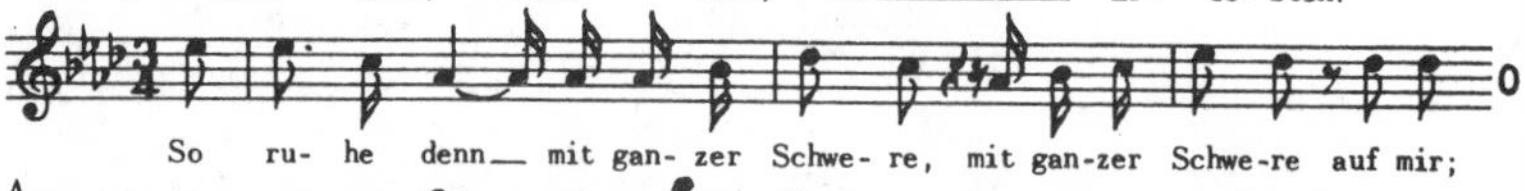

So ru- he denn__ mit gan-zer Schwe-re, mit gan-zer Schwe-re auf mir;

VI

A

In mei-nen A- dern wüh- len ge-rech-ter Zorn und Wuth

(Chorus) B

Auf, auf! er-grei-fet den Ver- rä-ther, wei-let hier nun län-ger__ nicht!

(Chorus) C

Wel- ten sin- gen, Wel- ten sin-gen, Wel- ten sin-gen Dank und Eh-re

(Chorus) D

Prei-set ihn, ihr En- gel-chö- re,_ laut im heil'- gen Ju-bel- ton,

SONGS:
Abendlied — A

Wenn die Son- ne nie-der- sin-ket, und der Tag zur Ruh' sich neigt

Adelaide, Op. 46 — B

Ein-sam wan- delt dein Freund im Früh-lings-gar-ten, mild von lieb-lich-en

Ah! Perfido, Op. 65 (Aria) — C

Per pie- tà, non dir- miad-di- o, non dir - - - - miad-di- o,

— D

Di- te voi, se in tan- to af-fan-no non_ son_ de- gna_ di_pie- tà?_

Andenken — E

Ich den- ke dein,_ wenn durch den Hain der Nach-ti-gal-len Ak- kor - - de schallen

An die ferne Geliebte, Op. 98, No. 1 — F

Auf dem Hü- gel sitz' ich, spä- hend in das blau-e Ne- bel-land

No. 2 — G

Wo die Ber- ge so blau aus dem ne - - bli-gen Grau schau-en her- ein,

No. 3 — H

Leich- te Seg- ler in den Hö- hen, und du Bäch-lein klein und schmal

No. 4 — I

Die- se Wol- ken in den Hö- hen, die-ser Vög-lein munt' rer Zug

No. 5 — J

Es keh-ret der Mai-en, es blü-het die Au'. Die Lüf-te, sie we-hen so mil-de, so lau,

No. 6 — K

Nimm sie_ hin denn, die- se Lie-der, die ich dir, Ge- lieb- te, sang,_

An die Geliebte — L

O dass ich dir vom stil-len Au- ge in sei-nem lie- be-vol-len Schein,

An die Hoffnung, Op. 32 — M

Die du so gern in heil'gen Näch- ten fei-erst und sanft und weich

Aus Goethe's Faust, Op. 75, No. 3 — N

Es war ein-mal ein Kö- nig, der hatt' ei- nen gros- sen Floh,

Clärchen's Song, from Egmont, Op. 84 — O

Die Trom- mel ge- rüh- ret! Das Pfeif- chen ge- spielt!

Freudvoll und leidvoll — P

Freud- voll und leid- voll, ge- dan- ken-voll sein;

Das Geheimniss — Q

Wo bluht das Blüm-chen, das nie ver-blüht? Wo strahlt das Stern- lein,

Gellert Lieder, Op. 48, No. 1 Bitten — R

Gott, dei- ne Gü- te reicht- so weit, so weit die Wol- ken ge- hen

No. 2 Die Liebe des Nächsten — S

So Je-mand spricht: Ich lie- be Gott!_ und hasst doch sei-ne Brü- der,

BEETHOVEN

SONGS: Gellert Lieder, Op. 48,
No. 3 Vom Tode

Mei- ne Le- bens-zeit ver-streicht, stünd-lich eil' ich zu dem Gra- be, A

No. 4 Die Ehre Gottes aus der Natur

Die Him-mel rüh-men des E- wi-gen Eh- re, ihr Schall pflanzt seinen Na-men_ fort B

No. 5 Gottes Macht und Vorse-hung

Gott ist mein Lied! Er ist der Gott der Stär- ke C

No. 6 Busslied

An dir al-lein, an dir hab' ich ge- sün-digt und ü- bel oft vor dir ge-than_ D

Ich liebe dich

Ich lie- be dich, so wie du mich, am A- bend und am Mor- gen, E

In questa tomba oscura

In que- sta tom- ba o- scu- ra la- scia-mi ri- po-sar; F

Irish Songs (voice and pianoforte trio)
The British Light Dragoons

'Twas a mar- e-chal of France, and he fain would hon- our gain, G

Morning a Cruel Turmoiler Is

Mor-ning a cru- el tur-moil-er is, ban-ish-ing ease and re-pose H

The Morning Air Plays on my Face

The morn- ing air_ plays on_ my face and, through_the gray mist peer- ing I

O Harp of Erin

O harp_ of E- rin thou art now_ laid low, J

O might I but my Patrick love

O might I but my Pat-rick love! My moth- er scolds se- vere- ly K

Oh! Who, my dear Dermot

Oh! who, my dear_ Der- mot, has dared to de- ceive thee, L

Once More I Hail Thee

Once more I_ hail thee, thou_ gloom- y De- cem- ber M

On the Massacre of Glencoe

Oh! tell me, Har-per, where-fore_flow_ thy way-ward notes of wail and woe N

The Pulse of an Irishman

The pulse of an I- rish- man ev- er beats quick-er,when war is the sto- ry O

The Return to Ulster

Once a- gain, but how_ chang'd, since my wan- d'rings be- gan P

Sad and Luckless Was the Season

Sad and luck-less was the sea-son, when to court fair_ El- len flew, Q

The Soldier

Then, Sol- dier!come_fill_ high the wine for we reck not of_ to- mor- row R

The Soldier in a Foreign Land

The_ pip- er who sat_ on his low_ mos- sy seat S

37

BEETHOVEN

SONGS:

Scotch Songs, Op. 108 (voice and
pianoforte trio)
No. 24. Again my Lyre

A- gain, my Lyre, yet once a- gain, with tears I wake — A

Welsh Songs: The Cottage Maid

I en- vy not the splen-dour fine that glit-ters in Sir Wat- kyn's hall; — B

Der Wachtelschlag

Horch, wie schallt's dor-ten so lieb-lich her-vor! Fürch- te Gott! — C

Wonne der Wehmut, Op. 83, No. 1

Trocknet nicht, trocknet nicht Thrä-nen der e-wi-gen Lie- be! — D

Symphony No. 9, "Choral", Op. 125: A
Finale

Freu- de schö-ner Göt-ter- fun- ken, Toch- ter aus E- ly- si-um — E

B

Seid um- schlun-gen, Mil- li- o-nen! Die-sen Kuss der gan- zen Welt! — F

C

Freu- - - - - - - de, Toch- ter aus E- ly- si- um — G

BELLINI, Vincenzo (1801-1835)

Norma (Opera) Act 1 A

I- te sul col- le O Dru- i-de i- te a spiar ne' cie - - - — I

B

Dell' au- ra tua pro- fe- ti- ca, ter- ri- bil Dio l'in- for- ma. — J

Me- co all'al-tar di ve- ne- re e- ra Adal- gi- sa in' Ro- ma — K

Ca - - - - - - sta Di - - va ca-sta Di va- che i nar-gen - - - - ti — L

Ah! bel- lo a me ri- tor- na del fi- do amor pri- mie - - - ro — M

No. 6 Duet

Ah! si fa co- re e ab- brac- cia mi — N

Act II

Mira o Nor- ma, a tuoi gi-noc- chi que-sti ca- ri tuoi pargo- let- ti — O

Si fi- ne all' o- re all' o- re e- stre- me com- pag-na tu- a — P

Ah! del Te- bro al gio- go in- de- gno frem- o io pu- re fremo — Q

Guer- ra, guer- ra le Gal- li-che sel- ve quan- te han quer- ce — R

Deh! non vo- ler- li vit- ti- me del mio fa- ta- le er- ro- re — S

40

BELLMAN, Carl Michael (1740-1795)

Blasen nu alla (Ulla's Trip to the Deer Park) (Fredmans Epistel No. 25)

Blow one and all, hear the thun-der's call, and the surg-ing sea;   B

Fjäriln vingad syns pa Haga (Butterflies at Haga) (Fredmans Sang No. 64)

But-ter-flies at Ha-ga soar-ing, Through the fog and dew-y___ mists,   C

Hör klokorna med ängsligt dan (Fredmans Sang No. 6)

Hör Kloc-kor-na med äng-sligt dan nu ringa för en Bacchi son   D

Joachim uti Babylon (Joachim at Babylon) (Fredmans Sang No. 41)

Jo-a-chim___ of___ Ba-by-lon, Had a wife Su-san-na,   E

Sa lunka vi sa smaningom (Fredmans Sang No. 21)

Sa lun-ka vi sa smaning-om fran bacchi buller ach tu-mult   F

Ulla min Ulla (The Little Fishing Town) (Fredmans Epistel No. 71)

Ul-la, my Ul-la, say, do you like my of-fer of straw-ber-ries   G

Villa vid denna Källa (Fredman's Farewell to Ulla) (Fredmans Epistel No. 82)

Come, love,___ and rest a while now,___ our break-fast we shall spread 'neath leaf-y   H

BEMBERG, Henri (1859-1931)

Un Ange est venu

Un ange est ve-nu_____ dans ma so-li-tu-de   J

Chant Hindou

Brahma,— Dieu des croy-ants,_____ Maî-tre des ci-tés sain-tes   K

Il a quit-té ce mon-de, m'ai-mant quand je l'ai-mais   L

Chant Vénitién

Le vent souf-fle et no-tre gon-do-le Sur l'eau s'en-vo-le   M

Il Neige

Il nei-ge, il nei-ge De gros flo-cons com-me du co-ton   N

Nymphes et Sylvains

L'air est lé-ger, la bri-se est pu-re,— un frais par-fum   O

Mar-quez___ la___ dan-se Bien en-ca-den-ce   P

BENEDICT, Sir Julius (1804-1885)

The Lily of Killarney (opera): Eily Mavourneen

Ei-ly Ma-vour-neen, I see thee be-fore me, fair-er than ev-er   R

Act I Duet

The moon has rais'd her lamp a-bove to light the way to thee,   S

La Capinera (The Wren)

Col ri- tor- nar___ Del dol ce a-pril___ Tu tor- ni pur,

Carnevale di Venezia (Carnival of Venice)

O me be- a- - - ta Ri- tor- na in Ciel. l'al-bo- re

La bru- na gon- do- let- ta ap- pres- ta o Bar- ca- rol

The Gypsy and the Bird

A gyp- sy roam- ing through the mead- ows,___ Spied a lin-net

BENJAMIN, Arthur (1893-1960)

Calm sea and mist

The slow___ heave of the sleep-ing sea, with pulse like mo-tion swells and falls

Hedgerow
Copyright 1925, Arthur Benjamin

The win- try winds are white; the wind seems fro- zen

The Wasp
Copyright 1925, Arthur Benjamin

Where the ripe pears droop heav- i- ly The yel- low wasp hums loud and long

BENNET, John (16th-17th cent.)

All Creatures Now

All crea- tures now are mer- ry. mer- ry, mer- ry mind- ed

Thyrsis, sleepest thou?

Thyr- sis, sleep- est thou? sleep-est thou? sleep-est thou? sleep-est thou

BERCHEM, Jachet Van (16th Cent.)

O Jesu Christe

O___ Je- su Chris- te, mi- se- re- re me- i, quum do- lo- re___

BERG, Alban (1885-1935)

Sieben frühe Lieder 1. Nacht
By permission Associated Music Publishers, Inc.

Däm- mern Wol- ken ü- ber Nacht und Thal

2. Schilflied

Auf ge- hei- men Wal- des- pfa- de schleich ich gern im A- - -bend-schein

3. Die Nachtigall

Das macht, es hat die Nach- ti- gall die gan- ze Nacht ge- sun- gen;

4. Traumgekrönt

Das war der Tag der wei- ssen Chry- san- the- men,

5. Im Zimmer

Herbst-son-nen-schein___ Der lie- be A-bend blickt so still her- ein

Sieben frühe Lieder
6. Liebesode

Im Arm der Lie- be schlie- fen wir se- lig ein____ A

7. Sommertage

Nun zie- hen Ta- ge ü- ber die Welt,____ B

Wozzeck (opera) Op. 7
(Three selections) I
By permission Associated Music
Publishers, Inc.

Sol- da- ten, Sol- da- ten sind schö- ne Bur- - - - schen C

II

Han-sel spann dei- ne sechs Schimmel an, Gib sie zu fressen auf's neu D

III

Rin- gel, Rin- gel Ro- sen- krantz, Rin- - - - - - - gel-reihn! E

BERLIOZ, Hector (1803-1869)

L'Enfance du Christ, Op. 25 (oratorio)
Part I. O misère des Rois

O mi- sè- re des Rois! Ré- gner____ et ne pas vi- vre! G

Part II. L'Adieu des Bergers

Il s'en va loin de__ la ter- re Où dans l'é- table il vit__ le jour H

Le Repos de la Sainte Famille

Les Pé- le- rins é-tant ve- nus En un lieu de bel- le ap-pa-ren- ce I

Les Nuits d'Été, Op. 7 (Songs)
No. 1 Villanelle

Quand vien-dra la sai- son nou- vel- le, Quand au- ront dis- pa- ru J

No. 2 Le Spectre de la Rose

Sou- le- ve ta pau- piè- re clo- se Qu'effleu- re un son- ge K

No. 4 L'Absence

Re-viens, re- viens__ ma bien ai- mé- e - - comme un-e fleur__ L

La Damnation de Faust, Op. 24 (opera)
Part II. Chanson de la Puce

U- ne pu- ce gen- til- le chez un prin- ce lo- geait M

Air de Roses

Voi-ci des ro-ses de cet-te nuit é- clo- ses, Sur__ ce lit en-bau-mé N

Part III.

Au- tre-fois un roi de Thu- lé Qui jusqu'au tom-beau fut fi- dè- le O

Mer- ci, doux cré- pus- cu- le! Oh! sois le bien-ve- nu! P

Sérénade de Méphistophélès

De- vant la mai- son De ce- lui__ qui t'a- do- - - - - re, Q

Part IV. Romance

D'a- mour l'arden- te flam- me Con- su- me__ mes beaux jours. R

Invocation à la nature

Na- ture im- men- se, in- pénétrable et fiè- re S

Les Troyens (Opera)
Act III. Scene I
Chers Ty- ri- ens,   tant de no- bles tra- vaux___

Act V. Scene II
A- dieu fiè- re ci- té   qu'un gé- né-reux ef- fort

I- nu- ti- les re-grets   je dois quitter Car-tha- ge

En un der- nier nau- fra- ge   Ah! puis- se___ je pé- rir

Requiem
1. Requiem aeternam
Re- qui- em___ ae- ter- - - - nam, re- qui- em aeter-nam do- na e- is,

Te de- cet hym- nus, De- us in___ Si- on,

2. Dies Irae
Di- es i- rae, di- es il- la, sol- vet sae- clum,

Et ___ i- te- rum___ ven- tu- rus est cum glo- ri- a

3. Quid sum miser
Quid ___ sum___ mi- ser   tunc dic- tu- - - - rus

4. Rex tremendae
Rex! Rex!   O rex tremendae ma- jes- ta-tis, rex tremendae ma- jes- ta- tis

5. Quaerens me
Quaerens me se- dis- ti las- - - sus quae- rens me,

6. Lacrymosa
La- - - - - - cry- mo- sa di- es il- - - - - - la,

7. Offertorium
Do- - - mi- ne,   Do- - - mi- ne Je- su Chris-te!

Accompaniment

9. Sanctus
Sanc- tus,   Sanc- tus,   Sanc- tus, Sanc- tus,

Ho- san- na in ex- cel- sis, ho- san- na in ex- cel- sis,

10. Agnus dei
Ag- nus de- i, qui tol-lis pec-ca-ta mun- di,   do- na e- is___

BERNARD, Paul (1827-1879)

Ça fait peur aux oiseaux
Ne par- lez pas tant, Li- san- dre, Quand nous ten-dons nos fi- lets;

BEYDTS, Louis (1895-)

C'est moi
Copyright 1944, Pierre Noel, Paris

Si ta marche at-tris- té- e   S'é-gare au fond d'un bois,___

Un cri

Hi- ron-delle, hi-ron-delle, Hi-ron-delle! Est-il au monde un coeur fi-dè- le?

En Arles
By permission Durand & Cie, Paris;
Elkan-Vogel Co., Inc., Phila.,
copyright owners

Dans Arle, où sont les A- lis-cams, Quand l'ombre est rou- ge

Theme in accompaniment (popular Fr. theme)

La Lyre et les Amours (Song Cycle)
No. 1 Le Bracelet
By permission Heugel & Cie, Paris,
copyright owners

A- mour en soit bé- ni!___   Le su-jet de mes voeux

No. 3 La belle esclave More

Beau mons- tre de na- tu- re, il est vrai, ton vi-sage est noir

No. 4 Les Baisers de Dorinde

La douce ha- lei-ne des zé- phirs   Et ces eaux qui se pré- ci- pi-tent

BILLINGS, William (1746-1800)

Chester

Let ty- rants shake their i- ron___ rod And slav- 'ry clank___

The dying Christian's last farewell

My friends, I am go-ing a- long jour-ney, nev- er___ to re-turn

Judea

A Vir- gin un- spot- ted by Proph- et fore-told

New Plymouth

O Lord our fa- thers oft have told, In___ our at- ten- tive ears___

Psalms and Fuguing Tunes:
Be Glad then, America

Be glad then A- mer- i- ca, be glad then A- mer-i-ca, shout, shout, shout

Creation

When I with___ pleas-ing won- der stand, and all___ my frame___ sur-vey,

When Jesus wept

When Je- sus wept___ the fall- ing tear in mer- cy flowed___ be-yond

The Shepherd's Carol (Shiloh)

Me- thinks I see an heav'n- ly Host of___ an-gels on the wing;

Let all___ your fears___ be ban- ished hence, Glad tid-ings I pro- claim,___

BIMBONI, Alberto (1882-)

Sospiri miei
By permission Galaxy Music Corporation, N. Y.

So- spi- ri mie- i an- da- te o- ve vi man- do   A

BINCHOIS, Gilles (1400-1460)

A Solis Ortu Cardine (motet)

A so- lis or- - - tu car- - - di- - - ne   C

De Plus en Plus (rondeau)

De plus en plus se re- nou- - - - vel- le   D

Files a marier

Fi- les a ma- ri- er, ne vous ma- ri- ez ja ne vous ma- ri- ez ja,   E

Inter Natos Mulierum

In-   F

Je loe amours

Je loe a- mours et ma- da- me mer- cy- - - - - - - - - e   G

Sanctus

San- - - - - - - - - ctus San- - - - - - - - ctus Do- mi- nus   H

BISHOP, Sir Henry (1786-1855)

Bid me discourse

Bid me dis- course I will en- chant thine ear   J

The Dashing White Sergeant

If I had a beau, for a sol- dier who'd go,   K

Echo Song (arr. Frank LaForge)
Copyright 1940, G. Schirmer, Inc.

Some spir- it seems - - - - to play, Some spir- it seems to play!   L

Still I hear the change- ful strain   M

Home Sweet Home, from Clari, or the Maid of Milan (opera)

Mid plea- sures and pal- a- ces, Though we may roam,   N

Lo, Here the Gentle Lark

Lo here the gen- tle lark wea- ry of rest   O

Love has eyes

Love's blind they say, O nev- er, nay Can words love's grace im- part   P

My Pretty Jane (The Bloom is on the Rye)

My pret- ty Jane, my pret- ty Jane - - - - Ah! nev- er, never look so shy   Q

Pretty Mocking Bird

Liv- - - ing e- - - - cho, liv- ing e- cho, bird of eve,   R

Pret- ty mock- ing bird, pret- ty mock- ing bird, pret- ty pret- ty, pret- ty   S

Should he upbraid

Should he up- braid, I'll own that he pre- vail___

BIZET, Georges (1838-1875)

Carmen (opera) Act I

Sur la pla- ce Cha-cun pas- se, Cha- cun vient, cha- cun va,___

Children's Chorus

A- vec la gar- de mon- tante,__ Nous ar- ri-vons, Nous voi- là!

Chorus of Cigarette Girls

Dans__ l'air_ nous sui- vons des yeux La fu- mé- e, La fu- mé- e

Habanera

L'a-mour est un oi- seau re- bel-le Que nul ne peut__ ap- pri-voi- ser.

L'a-mour est en- fant de Bo- hême, Il n'a ja- mais, ja-mais con-nu de loi.

Parle moi de ma mère (Duet Soprano and Tenor)

Tu vas, m'a- t- elle dit t'en al- ler a la vil- le:

Et__ tu lui di-rás que sa mè- re Songe nuit et jour___

Ma mè- re je la vois! Oui, je re- vois__ mon vil- la- ge

Seguidille

Pres des ram- parts de Sé- vil - - - - - - le,

Act II Chanson Bohème

Les tring-les des sistres tin- taient___ A- vec un é- clat

Toreador Song

Vo- tre toast je peux vous le ren- dre, Se- ñors, se- ñors__

To- ré- a- dor,__ en gar- de!__ To- ré- a- dor__

Quintet

Nous a- vons en tête une af- fai - - - - - - re.

Quand il s'a- git de trom- pe- ri-e, De du- pe- ri-e,

Carmen's Dance

La - - - - - la, la - - - - la__ La - - - - - - la, la - - la

Flower Song

La fleur que vous m'avais je- té- e, Dans ma prison___

Là- bas, là- bas dans la mon- ta- gne, Là- bas, là- bas

Songs:
Ouvre ton coeur (Spanish Serenade)

La Mar- gue-rite_____ a fer- mé sa co- rol - - - le

Pastorale

Un jour de prin-temps_____ Tout le long d'un ver-ger_____

Vieille Chanson

Dans les bois l'a-mou-reux Myr- til A-vait pris fau- vet- te lé- gè- re

BLAND, James A. (1854-1911)

Carry me back to old Virginny
Copyright by E. B. Marks
Music Corp., N. Y.

Car- ry me back to old Vir-gin- ny There's where the cot- ton

BLANGINI, F. (1781-1841)

Care pupille

Ca- re_____ pu- pil- le tra mil- le e mil_____

Per valli, per boschi

Per val- li, per bo- schi cer- can-do di ni- ce sol l'- co

BLOCH, Ernest (1880-1959)

Poèmes d'Automne
I. La Vagabonde
Copyright 1918, G. Schirmer, Inc.

Elle a pas- sé dans le vent d'au-tom-ne El- le che- mi-nait

II. Le Déclin

Dans le ver- ger pai- si- ble, bor- dé là- bas de peu-pli-ers

III. L'abri

J'é- cou- te la voix de mon rêve Pour al-ler à toi,

IV. Invocation

Les co- lon-nes du tem- ple s'a- ni- ment d'u-ne pa-leur plus chaude

Psalms
No. 22 (baritone and orchestra)
Copyright 1919, G. Schirmer, Inc.

E- lo-him! E- lo-him!___ Why hast thou thus for-sa- ken me?

No. 114

Snatched a- way by Jah- veh_____ from the land where they served_____

No. 137

Re-clined_ by the wa-ters of Ba- bel,_ Our harps were hung up-on the wil-lows

BLOW, John (1649-1708)

The Self Banished

It is not that_____ I love you less,— Than when_____ be- fore

BOATNER, Edward (1897-   )

Oh, What a beautiful city! (arr.)

Oh, what a beau- ti- ful ci- ty, Oh, what a beau- ti- ful ci- ty   **A**

BODENSCHATZ, Erhard (1576-1636)

Joseph, lieber Joseph mein (14th century German traditional Christmas song)

Jo-seph, lie-ber Jo-seph mein, hilf mir wie-gen mein Kin- de-lein,   **C**

BÖHM, Karl (1844-1920)

Still wie die Nacht, Op. 326, No. 27
By permission Associated Music Publishers, Inc.

Still wie die Nacht, tief wie das Meer,___ soll dei-ne Lie- be sein!___   **E**

Was i hab

Schö- ne Lied- le, ja die kenn i grad' drei an der Zahl   **F**

BOIELDIEU, François (1775-1834)

La Dame Blanche (Opera) Act I

Ah quel plai-sir d'ê- tre sol- dat.___ Ah quel plai-sir d'ê- tre sol- dat   **H**

Act II

Dé- jà la___ nuit, dé- jà la nuit plus som- bre sur nous ré- pand,   **I**

Viens gen-til- le da - - - me, viens___ gen-til- le da - - me,   **J**

Act III Song of Georges Brown (Reverie)

Al- lons___ gai- ment___ re- ce-vons leur hom-ma- ge de mon nou-vel é- tat   **K**

BOITO, Arrigo (1842-1918)

Mefistofele (opera) Prologue
Copyright by G. Ricordi & Co., Inc.

1   A- ve Si- gnor,_____ si- gnor de-gli an- ge- - - li   **M**

2   Sal- ve Re- gi- na! s'in-nal- zi un e- co dal mon-do cie-co   **N**

Il bel gio-va- net- to sen vie-ne al- la fes-ta   **O**

Da- i cam- pi, da-i pra-ti che in-non-da___ la___ not-te,   **P**

Act I

Son___ lo Spi- ri-to___ che ne-ga sem- pre tut- to; l'a-stro il fior   **Q**

(Duet) A

Se tu mi do- ni un' o- ra di ri- po- so,   **R**

B

Fin da sta not- te, fin da sta not- te nel-l'or-gie ghiotte del mio mes-ser   **S**

Mefistofele (opera)
Act II Scene I Garden Scene

Ca- va- lie-ro_il- lus-tre_e sag-gio, co- me mai vi può_al- le- tar

Scene II

Sta ben al nu- bi- le cor- rer gio-con-do,_in trac-cia d'i- la- ri venture

Act III

Rid- dia-mo, rid-dia-mo! che_il mon-do_è ca-du- to! Rid-dia-mo, rid- dia-mo!

(Duet)

L al- tra not- te_in fon-do_al ma- re il mio bim- bo han-no git-ta-to

Lon- ta- no, lon-ta-no, lon-ta- no, sui flut-ti d'un am-pio oce-à-no

Spun- ta' l'au-ro- ra pal-li-do, l'ul- ti-mo di già vie - - - ne

Act IV

For- ma ide- al pu- ris- si- ma del - - - la bel- lez-za_e- ter- na!

A- mo-re! mi- ste - - rio ce- leste pro-fon- do! già_il tempo di-le-gua

Epilogue

Guin- to sol pas- so_es-tre- mo del-la più_es-tre- ma e- tà,

Nerone (opera)   Act I
Copyright by G. Ricordi & Co., Inc.

A not-te cu- pa, quan- do ne-gli_an-tri del fu- ne - - reo suol

Act II

Ecco il ma- gi- co spec-chio in cui ri- fran-ge sua luce_a- stral___

Act III

Vi- ve-te_in pa- ce_in con-cen- to so- a - - - ve d'a-mor,

BOND, Carrie Jacobs (1862-1946)

I love you truly
Copyright by Boston Music Co.

I love you tru- ly, tru- ly, dear, Life with its sor- row

Just A-Wearyin' For You
Copyright by Boston Music Co.

Just a wear-y- in' for you, All the time a- feel- in' blue,

A Perfect Day
Copyright by Boston Music Co.

When you come to the end of a per-fect day and you sit a- lone

BORDES, Charles (1863-1909)

Dansons la gigue
By permission J. Hamelle Music
Publishers, Paris

Dan-sons la gi- gue J'ai-mais sur-tout ses jo- lis yeux

BORODIN, Alexander (1833-1887)

BORODIN

SONGS: The Sleeping Princess

Hush! Hush! with love- ly eyes Closed in sleep, the Prin- cess lies,

Song of the Dark Forest

Thro' the for- est's— moan, thro' the for- est's— sigh

BORTNIANSKY, D. S. (1751-1825)

Cherubim Song

Let— us, who fig - - - - ure forth— the Cher- u- bim,

Cherubim Song (No. 7)

Like— a choir of— an- gels glo - - - rious gath-'ring soft- ly

BOUGHTON, Rutland (1878-1960)

Faery Song, from The Immortal Hour (opera)
Copyright by Stainer & Bell, Ltd., London;
Galaxy Music Corporation, N. Y.,
U. S. Agents

How beau- ti-ful they are,— The lord-ly ones— Who dwell in the hills—

BOURGAULT-DUCOUDRAY, L. A. (1840-1910)

Chansons de Basse-Bretagne: L'Angelus

La clo- che son- ne l'an- gé- lus— La terre a donc un jour— de plus.

Dimanche à l'aube

Di- manche à l'aube, en me le- vant, Ho- ren drenn drenn Ho- la

Silvestrik

Saint Mi- chel en Grè- ve mon fils est- en- ga- gé—

BOURGEOIS, Louis (1510-1561)

Old Hundred

Praise God from whom all bless-ings flow, praise Him all creatures here be- low,

BOYCE, William (1711-1779)

The Song of Momus to Mars

Thy sword with- in the Scabbard keep, and let Man- kind— a- gree;

Tell me, lovely shepherd

Tell— me love- ly— shep- herd where, where, tell— me where thou feed'st

BRAGA, Gaetano (1829-1907)

Angel's Serenade

What sounds are those that wak- en me, Sweet ac- cents low and ten- der,

(Violin obbligato to above solo)

(violin obligato to above solo)

BRAHAM, John (1774-1856)

The Death of Nelson

O'er Nel-son's tomb with si-lent grief op-prest Bri-tan-nia mourns

'Twas— in Tra-fal-gar's bay we saw the foe-men lay

BRAHE, May H. (-1956)

Bless this House
By permission Boosey & Hawkes, Inc.,
copyright owners

Bless this house, O Lord we pray Make it safe by night and day

Down Here
By permission Boosey & Hawkes, Inc.,
copyright owners

Oh! it's quiet down here, yes as quiet as a mouse,

BRAHMS, Johannes (1833-1897)

Chorus and Solo Quartet: Songs for Women's Chorus, 2 Horns and Harp, Op. 17
No. 1. Es tönt ein voller Harfen-klang

Es tönt ein vol-ler Har-fen-klang,den Lieb und Sehn-sucht schwel-len

No. 2. Lied von Shakespeare (Come away, death!)

Komm her-bei, Komm her-bei, Tod! Und ver-senk in Cy-pres-sen

No. 3. Der Gärtner

Wo-hin ich geh und schau-e, in Feld und Wald und Tal,——

No. 4. Gesang aus Fingal

Wein' an den Fel-sen der brau-sen-den Win-de, wei-ne, O Mäd-chen

Der Gang zum Liebchen, Op. 31, No. 3 (Quartet)

Es glänzt der Mond nie-der, Ich soll-te doch wie-der

Ein Deutsches Requiem, Op. 45 (A German Requiem) No. 1

Se-lig sind, Se-lig sind, die da Leid tra-gen,

No. 2

Denn al-les Fleisch es ist wie Gras und al-les Herr-lich-keit

So seid nun ge-dul-dig, lie---ben Brü-der,

Die Er-lö-se-ten des Herrn wer-den wie-der kom-men

No. 3

Herr, leh-re doch mich, dass ein En--de mit mir ha-ben muss,

Der Ge-recht-en See-len sind— in— Got-tes Hand

No. 4

Wie lieb-lich sind dei-ne Woh-nun-gen, Herr Ze - - - - - ba-oth,

BRAHMS

Ein Deutsches Requiem, Op. 45 (A German Requiem)

No. 4

Wie lieb - - - - - - - - - lich sind dei - - ne Woh - nun - gen,

No. 5

Ihr - - habt nun Trau - - - - - - rig - keit, Trau - rig-keit,

Ich will euch trö - sten wie ei - nen sei - ne Mut - - - - ter

No. 6

Denn wir ha - ben hie kei - - - - - - ne blei - ben-de Statt

Denn es wird die Po - sau - - ne schal - - len und die To - ten

No. 7

Herr, du bist wür - dig zu neh - men Preis und Eh - - - re und Kraft

Se - - - - lig sind die To - ten, die in dem Her - ren ster - - - - - ben,

Rhapsody Op. 53, for Alto, Male Chorus and Orchestra

Dass sie ru - - hen von ih - rer Ar - - - - beit

Ach, wer hei - let die Schmer - zen des, dem Bal - sam zu Gift ward?

Schicksalslied, Op. 54, for Chorus and Orchestra (Song of Destiny)

Ist auf dei - nem Psal - ter, Va - ter der Lie - - - - be, ein Ton

Ihr wan - delt dro - - ben im Licht auf wei - chem Bo - den

O Heiland, reiss die Himmel auf, Op. 74, No. 2 (motet)

Doch uns ist ge - ge - ben, Auf kei - ner Stät - - - - te zu ruhn.

O Hei - land reiss die Him - mel auf, her - ab, her - auf vom Him - mel lauf,

Nänie, Op. 82, for Chorus and Orchestra

Auch das Schö - - - ne muss ster - - - - - - - - - - - - - ben,

A - ber sie steigt aus dem Meer mit al - len Töch - tern des Ne - reus

Gesang der Parzen, Op. 89, for Chorus and Orchestra (Song of the Fates)

Es fürch - te die Göt - ter das Men - schen- ge- schlecht!

Es wen - den die Herr - scher ihr seg - nen-des Au - ge von gan- zen Ge-schlechtern

Zigeunerlieder, Op. 103

No. 1

He, Zi - geu - ner, grei - fe in die Sai - ten ein

No. 2

Hoch- ge-türm - te Ri - ma-flut, wie bist - - - du so trüb,

55　　　　　　　　　　　　　　　　　　　　　　　　B R A H M S

Zigeunerlieder, Op. 103　　No. 3

Wisst ihr wann mein Kind- chen am al- ler- schönsten ist?

No. 4

Lie- ber Gott, du weisst, wie oft be- reut ich hab

No. 5

Brau- ner Bur- sche führt zum Tan- ze sein blau- äug- ig schö- nes Kind,

No. 6

Rös- lein drei- e in der Rei- he blühn so rot

No. 7

Kommt dir manch- mal in den Sinn, mein sü- sses Lieb

No. 8

Horch, der Wind_ klagt_ in den Zwei- gen_ trau- rig sacht;

No. 9

Weit und breit schaut Nie- mand mich an, und wenn sie mich has- sen,

No. 11

Ro- te A- bend- wol- ken ziehn am Fir- ma- ment_

Sandmännchen (The Little Sandman, or, The Little Dustman), from 14 Volkskinderlieder, No. 4

Die Blü- me- lein sie schla- fen schon längst im Mon- den- schein

Songs and Duets: Liebestreu, Op. 3, No. 1

O ver- senk, o ver- senk dein_ Leid, mein Kind, in die See, in die tie- fe See!"

In der Fremde, No. 5

Aus der Hei- mat_ hin- ter den Bli- tzen rot, da kom- men die Wol- ken her

Spanisches Lied, Op. 6, No. 1

In dem Schat- ten mei- ner Lo- cken schlief mir mein Ge- lieb- ter ein

Juchhe! No. 5

Wie ist doch die Er- de so schön, so schön! Das wis- sen die Vö- ge- lein,

Nachtigallen schwingen, No. 6

Nach- ti- gal- len schwin- gen lus- tig ihr Ge- fie- der

Treue Liebe, Op. 7, No. 1

Ein Mägd- lein sass am Mee- res- strand und blick- te voll Sehn- sucht ins Wei- te

Anklänge, No. 3

Hoch ü- ber stil- len Hö- - - hen stand in dem Wald ein Haus;

Heimkehr, No. 6

O brich nicht, Steg, du zit- terst sehr, o stürz nicht, Fels, du dräu- est schwer

Vor dem Fenster, Op. 14, No. 1

Soll sich_ der Mond_ nicht hel- ler schei- nen

Ein Sonett, No. 4

Ach könnt' ich, könn- te ver- ges- sen sie, ihr schö- nes, lie- bes

Songs and Duets:
Der Schmied, Op. 19, No. 4

Ich hör' mei-nen Schatz den Ham-mer er schwin-get, das rau-schet,

An eine Aeolsharfe, No. 5

An- ge-lehnt an die E-pheu-wand die-ser al-ten Ter-ras-se

Ihr kom-met, Win-de, fern her-ü-ber, ach von des Kna-ben,

Die Meere (Soprano and Alto Duet) Op. 20, No. 3

Al- le Win- de schla-fen auf_ dem Spie- - -gel der Flut;

Duets for Alto and Baritone, Op. 28
No. 1 Die Nonne und der Ritter

Da die Welt zur Ruh ge-gan-gen, wacht mit Ster- nen

No. 2 Vor der Tür

Tritt auf, tritt auf, den Rie- gel von der Tür

No. 3 Es rauschet das Wasser

Es rau- schet das Was- ser, und blei- bet nicht stehn;

No. 4 Der Jäger und sein Liebchen

Ist nicht der Him-mel so blau?_ Steh am Fen- ster und schau!

Nicht mehr zu dir zu gehen, Op. 32, No. 2

Nicht mehr zu dir zu ge-hen, be-schloss ich und beschwor ich

Bitteres zu sagen denkst du No. 7

Bit-te-res zu sa-gen denkst du; a-ber nun und nim- mer kränkst du;

Wie bist du, meine Königin No. 9

Wie bist du, mei- ne Kö- ni- gin, durch sanf-te Gü-te wonne- voll!_

Magelone Romanzen, Op. 33
No. 3. Sind es Schmerzen, sind es Freuden

Sind es Schmer-zen, sind_ es Freu-den, die durch mei-nen Bu- - - sen ziehn?_

No. 4. Liebe kam aus fernen Landen

Lie- be kam aus fer-nen Lan-den und_ kein We- sen_ folg-te ihr,_

No. 5. So willst du des Armen

So willst_ du des Ar- men dich gnä- dig er- bar- men?

No. 8. Wir müssen uns trennen

Wir müs- sen uns tren-nen, ge- lieb-tes Sai-ten-spiel, Zeit ist es,

No. 9. Ruhe, Süssliebchen

Ru- he, Süss- lieb- chen, im Schat- ten der grü- nen,

No. 11. Wie schnell verschwindet

Wie schnell ver- schwin-det so Licht_ als_ Glanz, der Mor- gen_ fin- det

No. 12. Muss es eine Trennung geben

Muss_ es ei- ne Tren-nung ge- ben, die_ das treu- e Herz_ zer-bricht

No. 14. Wie froh und frisch

Wie froh und frisch mein Sinn sich hebt, zu- rück bleibt al- les_

Magelone Romanzen, Op. 33, No. 15 Treue Liebe — A

Treu-e Lie-be dau-ert lan-ge ü-ber-le-bet man-che,man-che Stund

Von ewiger Liebe, Op. 43, No. 1 — B

Dun-kel, wie dun-kel in Wald und in Feld! A-bend schon ist es,

Die Mainacht, No. 2 — C

Wann der sil-ber-ne Mond durch die Ge-sträu-che blinkt

An die Nachtigall, Op. 46, No. 4 — D

Geuss nicht so laut der lieb-ent-flamm-ten Lie-der ton-rei-chen Schall

Botschaft, Op. 47, No. 1 — E

We-he, Lüft-chen lind und lieb-lich um___ Wan-ge der Ge-lieb-ten

Sonntag, No. 3 — F

So hab ich doch die gan-ze Wo-che mein fei-nes Lieb-chen

O liebliche Wangen, No. 4 — G

O lieb-li-che Wan-gen, ihr macht mir Ver-lan-gen

Der Gang zum Liebchen, Op. 48, No. 1 — H

Es glänzt der mond nie-der, ich soll-te doch wie-der

Der Überläufer, No. 2 — I

In den Gar-ten wol-len wir ge-hen, wo die schö-nen Ro-sen

Am Sonntag Morgen, Op. 49, No. 1 — J

Am Sonn-tag Mor-gen zier-lich an-ge-tan wohl weiss ich

Sehnsucht, No. 3 — K

Hin-ter___ je-nen dich-ten___ Wäl-dern weilst du,

Wiegenlied (Cradle Song), No. 4 — L

Gu-ten A-bend, gut Nacht mit Ro-sen be-dacht___

Wenn du nur zuweilen lächelst, Op. 57, No. 2 — M

Wenn du nur zu-wei-len lä-chelst, nur_ zu-wei-len

Es träumte mir, No. 3 — N

Es träum-te mir, ich sei dir teu - - - er doch zu er-wa-chen

Ach, wende diesen Blick, No. 4 — O

Ach, wen-de die-sen Blick, wen-de dies An-ge-sicht!

Die Schnur, die Perl an Perle, No. 7 — P

Die Schnur, die Perl an Per - - le um dei-nen___ Hals___

Blinde Kuh, Op. 58, No. 1 — Q

In Fin-stern geh ich su-chen, mein Kind, wo steckst du wohl?

O komme, holde Sommernacht, No. 4 — R

O kom-me, hol-de Som-mer-nacht, ver-schwie-gen;

Schwermut, No. 5 — S

Mir ist so weh ums Herz, mir ist,als ob ich wei-nen möch-te vor Schmerz

Songs

In der Gasse, Op. 58, No. 6

Ich bli- cke hin- ab in die Gas- se dort drü- ben hat sie ge- wohnt

Serenade, No. 8

Lei- se, um_ dich nicht zu we- cken, rauscht_ der Nacht- wind, teu- re Frau!

Dämm'rung senkte sich von oben, Op. 59, No. 1

Dämm- rung senk- te sich_ von o- ben, schon ist al- le Nä- he fern

Auf dem See, No. 2

Blau- er Him- mel, blau- e Wo- gen, Re- ben- hü- gel

Regenlied, No. 3

Wal- le, Re- gen, wal- le nie- der, we- cke mir

Agnes, No. 5

Ro- sen- zeit, wie schnell vor- bei, schnell vor- bei, bist du doch ver- gan- gen!

Eine gute, gute Nacht, No. 6

Ei- ne gu- te, gu- te Nacht_ pflegst du mir_ zu sa- gen

Mein wundes Herz, No. 7

Mein wun- des Herz ver- langt nach mil- der Ruh, O hau- che sie ihm ein

Dein blaues Auge, No. 8

Dein blau- es Au- ge hält so still, ich bli- cke bis zum Grund

Erinnerung, Op. 63, No. 2

Ihr wun- der- schö- nen Au- gen- bli- cke, die Lieb- lich- ste

An die Tauben, No. 4

Fliegt nur aus, ge- lieb- te_ Tau- ben! Euch als Bo- ten send_ ich hin

Meine Liebe ist grün, No. 5

Mei- ne Lie - - - be ist grün_ wie die Flie- der- busch,

O wüsst ich doch den Weg zurück, No. 8

O wüsst ich doch den Weg zu- rück, den lie- ben Weg

Klage I, Op. 69, No. 1 (from the Bohemian)

Ach mir fehlt, nicht ist da, was mich einst süss be- glückt;

Klage II, No. 2 (Slovak)

O Fel- sen, lie- ber Fel- sen was stürz- test du nicht ein,

Des liebsten Schwur, No. 4

Ei, schmoll- te_ mein_ Va- ter nicht_ wach_ und im Schlaf,

Tambourliedchen, No. 5

Den Wir- bel schlag ich gar so stark, dass euch er- zit- tert

Über die See, No. 7

Ü- ber die See, fern ü- ber die See ist mein Schatz ge- zo- gen,

Salome, No. 8

Singt mein Schatz wie ein Fink, sing ich Nach- ti- gal- len- sang;

BRAHMS

ngs

Mädchenfluch, Op. 69, No. 9

A Ruft die Mut- ter, ruft die Toch- ter ü- ber drei Ge- bir- - ge:

B Gä- be Gott im hel- len Him- mel dass er sich er- hän- - - ge

Lerchengesang, Op. 70, No. 2

Ae- the- ri- sche fer- ne Stim- men, der Lerchen himm-li- sche Grü- sse,

Es liebt sich so lieblich im Lenze, Op. 71, No. 1

Die Wel- len blin- ken und flie- ssen da- hin, es liebt sich so lieb- lich

An den Mond, No. 2

Sil- - - ber- mond, mit blei- chen Strahlen pflegst_ du Wald und Feld zu ma- len

Geheimnis, No. 3

O Früh- lings- a- bend- däm- me- rung! O lau- es lin- des Wehn,

Willst du dass ich geh? No. 4

Auf der Hei- de weht der Wind, her- zig Kind, her- zig Kind

Minnelied, No. 5

Hol- der klingt der Vo- gel- sang, wenn die En- gel- rei- - ne,

Alte Liebe, Op. 72, No. 1

Es kehrt_ die dunk- le Schwal- be aus fer- nem Land_ zu- rück

O kühler Wald, No. 3

O küh- ler Wald wo rau- schest du, in dem mein Lieb- chen geht?

Verzagen, No. 4

Ich sitz am Stran- de der rau- schen-den See und su- che dort_ nach Ruh,

Sommerabend, Op. 84, No. 1

Geh schla- fen, Toch- ter, schla- fen! Schon fällt der Tau aufs Gras,

Der Kranz, No. 2

Mut- ter, hilf mir ar- men Toch- ter, sieh nur, was ein Kna- be tat

Vergebliches Ständchen, No. 4

Gu- ten A- bend,mein Schatz, Gu- ten A- bend, mein Kind,

Mondenschein, Op. 85, No. 2

Nacht liegt auf den frem- den We- gen, Kran- kes Herz und mü- de Glie- der

Mädchenlied, No. 3

Ach, und du mein küh- les Was- ser! Ach, und du mein ro- tes Rös- lein!

In Waldeseinsamkeit, No. 6

Ich sass zu dei- nen Fü- ssen in Wal- des- ein- sam- keit;

Therese, Op. 86, No. 1

Du milch- jun- ger Kna- be, wie schaust du mich an?

Feldeinsamkeit, No. 2

Ich ru- he still im ho- hen grü- nen Gras und sen- de lan- - ge

BRAHMS

Songs

Über die Heide, Op. 86, No. 4

Ü-ber die Hei- de hal-let mein Schritt, dumpf aus der Er- de wan-dert es mit.

Todessehnen, No. 6

Ach, wer nimmt von mei-ner See-le die ge-hei-me, schwe-re Last,

Two Songs for Alto, Viola and Piano, Op. 91,
No. 1 Gestillte Sehnsucht (also theme of viola)

In gold-nen A- bend- schein ge- tau-chet, wie fei- er-lich

No. 2 Geistliches Wiegenlied (Viola theme; old German folk tune)

Was lis - - - peln die Win- de, die Vö - - - ge - - lein?

Jo- sef, lie- ber Jo- sef mein, hilf mir wieg'n mein Kind-lein fein

Die ihr schwe-bet um die- se Pal-men in Nacht und Wind

Mit vierzig Jahren, Op. 94, No. 1

Mit vier-zig Jah-ren ist der Berg ge-stie - - gen, wir ste- hen still

Steig auf, geliebter Schatten, No. 2

Steig auf, ge-lieb- ter Schat- ten, vor mir in to- ter Nacht

Sapphische Ode, No. 4

Ro- sen brach ich Nachts mir am dunk- len Ha - - - ge;

Kein haus, keine Heimat, No. 5

Kein Haus, Kei- ne Hei- mat, kein Weib und kein Kind,

Das Mädchen, Op. 95, No. 1

Stand das Mäd-chen, stand am Ber-ges-ab-hang, wi-der-schien der Berg

Bei dir sind meine Gedanken, No. 2

Bei dir sind mei- ne Ge- dan- ken und flat- tern, flat- tern

Der Jäger, No. 4

Mein Lieb ist ein Jä- ger, und grün ist sein Kleid,

Vorschneller Schwur, No. 5

Schwor ein jun - - ges Mäd-chen: Blu-men nie zu tra- gen,

Mädchenlied, No. 6

Am jüngsten Tag ich auf- er-steh und gleich nach mei- nem Lieb- sten seh

Schön war, das ich dir weihte, No. 7

Schön war, das ich dir weih- te, das gol- de- ne Ge- schmei- de

Der Tod, das ist die kühle Nacht, Op. 96, No. 1

Der Tod, das ist die küh- le Nacht, Das Le- ben ist der schwü- le Tag

Wir wandelten, No. 2

Wir wan- del-ten, wir zwei zu-sam- men Ich war so still

Es schauen die Blumen, No. 3

Es schau- en die Blu-men al- le zur leuch-ten-den Son- ne hin- auf;

B R A H·M S

Songs

Meerfahrt, Op. 96, No. 4 — A
Mein Lieb- chen, wir sassen bei-sa-men trau- lich

Nachtigall, Op. 97, No. 1 — B
O Nach-ti-gall, dein sü-sser Schall, er-drin-get mir

Auf dem Schiffe, No. 2 — C
Ein Vö-ge-lein fliegt ü-ber den Rhein und wiegt die Flü-gel

Dort in den Weiden, No. 4 — D
Dort in den Wei- den steht ein Haus, da schaut die Magd zum Fen-ster 'naus!

Komm bald, No. 5 — E
Wa-rum denn war-ten von Tag zu Tag? Es blüht im Gar-ten was blü-hen mag.

Wie Melodien zieht es mir, Op. 105, No. 1 — F
Wie Me-lo-di- en zieht es mir lei-se durch den Sinn

Immer leiser wird mein Schlummer, No. 2 — G
Im-mer lei-ser wird mein Schlum-mer nur wie Schlei-er

Auf dem Kirchhofe, No. 4 — H
Der Tag ging re-gen-schwer und sturm-be-wegt, ich war

Verrat, No. 5 — I
Ich stand in ei-ner lau-en Nacht an ei-ner grü-nen Lin-de

Ständchen, Op. 106, No. 1 — J
Der Mond steht ü-ber dem Ber-ge, so recht für ver-lieb-te

Es hing der Reif, No. 3 — K
Es hing der Reif im Lin-den-baum, wo-durch das Licht

Meine Lieder, No. 4 — L
Wenn mein Herz be-ginnt zu klin-gen und den Tö- nen

Ein Wanderer, No. 5 — M
Hier wo sich die Stra- ssen-schei-den, wo nun gehn die We-ge hin?

Das Mädchen spricht, Op. 107, No. 3 — N
Schwal- be, sing mir an `Ist's dein al-ter Mann

Maienkätzchen, No. 4 — O
Mai-en-kätz-chen er-ster Gruss, ich bre-che euch und ste-cke euch

Mädchenlied, No. 5 — P
Auf die Nacht in den Spinn-stubn, da sin-gen die Mäd-chen,

Vier ernste Gesänge (Four serious songs) Op. 121, No. 1 — Q
Denn es ge-het dem Men- schen wie dem Vieh,

No. 2 — R
Ich wand-te mich, und sa-he an al- le,

No. 3 — S
O Tod, O Tod, wie bit - - - ter, wie bit - - - ter bist du

„iebeslieder Waltzes, Op. 52, No. 3

O die Frau- en   O die Frau- en   wie sie Won- ne,

No. 4

Wie des A- bends schö- ne Rö- te   möcht ich ar- me

No. 5

Die grü- ne Hop- fen- ran- ke, sie schlän-gelt auf der Er- de hin

No. 6

Ein klei- ner, hüb- scher Vo- gel nahm den Flug zum Gar- ten hin,

No. 7

Wohl schön be- wandt war es vor- e- he mit mei- nem Leb- en

No. 8

Wenn so lind dein Au- ge mir   und so lieb - - - lich schau-et,

No. 9

Am Do- nau- stran- de,   Da steht ein Haus,

No. 10

O   wie sanft die Quel- le sich durch die Wie- se

No. 11

Nein, es ist nicht aus- zu- kom- men mit den Leu- ten;

No. 12

Schlos- ser auf! Schlos- ser auf, und ma- che Schlös- ser,

No. 13

Vö- ge- lein durch-rauscht die Luft, durch- rauscht die Luft,

No. 14

Sieh, wie ist die Wel- le klar, blickt der Mond her- nie- der

No. 15

Nach- ti- gall, sie singt so schön, wenn die Ster- ne

No. 16

Ein dun- ke- ler Schacht ist Lie- be, ein gar zu ge- fahr-li-cher Bron- nen;

No. 17

Nicht wand- le, mein licht; dort aus-sen im Flur- be- reich!

No. 18

Es be- bet das Ge- sträu- che, ge- streift hat es im Flu- ge

BRETON, Tomás (1850-1923)

Jota, from La Dolores (opera)

Gran- de co- mo el mis- mo sol Es la jo- ta

BREWER, A. Herbert (1865-1928)

The Fairy Pipers
By permission Boosey & Hawkes, Inc., copyright owners

When all the birds are gone to sleep and all the pi- pers still,

Come out! Come out! Lis- ten on the air! Up there! Down there!

BRIDGE, Frank (1879-1941)

Love Went A-Riding
Copyright by Boston Music Co.

Love____ went a- ri - - - - ding, Love____ went a- ri - - - - ding

O That It Were So

BRITTEN, Benjamin (1913-1976)

The Ash Grove (arr.)
By permission Boosey & Hawkes, Inc., copyright owners

Down yon- der green val- ley where stream- lets__ me - - an- der

Folk Songs:
By permission Boosey & Hawkes, Inc. copyright owners

La Belle est au jardin d'amour

La belle est au jar - din d'a- mour

The Bonny Earl o Moray

Ye Hie-lands and ye Low-lands,__O where hae ye been? They hae slain the Earl

Come you not from Newcastle

Come you not from New- cas- tle?__ Come you not there a- way?

The foggy, foggy dew

When I was a bach-elor I lived all a- lone and worked

Heigh ho, heigh hi!

Oh I lived with my dad- dy, an ap- prent- ice was I,

Little Sir William

Eas- ter day was a ho- li- day of all days in the year

Oliver Cromwell

Ol- i- ver Crom- well lay bur- ied and dead, Hee- haw

The Plough Boy

A flax- en head- ed cow- boy, as sim- ple as may be,

Le Roi s'en va-t-en chasse

Le roi s'en va_ t'en chas- se, dans le bois des_ Bour- bons____

The Sally Gardens

Down__ by the_ Sal- ly__ Gar- dens my_ love and_ I did meet,

Serenade for Tenor, Horn and Strings, Op. 31, No. 1 Pastoral (Cotton)
By permission Boosey & Hawkes, Inc., copyright owners

The Day's grown old; the faint- ing Sun Has but a lit-tle way____

Serenade for Tenor, Horn and Strings, Op. 31,

No. 2 Nocturne (Tennyson) — A
The splen - -dour falls— on cas-tle walls— and snow-y sum-mits

No. 3 Elegy (Blake) — B
O Rose, thou art sick; The in-vi-si-ble worm That flies— in the night,

No. 4 Dirge (anon. 15th cent.) — C
This ae nighte, this ae nighte e-ver-y night and alle,

No. 5 Hymn (Ben Jonson) — D
Queen and hunt-ress chaste and fair— Now the sun is laid to sleep

No. 6 Sonnet (Keats) — E
O soft— em-balmer of the still mid-night, Shutting with care-ful fin-gers

Seven Sonnets of Michelangelo, Op. 22 Sonetto XVI
By permission Boosey & Hawkes, Inc., copyright owners — F
Si co - me nel-la pe-na e nell' in-chio-stro

XXIV — G
Spir - to ben na - to, in cui si spec-chia e ve - de

XXX — H
Veg-gio co' bei— vo-stri oc-chi un dol-ce lu-me

XXXI — I
A che più debb' io mai l'in-ten-sa vog-lia— Sfo-gar con pian ti

XXXII — J
S'un casto a-mor, s'u-na pie-tà su-per-na, S'u-na for-tu-na

XXXVIII — K
Ren-de-te a gli oc-chi miei, O fon-te o fiu-me,— ren-de-te—

LV — L
Tu sa' ch'io so, si-gnior mie, che tu sai— Ch'i ven - -ni

BRUCH, Max (1838-1920)

Odysseus, Op. 41, No. 8
By permission Associated Music Publishers, Inc. — N
Ich wob— dies Ge-wand mit Thrä-nen am Ta- ge

BRUCK, Arnold Von (16th Cent.)

Aus tiefer Not (4-part chorus) — P
Aus tie-fer Not schrei ich zu dir, Herr Gott, er-hör

BRUCKNER, Anton (1824-1896)

Ave Maria (chorus)
By permission Associated Music Publishers, Inc. — R
A-ve Ma-ri-a gra-ti-a ple-na Do-mi-nus te-cum

Herbstlied (chorus) — S
Durch die Wäl-der streif' ich mun-ter, wenn der Wind die Stäm-me rüt-telt,

The Stein Song

For it's al-ways good wea-ther, when good fel-lows get to-geth-er,

Winter Song
Copyright by Oliver Ditson Co.
Used by permission

Ho,_ a song by the fire! Pass the pipes, pass the bowl!

BUNGERT, August (1846-1915)

Ich hab' ein kleines Lied erdacht,
Op. 49, No. 9

Ich hab ein klei-nes Lied er-dacht und hab' es ge-sun-gen

BUONONCINI, Giovanni (1670-1747)

Deh piu a me non v'ascondete

Deh piu a me non v'as-con-de-te lu-ci va-ghe del mio sol,

Per la gloria d'adorarvi

Per la glo - - - ria d'a - - - do-rar - - - vi

Pupille nere

Pu-pil-le ne-re, Se voi guar-da-te, Ce-der voi fa-te,

Vado ben spesso

Va-do ben spes-so can-gian-do lo-co,

BURLEIGH, Harry Thacker (1866-1949)

Arrangements of Negro Spirituals:
By an' By
Copyright by G. Ricordi & Co., Inc.

Oh by_ an' by by_ an' by, I'm goin' to lay down dis heavy_ load

Deep River

Deep _ riv-er, my home is o-ver Jor-dan_

Go down, Moses

When Is-rael was in E-gypt's lan' Let my peo-ple go,

Go down, Mo-ses, way down to E-gypt's lan'_

Hard Trials

Feen a-lis'-nin' all de night long, Been a-lis'-nin' all de day

Now ain't dem hard tri-als Great trib-u-la-tion,

Heav'n, Heav'n (I got a robe)

I got a robe, You got a robe, All of God's chil-dren got a robe

I don't feel no-ways tired

I am seek-in' for_ a ci-ty, Hal-le-lu - - - - - ja!

Lord,_ I don't feel no ways tir-ed, Chil-da-ren! Oh,_ Glo-ry

Arrangements of Negro Spirituals:
I want to be ready

I want__ to be read-y I want__ to be read-y

Nobody Knows de Trouble I've Seen

No-bod-y knows de trou-ble I've seen, No-bod-y knows but Je-sus

Oh, Didn't It Rain

Fo'-ty days fo'-ty nights when de rain kept a-fall-in

Oh, Peter, Go ring-a dem bells

Oh, Pe-ter, go ring-a dem bells, Pe-ter, go ring-a dem bells.

Sinner, please doan let dis Harves' Pass

Sin-ner, please doan let dis har-ves' pass;___ Sin-ner please

Swing Low Sweet Chariot

Swing low sweet char-i-ot,___ Com-ing for to car-ry me home

Were You There?

Were you there when they cru-ci-fied my Lord?___ Were you there

BUSCA, Padre Ludovico (17th Cent.)

Bionda, bionda Clori

Bion-da, bion-da Clo-ri bion-da Clo-ri che nel vol-to hai rac-col-to

Occhi belli

Oc-chi bel-li, non ful-mi-na-te, non ful-mi-na - - - - - - - - - - te,

BUTTERWORTH, George (1885-1916)

A Shropshire Lad
By permission of Augener, Ltd., London

With rue my heart__ is lad-en For gold-en friends__ I had,

When the lad for long-ing sighs, Mute__ and dull of cheer and pale,

Oh fair e-nough are sky and plain but I know fair-er far

Bredon Hill

In sum-mer-time on Bre-don the bells they sound so clear;___

Love-liest of trees, the cher-ry now is hung with bloom a-long the bough

Is my team plough-ing, That I was used to drive,

BUXTEHUDE, Dietrich (1637-1707)

CANTATAS:
Aperite mihi portas justitiae
(Ugrino No. 71)

(tenor) (alto)

A-pe-ri-te, a-pe-ri-te, a-pe-ri-te, a-pe-ri-té

CANTATAS:

Aperite mihi portas justitiae (Ugrino No. 71)

Be- ne- dic- tus, qui ven- it, qui ve- nit qui ve- nit

Jubilate Domino (Ugrino No. 19)

Ju- bi- la- te, Ju- bi- la- te, Ju- bi- la- te Do- mi- no,

O fröhliche Stunden (Ugrino No. 12)

O fröh- li- che Stun- den, o fröh- li- che Zeit, es hat ü- ber wun- den,

Singet dem Herrn (Ugrino No. 16)

Sin- - - - - - get, Sin- - - - - - get dem Her- ren— ein— neu- es Lied

Was mich auf dieser Welt betrübt (Ugrino No. 71)

Was mich auf die- ser Welt be- trübt, das wäh- ret kur- ze Zeit,

Missa Brevis (Ugrino No. 42)
Kyrie

Ky- ri- e- e- lei- - - - - - - - - - - - - - - - - son

Gloria

Et in ter- ra pax ho- mi- - - - - ni- bus

BUZZI-PECCIA, A. (1853-1943)

Colombetta
Copyright by G. Ricordi & Co., Inc.

La bel- la Co- lom- bet- ta Al cal- do si ri- po- sa,

Lolita
Copyright by G. Ricordi & Co., Inc.

A- mor, a- mor che lan- gue il cor,

BYRD, William (1543-1623)

MADRIGALS:

I thought that love had been a boy (5-part madrigal)

I thought that love had been a boy, I thought that love had— been a boy

Lullaby, my sweet little baby

Lul- la, lul- la, Lul- la, lul- la- by, lul- la- by—

Though Amaryllis Dance

Though A- ma- ry- lis dance in green, like fai- ry Queen

This sweet and merry month

This sweet and mer- ry, mer- ry month, and mer- ry, mer- ry month of— May

Mass (five voices)
I Kyrie Eleison

Ky- ri- e e- lei- - - - - - - - - - - - - - son

II Gloria in excelsis

Et in ter- ra pax ho- mi- - - - - - - - - - - ni- bus

III Credo

Pa- trem om- ni- po- ten- tem, fac- to- rem coe- - - - - li et ter- rae

IV Sanctus

Sanc- - - - - - - - tus, Sanc- - - - - - - tus, sanc- - - - - - tus,

Mass (five voices)
V Benedictus — Be- ne- dic- tus qui ve - - - - - - - nit   A

VI Agnus Dei — Ag- nus de- i qui tol- lis pec- ca - - - ta mun - - - - di,   B

MOTETS:
Ave Verum Corpus — A - - - - ve ve - - - - rum cor - - - - - - - pus   C

Justorum Animae — Ju- sto - - - rum a- ni- mae in ma - - nu De - - - - - i sunt   D

Non Vos Relinquam Orphanos — Non vos re- lin- quam or- pha- nos Al- le- lu - - - - - - ja   E

O Mistress Mine — O mis-tress mine, where are you roam-ing O___ mis-tress mine,   F

Sacerdotes Domini — Sa- cer- do- tes Do - - - - - - mi- ni in- cen - - - sum   G

CACCINI, Giulio (1548-1618)

Amarilli, mia bella — A- ma- ril- li mia bel- la, non cre- di o del mio cor   I

Dovrò dunque morire — Do- vrò dun- que mo- ri - re, Pria che di nuo- vo io mi ri   J

Non piango e non sospiro, from Euridice (opera) — Non pian- go, e non so- spi- ro O mia ca- ra Eu- ri- di- ce   K

Fere selvagge — Fe- re sel- vag- ge Che per mon- ti er- ra- te, il piè fer- ma- te   L

Occhi Immortali — Oc- chi im- mor- ta- li, D'a- mor glo- ria e splen- do - re;   M

Tu, ch'hai le penne amore — Tu ch'hai le pen- ne, A- mo- re, E sai spie- gar- le a vo- lo,   N

CADMAN, Charles Wakefield (1881-1946)

At Dawning, Op. 29, No. 1
Copyright by Oliver Ditson Co.
Used by permission — When the dawn flames in the sky I love you;   P

Far Off I Hear a Lover's Flute — Far off I hear a lo- ver's flute A- cry- ing thro' the gloom;___   Q

Four American Indian Songs, Op. 45, No. 1
Copyright by White Smith Co. — From the Land of the Sky- blue Wa-ter,___ They brought a cap- tive maid;___   R

No. 2 — The white dawn___ is steal- ing a- bove the dark ce- dar trees   S

our American Indian Songs,
Op. 45, No. 4

The moon drops low that once soared high as an ea-gle   A

A Moonlight Song, Op. 42, No. 2
Copyright 1933, G. Schirmer, Inc.

The moon-light shim-mers thro' the vine___ That to___ my___ porch   B

CALDARA, Antonio (1670-1736)

Come raggio di sol

Co- me rag- gio di sol   mi te e se- re- no   D

Mirti, Faggi

Mir- ti,   fag- gi tron- chi e fron- de   E

Selve amiche, ombrose piante

Sel- ve a- mi- che, om- bro- se pian- te, fi- do al- ber- go   F

CALLCOTT, Dr. John Wall (1766-1821)

To all you ladies now at land

To all you La- dies now at land We men at sea in- dite   H

Ye Mariners of England

Ye Ma- ri- ners of Eng- land that guard our na- tive seas   I

While the storm- y winds do blow,___ While the storm-y winds do blow___   J

CAMPBELL-TIPTON, Louis (1877-1921)

The Crying of Water
Copyright 1907, G. Schirmer, Inc.

O wa- ter,___ voice of my heart___ cry- ing in___ the sand,   L

A Spirit Flower
Copyright 1908, G. Schirmer, Inc.

My heart was fro- zen e- ven as the earth___   M

Down through the win- ter sun- shine snow flakes came, All shim-m'ring   N

CAMPION, Thomas (1567-1620)

The Cypress curtain of the night

The cy- press cur- tain of the night is spread   P

Follow thy fair sun

Fol- low thy fair sun, un- hap- py sha- dow. Though thou   Q

Follow your saint

Fol- low your saint, fol- low with ac- cents sweet;   R

My Sweetest Lesbia

My sweet-est Les- bia, let us live and love And though the sag-er sort

When to her lute Corinna sings

When to her lute Co- rin- na sings, her voice re- vives____

Never weather-beaten sail

Nev- er weath- er beat- en sail more will- ing bent to shore,

What if a day, or a month, or a year

What if a day, or a month or a year, crown thy de- lights

CAMPRA, André (1660-1744)

Charmant papillon, from Les Fêtes Vénitiennes

Char- mant pa- pil- lon dont l'ai - - - - le d'or pas- se

CANTELOUBE, Joseph (1879-1957)

Chants d'Auvergne:
Series I,
No. 2 Baïlèro
By permission Heugel & Cie, Paris, copyright owners

Pas- tré, dè dè- laï l'a- ïo, a gaï-ré de boun tèn dio__ lou bai- lè- ro

No. 3 (a) L'aïo de Rotso

L'a- ïo dè rot- so te fo- ro mou- rir fi- lho- to,

(b) Ound' onoren gorda?

Ound' o- no- ren gor- da pit- chou no droou- lè- to?

(c) Obal din lou Limouzi

O- bal din lou Li- mou- zi, pit- choun' o- bal din lou Li- mou- zi

Series II,
No. 2 L'Antouèno (L'Antoine)

Quond o- no- rèn__ o lo fiè- ïro, ié!____ Quond o- no- rèn__

No. 5 (a) Je n'ai pas d'amie

N'aï pas ïèu dè mi- o, soui qu'un pas- tou- rel

(b) Lo Calhé (La Caille)

E, dio mè tu, lo cal- hé, ound as toun nïou?

Series III,
No. 1 Lo Fiolaire (La Fileuse)

Ton qu'è- rè pit-chou- nè- lo Gor- da- vè loui mou- tous,

No. 2 Passo pel prat

Lo lo lo lo lo lo lo lo lo lo lo lo lo

Pas- so pel prat____ bè- lo- to____ Jeu pos- so- rai

No. 4 Brezaviola (Berceuse)

Soun, soun, bè- ni, bè- ni, bè- ni, soun, soun, bè- ni, bè- ni doun,

No. 5 Malurous qu'o uno fenno

Ma- lu- rous qu'o u- no fen- no, Ma- lu- rous qué n'o cat!

CAPLET, André (1878-1925)

Cinq Ballades françaises,
from La Ronde, No. 2
By permission Durand & Cie, Paris;
Elkan-Vogel Co., Inc., Phila.,
copyright owners

Si toutes les filles du monde____ vou-laient s'don-ner la main

Le Forêt
By permission Durand & Cie, Paris;
Elkan-Vogel Co., Inc., Phila.,
copyright owners

O____ Fo-rêt,____ toi____ qui vis pas-ser bien des a-mants

Les Prières
1. Oraison dominicale
By permission Durand & Cie, Paris;
Elkan-Vogel Co., Inc., Phila.,
copyright owners

Au nom du Père, du Fils, du Saint Esprit.____ Ain-si soit-il

2. Salutation angélique

Je vous sa-lue, Ma-ri-e, pleine de gra-ce

3. Symboles des Apôtres

Je crois en Dieu,____ le Pè-re tout puis-sant,

CAPUA, Eduardo di (1864-1917)

Maria, Marì (Oh, Marie)
Copyright by Mills Music, Inc., N. Y.

A-ra-pe-te fe-ne-sta,____ fam, m'af-fac-ciz a Ma-ri-a____

O Ma-rì!____ O Ma-rì!____ quan-ta suon-no ca per-de pe' te

O Sole Mio
Copyright by Boston Music Co.

Che bel-la co-sa 'na iur-na-ta'e so-le,____ n'a-ria se-re-na

Ma n'a-tu so-le-cchiù bel-lo ohi-ne',____ o so-le mi-o

CARDILLO, S.

Core'ngrato
Copyright by G. Ricordi & Co., Inc.

Ca-ta-rì,____ Ca-ta-rì,____ pec-chè me di-ce-sti pa-ro-le a-ma-re

CAREY, Henry (1690-1743)

A Pastoral

Flocks are sport - - - - - ing, doves are court - - - - ing

Sally in our alley: Two versions
No. 1, words by Carey
Tune "The Country Lass"

Of all the girls____ that are so smart, there's none like pret-ty Sal-ly;

No. 2, words and music by Carey

Of____ all the girls that____ are so smart, There's_none like pret-ty Sal-ly;

CARISSIMI, Giacomo (1605-1674)

A morire!

A-mo-ri-re, a mo-ri-re, a mo-ri--re!____

CARPENTER, John Alden (1876-1951)

CATALANI, Alfredo (1854-1893)

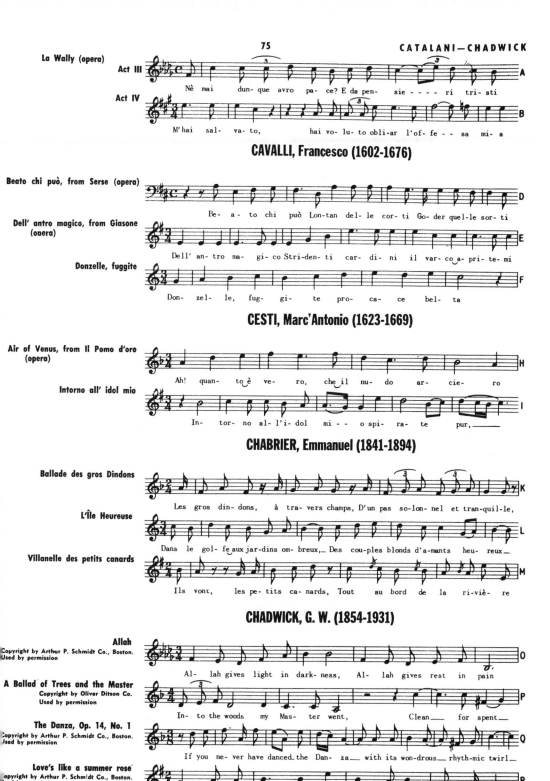

La Wally (opera)

Act III — Nè mai dun-que avrò pa-ce? E da pen-sie----ri tri-sti

Act IV — M'hai sal-va-to, hai vo-lu-to obli-ar l'of-fe--sa mi-a

CAVALLI, Francesco (1602-1676)

Beato chi può, from Serse (opera) — Be-a-to chi può Lon-tan del-le cor-ti Go-der quel-le sor-ti

Dell' antro magico, from Giasone (opera) — Dell' an-tro ma-gi-co Stri-den-ti car-di-ni il var-co a-pri-te-mi

Donzelle, fuggite — Don-zel-le, fug-gi-te pro-ca-ce bel-ta

CESTI, Marc'Antonio (1623-1669)

Air of Venus, from Il Pomo d'oro (opera) — Ah! quan-to è ve-ro, che il nu-do ar-cie-ro

Intorno all' idol mio — In-tor-no al-l'i-dol mi--o spi-ra-te pur,——

CHABRIER, Emmanuel (1841-1894)

Ballade des gros Dindons — Les gros din-dons, à tra-vers champs, D'un pas so-lon-nel et tran-quil-le,

L'Île Heureuse — Dans le gol-fe aux jar-dins om-breux,— Des cou-ples blonds d'a-mants heu-reux—

Villanelle des petits canards — Ils vont, les pe-tits ca-nards, Tout au bord de la ri-viè-re

CHADWICK, G. W. (1854-1931)

Allah
Copyright by Arthur P. Schmidt Co., Boston.
Used by permission
— Al-lah gives light in dark-ness, Al-lah gives rest in pain

A Ballad of Trees and the Master
Copyright by Oliver Ditson Co.
Used by permission
— In-to the woods my Mas-ter went, Clean— for spent

The Danza, Op. 14, No. 1
Copyright by Arthur P. Schmidt Co., Boston.
Used by permission
— If you ne-ver have danced the Dan-za— with its won-drous— rhyth-mic twirl—

Love's like a summer rose
Copyright by Arthur P. Schmidt Co., Boston.
Used by permission
— Love's like a sum-mer rose, whose fra-grant buds un-close,

CHAMINADE, Cécile (1857-1944)

L'Anneau d'Argent

Le cher an- neau d'ar- gent que vous m'a- vez don- né,

Chanson Slave

Dans mon_ beau pa- ys_ j'a- vais_ un a- mi_

Si J'Étais Jardinier
Copyright 1894, G. Schirmer, Inc.

Si j'é- tais_ jar- di- nier des cieux, Je te cueil- le- rais_ des é- toi- les!

CHARLES, Ernest (1895-   )

Let my song fill your heart
Copyright 1936, G. Schirmer, Inc.

Let my song_ fill your heart_ with its mel- o- dy oh so di- vine

When I Have Sung my Songs
Copyright 1934, G. Schirmer, Inc.

When I have sung my songs to you, _ I'll sing no more.

CHARPENTIER, Gustave (1860-1956)

A Mules (after "Impressions d'Italie")

Les_ yeux, la belle, hé- las! tes yeux fa- rou- ches

C'est l'heu - - - re où l'amant nous con- te fol- le- ment

La Chanson de Chemin

Qu'est-ce qui bril- le? Une au- ber- ge Ah!_ Ah!_

La route est lon- gue, lon- gue, bon pé- le- rin._

Les Chevaux de bois

Tour- nez, tour- nez,_ bons che-vaux de bois,_ Tour-nez_ cent tours,

Louise (opera)
Act I
By permission Heugel & Cie, Paris,
copyright owners

O coeur a- mi! O coeur pro- mis! Hé-las! si loin,_ si près!_

De- puis long- temps j'ha-bi-tais cet-te cham- bre, sans me dou- ter, hé- las!

Act II Scene II

Oh! moi quand je suis dans la ru- e, tout mon êt- re prend com- me feu!

Act III

De puis le jour où je me suis don- né- e,

Act IV

Les pau- vres gens peu-vent-ils être heureux?_ a qui le bon Dieu

Voir naître une en- fant, la fleur- ir des ca- res- ses,

Louise (opera)   Act IV

A   Res- te, re-pose-toi com- me ja-dis, toute pe- ti- te!

B   L'en-fant ser-ait sa- ge, tout à fait sa- ge, si son pè- re vou-lait

La ronde des compagnons

C   La cour se fleu- rit de sou- ci   Com- me le front de tous ceux- ci

Sérénade à Watteau

D   Votre âme____ est un pa-y-sa- ge choi-si____

Les Yeux de Berthe
By permission Heugel & Cie, Paris, copyright owners

E   Vous pou- vez mé- pri- ser les yeux les plus cé- lè- bres

CHAUSSON, Ernest (1855-1899)

Amour d'antan, Op. 8, No. 2
Copyright by Salabert, Paris, N. Y.

G   Mon a- mour d'an-tan, vous sou-ve-nez vous?   Nos coeurs ont fleu-ri

Apaisement, Op. 13, No. 1
Copyright by J. Hamelle Music Publishers, Paris

H   La lu- ne blan- - - che luit dans le bois____

La Caravane, Op. 14
Copyright by J. Hamelle Music Publishers, Paris

I   La ca- ra-vane hu- mai- ne au Sa-ha- ra du mon- - - de

La Chanson Bien Douce
Copyright by Salabert, Paris, N. Y.

J   E- cou- tez la chan-son bien dou- ce Qui ne pleu- re

Chanson d'Amour

K   Loin de moi, loin de moi ces lè- vres que j'a- do- re

Chanson de Clown

L   Fuis mon â- me fuis!____ Je meurs sous les traits

Chanson d'Ophélie

M   Il est mort ay- ant bien souf- fert, Ma-da- me;

Chanson Perpetuelle, Op. 37

N   Bois fris-son-ants,____ ciel____ é- toi-lé mon bien ai-mé s'en est al-lé

Le Charme, Op. 2, No. 2

O   Quand ton sou-ri- re me sur- prit je sen- tis fré- mir

Le Colibri, Op. 2, No. 7

P   Le vert co- li- bri, le roi des col- li-nes, Voy- ant la ro- sée

Dans la forêt du charme et de l'enchantement

Q   Sous vos som-bres ché-ve- lu- res pe- ti-tes fées____ Vous chan-tâ- tes____

La Dernière Feuille, Op. 2, No. 4

R   Dans la fo- rêt chauve____ et rouil- lé- e

Nanny, Op. 2, No. 1

S   Bois chers aux ra- miers,____ pleu-rez, doux feuil- la- ges,

Nocturne, Op. 8, No. 1
La nuit était pen- sive et té- né- breu- se

Nos Souvenirs, Op. 8, No. 4
Nos sou- ve- nirs tou- tes ces cho- ses Qu'à tous les vents

Les Papillons, Op. 2, No. 3
Les pa- pil- lons cou-leur de nei- ge vo- lent par es- saims

Printemps triste, Op. 8, No. 3
Nos sen- tiers ai- més s'en vont re- fleu- rir

Sérénade italienne, Op. 2, No. 5
Par- tons en bar- que sur la mer Pous pas- ser la nuit

Serres chaudes, Op. 24
No. 1 Serre chaude
Copyright by Salabert, Paris, N. Y.
O serre an mil-lieu des fo-rêts Et vos por-tes à ja-mais clo- ses!

No. 2 Serre d'ennui
O cet en-nui bleu dans le coeur a- vec la vi- si-on

No. 3 Lassitude
Ils ne sa- vent plus où se po- ser ces bai-sers,Ces lè-vres

No. 4 Fauves las
O les pas- si- ons en al- lées, Et les ri- res et les san-glots!

No. 5 Oraison
Vous sa- vez,Sei- gneur ma mi-sè- re! Voy-ez ce que je vous ap-por- te,

Les Temps de Lilas
Le temps des li- las et le temps des ro- ses

CHERUBINI, Maria Luigi (1760-1842)

J'ai vu disparaître l'espoir, from Les Abencerrages (opera)
J'ai vu dis- pa- raî- tre L'és- poir dont j'o- sais me nour- rir

Guide mes pas, from Les Deux Journées (opera)
Gui- de mes pas, ô pro- vi- den- ce! d'mon plan se- con- de

O Salutaris Hostia
O sa- lu- ta- ris, O sa- lu- ta-ris hos- ti- a qual coe- li

CHOPIN, Frédéric François (1810-1849)

Polish Songs, Op. 74
No. 1 The Maiden's Wish
Were I a sun, so high in Heav'n out- beam- ing,

Accompaniment Theme

No. 2 In Spring
Thro' the dew- y val- ley mur- mur brooks mé- an- d'ring

Polish Songs

No. 3 Troubled Waters — Tell me an-gry flow-ing tor- rent, why so tur- bid is thy cur-rent? — A

No. 4 Bacchanal — Poys, be jol- ly, grief is fol- ly, Drink then while you can! — B

No. 5 What a young maiden loves — Stream- let lov-eth the sedg- es, bird- ling lov-eth the hedg- es, — C

No. 6 Go Thou, and haste Thee — "Go thou, and haste thee!" I mute- ly o- bey thee — D

No. 7 The Messenger — Rills are bright- ly glit-t'ring, green the banks they__ fol- low — E

No. 8 My Sweetheart — When an eye like fire glow- ing, And a heart no guile__ know- ing, — F

No. 9 A Melody — Mute and re-sign'd, for pi- ty ne'er ap- peal- ing,__ — G

No. 10 The Trooper before the Battle — Why so rest-ive, so un-stead- y, Thou, my trust- y steed? — H

No. 11 Two Corpses — Fond were the lov- ers, Yet ne'er their love was plight- ed — I

No. 12 My Joys — When for a mo- ment thou dost speak, my dar- ling, — J

No. 13 Melancholy — Dew in the mead - - - - ow, mist in the val- ley — K

No. 14 The little Ring — Yet a child__ wert thou, O maid- en, when our faith__ we plight- ed — L

No. 15 The Return Home — Stran- ger in the storm swept for- est, Haste thee on, O Ri- der! — M

No. 16 Lithuanian Song — O- ver the mead- ow and home- ward I hied me, — N

No. 17 Poland's Dirge — By the storm they breast- ed Ev- 'ry leaf is wrest- ed — O

CIAMPI, Legrenzo Vincenzo (1719-1762)

Tre giorni son che Nina (2 different versions) (said to be by Pergolesi also)

1 — Tre gior-ni son che Ni- na, che Ni- na in let- to se ne sta ____ — Q

2 — Tre_ gior-ni son che Ni- na, che Ni- na, che Ni - - na — R

CILEA, Francesco (1866-1950)

Adriana Lecouvreur (opera)
Copyright by Sonzogno, Milan

Act I
I- o son' l'u- mi- le an-cel-la del Ge-nio cre-a-tor

La dol-cis-si-ma ef-fi-gie sor-ri-den-te

Act II
O va-ga-bon-da stel-la d'O-ri-en-te non tra-mon-tar,

L'a- ni-ma ho stan-ca, e la mè-ta è lon-ta-na:

I- o son su- a per l'a-mor ch'è più for-te del-la sor-te,

Act IV
Po- ve- ri fio- ri, gem-me de' pra-ti, pur ie- ri na-ti,

No, la mia fron- te, che pen-sier non mu- ta,

L'Arlesiana (opera)
Copyright by Sonzogno, Milan

Act I
Co- me due tiz-zi ac-ce- si, dal-l'al-to del di-ru- po

Act II
Vie- ni con me sui mon-ti, go-drai va- sti o-riz-zon- ti

Anch' i- o vor-re- i dor-mir co- si, nel son-no al-men

Act III
Ho da-to moglie al pa-dre del-lo spo-so e l'ho da-ta

Sa- i che gli ho da- to a bra- ni a bra-ni l'a-ni-ma

CIMARA, Pietro (1887-)

Canto di Primavera
Copyright by Forlivesi, Florence
A- pri- te tut-te le fi-ne-stra al So- le

Fiocca la neve
Copyright by C. W. Homeyer, Boston
Len- ta la ne- ve fioc- ca, fioc- ca, fioc- ca

Scherzo
Copyright by F. Bongiovanni, Bologna
U- na notte al da- van-za- le e- ro so- la o pur non e- ro?

Stornellata Marinara
Copyright by G. Ricordi & Co., Inc.
Ah! Al- ga di ma- re! Quan- do m'af-fo-sca qual-che gran do-lore

Stornello
Copyright by F. Bongiovanni, Bologna
Son co- me i chic- chi del- la me- lo- grana

CIMAROSA, Domenico (1749-1801)

Il Matrimonio Segreto (opera)

U- di- te, tut- ti u-di- te le or- rec- chie spa- lan- ca- te   B

È ve- ro che in ca- sa io so- no, io son la pa- dro- na,   C

Pria che spun- ti in ciel___ l'au- ro- ra in ciel___ l'au- ro- ra   D

Bril- lar mi sen- to il co- re, mi sen- to___ giu- bi- lar   E

Per- do- na- te, sig- nor mi- o, se vi lascio e fo___ par- ten- za   F

Se non___ ven- di- ca - - - ta con- ten- ta___ già___ so- no   G

CLARIBEL (1830-1869)

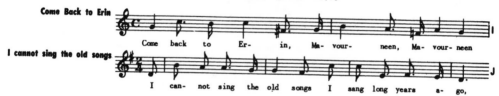

Come Back to Erin

Come back to Er- in, Ma- vour- neen, Ma- vour- neen   I

I cannot sing the old songs

I can- not sing the old songs I sang long years a- go,   J

CLARKE, Rebecca (1886-   )

The Seal Man
By permission Boosey & Hawkes, Inc.,
copyright owners

And he came by her ca- bin to the west of the road, call- ing   L

Shy One
By permission Boosey & Hawkes, Inc.,
copyright owners

Shy one, shy one, shy one of my heart, She moves___   M

CLARKE, Robert C. (1879-1934)

The Blind Ploughman

CLAY. Frédéric (1838-1889)

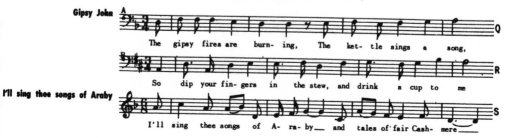

Gipsy John

The gipsy fires are burn- ing, The ket- tle sings a song,   Q

So dip your fin- gers in the stew, and drink a cup to me   R

I'll sing thee songs of Araby

I'll sing thee songs of A- ra- by___ and tales of fair Cash- mere___   S

The Sands o' Dee

Oh! Ma-ry go, and call the cat-tle home, and call the cat-tle home

CLEMENS Non Papa (1510-1555)

Aymer est ma vie

Ay- mer est__ ma vie Ay- -mer est ma vi- e____

COATES, Eric (1886-1957)

Bird Songs at Eventide

I heard you singing

Tell me where is fancy bred
By permission Boosey & Hawkes, Inc.,
copyright owners

Tell me where is fan- cy bred, Tell me where is fan- cy bred

COLERIDGE-TAYLOR, Samuel (1875-1912)

Eleanore, Op. 37, No. 6
Copyright by Novello & Co., Ltd., London

The for-est flow'rs are fad- ed all, The winds com-plain,

Life and Death

To look for thee, cry for thee, sigh for thee, un- der my breath,____

Onaway! Awake, beloved!
from Song of Hiawatha, Op. 30

"On- a- way! A- wake,_ be- lov- ed!___ Thou the wild-flow'r of the forest

She rested by the Broken Brook
Copyright by Oliver Ditson Co.
Used by permission

She_ rest- ed by the Bro- ken Brook, She drank of Wear- y Well___

COOKE, Thomas Simpson (1782-1848)

Love's Ritornella

Gen-tle Zi- tel-la, whi- ther a- way? Love's Ri-tor-nel-la, list while I play

Over Hill, Over Dale

O- ver hill, o- ver dale Tho- rough brush tho- rough brier

COQUARD, Arthur (1846-1910)

Haï luli
Copyright 1899, G. Schirmer, Inc.

Je suis tris- te je m'in-qui- è- te, Je ne sais plus

Ha- ï lu- li! Ha- ï lu- li! Ha- ï lu- li!

CORNELIUS, Peter (1824-1874)

Ave Maria — A - - - ve, a - - - ve, Ma - ri - a! Gra-ti-a ple-na

Der Barbier von Bagdad (The Barber of Bagdad) (comic opera)
Act I — Ach,___ das Leid hab ich er-tra-gen wie er-trag' ich nun das Glück?

Sanf-ter Schlum-mer wiegt ihn ein, lin-dert mil - de je - de Pein

Act II — O, hol-des Bild in En- gel- schö - ne, oft___ wenn in Träu - men

So mag kein and'res Wort___ er - klin-gen, als das die blüh'nde Ro - se

Ein Ton (The Monotone) Op. 3, No. 3 — Mir klingt ein Ton so wun-der-bar in Herz und Sin-nen im - mer dar,

Accompaniment Theme

Weihnachtslieder, Op. 8
No. 1 Christbaum — Wie schön geschmückt der fest- li - che Raum! Die Lich - ter fun-kehn

No. 2 Die Hirten — Die Hir- ten wa - chen Nachts in Feld; so still und dun-kel liegt die Welt,

No. 3 Drei Könige — Drei Kön' - ge wan-dern aus Mor - gen-land, Ein Stern-lein führt sie

COSTELEY, Guillaume (1531-1606)

Allon, gay, gay, gay, Bergères (madrigal) — Al- lon, gay, gay, gay, Ber- ge - res, Al- lon, gay, al- lon, gay

Mignonne, allon voir si la Roze — Mi - gnon- ne al- lon voir si la Ro-ze, Mi-gnon-ne al-lon voir

COTTRAU, Teodoro (1827-1879)

Addio a Napoli — Ad - dio mia bel- la Na- po- li, ad- di - o, ad - di - o!

Santa Lucia (Neapolitan) — Sul ma - re lu - ci - ca l'a- stro d'ar- gen - to

Ve - ni-te al l'ag- gi - le Bar chet- ta mi - a.

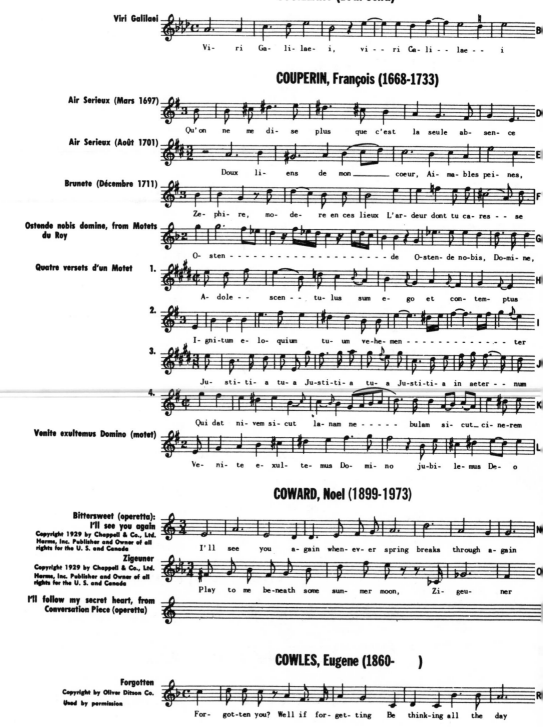

COUILLART (16th Cent.)

Viri Galilaei

Vi- ri Ga- li- lae- i, vi- ri Ga- li- - lae- - i

COUPERIN, François (1668-1733)

Air Serieux (Mars 1697)

Qu'on ne me di- se plus que c'est la seule ab- sen- ce

Air Serieux (Août 1701)

Doux li- ens de mon_____ coeur, Ai- ma- bles pei- nes,

Brunete (Décembre 1711)

Ze- phi- re, mo- de- re en ces lieux L'ar- deur dont tu ca- res- se

Ostende nobis domine, from Motets du Roy

O- sten- - - - - - - - - - - - - de O-sten- de no-bis, Do-mi- ne,

Quatre versets d'un Motet 1.

A- dole- - scen- - tu- lus sum e- go et con- tem- ptus

2.

I- gni-tum e- lo- quium tu- um ve-he- men- - - - - - - - - ter

3.

Ju- sti- ti- a tu- a Ju-sti-ti- a tu- a Ju-sti-ti- a in aeter- - num

4.

Qui dat ni- vem si- cut la- nam ne- - - - - bulam si- cut_ci- ne-rem

Venite exultemus Domino (motet)

Ve- ni- te e- xul- te- mus Do- mi- no ju- bi- le- mus De- o

COWARD, Noel (1899-1973)

Bittersweet (operetta): I'll see you again
Copyright 1929 by Chappell & Co., Ltd. Harms, Inc. Publisher and Owner of all rights for the U. S. and Canada

I'll see you a- gain when- ev- er spring breaks through a- gain

Zigeuner
Copyright 1929 by Chappell & Co., Ltd. Harms, Inc. Publisher and Owner of all rights for the U. S. and Canada

Play to me be-neath some sum- mer moon, Zi- geu- ner

I'll follow my secret heart, from Conversation Piece (operetta)

COWLES, Eugene (1860-   )

Forgotten
Copyright by Oliver Ditson Co. Used by permission

For- got-ten you? Well if for- get- ting Be think-ing all the day

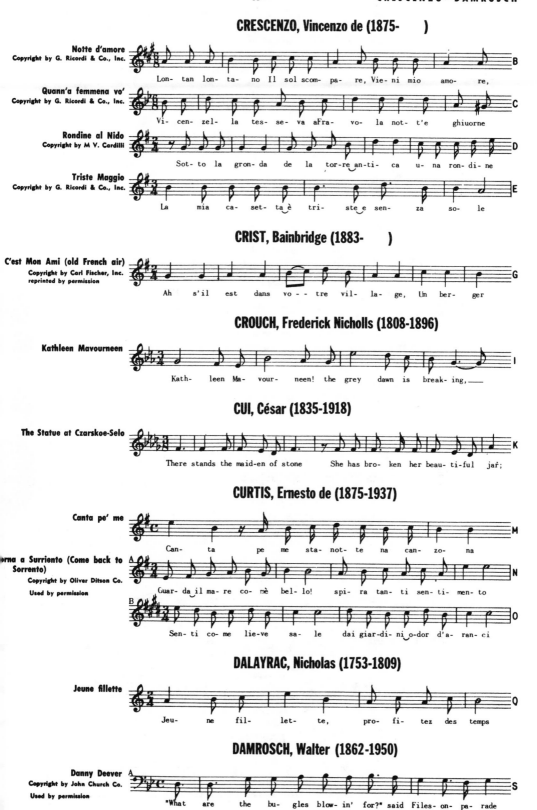

CRESCENZO, Vincenzo de (1875-   )

Notte d'amore
Copyright by G. Ricordi & Co., Inc.

Lon- tan lon- ta- no Il sol scom- pa- re, Vie- ni mio amo- re,

Quann'a femmena vo'
Copyright by G. Ricordi & Co., Inc.

Vi- cen- zel- la tes- se- va aFra- vo- la not- t'e ghiuorne

Rondine al Nido
Copyright by M V. Cardilli

Sot- to la gron- da de la tor- re an- ti- ca u- na ron- di- ne

Triste Maggio
Copyright by G. Ricordi & Co., Inc.

La mia ca- set- ta è tri- ste e sen- za so- le

CRIST, Bainbridge (1883-   )

C'est Mon Ami (old French air)
Copyright by Carl Fischer, Inc.
reprinted by permission

Ah s'il est dans vo- -tre vil- la- ge, Un ber- ger

CROUCH, Frederick Nicholls (1808-1896)

Kathleen Mavourneen

Kath- leen Ma- vour- neen! the grey dawn is break- ing,——

CUI, César (1835-1918)

The Statue at Czarskoe-Selo

There stands the maid-en of stone   She has bro- ken her beau- ti- ful jar;

CURTIS, Ernesto de (1875-1937)

Canta pe' me

Can- ta pe me sta- not- te na can- zo- na

Torna a Surriento (Come back to Sorrento)
Copyright by Oliver Ditson Co.
Used by permission

Guar- da il ma- re co- m'è bel- lo! spi- ra tan- ti sen- ti- men- to

Sen- ti co- me lie- ve sa- le dai giar- di- ni o- dor d'a- ran- ci

DALAYRAC, Nicholas (1753-1809)

Jeune fillette

Jeu- ne fil- let- te, pro- fi- tez des temps

DAMROSCH, Walter (1862-1950)

Danny Deever
Copyright by John Church Co.
Used by permission

"What are the bu- gles blow- in' for?" said Files- on- pa- rade

Danny Deever

For they're hang- in' Dan- ny Dee- ver, you can hear the Dead March play,

DARGOMIJSKY, Alexander (1813-1869)

I suffer

I suf- fer for I love thee from my in- most be- ing

The Lawyer's Clerk

There once was a clerk to a law- yer; So lit- tle and want- ing in grace,

The Miller

Said the mil- ler, home re- turn- ing Real- ly those are stran- ger's shoes

The Old Corporal

Chil-dren, keep step while you're march-ing! 'Ten-tion, your ri- fle hold fast!

Pretty Maiden

Oh,___ pret- ty___ maid- en, see the Boy - - - - ards are here!

Russalka (opera)
Act I Miller's Aria

Hey, Hey, you young ones, Hey, you_ pret-ty maid-ens, I'm on to all___

Act II Olga's Song

In our street it hap-pened that a hus-band asked his wife:

Act III Cavatina

Why am I drawn to these un- hap- py shores, What is their sec- ret?

All things here re- mind me of pleas-ures long o - - - ver.

Wherefore?

So full___ of grief, so waste_ and worn? And none_ who will help thee

The Worm

To my good wife I'm much in- debt- ed She taught me to be- come

DAVID, Félicien (1810-1876)

Lalla Roukh (opera)
Romance de Noureddin

Ma mai- tresse a quit- té la___ ten ┬ - - - te; Est elle al- lée

Couplets de Mirza

Si vous ne sa-vez plus___ char- mer Ne vous en pre- nez___

La Perle du Bresil (opera)
Couplets de Mysoli

Char- mant___ oi- seau qui sous___ l'om- bra- ge

DEBUSSY, Claude (1862-1918)

Cantatas
La Damoiselle Élue
By permission Durand & Cie, Paris;
Elkan-Vogel Co., Inc., Phila.,
copyright owners

La Da-moi- selle E- lue s'ap-puy- ait sur la bar-riè-re d'or du Ciel

DEBUSSY

La Damoiselle Élue

A
Au- tour d'el- le des a- mants, nou-vel-le-ment ré-u-nis,

B
Lorsq' au- tour de sa tê- te s'at-ta-che-ra L'au-ré- o- le,

L'Enfant Prodigue
By permission Durand & Cie, Paris;
Elkan-Vogel Co., Inc., Phila.,
copyright owners

C
L'an- né- e en vain chas- se l'an- né- e!

D
A cha- que sai-son ra- me- né- e, Leurs jeux et leurs e-bats

E
A- za- ël! A- za- ël Pour- quoi m'as tu quit- té- e?

F
Ce- pen-dant les_ soirs é-taient doux, dans la plai-ne d'or-mes plan-té- e

G
O temps à ja-mais éf- fa- cé,___ Où com-me eux j'a-vais l'â-me pu-re

H
Heu- res for-tu- né- es! A- près des an- né- es

Trois Chansons de Charles d'Orleans
'4-part unacc.)
By permission Durand & Cie, Paris;
Elkan-Vogel Co., Inc., Phila.,
copyright owners

I
Dieu! qu'il la fait bon re-gar-der La gra-ci- eu- se bonne et bel-le

J
Dieu qu'il la___ fait bon re- gar- der

K
Quant j'ai ou- y le ta-bou-rin Son- ner pour s'en al- ler au may,

L
Y- ver, vous n'es-tes qu'un vil- lain, Y-ver, Y- ver

SONGS:

Les Angélus
By permission J. Hamelle Music
Publishers, Paris

M
Chlo- ches chré- tien-nes pour les ma- ti-nes, Son-nant au coeur

Ariettes Oubliées
By permission Jean Jobert, Paris;
Elkan-Vogel Co., Inc., Phila.,
copyright owners

N
C'est l'ex-ta- se lan-gue- reu- se C'est la fa- tigue

O
Il pleu- re dans mon coeur comme il pleut dans la vil- le

P
L'om- bre des ar- - bres dans la ri- vière em-bru-mé- e

IV Paysages Belges—
Chevaux de Bois

Q
Tour- nez, tour- nez, bons che-vaux de boix Tour- nez cent tours

V Aquarelles (Green)

R
Voi- ci les fruits des fleurs des feuil- les et_ des bran- ches

VI Aquarelles (Spleen)

S
Les ro- ses é-taient tout- es rou- ges, Et les lier-res étaient tous noirs.

DEBUSSY

Ariettes Oubliées
VI Aquarelles (Spleen) — (actual theme of song) — A

Beau Soir
By permission Durand & Cie, Paris;
Elkan-Vogel Co., Inc., Phila.,
copyright owners — B
Lorsque au so-leil cou-chant les ri-viè-res sont ro-ses

La Belle au Bois Dormant — C
Des trous à son pour-point ver-meil, Un che-va-lier va __ par la

Chansons de Bilitis
I La Flûte de Pan
By permission Jean Jobert, Paris;
Elkan-Vogel Co., Inc., Phila.,
copyright owners — D
Pour le jour des Hy-a-cin-thies __ il m'a don-né u-ne sy-rinx

II La Chevelure — E
Il m'a dit: "Cet-te nuit, j'ai rê-vé J'a-vais ta che-ve-lure

III Le Tombeau des Naïades — F
Le long du bois cou-vert de gi-vre, je mar-chais;

Cinq Poëmes de Baudelaire
By permission Durand & Cie, Paris;
Elkan-Vogel Co., Inc., Phila.,
copyright owners
I Le Balcon — G
Mè-re des sou-ve-nirs maî-tres-ses des maî-tres-ses

II Harmonie du Soir — H
Voi-ci ve-nir les temps où vi-brant sur sa ti-ge

III Le Jet d'Eau — I
Tes beaux yeux sont las __ Pauvre a-man-te!

IV Recueillement — J
Sois sa-ge Ô __ ma dou-leur, et tiens toi plus tran-quille

V La Mort des Amants — K
Nous au-rons des lits pleins d'o-deurs lé-gè-res, Des di-vans pro-fonds

Deux Romances (words by P. Bourget)
By permission Durand & Cie, Paris;
Elkan-Vogel Co., Inc., Phila.,
copyright owners
1. (a) Romance — L
L'âme é-va-po-rée et souf-fran-te L'âme dou-ce, l'âme a-do-ran-te

(b) Romance — M
Voi-ci que le prin-temps, ce fils lé-ger d'A-vril

2. Les Cloches — N
Les feul-les s ou-vraient sur le bord des bran-ches dé-li-ca-te-ment

Fêtes Galantes:
First Series
1. En Sourdine
By permission Jean Jobert, Paris;
Elkan-Vogel Co., Inc., Phila.,
copyright owners — O
Cal-mes dans le de-mi jour Que les bran-ches hau-tes font

2. Fantoches — P
Sca-ra-mouche et Pul-ci-nel-la Qu'un mau-vais des-sein ras-sem-bla

3. Clair de Lune — Q
Votre âme est un pa-y-sa-ge choi-si Que vont char-mant mas-ques

Second Series
1. Les Ingénus
By permission Durand & Cie, Paris;
Elkan-Vogel Co., Inc., Phila.,
copyright owners — R
Les hauts ta-lons lut-taient a-vec les lon-gues ju-pes

2. Le Faune — S
Un vieux fau-ne de ter-re cui-te Rit au cen-tre des bou-lin-grins,

Trois Mélodies

No. 3

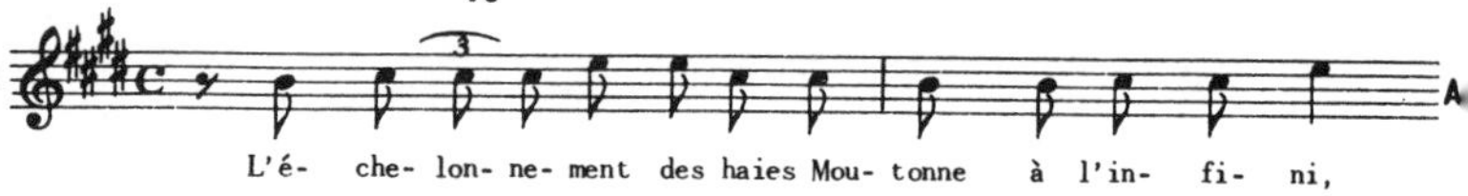

L'é- che- lon- ne- ment des haies Mou- tonne à l'in- fi- ni,

DEIS, Carl (1883-   )

Come down to Kew
Copyright 1916, G. Schirmer, Inc.

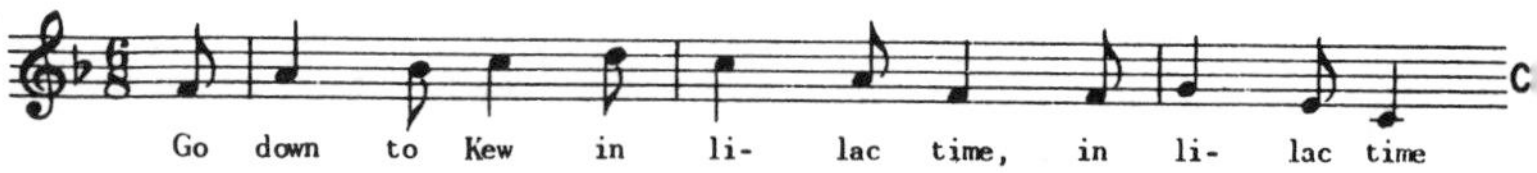

Go down to Kew in li- lac time, in li- lac time

DELANNOY, Marcel (1898-1962)

Le Galant Jardinier
By permission Heugel & Cie, Paris, copyright owners

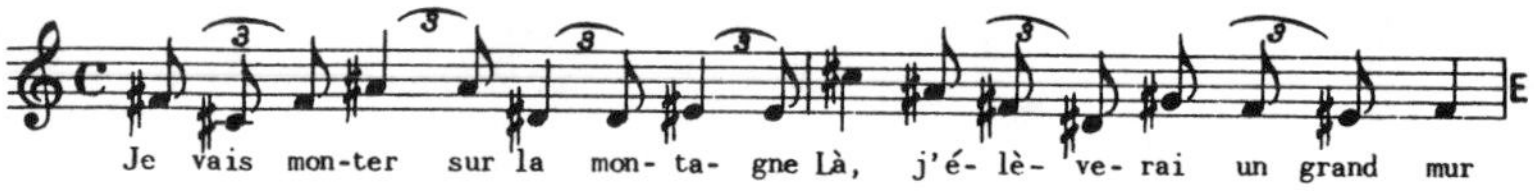

Je vais mon- ter sur la mon- ta- gne Là, j'é- lè- ve- rai un grand mur

DELBRUCK, Alfred

Un Doux Lien
Copyright 1902, G. Schirmer, Inc.

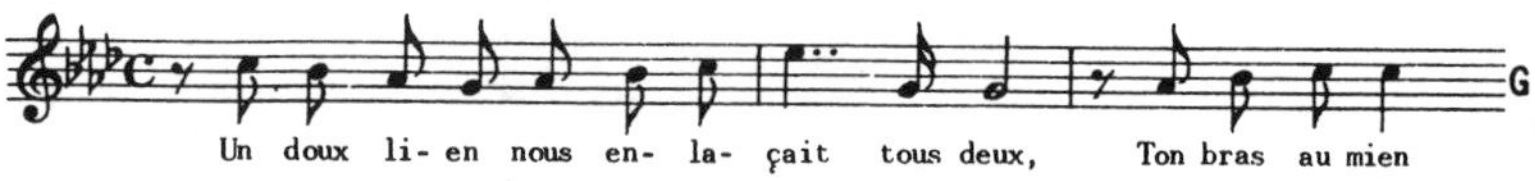

Un doux li- en nous en- la- çait tous deux, Ton bras au mien

DELIBES, Léo (1836-1891)

Arioso

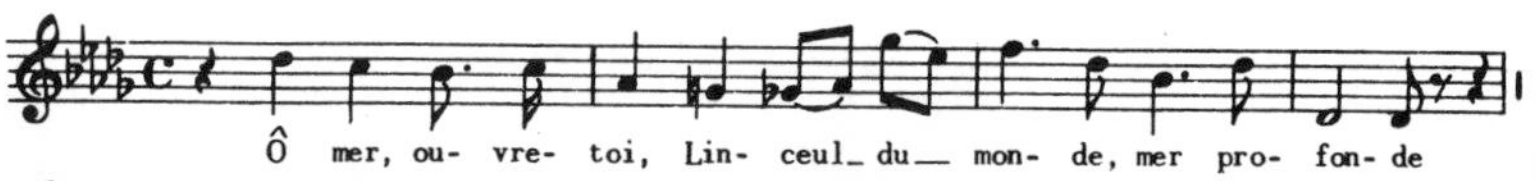

Ô mer, ou- vre- toi, Lin- ceul_ du_ mon- de, mer pro- fon- de

Bonjour, Suzon

Bon- jour, Su- zon, ma fleur des bois!_____ Es- tu tou- jours la plus jo- li- e?

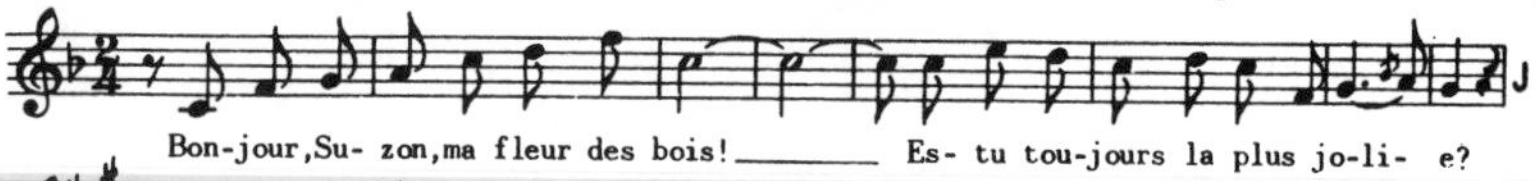

Les Filles de Cadix (Bolero)

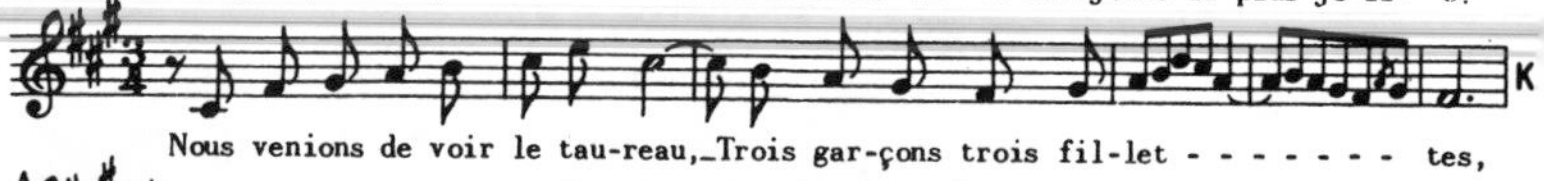

Nous venions de voir le tau- reau,_ Trois gar- çons trois fil- let - - - - - - tes,

Lakmé (opera)

Act I

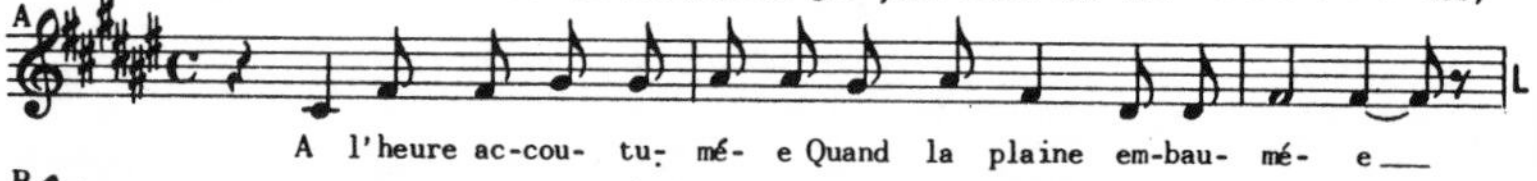

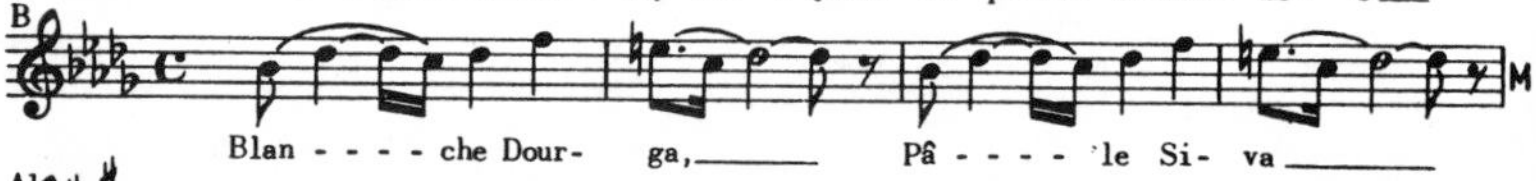

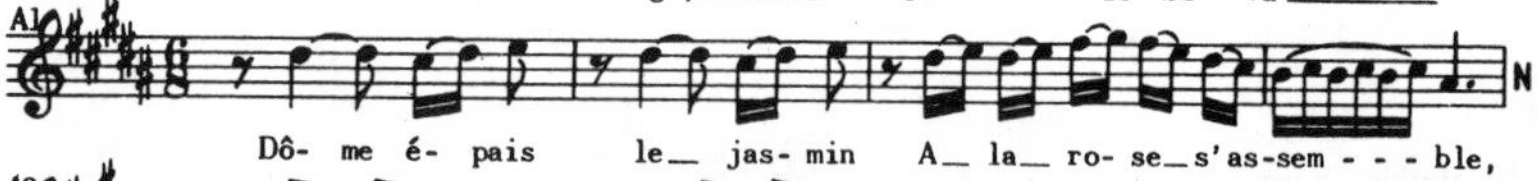

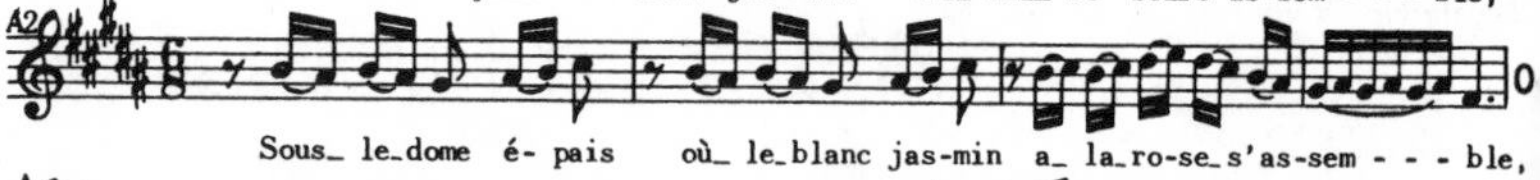

A l'heure ac- cou- tu- mé- e Quand la plaine em- bau- mé- e _

Blan - - - - che Dour- ga,_ Pâ - - - - le Si- va_

Dô- me é- pais le_ jas- min A la_ ro- se_ s'as- sem - - - ble,

Quintet

Sous_ le_ dome é- pais où_ le_ blanc jas- min a la- ro- se_ s'as- sem - - - ble,

Ah beaus fai- seurs de sys- te- mes, A- moureux_ du chan- ge- ment

Leur ver- tu bi- zar- re man- que d'ap- par- at_

Fan- tai- si- e aux div- ins men- son- ges Tu re- viens m'é- garer encore

Pour- quoi dans les grands bois ai- mé- je a m'é- ga- rer pour y pleu- rer?_____

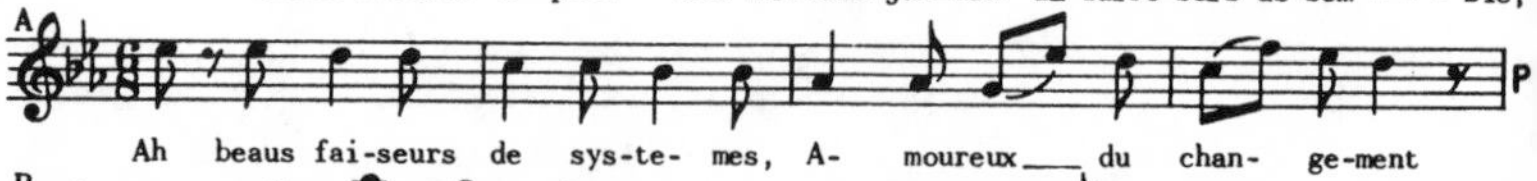

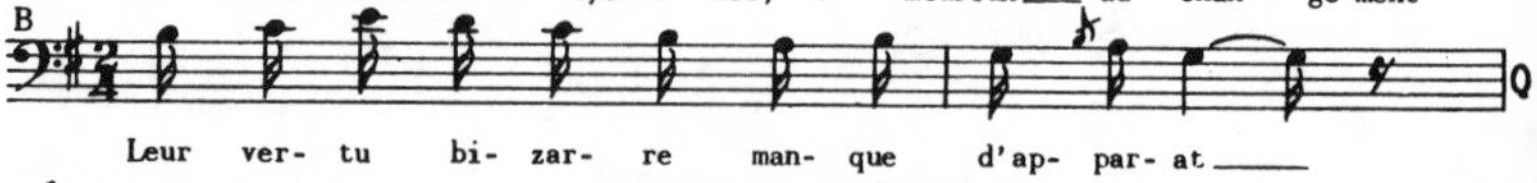

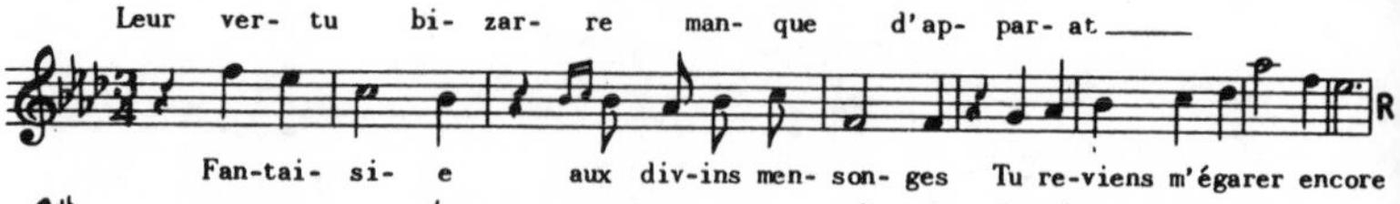

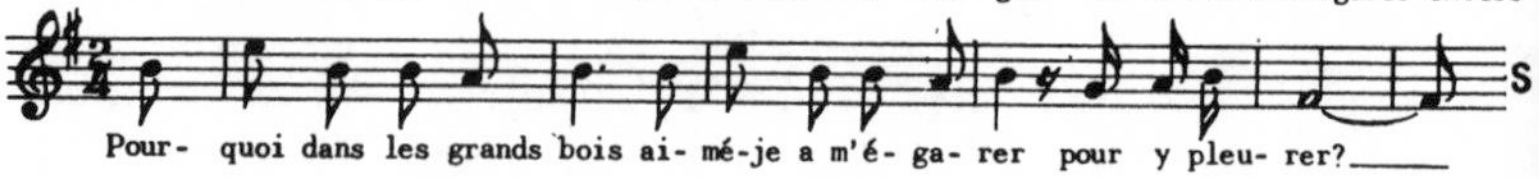

Lakmé (opera)

Act I Duet

Ou- bli- er que je t'ai vu-e, Te re- dres- sant toute é- mu- e

C'est le Dieu_ de la_ jeu- nes- se, C'est_ le Dieu du prin- temps,

Act II

Lak- mé, ton doux re- gard_ se voi- le, Ton sou- ri- re s'est at- tris- té_

Bell Song

Où va - - la jeune In- dou- e_ Fil- le des Pa- ri- as,

Là- bas dans la_____ fo - - - ret plus som- bre

Ah! Ah! Ah! Ah! Ah! Ah!_ Ah! Ah! Ah! Ah! Ah! Ah!_ Ah!_

Duet

Dans la fo- rêt près de nous, Se ca- che tou- te pe- ti- te,

Ah! c'est l'a- mour en- dor- mi Qui de son ai - - le l'ef- fleu- re,

Act III

Sous le ciel tout_ é- toi- lé Le ra- mier blanc au loin s'en_ est al- lé_

Ah! Viens,_ dans la fo- rêt pro- fon- de_ L'aile de l'a- mour a pas- sé

Tu m'as don- né le plus doux rê- ve Qu'on puisse a- voir sous notre ciel

Qu'au- tour de moi tout som- bre Je ne veux pas une om- bre

DELIUS, Frederick (1862-1934)

Appalachia (Variations on an old Slave Song) (chorus and orchestra)
By permission Boosey & Hawkes, Inc., copyright owners

Af- ter night has gone comes the day,_ the dark sha- dows will fade a- way

Cradle Song (Slumber Song)
By permission of Augener, Ltd., London

Das Kind- lein schlief ein Da schweb- te her- ein von En- geln

Hassan (closing chorus)
By permission Boosey &Hawkes, Inc., copyright owners

We take the gold- en road to Sa- mar- kand_

Indian Love Song
By permission Oxford Univ. Press, London, copyright owners

I a- rise from dreams of thee_ in the first sweet sleep of night,_

Irmeline Rose
By permission Boosey & Hawkes, Inc., copyright owners

There was a king in days of old_ and a- mongst his man- y gems

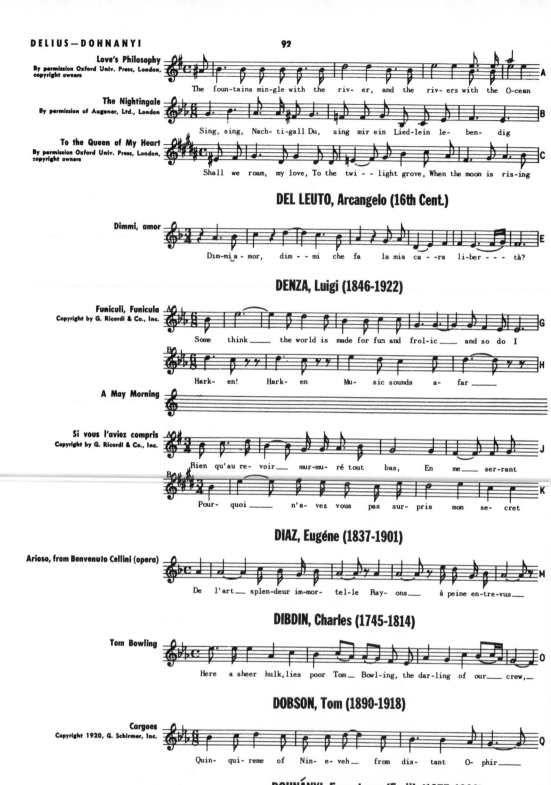

Love's Philosophy
By permission Oxford Univ. Press, London, copyright owners

The foun-tains min-gle with the riv- er, and the riv-ers with the O-cean **A**

The Nightingale
By permission of Augener, Ltd., London

Sing, sing, Nach-ti-gall Du, sing mir ein Lied-lein le- ben- dig **B**

To the Queen of My Heart
By permission Oxford Univ. Press, London, copyright owners

Shall we roam, my love, To the twi - - light grove, When the moon is ris-ing **C**

DEL LEUTO, Arcangelo (16th Cent.)

Dimmi, amor

Dim-mi a - mor, dim - -mi che fa la mia ca - -ra li-ber - - - tà? **E**

DENZA, Luigi (1846-1922)

Funiculi, Funicula
Copyright by G. Ricordi & Co., Inc.

Some think_____ the world is made for fun and frol-ic_____ and so do I **G**

Hark- en! Hark- en Mu- sic sounds a- far_____ **H**

A May Morning

Si vous l'aviez compris
Copyright by G. Ricordi & Co., Inc.

Rien qu'au re- voir_____ mur-mu-ré tout bas, En me_____ ser-rant **J**

Pour- quoi_____ n'a- vez vous pas sur- pris mon se- cret **K**

DIAZ, Eugéne (1837-1901)

Arioso, from Benvenuto Cellini (opera)

De l'art_____ splen-deur im-mor- tel-le Ray- ons_____ à peine en-tre-vus_____ **M**

DIBDIN, Charles (1745-1814)

Tom Bowling

Here a sheer hulk, lies poor Tom_____ Bowl-ing, the dar-ling of our_____ crew, **O**

DOBSON, Tom (1890-1918)

Cargoes
Copyright 1920, G. Schirmer, Inc.

Quin- qui-reme of Nin- e-veh_____ from dis- tant O- phir_____ **Q**

DOHNÁNYI, Ernest von (Ernö) (1877-1960)

Hungarian Folk Songs: Azok, Azok

Rain I thought it was that ran down drop by drop **S**

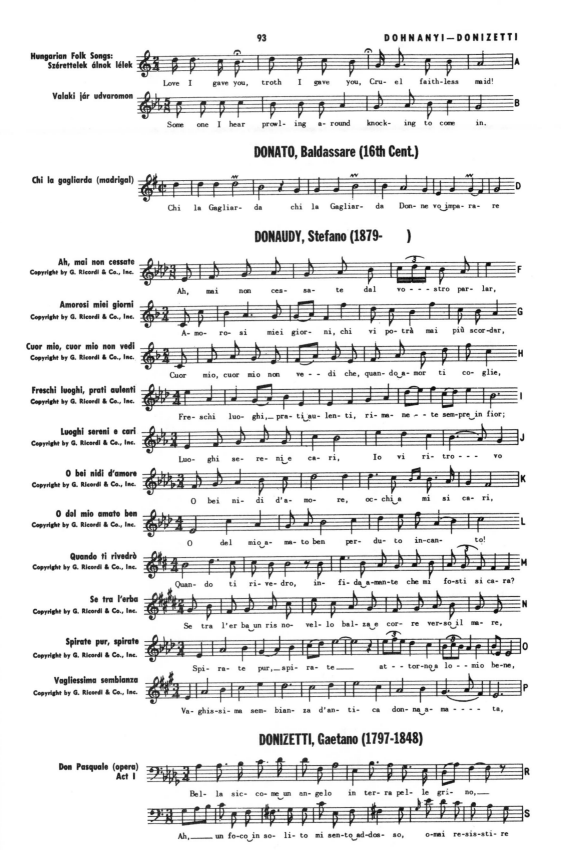

Hungarian Folk Songs:
Szérettelek álnok lélek

A — Love I gave you, troth I gave you, Cru-el faith-less maid!

Valaki jár udvaromon

B — Some one I hear prowl-ing a-round knock-ing to come in.

DONATO, Baldassare (16th Cent.)

Chi la gagliarda (madrigal)

D — Chi la Gagliar-da chi la Gagliar-da Don-ne vo impa-ra-re

DONAUDY, Stefano (1879-   )

Ah, mai non cessate
Copyright by G. Ricordi & Co., Inc.

F — Ah, mai non ces-sa-te dal vo - - stro par-lar,

Amorosi miei giorni
Copyright by G. Ricordi & Co., Inc.

G — A-mo-ro-si miei gior-ni, chi vi po-trà mai più scor-dar,

Cuor mio, cuor mio non vedi
Copyright by G. Ricordi & Co., Inc.

H — Cuor mio, cuor mio non ve-di che, quan-do a-mor ti co-glie,

Freschi luoghi, prati aulenti
Copyright by G. Ricordi & Co., Inc.

I — Fre-schi luo-ghi, pra-ti au-len-ti, ri-ma-ne - - te sem-pre in fior;

Luoghi sereni e cari
Copyright by G. Ricordi & Co., Inc.

J — Luo-ghi se-re-ni e ca-ri, Io vi ri-tro - - vo

O bei nidi d'amore
Copyright by G. Ricordi & Co., Inc.

K — O bei ni-di d'a-mo-re, oc-chi a-mi si ca-ri,

O del mio amato ben
Copyright by G. Ricordi & Co., Inc.

L — O del mio a-ma-to ben per-du-to in-can-to!

Quando ti rivedrò
Copyright by G. Ricordi & Co., Inc.

M — Quan-do ti ri-ve-dro, in-fi-da a-man-te che mi fo-sti si ca-ra?

Se tra l'erba
Copyright by G. Ricordi & Co., Inc.

N — Se tra l'er ba un ris no-vel-lo bal-za e cor-re ver-so il ma-re,

Spirate pur, spirate
Copyright by G. Ricordi & Co., Inc.

O — Spi-ra-te pur, spi-ra-te at-tor-no a lo - mio be-ne,

Vagliessima sembianza
Copyright by G. Ricordi & Co., Inc.

P — Va-ghis-si-ma sem-bian-za d'an-ti-ca don-na a-ma - - - ta,

DONIZETTI, Gaetano (1797-1848)

Don Pasquale (opera)
Act I

R — Bel-la sic-co-me un an-ge-lo in ter-ra pel-le gri-no,

S — Ah, ___ un fo-co in so-li-to mi sen-to ad-dos-so, o-mai re-sis-sti-re

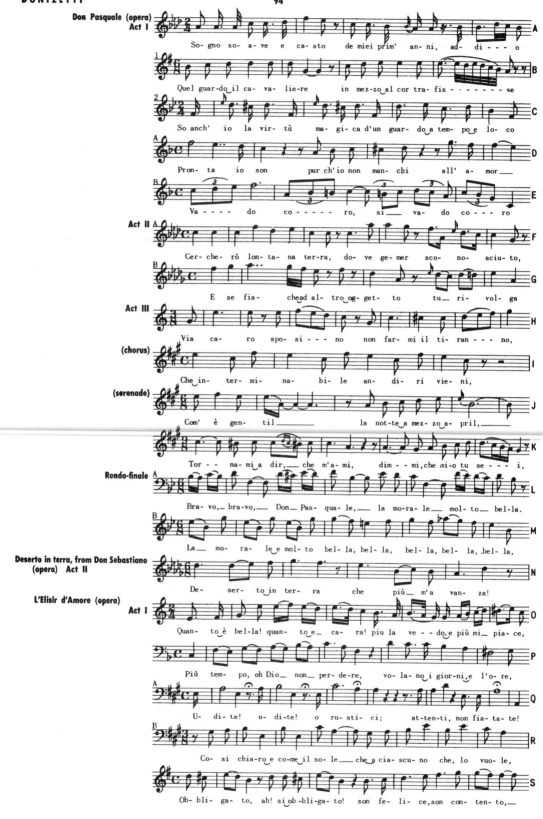

Don Pasquale (opera)
Act I

A — So- gno so- a- ve e ca-sto de miei prim' an- ni, ad- di- - - o

B — Quel guar-do il ca- va- lie-re in mez-zo al cor tra-fis - - - - - se

2 — So anch' io la vir- tù ma- gi-ca d'un guar-do a tem-po e lo-co   C

A — Pron- ta io son pur ch'io non man-chi all' a- mor___   D

B — Va- - - do co- - - ro, si_ va-do co- - ro   E

Act II
A — Cer-che- rò lon-ta-na ter-ra, do- ve ge-mer sco- no- sciu-to,   F

B — E se fia_ che ad al- tro og- get-to tu_ ri_ vol- ga   G

Act III
H — Via ca- ro spo- si- - no non far-mi il ti- ran- - no,

(chorus)
I — Che in- ter- mi- na- bi- le an- di- ri vie- ni,

(serenade)
J — Com' è gen- til___ la not-te a mez-zo a- pril,___

K — Tor- - na-mi a dir, che m'a-mi, dim- mi, che mi-o tu se- - - i,

Rondò-finale
A — Bra- vo,_ bra-vo,_ Don_ Pas- qua- le,_ la mo-ra- le mol- to_ bel-la.   L

B — La_ mo- ra- le e mol- to_ bel- la, bel- la, bel- la, bel- la, bel-la,   M

Deserto in terra, from Don Sebastiano (opera) Act II
N — De- ser- to in ter- ra che più_ m'a van- za!

L'Elisir d'Amore (opera)
Act I
O — Quan- to è bel-la! quan-to e ca- ra! piu la ve- do e più mi_ pia- ce,

P — Più tem- po, oh Dio_ non per- de- re, vo- la-no i gior-ni e l'o- re,

A — U- di- te! u- di- te! o ru- sti- ci; at- ten-ti, non fia- ta- te!   Q

B — Co- sì chia-ro e co-me il so- le___ che a cia- scu-no che, lo_ vuo-le,   R

S — Ob- bli- ga- to, ah! si ob- bli-ga- to! son fe- li- ce, son con- ten-to,___

L'Elisir d'Amore (opera)

Act I — A-di-na, cre-di-mi, te ne scon-giu-ro

Co-me Pa-ri-de vez-zo-so por-se il po-mo al-la più bel-la!

Act II — Io son ric-co e tu sei bel-la, io du-ca-ti e vez-zi hai tu

Ven-ti scu-di! E ben so-nan-ti. Quan-do? A-des-so?

U-na fur-ti-va la-gri-ma negl' occhi suoi spun-tò

Pren-di, pren-di, per me sei li-be-ro

La Favorita (opera)

Act I — U-na ver-gi-ne, un an-giol d'a-mo-re al Si-gno-re

An-giol ca-ro, so-a-ve, be-a-to, deh tu ve-glia

Bei rag-gi lu-cen-ti, bell' au-re be-a-te,

Ah! mio be-ne mio te-so-ro, il Cie-lo t'in-vi-a, vie-ni a vien

Fia ve-ro? la-sciar-ti! e tu il chie-di a me?

Act II — Vien, Leo-no-ra, a pie-di tuo-i, ser-to e so-glio il cor,

De' ne-mi-ci tuoi lo sde-gno di-sfi-dar sa-prò per te,

Quan-do le so-glie pa-ter-ne var-ca-i de-bil fan-ciul-la

In que-sto suo-lo a se-re-nar tuo cu-ra

Act III — A tan-to a-mor Leo-no-ra, il tuo ri-spon-da

O mio Fer-nan-do, del-la ter-ra il tro-no

Scrit-to è in ciel il mio do-lor, su, ve-ni-te ell'è u-na fe-sta,

Act IV — Splen-don più bel-le in ciel le stel le, ma lut-to or-ren-do

La Favorita (opera)
Act IV

Spir- to gen-til, ne' so-gni mie - - i bril la-sti un dì, ma ti per-de i

Preghiera

Pie- to - so al par del Nu— mi, pie- to - so— su per me

Vie-ni, ah vien,— io m'ab-ban- do - no— al- la gio - ja— che m'innebria

La Fille du Regiment (The Daughter
of the Regiment) (opera)   Act I

Au bruit de la guer- re j'ai re- çu le jour—

Cha- cun le sait, cha-cun le dit le re- gi-ment— par ex- cel-len-ce

Il est là, il est là, il est là, mor- bleu,

De-puis l'in-stant où dans mes bras je vous re- çus— tou-te trem-blan- te

De cet a- veu si ten-dre non— mon coeur en ce jour

Il faut par-tir— mes bons com-pag- nons d'ar-mes

Act II

Par le rang et— par l'o-pu- len-ce en vain l'on a cru m'é-blou-ir

Sa - - - lut à la Fran-ce à mes— beaux— jours—

Tous les trois ré- u- nis, quel plai-sir, mes a-mis, quel bon-heur, quel bon-heur,

Pour me rap- pro-cher— de Ma- ri- e, je m'en-rô- lai pau- vre sol- dat

Linda di Chamounix (opera)
Act I

Am- bo na- ti in que— sta— val- le

O lu- ce di quest' a - ni- ma de-li-zia a-mo-re e vi - ta

Love duet

Per sua ma-dre an-dò una fi- glia mi-glior sor-te a rin-trac- ciar;

Da quel dì, che t'in- con- tra- i ad a- mar— quel dì im-pa- ra- i

A con- so- lar mi af-fre- ti- si tal gior-no de- si- a- to

Prayer

O tu che re- go- li gli u- ma- ni e- ven - - - - - ti,

Linda di Chamounix (opera)
Act II
Se tanto in i - - ra a-gli uo-mi-ni è___ l'a-mor no - - stro,

Mad scene (duet)
No nom è ver, men-ti-ro nò tra-dir tu non mi puo___

Act III
Di tue pe-ne spar-ve il so - - gno al-le gio-je a-mor ti___ de - sta

Lucia di Lammermoor (opera)
Act I
Cru - da, fu - ne-sta sma - nia___ tu m'hai sve-glia-to in pet - - - to

Huntsmen's Chorus
Co - me vin - ti da_stan-chez - za, do-pa lun-go er-ra - re in-tor-no

La pie-ta - - de in suo fa-vo-re Mi ti sen-si in-van mi det - ta

Re-gna-va nel_si - len-zi-o al-ta la not-te e bru - - - na

Quan-do ra-pi-to in e-sta-si del più co-cen-te ar-do-re

Sul-la tom-ba che rin-ser-ra il tra-di-to ge-ni-to-re,

Ver - ran-no a te sul l'a - u-re i miei so-spi-ri ar-den - - ti,

Act II
Sof-fri - - - va nel pian-to, lan-gui - - a nel_ do-lo - re,

Se tra-dir-mi tu po-tra - i la mia_sor-te e già com-pi-ta;

Per te d'im-men-so giu-bi-lo tut-to s'av-vi-va in-tor- no

Sextet
Chi mi fre-na in tal mo-men - to? Chi tron-cò del-l'i-re il cor - so

E - - - sci,___ fug - - - gi il fu-ror___ che m'ac-cen-de

Act III
Qui del pa-dre an-cor___ re - spi-ra l'om-bra i-nul-ta e par che fre - - - ma

O so - le più rat - to a sor - ger t'ap-pre - sta,

Dal-le stan - ze, o - ve Lu - ci - a trat-ta a vea col suo con-sor-te

Oh qual fu - ne - sto av - ve - - ni- men-to!

Lucia di Lammermoor (opera)
Act III (Mad Scene)

Al- fin_ son tu - - - a al- fin_ sei mi - - - o,

Spar- gi d'a- ma- ro pian- to il mio ter- res- tre ve - - - lo,

Fra po- co a me ri- co- ve- rò da- rà ne- glet- to a ve - lo _

Tu che a Dio spie- ga- sti l'a- li o bel- l'al- ma in- na- mo- ra- ta,

Lucrezia Borgia (opera)
Prologue

Com' è bel- lo qua- le in- can- to In quel vol- to o- nes- to e al- te- ro,

Di pe- sca- to- re i- gno- bi- le Es- ser fi- gliuol cre- de - - - i

Act I

Vie- ni! la mia ven- det - - - - ta È me- di- ta- ta e pron- ta

Act II

Il se- gre- to per es- ser fe- li - - - - - ci

M'o- di, oh! m'o- di, Io non t'im- plo- ro Per vo- ler _

Fra l'erbe, from La Zingara (opera)

Fan- ciul- la sui grep- pi le ca- pre e- mu- la - - - - - i

Un gior - - - no la ma - - - no mi por - - - se un don- zel- lo

DOURLEN, Victor Charles (1780-1864)

Je sais attacher des rubans,
from Le Frère Philippe (opera)

Je sais at- tach- er des ru- bans, Je sais com- ment vien- nent

DOWLAND, John (1563-1626)

First Book of Ayres:
Awake, sweet love

A- wake, sweet love, thou art re- turned. My heart, which long

Come again! Sweet love

Come a- gain! Sweet love doth now in- vite Thy grac- es, that re- frain

Come, heavy sleep

Come, hea- vy Sleep the im- age of true Death

Go, crystal tears

Go, crys- tal tears, like to the _ morn- ing showers,

Second Book of Ayres:
Fine knacks for ladies

Fine knacks for la- dies cheap, choice, brave and new! Good pen- ny worths!

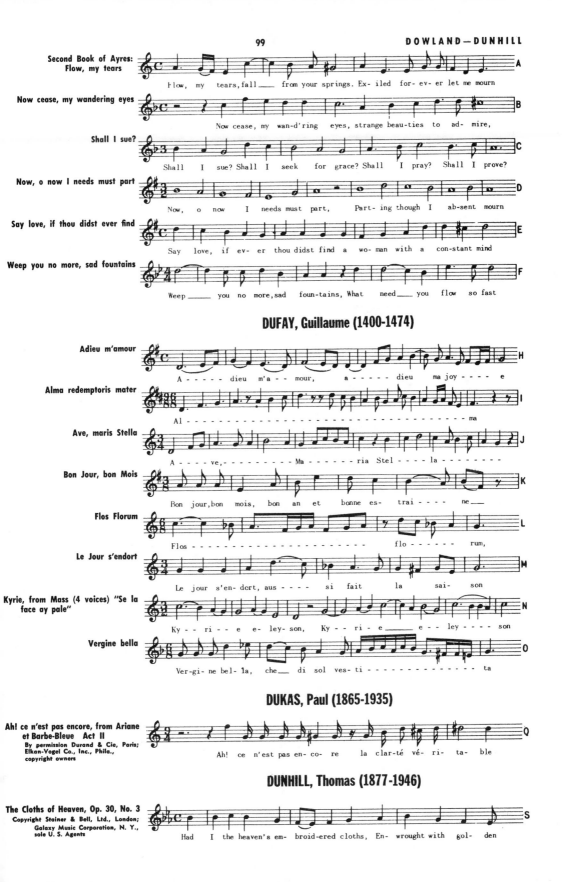

**Second Book of Ayres:
Flow, my tears**
Flow, my tears, fall from your springs. Ex-iled for-ev-er let me mourn

Now cease, my wandering eyes
Now cease, my wan-d'ring eyes, strange beau-ties to ad-mire,

Shall I sue?
Shall I sue? Shall I seek for grace? Shall I pray? Shall I prove?

Now, o now I needs must part
Now, o now I needs must part, Part-ing though I ab-sent mourn

Say love, if thou didst ever find
Say love, if ev-er thou didst find a wo-man with a con-stant mind

Weep you no more, sad fountains
Weep you no more, sad foun-tains, What need you flow so fast

DUFAY, Guillaume (1400-1474)

Adieu m'amour
A - - - - - dieu m'a - - mour, a - - - - - dieu ma joy - - - - e

Alma redemptoris mater
Al - ma

Ave, maris Stella
A - - - ve, - - - - - - - Ma - - - - - - ria Stel - - - - la - - - - - - -

Bon Jour, bon Mois
Bon jour, bon mois, bon an et bonne es - trai - - - - ne

Flos Florum
Flos - - - - - - - - - - - - - - - - flo - - - - - - rum,

Le Jour s'endort
Le jour s'en-dort, aus - - - - si fait la sai - - son

**Kyrie, from Mass (4 voices) "Se la
face ay pale"**
Ky - - ri - e e - ley-son, Ky - - ri - e - - - - - e - ley - - - - son

Vergine bella
Ver-gi-ne bel-la, che - - di sol ves-ti - - - - - - - - - - - - - ta

DUKAS, Paul (1865-1935)

**Ah! ce n'est pas encore, from Ariane
et Barbe-Bleue Act II**
By permission Durand & Cie, Paris;
Elkan-Vogel Co., Inc., Phila.,
copyright owners
Ah! ce n'est pas en-co-re la clar-té vé-ri-ta-ble

DUNHILL, Thomas (1877-1946)

The Cloths of Heaven, Op. 30, No. 3
Copyright Stainer & Bell, Ltd., London;
Galaxy Music Corporation, N. Y.,
sole U. S. Agents
Had I the heaven's em-broid-ered cloths, En-wrought with gol-den

To the Queen of Heaven
Copyright 1926, T. F. Dunhill

Queen of heav-en, bless'd may thou be, for God-ës Son born — A.

DUNSTABLE, John (15th Cent.)

Quam pulchra es

Quam — pul - - chra és, et quam de-cor-ra, ca-ris-si-ma, — C.

DUPARC, Henri (1848-1933)

Au pays où se fait la guerre
Copyright by Salabert, Paris, N. Y.

Au pa- ys où se fait la guer - - - - re mon bel _ a- mi — E.

Chanson Triste
Copyright by Salabert, Paris, N. Y.

Dans ton coeur dort un clair de lu- ne, un doux clair de lu- ne — F.

Élégie
Copyright by Salabert, Paris, N. Y.

Oh! ne mur- mu- rez pas _ son nom! qu'il dor-me dans l'om-bre, — G.

Extase
Copyright by Salabert, Paris, N. Y.

Sur un lys pâ- le mon coeur dort D'un som-meil doux comme la mort _ — H.

L'Invitation au Voyage
Copyright by Salabert, Paris, N. Y.

Mon en-fant, _ ma sœur Songe _ a la dou-ceur D'al-ler là- bas — I.

Lamento
Copyright by Salabert, Paris, N. Y.

Con- nais-sez vous la blan-che tom- bé Où flotte a-vec un son plain- tif — J.

Le Manoir de Rosamunde
Copyright by Salabert, Paris, N. Y.

De sa dent soudaine _ et vo-ra- ce Comme un chien l'amour — K.

Phidylé
Copyright by Salabert, Paris, N. Y.

L'herbe est molle _ au sommeil _ sous les frais peupliers, _ — L.

Re- po- se _ ô Phidy- lé — M.

Sérénade Florentine
Copyright by Salabert, Paris, N. Y.

É- toi- le dont la beau- té luit _ comme un di- a- mant dans la nuit, — N.

Soupir
Copyright by Salabert, Paris, N. Y.

Ne ja-mais la voir ni l'en-ten- dre, Ne ja-mais tout haut la nom- mer, — O.

Testament
Copyright by Salabert, Paris, N. Y.

Pour que le vent te les ap- por- te Sur l'ai-le noi-re d'un re-mord, _ — P.

La Vague et la Cloche
Copyright by Salabert, Paris, N. Y.

U- ne fois, ter-ras-sé par un puis-sant _ breu- va- ge J'ai rê-vé — Q.

La Vie Antérieure
Copyright by Salabert, Paris, N. Y.

J'ai long- temps ha- bi- té sous de vas- tes por- ti- ques — R.

DUPONT, Gabriel (1878-1914)

Mandoline
Copyright 1946, G. Schirmer, Inc.

Les don-neurs de sé-ré-na-des Et les bel-les é-cou-teu-ses

DURANTE, Francesco (1684-1755)

Danza. danza. fanciulla gentile

Dan-za,— dan-za, fan-ciul-la,— al— mi-o can-tar,

Vergin, tutta amor

Ver-gin, tut-ta a-mor,— O Ma-dre di bon-ta-de, O Ma-dre pi-a,

DVOŘÁK, Antonin (1841-1904)

The Devil and Kate, Op. 112 (opera)
Act III   The Countess's Aria

Wie trau-rig rings-um öd' die Hal-len, wo-rin einst Freu-de

Dimitrij Op. 64 (opera)
Act II Dimitrij's Aria

Zdi-voké-ho ži-tí vi-ru du-še mo-je stou-hou spě-la

Act III Dimitrij's Aria

Vi-děl jsem je Xe-ni-i jsem zrel, my-slí ti-chým blahem o-po-je nou

Rusalka (opera)
Act I O lovely moon (Rusalka's Song)

Glei-ten-der Mond du, so sil-ber-zart,— Sendest weit-hin deine Blik-ke—

Act I A strange vision (Prince's Air)

Weiss, dass ein Trug-bild du, dass wohl schwindet, wie vor der Nacht

Act II

Was im saal, in je-dem Stüb-chen heut' im Schloss für Mord-ru---mor?

Act II Alas, alas

Hast du dir als Theil er-ko-ren,— Im-mer wird dir Lust, nim-mer Lust und Schmerz_

Act II White flowers along the way

Blü-me-lein weiss am Wie-ges-rand, blüh-ten wohl still be-schei-den,

Act III I have golden hair

Mein, mein gold' nes Haar ist mein, mein, mein gold' nes Haar ist mein

The Sly Peasant, Op. 37 (opera)
Act I Prince's Song

Wer kann's mit Wor-ten sa-gen auch, was drinn im Her-zen

Biblical Songs, Op. 99 (duets)
No. 1 Clouds and darkness are round about
By permission Associated Music Publishers, Inc.

Clouds and dark-ness are round a-bout Him Right-eous-ness and judgment

No. 2 Lord, thou art my refuge

Lord, thou art my re-fuge and my shield, and in thy word put I my trust

No. 3 Hear my prayer, O Lord

Hear my prayer, O Lord, my— God O hide— not thy face

Biblical Songs:
No. 4 God is my Shepherd

God is my shep - - herd, I want for no - thing.

No. 5 I will sing Jehovah's praises

I will sing new songs of glad-ness, I will sing Je-ho-vah's prai-ses

No. 6 Hear my prayer, O Lord

Hear my prayer O Lord ___ give ear un-to my ___ cry!

No. 7 By the Waters of Babylon

By the wa-ters of Ba-by-lon, ___ there we sat us down ___ and wept

No. 8 Turn Thee to Me

Turn Thee to me and have ___ mer-cy for I am de-so-late

No. 9 I will lift mine eyes up to the mountains

I will lift mine eyes up to the moun-tains,

No. 10 Sing ye a joyful song

Sing ye a joy-ful song un-to the Lord ___

Goin' Home, from New World Symphony, Op. 95, Largo (arr. William Arms Fisher)
Copyright 1922, Oliver Ditson Co.
Used by permission.

Go - in' home, go - in' home, I'm a-go - in' home

Gypsy Songs, Op. 55
No. 1 Mein Lied ertönt

Mein Lied er-tönt, ein Lie-bespsalm, be-ginnt der ___ Tag zu ___ sin-ken,

No. 2 Ei, wie mein Triangel

Ei, wie mein Tri-an-gel wun-der-herr-lich läu-tet!

No. 3 Rings is der Wald so stumm

Rings ist der Wald so stumm und still, das Herz schlägt mir so ban - - ge,

No. 4 Als die alte Mutter (Songs my mother taught me)

Als die al-te ___ Mut - - - ter mich noch lehr-te ___ sin - - - gen,

No. 5 Rein gestimmt die Saiten!

Rein ge-stimmt die Sai-ten! Bur-sche, tanz' im Krei-se!

No. 6 In dem weiten, breiten (Freer is the gypsy)

In dem wei-ten, ___ brei-ten, ___ luft' gen Lei-nen-klei-de ___

No. 7 Darf des Falken Schwinge Tatra (Cloudy heights of Tatra)

Darf des Fal-ken Schwin-ge Tat-ra-höh'n um-rau - - -schen

Lasst mich allein (Leave me alone) Op. 82, No. 1

Lasst mich al-lein in mei-nen Träu-men geh'n, stört mir die Wol-lust nicht

The Mower, Op. 73, No. 2

Nah ___ bei ___ Te-mes-var, dem Städt-chen mah-te ___ Gras ein her-zig Mäd-chen

Thirteen Moravian Duets, Op. 31, No. 1 The Fugitive

Where blue the Danube flows, far will I fly from thee Where blue the Danube flows

No. 2 Speed thee, Birdie

Speed thee, bir-die, fly a-cross the pur-ple moun-tain

Moravian Duets
No. 3 The Slighted Heart

Oh that now I held the scythe well sharpen'd, and the grass were wav-ing high

No. 4 Parting without sorrow

Gai-ly as I met thee, let us part to-mor-row, fear not that I e'er forget thee

No. 5 The pledge of love

Dost thou see the stars shi-ning yon-der? Thus are we and joy a-sun-der

No. 6 Forsaken

Lo, the dove from her cot hath flown, sits on the al-der and makes her moan,

No. 7 Sad of heart

By the for-est sha-dy flows a brooklet clear, thither lead my steed, thou damsel young

No. 8 The modest maid

Swee-ter than the vio-let is my gen-tle mai-den, with the__ ro-se's dawning_blushes

No. 9 The Ring

Let us sing to day joy-ous roun-de-lay! Let us sing to-day

No. 10 Omens

Thrive and grow, thou come-ly grass, thrive on the sun-ny mea-dows!

No. 11 The Maid imprisoned

Mai-den journeys forth a-mow-ing, by the vineyard stands and pon-ders.

No. 12 Comfort

Thou fo-rest dear, fare-well, ah, who will tend thee now?

No. 13 The Wild Rose

Forth went a come-ly lass mov-ing the Au-tumn grass;

EAST, Michael (17th Cent.)

How Merrily We Live

How mer-ri-ly we live that shep-herds be, we live

EDWARDS, Clara (-1974)

By the Bend of the River
Copyright 1927, G. Schirmer, Inc.

The gold-en moon-light,__ the gloam, My thoughts re-turn-ing

By the bend of the riv-er____ Where rush-es are grow-ing

Into the Night
Copyright 1939, G. Schirmer, Inc.

Si-lent-ly in-to the night I go, In-to the frag-rant night,

EDWARDS, Richard (c.1523-1566)

In going to my naked bed

In go-ing to my nak-ed bed as one that would have slept

ELGAR, Sir Edward (1857-1934)

As torrents in summer, from King Olaf, Op. 30
By permission Novello & Co., Ltd., London

As tor-rents in sum-mer, Half dried in their chan-nels

The Dream of Gerontius
By permission Novello & Co., Ltd., London

Sanc-tus for-tis, Sanc-tus De-us De pro-fun-dis o-ro te

Praise to the ho-li-est in the height, and in the depth be praise;

O lov- ing wis-dom of our God When all was sin and shame,

Soft - - - ly and gen-tly dear-ly ran-somed soul

Lament, from Caractacus, Op. 35
By permission Novello & Co., Ltd., London

O my war- riors, tell me tru-ly O'er the red groves where ye lie,

The Light of Life, Op. 29 (oratorio)
By permission Novello & Co., Ltd., London

Be not ex-treme, O Lord, to mark a-miss those se-cret sins

As a spi-rit didst thou pass be-fore mine eyes, I saw thee not,

Thou on-ly hast the words of life! Be pro-phet to my heart,

I am the good Shep-herd, and know my sheep, and am known by them

The Pipes of Pan
By permission Boosey & Hawkes, Inc.,
copyright owners

When the woods are gay in the time of June with the chest-nut flow'r and fan,

Pleading, Op. 48, No. 1
By permission Novello & Co., Ltd., London

Will you come home-ward from the hills of Dream-land, Home in the dusk,

Sea-Pictures, Op. 37
No. 1 Sea Slumber Song
By permission Boosey & Hawkes, Inc.,
copyright owners

Sea-birds are a- sleep, The world for-gets to weep

No. 2 In Haven

Close-ly let me hold thy hand, Storms are sweep-ing sea and land;

No. 3 Sabbath Morning at Sea

The ship went on with so-lemn face: To meet the dark-ness on the deep,

No. 4 Where Corals Lie

The deeps have mu-sic soft and low When winds a-wake the air-y spry,

No. 5 The Swimmer

With short, sharp, vi-o-lent lights made vi-vid, To south-ward

Coronation Ode, Op. 44, No. 6
(Trio of Pomp and Circumstance,
No. 1)
By permission Boosey & Hawkes, Inc.,
copyright owners

The Sun goeth down, from The Kingdom, Op. 51, No. 4 (oratorio)
By permission Novello & Co., Ltd., London

Land of hope and glory Moth - - er of the free,

The sun go - eth down;___ Thou mak-est dark-ness, and it is night:

ERLEBACH, Philipp Heinrich (1657-1714)

Ihr Gedanken

Ihr Ge - dan - ken, Ihr Ge - dan-ken, quält mich nicht!

Nur getrost

Nur ge-trost nur ge-trost, lass al - les ge - hen,

Schwaches Hertz

Schwa - ches Hertz, du bist be - sie - get, du bist be - sie - get,

EULENBURG, Philipp zu (1847-1921)

Rosenlieder (song cycle)
No. 1 Monatsrose

Aus des Nach-bars Haus trat mein Lieb hin-aus, hielt ein Rös-lein in der Hand

No. 2 Wilde Rose

Bei dem Wal - des-saum im Wie - sen-hang stand am Ro-sen-strauch

No. 3 Rankende Rose

Sagt, ihr wei-ssen Rank- rö- se-lein, Was treibt ihr am Hau-se des Lieb-chens mein?

No. 4 Seerose

Der a - bend ist still und dun- kel der See, im Schil-fe leuch-ten

No. 5 Weisse und rothe Rose

Mein Schatz der liegt auf der Tod- ten-bahr, hat wei-sse Ro-sen

FALCONIERI, Andrea (c. 1600-1650)

Bella porta di rubini

Bel- la por-ta di ru- bi- ni ch'a-pri il var-co ai dol- ci ac-cen-ti,

Non più d'amore (villanella)

Non più d'a - mo - re, Non più d'ar - do - re, Pe- ne e tor- men- ti,

O Bellissimi capelli

O bel-lis- si- mi ca- pel- li, miei dol-cis- si- mi di- let- ti,

Occhietti amati

Oc- chietti a - ma-ti che m'in-cen- de-te per-chè spie-ta-ti o-mai più sie-te

Segui, segui dolente core

Se-gui, se-gui, do-len- te co- re, gli oc-chi fon-ti del vi-vo ar-do- re;

Vezzosette e care

Vez- zo-set- te e ca-re pu- pi-let-te ar-den-ti, chi v'ha fat-to a- va-re

FALLA, Manuel De (1876- 1946)

El Amor Brujo (ballet)
Canción del amor dolido
By permission J. & W. Chester, Ltd., London, copyright owners

Yo no sé — qué sien-to, ni sé qué me pa-sa,

Canción del fuego fatuo

Lo mis-mo que_es fue-go fa-tuo, lo_-mis- mi-to_es er-que-ré.

Danza del juego de amor

Tú_e-res a-quel mal gi-ta — no

Quien lo_ha-bi- a de de-ci que con o-tra la ven-di - - - as!

Las Campanas del Amanecer

Ya_es-ta des pun-tan-do_el dí - - - a! Can-tad, cam-pa-nos, can-tad,

Les Colombes
Copyright by Salabert, Paris, N. Y.

Sur le co-teau, là- bas où sont les tom-bes

Seguidilla
Copyright by E. B. Marks Music Corp., N. Y.

Un ju-pon ser-ré sur les han - -ches Un pegne é-norme à son chi-gnon

Seven Popular Spanish Songs
No. 1 El paño moruno
By permission Associated Music Publishers, Inc.

Al pa-ño fi-no_en la tien-da, Al pa-ño fi-no_en la tien-da,

No. 2 Seguidilla Murciana

Cualquie-ra que_el te-ja - - - do len-ga de vi - - - drio.

No. 3 Asturiana

Por ver si me con-so-la-ba, A-rri-me-me à_un pi - no ver-de

No. 4 Jota

Di- cen que no nos que-re- mos

No. 5 Nana (Berceuse)

Duér- me-te, ni-ño, duer-me, Duer-me, mi al-ma,

No. 6 Canción

Por trai-do-res, tus o-jos, Voy á_en-te-rrar los;

No. 7 Polo

Guar-do_u-na - - - "A - - - y!" Guar-do_u-na "A - - - y!"

Soneto a Córdoba
By permission Oxford Univ. Press, London, copyright owners

Oh_ex-cel- so mu-ro, oh to-rres co-ro-na-das De ho-nor

Tus Ojillos Negros

Yo no sé qué tie- nen tus o-ji- llos ne- gros

Mas, por o-tra par-te, son tan em-bus-te- ros

La Vida Breve
By permission Associated Music Publishers, Inc.

Vi-van los que ri - - - en! Mue-ran los que llo- ran!

FARMER, John (c. 1565-c. 1600)

Fair Phyllis I saw sitting all alone

Fair Phyl-lis I saw sit-ting all a-lone Feed-ing her flock near to the mountain

FARNABY, Giles (c. 1560-c. 1600)

Simkin said that Sis was fair

Sim-   kin said that Sis   was   fair, and   that   he meant to   love her,

Some time she would

Some-   time   she   would and some-time   not, and   some-   time   not

FAURÉ, Gabriel (1845-1924)

Dans les ruines d'une abbaye, Op. 2, No. 1
By permission J. Hamelle, Paris

Seuls tous deux, ra-   vis, chant-ants, comme   on s'ai - - - me;

Seule! Op. 3, No. 1
By permission J. Hamelle, Paris

Dans un bai-ser l'onde au ri-va-   ge   dit ses dou-leurs!

Sérénade Toscane, No. 2

O   toi   qui ber-ce un   rêve   en-chan-teur

Chanson du Pêcheur, Op. 4, No. 1
By permission J. Hamelle, Paris

Ma belle a-mi est morte   Je pleurerai   tou-jours!

Lydia, No. 2

Ly- di- a,   sur tes roses jou-   es   Et sur ton col frais et si   blanc.

Chant d'Automne, Op. 5, No. 1
By permission J. Hamelle, Paris

Bien- tôt   nous plon-ge-rons   dans les froi-des té-nè-bres,

L'Absent, No. 3

Sen- tiers où l'herbe se ba-lan-ce,   Va-lons, côteaux, bois cheve-lus,

Tristesse, Op. 6, No. 2
By permission J. Hamelle, Paris

Av- ril est de re-tour, La pre-mière des ro-ses

Sylvie, No. 3

Si tu veux sa-voir, ma bel-le, Où s'en-vo-le à ti-re d'ai-le

Après un rêve, Op. 7, No. 1
By permission J. Hamelle, Paris

Dans un som-meil que char-mait ton i-ma-ge   Je rêvais le bon-heur

Barcarolle, No. 3

Gon- do- dier du Ri-al-to   mon Châ-teau, c'est la la-gu-ne

Au bord de l'eau, Op. 8, No. 1
By permission J. Hamelle, Paris

S'asseoir   tous deux au bord du flot qui pas-se

La Rançon, No. 2

L'hom- me a, pour pay-er sa ran-çon Deux chaumps au tuf

Ici-Bas! Op. 8, No. 3

I- ci-bas! tous les li-las meu-rent, Tous les chants des oi-seaux sont courts — A

Nell, Op. 18, No. 1
By permission J. Hamelle, Paris

Ta ro-se de pour-pre a ton clair so-leil O juin, é-tin-celle en-i-vré-e, — B

Le Voyageur, No. 2

Voy- a-geur, où vas tu, mar-chant dans l'or vi-brant — C

Automne, No. 3

Au-tom- - - ne au ciel bru-meux aux ho- ri-zons na-vrants, — D

Poèmes d'un Jour Op. 21
No. 1 Rencontre
By permission J. Hamelle, Paris

J'é-tais triste et pen- sif quand je t'ai ren-con-tré - - - e, — E

No. 2 Toujours

Vous me de-man-dez de me tai- re, De fuir loin de vous pour ja-mais, — F

No. 3 Adieu

Com- me tout meurt vi- te, la ro-se dé- clo- se, — G

Les Berceaux, Op. 23, No. 1
By permission J. Hamelle, Paris

Le long du Quai_ les grands_vaisseaux, Que la houle in-cli-ne en si-len-ce — H

Notre Amour, No. 2

Notre a-mour est cho-se lé-gè- re, Com-me les par-fums que le vent prend aux — I

Le Secret, No. 3

Je veux que le ma-tin l'i-gno- re Le nom que j'ai dit à la nuit, — J

La Fée aux Chansons, Op. 27, No. 2
By permission J. Hamelle, Paris

Il é-tait u- ne Fé- e D'her-be fol- le coif-fé- e, — K

Aurore, Op. 39, No. 1
By permission J. Hamelle, Paris

Des jar-dins de la nuit s'en-vo-lent les é- toi - - les — L

Fleur jetée, No. 2

Em-por-te ma fo-li- e au gré du vent Fleur en-chan-tant cueil-li- e — M

Les Roses d'Ispahan, No. 4

Les ro- ses d'Is-pa- han dans leur gaî- ne de mous- se, — N

Noël, Op. 43, No. 1
By permission J. Hamelle, Paris

La nuit de-scend du haut des cieux, le givre au toit suspend ses fran-ges. — O

Nocturne, No. 2

La nuit, sur le grand mys- tè- re, entr'-ou-vre ses é-crins bleus:__ — P

Clair de Lune, Op. 46, No. 2
(Menuet)

1.
Vo-tre â-me est un pa- y- sa-ge choi-si qui vont char-mant mas-ques — Q

2. Accomp. theme

— R

Requiem, Op. 48
I Kyrie
By permission J. Hamelle, Paris

Ky- ri- e, Ky- ri- e, Ky- ri- e e- le- i-son Ky-ri-e e-le-i-son — S

Horizon Chimérique, Op. 118, No. 3

Di- a- ne, Sé-lé-ne___ lu- ne de beau métal,___ Qui re-flé-tes vers nous,

No. 4

Vais- seaux, nous vous au- rons ai- més en pu- re per- te;

En Prière
By permission J. Hamelle, Paris

Si la voix d'un en- fant peut mon- ter jus-qu'a Vous, Ô mon Pè- re

FAURE, Jean Baptiste (1830-1914)

Charité

Voi- ci l'hi-ver et son tris-te cor-tè- ge, Les malheur-eux souffrent beaucoup,

Va,___ cha- ri- té___ vier- ge pu- re et fé- con- de,

Crucifix! (duet)
By permission Heugel & Cie, Paris,
copyright owners

Vous qui pleu- rez, ve- nez à ce Dieu, car il pleu- re

Les Rameaux (The Palms)

Sur nos che- mins les ra-meaux et les fleurs___

Ho- san- na! Gloire au Seigneur! Bé- ni ce-lui qui vient sauver le mon - - - - de!

Sancta Maria

J'ai vu les Sé- ra- phins en son- ge Chanter dans leurs divins con-certs___

Vi- brez en- cor, sainte har-mo-ni- e, Vi- brez en- cor, hymne é- ternel!

FERRABOSCO, Alfonso (The Younger) (c. 1557- 1628)

Come, my Celia

Come, my Ce - - - lia, let us prove, while we may,

O eyes, o mortal stars

O eyes, O mor-tal stars, The au-thors of my harms,

FERRARI, Gustav (1872-1948)

Le Miroir
Copyright 1949, G. Schirmer, Inc.

L'o-deur de vous flot-tait dans l'air si- len-ci- eux

FEVRIER, Henry (1875-1957)

Elle avait trois couronnes d'or
By permission Heugel & Cie, Paris,
copyright owners

Elle a-vait trois cou- ron-nes d'or.___ A qui les don-na-t-el- le?

L'Intruse
By permission Heugel & Cie, Paris,
copyright owners

Elle est ve- nu- e vers le palais Le soleil se le-vait

FIBICH, Zdenko (1850-1900)

My Moonlight Madonna
(Words by Paul Webster)
Copyright by Carl Fischer, Inc.
reprinted by permission

Where are you____ beau-ti-ful moon-light Ma-don-na____ Like the dew

Sarka, Op. 51 (opera) Act I

Ja-ko bla-hý o-hlas do-by za-šlé vdu-še zvu-čí slo-va

Act II

Jsi krás-ná, ja-ko let-ní noc, jíž hvězd-ná zdo-ba v kšti-ci pla-ne!

(duet)

Jak jsi krás-na Cé-tiš žár jenž z na-der šle-há?

Act III

Já ne-le-kám se, smr-ti chlad-ná, muk-ni sti-nů____ tvých

FIELITZ, Alexander Von (1860-1930)

Eliland, Op. 9,
No. 1 Stilles Leid
Copyright 1910, G. Schirmer, Inc.

Ei- ne stil-le Zel-le an____ blau-er Wel-le

No. 2 Frauenwörth

Das war ein Tag' voll Mai-en-wind, da ist____ auf blau-en

No. 3 Rosenzweige

Wohl man-chen Ro-sen-zweig brach ich von Pfa-de

No. 4 Heimliche Grüsse

O Ir-men-gard, wie schön bist du hold--- se-li-ger ist Kei-ne

No. 5 Am Strande

Mein Lieb-ling ist ein Lin-den-baum der steht am Strand;

No. 6 Kinderstimmen

Mit un-sern Fi-schern war ein Kind ge-kom-men

No. 7 Mondnacht

Ich lieg'____ an mei-nes La-gers End' und lug'____ in stille Ster-ne

No. 8 Wanderträume

O, der Al-pen blan-ke Ket-te, wie sie glänzt

No. 9 Anathema

Nun ist wohl San-ges En-de! Wie hart ich da-von schied,

No. 10 Ergebung

Ge-hor-chen ist das Er-ste! Ich hab' mich stumm ge-neigt,

Die stille Wasserrose, Op. 18, No. 1

Die stil-le Was-ser-ro-se steigt aus dem blau____ en See____

Frülingslied, Op. 26, No. 1

Und ein Duf-ten zieht ü-ber die Er-den-welt,

FINCK, Heinrich (1445-1527)

Ach herzigs Herz

Ach her-zigs Herz_ mein Schmerz er-ken-nen tu, ich hab_ kein Ruh

FISCHER, Ludwig (1745-1825)

Im tiefen Keller

In tie-fen Kel-ler sitz' ich hier auf ei-nem Fass voll Re-ben,

FLÉGIER, Ange (1846-1927)

Le Cor
Copyright 1898, G. Schirmer, Inc.

J'ai-me le son du cor, le soir_ au fond des bois,_

Que de fois seul_ dans l'om-bre à mi-nuit de-meu-ré,

FLOTOW, Friedrich Von (1812-1883)

Martha (opera)
Act I (duet)

So-lo, pro-fu-go, re-jet-to, Di mia vi-ta sul mat-tin

Act II

Siam giun-ti o gio-vi-net-te, al nos-tro ca-solar!

The Last Rose of Summer

Qui so-la ver-gin ro-sa, come_ puoi_ tu fio-rir

Goodnight Quartet

Dor-mi pur, ma il mio ri-po-so, tu m'hai tol-to in-gra-to cor

Che vuol dir cio? l'of-fen-do, son col-mo di stu-por!

Pres-to, pres-to an-diam pren-de-te roc-ca e fu-so

Di ve-der-lo ah - - - - - - -

Act III Porter's Song

Chi mi di-rà di che il bic-chier col-ma - - - to va,

M'ap-pa-ri tutt' a - - mor, il_ mio squar-do l'in-con - - tro;

Ah! che a voi_ per-do ni Id-dio-O, la mia pena il mio do-lor:

Act IV (This number not in Italian edition)

Den Theu-ren zu ver-söh-nen durch wah-re Reu, durch wah-re Reu,

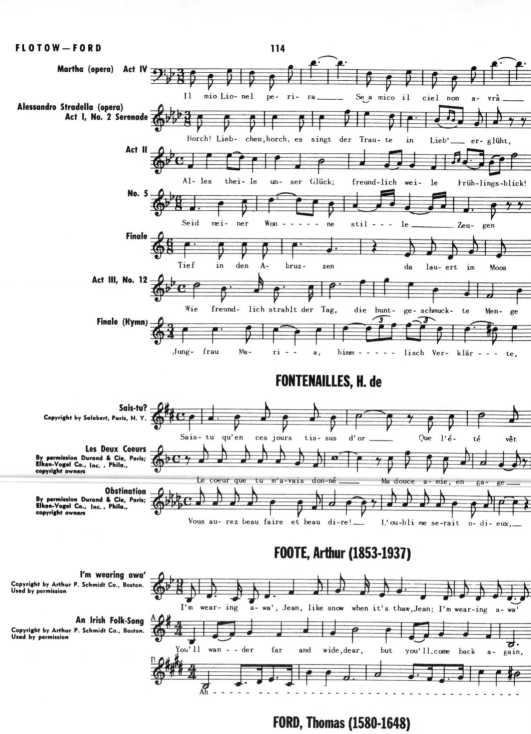

Martha (opera) Act IV

Il mio Lio-nel pe-ri-ra____ Se a mico il ciel non a-vrà

Alessandro Stradella (opera)
Act I, No. 2 Serenade

Horch! Lieb-chen, horch, es singt der Trau-te in Lieb'___ er-glüht,

Act II

Al-les thei-le un-ser Glück; freund-lich wei-le Früh-lings-blick!

No. 5

Seid mei-ner Won___ne stil - - le Zeu-gen

Finale

Tief in den A-bruz-zen da lau-ert im Moos

Act III, No. 12

Wie freund-lich strahlt der Tag, die bunt-ge-schmuck-te Men-ge

Finale (Kymn)

Jung-frau Ma-ri - - a, himm - - - - - lisch Ver-klär - - - te,

FONTENAILLES, H. de

Sais-tu?
Copyright by Salabert, Paris, N. Y.

Sais-tu qu'en ces jours tis-sus d'or___ Que l'é-té vêt

Les Deux Coeurs
By permission Durand & Cie, Paris;
Elkan-Vogel Co., Inc., Phila.,
copyright owners

Le coeur que tu m'a-vais don-né___ Ma douce a-mie, en ga-ge___

Obstination
By permission Durand & Cie, Paris;
Elkan-Vogel Co., Inc., Phila.,
copyright owners

Vous au-rez beau faire et beau di-re! L'ou-bli me se-rait o-di-eux,___

FOOTE, Arthur (1853-1937)

I'm wearing awa'
Copyright by Arthur P. Schmidt Co., Boston.
Used by permission

I'm wear-ing a-wa', Jean, like snow when it's thaw, Jean; I'm wear-ing a-wa'

An Irish Folk-Song
Copyright by Arthur P. Schmidt Co., Boston.
Used by permission

You'll wan-der far and wide, dear, but you'll come back a-gain,

Ah - - - - - - - - -

FORD, Thomas (1580-1648)

Since first I saw your face

Since first I saw your face I re-solved to hon-our and re-nown ye,

There is a lady sweet and kind

There is a la-dy sweet and kind, was nev-er face so pleased my mind

FOSTER, Stephen (1826-1864)

Ah! may the red rose live alway
Ah! may the red rose live al-way, To smile up-on earth and sky!___ B

Angelina Baker A
'Way down on de old plan-ta-tion, Dat's where I was born, C

B
An- ge-li- na Ba-ker An- ge-li- na Ba-ker's gone D

Beautiful Dreamer
Beau-ti- ful dream-er, wake un-to me___ Star-light and dew-drops E

Camptown Races
De Camp-town la- dies sing dis song, Doo-dah, doo-dah! F

Come where my love lies dreaming
Come where my love lies dream-ing Dream-ing the hap-py hours a-way, G

Gentle Annie
Thou wilt come no more, gen- tle An- nie, Like a flow'r H

Hard Times (chorus)
T' is the song, the sigh of the wear- y; Hard times, hard times, I

Jeanie with the light brown hair
I dream of Jea- nie with the light brown___ hair, J

Katy Bell
Go- ing down the Sha- dy dell where the hon- ey-suck-les grow, K

Laura Lee
Why has thy mer- ry face Gone from my side Leav- ing each cherished place L

Little Belle Blair
We have made a grave for lit-tle Belle Blair, in the fields be-yond the town M

Lou'siana Belle
Oh! Lou'- si- an-a's de same old state, Where Mas- sa used to dwell N

Massa's in de cold, cold ground
Round de meadows am a ring- ing De dar-keys mourn- ful song O

My old Kentucky Home
The sun shines bright in the old Ken- tuck- y home, P

Nell and I
We part- ed in the spring time of life, Nell and I Q

Nelly Bly A
Nel- ly Bly! Nel- ly Bly! Bring de broom a- long, R

B
Heigh, Nel- ly, Ho! Nel- ly, lis- ten, lub, to me S

Nelly was a lady
Down in de Mis-sis-sip-pi float-ing, Long time I trab-ble on de way

Oh boys, carry me 'long
Oh! car-ry me 'long;____ Der's no more trouble for me ____

Oh, boys, car-ry me 'long; Car-ry me till I die ____

Oh, Lemuel
Oh Lem-u-el, my lark, Oh, Lem-u-el, my beau

Go down to de cot-ton-field! Go down I say!

Oh, Susanna
I ____ come from Al-a-ba-ma wid my ban-jo on my knee

Old Black Joe
Gone are the days when my heart was young and gay

I'm com-ing I'm com-ing, for my head is bend-ing low

Old Dog Tray
The morn of life is past And ev'-ning comes at last

Old dog Tray's ev-er faith-ful Grief can-not drive him a-way

Old Folks at Home
Way down up-on de Swa-nee Rib-ber, Far, far a-way

Open thy lattice, love
O-pen thy lat-tice, love, lis-ten to me! The cool bal-my breeze is a-broad

Ring, ring de banjo
De time is neb-ber drea-ry, If de dar-key neb-ber groans;

Ring, ring de ban-jo, I like dat good old song

Some folks like to sigh
Some folks like to sigh Some folks do, some folks do

Sweetly She Sleeps
Sweet-ly she sleeps,__ my Al-ice fair, Her cheek on the pil-low pressed __

Uncle Ned
There was an old dar-key, his name was Un-cle Ned,

The Village Maiden
The vil-lage bells are ring-ing, and mer-ri-ly they chime

FOURDRAIN, Felix (1880-1923)

La Belle au Bois Dormant
Copyright by G. Ricordi & Co., Inc.

Comme elle avait dor-mi cent ans Dans son lit fleu-rant la bruyère, ___

Carnaval
Copyright by G. Ricordi & Co., Inc.

Car-na-val! ___ joy-eux Car-na-val! ___ On s'é-lan-ce

Chanson Norvégienne
Copyright by G. Ricordi & Co., Inc.

Je suis pri-se d'u-ne tris-tes--se Qui pè-se, pè-se lour-dement

Le papillon
Copyright by G. Ricordi & Co., Inc.

Gai ___ pa-pil-lon, pa---pil-lon d'or Qui t'en-vo-les rapide

FOX, Oscar J. (1879-   )

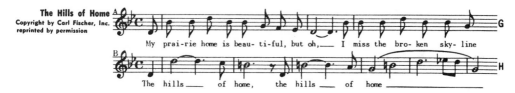

The Hills of Home
Copyright by Carl Fischer, Inc.
reprinted by permission

My prai-rie home is beau-ti-ful, but oh, ___ I miss the bro-ken sky-line

The hills ___ of home, the hills ___ of home ___

FRANCHETTI, Alberto (1860-1942)

Germania (opera)
Prologue
Copyright by G. Ricordi & Co., Inc.

Stu-den-ti! U-di-te, o voi, an-ti-chi e no-vi a-mi-ci

Act I

No, non chiu-der gli oc-chi va-glie ci-le-stri-ni ___ co-me la-ghi,

Fe-ri-to prigio-nier, vol-li fug-gir per non mo-rir fra col-tri

FRANCK, César (1822-1890)

L'Ange Gardien

Veil-lez sur moi quand je m'é-veil-le Bon an-ge, puis-que Dieu ___ l'a dit

Les Béatitudes (oratorio)
No. 4 Heureux les coeurs

Puis-que par-tout où nous en-traîne ___ un sort fa-tal

Heu-reux les coeurs al-té-rés de jus-ti-ce

No. 8 Mater dolorosa

Moi du Sau-veur ___ je suis la mè--re; Sept glai-ves

Les Cloches du Soir

Quand les clo-ches du soir dans leur len-te vo-lé-e,

Lied

Pour moi sa main cueil-lait des ro-ses A ce buis-son ___

Le Mariage des Roses
Mi-gnon- ne, sais tu com- ment S'é-pou- sent les ro- ses?

Ninon
Ni- non! Ni- non! que fais tu de la vi- e?

Nocturne
O frai- che nuit, Nuit transpar- en-te, Mys-te- re sans ob-scu-ri- té

Panis Angelicus, from Messe Solonnelle, Op. 12
Pa- nis an-ge- li-cus Fit pa- nis ho- mi-num Dat pa-nis coe-li-cus

La Procession
Dieu s'a-vance à tra- vers les champs! par les lan- des, les_ prés

Psalm 150
Lou- ez le Dieu ca- ché dans des saints ta- ber- na- cles

La Terre a tressailli, from The Redemption
La terre a tres-sail- li d'une ex- ta- se pro- fon- de

S'il est un charmant gazon
S'il est un char-mant ga- zon que le ciel ar- ro- se

Souvenance
Com- bien j'ai dou- ce sou- ve- nan- ce Du jo- li lieu

Le Vase Brisé
Le vase où meurt cet- te ver-vei- ne D'un coup d'even-tail fut fé-lé

La Vierge à la Crèche
Dans les lan- ges blancs fraîche-ment cou-sus, La__ Vierge ber- çait

FRANCK, Johann Wolfgang (17th Cent.)

Auf, auf zu Gottes Lob
Auf, auf zu Got- tes Lob, ihr hol- den Che- ru- bim

Jesus neigt sein Haupt und stirbt
Je- sus neigt_ sein_ Haupt und_stirbt,seht am Kreu-ze ihn ent-schlafen

Sei nur still
Sei nur_ still, sei nur_still und harr'_ auf_ Gott,er weiss alles

FRANCK, Melchior (1573-1639)

Ach treuer Gott, Herr Jesus Christ
Ach, treu-er Gott, Herr Je- su Christ,der du al-lein mein Hei-land bist;

FRANZ, Robert (1815-1892)

Er ist gekommen, Op. 4, No. 7
Er ist ge-kom- men in Sturm____ und Re- gen

FRANZ

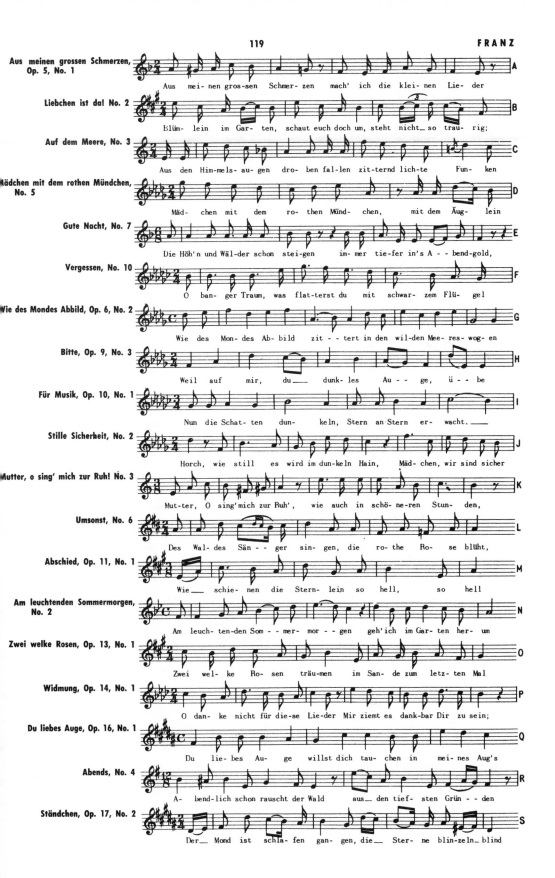

Aus meinen grossen Schmerzen, Op. 5, No. 1

Aus mei-nen gros-sen Schmer-zen mach' ich die klei-nen Lie-der

Liebchen ist da! No. 2

Blüm-lein im Gar-ten, schaut euch doch um, steht nicht so trau-rig;

Auf dem Meere, No. 3

Aus den Him-mels-au-gen dro-ben fal-len zit-ternd lich-te Fun-ken

Mädchen mit dem rothen Mündchen, No. 5

Mäd-chen mit dem ro-then Münd-chen, mit dem Äug-lein

Gute Nacht, No. 7

Die Höh'n und Wäl-der schon stei-gen im-mer tie-fer in's A--bend-gold,

Vergessen, No. 10

O ban-ger Traum, was flat-terst du mit schwar-zem Flü-gel

Wie des Mondes Abbild, Op. 6, No. 2

Wie des Mon-des Ab-bild zit--tert in den wil-den Mee-res-wog-en

Bitte, Op. 9, No. 3

Weil auf mir, du dunk-les Au-ge, ü--be

Für Musik, Op. 10, No. 1

Nun die Schat-ten dun-keln, Stern an Stern er-wacht.

Stille Sicherheit, No. 2

Horch, wie still es wird im dun-keln Hain, Mäd-chen, wir sind sicher

Mutter, o sing' mich zur Ruh! No. 3

Mut-ter, O sing'mich zur Ruh', wie auch in schö-ne-ren Stun-den,

Umsonst, No. 6

Des Wal-des Sän-ger sin-gen, die ro-the Ro-se blüht,

Abschied, Op. 11, No. 1

Wie schie-nen die Stern-lein so hell, so hell

Am leuchtenden Sommermorgen, No. 2

Am leuch-ten-den Som--mer-mor--gen geh'ich im Gar-ten her-um

Zwei welke Rosen, Op. 13, No. 1

Zwei wel-ke Ro-sen träu-men im San-de zum letz-ten Mal

Widmung, Op. 14, No. 1

O dan-ke nicht für die-se Lie-der Mir ziemt es dank-bar Dir zu sein;

Du liebes Auge, Op. 16, No. 1

Du lie-bes Au-ge willst dich tau-chen in mei-nes Aug's

Abends, No. 4

A-bend-lich schon rauscht der Wald aus den tief-sten Grün--den

Ständchen, Op. 17, No. 2

Der Mond ist schla-fen gan-gen, die Ster-ne blin-zeln blind

Im Herbst, Op. 17. No. 6

Die Hai- de ist braun, einst blüh-te sie roth;___ die Bir- ke ist kahl,

Marie, Op. 18, No. 1

Ma- rie, am Fen-ster sit-zest du, du lie-bes sü - - sses Kind___

Im Rhein, im heiligen Strome, No. 2

Im Rhein, im hei- li-gen Stro- me, da spie-gelt sich in den Well'n___

Die blauen Frühlingsaugen, Op. 20, No. 1

Die blau-en Früh-lungs- au - - gen schau'n aus_ dem Gras her- vor___

Das macht das dunkelgrüne Laub, No. 5

Das_ macht das dun-kel- grü- ne Laub, dass der Wald so schat-tig ist;

Im wunderschönen Monat Mai, Op. 25, No. 5

Im wun- der- schö-nen Mo- nat Mai, als al- le Knos- pen spran-gen

Lieber Schatz, sei wieder gut mir, Op. 26, No. 2

In dem Dornbusch blüht ein Rös-lein, ist ein Lust, es an- zu- sehn

Sterne mit den gold'nen Füsschen, Op. 30, No. 1

Ster- ne mit den gold'- nen Füss- chen wan-deln dro- ben

Wonne der Wehmut, Op. 33, No. 1

Trock- net nicht,___ trock- net nicht_ Thrä-nen der e-wigen Liebe

Es ragt in's Meer der Runenstein, Op. 39, No. 2

Es ragt in's Meer der Ru- nen-stein, da sitz' ich

Wandl' ich in dem Wald des Abends, No. 4

Wandl' ich in dem Wald_ des A-bends, in dem träu-me- ri- schen Wald

Die helle Sonne leuchtet, Op. 42, No. 2

Die hel- le Son- ne leuch- tet auf's_ wei- te Meer her- nie - - - der

Es hat die Rose sich beklagt, No. 5

Es hat die Ro- se sich__ be- klagt, dass gar zu schnell

Ach Elslein, liebes Elselein

Ach Els-lein, lie-bes El- se-lein mein, wie gern wär' ich bei dir!

Dich meiden

Dich mei- den nein,_____ ach nein!

Es taget vor dem Walde

Es ta- get vor dem Wal- de; stand auf Kä- ther- lein___

FRASER-SIMSON, Harold (1878-1944)

Vespers (Christopher Robin is saying his prayers)

Lit- tle boy kneels at the foot of the bed, Drops on the lit- tle hands

FRESCOBALDI, Girolamo (1583-1643)

Non mi negate, ohimè

Non mi_____ ne- ga- te, ohi- mè, Lu-- mi se-re-ne,

Se l'Aura spira

Se l'Au- ra spi-ra tut-ta vez - - - zo-sa, La fres-ca Ro- sa ri-den-te____ stà

Voi partite mio Sole

Voi par- ti- te mio So- le E por-ta il vo-stro lu-me al tro-ve il gior- no;

FRIML, Rudolf (1881-1972)

L'Amour-Toujours—l'Amour
Copyright 1922, Harms, Inc.

L'a-mour____ tou-jours____ l'amour, Love, now at last, you've found me____

Giannina Mia, from The Firefly (operetta)
Copyright 1912, G. Schirmer, Inc.

In my gon-do-la, love, let us glide____ O'er the drow- sy blue la-goon____

For____ I a- dore, I a-dore you Gian- ni- na mi- a

Give me one hour, from The White Eagle (operetta)
Copyright by Mills Music Inc., N. Y.

Give me one hour whose pas-sion re- pays The death of power,

Rose Marie (operetta)
Copyright 1924 Harms, Inc.
Indian Love Call

When I'm call- ing you - - - - oo - - oo - - - oo- oo- oo!

Rose Marie

O Rose Ma- rie, I love you____ I'm al- ways dream- ing of you

Vagabond King (operetta)
Only a Rose

Song of the Vagabond

FUENLLANA, Miguel de (16th Cent.)

Paseábase el Rey moro

Pa- se- á- ba- se el rey mo- re Por la ciu- dad

GABRIELI, Giovanni (1557-1612)

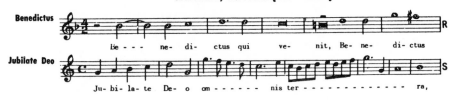

Benedictus

Be - - ne- di- ctus qui ve- nit, Be- ne- di- ctus

Jubilate Deo

Ju- bi- la- te De- o om - - - - - nis ter - - - - - - - - ra,

GADE, Niels W. (1817-1890)

Elverskud (The Erl-King's Daughter)
(cantata)
Part I Oluf's Ballade

When- e'er I ride through the ten- der grove, A- glow with the sun- beams

Part III The sun now mounts the eastern sky

The sun now mounts__ the eas- tern sky, To clouds bright hues he lends

Farvel, Lille Grete

Ak, kjae- re- ste, Hr. Guld- smed jeg har kun Sorg og Saon

Knud Lavard

Herr Mag- nus han stir- ren i Vin- ter- nat- ten ud:

GALUPPI, Baldassare (1706-1785)

Adriano in Siria (opera)

E in- gra- to, lo veg- gio, ma sie- de nel so- glio, ma sie- de nel so- glio,

Pri- gio- ni- e- ra, ab- ban- do- na- ta,

Son troppo vezzose, from Enrico (opera)

Son trop- po vez- zo- se Del vol- to le ro- se, Son ca- re

GANZ, Rudolph (1877-)

A Memory
Copyright 1919, G. Schirmer, Inc.

Some- how I feel that thou__ art near, Though there is naught a- round;

GARNIER, François (16th Cent.)

Resveillez-moy

Res- sveil- lez moy, re- sveil- lez moy mon bel a- my.__

GASPARINI, Francesco (1668-1727)

Adoramus Te, Christe (wrongly ascribed to Mozart)

Ad- o- ra- - - - - - - mus te, Chri- - - ste, et be- ne- di- ci- mus.

Caro laccio, dolce nodo (cantata)

Ca- ro lac- cio, dol- ce no- do, che le- ga- sti, le- - ga- sti

Lasciar d'amarti

Lasciar d'a- mar- ti per non pe- nar, ca- ro mio be- ne,

GASTOLDI, Giovanni Giacomo (1550-1619)

Maidens fair of Mantua's city

Mai- dens fair of Man- tua's ci- ty, none so grace- ful, none so pret- ty

GEEHL, Henry E.

For you alone
Copyright by Schuberth Music Pub. Co., Inc., N. Y.

Take thou this rose, this lit-tle ten-der rose;—   B

GENTIAN, (16th Cent.)

La Loy d'Honneur

La loy d'hon-neur qui nous dict et com-man-de,   D

GERMAN, Edward (1862-1936)

Charming Chloe
Copyright by Novello & Co., Ltd., London

It was the charm-ing month of May— When all— the flow'rs were fresh   F

Merrie England (opera) Act I

The Yeomen of England

Act II The English Rose

Rolling Down to Rio
Copyright by Novello & Co., Ltd., London

I nev-er sailed the A-ma-zon, I've nev-er reached— Bra-zil;   K

Waltz Song, from Tom Jones (operetta)

Who'll buy my lavender?
By permission Boosey & Hawkes, Inc., copyright owners

La-dies fair, I— bring to you La-ven-der with spikes of— blue   M

GERSHWIN, George (1897-1937)

Porgy and Bess (opera) Act I, Scene I Summertime

A woman is a sometime thing

Act I, Scene II My man's gone now

Act II, Scene I It takes a long pull to get there

Porgy and Bess (opera)
Act II, Scene I It takes a long pull to get there

I got plenty o' nuttin'

Buzzard Song

Bess, you is my woman now

Scene II, It ain't necessarily so

There's a boat dat's leavin' for New York

Act III, Scene III Oh, Bess, oh, where's my Bess

Oh Lawd, I'm on my way

GESUALDO, Carlo (Prince of Venosa) (1560-1613)

Dolcissima mia vita

Dol - cis - si - ma mia vi - ta   mia vi - ta   J

Io tacerò

Io ta - ce - rò;   ma, nel si - len - zio mi - o,   K

Moro lasso (madrigal)

Mo - ro las - so al   mio duo - lo   L

E chi mi può dar vi - - - - - - - - - ta   M

Resta di darmi noia (madrigal)

Re - sta di dar - - mi no - ia, re - sta di dar - - mi no - ia   N

GHERARDELLO, da Firenze (15th Cent.)

Tosto che l'alba; caccia

To-sto che l'al-ba del_bel_gior-no   P

GHIZEGHEM, Hayne Van (15th Cent.)

Les grans regrets

Les____ grans re - - grets que____ sans____ ces - - - - - ser   R

GIANNINI, Vittorio (1903-1966)

Tell me, Oh blue, blue Sky
Copyright by G. Ricordi & Co., Inc.

Sum-mer has flown, the leaves are fall-ing, I hear a voice

GIBBONS, Orlando (1583-1625)

Ah, dear heart (madrigal)

Ah,___ dear heart___ why do you rise? The light that shines comes from your___ eyes

Dainty fine bird

Dain-ty fine Bird, that art en-cag-ed there

Hosanna to the son of David

Ho-san-na to the Son of Da-vid, of___ Da-vid

The Silver Swan (madrigal)

The sil-ver swan, who, liv-ing, had no note, when death ap-proached

What is our life? (madrigal)

What is our life?___ our___ life? A play of___ pas-sion

GIBBS, Cecil Armstrong (1889-1960)

Five Eyes, Op. 9, No. 3

In Hans' old mill his three black cats Watch the bins

Padraic the fidiler
Copyright 1931, A. Gibbs

Pod-raic sits in the gar-den In un-der the bright new moon___

Take heed, young heart
Copyright 1926, A. Gibbs

Take heed, young heart, to Time How soft his foot-fall is

To One Who Passed Whistling Through the Night
Copyright 1921, A. Gibbs

Some-thing hath called me, Called me from far dreams___
Ah

GILBERT, Henry F. (1868-1928)

Pirate Song
Copyright by Novello & Co., Ltd., London

Fif-teen men on the dead man's chest, Yo! ho! ho and a bot-tle of rum

GIORDANI, Giuseppe (1744-1798)

Caro mio ben

Ca-ro mio ben, cre-di-mi al-men, sen-za di te lan--gui-sce il cor___

GIORDANO, Umberto (1867-1948)

Andrea Chenier (opera)
Copyright by Sonzogno, Milan

Fedora (opera)
Copyright by Sonzogno, Milan

Act I — Son ses-san-t'an-ni, o vec-chio, che tu ser-vi

Un di al-l'az-zur-ro spa-zio guardai pro-fon-do

O Pa-sto-rel-le, ad-di-o, ad-di-o, ad-di-o

Act II — Vi-ve-re in fret-ta di que-sta feb-bre ga-ja d'un go-de-re

Io non ho a-ma-to an-cor Pu-re só-ven-te nel-la vi-ta

Act III — Ne-mi-co del-la pa-tria? È vecchia fia-ba che be-a-ta-men-te

Un dì m'e-ra di gio-ia pas-sar fra gli od¹ e le ven-det-te.

La mam-ma mor-ta m'hanno a la por-ta del-la stan-za mi-a; mo-ri-va

Si fui sol-da-to e glo-ri-oso af-fron-ta-to

Act IV — Come un bel dì di mag-gio che con bacio di ven-to

Vi-ci-no a te s'ac-que-ta l'ir-re-quie-ta a-ni-ma mi-a;

La no-stra mor-te è il trion-fo del-l'a-mor

Act I — O gran-di oc-chi lu-cen-ti di fe-de! O va-sta fron-te di me

Act II — Ve-di io pian-go ma, se pian-go, no, non è per la mia vi-ta

A-mor ti vie-ta di non a-mar

Mia ma-dre, la mia vec-chia ma-dre, so-lin-ga vi-ve

La don-na rus-sa è fem-mi-na due vol-te,

Act III — Dio di giu-sti-zia scru-ti le an-go-scie

Brilla sulla mia fronte, from Il Re (opera) Act 3
Copyright by Sonzogno, Milan

Bril - la sul - - la mia fron - - te___ ri - splen - - de

Siberia (opera) Act I
Copyright by Sonzogno, Milan

T'in - con - trai per via! L'occhio pen-so-so_e gra - ve è pe - ne - tra - to

Nel suo_a - mo - re ria - ni - ma - ta la co - scien - za

Act II

Or - - ri - de step - - pe! Tor - ri - da l'e - sta - - te!

Act III

Non o - di là il mar - tir d'an - go - scia fie - ra?

GLAZOUNOV, Alexander (1865-1936)

Romance

Wenn ich in dei - ne Au - gen seh', so schwindet all' mein Leid

Romance Orientale

Dans le sang brû - - - le_ ar - den - te_ flam - - me___

GLIÈRE, Reinhold (1875-1956)

Ah, twine no blossoms (Oh, do not wreathe) Op. 18, No. 7

Ah___ twine no blos-soms fair and frag-rant To weave a-new my crown of woe,

Over the Depths of the Sea, Op. 59
Copyright 1923, G. Schirmer, Inc.

O - ver- hang-ing the fath-om-less o - cean, a cliff tow-ers high

GLINKA, Michael (1804-1857)

A Life for the Czar (Ivan Sussanin) Act I Introduction

Fou - - dre et vent gron - - dent en vain,___ Le___ fau - con___ fran - chit___

Le___ doux prin - temps pa - rait___ Le___ beau prin-temps re - nait___

Rondo of Antonida

Au vil - la - ge sur la ri - viè - re, L'on_at - tend l'ai - mé,

Act IV Bogdan Sobinjin's Aria

Frè - res, le froid, l'hor - - - - reur des bois pro - fonds,

Tris - te et_ dans_ l'an-gois-se,___ la___ fil-le at - tend_cher_coeur!

Sussanin's Aria

Pâle au - ro - re,___ tu vien-dras Bai - gner_ mes yeux_ las - sés

Russian and Ludmilla Act I Song of the Bard

Dort, gen Mit - ter - nacht liegt ein wüs - tes___ Land

Russlan and Ludmilla (opera)
Act II Farlaf's Rondo
Nah ist die Stun- de schon mei- nes Tri- umph's und Russ- lan der ge- hass- te   A

Russlan's Aria
Gieb, o Kriegs- gott, mir ein Schwert nach mei- ner Hand   B

O Lud- mil- la! bald wird uns die Freu- de   C

Act III Persian Chorus
Schon deckt die Fel- der dunk- le Nacht.   D

Gorisslava and Chorus
O mein Rat- mir, dich seh' ich wie- der hier! vereint auf's neu' mit dir   E

Cherubim Song
Like glad Cher- u- bim in heav'n- ly cho- rus,   F

Doubt
Be si- lent de- spair of af- fec- tion, Oh heart without hope   G

In my blood the fire of desire burns
(Now am I all with fever shaken)
Now am I all with fe- ver sha- ken, Grief in my soul   H

I remember
The mo- ment I re- mem- ber clear- ly Thou didst ap- pear   I

The Lark
High o'er earth in Hea- ven, floats the sound of sing- ing   J

Midnight Review
When mid- night is strik- ing the hour The drum- mer from grave- yard   K

The North Star
'Neath a mar- vel- lous roof man- y man- sions a- rise   L

Venetian Night (Barcarolle)
Fann'd by South- ern winds that chast- en, In the balm- y sum- mer night   M

GLUCK, Christoph Willibald (1714-1787)

Alceste (opera)
Act I
Grands Dieux! du des- tin, qui m'ac- ca- ble sus- pen- dez du moins   O

Pa- rez vos fronts des fleurs nou- vel- les, ten- dres a- mants,   P

Di- vi- ni- tés du Styx, di- vi- ni- tés du Styx,   Q

Non! ce n'est point un sac- ri- fi- ce!   R

Act II
Ban- nis la crainte et les a- lar- mes   S

Iphigénie in Aulis (opera)

Act II, No. 20 — A
Par la crainte et par l'es-pé-rance, Ah, que mon coeur est tour-men-té!

No. 24 — B
Chan-tons, cé-lé-brons no-tre Rei-ne! L'hy-men,— qui sous— ses lois

No. 31 — C
Par son pè-re cru-el á la mort con-dam-né - - - e

No. 37 — D
O toi, l'ob-jet le plus ai-ma-ble, que tant de ver-tus font ché-rir

Act III, No. 40 — E
Il faut de mon de-stin— su-bir la loi su-prê - - me,

No. 42 — F
A-dieu, con-ser-vez dans— votre â-me le sou-ve-nir

No. 44 — G
Cal-chas, d'un trait mor-tel bles-sé se-ra ma pré-mie-re vic-ti-me

No. 47 — H
Ju-pi-ter, lan-ce ta fou-dre, lan-ce, lan-ce ta fou-dre

No. 53 — I
Heu-reux guer-riers, vo-lez à la vic-toi-re

Iphigénie en Tauride (opera)

Act I — J
O toi, qui pro-longe-as mes jours,— re-prends—un bien que je dé-tes-te,

Act II — K
Dieux qui me pour-sui-vez, Dieux, au-teurs de mes cri-mes

— L
U-nis dès la plus ten-dre en-fan-ce nous n'a-vions qu'un mê-me de-sir,

Act III — M
D'une i-mage hé-las! trop ché-ri-e j'aime en-core à m'en-tre-te-nir,

— N
Ah! mon a-mi,— j'im-plo-re ta pi-tié—

— O
Di-vi-ni-té des gran - -des â-mes A-mi-tié

Act IV — P
Je t'im-plo-re,et je trem-ble, ô Dé-es-se im-pla-ca-ble!

Orfeo ed Euridice (Orpheus) (opera)

Act I, No. 1 — Q
Ah! se in-to-no a quest'— ur-na fu-ne-sta

No. 7 — R
Chiamo il mio ben co-sì, Quan-do si mo-stra il dì

No. 13 — S
Dal-la ce-tra tua dol-ci tuo-ni ar-mo-ni-ci— fa ri-so-nar;

GLUCK

Orfeo ed Euridice (Orpheus) (opera)
Act I, No. 15

A — Gli squar- di trat- tie- ni, af- fre- na gli ac- cen- - ti,

No. 17

B — Ad- dio, ad- dio, o miei so- spi- ri, han spe- me i miei de- si- ri;

No. 19 and 21 (chorus)

C — Chi mai dell' E- re- bó fra le ca- li- gi- ni sull' or- me d'Er- co- le

Act II, No. 22

D — Deh pla- ca- te- vi con me! Fu- rie, No, Fu- rie, No,

No. 23

E — Mi- se- ro gio- va- ne, che vuoi, che me- di- ti

No. 24

F — Mil- le pe- - - ne om- bre sde- gno- - se

No. 25

G — Ah! qua- le in- cog- ni- to af- fet- to fle- bi- le

No. 26

H — Men ti- ran- ne, voi sa- re- ste al mio pian- to, al mio do- lor

No. 32

I — E quest' a- si- lo a- me- no e gra- to del ri- po- so il ter- ren,

No. 33

J — Che pu- ro ciel! che chia- ro sol! che mio va luce

No. 34

K — Vie- ni a re- gni del ri- po- - so, grande E- ro- e, te- ne- ro spo- so

Act III, No. 39 Duet

L — Su e con me vie- ni, ca- ro su e con me vie- ni,

No. 41 A

M — Che fie- ro mo- men- - - to che bar- ba- ra sor- - - te

B

N — Av- - vez- zo al con- ten- to d'un pla- ci- do ob- bli- o

No. 43

O — Che fa- ró sen- za Eu- ri- di- ce, do- ve an- drò sen- za il mio ben!

A

P — Tri- on- fi A- mo- re, e il mon- do ser- va in- tie- ro all' im- pe- ro del- la bel- ta

B

Q — Tal di- spe- ra, tal af- fan- na d'u- na ti- ran- na

A

R — Gau- dio, gau- dio son al cuo- re que- ste pe- ne dell' a- mor

B

S — Qual pia- ce- - re, qual dol- cez- za l'a- mor ci ren- de,

Paris et Helena (opera)

O del mio dol-ce ar- dor___ bra-ma-to og-get - - - - to,

Spiag- ge_a-ma- te, o-ve ta-lo-ra l'I-dol mi - o

Un ruisselet, bien clair, from La Rencontre Imprévue (opera)

Un ruis-se- let, bien clair, bien net, Qui dans la plai-ne ri-an-te

Vieni, che poi sereno, from La Semi-ramide (opera)

Vie- ni che poi se-re - - - - -no, al- ta tua bel-la in son - - - - no

GODARD, Benjamin (1849-1895)

Nous allons partir, from Dante (opera) Act IV, Scene II

Nous al- lons par- tir___ tous deux, Par-tir___ tous deux

Berceuse, from Jocelyn (opera)

A

Ca- chés dans cet a- sile où Dieu nous a con- duits

B

Oh! ne t'é- veille pas en- cor___ Pour qu'un bel an-ge de ton rê- ve

La Vivandière (opéra-comique)

Viens a- vec nous pe-tit,___ Viens a-vec nous, viens!___

(The Letter)

Mon p'tit gars,___ si nous t'é-cri-vons C'est pour te bien di-re sans ces-se

Chanson de Florian

Ah! s'il est dans vo-tre vil- la - - ge Un ber- ger sen-sible

Embarquez-vous!

Em- bar- quez- vous! 'qu'on se dé- pê - - - - che;

Te souviens-tu? Op. 19, No. 6

Le souviens-tu de ta pro- mes - - se? Te souviens-tu des ans pas- sés?

GOETZ, Hermann (1849-1878)

Die Kraft versagt, from The Taming of the Shrew (opera)

A

Die Kraft ver- sagt des Kam- pfes des Kam-pfes bin ich mü-de

B

Es schwei- ge die Kla- ge In De-muth es tra - - - ge,

GOLDMARK, Carl (1830-1915)

The Queen of Sheba (opera) Act I

Der Freund ist dein,___ der Freund ist dein___ der un-ter Ro - - sen wei-det,

Act II

Lift thine eyes to worlds a-bove thee, to the throne___ of God most high

The Queen of Sheba (opera)
Act II

Ma - gi-sche Tö - - ne, be - rau-schen-der Duft___ kü - - - sse mich

Act III

doch eh' ich in des To - des Thal zur ew' gen Ru - he zie - he

GOMES, Antonio Carlos (Gomez) (1836-1896)

Il Guarany (opera) Act I

Gen - ti - le di cuo - re - - - leg - gia - dra di vi - so

Sen - to una for - za in-do-mi - ta che ognor mi trag - ge a te___

Qua - lunque via di - schiuda - si al li - be - ro tuo piè___

Act II

C'era u - na vol - ta un prin - ci - pe me-sto, pen-so-so e bel - - - - - lo

Salvator Rosa (opera) Act I
Copyright by G. Ricordi & Co., Inc.

Mia pic - ce - rella deh! vie-ni al-lo ma - re, nel - la bar - chetta

Act II

Di spo - so di pa - dre le gio - je se - re - ne

Romanza (Quando nascesti tu), from
Lo Schiavo (opera)

Quan - do nasces - ti tu nasciano i fior___ che il ciel baciò___

GOUBLIER, Gustave

L'Angélus de la Mer
By permission Boosey & Howkes, Inc.,
copyright owners

Au loin c'est l'An - ge - lus___ c'est l'An - ge - lus qui son - ne

Le Credo du Paysan
Copyright by Jacquot & Fils, Paris

L'im men - si - té,___ les cieux, les monts, la plai - ne,

La Voix des Chênes
Copyright by Eveillard, Paris

Quand le soleil s'en - fuit à l'ho - ri - zon,___ Se - mant la nuit

GOUDIMEL, Claude (1510-1572)

Psalm 19

Der Him - mel zahl - los Heer Er - zählt von Got - tes Ehr

Psalm 25

A toi, mon Dieu, mon___ cœur mon - te, En toi mon es - poir j'ai mis;

Psalm 123

D'où vient, Sei - gneur, que tu nous as es - pars Et si long - temps

GOUNOD, Charles François (1818-1893)

Messe Solennelle (St. Cecilia Mass)
Agnus Dei
Ag - - - nus De - i, Ag - - - nus De - i qui tol-lis, qui tol-lis

Benedictus
Be - ne-dic-tus qui ve - - - nit — in no - - mi - ne Do - - - - mi - ni

Credo
Cre - do — in u-num De - um Pa - trem — o - mni - po - ten-tem

Sanctus
Sanc - tus, sanc - tus, — sanc-tus Do - mi - nus Sanc-tus, sanc - tus,

Mors et Vita (oratorio)
Hosanna
Ho - san - na in ex - - cel - sis De - - - - - - - o,

Judex
Se - den - ti in Thro - no et Ag - - no, — be - ne - dic - ti - o

Faust (opera)
Act I
Sa - lut! ô mon der-nier ma-tin! Sa - lut! ô mon der-nier ma-tin!

Pa - res- seu - se fil - le Qui som-meille en-core, —

À moi — les plai-sirs, les jeu - - - - nes maî - tres - ses!

Act II Kermesse
Vin ou biè - re, Bière ou — vin, que mon — ver - re soit — plein!

Cavatina
A- vant de quit - ter ces lieux, — Sol na-tal de mes a-ieux —

The Golden Calf
Le veau d'or — est tou-jours de-bout! On en-cen - se sa puis-san - - - - - - ce,

De l'en-fer qui vient é-mous-ser nos ar - mes;

Chorale
C'est u - ne croix qui de l'en-fer nous gar - de,

Waltz
Ain - si que la brise — le-gè - re Sou - lève en é-pais tour-bil-lons,

(accompaniment theme)

Act III Flower Song
Fai - tes-lui mes a-veux — Por-tez — mes voeux! — Fleurs é-closes près d'el-le

Cavatina
Sa - lut! de-meu-re chaste et pu - re, Sa - lut! de-meu - re chaste et pu - re,

GOUNOD

Faust (opera)
Act III The King of Thule
Il e-tait un Roi de Thu-lé___ Qui jus- qu'à la tom- be fi- dè- - le **A**

Jewel Song
Ah! Je ris___ de me voir Si belle en ce mi- roir **B**

Quartet
Pre- nez mon bras___ un mo- ment! Lais- sez,___ je vous en con- ju- re **C**

Duet
Lais- se- moi, Lais- se- moi con- tem- pler ton vi- sa- ge, **D**

Ô nuit d'a- mour!___ ciel ra- di- eux___ Ô douces flam- mes **E**

Il m'ai- me! il m'ai- me!___ Quel trouble en mon coeur!___ **F**

Act IV
Il ne re- vient pas,___ Il ne re- vient pas! J'ai peur,__ je fris- son- ne; **G**

Si le bon- heur___ à sou- ri- re 't'in- vi- te **H**

Scene in the church
Seig- neur, daignez per- mettre à votre humble ser- van- te **I**

Sou- viens- toi du pas- sé, quand sous l'ai- le des an- ges **J**

Soldiers' Chorus
Gloire im- mor- tel- le de nos a- ieux,___ Sois nous fi- dè- le, Mou- rons comme eux **K**

Mephistopheles' Serenade
Vous qui fai- tes l'en- dor- mi- - e, N'en- ten- dez- vous pas, **L**

Death of Valentine
É- cou- te- moi bien,___ Mar- gue- ri- te Ce que doit ar- ri- ver___ **M**

Act V
An- ges purs, an- ges ra- di- eux,___ Por- tez mon âme au sein des cieux! **N**

Oui c'est toi je t'ai- me, oui, c'est toi je t'ai- me **O**

Mireille (opera) Act I
Chan- tez, chan- tez, mag- na- na- relles, Car la cueillette ai- me les chants! **P**

Valse
O lé- gère hi- ron- del - - le,___ Mes- sagè - - re fi- dè - - le **Q**

Act II
La fa- ran- do- le Joy- euse et folle En- traine au bruit des chan- sons **R**

Chanson de Magali
La brise est douce et par- fu- mée___ L'oi- seau s'en- dort **S**

Mireille (opera)
Act II Chanson

Voi- ci la sai- son, mi- gnonne, Voi- ci la sai- son

Mon coeur ne peut chan- ger!_ Sou- viens- toi que je t'ai- me!

A toi mon â- me Je suis ta fem- me! Mal- gré leur blâ- - - me

Si les fil- les_ d'Ar- les sont rei- nes

Act IV Scene II

Le jour se lève Et fait pa- lir la som- bre nuit!

Heu- reux pe- tit ber- ger! Heu- reux pe- tit ber- ger!

Act V Chorus of Sainte-Marie

Vous qui du haut des cieux_ Vo- yez les pleurs de nos yeux_

An- ges du pa- ra- dis cou- vrez- la de votre ai- le_

La foi, de son flam- beau di- vin, Gui- dait par le che- min,

Philémon et Baucis (opera)
Act I

Ah, si je re- de- ve- nais bel- le, Si son front pou- vait ra- jeu- nir,_

Au bruit des lourds mar- teaux d'ai- rain_ Au sombre é- clat

Que les songes heu- reux_ pla- nant sur votre tê- te

Act II

Phi- lé- mon m'aimerait en- co- re, J'aime- rais en- core Phi- lé- mon,

Ô_ ri- an- te na- tu- re Ô jar- dins em- bau- més_

Polyeucte (opera)
Act II

A Ves- ta, por- tez vos of- fran- des; Devant el- le je vais m'in- cliner

Nym- - - - - - phes at- ten- ti- - - ves_ Dans les ro- seaux!

Act IV

Sour- ce dé- li- ci- eu- se en mi- sé- - res fé- con- de

La Reine de Saba (Queen of Sheba)
(opera)

Sous les pieds d'u- ne fem- - me A- bais- sant de son â- me

Act II

In- spi- rez moi, ra- ce di- vi- - - ne! no- bles a- ieux_ en qui j'ai foi!_

GOUNOD

Reine de Saba (Queen of Sheba) (opera) Act III

Plus grand, dans son ob-scu-ri-té,__ Qu'un roi pa-ré du di-a-dè-me — A

Roméo et Juliette (opera) Act I Ballade of Queen Mab

Mab, la rei-ne des__ men-son-ges, Pré-side aux son- ges, — B

"Waltz song"

Je veux vi - - vre__ dans le rê - - ve — C

Madrigal

Ange a-do-ra-ble, ma main cou-pa-ble Pro-fane, en l'o-sant tou-cher__ — D

Al- lons! jeu-nes gens ___ Al- lons! bel-les da- mes — E

Act II Cavatina

Ah! lè- ve-toi, so- leil! fais pa-lir les é- toi- les — F

Act III

Que fais tu, blan-che tour-te- rel-le, Dans ce nid de vau-tours?__ — G

Act IV Love duet

Nuit d'hy- mé- né - - e! Ô__ dou-ce nuit d'a-mour! — H

Que l'hym- ne nup-ti- al__ suc- cède aux cris d'a-lar-mes — I

C'est- là qu'après un jour vo- tre corps et votre â- me — J

A- mour,__ ra-ni- me mon cou- ra-ge, Et de mon coeur chas - -se l'ef-froi — K

O ma lyre immortelle, from Sappho (opera)

O__ ma lyre im-mor-tel- le Qui dans les tris- tes jours__ — L

Aimons-nous!

Au fleuve le ruisseau se mêle Et le fleuve à la mer!__ — M

Au Printemps

Le printemps chas-se les hi-vers Et sou-rit dans les ar- bres verts — N

Au Rossignol

Quand ta voix cé- les-te pre-lude au si-len-ce des bel-les nuits__ — O

Ave Maria (Meditation on Bach Prelude in C, Well-tempered Clavichord, Book I, No. 1)

A- ve Ma-ri-a __ Gra- ti-a ple-na, Do- minus te - -cum — P

Ce que je suis sans toi

Ce qu'est le lier-re sans l'or-meau,Qui fut l'ap-pui de son en- fan - -ce — Q

Le Ciel a visité la terre

Le ciel a vi-si-té la ter- re, mon bien ai- mé re-pose — R

Entreat me not to leave thee

En- treat me not to leave thee, En- treat me not to leave thee — S

Envoi de Fleurs
Si l'on veut sa- voir qui m'en-voi - - - e ces bel-les fleurs,

La Glu
Y a- vait un fois un pauv' gas et lon lon lair- e e lon

Hymne à la Nuit
Viens, lorsque dans l'a- zur les as- tres ra- di- eux

Medjé (Chanson Arabe) A
O Medjé, qui d'un sou- ri- re En-chainas ma li-ber- té

B
La voix de l'a-mour mê- me De- vrait te dé-sar- mer

Nazareth
Né dans u- ne crè- che, Di- vin Ré- -demp- teur

Oh, That We Two Were Maying
Oh, that we two were may- ing O- ver the fra- - grant grass

O ma belle rebelle
O ma bel- le re- bel- le, Las que tu m'es cru-el- le

Où voulez-vous aller (Bacarolle)
Di- tes la jeu- ne bel- le où vou- lez vous al- ler?

Repentir (O Divine Redeemer) A
Ah! ne re- pous-se pas mon â- me pé-che-res- se!

B
O Di- vin Ré-demp- teur O Di- vin Ré-demp- teur

Ring out, wild bells
Ring out, wild bells, to the wild sky The fly-ing cloud,

Sérénade
Quand tu chan - - - tes ber-cé-e le soir, en-tre mes bras

Le Soir
Le soir ra- mè- ne le si- len- ce, As- sis sur ces ro-chers dé-serts,

There is a green hill far away (Le Calvaire) A
There is a green hill far a- way, With- out a ci- ty wall

B
There was no oth- er good e- nough To pay the price

Le Vallon A
D'i- ci je vois la vi- e à tra-vers un nu-a- ge

B
Re- po- se- toi, mon â- me, en ce der- nier a- si- le

Venise
Dans Ve- ni - - - se la rou- ge, Pas un bateau qui bou- ge;

GRAENER, Paul (1872-1944)

Philantropisch, Op. 43 b, No. 6 — B
Ein ner-vö-ser Mensch auf ei-ner Wie-se Wä-re bes-ser oh-ne sie

Palmström, No. 7 — C
Palm-ström steht an ei-nem Tei-che und ent-fal-tet gross ein rotes Taschentuch

Der Page sprach, Op. 49, No. 1 — D
Mei-ne wun-der-schö-ne Kö-ni-gin, du sollst wis-sen

Der alte Herr, No. 3 — E
Kennst du nur den al-ten Her-ren der zur sel-ben Mit-tag-stunde

Der König, Op. 71, No. 3 — F
By permission Associated Music Publishers, Inc.
Das war der jun-ge Kö-nig, der Kö-nig oh-ne Land,

Verspruch, No. 9 — G
Wir sind ein-an-der zu - - ge-sellt für al-le E-wig-keit,

GRAINGER, Percy (1882-1961)

Brigg Fair (arr.) — I
Copyright by Percy Grainger
It was on the fift' of Au-gust, er the wea-ther fine and fair

GRANADOS, Enrique (1867-1916)

Amor y odio — K
Copyright by Union Musical Española
Pen-se que yo sa-bri-a o-cul-tar la pe-na mi-a

Callejes — L
Copyright by Union Musical Española
Dos ho-ras ha que calle-je - - o, pe-ro no ve - o

Las Currutacas modestas — M
Copyright by Union Musical Española
De-cid que da-mi se-las se ven por a-hí que luz-can a-si

El Majo discreto — N
Copyright by Union Musical Española
Di-cen que mi ma-jo es fe-o, Es po-si-ble que si

La Maja Dolorosa, No. 1 — O
Copyright by Union Musical Española
¡Oh muer-te cruel ¿Por-qué tu á trai-ción

No. 2 — P
¡Ay ma-jo de mi vi-da, no no, tu no has muer-to;

No. 3 — Q
De a-quel ma-jo a-man-te que fué mi glo-ria guar-do an-he-lan-te

La Maja de Goya — R
Copyright by Union Musical Española
Yo no ol-vi - - da-re en mi vi-da de Go-ya la i-magen

The Maiden and the Nightingale, from Goyescas (opera) (La Maja y el Ruiseñor) — S
Copyright 1915, G. Schirmer, Inc.
Por-qué en-tre som-bras el rui-se-ñor en-to-na su ar-mo-nio-so can-tar?

El Majo Olvidado
Copyright by Union Musical Española

Cuan- do re-cuer- des los di- as pa- sa- dos pien-sa___ en mi,

El Majo Tímido
Copyright by Union Musical Española

Lle-ga á mi re-ja y me mi- ra por la no-che un ma- jo

El Mirar de la Maja
Copyright by Union Musical Española

Por- que es en mis o- jos___ tan hon-do el mi- rar___

El Trá-lá-lá y el Punteado
Copyright by Union Musical Española

Es en bal- de ma- jo mí- o que si- gas ha- blan- do

GRENON, Nicolas (15th Cent.)

Je ne requier de

Je ne re- qui- er de ma - - - - dame et ma mi

Nova vobis gaudia

No- va vo- bis gau- di- a___ re- fe- ro

GRETCHANINOV, Alexander (1864-1956)

The Wounded Birch, Op. 1, No. 2

By the hatch- et wound-ed, See the birch-tree lan-guish;

My Native Land (My Country) No. 4

Home - - land mine, my na- tive land! Beat- ing hoofs of hors- es,

Berceuse (Cradle Song) No. 5

Sleep, my dar- ling sleep, my star- ling, Bye, my ba- by, bye___

Over the Steppe, Op. 5, No. 1

Sad lies the Steppe___ in its sol- i-tude Night comes on shad- ow-y wings;

Night No. 2

Stil - - le Schlaf und nächt-lich Dun- kel al- les zau- be-risch

Hushed the song of the Nightingale, Op. 20, No. 2
Copyright by Oliver Ditson Co.
Used by permission.

Hushed the song of the night- in- gale, Yon- der star fall-ing trails thro' the blue

The Captive No. 4

Je suis dans ma ca- ge dans l'om- bre gla- cée

(Children's Songs), Op. 47, No. 1 Snowflakes
By permission Associated Music Publishers, Inc.

We- het, weht ihr Flock-en-ster- ne, uns nur bleibt hübsch fer - - - - ne!

No. 9 The Snowdrop

Im Wal- de wo Bir-ken sich drän- gen zu Hauf,___

Death (La Morte), Op. 48, No. 5
By permission Associated Music Publishers, Inc.

O mort vieux ca- pi- tai- ne, il est temps! le- vons___ l'an-cre

Ob ich gehe, ob ich stehe, Op. 120, No. 2
By permission Associated Music Publishers, Inc.

Ob ich ge- he, ob ich ste- he ob- ich ge- he, ob ich ste- he,

GRETRY, André (1741-1813)

Jugement de Midas (opera)
Doux char-me de la vi-e, Di-vi-ne mé-lo-di-e

Par _____ u-ne grâ - - ce tou-chan-te u-ne mine in-té-re-san-te

Naissantes fleurs, from Céphale et Procris (opera)
Nais - - san-tes fleurs, _____ ces - - - - sez d'é-clo - - re

Plus de dépit, plus de tristesse, from Les Deux Avares (opera)
Plus de dé-pit, _____ plus de_ tris- tes-se

Qu'il est cruel d'aimer, from Les Évènements Imprevues (opera)
Qu'il est cru-el d'ai-mer, _____ D'ai-mer sans o-ser di - - re,

Richard Coeur-de-Lion (opera) Act I, No. 2
La dan-se n'est pas ce que j'ai-me, Mais c'est la fille

Duet
U-ne fiè-vre brû-lan - - te Un jour me terras-sait

Je crains de lui par-ler la nuit, J'é-cou-te trop tout ce qu'il dit

Song of Blondel
O Ri-chard, ô mon Roi! L'u-ni-vers t'a-ban-don-ne

Si l'u-ni-vers en-tier m'ou-bli-e S'il faut i-ci pas-ser ma vi-e

Serenade, from L'Amant Jaloux (opera)
Tan-dis que tout som-meil-le dans l'om-bre de_ la nuit _____

Vous étiez ce que vous n'êtes plus, from Le Tableau Parlant (opera)
Vous é-tiez ce que vous n'ê-tes plus, Ce que vous n'ê-tes_ plus _____

Zémiré et Azor (opera)
Ah, quel tour-ment d'ê-tre sen-si - - - ble, D'a-voir un_ coeur

Du mo-ment qu'on_ ai-me, L'on de-vient_ si doux _____

La fau-vet-te a - - - vec ses pe-tits _____

Ro-se ché-ri - - - e, Ai-ma-ble fleur! Ro-se ché-ri - - - e

GRIEG, Edvard Hagerup (1843-1907)

To brune Øjne, Op. 5, No. 1 (Two Brown Eyes)
To bru-ne Øj-ne jeg ny-lig saa, i dem mit Hjem

Ich liebe dich (I Love Thee), Op. 5, No. 3

Du mein Ge- dan- ke, du mein Sein und Wer- den!

Vuggesang, Op. 9, No. 2

Sov min Søn, o slum- re sødt end- nu gar din Vug- ge blødt

Ausfahrt (Outward Bound), No. 4

Es war ei- ne dämmernde Som- mer-nacht, ein Schiff am U- - fer lag,

Love, Op. 15, No. 2

The sun like vi-sions of love doth glow; he cooleth his face

The Poet's Last Song, Op. 18, No. 1

Thou Gi- ant Death O hear me high, To Spi-rit land swift fly- - ing!

Vandring i skoven No. 2

Min sø- de Brud, min un- ge Vio, min kjaer- lif hed, mit Liv

Hytten No. 3

Hvor Bøl- gen hejt mod ky-stens slaar en gan- ske lil- le

Herbststurm (Autumn Storm) No. 4

Im Som- mer wie war da so grün der Wald, als Zwit-schern von je-dem Zweig

Erstes Begegnen (First Meeting), Op. 21, No. 1

Des er- sten Se- hens Won- ne ist wie der Duft im Wal- de

Dein Rat ist wohl gut (Your Advice is Good) (Thanks for the Rede) No. 4

Dein Rat ist wohl gut, der mich warnt vor der Flut,

Kvad, Op. 22, No. 1

Nor- rø- na fol- ket det vil fa- re, det vil fa- re

Peer Gynt (drama with music) Solveig's Song, Op. 23, No. 1

A

Der Win-ter mag schei-den, der Früh- ling ver-geh'n,der Früh-ling ver-geh'n,

B

Ah - - - - - - - - - - - - -

Solveig's Slumber Song, No. 2

Schlaf', du theu-er- ster Kna- be mein! Ich will wie-gen mein Kind

Ein Schwan (A Swan), Op. 25, No. 1

Mein Schwann, mein stil-ler, mit wei-ssem Ge-fie-der,dei-ne wonnigen

Glücksbote mein, No. 3

Glücks- bo- te mein, so nannt ich dich, ver-glich dich einem Ster- ne

Mit einer Wasserlilie, No. 4 (With a Water-Lily)

Sieh, Ma- rie, was ich dir brin - - - - - ge:

Am schonsten Sommerabend war's (It was a lovely summer eve) Op. 26, No. 2

Am schön- sten Som-mer- a- bend war's,ich ging durch ein ein-sam Thal,

Zur Johannisnacht (St. John's Eve), Op. 60, No. 5

Ei- ne We-ste wünsch ich von Sei- de mir, ja,— ja, von Sei- de— mir.

Fisher's Song, Op. 61, No. 4

Ere day-light a- wak-eth, the fi-sher-man tak-eth his boat on the main

Haugtussa, Op. 67, No. 1 Det syng (Det synger)

Og vad du den Dröm og vad du den Sang sä vil du To- ner-ne gemme—

No. 2 Veslemöy (Ungmöen)

Hun er ma-ger og mörk og myg med— bru- ne og re- ne Drag,—

No. 3 Blåbaer-Li (I Blåbaer-Tuerne)

Nei se, hvor det blå-ner her! Nu vil en Hirl vi os ta- ge!

No. 4 Møte (Möde)

En stil- le Sön- dag sid-der hun i Li; — det strömmer på

No. 5 Elsk (Elskoe)

Den vil-de Gut-ten mit Sind har då- ret, som Fugl i Sna-ren jeg sid-der sa-ret;

No. 6 Killingdans (Kiddenes Dans)

A hipp og hop-pe og tipp og top-pe på den ne— Dag;—

No. 7 Vond Dag (Ond Dag)

Hon toel-ler Dag og Stund og se- ne kvoeld til Sön-dags- tid

No. 8 Ved Gjaetle-Bekken (Ved Gjatle-Bakken)

Du ris-len-de Boek, du heis-len-de Boek, her lig-ger i Sol du så klar

A Boat on the Waves is Rocking, Op. 69, No. 1

A boat on the waves is rock- ing, There sit-ting a- lone on board—

Eros, Op. 70, No. 1

Hört mich, ihr frö- sti- gen Her - - - - zen im Nord,

Lichte Nacht (Radiant Night), No. 3

Sank nicht die Son-ne kaum erst zum Meer in duf-ti-ger däm_mernder Fer-ne,

GRIFFES, Charles Tomlinson (1884-1920)

In a Myrtle Shade, Op. 9, No. 1
Copyright 1918, G. Schirmer, Inc.

To a love- ly myr- tle bound, Blos-soms_show-'er-ing all a- round

Waikiki No. 2

Warm per- fumes like a breath from vine and tree

An Old Song Re-Sung, No. 4

I saw a ship a sail-ing, a- sail- ing, a-sail-ing,

Sorrow of Mydath, No. 5

Wear - - - y the cry— of the wind— is

A Feast of Lanterns, Op. 10, No. 5
Copyright 1917, G. Schirmer, Inc.

In Spring for sheer de-light— I set the lanterns swinging through_the trees

The Lament of Ian the Proud, Op. 11, No. 1
Copyright 1918, G. Schirmer, Inc.

What is this cry-ing___ that I hear in the wind?___   A

Thy Dark Eyes to Mine,   No. 2

Thy dark eyes to mine, Ei - lidh,___ Lamps of de- sire!___   B

By a lonely forest pathway
Copyright 1909, G. Schirmer, Inc.

By a lone - ly for-est path-way I am fain___ at eve to flee___   C

The Dreamy Lake
Copyright 1909, G. Schirmer, Inc.

An o- pal dream___ en- chants the lake, Where wa- ter lil- ies gent-ly lie   D

O'er the tarn's unruffled mirror
Copyright 1909, G. Schirmer, Inc.

O'er the tarn's un-ruf- fled mir- ror lies the moon - light's sil-ver sheen,   E

Time was when I in anguish lay
Copyright 1909, G. Schirmer, Inc.

Time was when I in an- guish lay, While day and night I wept;   F

GROTTE, Nicolas de la (16th Cent.)

Je suis amour

Je - - - - - - - - - suis a-mour___ le grand mais- tre des dieux   H

GRUBER, Franz Xavier (1787-1863)

Stille Nacht, Heilige Nacht (Silent Night, Holy Night)

Stil - le Nacht, Hei- li- ge Nacht! Al- les___ schläft, Ein- sam___ wacht   J

GRUENBERG, Louis (1884-1964)

standin' in de need of Prayer (based on a spiritual), from Emperor Jones (opera)
Copyright 1932, Cos Cob Press, Inc.

It's a- me,___ It's a- me, Oh Lawd,___ stan-din' in de need of prayer   L

GUARNIERI, Camargo (1907-   )

Den Báu
Copyright 1947, Mercury Music Corp.
Used by permission.

Den báu den báu den col ma- ri- ol- den mi- ne- ról den,   N

Quebra O Côco, Menino (Break the cocoanut)
Copyright 1947, Mercury Music Corp.
Used by permission.

Fol- gue, .fol-gue mi- nha gen- te, Que u-ma noi- te não é na- da   O

Que- bra cô- co, me- ni- na Du- ro esta! Ai com for-ca no cô- co   P

GUION, David W. (1895-   )

All day on the Prairie (arr.)
Copyright 1930, G. Schirmer, Inc.

All day on the prai-rie in the sad-dle I ride, not e- ven a dog,boys   R

At the cry of the First Bird
Copyright 1924, G. Schirmer, Inc.

At the cry___ of the first bird___ they be-gan to cru-ci- fy thee   S

Home on the Range (Cowboy Song) (arr.)
Copyright 1930, G. Schirmer, Inc.

Oh, give me a home where the buf-fa-lo roam, Where the deer

A

What shall we do with a Drunken Sailor (arr.)
Copyright 1933, G. Schirmer, Inc.

What shall we do with a drun-ken sai-lor, What shall we do with a drun-ken sai-lor;

B

HAGEMAN, Richard (1882-   )

At the Well
Copyright 1919, G. Schirmer, Inc.

When the two sis-ters go to fetch wa-ter They come to this spot

D

Christ went up into the hills
Copyright by Carl Fischer, Inc.
Used by permission

Christ went up in-to the hills a-bove, Walk-ing slow-ly

E

The Donkey
By permission Boosey & Hawkes, Inc., copyright owners

When fish-es flew and for-ests walked and figs grew up-on thorn

F

Do not go, my love
Copyright 1917, G. Schirmer, Inc.

Do not go, my love, with-out ask-ing my leave

G

Miranda
By permission Galaxy Music Corporation, N. Y.

Do you re-mem-ber an Inn, Mi-ran - - - - - - - - - da,

H

Music I heard with you
By permission Galaxy Music Corporation, N. Y.

Mu-sic I heard with you was more than mu-sic,

I

HAHN, Reynaldo (1875-1947)

À Chloris
By permission Heugel & Cie, Paris, copyright owners

S'il est vrai, Chlo-ris___ que tu m'aimes,(Mais j'entends que tu m'aimes bien),

K

L'Air
By permission Heugel & Cie, Paris, copyright owners

Dans l'air s'en vont les ai-les Par le vent ca-res-sé-es

L

La Barcheta
By permission Heugel & Cie, Paris, copyright owners

La no - - te, è be-la,___ Fa pres-to, o Ni-ne-ta

M

Chanson au Bord de la Fontaine
By permission Heugel & Cie, Paris, copyright owners

C blan-ches co-lom-be du soir, que je vien-drai m'as-seoir___

N

Ciboulette (operetta)
Ce n'était pas la même chose
Copyright by Salabert, Paris, N. Y.

Bien des jeu-nes gens ont vingt ans___ Dont la sai-son n'a pas de ro-ses

P

Dans une charrette

C'est le prin-temps qui m'a sur-pri-se, Ce ciel trop bleu,___

Q

Moi j'm'appell' Ci-bou-let-te! Ça sonn' clair comme un' chan-son

R

Comme frère et soeur A

Les pa-rents, quand on est bé-bé tout dé-fend-ent,dé-fend-ent,dé-fend-ent.

B

Comm' la vie vous semble a-voir d'la dou-ceur___ Quand on est en-semble

S

Mozart (operetta)
Act II Letter Song

De-puis ton dé- part, mon a-mour,___ De-puis, hé-las, de si longs jours

Act III Air des Adieux

Sois cou-ra-geu- se,O ma maî-tres-se, Pen-dant que je te dis a-dieu

Nocturne
By permission Heugel & Cie, Paris,
copyright owners

Sur ton sein pâ- le, mon coeur dort D'un som- meil doux___ com-me la mort.

Offrande
By permission Heugel & Cie, Paris,
copyright owners

Voi- ci des fruits, des fleurs,des feuilles et des branches Et puis voi-ci mon coeur

Paysage
By permission Heugel & Cie, Paris,
copyright owners

A deux pas de la mer qu'on en-tend bour-don- ner,

Paysage Triste

L'om- bre des ar- bres dans la ri-viere em-bru- mé___ meurt

Phyllis
By permission Heugel & Cie, Paris,
copyright owners

De-puis neuf ans et plus dans l'am- pho-re scel-lé- - e

Le Plus Beau Présent
By permission Heugel & Cie, Paris,
copyright owners

Tu m'as don-né un cous-sin de soi- e, Un brû-le-par-fum d'un art per- san;

Le Printemps
By permission Heugel & Cie, Paris,
copyright owners

Te voi-là,___ ri- re du Prin-temps___ Les thyr-ses des li-las.

Quand je fus pris au pavillon
By permission Heugel & Cie, Paris,
copyright owners

Quand je fus pris au pa-vil-lon de ma da- me très gente et bel - - le

Rêverie
By permission Heugel & Cie, Paris,
copyright owners

Puisqu' i-ci vas toute â-me Donne à quel- qu'un Sa mu-si-que,sa flamme

Le Rossignol des Lilas
By permission Heugel & Cie, Paris,
copyright owners

O pre-mier ros-si- gnol qui viens dans les li-las, sous ma fe- nê-tre,

Seule
By permission Heugel & Cie, Paris,
copyright owners

Dans un bai-ser, l'onde,au ri- va- ge, Dit ses dou- leurs___

Si mes vers avaient des ailes

Mes vers fui-raient doux et frêles vers vo-tre jar-din si beau,

Le souvenir d'avoir chanté
By permission Heugel & Cie, Paris,
copyright owners

Le sou-ve-nir d'a-voir chan- té Au so- leil,sous l'a-zur cé- les- - te,

Sur l'eau
By permission Heugel & Cie, Paris,
copyright owners

Je n'en-tends que le bruit de la rive et de l'eau___

Tyndaris
by permission Heugel & Cie, Paris,
copyright owners

O___ blan- che Tyn- da- ris, les Dieux me sont a- mis

HALÉVY, Jacques François (1799-1862)

La Juive (opera)   Act I

Si la ri-gneur et la ven-gean-ce leur font ha- ir___ la sain-te loi

La Juive (opera)

Act II — O Dieu, Dieu de nos pè-res, par-mi nous dé-scends!

Si tra-hi-son ou per-fi-di e o-sait se glisser par-mi nous,

Cavatine — Dieu,__ que ma voix trem-blan-te s'é-lè----ve jusqu'aux cieux,

Il va ve-nir! et d'éf-froi je me sens fré-mir

Act III — Vous qui du Dieu vi-vant ou-tra-gez la puis-san-ce

Act IV — Ra-chel, quand du Seig-neur la grâ-ce tu-té-lai-re

HAMMERSCHMIDT, Andreas (1612-1675)

Sei nun wieder zufrieden — Sei nun wie-der zu-frie-den, mei-ne See-le,

HANDEL, George Frideric (1685-1759)

Arioso (cantata con stromenti)
(Questionable authenticity) — Dank_____ sei Dir, Herr, Dank_____ sei Dir, Herr Du hast Dein

O come, let us worship, from Chandos Anthem — O come,__ let us wór-ship, let us wor-ship and fall down,__

Di Cupido impiego — Di Cu-pi-do im-pie-go i van-----ni

Il dolce dell' oblio (cantata for solo voice—secular) Aria — Giacchè il son-no a lei di-pin-ge la sem-bian-za del suo be--ne,__

Aria — Ha l'in-gan-no il suo di-let-to se i pen-sier mos-si d'af-fet-to

Praise of Harmony — Look down, look down, har-mo-----------nious Saint,

Süsse Stille — Sü-sse__ Stil-le, sanf-te Quel-le__ ru----hi-ger

Te Deum (Dettingen) — Vouch-safe, O Lord! Vouch-safe, O Lord! to keep us this day with-out__ sin

When thou took-est up-on thee to de-li-ver man

ODES: Alexander's Feast — Bac-chus e-ver fair and__ young, drink-ing days did first or-dain

Alexander's Feast: Revenge, Timotheus cries

A — Re- venge, re- venge, re- venge, Ti-mo-theus cries, revenge, Timotheus cries

L'Allegro

B — But, oh! sad vir- gin that thy power might raise Mu-sae - us from his bower!

C — Come and trip_ it as_ you go, on the light fan-tas-tic toe, trip it, trip it

D — Come, come, thou god-dess_ fair and free, fair_ and free in heav'n yclep'd Eu-phro-sy-ne,

E — Come with na- tive lus-tre shine, Mo- de- ra- tion, grace di- vine

F — Hide me_ from day's gar-ish_ eye, While the bee with hon- -ied_ thigh

G — A — Let me wan- -der not_ un- seen, by hedge-row elms on hill-locks green.

H — B — Or let the mer- ry bells ring round, And the jo-cund re-beck's_ sound

I — Mirth, ad- -mit me of thy crew, Mirth, ad-mit me of thy crew, Mirth, ad-mit me,

J — Mirth, ad-mit me of thy crew!_ Mirth, admit me of_ thy crew, Mirth, admit me,

K — Oft on a plat of ris-ing ground I hear the far off cur- few_ sound

L — Sweet bird,_ Sweet bird, that shun'st the noise of folly,

Ode to St. Cecilia

M — But oh!_ What art can teach, what hu- man voice_ can reach

N — The soft com- plain - - - - -ing Flute in dy- ing notes dis-co- -vers

OPERAS
Admeto

O — Can-gio d'aspet- to il cru-do fa- to e nel mio pet- to

P — Lu- ci ca-re, ad-di- o, po- sa-te! Lu-ci ca-re, ad- di- o,

Q — Si- gnor, lo cre-di-a me: ti ser- ba-a- mo- re e fè

R — Spe- - ra, si, mio ca- ro_ be- ne, ch'io per te_

S — Quan- to god-rà, al- lor-che mi ve-drà l'a-ma-to spo-so mi-o,

HANDEL

Agrippina

Del pia - ce - re___ è go - de - re fi - do a - - - mor!

Col rag-gio pla - ci - do___ del - la spe-ran - za la___ mi a

In - gan - na-ta u-na sol vol - ta es - ser pos-so, mà non più

Io di Ro-ma il Gio - - ve so-no, nè v'è già___ chi me-co___

O - - - gni ven-to, o - o-gni ven-to ch'al por-to lo spin- ga,

Alcina

Ah!___ mio___ cor! scher-ni-to se i! Stel-le! De i!

La boc-ca va - ga, quell' oc-chio ne-ro lo sò, t'im - pia-ga;

Mi re - sta-no le la-gri-me, di-rei dell' al - ma i vo ti

Sem - pli-cet - to! a don - na cre-di? a don - na cre-di?

Ver-di pra - ti, sel-ve a-me - ne, per-de - - re-te la___ bel-ta

Al sen ti stringo e parto,
from Ariodante

Al sen ti strin - go e par-to al sen ti stringo e par-to,

Amadigi

Ah spie - ta - - - to! e non ti muo - - - ve

Siciliana

Gio - - - ja, ve - ni-te in sen; bril - la - te nel___ mio cor

O ren-de-te-mi il mio be - - ne, a - stri in-fi - di

Pe-na ti-ran - na io sen-to al co-re, nè spe-ro ma i

Tu mia spe - - ran-za, tu mio___ con - for-to,

Atalanta

Ben' io sen - to l'in-gra-ta, spie-ta - - ta fu-ria a-tro-ce,

Ca - - - - - - re sel - ve ca-re, ca-re sel-ve, om-bre be-a - te,

Co - me al-la tor-to-rel - la lan-gue al suo ca-ro ap-presso

OPERAS
Atalanta

Di ad I- re- ne,— ti- ran- na_in- fe- de- le,

La- scia_ ch'io par- ta so- lo, e tu ri- man- ti,oh bel- la,

M'al- lon - - - - - - - - ta- no, sde- gno- se pu- pil- le,

Ri- por- tai,— glo- rio- sa pal- ma,

S'è tuo_ pia- cer,ch'io mo.ra va- do_a mo- rir, I- re- - ne

Sof- fri in pa- ce_il tuo do- - re, se_il mio_a- mor tu di- sprez- za- sti

Berenice

Si, tra_i cep- pi e le ri- tor- te La mia fè ri- splen- de- rà,—

No, sof- frir non può_il mio_a- mo- re, che non re- gni tua bel- tà,

Caro amor, from Il Pastor
Fido   Act II

Ca- ro_A- mor, Ca- ro_A- mor, sol per mo- men- - - ti

Deidàmia

Due bell' al- me_in- na- mo- ra- te, ca- re, fi- de_a- man- ti

Nel ri- po- so_e nel con- ten- to Go- do_e sen- to Lie- ve_il pe- so

Se pen- si_a- mor tu so- - lo per vez- zo_e per_ bel- ta

Ezio

Na- sce al bos- co_in roz- - za cu- na un fe- li- ce pa- - - sto- rel- la

Quan- to mai fe- li- ce sie- te, in- no- cen- ti pas- to- rel- le,

Se_un bell' ar- di- - - - re Può_in- na- mo- rar- ti

Vi fi- - da lo spo- - so, vi fi- da_i! re- gnan- te,

Flavio

A- mor,— nel mi- o pe- nar— deg- - gio spe- rar,

L'ar- - mel- lin— vi- ta non cu- ra se d'of- fen- de- re ha ti- mo- - re

Chi può_ mi- ra- re e non a- - ma- re, e non a- - ma- re

HANDEL

OPERAS

Flavio

A

Quan-to dol-ci, quan-to ca-re son le gio-je nel mio sen,

Floridante

B

Al - - - ma mi-a, sì, sol tu se-i la__ mia glo-ria, il mio dilet-to,

C

A-mor com-man-da o-no-re in-vi-ta, più bel im-pe-gno__

D

Finche lo strale non giun-ge al segno, pen-sier re-ga-le, no, non si__ sa

E

Non las-ciar Op-pres-sa del-la sor-te Pe-rir quell' alma for-te

F

Se dol - - ce m'e - ra già vi - ver, cor mio, con te,

Giulio Cesare (Julius Caesar)

G

Da tem-pe - - - - ste il le - - gno in-fran - - - - - - - - - to,

H

Dal_ ful-gor__ di que - sta spa - - da

I

Pian-ge-rò, pian-ge-rò la__ sor-te mi-a,

J

Se pie-tà di me non sen-ti giu-sto ciel, io mo-ri-rò,

K

V a - do-ro, pu-pil-le, sa-et - - te__ d'a-mo - re,

Lotario

L

Già mi sem-bra al ca - - - ro av-vin-to Trar l'au-da-ce,

M

Per_ sal-var-ti, i - do-lo mi-o so__ ben i - o,

Lusinghe più care, from Alessandro

N

Lu-sin-ghe più_ ca-re d'A-mor ve-ri dar-di

Muzio Scevola

O

Pu-pil-le sde-gno-se! sa-re - - ste pie-to-se,

P

Vo-la-te più dei ven-ti, mo-men-ti che scor-re-te,

Nel mondo e nell' abisso, from Riccardo primo

Q

Nel mon-do e nell' a-bis-so io non pa-ven - - - - - - - to

Orlando

R

La-scia A-mor, e sie-gui Mar-te,__ va! com-bat-ti, com-bat-ti

S

Sor-ge in-fau sta u-na pro-cel-la, Che'o-scu-rar fa il cie-lo e il mare

OPERAS

Orlando

Va- ghe_ pu- pil- le, no, non pian- ge- te,___ no,

Ottone

Af- fan- ni del pen- sier, un sol mo- men- to da- te- mi pa- ce_ almen

Ah! tu non sai, quant'_ il mio cor so- spi- ra_ e_ sen- te

Del mi- nac- ciar del ven - - - - - - - - - - - - - - - to

Un di- sprez- za- to af- fet- to, un mi- se- ro so- spet- to

Io spe - - - - ra - - i, io sperai tro- var ri- po - - so

S'io dir po- tes- si al mio cru- de- le la tua fe- de- le

La spe- ran- za e giun - - - - - ta_ in por- to

Ve- ni, o fi - - - glio! ve- ni, o fi - - glio, e mi con- so- la,

Partenope

Fu- ri- bon - do spi- ra_ il ven- to

Sei mia_ gio- ja sei_ mio be- ne, sei mia pa- ce_ e mia spe- ran- za

Qual far- fal- let- ta___ gi- ra_ a_ quel_ lu- me,

Poro

Chi vi- ve_ a man- te sai che de- li - - ra, sai che de- li- ra,

E prez- zo leg- gie- ro D'un sud- di- to il san- gue

Son con- fu- sa pa- sto- rel- la, che_ nel_ bo- sco_ a notte_ o- scu- ra,

Radamisto

Ca- ra spo- sa_ a- ma- to be- ne pren- di spe- ne

Già che mo- rir non pos- so: fu- rie che cie- co_ a- bis- so

Om - - bra ca- ra, Om - - - - - bra ca- ra di_ mia spo- sa

Per- fi- do! per- fi- do, di a quell' em- pio ti- ran- no

HANDEL

OPERAS

Radamisto

Qual na-ve smar-ri-ta trà sir-ti e tem-pe-sta,

Quan-do mai spie-ta-ta sor-te, spie-ta-ta sor-te,

Som-mi De-i, som-mi De-i, che scor-ge-te

Rinaldo

Ca - - - ra spo-sa, a-man-te ca-ra, Do-ve se-i?

Del vostro E-re-bo sull' a-ra, Col-la fa-ce del mio sdegno

Las-cia ch'io pian-ga mia cru-da sor-te,

Il Tri-cer-bero hu-mi-lia-to al mio bran-do ren-de-rò

Vò far guer-ra, e vin-cer vo-glio, e vin-cer vo-glio

Rodelinda

Con-fu-sa si mi-ri l'in-fi-da con-sor-te,

Con rau-co mor-mo-ri o Pian-go-no al pian-to mi-o

Do - ve se-i, a-ma-to be-ne? Vie-ni, l'al-ma

L'em - pio ri-gor del fa-to vi - le non po-trà far-mi

Ho per - du-to il ca-ro spo-so,

Mio ca-ro be-ne! ca-ro, ca-ro! mio ca-ro be-ne!

Mor-rai sì, l'em-pia tua te-sta, già m'ap-pre-sta

Om-bre, pian-te ur-ne fu-ne-ste! Voi sa-re-ste

Pa-sto-rel-lo d'un po-ve-ro ar-men-to pur dor-me con-ten-to

Pri-gio-nie-ra hò l'al-ma in pe-na mà si bel-la

Ri-tor-na, oh ca-ro e dol-ce mio te-so-ro,

OPERAS

Rodelinda

Scas - cia - ta dal suo ni - do sen__ vo - la in al - tro li - do,

Spieta- ti, Io vi giu-rai, se_al mio fi-glio il cor-do-na- i,

Rodrigo

Al- lor- chè sor- ge___ a- stro lu- cen- te,

Begl' oc - - - - - chi begl' oc - - chi del__ mio ben,

Il dol- ce fo-co mi - - o, il dol-ce fo - co mi - - ò

Scipione

Dim- mi, ca- ra dim-mi_tu_ dei mo-rir," mà oh ca-ra,_ non mi dir:

Ge- ne - - ro - so chi sol__ bra - ma quel che pia-ce_al ben ch'e-glia-ma

Par- to, fug- go, re- sta, e___ go- di de tue fro-di

Pen - - - - - - sa,oh__ bel- la, al- la mia___ spe- me___

Se mor- mo- ra ri-vo_o fron-da, su-sur-ran___ ven-ti - -cel- li

Son pel- le-gri- no che d'al-to ve-de il con-fi- ne del suo cam- mi-no

Tut- ta rac-col-ta_an-cor nel pal-pi-tan-te cor tre-man- te ho l'al-ma,

Sento che un giusto sdegno,
from Faramondo

Sen- to che_un gius-to sde- gno mi spro-na_a ven-di- car - - mi,

Serse (Xerxes)

Ca- ro voi sie-te all' al - -ma, dol- ce voi sie-te_al cor,

Del mio ca- ro ba- co_a-ma- bi- le nell' im-pe- ro suo

Di- rà che_a-mor per me pia- ga- to il cor non gli_ha

Nè men con__ l'om-bre d'in- fe-del- tà vo-glio tra-di- re l'a-ni-ma

Non so se sia la spe- me, che mi so-stie-ne_in vi - - -ta

(accompaniment)

Om - - - - - -bra mai__ fu__ Di ve-ge- -ta- bi- le

HANDEL

OPERAS

Serse (Xerxes)

A. Quel- la che tut- ta fè per me__ lan-guia__ d'a-mo-re

B. Va go----den-do vez-zo-so e bel-lo quel ru-scel-lo la li-ber ta

Siroe

C. Ch'io mai__ vi__ pos-sa la-sciar d'a-ma-re

D. Deg-gio mo-ri-re o stel-le, nè all in-no-cen-za mi a

E. Ge-li-do, in o-gni ve-na scor-rer mi sen-to il san-gue:

F. Mi la-gne-rò ta-cen-do del mio de-sti-no a-va-ro,

G. Non vi piac-que in-giu-sti De- i, ch'io na-sces-si pa-sto-rel-la;

H. La sor- te mia ti-ran-na far-mi di più non può

I. Tor-ren--te cre-sciu--to per tor-bi-da pie-na,

Sosarme

J. Ren-di'l se-re-no al ci----glio, Ma-dre, non pian-ger più,

K. Si, si, si si, mi-nac-cia, e__ vin-ta li-ra in si gran pe-ri-glio

Tamerlano

L. A suoi pie-di pa-dre e san-gue la su--per-ba mi ve-drà,

M. Bel- la A-ste--ria, bel- la A-ste-ria il tuo cor mi di-fen-da,

N. Cor di__ pa-dre e cor d'a-man-te, Sal-da fe- de o-dio co-stan-te,

O. Deh! la-scia-te-mi il ne-mi- co, se to-glie-ste a me l'a-man-te

P. Em- pio, em- pio, per far-ti guer- ra, dal re-gno di sot-ter-ra

Q. Fi-glia mi- a, non pian-ger, no, no, fi-glia, no, non pianger,

R. For- te e lie-to a mor-te an-drei,__ se ce-las-si ai pen-sier mie- i

S. Nò, nò, il tuo__ sde- gno__ mi pla----co,

OPERAS
Tamerlano
Par che mi nasca in se - - no un_ rag - - gio di spe-ran - - za,

Teseo
Più non cer-ca li-ber-ta,___ mà l'a-mor, la fe-del-ta,___

Ri - cor - da-ti, oh bel - la, che tu___ sol sei quel-la per cui_ pe-na il cor

Vie - ni, tor - - na, i-do-lo mi - - - - o, que-sto cor___ a con-so-lar!

Tolomeo
Non lo di - rò col lab-bro, che tan-to ar-dir non ha___

Stil-le a - ma - - re, gia vi sen-to tut-te in se-no, la mor-te a chiamar

Voi dol - ci au-ret-te al cor, mo-stra-te o-ve_ s'ag-gi-ra,

Vado a morir, from Arminio
Va - - - - - do, va-do a mo-rir va-do a mo-rir vi la-scio

Zweier Augen Majestät
from Almira
Zwei-er_ Au-gen Ma-je-stät zwei-er_ Au-gen Ma-je-stät

ORATORIOS
Acis and Galatea
As when___ the___ dove___ la-ments_ her_ love,_

Love in her eyes sits play-ing, and sheds_ de-li - - cious death;

Love sounds th'a-larm,___ love sounds th'a-larm, and fear is a fly-ing

O rud-dier than the cher-ry o sweet-er than the ber-ry,

Would_ you gain_ the ten-der crea-ture, soft - - ly, gent-ly, kind - - ly

Alexander Balus
Con-vey me to some peace-ful shore, where no tu-mul-tuous bil-lows roar,

Here a-mid_ the sha-dy woods Fra-grant flow'rs and crys-tal floods,

Sub-tle_ love with fan - - cy view-ing, rapt'-rous joys_ on_joys ensu-ing,

Athalia
Gen-tle airs me-lo-dious strains,_ Call for rap - - tures out of woe

Oh_ Lord Oh Lord whom_we a - - dore, whom we a - - dore

ORATORIOS

Athalia — A

Will God, whose mer-cies ev-er flow Ex-pose his chil-dren's youth to woe?

Belshazzar — B

Great God! who yet but dark-ly known___ Thus far hast deigned my arms to___

C

O sa — — — cred, sa-cred o-ra-cles of___ truth,

D

Thus saith the Lord to Cy-rus his a-noint-ed Whose right hand I have holden

Deborah — E

All dan-ger dis-dain-ing, all dan-ger dis-dain-ing for bat-tle I glow

F

Impious mor-tal, cease to brave_ us, Great Je-ho-vah soon_ will save_ us,

G

In___ the bat-tle fame___ pur-su-ing

H

Tears, tears such as ten-der fa-thers shed

Esther — I

Al- le- lu -ja, al-le-lu — — — — — — — — — — — ja

J

O beau-teous Queen un-close_those eyes, My fair-est shall_not bleed,

K

Pluck root and branch from out the land: Shall I the God of Is-rael fear,

L

Sing songs of praise,___ bow down the knee, bow down the knee,___

M

Turn not, O Queen, thy face___ a- way___

Hercules — N

From ce-les-tial_seats de-scend-ing, joys di-vine a-while sus-pend- ing

O

My fa-ther! ah! me-thinks I see the sword inflict the deadly_wound

P

The smil-ing___ hours___ a joy-ful___ train,

Q

The world when_ day's ca- — — reer___ is_ run

Israel in Egypt
Part I, No. 10 — R

But as for his peo-ple, but as for his peo-ple,

Part II, No. 17 — S

Mo- ses and the chil-dren of Is-rael sung this song un-to the Lord

ORATORIOS
Israel in Egypt
Part II, No. 35

The Lord shall reign for e- ver and e- ver,

No. 39

Sing ye to the Lord, for He hath tri- umph- ed glo- rious- ly;

The e- ne- my said: I will pur- sue I will o- ver take,

The Lord is a man of war, the Lord, the Lord is a__ man of war

Thou_shalt bring_them in and plant them in the moun - - - - - - - tain

Jephtha
Recitative

Deep- er and deep-er still thy good-ness, child, Pier-ceth a fa-ther's bleeding heart,

Aria

Waft her, an-gels, through the skies, Far a-bove yon a- zure plain

Fare- well, fare-well, ye lim - - - pid springs__ and floods,

Bright-er scenes I seek a- bove In__the realms of peace and love____

In gen- tle__ mur-murs will____ I mourn, As mourns____ the mate

Pour forth no more un- heed- ed prayers To i-dols deaf and vain

The smi- ling____ dawn of hap- py days Pre - - sents a prospect clear,

Joseph

The pea-sant tastes_the sweets of life,__ un - - wound- ed by its__ cares

What's sweet- er than the new - - blown rose or bree-zes from the new mown close?

Joshua

Aw- ful pleas-ing Be-ing, say, If from heav'n thou wing'st

Hark, hark! 'tis the lin-net and the thrush, In dul - cet__ notes

He-roes, when with glo- ry__ burn- ing, all their toil with plea-sure bear

Oh, had I Ju- bal's lyre, or Mi- riam's__ tune- ful __ voice:

See the ra-ging flames a- rise____

ORATORIOS
Joshua — A
Shall I in Mam-re's fer-tile plain the remnant of my days re-main

Judas Maccabeus
No. 2 — B
Mourn, mourn, mourn, ye af-flict-ed chil-dren, the re-mains

No. 9 — C
Oh Fa - - - - ther, whose al- might - - y pow'r

No. 11 b — D
We come, we come, we come, in bright ar-ray, in bright ar-ray,

No. 22 — E
Pi- ous or - - gies, pi- ous airs, de - - - cent sor- row,

No. 23 — F
Fall'n is the foe Fall'n is the foe: so fall thy foes

No. 26 — G
Zi- on now her head shall raise, tune your harps,

No. 28 — H
Hail, hail, hail Ju- de- a, hap-py land, Ju- de- a, hap-py land,

No. 35 — I
Arm, arm ye brave! arm, arm ye brave! a no -ble cause, a no - ble cause

No. 43 — J
Call forth thy pow'rs, my soul, and dare the con-flict, the con-flict

No. 45 — K
Sing un- to God and high af- fec- tions raise,

No. 46 — L
Oh li- ber-ty thou choicest treasure, seat of virtue source of pleasure!

No. 51 — M
'Tis li - - - - - - ber-ty, dear li- ber-ty a- lone

No. 52 — N
Hal- le- lu- jah, A- men, a- men, Hal- le- lu- ja, a- men

No. 54 — O
Come, e- ver smil-ing li-ber-ty, come, smil-ing li-ber-ty, and with thee bring

No. 66 — P
No, no un- hal-low'd de- sire our breasts shall in- spire,

No. 92 — Q
So ra- pid thy course is, not num- ber- less for- ces

No. 110 — R
From might - - y kings he took the spoil, and with his acts made Judah

No. 120 — S
How vain is man who boasts in fight

Judas Maccabeus
No. 132 — The Lord work-eth won - - - - - - - - - - - - - - - - - ders — A

No. 136 — Sound an a-larm, sound an a-larm! your sil - ver trum-pets sound, — B

No. 148 — With pi-ous hearts and brave as pi-ous, Oh Si-on, we thy__ call at - - - tend; — C

No. 152 — Wise__ men,_____ flat - - t'ring, may__ de - - - - - ceive__ us — D

No. 172 — Fa - ther of__ Heav'n! from Thy e-ter-nal throne, From Thy e - ter - - nal__ throne — E

No. 178 — So shall the lute__ and__ harp a-wake, and sprightly voice sweet descant__ run, — F

No. 186 — See, the _____ con- qu'ring he - - - - - - ro comes! sound _____ the trum-pets, — G

No. 199 — With ho-nour let de-sert be crown'd the trum-pet ne'er in vain shall sound, — H

No. 210 — Oh love-ly peace, with plen-ty crown'd,__ oh, love-ly love-ly peace_____ — I

Messiah
No. 2 — Com- fort ye, Com - - - fort__ ye_____ my peo- ple, — J

No. 3 — Ev-'ry val - - ley, ev-'ry val - ley__ shall_be ex-alt-ed — K

No. 4 — And the glo-ry, the glo-ry of the Lord, And the glo-ry, the glory of the Lord — L

No. 6 — But who may a- bide the day of his com- ing, — M

No. 6 (cont.) — For he is like_____ a re- fi - - - - - - - ner's fire_____ — N

No. 7 — And he shall pu-ri-fy, and he shall purify_____ — O

No. 9 — O, thou that tell- est good tid- ings to Zi- on, — P

No. 11 — The peo - - ple that walk - - ed in dark - - - - - - - - ness, — Q

No. 12 — For un- to us a child is born,__ un-to us a son is giv- en, — R

No. 18 — Glo- ry to God, Glo- ry to God in the high- est, — S

HANDEL

ORATORIOS
Messiah
No. 45

I know that___ my Re- deem --- er liv- eth

No. 48

The trum- pet shall sound_____ and the dead shall_ be__ raised

No. 50

O death, o death, where, where is thy sting? O death, where is thy sting?

No. 51

But thanks___ but thanks, thanks, thanks be to God, but thanks, thanks, thanks,

No. 52

If God____ be for us, who can be a- gainst us?

No. 53

Wor- thy is the lamb that was slain, and hath re- deem- ed us to God

Amen Chorus

A - - - - - - - men, A - - - - - - - - men, A - - - - - - - - - men

Occasional Oratorio

His sceptre is the rod of righteousness, his sceptre is the rod

Je- ho- vah, to my words_ give ear, To my words_ give ear,

Then will I___ Je- ho - - vah's praise ac- cord - ing_ to his jus- tice_ raise,

Samson

A- wake the trum- pet's loft- y sound, A- wake, a- wake

Honour and arms_____ scorn such a foe, scorn such a foe

How will- ing_ my pa- ter- nal_ love the weight_ to share_ of fil - ial care,

Let the bright Se- ra- phim in burn - - - - ing row,

Re- turn, re- turn, Oh_ God____ of hosts! oh God re - - turn,

Thus when the sun from's wa - - t'ry__ bed all cur- tain'd_ with_ a clou - - dy red,

Thy glo- rious deeds in - spir'd_ my_ tongue, whilst airs of joy from_ thence_ did flow

To- tal e - clipse! No sun, no moon, all dark,_____ all dark_____

Why does the God of Is- rael sleep? A- rise with dread- ful sound,

ORATORIOS
Samson — A

Ye sons of Is-rael, now la - ment; your spear is__ broke, your bow's un - bent

Saul — B

Brave Jo - na - than his bow ne'er__ drew. but wing'd with death,

— C

Fell rage and black des-pair_ pos- sessed, with hor-rid sway the mon-arch's breast,

— D

Oh__ god-like youth!_ by all__ con-fess'd of hu-man race _____ the pride!

— E

Oh Lord, whose mercies num- ber-less o'er all thy works _____ pre - vail,

— F

Sin not, O King, a- gainst the youth   Who ne'er-of-fend - - - ed_ you,

Semele — G

End- less plea - - sure   End- less plea - sure, endless love

— H

Hence, hence, I- ris, hence a- way,   I- ris, hence a- way, a- way,

— I

Hy-men, haste,   Hy-men, haste! thy torch prepare! Love al-read-y his has lighted,

— J

Leave__ me,   leave me, loath - some light! re-ceive me, re - ceive me,

— K

Oh _____ sleep,   Oh_ sleep why dost thou leave me?

— L

Where 'er you_ walk, cool gales shall fan the glade; trees, where you sit, shall crowd

Solomon Chorus — M

May no rash in- tru- der dis- turb their soft hours;

— N

What though I trace each herb and_ flow'r that drinks the morning dew,

— O

With thee th'un-sheltered moor I'd__ tread, nor once of fate_ com- plain,

Susanna — P

Ask if yon damask rose_ be sweet, that scents the__ am- bient air?

— Q

Be- neath the cy- press gloom- y shade where silver lil-lies paint the glade

— R

Crys-tal_ streams in mur - murs_ flow- ing in mur - murs_ flow - - ing,

— S

If guiltless blood be your in - - tent, I here re- sign it all

ORATORIOS
Susanna

A — The parent bird in search of food a- while de-serts her cal- low brood,

B — When first__ I saw my love-ly maid, be- neath__ the cit - ron's shade

C — Ye ver- dant hills, ye balm- y vales bear wit- ness of my pain

Theodora

D — An-gels e- ver_ bright and_ fair, an-gels e- ver_ bright and fair, take, oh, take me,

E — As with ro- sy steps the morn ad- vanc-ing, drives the shades of night

F — De- fend her, Heaven, let an-gels spread _____

G — Lord, to__ thee, each_ night and__ day, strong in hope we sing and__ pray

The Triumph of Time and Truth

H — False, de-struc-tive ways of__ pleasure Leave, and court a no-bler__ treasure

I — Loath-some urns,__ dis-close your treas-ure, Pride and pleasure Un-veil to me

HANDL, Jacob (1550-1591)

Adoramus te, Jesu Christe

K — A- do- ra- mus te, Je- su Chris- te

Ecce quomodo moritu, justus

L — The right- eous, the right-eous per - - ish-eth, per- ish-eth

HANSON, Howard (1896-)

Oh, 'tis an earth defiled, from Merry
Mount (opera)
(pseud., Helen Guy Rhodes)
Copyright 1933, Harms, Inc.

N — Oh, 'tis an earth de- filed where-on we live! There is no leaf- y bow'r,

HARDELOT, Guy d' (1858-1936)

Because

I know a Lovely Garden

Sans Toi

HARRISON, Annie Fortescue (d. 1944)

In the Gloaming

In the gloam-ing o my dar-ling! When the lights are dim and low

HARTMANN, Johann Peter (1805-1900)

Flyv, Fugl, Flyv

Flyv, Fugl, flyv o-ver Fu-re-sø-ens Vo-ve!

Frejas Stjerne (choral)

Kun een er Frej-as Stjer-ne, men rundt den sen-der sin Glans

Jaegersang (choral)

Snart er Nat-ten svun-den, Da-gen bry-der frem

Jeg synge skal en Vise

Jeg syn-ge skal en Vi-se; vel-an jeg er be-red

Laer mig!

Laer mig, Nat-tens Stjer-ne, at ly-de fast og ger-ne

Mindnesang over de faldne

Slum-rer sødt i Sles-vigs Jord, dy-re-købt den blev ved e-der!

Rejsen til Vinlandene (choral)

Vort Dag-waerk er til En - - - de; som fri og mun-tre Sven-de

Sange af "Ambrosius"

Den ked-som Vin-ter gik sin Gang, den Dag saa kort, den Nat saa lang

Studentersang (choral)

Vi er et ly-stigt Fol-ke-faerd fra al-le Ver-dens Kan-ter

Ved Jaegerhuset

Du, som har Sorg i Sin-de gak ud i Mark og Lund,

HARTY, Hamilton (1879-1941)

My Lagan Love (arr.)
By permission Boosey & Hawkes, Inc., copyright owners

Where Lagan stream sings lull-a-by There blows a li-ly fair:

Three Irish Folksongs (arr.)
1. The Lowlands of Holland
By permission Oxford Univ. Press, London, copyright owners

The first night I was mar-ried, a hap-py hap-py bride

2. The Faery King's Courtship

On the first day of May at the close of the day

3. The Game Played in Erin-go-Bragh

In London one day as I walked up the street, An im-pu-dent fel-low

HASSLER, Leo (1564-1612)

Feinslieb, du hast mich g'fangen

Feins-lieb, du hast mich g'fan-gen mit dein zwei Äug-lein schon

Jungfrau, dein schöne G'stalt

Jung-frau, dein schö-ne G'stalt er-frent mich sehr je länger je mehr

Mein Lieb' will mit mir kriegen

Mein Lieb' will mit mir krie-gen, hat sich ge-rist zur Schlacht

Tanzsen und Springen

Tan-zen und Sprin-gen, Sin-gen und Klin-gen, fa la la la

HATTON, John L. (1809-1886)

Goodbye, sweetheart, goodbye

The bright stars fade, the morn is break-ing, The dew-drops pearl

Simon the Cellarer

Old Si- mon the Cel- lar- er keeps a rare store.

HAYDN, Franz Josef (1732-1809)

The Apothecary (opera)

Al- le Ta- ge, Al- le Ta- - ge klop-fen, rei-ben

Sitzt Ei- nem hier im Kopf das Weh' so neh-men_ wir von_ die-sem Thee

Wo Lie- bes- göt - - - - ter_ lach-ten, stürmt Hass auf Hass

Es_ kam_ ein Pa- scha aus Tür- -ken-land

Die- se Püpp-chen sind nicht zu er-grün-den, sind nicht zu er-grün-den

Wie Schlei- - er seh'_ ichs nie- - der_ schwe-ben

Mass No. 11 (Nelson Mass)
I Kyrie

Ky- ri- e, Ky-ri- e e-lei- son Ky-ri-e e- lei-son

II Gloria

Glo- ri- a in ex- cel- - - - sis De- o

Lau- da- mus_ te, be- ne- di- ci- mus te

III Qui Tollis

Qui tol-lis, qui_ tol- lis pec- ca- ta

HAYDN

Mass No. 11 (Nelson Mass) IV Quoniam Tu Solus — A
Quo- ni- am tu so- lus so - - - - - lus sanc- tus tu

V Credo — B
Cre- do in u- num De - - - - um, Pa - - - - trem om-ni-po-ten-'tem

VI Et Incarnatus — C
Et in- car-na- tus est de Spi- ri- - tu__ san- cto

VII Et Resurrexit — D
Et, et re- sur- rex- - it ter- ti- a di - - e

VIII Sanctus — E
Sanc - - - tus __ Sanc - - - tus, __ san-ctus Do-mi-nus

IX Benedictus — F
Be- ne- di- ctus qui ve-nit', be- ne- di- - ctus qui ve- nit

X Osanna — G
O- san- na in ex- cel - - - - - - - - - - - - - - - - - sis,

XI Agnus Dei — H
A- gnus __ De- i qui tol- lis pec- ca- ta mun- di

XII Dona Nobis — I
Do- na __ no- bis pa- cem pa- cem, pa - cem,

The Creation (Die Schöpfung) (oratorio) Part I, No. 6 — J
Roll- ing in foam- ing bil-lows up- lift-ed, roars the boist'rous sea

— K
Soft- ly purl- ing,_ glides on through si- lent vales the lim-pid brook

No. 8 — L
With ver-dure clad the fields ap- pear de-lightful to_____ the ra- vish'd sense__

No. 10 — M
Stummt an die Sai-ten ergreift die Leier, lasst eu-er Lob- ge- sang

(Same theme, text in English) — N
A-wake the Harp, the lyre a-wake! In shout and joy your voi-ces

No. 13 — O
The hea- vens are tell- ing the glo- ry of God____

Part II, No. 15 — P
On might- y_ pens up- - lift- ed_ soars_ the_ eagle a-loft

No. 18 — Q
Most beau- ti- ful ap- pear, with_ ver-dure young a- dorn'd

No. 21 — R
The cattle in herds al- rea-dy seeks his food on fields and meadows green

No. 22 — S
Now heav'n in full- est glo - - - - - - - ry_ shone__

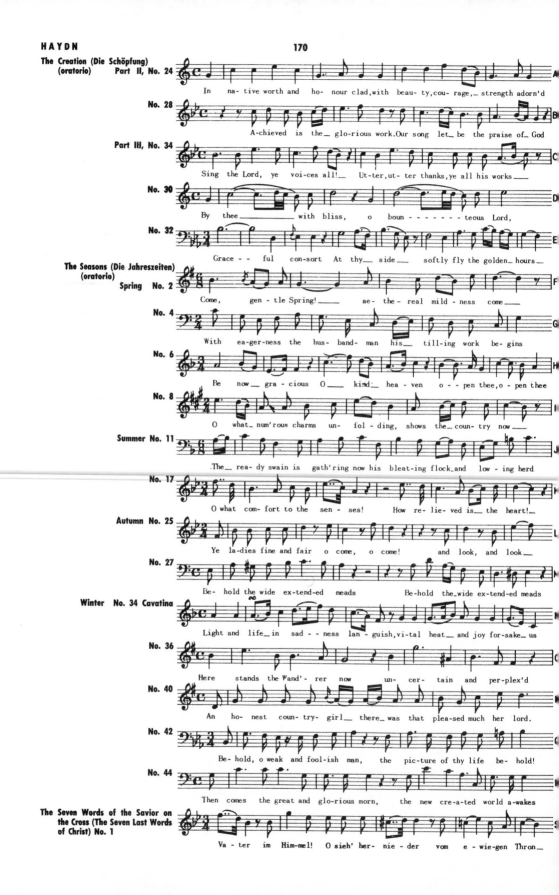

The Creation (Die Schöpfung)
(oratorio)   **Part II, No. 24**

In na-tive worth and ho-nour clad, with beau-ty, cou-rage,— strength adorn'd

No. 28

A-chieved is the— glo-rious work. Our song let— be the praise of— God

Part III, No. 34

Sing the Lord, ye voi-ces all!— Ut-ter, ut-ter thanks, ye all his works—

No. 30

By thee——— with bliss, o boun- - - - - -teous Lord,

No. 32

Grace - - ful con-sort At thy— side— softly fly the golden— hours—

The Seasons (Die Jahreszeiten)
(oratorio)
Spring   No. 2

Come, gen - tle Spring!— ae-the-real mild - ness come—

No. 4

With ea-ger-ness the hus-band- man his— till-ing work be- gins

No. 6

Be now— gra-cious O— kind:— hea-ven o - -pen thee, o - pen thee

No. 8

O what— num'rous charms un- fol-ding, shows the— coun-try now—

Summer No. 11

.The— rea-dy swain is gath'ring now his bleat-ing flock— and low - ing herd

No. 17

O what com- fort to the sen- ses! How re- lie-ved is— the heart!—

Autumn No. 25

Ye la-dies fine and fair o come, o come! and look, and look—

No. 27

Be-hold the wide ex-tend-ed meads Be-hold the wide ex-tend-ed meads

Winter No. 34 Cavatina

Light and life— in sad - -ness lan- guish, vi-tal heat— and joy for-sake— us

No. 36

Here stands the Wand'- rer now un- cer- tain and per-plex'd

No. 40

An ho- nest coun-try- girl— there was that plea-sed much her lord.

No. 42

Be- hold, o weak and fool-ish man, the pic-ture of thy life be-hold!

No. 44

Then comes the great and glo-rious morn, the new cre-a-ted world a-wakes

The Seven Words of the Savior on
the Cross (The Seven Last Words
of Christ) No. 1

Va- ter im Him-mel! O sieh' her- nie- der vom e- wie-gen Thron—

The Seven Words of the Savior on The Cross (The Seven Last Words of Christ) No. 2
Ganz Fr- bar-men, Gnad und Lie-be, ganz Fr- bar-men, ganz Er- bar-men

No. 3
Mut-ter Je-su, die du trost-los, Mutter Je- su, die_ du_ trostlos,

No. 4
„Wa- rum hast Du mich ver-las-sen?" Wer - - sieht hier der Gottheit Spur?

No. 5
Je-sus ru - - - fet: Je-sus ru - fet ach, mich dür- stet

No. 6
Es ist voll- bracht! An das Op- fer-holz ge- hef-tet,

No. 7
In dei-ne Händ, O Herr, empfehl' ich mei- nen Geist, mei-nen Geist

Die Beredsamkeit
Freun- de, was- ser mach- et stumm, was-ser ma-chet stumm, stumm, stumm,

Deutschland über Alles (Gott erhalte Franz den Kaiser)
Gott er- hal- te Gott be schü- tze un- sern Kaiser

Der erste Kuss
Lei- se nannt ich dei - - nen Namen.und mein au- ge wart_ um dich

Die Harmonie in der Ehe
O wun-der-ba- re Har- mo-nie, was Er_ will, will auch Sie

Jeder meint, das holde Kind
Je- der meint, das hol- de Kind, das ich mir er- wäh- le

Jeder meint, der Gegenstand
Je- der meint, der Ge-gen-stand, den er sich er- wäh-let

Liebes Mädchen, hör' mir zu
Lie- bes Mad- chen hör mir zu, öff- ne leis, das Git- ter;

Lob der Faulheit
Faul- heit, end-lich muss ich dir auch ein kleines Lob- leid_ bringen!

The Mermaids' Song
Now the_____ danc- ing sun - - beams play

My Mother bids me bind my hair
My moth- er- bids.me bind_ my hair_ with bands_ of_ ros - y hue

Pensi a me
Pen- si a me si fi- do,a-man- te co- me a te_ sempr' io co-stante?

The Sailor's Song
High on the gid-dy_ bend-ing mast, The sea- man furls_ the_ rend-ing_ sail

She never told her love
She ne- ver told' her love, she ne- ver told her_ love

The Spirit's Song

Hark! Hark! What I tell to thee no sor-row o'er the tomb,

Un tetto umil

Un tet — — to u- mil cui cinge il fag-gio e il pin,

The Wanderer

To wan-der a- lone__ when the moon faint-ly__ beam-ing

HEAD, Michael (1900-   )

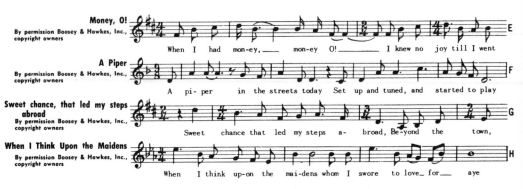

Money, O!
By permission Boosey & Hawkes, Inc.,
copyright owners

When I had mon-ey, mon-ey O! I knew no joy till I went

A Piper
By permission Boosey & Hawkes, Inc.,
copyright owners

A pi- per in the streets today Set up and tuned, and started to play

Sweet chance, that led my steps
abroad
By permission Boosey & Hawkes, Inc.,
copyright owners

Sweet chance that led my steps a- broad, Be-yond the town,

When I Think Upon the Maidens
By permission Boosey & Hawkes, Inc.,
copyright owners

When I think up-on the mai-dens whom I swore to love_ for__ aye

HEISE, Peter (1830-1879)

Ak, hvem der Havde en Hue

Ah__ who once wore a fine bon- net with plume and bro-cade so__ gay

Arnes Sang

Ör- nen löf-ter med stoer-ke Slag o- ver de hör- e Fjel-de

Dengang jeg var Kun saa
(Helligtrekongersaften)

Den- gang jeg var kun saa stor som saa, saa stor som saa__

It Rises (Det Stiger)

It ri-ses, it ri-ses, it ri-ses so high Riv-er wanders 'gainst mountain

Jylland mellem tvende Have

Jyl-land mel-lem tven-de Ha-ve som en Bu- ne-stav er lagt,

Liden Karen

Hus-ker Du i Höst, da vi hjemod fra Mar-ken gik

Woodland Stillness

Through aisles__ of birch — -en for-est I led_ thee, coy_ but willing;

HENSCHEL, Sir George (1850-1934)

Morning Hymn, Op. 46, No. 1
Copyright by John Church Co.
Used by permission

Soon night will pass; Through field and grass What o-dors sweet

HERBERT, Victor (1859-1924)

Babes in Toyland (operetta) Act II, No. 13 Toyland
Copyright 1903, M. Witmark & Sons
Toy- land! Toy- land! Lit - tle girl and boy-land,

The Fortune Teller (operetta)
Copyright 1898, M. Witmark & Sons
Gypsy Love Song
The birds of the for-est are call-ing for thee__ and the shades, and the glades__

Slum-ber on, my lit-tle gyp-sy sweet-heart, Dream of the field and the grove

Romany Life
We have a home 'neath the for-est shade Nev-er an-y oth-er__

Kiss in the Dark, from Orange Blossoms (operetta)
Copyright 1922, M. Witmark & Sons
I re-call the mad de-light of a love-ly dance__

Oh that kiss in__ the dark was__ to him just__ a lark,

Kiss Me Again, from Mlle. Modiste (operetta)
Copyright 1915, M. Witmark & Sons
Sweet sum-mer breeze, Whis-per-ing trees, Stars shining brightly a-bove

Naughty Marietta (operetta)
Copyright 1910, M. Witmark & Sons
Ah! Sweet Mystery of Life
Ah! sweet mys-ter-y of life at last I've found thee

I'm falling in love with someone
For I'm falling in love with some-one, some one girl;__

Italian Street Song
Oh! my heart is back in Na-po-li, dear Na-po-li__

Zing, Zing, ziz-zy, ziz-zy, zing, zing, Boom, boom aye, Zing, Zing

'Neath the Southern Moon
'Neath the South-ern moon, Oh, love so warm and ten-der

Tramp, Tramp, Tramp along the Highway
Tramp, tramp, tramp a-long the high-way, Tramp, tramp, tramp, the road is free

Neapolitan Love Song, from Princess Pat (operetta)
Copyright 1915, M. Witmark & Sons
Sweet one!__ How my heart is yearn-ing__ Ev-er__ with you to be__

The Red Mill (operetta)
Copyright 1906, M. Witmark & Sons
Because You're You
Not that I am fair, dear, Not that I am true. Not my gold-en hair, dear

Isle of Our Dreams
In the beau-ti-ful isle of our dreams, dear, there is nev-er a sorrow or pain

The Streets of New York
In old New York! In old New York! The peach crop's al-ways fine__

Thine Alone, from Eileen (operetta)
Copyright 1917, M. Witmark & Sons
In thine arms en-fold me, my be- lov-ed! Lift thine eyes look fondly in-to mine

Waltz, from Sweethearts (operetta)
Copyright 1913, G. Schirmer, Inc.
Sweet-hearts make love their ver-y own, Sweethearts can live on love a-lone   A

When You're Away, from The Only Girl (operetta)
Copyright 1914, M. Witmark & Sons
When you're a- way, dear, how wear-y the lone-some hours   B

HERMANN, Hans (1870-1931)

Drei Wandrer, Op. 5, No. 4
Drei Wan- drer sind ge-gan- -gen, und als der A-bend fiel   D

HEROLD, Louis (1791-1833)

Le Pré aux Clercs (opera)
Act I. No. 2
Le ren- dez- vous de nob-le com- pa- gni- e se don-nent tous   F

Dans la prai-ri- e fraiche et fleu-ri- e da-me jo- li- e viendra   G

No. 3
O ma ten-dre a- mi- e   je suis près de toi   H

O toi de qui l'ab- sen- ce tou- jours me fait gé- mir   I

No. 5
Sou- ve- nir du jeune â- ge sont gravés dans mon coeur   J

Act II, No. 6
Jours de mon en- fan- - ce o jours d'in- no- cen- - - - ce   K

Oui Mar-gue- rite en qui j'es-pè- re pro-tège u- ne pauvre   L

Act III
À la fleur du bel â- - ge Geor-get- te cha-que jour di- sait   M

Perchè Tremar, from Zampa (opera)
Act III, No. 34
Per-chè tre- mar per- chè? son i- o che pre- go   N

HILDACH, Eugen (1849-1924)

Im Volkston
Was leuch- tet ihr Ster- ne so hell in der Nacht?   P

Der Lenz, Op. 19, No. 5
Die Fin- ken Schlagen, der Lenz ist da, und kei- ner kann sa-gen,   Q

Der Spielmann, Op. 15, No. 1
Du mit dei- ner Fie- del blei- be hier nicht stehn,   R

Wo du hingehst, Op. 8
Wo du hin- -gehst, da will auch ich, auch ich hin- ge- hen   S

HIMMEL, Friedrich (1765-1814)

Gebet während der Schlacht

Va- ter, ich ru- fe dich! Brül- lend um- wolkt mich der Dampf

HINDEMITH, Paul (1895-1963)

Eight Songs, with piano, Op. 18, No. 2
By permission Associated Music Publishers, Inc.

Wie Sankt Fran- cis- cus schweb'ich in- der Luft mit bei- den Fü- ssen

No. 4

Auf der Trep- pe sit- zen mei- ne Öhr- chen wie zwei Kätzchen die die Milch

No. 8 Trompeten

Un- ter verschnit- te- nen Wei- den wo brau- ne Kin- der spie- len

Five songs on old Texts: Of Household Rule
By permission Associated Music Publishers, Inc.

Es ist_ ge- - wiss ein from- mer Mann, ein from- mer Mann,

Lady's Lament

Nun heis- sen sie mich mei- - - - - - - - - den

The Devil a Monk Would Be!

Ein wolf, ein wolf_ der Sün- den- angst be- wog,

True Love

Tris- tan muss- - te oh- ne Dank Treu- e wahr'n der Kö- ni- gin

Troopers' Drinking Song

Tum- mel dich, tum- mel dich, guts Wein- lein, tum- mel dich, tum- mel dich

Frisch_ auf,_ gut_ Gsell, lass rum- mer gahn,

Das Marienleben, Op. 27, No. 1 Geburt Maria
By permission Associated Music Publishers, Inc.

O was muss es die En- gel ge- ko- stet ha- ben,

Schwin- gend ver- schwie- gen sie sich und zeig- ten die Rich- tung

No. 5 Argwohn Josephs

Und der En- gel sprach_ und gab sich Müh an dem Mann

No. 7 Geburt Christi

Hät- test du der Ein- falt nicht, wie soll- te die ge- schehn_

No. 11 Pieta

Jetzt wird mein E- lend voll und na- men- los er- füllt es mich

Six Chansons No. 1 The Doe
By permission Associated Music Publishers, Inc.

O thou doe,_ what vis- tas of sec- u- lar for- ests ap- pear in thine eyes

No. 2 The Swan

A swan is breast- ing the flow all in him- self_ en- fold- ed

Six Chansons
No. 3 Since all is passing

Since all is pass-ing, re- tain The mel- o- dies that wan-der by us

No. 4 Springtime

O song that from the sap art pour-ing and through the sounding board

No. 5 In Winter

With the win- ter, Death, gris-ly guest through the door-way steals in

No. 6 Orchard

The earth is no- where so real a pres-ence As mid thy branches, O orchard

HOLBROOKE, Joseph (1878-1958)

Noden's song, from Children of Don (opera)
By permission Novello & Co., Ltd., London

Deep is my bon- dage and a dread-ful sleep__ the gods have set me

Sea King's Song, from Dylan (opera)
By permission Novello & Co., Ltd., London

The night that bounds my sub- ject spa- ces has no fierc- er gloom

HOLLMAN, J. (1852-1927)

Chanson d'Amour

Te sou- vient il des mar- ron- niers fleu- ris

HOLMÈS, Augusta (1847-1903)

Au pays
Copyright by L. Grus, Paris

Sur la route, Et gaie-ment, Sans u- - - ne crou- te!

Noël

Trois an- ges sont ve- nus ce soir M'ap- por- ter de bien

HOLST, Gustav (1874-1934)

Four Songs for Voice and Violin, Op. 35,
No. 1
By permission J. & W. Chester, Ltd., London, copyright owners

Je- su Sweet, now will I sing to thee a song of love long- ing

No. 2

My soul has nought but fire and ice and my bo- dy earth and wood:

No. 3

I sing of a mai- den that match-less is: King of all Kings

No. 4

My Le- man is so true of love and full stead- fast

The Heart Worships
By permission Galaxy Music Corporation, N. Y., sole U. S. agents for Stainer & Bell, Ltd., London

Si- lence in Heav'n Si- lence on Earth Si- lence within

Hymn to the Waters (Choral Hymn, from the Rig-Veda)

Flow- - ing from the fir- ma- ment Forth to the o- cean.

I Love My Love (arr.)
Copyright 1917, J. Curwen

A- broad as I was walk- ing one eve-ning in the spring   **A**

Midwinter
By permission Oxford Univ. Press, London, copyright owners

Our God, heaven can- not hold Him nor earth sus- tain   **B**

The Sergeant's Song
Copyright by Edwin Ashdown, London

When Law- yers strive to heal a breach, and Par- sons prac-tice   **C**

This Have I Done for My True Love
By permission of Augener, Ltd., London

To- mor-row shall be my danc-ing day, I would my true love   **D**

Turn Back O Man (melody from the German Psalter, 124th Psalm)
By permission Galaxy Music Corporation, N. Y., sole U. S. agents for Stainer & Bell, Ltd., London

Turn back O Man, for- swear thy fool- ish ways. Old now is Earth   **E**

Wassail Song (arr.)
Copyright 1931, G. Holst

The was- sail, the was- sail through - out all the world   **F**

HOMER, Sidney (1864-1953)

Requiem, Op. 15, No. 2
Copyright 1904, G. Schirmer, Inc.,

Un- der the wide and star- ry sky Dig the grave and let me lie.   **H**

A Banjo Song, Op. 22, No. 4
Copyright 1910, G. Schirmer, Inc.

I plays de ban- jo bet- ter now Dan him dat taught me do   **I**

Dearest, Op. 24
Copyright 1910, G. Schirmer, Inc.

Dear- est, when I am dead, make one last song for me   **J**

Sheep and Lambs, Op. 31
Copyright 1914, G. Schirmer, Inc.

All in the A- pril morn- ing A- pril airs were a- broad   **K**

HONEGGER, Arthur (1892-1955)

"Alcools" Six Poèmes de G. Apolli- naire

No. 1. A la "Santé"
Copyright by Salabert, Paris, N. Y.

Que len-te-ment passent les heu-res Com-me passe un en-ter- re- ment   **M**

No. 2. Clotilde

L'a-nè-mone et l'an-co- li- e Ont poussé dans le jar- din   **N**

No. 3. Automne

Dans le brouillard s'en vont un pa- y- san ca- gneux et son boeuf   **O**

No. 4. Saltimbanques

Dans la plai-ne les ba- la- dins S'e- loi-gnent au long des jar-dins   **P**

No. 5. L'Adieu

J'ai cueil- li ce brin de bru- yè- re L'au-tomne est mor- te   **Q**

No. 6. Les Cloches

Mon beau tzi-ga-ne mon a-mant É- cou-te les clo-ches qui son-nent   **R**

Berceuse de la Sirène
Copyright by Salabert, Paris, N. Y.

Danse a- vec nous dans le bel o- ce- an   **S**

HONEGGER

Judith (opera)
Act I, No. 3 Prière
Copyright by Salabert, Paris, N. Y.

Seigneur___ Dieu de mes pères, e-cou-te-moi et viens à mon se-cours

No. 4 Cantique funèbre

O Béthu-li-e Béthu-lie a-ban-don-né-e nous te tendons les mains

Act II, No. 6 Incantation

Is-tar___ Is-tar___ Dé-es-se des ba-tail-les Mar-douk_ Mardouk_

Act III, No. 11 Cantique de la bataille

Ho Ho Ho_ Ho_ Ho Ho Ho_ Ho_ Ho___

Je crie à toi___ dans le ba-taille_ Je crie à toi_ dans le dan-ger

No. 12 Cantique des Vierges

Com- me le jour d'é-té met en fui-te la nuit l'É-ter-nel s'est levé

No. 13 Cantique de la victoire

Son non est Je-ho-vah___ c'est un vail-lant guerrier

Gloire au Dieu Tout Puis-sant Je-ho-vah des ar- mé- es

Mimaamaquim (Psalm 130)
Copyright by Salabert, Paris, N. Y.

Mi- ma- a- ma-quim que-ra-ti kha_ A- do - - - - - - - nai

4 Chansons pour voix grave
No. 1 (Tchobanian)
Copyright by Salabert, Paris, N. Y.

La douceur de tes yeux peut gue-rir___ la plus mortel - - le

No. 2 (William Aguet)

Der- rière_ Marcie en fleurs je con-nais un che- min qui mè- ne jusqu'à toi

No. 3 (Verlaine)

Un grand som-meil noir tom- be sur ma vi-e: Dor-mez tout es-poir

No. 4 (Ronsard)

La ter- re les eaux va bu-vant L'ar-bre la boit par sa ra- ci-ne

Le Roi David (Symphonic Psalm)
No. 2 Cantique du berger David
Copyright by E. C. Schirmer, Boston

L'É-ter- nel est mon ber- ger. Je ne suis que son a- gneau

No. 3 Psalm

Lou- é soit le Sei-gneur plein de gloi- re Le Dieu vi-vant,

No. 4 Chant de Victoire

Vi- ve Da- vid, vain- queur des Philis- tins, L'E-ter-nel l'a choi-si;

No. 7

Ah, si j'a-vais des ai- les de co- lom-be, Je vo-le-rais bien loin

No. 8 Cantique des Prophètes

L'hom-me né de la fem-me a peu de jours a vi-vre.

No. 11 Psalm

L'É- ter- nel est ma lu- mière___ in-fi- ni- e___

Le Roi David (Symphonic Psalm)
No. 17 Cantique
De mon coeur jail- lit un can-ti-que Je dis, mon oeu-vre pour le Roi   A

No. 18 Chant de la Servante
Bien ai- mé, prends ma main, des- cen- dons la col- li- ne   B

No. 22 La Chanson d'Ephraim
O fo- rêt d'Eph- ra- im où tour- nent les cor- beaux   C

No. 24
Je t'ai- me- rai, Sei- gneur____ d'un a- mour ten- dre   D

No. 27 La Mort de David
Dieu le dit: un__ jour vi- en- dra où u- ne fleur fleu- ri- ra   E

Al - - - - - - - le - - lui- a, Al - - - - - - - - - le - - lui- a ____   F

Saluste du Bartas
No. 1 Le Château du Bartas
permission Henri Lemoine, Paris; Elkan-
ogel Co., Inc., Phila., copyright owners
Un Gas- con à mi- ne fiè- re É- crit de beaux vers pom- peux   G

No. 2 Toute le long de la Baïse
Tout le long de la Ba- ï- se C'est Sa- lus- te du Bar- tas   H

No. 3 Le Départ
A- vec sa bel- le pres- tan- ce Lè- vre rou- ge regard noir,   I

No. 4 La Promenade
Mar- gue- ri- te de Na- var- re Par un jour brû- lant d'é- té   J

No. 5 Nérac en Fête
Qu'est ce donc sur la ga- ren- ne Le peu- ple dan- se gai- ment   K

No. 6 Duo
La- mour auquel tout in- vi- te Va ré- u- nir à la fin   L

Six Poésies de Jean Cocteau
No. 1 Le Nègre
Copyright by Salabert, Paris, N. Y.
Le nè- gre mi- neur de l'a- zur que ja- mais pleu- voir ne mouille   M

No. 2 Locutions
Fraî- che comme u- ne ro- - se Sa- ge comme une i- ma- - - ge   N

No. 3 Souvenirs d'enfance
Pen- dant la nuit u- ne ro- se a- van- ce sous feux é- teints   O

No. 4 Ex-voto
Au- tour de la Sain- te Vi- erge il fait chaud ce sont les cier- ges   P

No. 5 Une danseuse
Le crabe sort sur ces pointes A- vec ses bras en cor- beil- le   Q

No. 6 Madame
O Ma- da- - me voi- là ce qu'il fau- drait com- pren- - dre   R

Three Psalms: 1. Psalm 34
Copyright by Salabert, Paris, N. Y.
Ja- mais ne ces- se- rai De ma- gni- fi- er le Sei- gneur   S

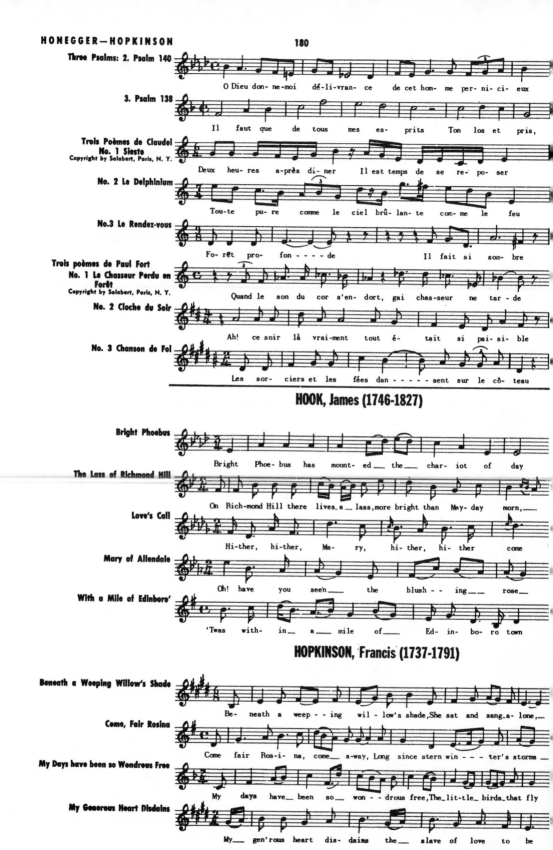

Three Psalms: 2. Psalm 140

O Dieu don- ne-moi dé-li-vran- ce de cet hom- me per-ni-ci- eux

3. Psalm 138

Il faut que de tous mes es- prits Ton los et pris,

Trois Poèmes de Claudel
No. 1 Sieste
Copyright by Salabert, Paris, N. Y.

Deux heu- res a-près di- ner Il est temps de se re- po- ser

No. 2 Le Delphinium

Tou-te pu- re comme le ciel brû- lan-te com-me le feu

No.3 Le Rendez-vous

Fo- rêt pro- fon - - - - de Il fait si som- bre

Trois poèmes de Paul Fort
No. 1 Le Chasseur Perdu en Forêt
Copyright by Salabert, Paris, N. Y.

Quand le son du cor s'en-dort, gai chas-seur ne tar- de

No. 2 Cloche du Soir

Ah! ce soir là vrai-ment tout é- tait si pai-si- ble

No. 3 Chanson de Fol

Les sor- ciers et les fées dan - - - - sent sur le cô- teau

HOOK, James (1746-1827)

Bright Phoebus

Bright Phoe- bus has mount-ed __ the __ char- iot of day

The Lass of Richmond Hill

On Rich-mond Hill there lives_a __ lass,more bright than May- day morn,—

Love's Call

Hi-ther, hi-ther, Ma- ry, hi- ther, hi- ther come

Mary of Allendale

Oh! have you seen __ the blush - - ing __ rose—

With a Mile of Edinboro'

'Twas with- in a __ mile of __ Ed- in- bo- ro town

HOPKINSON, Francis (1737-1791)

Beneath a Weeping Willow's Shade

Be- neath a weep - - ing wil- low's shade,She sat and sang_a- lone,—

Come, Fair Rosina

Come fair Ros-i- na, come __ a-way, Long since stern win - - - ter's storms

My Days have been so Wondrous Free

My days have_ been so_ won - - drous free,The_lit-tle_ birds_that fly

My Generous Heart Disdains

My__ gen'rous heart dis- dains the__ slave of love to be

O'er the Hills

O'er the hills far a-way at the_birth of the morn, I heard the full_tone

The Traveller Benighted

The trav-'ler be-night-ed and lost O'er the moun-tain pursues his lone way;

HORN, Charles Edward (1786-1849)

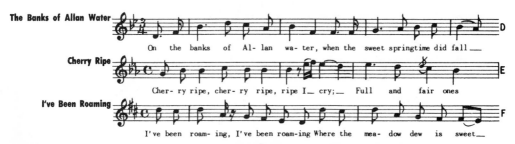

The Banks of Allan Water

On the banks of Al-lan wa-ter, when the sweet springtime did fall_

Cherry Ripe

Cher-ry ripe, cher-ry ripe, ripe I_cry;_ Full and fair ones

I've Been Roaming

I've been roam-ing, I've been roam-ing Where the mea-dow dew is sweet_

HORSMAN, Edward (1873-1918)

The Bird of the Wilderness
Copyright 1914, G. Schirmer, Inc.

My heart,_ the bird_ of the wil - - der-ness

HUE, Georges (1858-1948)

À des Oiseaux
Copyright by A. Leduc Music Publishers, Paris

Bon-jour, bon-jour les fau-vet-tes Bon-jour les joy-eux pin-sons_

L'Âne Blanc
By permission Heugel & Cie, Paris, copyright owners

Je ne t'en- voie ni va-se, ni ro-ses ce soir, Mi-gnon-ne Mir-za

Les Clochettes des Muguets
Copyright by Salabert, Paris, N. Y.

Les clo-chet-tes des mu-guets, Fris-son-nan-tes sous la bri-se

La Fille du Roi de Chine
By permission Heugel & Cie, Paris, copyright owners

Je suis fou de la fil-le de roi de Chi-ne

Il a Neigé des Fleurs
Copyright by Salabert, Paris, N. Y.

Il a nei-gé des fleurs_cet-te nuit; Les sen-tiers et les al-lées_

J'ai Pleuré en Rêve
Copyright by A. Leduc Music Publishers, Paris

J'ai pleuré en rê-ve: J'ai rê-vé que tu é-tais mor-te

Sonnez les Matines
By permission Heugel & Cie, Paris, copyright owners

Pour-quoi ne me ber-cez-vous plus Ô chan-son de Ro-se Ma-ri-e?

Sur l'Eau
By permission Heugel & Cie, Paris, copyright owners

Sur l'eau mu-si-ca-le qui pas-se U-ne ro - - - - se se berce

Tête de Femme est Légère
By permission Heugel & Cie, Paris, copyright owners

Tê-te de femme est lé-gè-re Et tourne au-tant que plume au vent

HUGHES, Herbert (1882-1937)

ARRANGEMENTS:
By permission Boosey & Hawkes, Inc.,
copyright owners

A Ballynure Ballad (Antrim)

As I was goin' to Bal-ly-nure, the day I well___ re-mem-ber___

I know my love (Irish tune)

I___ know my love by his way o' walk-in and I know my love

I know where I'm goin' (Antrim)

I know where I'm go-in, And I know who's go-in with me

I will walk with my love (Dublin)

I once loved a boy and a bold I-rish boy who would come and would go

The next market day (Ulster)

A maid goin' to Com-ber her mar-kets to larn, To sell for her mam-my

The Old Turf Fire

Oh, the old turf___ fire and the hearth swept clean, There is no one

She moved thro' the fair (Donegal)

My_____ young love said to me___ "My mother won't mind and my father___

HUHN, Bruno (1871-   )

Invictus
Copyright by Arthur P. Schmidt Co., Boston.
Used by permission

Out of the night that cov-ers me, Black as the pit from pole to pole

HULLAH, John Pyke (1812-1884)

Three Fishers Went Sailing

Three fish-ers went sail-ing out in-to the west

HUME; Alexander (1811-1859)

Flow Gently, Sweet Afton

Flow gent-ly, sweet___ Af-ton, a-mong thy green braes

HUMPERDINCK, Engelbert (1854-1921)

Hänsel und Gretel (opera) Act I

A   Su-sy, lit-tle Su-sy, pray what is the news?

B   Cross-patch a-way, Leave me I pray! Just let me reach you

A   Bro-ther come and dance with me, both my hands I of-fer thee

B   With your foot you tap, tap, tap, With your hand you clap, clap, clap

Konigskinder (opera)

Act I — Va-ter! Mut-ter! Hier will ich knien!— Bit-ten! Flehn!

Act III — Weisst noch das gro-sse Nest aus Moos und Laub ge-äst

Lie-ber Spiel-man, al-le Kin-der und ich, wir ha-ben ge-be-ten

Am Rhein — Wenn im son-ni-gen Herb-ste die Trau-be schwillt—

Wiegenlied — Es schau-keln die Win-de das Nest in der Lin-de

HUMPHREY, Pelham (1647-1674)

I pass all my hours — I pass all my hours in a sha-dy old grove

O the sad day — O— the sad— day when men shall shake their heads and say

INDY, Vincent d' (1851-1931)

Madrigal dans le style ancien, Op. 4 — Qui ja-mais fut de plus char-mant vi-sa-ge, De col plus blanc,

Mirage, Op. 56
By permission J. Homelle Music Publishers, Paris — De loin, tu pa-rais-sais très gran-de Et très grave aus-si—

ARRANGEMENTS:
Le Roy Loys, Op. 90, No. 1
Copyright by Salabert, Paris, N. Y. — Le Roy Lo- ys est sur son pont, Ten-ant sa fille en son gi-ron.

Le Vingt-cinq d'Août, Op. 100, No. 1
Copyright by Salabert, Paris, N. Y. — C'etait vers le vingt-cinq d'A- oût voi-ci ve-nir, sous l'vent à nous—

En Passant par la Lorraine, No. 2 — En pas-sant par la Lor-rai-ne, a-vec mes sa-bots—

À La Pêche des Moules, No. 3 — À la pê-che des mou-les, je ne veux plus al- ler, ma-man,

Gentil Coqu'licot, No. 4 — Je des-cen-dis dans mon jar-din; Je des-cen- dis dans mon jar-din

Cadet Rousselle, No. 5 — Ca-det Rous- selle a trois mai-sons qui n'ont ni pou-tres ni che-vrons

Compère Guillery, No. 6 — Il é-tait un p'tit hom-me, qui s'app'lait Guil-le- ry, ca-ra-bi,

Lied Maritime — Au loin dans la mer s'é-teint le so-leil— et la mer est calme

IPPOLITOV-IVANOV, Michael (1859-1935)

Bless the Lord, O my Soul
Copyright by Boston Music Co.

Bless the Lord, O___ my soul.__ Blessed art Thou,___ O___ Lord___

Parting (Adieu)
permission J. & W. Chester, Ltd., London,
opyright owners

We've trod one road, long years in ev-'ry wea-ther

IRELAND, John (1879-1962)

The Bells of San Marie
By permission of Augener, Ltd., London

It's plea-sant in Ho-ly Ma-ry By San Ma-rie la-goon,

The Heart's Desire
By permission Boosey & Hawkes, Inc.,
copyright owners

The boys_ are up the woods_with day to fetch_the daf-fo-dils___

Hope the Hornblower
By permission Boosey & Hawkes, Inc.,
copyright owners

Hark ye, hark to the wind-ing horn, Slug-gards, a-wake and front the morn!___

If there were dreams to sell
By permission Boosey & Hawkes, Inc.,
copyright owners

If there were dreams to sell,___ What would you buy?

I have twelve oxen
By permission Boosey & Hawkes, Inc.,
copyright owners

I have twelve ox-en that be fair and brown

The Lent Lily
By permission of Augener, Ltd., London

'Tis spring; come out to ram-ble the hill-y brakes a-round,

The Salley Gardens
By permission Associated Music
Publishers, Inc.

Down by the sal-ley gar-dens my love and I did meet

Sea Fever
By permission of Augener, Ltd., London

I must go down to the seas a-gain, to the lone-ly sea and the sky,

The Soldier
By permission Boosey & Hawkes, Inc.,
copyright owners

If I should die, think on-ly this of me: that there's some cor-ner

Vagabond
By permission of Augener, Ltd., London

Dun-no a heap a-bout the what an' why

We'll to the woods no more
By permission Oxford Univ. Press, London,
copyright owners

We'll to the woods no more, The lau-rels are all cut

ISAAC, Heinrich (1450-c. 1517)

Innsbruck, ich muss dich lassen

Inns-bruck, ich muss dich las-sen, ich fahr da-hin mein Stra-ssen

IVES, Charles (1874-1954)

Ann Street

Quaint name Ann - - street. Width of same___ ten feet Bar-num's mob___

Charlie Rutlage
Copyright 1932, Cos Cob Press, Inc.

An- oth-er good cow-punch- er has gone to meet his fate,

Evening
Copyright 1932, Cos Cob Press, Inc.

Now came still Eve-ning on, and Twi-light gray had in her so-ber liv-ery

General William Booth enters into heaven
Copyright 1935, Charles Ives

Booth led bold- ly with his big bass drum (Are you washed in the blood

The Greatest Man

My teacher said us boys should write a- bout some great___ man___

Resolution

Walk- ing strong- er un- der dis- tant skies,

Two little flowers

On sun- ny days in our back yard, Two lit-tle flowers are seen

JACKSON, Marylou

Trampin' (Try'n a make Heav'n my home) (Negro spiritual) (arr.)

I'm tram- pin', tram- pin', try'n a make heav'n my home

JACOBSON, Myron

Chanson de Marie Antoinette (arr.)
Copyright 1927, Carl Fischer, Inc.
Used by permission

On dit que le plus fier c'est moi Moi pau-vre jar-di-nier

JACQUES-DALCROZE, Emile

Le Coeur de ma mie
Copyright by Jobin & Cie, Paris

Le coeur de ma mie est pe- tit, tout pe- tit, pe- tit;

JANACEK, Leos (1854-1928)

Jenufa (opera)
Act II, Scene 5
By permission Associated Music
Publishers, Inc.

Co chví - - - la co chví - la a já si mám - - -

Act III, Scene 12

O- de- sli Jdi ta- ke! Vsak'včil vi- diš, že smým

JANNEQUIN, Clement (c.1472-c.1560)

A ce joly moys

A ce jo- ly moys, jo- ly moys, jo- ly moys de mays

L'Alouette

Or sus, or sus, vous dor- mez trop Ma- da- me Jo-li- et - - - - - - - - - - te

Au joly jeu

Au jo- ly, jo-ly, jo- ly jeu du pous-se a- vant, du pous-se a-vant

Au premier jour du joly moys de may — A
Au premier jour du jo-ly moys de may_____

Au verd boys — B
Au verd boys je m'en i-ray je m'en i-ray seu-le, au verd boys,

La Bataille de Marignan (La Guerre) — C
É-cou-tez, é-cou-tez é-cou-tez tous__ gentils gal-----lois__

Ce moys de may — D
Ce moys de may, ce moys de may, Ce moys de may ma ver-te

Ce sont gallans — E
Ce sont gal-lans qui s'en vont res-jou-yr

Le Chant des Oiseaux A — F
Re-veil-lez- vous coeurs en-dor-mis Le__ dieu d'a-mour vous son-ne,

B — G
Les oi-seaux quand sont ra-vis, En leur chant font mer-veil-les.

Las, povre coeur — H
Las,____ po-vre coeur___ tant tu as de tri-----stes---se

Petite Nymphe folastre — I
Pe-ti-te Nym-phe fo-la-stre, Nym-phet-te que l'i-do-la-stre

Quand j'ay esté — J
Quand j'ay es-té quinze heu-res a-vec vous

Quand je boy — K
Quand je boy du vin cla-ret, Tout tour_____

JARNEFELT, Armas (1869-1958)

Sunnuntaina (Sunday) — M
Kau-nis Kir-kas__ nyt on aa-mu, Aa-mu ar-mas__ sun-nun-tain

JENSEN, Adolf (1837-1879)

Lehn' deine Wang', Op. 1, No. 1 — O
Lehn' dei-ne Wang an mei-ne Wang', dann flie-ssen die Trä-nen

Marie, No. 2 — P
Ma-rie, am Fen-ster sit-zest du, du lie-bes, sü-sses Kind,___

Waldesgespräch, Op. 5, No. 4 — Q
Es ist schon spät es wind schon kalt,__ was reit'st du ein-sam durch den Wald?

Murmuring Breezes, Op. 21, No. 4 — R
Mur---meln-des Lüft-chen, Blü-ten-wind,___ der die schö-ne Welt_____

Am Ufer des Flusses, des Manzanares, No. 6 — S
Am U-fer des Flusses, des Man-za-na-res, Spült Lin-nen das Mäd-chen

Der Schmied, Op. 24, No. 6

Ich hör mei - nen Schatz den Ham-mer er schwin- get,das rauschet,das klin-get,

Mein Herz ist im Hochland, Op. 49, No. 1

Mein Herz ist im Hochland,mein Herz ist nicht hier!Mein Herz ist im Hochland

Wenn durch die Piazzetta, Op. 50, No. 3

Wenn durch die Piaz-zet-ta die A - - -bendluft weht, dann weisst du

Leis' rudern hier, mein Gondolier! No. 4

Leis' ru-dern hier, mein Gon-do- lier! Die Flut vom Ru-der sprühn

Wiegenlied, Op. 53, No. 2

Süss und sacht,sach- te weh', Wind du vom west-li-chen Meer;

O lass dich halten, gold'ne Stunde

O lass dich hal- ten, gold'- ne Stun-de, die nie so schön

JOHN of Fornsete (13th Cent.)

Sumer is icumen in (Reading rota)

Sum- er is i- cum- en in, Loud now sing cuck- oo

JOHN IV, King of Portugal (1604-1656)

Crux fidelis

Crux fi- de- lis in - - - ter om- nes

JOMMELLI, Niccolo (1714-1774)

Chi vuol comprar

Chi vuol com-prar la bel- la ca- ian-dri - - - na

JONES, Robert (1597-1617)

Farewell, dear Love

Fare-well, dear love,since thou will needs be gone Mine eyes do show

Go to bed, sweet muse

Go to bed,sweet Muse, take thy rest, Let not thy soul be so op- prest

Love is a bable

Love, love, love, love, love is a ba- ble, love is a ba-ble

Love's god is a boy

Love's god is a boy; None but cow-herds re-gard him; His dart is a toy

My love bound me with a kiss

My love bound me with a kiss That I should no long-er stay

What if I sped?

What if I sped where I least ex- pect- ed? What shall I say?

JOSQUIN des Prés (c. 1445-1521)

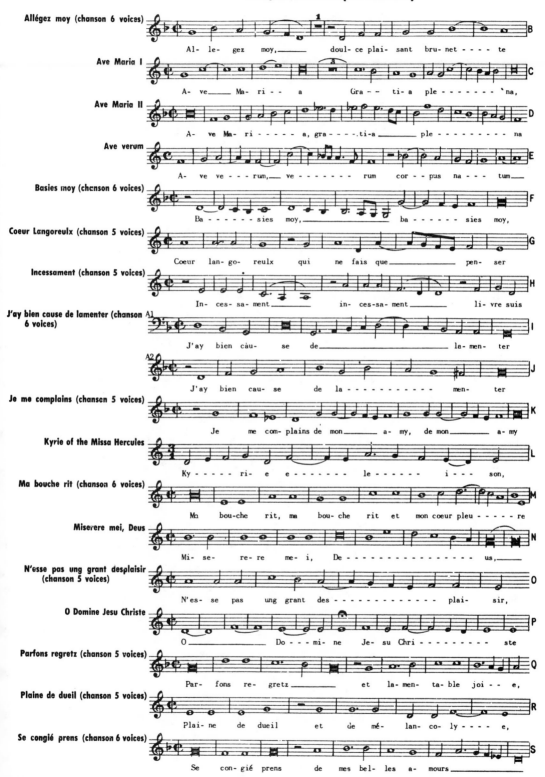

Stabat Mater

Part I — Sta- bat ma- ter do- lo- ro- sa Jux- ta- cru-cem

Part II — E- ia Ma- ter fons a- mo- ris,

Tenez moy en voz bras (chanson 6 voices) — Te- nez moi en voz bras, Mon a- my, je suis

Tu pauperum refugium — Tu pau-pe- rum re- fu- gi- um, Tu lan- guo-rum

KAHN, Percy B.

Ave Maria
Copyright 1913, G. Schirmer, Inc. — A- ve Ma- ri- a, gra- ti- a ple- na

KENNEDY-Fraser, Marjory (1857-1930)

Songs of the Hebrides (arrangements)
By permission Boosey & Hawkes, Inc., copyright owners
Aillte — The Queen of Loch- lin of the brown shields Deep love gave,

An Eriskay Love Lilt — Bheir mi ò- ro bhan o Bheir mi ò- ro bhan

The Bens of Jura — Like wa- ter- cress ga-ther'd fresh from cool streams Thy kiss, dear love,

Bloweth the West Wind — Lad down yon- der, Ho-i- o, Keep'st thou watch there? Ho-ro Yal- lo- vi,

A Fairy's Love Song — Why should I sit and sigh, Pu- in brack- en, pu- in brack-en,

Islay Reaper's Song — A day in the corn field I a reap- in' Cut-tin' my sheaf

Kishmul's Galley — High from the Ben a Hay- ich On a day of days Sea-ward I gaz'd

Land of Heart's Desire — Land of Heart's De-sire, Isle of Youth, dear Western Isle, gleaming in sun-light!

The Mull Fisher's Love Song — O Mhairead og! Mhairead, my girl, Thy sea-blue eyes

The Road to the Isles — A far croon- in is pull- in' me a- way

— Sure, by Tummel and Lech Rannoch and Lock- a- ber I will go,

Sea Sorrow (arr. by Bantock) — Mouth of glad- ness! Mu-sic's laughter Sad that I am not be-side thee.

Songs of the Hebrides (arrangements)
Skye Fisher's Song

Far the rug-ged mis-ty Isle The Isle of Skye doth show   A

Sleeps the Noon

Sleeps the noon in the deep blue sky While bright the sun shines on Co-na's steep   B

The Wild Swan

Swan o' the West, Mate o' my heart, West-ward I'd fly toward Ju-ra   C

KERN, Jerome (1885-1946)

All the things you are, from Very Warm for May

All through the Day, from Centennial Summer (film)

I dream too much, from I Dream too Much (film)

Show Boat:
Bill

Can't Help Lovin' Dat Man

Make Believe

Ol' Man River

Smoke gets in your eyes, from Roberta

The Song is you, from Music in the Air

KIENZL, Wilhelm (1857-1941)

Der Evangelimann, Op. 45 (opera)
Act II
By permission Associated Music Publishers, Inc.

O schö - - ne Ju- gend- ta- ge mit eu'- rem stil - len Glück   Q

Se- lig sind, die Ver- fol- gung lei - den um der Ge- rech- tig-keit   R

Der Kuhreigen, Op. 85 (opera)
Act I
Copyright by Josef Weinberger, Ltd., London

Lug', Dursel, lug';— der A-bend bricht her-ein.— Lug' wie der Son-ne   S

Der Kuhreigen, Op. 85 (opera)
Act I

Zu Stras-burg auf der Schanz', da ging mein Trauern an;

KILPINEN, Yrjo (1892-1959)

Von zwei Rosen, Op. 59, No. 3
By permission Associated Music Publishers, Inc.

Von zwei Ro-sen duf-tet ei-ne an-ders als die and-re Ro-se,

Siehe, auch ich—lebe, Op. 59, No. 5

Al-so ihr lebt noch, al-le, al-le, ihr, am Bach ihr Wei-den

Thalatta! Op. 59, No. 6

Es stür-zen der Ju-gend Al-tä-re zu-sam-men,

Lieder der Liebe, Op. 60, No. 1
By permission Associated Music Publishers, Inc.

Mein Herz ist leer, ich lie----be dich nicht mehr

No. 2

Es ist Nacht, und mein Herz kommt zu dir, hält's nicht aus,

No. 3

Die--se Ro--se von heim-li-chen Küs--sen schwer

No. 4

Wir sit-zen im Dun-keln. Der Vor-hang rauscht lei--se

No. 5

Wir sind zwei Ro-sen, dar-ü-ber der Sturm fuhr und sie ab-riss.

Lieder um den Tod, Op. 62, No. 1 Vöglein Schwermut
By permission Associated Music Publishers, Inc.

Ein schwar-zes Vög-lein fliegt ü-ber die Welt,

No. 2 Auf einem verfallenen Kirchhof

Was gehst du, ar-mer blei-cher Kopf, mich an Es ist kein Grund

No. 3 Der Tod und der einsame Trinker

Gu-ten A-bend, Freund! Dein Wohl! Wie geht's? Dein Wohl!

No. 4 Winternacht

Flok-ken-dich-te Win-ter-nacht. Heim-kehr von der Schen-ke

No. 5 Der Säeman

Durch die Lan-de auf und ab schrei-tet weit Bau--er Tod

No. 6 Unverlierbare Gewähr

Ei-nes gibt's dar-auf ich mich freu----en darf

Vorfrühling, Op. 79, No. 3
By permission Associated Music Publishers, Inc.

Durch ho-he Tan-nen träu-felt schon in schwin-den-den Schnee das Licht.

Venezianisches Intermezzo, Op. 79, No. 4

Durch al-te Mor-mor-hal-len streift weicher Wind von Meer

Marienkirche zu Danzig im Gerüst, Op. 79, No. 7

Du Trotz des Glau-bens! Du be-helm-tes Haupt Burg Got-tes-

KJERULF, Halfdan (1815-1868)

Aftenstimmung (Twilight musing)
The prin-cess sat high in her loft-y bow'r,

Detvar da
Hear how the break-ers An-gri-ly lash the sand,

Ingrids Vise (Ingrid's Song)
The fox lay low neath the birchtree root By the hea-ther, by the heather

Laengsel (Longing)
Last night the night-in-gale woke me, When all the world was still,

Mit Hjerte og miss Lyre
I give thee all, I can no more, Tho' poor the off'-ring be,—

Sing, Sing!
Sing, sing Night-in-gale, sing, Sing as we watch to- geth-er,

Synnöve's Sang (Synnöve's Song)
Grate-ful am I for the 'hap-py time We two, from child-hood

KNIGHT, J. P. (1812-1887)

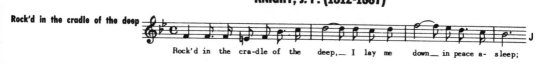

Rock'd in the cradle of the deep
Rock'd in the cra-dle of the deep,— I lay me down— in peace a- sleep;

KODALY, Zoltan (1882-1967)

Hary Janos, Op. 15, (opera) No. 5
By permission Boosey & Hawkes, Inc., copyright owners
Sej! verd meg Is-ten, a ki ez-tet csi-nál-ta!

No. 6
La—la la— la la la la la la la la la—— la la la la— la la la

No. 7
Pi-ros al-ma le-e-sett a sár-ba Ki felve-szi nem e-sik hi- á-ba

No. 8
Óh,mely sok hal te-rem oz nagy Ba-la-ton bah- ha- rah- ha- ra

No. 9
Ti-szán in-nen Du-nán túl, túl_ a Ti szán, van egy esikós—_ nyá-jas- túl

No. 11
Ku- ku- ku-kus- kám, Szállj le hoz- zám madár- kám!

No. 13
Ho-gyan tud- tál ró-zsám, i- de jön- ni? Ár- kot kel-tett né-ked

No. 14
Hej két ti- kom ta- va-li, há- rom har- mad- é- vi

KODALY 194

Hary Janos, Op. 15 (opera) No. 15 A

Sej, be-so-roz-tak, sej, be-so-roz-tak en-ge-met ka to-no-tak,

B

Nagy- a bony- ban csak kit to- rony lát szik

No. 21

Hagyj bé-két, vi-   as-ko-dó, óh! Mi-don nem vagy hasz nos hó óh

No. 22

A- jo lo-vas ka-to-ná-nak, de jo va-gyon dol- ga

No. 23 A

Gyíy- tot- tam gyer-tyát a-vó- le gén- nek, Lát-tam sze- me-lit

B

Mar en-gem, mat kam, ti zen ké- ret-tek! Adj jó ta- ná-csot

No. 26

Á- bé- cé- dé, Raj-tam kez- dé, A nagy böl cses-sí- get,

No. 28

Sze- geny va- gyok, sze- gény- nek szü- let- tem,

No. 29

Fel- szán tom a csá- szár ud- va-rát, Be- le- ve- tem ha-zam

Hungarian Folksongs:
By permission Oxford Univ. Press, London,
copyright owners
(except where otherwise noted)

A Növérek (The Sisters)

Frei- er kam zum Schwester-lein; rei- cher Schneider Gün-ther,

Arról Alúl (Over Yonder)

O- ver yon-der clouds are spread-ing dull and grey, Where my sweet- heart sits

Aszszony, Aszszony (Woman, Woman)

Wo- man, wo- man, out of your bed! From the drink-ing par-ty I'm back

A rossz feleség (The heartless wife)

Come home quickly, mother dearest   Fath-er on his deathbed's lying

Az hol ên elmênyêk (I rove, I look around)

I rove, I look a-round,___ See eve- ry tree weep-ing___

Akkor szep az erdö (Lovely is the forest)

Love- ly is the for- est, forest green, Tur- tle doves a- woo-ing,

Apró alma lehulott (From the tree an apple fell)

From the tree an ap-ple fell, high,dil- ly, He who finds it, picks it up,

Cigány nóta (Gypsy Song)

E- gész fa- lut ösz-sze- jár- tam, Még- is sem- mit sem Kop- hat-tam,

Elkiáltom magamat (Far across the village green)

Far a-cross the vil-lage green There's my sweetheart passing, Ea-ger-ly I wave

Egy nagyórú böha (Long-nose Flea)

Long___ Nose comes a- call- ing, Dai-ly comes a- call-ing, Comes to lunch,

Hungarian Folksongs:

Egy kicsi madarka (Came a bird a-flying) — A
Came a bird a fly - - - - - ing To my flow - - er gar - den

Hej, a Mohi hegy borának (Hey! The wine of Mohi)
By permission Boosey & Hawkes, Inc., copyright owners — B
Hey! the wine of Mo - hi vin - tage__ now costs flo-rins twen-ty

Három Árva (The Three Orphans) — C
Trudged a-long the road__ three or - phans, Way-worn, wea - ry,__

Kitrákotty mese (Tale of the clucking) — D
Once I went to mar-ket with one groat to spend, And up-on a roos-ter

Kádár Kata (Dear Mother) — E
Gyu- la-i-né, é-des a-nyám!__ En-ged-je-meg__ azt az e-gyet,

Körtéfa (The Pear Tree)
By permission Boosey & Hawkes, Inc., copyright owners — F
Still you stand, O, Peartree, As of old, green Pear Tree! Once your spreading

Kocsi, szekér (Wheelcart, barrow) — G
Wheel-cart,bar-row wheelcart,sleigh, I'm a spin-ster, Fol-de-rol de rid-dle

Kádár István (Ballad of Stephen Kádár)
By permission Boosey & Hawkes, Inc., copyright owners — H
Once Pa- no- nia lay in dire dis-tress and pe- ril,__

Katona vagyok én (Called to serve) — I
Called to serve my country all I love I'm leaving__ Sad-ly weeps my mo-ther

Kit Kéne elvenni (Which one should I marry) — J
Wise it were and time- ly ev- en now to mar- ry.

Labanc gúnydal a Kuruczra ("Labantz" mocking "Kurutz")
By permission Boosey & Hawkes, Inc., copyright owners — K
Look out, Ku- rutz, run a-way now, Rough haired Ger- mans

Megégett Rácország (All our homes)
By permission Boosey & Hawkes, Inc., copyright owners — L
All our homes__ charred ruins, Three a-lone scaped burning, One is our King's palace

Meghalok, Meghalok (Woe is me) — M
Woe is me, woe is me, so young and hale, I die. Let me for-e-ver sleep

Mónár Anna (Ballad of Annie Miller) — A N
Come, my darling An-nie Mil - ler, Let us go forth, both to-gether,

B O
No, I come not, reckless Mar-tin! I won't leave my home my hus-band

Most jöttem Erdélyböl (I've just arrived) — P
Bin e-ben an- ge- langt, Aus Sie- ben- bur- gen's Land,

Öreg vagyok már én (I am old now)
By permission Boosey & Hawkes, Inc., copyright owners — Q
I am old and bold now I don't work at all now,

Puciné
By permission Boosey & Hawkes, Inc., copyright owners — R
One small loaf is all my liv- ing, This to Pu- ci- ne I'm giv-ing, Hey!

Rákóczi kesergöje (Rakoczi's Lament)
By permission Boosey & Hawkes, Inc., copyright owners — S
Hear- ken un- to me my Magyars! All my words are__ true,

Hungarian Folksongs:

Siralmas volt nekem (All my days are clouded)
By permission Boosey & Hawkes, Inc., copyright owners

All my days are cloud-ed___ Joy - - - less___ dawns___ each mor-row

Szölöhegyen keresztül (Through the vineyard)

Through the vine-yard fair Kit-ty With her bro-ther walk'd one day

Szomoru füzfänak (The weeping willow)

See the weep-ing wil-low's three and thir-ty bran-ches

Tölem a nap (Shades of eve)

Shades of eve are slow-ly fall-ing,___ No re-lief

Tücsök lakodslom (Wedding of the Cricket)

Gril-le ist ein ar-mer Wicht, Möch-te sich ver-mäh-len,

Vasárnap bort inni (Sit and drink all Sunday)
By permission Boosey & Hawkes, Inc., copyright owners

Sit and drink, all___ Sun-day, Id-le rest all___ Mon-day,

Verbunk (Recruiting)

All Hus-sars are splendid fellows Al-ways___ gay and___ chee-ry,

Virágos kenderem (All the hemp)

All the hemp lies wast-ed, far too long lay sleep-ing My be-loved

Zöld erdöben (In the forest)

Tief im Wal-de, auf der Hal-de, Tief im Wal-de auf der Hal-de

KOECHLIN, Charles (1867-1950)

La Nuit
Copyright by Bordoux, Paris

Nous bé-nis-sons la dou-ce Nuit, Dont le frais bai-ser

Si tu le veux
Copyright by Boston Music Co.

Si tu le veux, ô mon a-mour, ce soir des que la fin du jour

Le Thé
Copyright by Boston Music Co.

Miss El-len, ver-sez-moi le thé___ Dans la bel-le tas-se chi-noise

Villanelle, Op. 21, No. 1
Copyright by Philippo, Paris

Le temps, l'é-ten-due et le nom-bre Sont tom-bés du noir fir-ma-ment

KOENEMAN, Theo (-1938)

When the King went forth to war, Op. 7, No. 6
By permission J. & W. Chester, Ltd., London, copyright owners

When the King went forth to war To a coun-try strange and far

KORBAY, F. (1846-1913)

Hungarian Folksongs (arrangements):
Had a horse

Had___ a horse, a fi-ner no one ev-er saw

But the she-riff sold him in the name of law.

Hungarian Folksongs (arrangements):
Rosebud, to the fields art going

Rose-bud, to the fields art go - ing Ten-der are thy hands for mow - ing

Shepherd, see thy horse's foam-
ing mane

Shep-herd see thy hor-se's foam-ing mane Why dost ride so wild-ly

KORNGOLD, Erich Wolfgang (1897-1957)

Die tote Stadt (The Dead City), Op.
12 (opera)
Act I Marietta's Song

By permission Associated Music
Publishers, Inc.

Glück, das mir ver - blieb, rück zu mir, mein treu-es Lieb

Marietta's Lute Song

O Tanz, __ O Rausch! __ Lust __ quillt aus mir, braust __ in mir, jagt den Puls

Act II Pierrot Song

Mein Seh-nen, __ mein Wäh-nen, __ es träumt sich zu - rück

Act III Ich werde sie nicht
Wiedersehen

O Freund, ich wer-de sie nicht mehr wie-der-sehn __

Ich wer-de sie nicht mehr wie - - der-sehn __

Ich ging zu ihm, from Das Wunder
der Heliane (opera) Act II

By permission Associated Music
Publishers, Inc.

Ich ging zu ihm der mor - gen-ster ben - - - - soll __

Doch schön war __ der Kna - be, schön wie ein Stern im Ver - ge - hen

DE KOVEN, Reginald (1859-1920)

At Parting

Copyright by John Church Co.
Used by permission

To-night the dew will kiss the rose __ The song bird shel-ter on the tree __

Robin Hood (operetta) Oh, promise me

Oh, prom-ise me that some day you and I will take our love to-geth-er

Act II, No. 10 Brown October
Ale

And it's will ye quaff with me, my lads, And it's will ye quaff with me? __

So laugh, lads, and quaff, lads- 'Twill make you stout __ and hale __

Act III, No. 16 Armorer's Song

Let ham-mer on an-vil ring, __ And the forge-fire bright-ly shine __

Clang! clang! clang! Then huz - zah for the an-vil, the forge and the sledge,

KRAMER, A. Walter (1890-1969)

The Last Hour

Copyright by John Church Co.
Used by permission

Sup-pose, be - lo-ved, that the gods should say:

The Last Hour

And you should gaze deep down in my eyes

KREISLER, Fritz (1875-1962)

The Old Refrain
Copyright by Charles Foley, New York

I of- ten think of home, Dee- oo- lee- ay, When I am all a- lone

You are free, from Apple Blossoms (operetta)
Copyright 1919, Harms, Inc.

Free as the birds in the air____ Fly- ing with nev- er a care____

Love is just a game we two are play- ing

KREMSER, Eduard (1838-1914)

Berg op Zoom (arr.)

Sieh, wel- che Macht sie ge- bracht uns zur Schlacht! Wie grim- me Lev'n

Wir treten zum Beten

Wir tre- ten zum Be- ten vor Gott, den Ge- rech- ten,

KŘENEK, Ernst (1900-   )

Jonny spielt auf, Op. 45 (opera) Swanee River Song
By permission Associated Music Publishers, Inc.

Oh!____ Das wur- de mir nun doch zu dumm! Das ist kein Le- ben

Triumphlied

Jetzt ist die Gei- ge mein, und ich will drauf spie- len,

KREUTZER, Konradin (1780-1849)

Das Nachtlager in Granada (opera) Act I

Sei- ne from- me Lie- bes- ga- be ist auf e- wig nun da- hin

Ein Schütz_ bin ich in des Re- gen- ten Sold In Deutschlands Gau- en

No. 11

Schon die A- bend- glo- cken klan- gen, und die Flur

Act II

Für- wahr,_ für- wahr_ es ist_ ein A- ben- teu- - er, das mir je mehr_

Es zieht aus je- ner Welt von gold'nen_ hei- tern_ Ster- nen- zelt

Lei- se we- het, lei- se wal- let rings der Tau, rings der Tau,

No. 18

Tren- ne nicht das Band____ der Lie- be,

Schäfers Sonntagslied

Das ist der Tag des Herrn, das ist der Tag des Herrn

Hobellied, from Der Verschwender
(Fairy opera) Act III

Da strei-ten sich die Leut her-um oft um den Wert des Glücks

KŘIČKA, Jaroslav (1882-)

L'Albatros, Op. 14, No. 1

Tout là- haut dans le ciel— pro-fond au des-sus de la va- gue,

KRIEGER, Johann Philip (1649-1725)

Die Gerechten werden weggerafft

Die Ge-rech-ten wer-den. weg-ge-rafft vor dem Un-glück,

KÜCKEN, Friedrich (1810-1882)

How Can I Leave Thee (Ach! Wie ist
möglich dann)

How can I leave thee! How can I from thee part!

LA FORGE, Frank (1879-)

An einen Boten
Copyright 1909, G. Schirmer, Inc.

Wenn— du zu mei'm Schat- ze kommst,— sag':—

Come unto these yellow sands
Copyright 1907, G. Schirmer, Inc.

Come un-to these yel - - - - - - - - - - - low sands

Hills
Copyright by G. Ricordi & Co., Inc.

I want my hills! Hills! The trail— that scorns the hol-lows

Song of the Open
Copyright by Oliver Ditson Co. Used by
permission.

To your soul is it wine,— As it is— to mine—

Take, O take those lips away
Copyright 1909, G. Schirmer, Inc.

Take, o take those lips a - way that so sweet-ly were for-sworn

LALO, Edouard (1823-1892)

Ballade à la lune

C'é- tait dans la nuit bru-ne, sur le clocher jau-ni— la lu-ne—

Guitare

Com- ment, disaient ils,— a- vec nos na- celles—fuir les al-gua- zils?

Oh, quand je dors

Oh quand je dors, viens au-près de ma cou-che!

Le Roi d'Ys (opera)
Act I (Breton theme)

Les— guerres— sont ter - mi-né-es, Voi-ci pour—nous dé-sor-mais—

Le Roi d'Ys (opera)
Act I

En si- len- ce pour-quoi souf-frir?_ Dans mon coeur___ é-pan-che ta pei-ne!

Act II

Le sa- lut nous est pro- mis, c'est à nos seuls en- ne- mis

Ah! si j'a- vais souf- fert de la mê- me tor- tu- re,

Act III Aubade

Vai-ne- ment___ ma bien ai- mé- - e On croit me dé- ses- pé- rer

A l'au-tel j'al-lais rayon- nant___ mon amour é-tait "ma pri-è- re___

L'Esclave

Cap- ti- - ve___ et peut- ê-tre ou-bli- é- e je songe

LAMBERT, Constant (1905-1951)

The Rio Grande
By permission Oxford Univ. Press, London,
copyright owners

By the Ri- o Grande___ they dance a sa- ra- bande___

But they dance in the ci- ty down the pub- lic squares

The Com- men- da- dor and Al- qua- cil___ are there on horse-back

The noi- - sy streets are emp- ty and hushed is the town___

Such a space of si- lence through the town___ to the ri- ver

LAMBERT, Frank

She is far from the land

LANDINO, (Landini) Francesco (1325-1397)

Benche ora piova

Ben-che o- ra___ pio- va pur buon tem-po

Gram piant'agli occhi

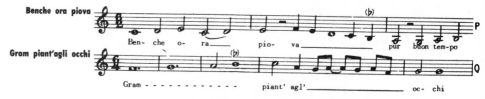

Gram - - - - - - - - - piant' agl' oc- chi

LANG, Margaret Ruthven (1867-   )

Irish Love Song, Op. 22
Copyright by Arthur P. Schmidt Co., Boston.
Used by permission

O, the time is long Ma- vour- neen, Till I come a- gain,

LANGE-MÜLLER, Peter Erasmus (1850-1926)

Efteraar (Autumn), Op. 61, No. 3
Copyright by Oliver Ditson Co. Used by permission.

Skin ud, du Klare Solskin (Bright Sunshine), Op. 18, No. 4
Copyright by Oliver Ditson Co. Used by permission.

Fa-ther, swans fly-ing — where do they go? Hence! Hence!

Shine bright and clear, O sun, shine, and lead us on to__ Spring

LASSEN, Eduard (1830-1904)

Allerseelen

Ich hatte einst ein schönes Vaterland

Mit deinen blauen Augen

Stell auf dem Tisch die duf-ten-den Re-se-den

Ich hat-te einst ein schönes Va-ter-land;— der Ei-chen-baum wuchs dort

Mit dei-nen blau-en Au-gen siehst du mich lieb-lich an___

LASSUS, Orlando de (1530-1594)

**Chansons Françaises
A ce matin**

A ce ma-tin ce se-rait bon-ne e-strei-ne

Amour, donne moy payx

A-mour, A-mour, don-ne moy payx

Bon jour, bon jour

Bon jour, Bon jour, Bon jour, Bon jour, Bon jour, Bon jour

Dessus le marché d'Arras

Des-sus le mar-ché d'Ar-ras, mi-re-li, mi-re la bon ba,

Guerir ma douleur

Gue-rir ma dou-leur mon mal et tour-ment,

Hélas, quel jour

Hé-las, quel jour se-ray-je à mon___ vou-loir

J'ay cherché la science

J'ay cher-ché la sçi-en-ce, j'ay cher-ché la sçi-en-ce

Margot, labourez les vignes

Mar-got, la-bou-rez les vi-gnes, Vi-gnes, vi-gnes, vi-gno-let,

La nuit froide

La nuit froi-de et som-bre___ Cou-rant d'ob-scu-re om-bre

O Mère des Amours

O Mè-re des a-mours,___ Ci-pri-ne, O gran-de dé-es-se

Tu sais, Tu sais, o gen-ti-le dé-es-se

LEGRENZI, Giovanni (1626-1690)

Che fiero costume

Che fie-ro co-stu-me d'a-li-ge-ro nu-me, che a for-za di pe-ne

LEHÁR, Franz (1870-1948)

Friederike (operetta)
Act I

Sah ein Knab' ein Rös-lein stehn, Rös-lein auf der Hei-den

Act II

O Mäd-chen, mein Mäd-chen wie lieb ich dich!

Wa-rum hast du mich wach ge-küsst? Hab nicht ge-wusst

Lie - be, se-li-ger Traum aus himm-li-schen Höh'n, du kannst nicht vergehn

Giuditta (operetta)

Du bist mei-ne Son-ne, du bist ein Traum voll süsser Won-ne!

Freun- de, das Le- ben ist le- bens- wert

Mei-ne Lip-pen, sie Küs-sen so heiss Mei-ne Glie-der sind schmiegsam

Hab' ein blaues Himmelbett, from Frasquita (operetta) Act II

Schatz, ich bitt' dich, komm heut Nacht Al-les ist be-reit ge-macht

Ein Glück dir winkt so wie noch nie, Kein Laut uns stört,

Im heimlichen Dämmer, from Eva (operetta) Act I
Copyright 1912, G. Schirmer, Inc.

Im heim-li-chen Däm-mer der sil-ber-nen Am-pel,

Wär' es auch nichts als ein Au-gen-blick, wär' es auch nichts

Das Land des Lächelns (The Land of Smiles)
Act I Immer nur lächeln

Ich tre-te ins Zim-mer, von Sehn-sucht durch-bebt.

Von Ap-fel-blü-ten ei-nen Kranz, ah

Du bist das traum-süs-se Le- ben, Du al-lein

Act II

Wer hat die Lie-be uns ins Herz ge-senkt, uns den sü-ssen Rausch

Dein ist mein gan-zes Herz! Wo du nicht bist, Kann ich nicht sein,

The Merry Widow
Act II Vilia Song
Es lebt ei- ne Vil- ja, ein Wald- mäg- de- lein,

Vil- ja, O Vil- ja, du Wald- mäg- de- lein, fass' mich und lass' mich

Act III
Lip- pen schwei- gen, 'sflü- tern Gei- gen: Hab mich lieb

Paganini (operetta) Act II
Gern hab' ich die Frau'n ge- küsst, hab' nie ge- fragt

Lie- - - be, du Him- mel auf Er- den, e- - - - wig be- steht

Waltz, from The Count of Luxemburg
(operetta)

Was ich längst erträumte, from Der Göttergatte
Was ich längst er- träum- te, was ich lang ver- säum- te

Wenn sich zwei lieben, from Der Rastelbinder Act I
Wenn sich zwei lie- ben, so steht's ge- schrie- ben, sind sie ein Herz,

Der Zarewitsch (operetta) Act I
Ei- ner wind Kom- men der wird mich be- geh- ren

Mir ist so bang, als hielt mich ein Traum be- fan- gen

Volgalied
Hast Du dort o- ben ver- ges- sen auf mich? Es sehnt doch mein Herz

Act II
Hab' nur dich al- lein, die gan- ze Welt sollst du mir sein,

Act III Napolitana
Wa- rum hat je- der Früh- ling ach nur ei- nen Mai

Zorika, kehre zurück, from Zigeuner-liebe Act II
Zo- ri- ka, Zo- ri- ka, keh- re zu- rück, lass uns zur Hei- mat

LEHMANN, Liza (1862-1918)

The Cuckoo
By permission Boosey & Hawkes, Inc., copyright owners
The Cuc- koo sat in the old pear tree. "Cuc- koo"

Go, lovely Rose

In a Persian Garden (song cycle)
Ah, moon of my delight
Copyright by Boston Music Co.
Ah, moon of my de- light that knows no wane

Alas! that Spring should vanish with the rose
Copyright by G. Schirmer, Inc.
A- las! That Spring should va- nish with the Rose

205 LEHMANN—LEONCAVALLO

In a Persian Garden (song cycle)
Myself when young
Copyright by Boston Music Co.

My- self when young did ea- ger- ly fre- quent Doc- tor and Saint

Magdalen at Michael's gate

There are Fairies at the Bottom of our Garden

LEJEUNE, Claude (1530-1600)

O occhi manza mia

O oc- chi man- za mi- a, o oc- chi man- za mia

Revecy venir du Printans

Re- ve- cy ve- nir du Prin- tans L'a- mou- reuz' et bel- le sai- son

LEMAIRE, Gaston (1854-1928)

Vous dansez, marquise (Gavotte des Mathurins)

Vous dan- sez, mar- qui- se, D'un pas si lé- ger

LEONCAVALLO, Ruggiero (1858-1919)

La Bohême (opera)
Act II
Copyright by Sonzogno, Milan

Io non ho che u- na po- ve- ra stan- zet- ta

Da quel suon so- a- ve- men- te Già le cop-pie i-ne-bri-a- te

Act III

Tes- ta a- do- ra- ta, più non tor- ne- ra- i,

Pagliacci (opera) Prologue
Copyright 1906, G. Schirmer, Inc.

Si può? Si può? Si- gno- re! Si- gno- ri! Scu- sa- te- mi

Poi- chè in iscena ancor le an- tiche ma-schere met- te l'au-to- re;

Un ni- do di me- mo- rie in fon-do a l'a-ni- ma can-ta-va un gior- no,

E vo- i, piut- to- sto che le no-stre po- ve- re ga- ba- ne

Act I

Un gran- de spet- ta- co- lo a ven- ti- tre o- re

Un tal gio- co, cre- de- te- mi è meglio non gio- car-lo con me,

Bell Chorus

Din, don, suo- na ve- spe- ro, ra- ga- ze e gar- zon,

Ballatella

Stri- do- no las- sù, li- be- ra- men- te lan- cia-ti a vol,

Pagliacci (opera)

Act I Ballatella

Van- no lag- giù_____ ver-so un pa-e- se stra- no

Duet: Tonio and Nedda

So ben che dif-for- me, con- tor-to son i- o;

Duet: Silvio and Nedda

Hai tem-po a ri- dir- me- lo stas-se-ra, se bra-mi

De- ci- di il mio de- stin, Ned- da! Ned-da, ri- ma- ni

Non mi_____ ten- tar! Vuoi tu per- der la vi- ta mia?

E al-lor per-che, di',_____ tu m'hai stre-ga- to se vuoi la- sciar- mi

Tut- to - - - scor- diam!_____ Tut- to scor- diam _____

Vesti la giubba

Ve- sti la giub- ba e la fac- cia in fa- ri- na

Act II Serenade

O_____ Co-lom-bi-na il te-ne- ro fi-do Al-lec-chin è a te vi- cin!_____

Guar- do, amor mio, che splen-di- da ce- net- ta pre- pa- ra- i!

No! Pa-gliac- ci non son; se il vi- so è pal- li- do,

Spe- rai tan-to il de- li-rio ac- ce- ca- to m'a- ve- va,

Zaza (opera)

Act II
Copyright by Sonzogno, Milan

Buo- na Za- za del mio buon tem- po, a- scol- ta:

Act III

O mio pic- co- lo ta- vo- lo in-gom- bra- to

Act IV

Za- za, pic- co- la zin- ga- ra, schia- va d'un fol- le a- mo- re

Mattinata
Copyright by G. Ricordi & Co., Inc.

A beau-ti-ful morn- ing is break-ing With won-der and light, now the sun_____

LEROUX, Xavier (1863-1919)

Le Nil
Copyright 1905, G. Schirmer, Inc.

Les eaux du Nil_____ tou-tes pâ- les, s'é- cou- lent _____

Le bien ai- mé_____ s'ac- cou- dant sur la prou- e

LEVERIDGE, Richard (c. 1670-1758)

The Beggar's Song — B

How jol-ly are we beg-gars Who nev-er toil for treas-ure

Black-ey'd Susan — C

All in the Downs the fleet was moor'd, The streamers wav-ing in the wind

When Dull Care — D

This great world is a trou-ble Where all must their for-tunes bear;

LIE, Sigund (1871-1904)

Sne (Snow) — F
Copyright by Oliver Ditson Co. Used by permission.

There is nought on earth so still as the snow

LIEURANCE, Thurlow (1878-)

By the Waters of Minnetonka (Indian Love Song) — H
Copyright by Theodore Presser Co. Used by permission.

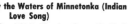

Moon Deer How near your soul di - - - vine

LILLIJEBJORN, H. (1797-1875)

When I Was Seventeen (När jag blef sjutton år) (arr.) — J

Four-teen years I had seem'd just to be Lit-tle maid-en so hap-py

LINLEY, William (1771-1835)

Lawn as white as driven snow, from "A Winter's Tale" — L

Lawn as white as dri- ven snow; Cy- press, black as a- ny crow;

LISZT, Franz (1811-1886)

Christus vincit, from Christus (oratorio) — N

Chris-tus vin-cit, Chris-tus reg-nat, Chris-tus im-pe-rat

Comment, disaient-ils — O

Com- ment, di-saient- ils, A- vec nos na-cel-les Fuir les al-gua-zils?

Die drei Zigeuner — A P

Drei Zi- geu- ner fand ich ein- mal lie - - - gen an ei-ner Wei - - de

B — Q

Hielt der Ei- ne für sich al-lein in den Hän- den die Fie- del,

Du bist wie eine Blume — R

Du bist wie ei-ne Blu- - me, so hold so schön und rein

Es muss ein Wunderbares sein — S

Es muss ein Wun-der-ba-res sein Um's Lie- ben zwei-er See- len

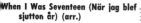
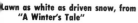

Freudvoll und Leidvoll

Freud- voll und leid- voll ge- dan- ken- voll_ sein,

Ich liebe dich

Ich lie-- be dich weil ich dich lie- ben muss;__

Im Rhein, im schönen Strome

Im Rhein, im schö- nen Stro- me, Da spie-gelt sich in den Wel- len

Die Lorelei

A

Ich weiss nicht, was soll's be- deu- ten, dass ich so trau- rig,

B

Die Luft ist kühl, und es__ dun - - kelt,

Mignons Lied (Kennst du das Land)

Kennst du das Land, wo die Zi- tro- nen blühn,

Missa Choralis
I Kyrie

Ky - - ri- e e- le - - - - - - - i- son e- le - - - - - - i- son

II Gloria

Glo - - - - - ri- a in ex-cel-sis De- o Et in ter- ra pax

III Credo

Cre- do in u-num De - - - um Pa-trem om-ni-po- ten - - tem

IV Sanctus

San- ctus, San- ctus, San-ctus Do- mi- nus De - - us Sa - ba- oth

V Benedictus

Be - - ne- di- ctus, be - - ne- di - - - - - ctus

VI Agnus Die

A- gnus De - - i qui_ tol - - lis pec- ca- ta mun- di

Nimm einen Strahl der Sonne

Nimm ei- nen Strahl der Son- ne, vom A- bend-stern das Licht,

Oh! quand je dors

Oh! quand je dors, viens au- près de ma cou- che

O Lieb (original version of Liebestraum, No. 3)

O lieb', o lieb,__ so lang du lie- ben kannst.

Wieder möcht' ich dir begegnen

Wie- der möcht' ich dir be- geg-nen, Wie- der schau-en dei- nen Blick;

LOEWE, Karl (1796-1869)

Edward, Op. 1, No. 1

A

Dein Schwert, wie ist's von Blut so rot? Ed- ward, Ed- ward!

B

Ich hab' ge-schla-gen mei-nen Gei- er tot Mut- ter, Mut- ter!

LOEWE

Archibald Douglas, Op. 128

Denk' nicht an den al-ten Dou - - glasneid, der trotzig dich be-kriegt,

Der Nöck, Op. 129, No. 2

Es tönt des Nö - cken Har- fen- schall

Tom der Reimer, Op. 135

Der Rei- mer Tho- mas lag am Bach, am Kie- sel- bach

Da sah er ei- ne blon- de Frau, die sass auf ei- nem wei- ssen Ross

Canzonetta

War schö - - - - ner als der schön - - - - ste Tag,

Das Erkennen

Ein Wan- der-bursch, mit dem Stab in der Hand, Kommt wie- der heim

Die nächtliche Heerschau

Nachts um die zwölf- te Stun- de ver- lässt der Tam-bour sein Grab

Der Zahn

Vic- to- ri- a! Vic- to- ri- a! Der klei- ne weis- se Zahn ist da,

LOGAN, Frederic Knight

Pale Moon
Copyright by Foster Music Co., Chicago

Out of my lodge at e-ven- tide 'Mong the sob- bing pine

LORTZING, Gustav Albert (1801-1851)

Undine (opera)

Act II

Es wohnt am See- ge- sta- de ein ar- mes Fis- cher- paar,

Act III

Va- ter, Mut- ter, Schwes-tern, Brü- der, hab' ich auf der Welt nicht mehr

O kehr' zu- rück, mein ei- tel Seh- nen ist nun ge- stillt,

Act IV

Ich war in mei- nen jun- gen Jah- ren ein feu- ri- ges, ver- lieb- tes Blut,

Im Wein ist Wahr-heit nur al- lein, Im Wein ist Wahr-heit nur al- lein

Auch ich war ein Jüngling, from Der Waffenschmied (opera)
Act III

Auch ich war ein Jüng- ling mit lo- cki- gem Haar,

Der Wildschütz (opera)
Act I Duet and Chorus

A B C D, der Jung-ge-sel-len-stand tut weh, E F G H,

Act II

Fünf- tau-send Tha- ler! Fünf- tau-send Tha- ler Träum o-der wach ich?

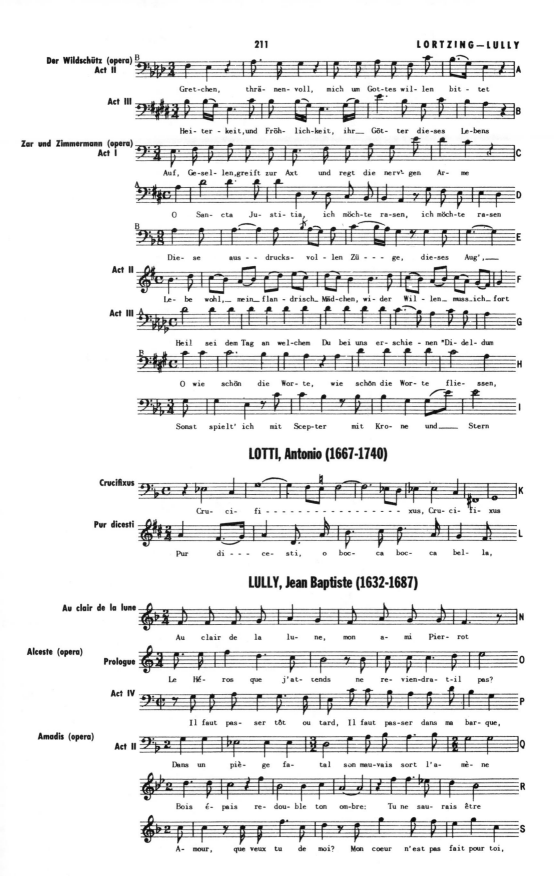

Der Wildschütz (opera) — Act II
Gret-chen, thrä-nen-voll, mich um Got-tes wil-len bit-tet

Act III
Hei-ter-keit, und Fröh-lich-keit, ihr__ Göt-ter die-ses Le-bens

Zar und Zimmermann (opera) — Act I
Auf, Ge-sel-len, greift zur Axt und regt die nerv'-gen Ar-me

O Sanc-ta Ju-sti-tia, ich möch-te ra-sen, ich möch-te ra-sen

Die-se aus--drucks-vol-len Zü--ge, die-ses Aug',__

Act II
Le-be wohl,__ mein__ flan-drisch Mäd-chen, wi-der Wil-len muss-ich_ fort

Act III
Heil sei dem Tag an wel-chem Du bei uns er-schie-nen "Di-del-dum

O wie schön die Wor-te, wie schön die Wor-te flie-ssen,

Sonst spielt' ich mit Scep-ter mit Kro-ne und__ Stern

LOTTI, Antonio (1667-1740)

Crucifixus
Cru-ci-fi - - - - - - - - - - - - - xus, Cru-ci-fi-xus

Pur dicesti
Pur di - - ce-sti, o boc-ca boc-ca bel-la,

LULLY, Jean Baptiste (1632-1687)

Au clair de la lune
Au clair de la lu-ne, mon a-mi Pier-rot

Alceste (opera) — Prologue
Le Hé-ros que j'at-tends ne re-vien-dra-t-il pas?

Act IV
Il faut pas-ser tôt ou tard, Il faut pas-ser dans ma bar-que,

Amadis (opera) — Act II
Dans un piè-ge fa-tal son mau-vais sort l'a-mè-ne

Bois é-pais re-dou-ble ton om-bre: Tu ne sau-rais être

A-mour, que veux tu de moi? Mon coeur n'est pas fait pour toi,

Amadis (opera)
Act V
Fer- mez- vous pour ja- mais, mes yeux, mes tris- tes yeux

Armide (opera)
Act I
Al- lez, al- lez rem- plir ma pla- ce aux lieux d'où mon mal- heur

Act II
Plus j'ob- ser- ve ces lieux, et plus je les ad- mi- re

Act III
Ah! si la li- ber- té me doit ê- tre ra- vi- e

Act IV
Que vois-je? O spec-tacle effro- ya- ble O trop fu-nes- te sort

Cadmus et Hermione
Act II
A- mour, vois quels maux tu nous fais, où sont les biens que tu pro- mets?

Act V
Belle Her- mi- o- ne, He- las! He-las! puis-je être heu- reux sans vous?

Dormons tous, from Atys (opera)
Act III
Dor- mons dor- mons tous, ah! ah! Que le re-pos est

Persée (opera)
Act III
A
J'ai per- du la beau- té qui me ren-dit si vai- ne

B
Je por - - te l'e- pou- vante et la mort en tous lieux.

Act V
Ô mort! Ve- nez fi- nir mon des-tin dé- plo- ra- ble

Thésée (opera)
Prologue
Re- ve- nez, re- ve- nez A- mours re- ve- nez Re- ve- nez, A- mours

Que rien ne trouble i- ci Vé- nus et les a- mours

Act V
Ah! Ah! faut- il me ven- ger, En per- dant ce que j'ai - - me!

LUTHER, Martin (1483-1546)

A mighty fortress is our God (Eine feste Burg)
A might- y fort-ress is our God, A bul-wark nev-er- fail - ing

Vom Himmel hoch
Vom Him- mel hoch da Komm' ich her, ich bring' euch

MAC DOWELL, Edward (1861-1908)

Deserted, Op. 9, No. 1
Ye banks and braes o' bon- nie Doon, how can ye bloom sae fair!

The Blue Bell, Op. 26, No. 5

In love__ she fell, My shy__ Blue-bell, With a stroll-ing Bum-ble-Bee   A

Cradle Hymn, Op. 33, No. 2
Copyright by Arthur P. Schmidt Co., Boston.
Used by permission

Dor- mi Je - - - - - su! dor-mi Je - - su, Ma-ter ri-det   B

Menie, Op. 34, No. 1
Copyright by Arthur P. Schmidt Co., Boston.
Used by permission

In vain to__ me the cow-slips blaw, In vain to me__ the vi-o-lets spring   C

Thy beaming eyes, Op. 40, No. 3
Copyright by Arthur P. Schmidt Co., Boston.
Used by permission

Thy beam-ing eyes, Are Par- a-dise, to me, my love, to me,   D

The Sea, Op. 47, No. 7

One sails__ a-way to sea, to sea, One stands on the shore_and cries__   E

Long Ago, Op. 56, No. 1
Copyright by Arthur P. Schmidt Co., Boston.
Used by permission

Long a-go_____ sweet-heart_mine, Ros-es bloomed as ne'er be- fore,   F

The Swan bent low, No. 2

The Swan bent low to the Lil- y, Mid wav'-ring shad-ows green__   G

A maid sings light, No. 3

A maid sings light, And a maid sings low, With a mer-ry, mer-ry laugh   H

As the gloaming shadows creep, No. 4

As the gloam - - ing shad-ows creep Through__ the for-est deep   I

Fair Springtide, Op. 60, No. 2
Copyright by Arthur P. Schmidt Co., Boston.
Used by permission

Fair Spring-tide com- eth once a- gain_____ Stirs_the sap in_lone-ly trees__   J

MAC GIMSEY, Robert (1898-)

Shadrack
Copyright 1937, Carl Fischer, Inc.
Used by special permission.

Thah was three chill- un frum nuh lan' uv Is- ri-el Shad - - rack   L

MACHAUT, Guillaume De (c. 1300-1377)

De tout sui si confortée (Virelai)

De tout sui si con- for- té- e Que je-mais n'iert hoste- lé- e   N

Je puis trop bien (ballade)

Je - - - - - - - - - - puis_trop__ bien ma - - - - - - - - - da-me com- pa-rer   O

Mass

1. Kyrie

Ky- ri - - - - - e   e - - - - - - - -   P

2. Qui propter nos

Qui pro- pter_____ nos_____ ho- mi- nes,_____   Q

3. Agnus Dei

A - - - - - - - - - - - gnus De - - - - - - - - - - - i   R

A - - - - - - - - - - - - - - - - - - - gnus De - - - - - - - i   S

Quant Theseus (ballade)

Quant The- - - - - se- - - - us, Her- cu- - les et- Ja-zon

Ne quier ve- - - - oir la- - - beau-té d'Ab-sa- lon

Rose lys (rondeau)

Ro- se lys- printemps ver-du-re

MAHLER, Gustav (1860-1911)

Blicke mir nicht in die Lieder

Blik- ke mir- nicht in die Lie- der! Mei- ne- Au- - gen-

Ich atmet' einen linden Duft

Ich at- met' ei- nen lin- den Duft Im Zim- mer stand-

Ich bin der Welt abhanden gekommen

Ich bin der Welt- ab- - han- - den ge- kom- men

Kindertotenlieder (song cycle) No. 1
By permission Associated Music
Publishers, Inc.

Nun will die Sonn' so hell auf- geh'n als sei- kein Un- glück,

No. 2

Nun seh' ich wohl war- um so dunk- le Flam- men

No. 3

Wenn dein Müt- ter- lein tritt zur Tür her- ein und den Kopf ich dre- he,

No. 4

Oft denk ich sie sind nur aus ge- gan- gen!

No. 5

In die- sem Wet- ter, in die- sem Braus, nie hätt' ich ge- sen- det

In die- sem Wet- ter, in die- sem Saus in die- - sem Braus,

Des Knaben Wunderhorn (song cycle)
Des Antonius von Padua Fisch-
predigt
By permission Boosey & Hawkes, Inc.,
copyright owners

An- to- nius zur Pre- digt die Kir- che findt- le- dig!

Das irdische Leben

Mut- ter, ach Mut- ter, es hun- gert- mich! Gib mir Brot,

Lob des hohen Verstandes

Einst- mal in ei- nem tie- fen Thal Ku- kuk und Nach- ti- gall

Rheinlegendchen

Bald- gras' ich am Nek- kar,- bald gras ich am Rhein

Wer hat dies Liedlein erdacht?

Dort- o- ben am Berg in dem hoh- - - en- Haus, in dem Haus,

Wo die schönen Trompeten
blasen

Wer ist denn draussen und wer klop- fet an der mich- so- lei- - se,

MAHLER

Des Knaben Wunderhorn (song cycle)
Wo die schönen Trompeten blasen

Das ist der Herz-al-ler-lieb-ste dein, steh auf_ und lass_mich zu dir ein

Sieben Lieder aus letzter Zeit
Der Tamboursg'sell

Ich_ ar- mer Tam- bours- g'sell   Man_ führt mich aus dem G'wölb_

Revelge

Des_ Mor- gens zwi- schen drei'n und_____ vie- ren,

Ach Bru- der, ach Bru- der, ich kann dir nicht tra- gen

Liebst du um Schönheit

Liebst du um Schön-heit, O nicht mich lie- be! Lie- be die Son- ne

Das Lied von der Erde (song cycle)
By permission Boosey & Hawkes, Inc., copyright owners
No. 1 Das Trinklied vom Jammer der Erde

Schon winkt der Wein_____ im gold' - -nen Po- ka- le,

Dun- kel ist das Le- ben, ist der Tod

No. 2 Der Einsame im Herbst

Herbst- ne- bel wal- len bläu- lich ü- berm See

No. 3 Von der Jugend

Mit- ten_ in_ dem klei-nen Tei-che steht ein Pa-vil- lon aus grü- nem

In dem Häus-chen sit-zen Freun- de, schön ge-klei-det, trin-ken, plau-dern

No. 4 Von der Schönheit

Jun- ge Mäd- chen pflük-ken Blu-men, pflük-ken Lo-tos-blu- men_an dem_U-fer

No. 5 Der Trunkene im Frühling

Wenn nur ein Traum das_Le- ben ist   war- um denn Müh' und Plag'

der Lenz ist da, sei kom- men ü- ber Nacht!

No. 6 Der Abschied

Die Son- ne schei-det hin- ter dem Ge-bir- ge. In al- le Tä-ler

Lieder eines fahrenden Gesellen (song cycle)
No. 1

Wenn_ mein_ Schatz Hoch- zeit macht   froh- li-che Hoch-zeit macht

No. 2

Ging heut' mor-gens ü- ber's Feld, Tau noch_ auf den Grä-sern hing;

No. 3

Ich hab ein glü-hend Mes- ser, ein Mes-ser in mei-ner Brust, O weh

No. 4

Die zwei blau- en Au- gen von mei-nem Schatz, die ha- ben mich

Symphony No. 2: 4th movement "Urlicht"
By permission Boosey & Hawkes, Inc., copyright owners

Der Mensch liegt in gröss- ter Noth! Der Mensch liegt in grösster Pein

Symphony No. 2, 5th movement
(Chorus)

Auf- er- steh'n, ja auf- er- steh'n, wirst du, mein Staub, nach kur- zer Ruh!

Symphony No. 4, 4th movement
By permission Boosey & Hawkes, Inc.,
copyright owners

Wir ge- nie- ssen die himm - - - - - - - li- schen Freu- den

Jo- han- nes das Lämm- lein aus- las- set, der Metz- ger He- ro- des drauf pas- set

Um Mitternacht
By permission Boosey & Hawkes, Inc.,
copyright owners

.Um Mit - - ter- nacht hab' ich ge- wacht und auf- ge- blickt zum Him- mel

MAILLART, Louis (1817-1871)

Les Dragons de Villars (opéra-
comqive)
Act I No. 3

Ne par- le pas. Ro- se, je t'en sup- li- e, car me tra- hir

Act I No. 5

Grâce à ce vi- lain er- mi- te, a sa clo- che mau- di- te,

Act III No. 13 bis
Soldatenart (this aria by Franz
Abt)

Wenn mann beim Wein sitzt, wenn man beim Wein sitzt, was ist da das Bes- te

MALOTTE, Albert Hay (1895-   )

The Lord's Prayer
Copyright 1935, G. Schirmer, Inc.

Our Father,___ Which art in heaven,___ Hal- low- ed be___ thy Name.___

Song of the Open Road
Copyright by A B C Music Corp., N. Y.

What in the world could be so sweet, As the thun- der- ing clat- ter

MANA-ZUCCA (1890-   )

I love life, Op. 83
Copyright by John Chuch Co.
Used by permission

I love life___ and I___ want to live___ and drink of life's full- ness

Rachem, Op. 60, No. 1
Copyright by John Chuch Co.
Used by permission.

O- vi- nu mal- ke- nu O- vi- nu O- vi- nu A- do- nai- nu

Wie lang wet men ins___ stick- en, Wie lang wet men ins er- drick- en

MANNING, Katherine Lockhart

In the Luxembourg Gardens
Copyright 1925, G. Schirmer, Inc.

When sha- dows fall I wan- der thro' the gar- dens,

MANZOLO, Domenico (17th Cent.)

Quando tu mi guardi e ridi

Quando tu mi guar- di e ri- di, o mio be- ne, o mio co- re,

Se vedeste le piaghe

Se ve- de- ste le pia- ghe ch'io por- to nel cor,

MARCELLO, Benedetto (1686-1739)

Quella fiamma che m'accende
Recitative

Il mio bel fo- co o lon- ta- no o vi- ci- no ch'es-ser pos- si- o

Aria

Quel- la____ fiam- ma____ che m'ac - - - cen - - de

MARENZIO, Luca (1550-1599)

Già torna

Già tor- na a ral- le- grar____ l'a- ria e la ter- ra

O Rex Gloriae (O King of Glory)

O King of Glo- ry Lord__ of all__ pow- er, Lord of all__ pow'r,

Perche di pioggia

Per- che di piog - - - - gia'l ciel non si de-stil - - - - - - le,

Strider faceva

Stri- der fa- ce- va le zam- po- gne a l'au - - - - - - - - - ra,

MARSCHNER, Heinrich (1795-1861)

An jenem Tag, from Hans Heiling
(opera) Act I

An je- nem Tag da du mir Treu - - - - e ver- spro- chen

O lass die Treu- e nie-mals wan-ken, o lass die Treu- e

MARSHALL, Charles (1887-1927)

I Hear You Calling Me
By permission Boosey & Hawkes, Inc.,
copyright owners

I hear you call-ing me. You call'd me when the moon had veil'd her light,

MARTIN, Easthope (1887-1925)

Come to the Fair
By permission Boosey & Hawkes, Inc.,
copyright owners

The sun is a shin-ing to wel-come the day__ Heigh- ho! come to the fair!__

MARTINI, Giovanni (1741-1816)

Plaisir d'Amour

Plai- sir d'a- mour____ ne du- re qu'un__ mo-ment;__ cha-grin d'a-mour

MARX, Joseph (1882-1964)

Ein junger Dichter denkt an die Geliebte
By permission Associated Music Publishers, Inc.

Der Mond steigt auf- wärts, ein ver-lieb-ter Träu- mer,

Hat dich die Liebe berührt
By permission Associated Music Publishers, Inc.

Hat Dich die Lie- - be be-rührt, still un-ter lär-men-dem Vol-ke

Marienlied
By permission Associated Music Publishers, Inc.

Ich se-he dich in tau-send Bil-dern Ma-ri-a lieb-lich aus-gedrückt,

Nocturne
By permission Associated Music Publishers, Inc.

Süss duf-ten-de Lin-den-blü-te in quel-len-der Ju-ni-nacht,

Regenlied
By permission Associated Music Publishers, Inc.

Wo ich fer-ne des Mi-ka-ne ho-hen Gip-fel ra-gen seh,

Selige Nacht
By permission Associated Music Publishers, Inc.

Im Arm der Lie- be schie-fen wir se- -lig ein

Una gestern hat er mir Rosen gebracht
By permission Associated Music Publishers, Inc.

Und ge-stern hat er mir Ro-sen ge-bracht, Sie ha-ben ge-duf-tet

Valse de Chopin
By permission Associated Music Publishers, Inc.

Wie ein blas-ser Trop-fen Blut's färbt die Lip-pen ei-ner Kran-ken

Venetianisches Wiegenlied
By permission Associated Music Publishers, Inc.

Ni- na ni-na- na, will ich Dir sin- gen Um Mit-ter-nacht

Waldseligkeit
By permission Associated Music Publishers, Inc.

Der Wald be-ginnt zu rau-schen, den Bäu-men naht die Nacht

MASCAGNI, Pietro (1863-1945)

L'Amico Fritz (opera)
Act I
Copyright by Sonzogno, Milan

Son po-chi fio-ri, po-ve-re vi-o-le, Son l'a-li-to d'A-pri-le,

Noi sia--mo fi-glie ti-mi-de e pu-di-che di pri-ma-ve-ra

La-ce-re, mi-se-ri, tan-ti bam-bi-ni lan-guia-no qua

Per voi, ghiot-to-ni j-nu-ti-li, la vi-ta è nel go- der

Act II Duetto delle ciliege

Suzel, buon dì. D'un gai-o ro-si-gnuo-lo la vo-ce mi sve-glio

Han del-la por-po-ra vi-vo il co-lo-re, Son dol-ci e te-ne-re,

Tut-to ta-ce, e-pur tut-to al cor mi par-la; que-sta pa-ce,

MASCAGNI

Amico Fritz (opera)
Act II Duetto delle ciliege

Tut-to il pra--to d'un tap-pe-to s'è smal-ta-to,

Act III

O pal-li-da, che un gior-no mi guar-da-sti, in so-gno tor-na-mi!

O a-mo-re, o bel-la lu-ce del co-re, fiam-mel-la e-ter-na,

Non mi re-sta che il pian-to ed il do-lo-re, _____

Cavalleria Rusticana (opera)
Siciliana: O Lola

O Lo-la, bian-ca co-me fior di spi-no, _____

Opening Chorus

Gli a-ran-ci o-le-za-no sui ver-di mar-gi-ni,

Tem-po è si mor--mo-ri da o-gnu-no il te-ne-ro can--to

In mez-zo al cam-po tra le spi-che d'o-ro giun-ge il ru-mo-re

Il ca-val-lo scal-pi-ta i so-na-gli squil-la-no,

O che bel me-stie-re fa-re il car-ret-tie-re

Re-gi-na Coe----li, lae-ta--re (Al-le-lu-ja!)

In-neg-gia-mo, il Si-gnor non è mor-to! Ei ful-gen-te ha di-schiu-so

In-neg-gia----mo il Si-gnor non è mor----to

Voi lo sa-pe-te, o mam-ma, pri-ma d'an-dar sol-da---to

Turriddu-Santuzza Duet

E sta-mat-ti-na al-l'al-ba t'han-no scor-to pres-so

Ba-da, San-tuz-za, schiavo non so-no di que-sta va-na

Lola's Ditty

Fior di giag--gio--lo _____ gli an-ge-li bel-li stan-no a mille

Turiddu-Santuzza Duet (2nd part)

No, no, Tu-rid---du, ri-ma-ni, ri-ma-ni an-co-ra

La tu-a San-tuz-za pian-ge e t'im-plo-----ra _____

MASCAGNI

220

Cavalleria Rusticana (opera)
Duet: Santuzza-Alfio

A — Tu - - rid-du, mi tol - - se, mi tol-se l'o - no - - - - - - - - - - ré,

Intermezzi

B — A- ve Ma-ri - - - - a____ Gra-tia ple - na

Chorus

C — A ca-sa, a ca-sa, a- mi - ci, o-ve ci a-spet-ta-no

Brindisi A

D — Vi-va il vi no spu- meg- gian-te, nel bic-chie-re scin-til- lan- te

B

E — Vi-va il vi - no ch'è sin- ce- ro che ci al- lieta o-gni

Addio al mamma
(Turiddu's Farewell)

F — Voi__ do-vre- te fa- re da ma - - - - dre a San-ta,

Il Piccolo Marat (opera) Act II Duet
Copyright by Sonzogno, Milan

G — Va nel- la tua stan-zet- ta, Pre - - - ga ed a- spet- ta_

E sempre il vecchio andazzo, from
Guglielmo Ratcliff, (opera)
Act I
Copyright by Sonzogno, Milan

H — E sem-pre il vec-chio an -daz-zo. Vi- si cor-re a ca- val- lo

Iris (opera)
Act I Inno al sole
Copyright by G. Ricordi & Co., Inc.

I — Son I- o! Son Io la Vi- ta! Son la Bel-tà in-fi- ni- ta

J — A-pri la tua fi- ne-stra! For son i- o - - - che ven-go al tuo chia-mar,

K — In pu- re stil- le, ga- ie scin- til- le scen-de la vi- ta!

Act II

L — Io pin-go, pin- go, ma il mio pen-nel-lo in-vano stendo in-tin-go

M — Un dì (e - ro pic-ci- na) al tem-pio vi- di un bon- zo

N — Or dam-mi' il brac- cio tu- o, brac-cio di ne- ve e a- vo- rio

Isabeau (opera)
Act I
Copyright by Sonzogno, Milan

O — Tu ch'o-di lo mio gri-do scru-ta le vi- e del cie- lo

P — Non co- lom-bel- le! Il do-no mi- o chiama- re vo-glio dal cie- lo

Act II A

Q — Or so-lo in-tor- no i- na- ni- ma- te co- se

B

R — E pas-se- rà la vi- va cre- a-tu- ra entro il si- lenzio

Act III

S — Fu vi-le l'E- dit- to che vi- li fè gli uo- mi- ni

Isabeau (opera) Act III — I tuo- i oc-chi!__ Gli a-per-ti occ-hi sol-tan-to col- pe- vo- li! A

Lodoletta (opera) Act III — Copyright by Sonzogno, Milan — Ah! ri- tro- var-la nel-la sua ca- pan- na tut- ta pian- gen- te B

Flam- men, per- do- na- mi__ non pian-ger più! Son i- o! C

Il Canto del Lavoro — Quan- do la Pa- trie si chia-ma- va Ro- ma, I- ta- li- a- no, D

Serenata — Co- me col ca- po sot- to la- la bian- ca _____ E

MASSÉ, Victor (1822-1884)

Les Noces de Jeannette (opera) No. 1 Air de Jean — Qu'un au- tre se ma- ri- e, moi, je re-prends ma foi, G

No. 2 Romance — Par- mi tant d'a- mou- reux__ em- pressés à me plai- re, H

No. 3 — Ah! jar- ni- gué! Ca' n'est pas gai, le bon-homme est par- fois bru- tal. I

No. 5 — Cours, mon ai- guille, dans la lai- ne, ne te casse pas dans ma main! J

Les voi- là, ces meubles joy- eux, les voi-là, ces meubles joy-eux K

No. 6 Air du Rossignol A — Au bord du che- min qui passe à ma por - - - - - - - te L

B — Voix lé- gè- re chan-son pas- sa- ge- re, ba- bil gra- ci- eux M

Song of the Tiger, from Paul et Virginie (opera) Act I — Mid the thick li- a - - - - - - - - - - na _____ N

MASSENET, Jules (1842-1912)

Le Cid (opera) Act I — O no-ble la - - me é- tin- ce- lan- te Pu-re comme un__ re-gard P

Act II — Plus de tour- ments__ et plus__ de pei- ne au jour__ at- ten- du Q

Act III — Pleu- rez! pleu- rez mes yeux__ tom- bez tris- te ro- sé- e R

O sou- ve- rain,__ ô ju- ge, ô pe- re, Tou-jours voi- lé__ S

MASSENET

222

Don Quichotte (opera)
Act I

Quand la femme a vingt ans,___ La ma- jes- té su- prê - - - - me

Quand ap- pa- rais- sent les___ é- toi- les Et quand la nuit___

Act V Morte de Don Quichotte

O mon maitre, ô mon Grand! dans des splen- deurs de son- ge

Prends cette i- le qu'il est tou- jours en mon pou- voir De te don- ner___

Grisélidis (opera)
Prologue
By permission Heugel & Cie, Paris, copyright owners

Ou- vrez- vous sur mon front, por- tes du pa- ra- dis!___

Act I

Oi- seau___ qui pars___ à- ti- re- d'ai- le Qui là- bas me par- le- ra

Act II

Il par- tit___ au prin- temps___ Voi- ci ve- nir___ l'au- tom- ne

Je suis l'oi- seau que le fris- son D'hi- ver chas- se de la ra- mé- e

Hérodiade (opera)
Act I

Il est doux,___ il est bon,___ sa pa- role___ est se- rei- - ne:

Sa- lo- mé!___ Sa- lo- mé! ah! reviens! je te veux! c'est ma voix qui t'implore

Ne me re- fu- se pas! Toi, mon seul bien!___ Pour qui j'ai tout quitté

Duet: Salomé and Jean

Ce que je veux te di - - - re que je t'ai- me,

Act II

Vi - - si- on fu - - - gi- tive et tou- jours pour- sui- vi- e,

Act III

As- tres é- tin- ce- lants que l'in- fi- ni pro- mè- ne

De- mande au pri- son- nier qui re- voit la lu- miè- re,

Act IV

A- dieu donc,___ Vains ob- jets qui nous charment sur ter- re!

Quand nos jours s'é- tein- dront com- me une chas- te flam- me

Le Jongleur de Notre-Dame (opera)
Act I
By permission Heugel & Cie, Paris, copyright owners

O Li- ber- té, m'ami - - - - e In- sou - - ci- eu- se fé- e

Par son charme di- vin,___ tout me rit, tout m'en- chan - - - - te

MASSENET

Le Jongleur de Notre-Dame (opera)
Act I

Pour la Vièr - - - ge D'a-bord voi - ci les fleurs qu'elle ai - - me,

Act II Légende de la sauge

(orchestral theme)

Fleu - ris - sait u - ne Ro - se au bord du che - min,

Manon (opera)
Act I

Je suis en-core tout é-tour-di-e, Je suis en-core tout en-gour-di-e!

Re-gar-dez-moi bien dans les yeux! Je vais tout près, à la ca-ser-ne,

Ne bron-chez pas, Soy-ez gen-tille, Et n'ou-bli-ez pas

Voy-ons, Ma-non, plus de chi-mè-res, Où va ton es-prit en re-vant?

Duet

Nous vi-vrons à Pa-ris, Tous les deux, Tous les deux,

accompanying figures of duet and also Letter Duet in Act II

Act II Letter Dust

J'é-cris à mon pè-re: et je trem-ble que cet-te lettre

On l'ap-pel-le Ma-non, elle eut hi-er seize ans

A-dieu, no-tre pe-ti-te ta-ble, Qui nous ré-u-nit si sou-vent!

Des Grieux's Dream

En fer-mant les yeux, je vois Là-bas u-ne hum-ble re-trai-te,

Act III Scene 1

La char-man-te pro-me-na - - - - - - - de

O Ro-sa-lin-de, Il me fau-drait gra-vir le Pin-de,

Je mar-che sur tous les che-mins Aus-si bien

Gavotte

O- bé- is-sons quand leur voix ap-pel-le Aux tendres a-mours, tou-jours,

Pro - - - fi-tons bien de la jeu-nes-se,

Fabliau

Oui, dans les bois et dans la plai-ne Rien que pour ri-re et sans raison

Manon (opera)
Act III Scene 1

A — Par- don! mais j'é-tais là près de vous, à deux pas

B — Faut- il donc sa- voir tant de cho- ses? Que de- vien- nent

Scene 2

C — É- pou- se quel-que bra- ve fil- le, Di-gne de nous, di- gne de toi__

D — Ah! fuy- ez, dou- ce i- ma- ge, à mon â- me trop chè- re

E — N'est-ce plus ma main que cet- te main pres- se? N'est-ce plus ma voix?__

Act IV

F — A nous les a- mours et les ro - - - - - - ses! Chan- ter, ai- mer,

Marie-Magdeleine (sacred drama)
Act I (La Magdaléenne à la fontaine)
By permission Heugel & Cie, Paris, copyright owners

G — C'est i- ci même__ en cet- te pla - - ce, C'est i- ci, Qu'il daigna m'apparaitre

Act III (La Magdaléenne à la croix)

H — O Bien- ai- mé, Ô Bien ai- mé, sous ta som- bre cou- ron- ne

Promesse de mon avenir, from Le Roi de Lahore (opera) Act IV
By permission Heugel & Cie, Paris, copyright owners

I — Pro- mes- se de mon a- ve- nir, O Si- tâ, rê- ve de ma vi- e,

Sapho (opera)
Act I
By permission Heugel & Cie, Paris, copyright owners

J — Ah!__ qu'il est loin mon pa- ys!__ Ah!__ qu'il est loin

Act II

K — Ce que j'ap- pel- le beau__ c'est d'a-voir_____ tes vingt ans,

Act IV

L — Pen-dant__ un an__ je fus__ ta femme,__ et j'entends res-ter à toi

Thais (opera)
Act I
By permission Heugel & Cie, Paris, copyright owners

M — Hé- las!____ en-fant en- co- re, a- vant qu'à mon coeur__

N — Voi- là donc la ter- ri- ble ci- té__ A- le-xan- dri- e!

O — Qui te fait si se- vè - - re, et pour-quoi démens- tu la flam- me

Act II

P — Dis-moi que je suis bel- le et que je se- rai belle__ é- ter- nel- le- ment!

Q — L'a- mour__ est un- e ver- tu ra- re, J'ai pé-ché non par lui,

Act III

R — O__ mes- sa- ger de Dieu,__ si bon dans ta ru- des- se, sois be- ni,

S — Bai- gne d'eau mes mains et mes lè - - vres, don- ne ces fruits, donne ces fruits,

Sérénade du Passant — Mi-gnon - - - ne, voi-ci l'A-vril! Le so-leil re-vient — d'e-xil; — A

Si tu veux, Mignonne — Si tu veux, Mignonne, au prin-temps Nous ver-rons fleu-rir — B

MAUDUIT, Jacques (1557-1627)

A la fontaine — A la fon-tai-ne je vou-drais a-vec ma bel-le al-ler jou-er, — D

En son temple sacré, Psalm 150 — En son tem-ple — sa-cré — lou-ez le grand Dieu — E

Si d'une petite oeillade — Si d'u-ne pe-ti-te oeil-la-de tou-te d'a-mour et de-sir — F

MC GILL, Josephine (1877-1919)

Duna
By permission Boosey & Hawkes, Inc.,
copyright owners — When I was a lit-tle lad with fol-ly on my lips — H

MEHUL, Etienne Henri (1763-1817)

Chant du Depart A — La vic-toire en chan-tant nous ou-vre la bar-riè-re — J

B — La Ré-pub-li-que vous ap-pel-le, sa-chez vaincre ou sachez pé-rir, — K

Champs paternels, from Joseph (opera) Act I — Champs pa-ter-nels, Hé-bron, dou-ce val-lé-e, loin de vous — L

Romance du barde, from Ariodant (opera) Act II — Fem-me sen-sible, en-tends tu le ra-ma-ge de ces oi-seaux — M

MENDELSSOHN, Felix (1809-1847)

Elijah, Op. 70 (oratorio)
No. 4 — If with all your hearts ye tru-ly seek me, ye shall e-ver sure-ly find me, — O

No. 9 — Blessed are the men who fear him, they e-ver walk in the ways of peace — P

No. 14 — Lord God of A-bra-ham, I-saac and Is-ra-el, this day let it be known — Q

No. 17 — Is not His word — like a fire? — and like a ham-mer — R

No. 18 — Woe, woe un-to them who for-sake Him! De-struction shall fall up-on them — S

MENDELSSOHN

Elijah, Op. 70 (oratorio)

No. 20 — Thanks be to God! He_ la-veth the thirsty land, the thirs_ _ ty land_ A

No. 21 — Hear ye, Is- ra- el, hear what the Lord_ speak- eth! B

No. 22 — I, I am he that com- fort- eth! Be not a-fraid, C
Be not a-fraid, saith God the Lord, be not a- fraid; thy help is near D

No. 26 — It is e- nough! O Lord, now take a- way my life_ E

No. 28 — Lift thine eyes, o lift thine eyes to the moun-tains whence com-eth F

No. 29 — He, watch-ing o- ver Is- ra- el slum- bers not nor sleeps G

No. 31 — O rest in the Lord, wait pa- tient- ly for Him H

No. 37 — For the moun-tains shall_ de-part_ and the hills,_the hills be remo- ved I

No. 39 — Then, then_shall the righteous shine forth as the sun in the heav'nly father's realm J

No. 41 — O come, ev' - - ry one that thirst-eth, o come to the wa-ters, K

St. Paul, Op. 36 (oratorio)

No. 7 — Je- ru- sa- lem, Je- ru- sa- lem, thou that kill - est the Pro-phets, L

No. 11 — Hap- py and blest are they who have en- dur - - - - - - - - ed M

No. 12 — Con- sume them all, Lord Sa-ba- oth, con-sume all these thine en-e- mies N

No. 13 — But the Lord is mind-ful of His own_ He- re- mem - bers His chil-dren O

No. 15 — Rise! up! a- rise! rise,and shine,_ rise, and shine! Rise up! A- rise!_ P

No. 18 — O God, have mer- cy, have mer- cy up- on_ me, Q

No. 20 — I praise Thee O Lord_ my God, with all_ my_ heart_ R

No. 22 — O great is the depth of the rich- es of wis- dom and knowledge S

MENDELSSOHN

Minnelied, Op. 47, No. 1
Wie der Quell so lieblich klin-get, und die Zar-ten Blu-men küsst,

Morgengruss No. 2
Ü- ber die Ber- ge steigt schon die Son- ne, die Läm -mer-heer-de läu- tet

Frühlingslied No. 3
Durch den Wald,— den dun-keln, geht hol- de Früh - -ling-mor-gen-stun-de,

Volkslied No. 4
Es ist be-stimmt in Got- tes Rath, dass man von Lieb-sten

Der Blumenstrauss No. 5
Sie wan-delt im Blu-men- gar-ten und mus-tert den bun - ten Flor,—

Bei der Wiege No. 6
Schlumm - - - re! Schlumm- re und träu-me von kom-men-der Zeit

Der Jager Abschied, Op. 50, No. 2
Wer hat dich, du schö-ner Wald, auf-ge- baut so hoch da dro-ben?

Lobgesang (Hymn of Praise) Op. 52, No. 2
Al- les, Al- les, Al- les was O- dem hat Al- les, Al- les

No. 3
Er zäh- let uns'- re Thrä- nen in der Zeit der Noth,

No. 5
Ich har- re- te des Herrn, und er neig- te sich zu mir,

No. 6
Die Strich- e des Tod- es hat- ten uns emp- fan- gen,

Altdeutsches Lied, Op. 57, No. 1
Es ist in den Wald ge-sun-gen, wenn— ich dir mein Lei- den sa- ge

Hirtenlied No. 2
O Win- ter, schlimmer— Win-ter, wie ist die Welt so klein!

Suleika No. 3
Was be- deu- tet die Be- we-gung? bringt der Ost mir fro- he Kun- de?

O Jugend, O schöne Rosenzeit, No. 4
Von al- len schö-nen Kin-dern auf der Welt— mir ei- nes doch am meisten

Venetianisches Gondellied No. 5
Wenn durch— die Piaz- zet - - - ta die A- bend - luft weht,—

Abschied vom Wald, Op. 59, No. 3
O, Thä- ler weit o Hö- hen, O schö-ner grü- ner Wald,

Die Nachtigall No. 4
Die Nach- ti-gall,sie war ent- fernt, der Früh-ling lockt sie wie-der

Ich wollt' meine Lieb' ergösse sich, Op. 63, No. 1
Ich wollt'— mei-ne Lieb' er- gös- se sich all'— in ein ein-zig Wort,

Abschiedslied der Zugvögel, Op. 63, No. 2 — A
Wie war so schön doch Wald und Feld! Wie ist so trau-rig jetzt die Welt!

Gruss No. 3 — B
Wo-hin ich geh', und schau-e, in Feld und Wald und Thal

Herbstlied No. 4 — C
Ach, wie so bald verhal-let der Rei-gen

O säh' ich auf der Haide dort (O wert thou in the could blast) No. 5 — D
O säh' ich auf der Hai-de dort im Stur-me dich, im Stur-me dich!

Festgesang, Op. 68, No. 2 (male chorus) (Hark the Herald Angels sing) — E
Va-ter-land, in dei-nen Gau-en brach der gold'-ne Tag einst an

Tröstung Op. 71, No. 1 — F
Wer-de hei-ter mein Ge-mü-the und ver-giss der Angst und Pein!

An die Entfernte No. 3 — G
Die-se Ro-se pflück' ich hier in der wei-ten Fer-ne,

Schilflied No. 4 — H
Auf dem Teich, dem re-gungs-losen, weilt des Mon-des hol-der Glanz,

Nachtlied No. 6 — I
Ver-gan-gen ist der lich-te Tag, von fer-ne kommt der Glo-cken Schlag;

Lauda Sion, Op. 73, No. 6 — J
Ca-ro ci-bus, san-guis po-tus, ma-net ta-men Christus to-tus

Der frohe Wandersmann, Op. 75, No. 1 — K
Wenn Gott will rech-te Gunst er-wei-sen, den schickt er in die Wei-te Welt

Sonntagsmorgen, Op. 77, No. 1 — L
Das ist der Tag des Herrn, das ist der Tag des Herrn. Ich bin al-lein

Lied aus Ruy Blas No. 3 — M
Wo-zu der Vög-lein Chö-re be-lau-schen fern und nah?

Jagdlied Op. 84, No. 3 — N
Mit Lust thät ich aus-rei-ten durch ei-nen grü-nen Wald

Die Liebende schreibt, Op. 86, No. 3 — O
Ein Blick von dei-nen Au-gen in die mei-nen

Der Mond No. 5 — P
Mein Herz ist wie die dunk-le Nacht, wenn al-le Wi-pfel rau-schen;

Neujahrslied, Op. 88, No. 1 — Q
Mit der Freu-de zieht der Schmerz trau-lich durch die Zei-ten,

Heimkehr aus der Fremde, Op. 89, No. 4 (Son and Stranger) — R
Ich bin ein viel-ge-reis-ter Mann, der al-ler Län-der Tän-ze kann

Concert Aria, Op. 94 (Infelice! Gia' del mio sguardo) — S
Ah, ri-tor-na,e-tà fe-li-ce quando_ac-can-to del mio be-ne

Die Lorely, Op. 98, No. 2 Ave Maria
Horch der A- bend- glo- cke Ton! A- ve Ma- ri- a!

Lieblingsplätzchen, Op. 99, No. 3
Wisst ihr wo ich ger- ne weil' in der A- bend- küh- le?

Wenn sich zwei Herzen scheiden, No. 5
Wenn sich zwei Her- zen schei- den, die sich der- einst ge- liebt,

Beati Mortui, Op. 115, No. 1 (male chorus)
Be- a- ti mor- tu- i in Do- mi- no mo- ri- en- tes,

Der Blumenkranz (By Celia's Arbour)
An Ce- lia's Baum in stil- - - ler Nacht___

Drei Volkslieder (Three Folksongs)
No. 1 Wie kann ich froh
Wie kann ich froh und lus- tig sein? Wie kann ich geh'n mit Band und Strauss

No. 2 Abendlied
Wenn ich auf dem La- ger lie- ge, in Nacht___ ge- hüllt,

No. 3 Wasserfahrt
Ich stand ge- leh- net an den 'Mast,___ und zähl- te je- de Wel- le,

Hear My Prayer (Hymn) A
Hear my prayer___ O God, in- cline thine ear! Thy- self from my pe- ti- tion

B
O___ for the wings,___ for the wings___ of a dove! Far a- way

Two Songs after Eichendorff
1. Pagenlied
Wenn die Son- ne lieb- lich schie- ne wie in Wälsch- land, lau und blau___

2. Das Waldschloss
Wo noch kein Wand- rer- ge- gan- gen, hoch ü- ber Jä- ger und Ross

Warnung vor dem Rhein
An den Rhein, an den Rhein, zieh nicht an den Rhein,

MENOTTI, Gian-Carlo (1911-   )

The Consul
The Empty-handed Traveler
Copyright 1950, G. Schirmer, Inc.
I'm not cry- ing for him not for us; but for John

Lullaby
I shall find for you shells and stars. I shall swim for you

Magda's Aria A
To this we've come: that men with- hold the world from men

B
If to men, not to God, we now must pray, tell me,

What is your name? Mag- da Sor- el Age? Thir- ty three.

The Medium (opera)
Act I
Copyright 1947, G. Schirmer, Inc.

Where, oh, where____ is my new gol-den spin-dle and thread?____ — A

Mo-ther, mo-ther, are you there? Mo-ther, mo-ther, are you there? — B

Black Swan Song

The sun has fallen and it lies in blood, The moon is weav-ing — C

O black swan, where, oh, where____ is my lov-er gone — D

Act II

Up in the sky some one is play-ing a trom-bone and a gui-tar — E

Mon-i-ca, Mon-i-ca, dance the waltz, Mon-i-ca, Mon-i-ca, dance the waltz. — F

A-fraid, am I a-fraid? Madame Flo-ra a-fraid! — G

The Telephone
Copyright 1947, G. Schirmer, Inc.

Hel-lo! Hel-lo? Oh Margaret, it's you, I am so glad you called, — H

And how are you? And how is John? And how is Jean? You must tell them — I

It all be-gan on a Sun-day, when John and I went skat-ing — J

Duet

Hel-lo? Hel-lo? Where are you, my dar-ling? I'm ter-ri-bly near you — K

MESSAGER, André (1835-1929)

Fortunio (opera)
Act II La Maison Grise
Copyright by Choudens fils, Paris

J'ai-mais la vieil-le mai-son gri--se Où j'ai gran-di — M

Act III Chanson de Fortunio

Si vous croy-ez que je vais di-re Qui j'ose ai-mer — N

Le jour sous le soleil béni, from Madame Chrysanthème (opera)
Act III
Copyright by Choudens fils, Paris

Le jour, sous le so-leil bé-ni,__ La nuit, sous L'é-toi-le qui rê----ve, — O

Véronique (opéra-comique)
Act 1, No. 7
Copyright by Choudens fils, Paris

Pe-ti-te dinde: Ah! quel ou-tra-ge! Vrai-ment je suf-fo-que — P

Ah Monsieur Flo-res-tan! A nous deux main-te-nant! — Q

Act III, No. 20

Ma foi! pour ve-nir de pro-vin-ce Le tour n'est pas trop mal,

METCALF, John W.

Absent

Copyrigrt by Artrur P. Schmidt Co., Boston.
Used by permission

Some-times be-tween long shad-ows on the grass

MEYERBEER, Giacomo (1791-1864)

L'Africaine (opera)
Act I

A-dieu, mon doux ri-va-ge, a-dieu, mon seule a-mour!

Act II

Pour cel-le qui m'est chè-re qui m'est chè-re,

Sur mes ge-noux fils du so-leil, Vainqueur au champ d'a-lar-mes

Fil-le des Rois, à toi l'hom-ma-ge à toi l'hom-ma-ge

Act III

Je vois dans la gran-de î-le, en nos jours for-tu-nés,

A-da-mas-tor, roi des va-gues pro-fon-des

Act IV

Aux voi-les, aux cor-da-ges De van-cez les o-ra-ges

Ô pa-ra-dis sor-ti de l'on-de

Con-dui-sez-moi vers ce na-vi-re Dont la voi-le bril-le à vos yeux

L'a-voir tant a-do-ré-e Et dans ce jour fa-tal

Dinorah (Le Pardon de Ploërmel)
(opera)
Act II

De-puis lors, quand la nuit ga-gne Le vil-lage et la mon-ta-gne,

Om-bre lé-gè-re Qui suis mes pas Ne t'en va pas! non, non, non!

Act III

Le jour est le-vé, La pluie a la-vé Les cieux et la plai-ne,

Ah! mon re-monde te ven-ge De mon fol a-ban-don

L'Etoile du Nord (opera) Act I (Finale)

Veil-le sur eux tou-jours, Mè-re, mè-re,

O jours heu-reux de joie et de mi-sè-re

La, la, la, air ché-ri la, la, la la c'est lui,

Les Huguenots (opera)

Act I

Plus blan- che_ que la blan--che_her-mi------ne

(Tune of "Eine feste Burg" of Martin Luther)

Sei- gneur rem-part_et seul_sou- tien_ du fai-ble qui t'im-plo- re,

Piff, paff, piff, paff, Pour les cou- vents c'est fi-ni,

U- ne da-me noble et sa- ge Dont les rois se-raient_ja- loux_

Finale (recitative) Act II

Nobles Sei- gneurs, sa-lut! nobles Sei-gneurs, sa- lut!

Act II

O beau_pa- ys_ de la Tou- rai- ne, ri-ant_ jar- dins,

Act IV

Par-mi les pleurs mon rê- ve se ra- ni- me c'est_ à_ lui seul_

Gloi--------re, gloire au grand Dieu ven- geur!

Finale duet (Raoul and Valentine)

Le dan- ger pres- se et le temps vo- le,

Cavatina

Tu l'as dit: oui tu m'ai---- mes!

Stretto

Plus d'a- mour, plus d'i-vres- se, ô re-mords qui m'op-pres- se

Act V

A la lu- eur de leurs tor- ches fu- nè- bres

Le Prophète (opera)

Act I

Mon coeur s'é-lan--------ce et pal- pi- te

Act II

Pour_Ber-tha_ moi je_soupi- re, je_ne veux_ pas aut-re empi- re;

Ah! mon fils, sois bé- ni! ta pau-vre mè- re te fus plus

Act III

Aus- si nom-breux_ que les é-toi- les où bien que les flots,

Roi du Ciel_et des_ an- ges, je di- rai_tes_ lou- an-ges

Act IV

Don- nez,_ don- nez pour u--ne_ pau- vre â- me,

Je_ suis, hé- las! je_ suis la pau-vre fem- me

Act V

O toi qui m'a-ban-don-nes. mon_coeur,mon coeur est dé- sar- mé,

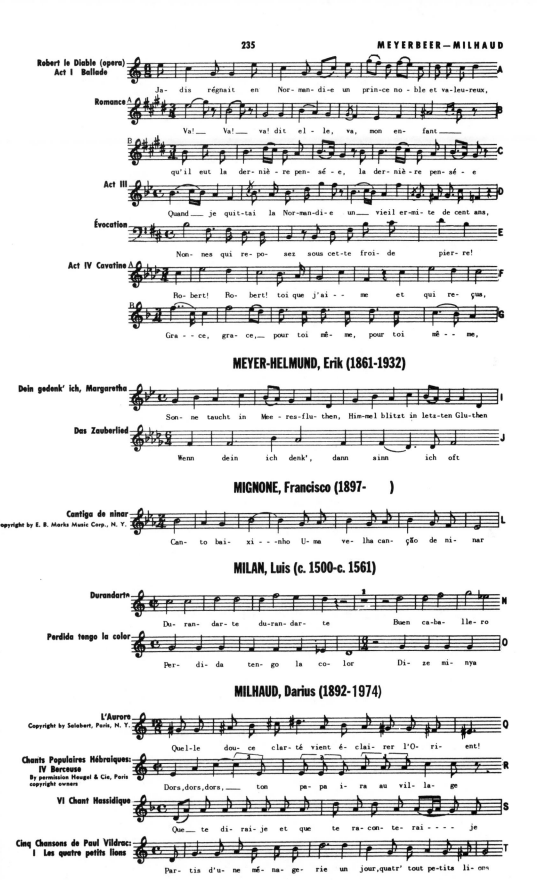

Robert le Diable (opera)
Act I Ballade

Ja- dis régnait en Nor- man- di-e un prin-ce no- ble et va-leu-reux,

Romance

Va! Va! va! dit el- le, va, mon en- fant

qu'il eut la der- niè- re pen- sé- e, la der- niè- re pen- sé- e

Act III

Quand __ je quit-tai la Nor-man-di-e un __ vieil er-mi- te de cent ans,

Évocation

Non- nes qui re- po- sez sous cet-te froi- de pier- re!

Act IV Cavatine

Ro- bert! Ro- bert! toi que j'ai - - me et qui re- çus,

Gra- ce, gra-ce,__ pour toi mê- me, pour toi mê- - me,

MEYER-HELMUND, Erik (1861-1932)

Dein gedenk' ich, Margaretha

Son- ne taucht in Mee- res-flu- then, Him-mel blitzt in letz-ten Glu-then

Das Zauberlied

Wenn dein ich denk', dann sinn ich oft

MIGNONE, Francisco (1897-   )

Cantiga de ninar
Copyright by E. B. Marks Music Corp., N. Y.

Can- to bai- xi- - nho U- ma ve- lha can- ção de ni- nar

MILAN, Luis (c. 1500-c. 1561)

Durandarte

Du- ran- dar- te du-ran-dar- te Buen ca-ba- lle- ro

Perdida tengo la color

Per- di- da ten- go la co- lor Di- ze mi- nya

MILHAUD, Darius (1892-1974)

L'Aurore
Copyright by Salabert, Paris, N. Y.

Quel-le dou- ce clar- té vient é- clai- rer l'O- ri- ent!

Chants Populaires Hébraiques:
IV Berceuse
By permission Heugel & Cie, Paris
copyright owners

Dors,dors,dors,__ ton pa- pa i- ra au vil- la- ge

VI Chant Hassidique

Que te di- rai-je et que te ra-con-te-rai - - - - je

Cinq Chansons de Paul Vildrac:
I Les quatre petits lions

Par- tis d'u- ne mé- na- ge- rie un jour,quatr' tout pe-tits li- ons

Cinq Chansons de Paul Vildrac:
II Poupette et Patata

Au beau mi-lieu de l'i-le ver-te Il y a un cha-teau de bois

III La pomme et l'escargot

Il y a-vait u-ne pom-me A la ci-me d'un pom-mier

IV La Malpropre

Un fer-mier du voi-si-na-ge Qui boit plus que de rai-son

V Le Jardinier Impatient

Dans son po-ta-ger ma grand mè-re m'a ré-ser-vé un pe-tit coin

Poèmes Juifs
I Chant de Nourrice
By permission Associated Music
Publishers, Inc.

Dors, ma fleur, mon fils ché-ri pendant que je ba-lan-ce-rai ton ber-ceau;

II Chant de Sion

Ce n'est_ la ro-sée_ ni la pluie, ce sont_ mes lar-mes

III Chant du Laboureur

Mon es-pé-ran-ce n'est pas en-core per-due

IV Chant de la pitié

Dans les champs de Beth-le-em_ u-ne pier-re se dres-se

V Chant de resignation

Prends mon à----me fais en u-ne ly-re bril-lan-te

VI Chant d'amour

En mê-me temps que tous les bourgeons la Ro--se de mon coeur

VII Chant de forgeron

Près du Jourdain il y a u-ne mai-son de for-ge-ron

VIII Lamentation

Au ciel_ sept ché-ru-bins si-len-ci-eux com-me les rêves

La Tourterelle
By permission Durand & Cie, Paris;
Elkan-Vogel Co., Inc., Phila.,
copyright owners

Ma co-lom-be, Ô ma tour-te-rel-le, Est-ce vous dont j'entends

Tros Poèmes de Jean Cocteau
I Fumée
Copyright by Ed. de la Sirene, Paris

C'est per-mis de fu-mer_ ga--re L'e-cu-yer de Me-dra-no

II Fête de Bordeaux

La ma-nège a va-peur_ re-gar-de s'en al-ler

III Fête de Montmartre

Ne vous ba-lan-cez pas si fort le Ciel est à tout le mon-de

MILLOECKER, Karl (1842-1899)

The Beggar Student (Der Bettel-
student) (operetta)   No. 2

Yet this he-ro_ all vic-to-rious_ whom re-vere_ high and low

Noth-ing I have ev-er heard worse than that up-on my word, worse than that

No. 3

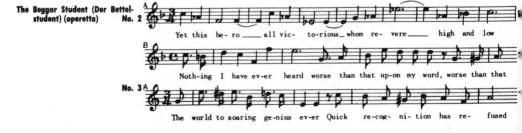

The world to soaring ge-nius ev-er Quick re-cog-ni-tion has re-fused

The Beggar Student (Der Bettel-student) (operetta)   No. 3
From clouds of pet- ty woe jol-li-ty breaks forth ra-diant- ly

No. 6
I've of-ten felt the pas-sion ten-der at Paris the gri- sette I knew

No. 10
I'll put the case that I were not of stock pa- tri- cian

Gasparone (operetta)   Act I No. 3
O dass ich doch der Räu- ber wä- re, ich streb-te nicht

No. 6
An- zo- let- ta sang:Komm mi- a bel- la!__ Un- ter'm Fen-ster

Act III Waltz
Er soll dein Herr sein!Wie stolz das klingt! Geltung hat's leider nur sehr bedingt

Der Arme Jonathan (operetta)   Act I, No. 5
In me__ you see__poor Jon- a-than, How shall__I bear__ my life be- gun?

MOERAN, Ernest John (1894-1950)

Diaphenia
By permission Boosey & Hawkes, Inc., copyright owners
Di - - a- phe- nia,__ like the daf- fa- down- dil- ly,

The Sweet o' the Year
By permission of Augener, Ltd., London
When da- fo-dils be- gin to peer,with heigh!__ The do- xy o- ver the dale,

MOLLOY, J. L. (1837-1909)

The Kerry Dance
O the days of the Ker- ry danc-ing O the ring of the pi-per's tune

Love's Old Sweet Song
Once in the dear dead days be-yond re- call, When on the world

Just a song at twi-light, when the lights are low,

MONRO, George (18th Cent.)

My Lovely Celia
My love - - - ly__ Ce - - lia, heav'n - - - ly__ fair,

MONSIGNY, Pierre Alexandre (1729-1817)

Adieu, chère Louise, from Le Déserteur (opéra-comique)
A- dieu, chè-re Lou- i- se! Chè- re Lou-ise, a- dieu!__

Il regardait mon bouquet, from Le Roi et le Fermier
Il re- gar- dait mon bou-quet, Sans doute il le dé- si- rait,

La sagesse est un trésor, from Rose et Colas (opera)
La sa-gesse est un__ tré- sor,un tré-sor c'est la sa-ges- - se

MONTEMEZZI, Italo (1875-1952)

Son quarant' anni, from L'Amore dei tre re (opera) Act I
Copyright by G. Ricordi & Co., Inc.

Son quarant' an- ni   che di- sce-si in questa bel-la   ser-ra

MONTEVERDE, Claudio (1567-1643)

Amor (Lamento della Ninfa)

A- mor Di- ce a- mor il ciel mi- ran-do il pie fer-mò

Ardo

Ar- do   Ar- do   Ar- do   Ar-   do   e scoprir ahi_ lasso

Ardo si ma non t'amo

Ar- do   si   ma non t'a - - - - - mo__   Da un si le-al a- man- - te

Il Balletto delle Ingrate

Ahi trop- - po Ahi   trop-po è   du- ro   cru- del sen-ten-za

Chiome d'oro

Chio-me d'oro bel the-so-ro tu mi leghi in mille   mo-di_____

Ch'io t'ami

Ch'io t'a- mi   e t'a-mi più de   la mia vi - - - - - ta

Cor mio mentre vi miro

Cor   mio   men-tre vi   mi - - - - - - - - - ro

Ecco mormora l'onde (madrigal, 5-part)

Ec- co mor - - mo- ra l'on- de   e tre-mo-lar le ron-de

Hor ch'el ciel e la terra (madrigal, 6-voice)

Hor ch'el ciel e la ter-ra el ven-to ta- ce E le fe-re e gli angeli

Guer-ra è il mio sta- to Guer- ra guer-ra guer-ra guer-ra   guer-ra guer-ra

Lagrime d'Amante al Sepolcro dell' Amata:

In - - ce-ne-ri- te spo-glie   a- va-ra tom - - ba _____

Di-te- lo o fiu-mi, o fiu- mi   O fiu- mi   O fiu-mi e voi che udeste

Da- rà   la notte il sol lu- me alla ter- ra Splenderà Cin - - tia il dì

Ma te rac-co-glie o Nin fa   ma te rac-co-glie o Nin- fa

O chio-me d'or ne - - ve gen-til   ne - - ve gen-til___ del se- no

Dun - - - que a- ma- te re- li-quie un mar di   pian- to

MONTEVERDE

Lasciatemi Morire
La-scia--te-mi mo--ri-re, La-scia-te-mi mo--ri--re A

Lettera amorosa
Se i lan-gui-de miei sguar-di se i sos-pir in-ter-rot-ti B

Maledetto sia l'aspetto
Ma--le-det-to sia l'as-pet-to che m'ar-de tris-to mé C

Ohimè ch'io cado
Ohi-mè ch'io ca-do ohi-mè ch'in-ciam-po an co-ra il piè D

Ohimè dov è il mis ben
Ohi Ohi--mè dov'è il mio ben do-v'è il mio co-re E

O Mirtillo
O Mir--til--lo Mir--til-l'a---ni-ma mi--a F

La piaga c'ho nel core
La pia--ga c'ho nel co--re Don-na Don--na G

Si dolce è'l tormento
Si dol-ce è'l tor--men-to Che in se-no mi sta, H

Su su Pastorelli vezzosi
Su su su pa-sto--rel-li vez--zo-si vez--zo-si I

Zefiro torna (duet for 2 tenors)
Ze--fi-ro ze-fi-ro ze--fi-ro tor---na, J

L'Incoronazione di Poppea (opera)
Act II
Sen-to un cer--to non so che che mi piz-zi-ca e di-let-ta K

O-bli-vi-on so-a---ve i dolci L

Orfeo (opera)
Prologue
Dal mio per-messo a--ma-to a voi ne ve-gno in-cli-ti e-roi M

Act I (Chorus)
Vie-ni I-me-neo deh vie-ni e la tua fa-ce ar-din-te N

(Chorus) A
Lascia-te i mon-ti lascia-te i fon----ti Nin----fe O

B
Qui mi-ri il so-le vo-stre ca-ro-le più va-ghe as-sai P

(Orfeo)
Ro-sa del ciel vi-ta del mon-do e de-gna pro-le di lui Q

(Chorus)
Ecco Or-feo Ecco Orfeo cui pur dian-zi fu-ron ci-bo i so-spir R

Act II
Ec-co pur ch'a voi ri-tor-no ca-re sel---ve e piagge a-man-te S

Orfeo (opera)
Act II (Shepherds)

In questo prato a- dor-no___ o- gni sel- vag- gio nu- me___

Qui le Na- pee vez- zo- se schie- ra sem- pre fio- ri- ta

(Orfeo)

Vi ri- cor- da o bo-schi om-bro- si Vi ri- cor- da o bo-schi om-bro- si

Lament (Orfeo)

Tu___ sè mor- ta se' mor- ta mia vi- ta ed io re- spi- ro

(Chorus)

Ahi ca- so a- cer- bo, Ahi fat' em---- pio e cru- de- le,

(Chorus)

Chi___ ne con- so la ahi las- si O pur chi ne con- ce- de

Act III (Orfeo)

Pos-sen--- te spir- to e for-mi-da---bil nu--me

(Orfeo)

Sol tu no- bi- le Dio puoi dar-mi a- i- ta

(Orfeo)

Ahi sven-tu-ra-to a-man-te, sperar dun- que non li- ce ch'o- dan miei prie- ghi

(Chorus)

Nul-la im-pre- sa per huom si ten-ta in va----- no

Act IV (Proserpina)

Si-gnor quel in- fe- li- ce che per queste di morte am---pie cam-pa- gne

(Orfeo)

Qual ho- nor___ di te sia de- gno mia cetra on- ni- po- ten- te,

(Chorus)

È la vir- tu- te rag-gio di___ ce- le- ste be- lez- za

Act V (Orfeo)

Que- sti i cam-pi di Tra- cia lo- ve pas- somm'il co- re

(Orfeo and Apollo)

Sa- liam,___ sa- liam___

(Chorus)

Van- ne Or-feo fe- li- ce a pie- no, a go- der ce- le-ste ho- no- re,

MORALES, Cristóbal de (c. 1500-1553)

O vos omnes

O___ vos o--------mnes___ qui tran- si- tis___

MORLEY, Thomas (1557-c. 1603)

April is in my mistress' face

A-pril is in my Mis-tress' face, April is in my Mis-tress' face,

Dainty fine sweet nymph

Dain-ty fine sweet nymph de - light-ful, while the sun a - loft is mount-ing

Fire, fire

Fire fire, Fire, fire Fire, fire, Fire, fire, my heart

Hard by a crystal fountain

Hard by a Crys-tal fount - - - - - - - - - - - - - - - - - - ain

I follow, lo, the footing

I fol-low, lo, the foot-ing I fol- low, lo, the foot- ing

It was a Lover and his Lasse

It was a lov-er and his lasse with a hey, with a hoe

My bonny lass she smileth

My bon-ny lass she smil-eth When she my heart be- guil-eth

Now is the gentle season

Now is the gen- tle sea- son fresh-ly flow'r- ing

Now is the month of Maying

Now is the month of May- ing when mer- ry lads are play-ing

Shoot, false love, I care not

Shoot false love I care not, spend thy shafts, and spare not,

Since my tears and lamenting

Since____ my tears and la- ment-ing, false love breed thy con-tenting

Sing we and chant it

Sing we and chant it, While love doth grant it, Fa la la la la la la la

Sweet nymph

Sweet Nymph, come to _____ thy lo-ver, to _____ thy lov- er,

MOZART, Wolfgang Amadeus (1756-1791)

Bastien and Bastienne (opera) K. 50
No. 1

Mein lieb-ster Freund hat mich ver - lassen, mit ihm ist Schlaf__

No. 2

Ich geh' jetzt auf die Wei-de be - täubt und__ ganz ge - dan - ken__ leer,

No. 4

Be - fra- get mich ein zar - tes__ Kind um sein zu- künftges Glücke

No. 5

Wenn mein Ba- stien einst__ im Scherze mir ein__ Blüm-chen__ sonst ent- wand

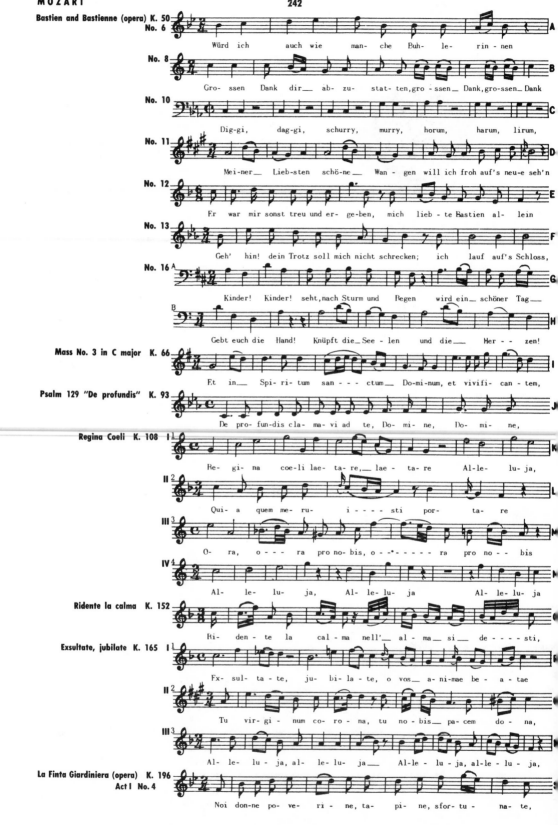

Bastien and Bastienne (opera) K. 50
No. 6
Würd ich auch wie man-che Buh-le-rin-nen

No. 8
Gro-ssen Dank dir ab-zu-stat-ten, gro-ssen Dank, gro-ssen Dank

No. 10
Dig-gi, dag-gi, schurry, murry, horum, harum, lirum,

No. 11
Mei-ner Lieb-sten schö-ne Wan-gen will ich froh auf's neu-e seh'n

No. 12
Er war mir sonst treu und er-ge-ben, mich lieb-te Bastien al-lein

No. 13
Geh' hin! dein Trotz soll mich nicht schrecken; ich lauf auf's Schloss,

No. 16 A
Kinder! Kinder! seht, nach Sturm und Regen wird ein schöner Tag

B
Gebt euch die Hand! Knüpft die See-len und die Her-zen!

Mass No. 3 in C major K. 66
Et in Spi-ri-tum san - - - ctum Do-mi-num, et vivifi-can-tem,

Psalm 129 "De profundis" K. 93
De pro-fun-dis cla-ma-vi ad te, Do-mi-ne, Do-mi-ne,

Regina Coeli K. 108 I
Re-gi-na coe-li lae-ta-re, lae-ta-re Al-le-lu-ja,

II
Qui-a quem me-ru-i - - - -sti por-ta-re

III
O-ra, o - - - ra pro no-bis, o - - • - - - - ra pro no - - bis

IV
Al-le-lu-ja, Al-le-lu-ja Al-le-lu-ja

Ridente la calma K. 152
Ri-den-te la cal-ma nell' al-ma si de - - - -sti,

Exsultate, jubilate K. 165 I
Ex-sul-ta-te, ju-bi-la-te, o vos a-ni-mae be-a-tae

II
Tu vir-gi-num co-ro-na, tu no-bis pa-cem do-na,

III
Al-le-lu-ja, al-le-lu-ja Al-le-lu-ja, al-le-lu-ja,

La Finta Giardiniera (opera) K. 196
Act I No. 4
Noi don-ne po-ve-ri-ne, ta-pi-ne, sfor-tu-na-te,

MOZART

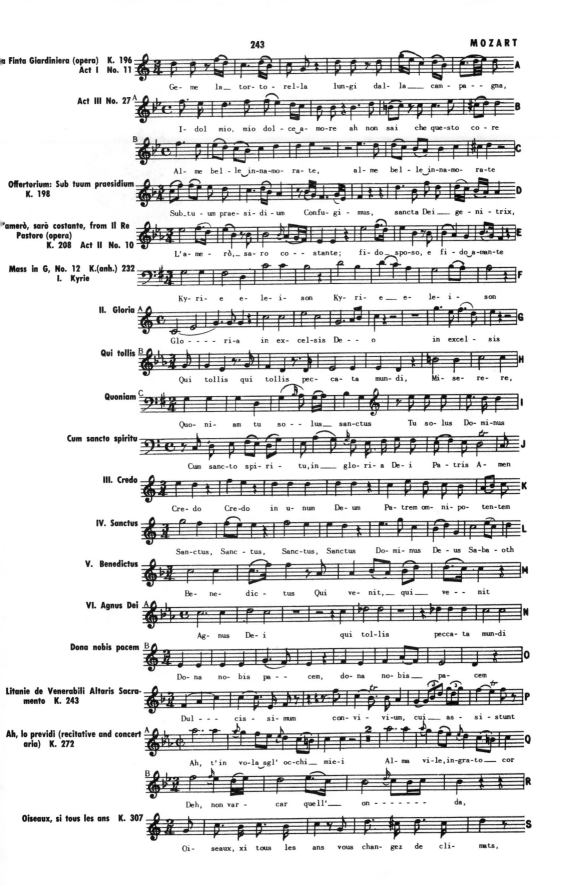

a Finta Giardiniera (opera) K. 196
Act I No. 11

Ge- me la__ tor- to- rel- la lun- gi dal- la__ cam- pa- gna,

Act III No. 27

I- dol mio, mio dol- ce_a- mo- re ah non sai che que- sto co- re

Al- me bel- le_in- na- mo- ra- te, al- me bel- le_in- na- mo- ra- te

Offertorium: Sub tuum praesidium K. 198

Sub_tu- um prae- si- di- um Con- fu- gi- mus, sancta Dei__ ge- ni- trix,

'amerò, sarò costante, from Il Re Pastore (opera) K. 208 Act II No. 10

L'a- me- rò,_ sa- ro co- - stante; fi- do spo- so, e fi- do_a- man- te

Mass in G, No. 12 K.(anh.) 232 I. Kyrie

Ky- ri- e e- le- i- son Ky- ri- e e- le- i- son

II. Gloria

Glo- - - - ri- a in ex- cel- sis De- - o in excel- sis

Qui tollis

Qui tollis qui tollis pec- ca- ta mun- di, Mi- se- re- re,

Quoniam

Quo- ni- am tu so- - lus__ san- ctus Tu so- lus Do- mi- nus

Cum sancto spiritu

Cum sanc- to spi- ri- tu, in__ glo- ri- a De- i Pa- tris A- men

III. Credo

Cre- do Cre- do in u- num De- um Pa- trem om- ni- po- ten- tem

IV. Sanctus

San- ctus, Sanc- tus, Sanc- tus, Sanctus Do- mi- nus De- us Sa- ba- oth

V. Benedictus

Be- ne- dic- tus Qui ve- nit,_ qui ve- - nit

VI. Agnus Dei

Ag- nus De- i qui tol- lis pecca- ta mun- di

Dona nobis pacem

Do- na no- bis pa- - cem, do- na no- bis__ pa- cem

Litanie de Venerabili Altaris Sacra- mento K. 243

Dul- - - cis- si- mum con- vi- vi- um, cui__ as- si- stunt

Ah, lo previdi (recitative and concert aria) K. 272

Ah, t'in vo- la_agl' oc- chi__ mie- i Al- ma vi- le, in- gra- to__ cor

Deh, non var- car quell'__ on- - - - - - da,

Oiseaux, si tous les ans K. 307

Oi- seaux, xi tous les ans vous chan- gez de cli- mats,

Dans un bois solitaire K. 308

Dans un bois so-li- tai-re et som-bre je __ me pro-me- nais __

Popoli di Tessaglia K. 316

Io non __ chie- do e-ter- ni Dei, tut- to il ciel per me se- re- no

Mass in C ("Krönungs Messe")
(Coronation Mass) K. 317
Agnus Dei

A- gnus De- i, a- gnus De- i, qui tol - lis pec- ca - - ta,

Adoramus te K. 327

Ad- o- ra - - - - mus te, Chri - - ste, et be-ne-dici - - mus ti- bi,

Vesperae solennes de confessor
K. 339 No. 5

Lau - - - - da - - - - - - - - te Do- mi-num o - - mnes gen - tes

Wiegenlied K. 350 (K.anh. 284 f)
(attributed to Mozart. Actually
by Bernard Flies, a contemporary
of Mozart)

Schlafe mein Prinzchen schlaf' ein, es ruh'n nun Schäfchen und Vö- ge- lein

Komm, liebe Zither K. 341

Komm, lie- be Zi- ther, komm, du Freund in stil - ler Lie- be,

Idomeneo (opera) K. 366 **Act I**

Pa- dre! Ger- ma-ni ad-di- o voi foste io vi per-de- i

A

Non ho col-pa e mi con- dan- ni e mi con- dan- ni

B

Col-pa è vos-tra o Dei__ ti - ran- ni è di pe- na

Tut- te nel cor vi sen-to, vi sen-to, vi sen-to

Ve- drom-mi in-tor- no l'om-bra do- len-te, l'om-bra, l'om-bra

Il Pa- dre__ ado- ra - to ri tro-vo, e lo per-do

Act II

Se __ il tuo duol, se il mio de - - si - o s'in-vo-las __

Se __ il pa- dre per- de- i la Patria, il ri - po- so,

Fuor del mar ho un mar in seno che __ del pri-mo è più fu- nesto

I - - - dol mi-o se __ ri - tro-so al tra A- man-te

Act III

Zef- fi- ret- ti lu - - sin- ghie- ri

Se co - - - là __ nè fa - - tiè scrit-to

Idomeneo (opera) K. 366 Act III

D'O- re- ste, d'A- ja- ce ho in se- no i tor- men- ti D'O-re-ste

Tor - - - - na la pa- ce al co- re, al co- re,

Ma che vi fece, o stelle K. 368

Spe- rai vi- ci- no, vi- ci- no il_ li- do,

Ma tra- por- tar _____ mi sen- to,

Misera, dove son! K. 369

Ah! non son io che par- lo, Ah,_ non son io che par- lo

Non cu- ra il ciel ti- ra- no l'af- fan no in cui mi ve- do

A questo seno deh vieni K. 374

Or che il cie- lo a me ti ren- de, ca- ra par- te del mio cor,_

Entführung aus dem Seraglio (The Abduction from the Seraglio) (opera)

K. 384 Act 1

Hier soll ich dich denn se- hen, Kon- stan- ze, dich, mein_ Glück_

Wer ein Lieb- chen hat ge- fun- den, das es treu und red- lich meint,

Sol- che her- ge- lauf'ne Laf - - - - - - - - - - - - - - - fen

O wie ängstlich, o wie feurig Klopft mein lie- be- vol- les Herz_

Ach ich liebte, war so glücklich, kann- te nicht der Lie- be Schmerz

Doch wie schnell schwand_ mei- ne Freude, doch wie schnell schwand meine Freude!

Act II

Durch Zärt- lich- keit und_ Schmeicheln Ge- fäl- lig- keit_ und Scherzen

Ich ge- he, doch rathe ich dir, den Schurken Ped- ril- lo zu mei- den

Trau- rig- keit ward mir zum Lo- se, ward mir zum Lo- se,

Mar- tern al- ler Ar- ten al- ler Ar- ten mö- gen mei- ner_ war- ten,

Wel- che Won- ne, wel- che Lust regt sich nun in mei- ner Brust

Frisch zum Kampfe! Frisch zum Streite! Nur ein fei- ger Tropf verzagt,

Die Entführung aus dem Seraglio (The Abduction from the Seraglio) (opera)

K. 384 Act II Duet

Vi - vat_ Bac-chus! Bac-chus le - be! Bac-chus war ein bra-ver Mann.

Wenn der Freu-de Thrä - nen fliessen, lä - chelt Lie-be_ dem Ge-liebten hold_

Act III (Romanze)

Ich bau-e_ ganz ___ auf_ dei - ne Stär - - ke,

Im Moh - ren - land ge - fan - gen war_ ein Mäd-chen hübsch_ und fein,

O! wie will ich tri-um- phi - ren, wenn sie euch zum Richt-platz füh- ren,

Nie werd' ich dei - ne Huld ver - ken - nen, mein Dank bleibt e - wig dir_ ge - weiht.

Ich würd auf meinem Pfad   K. 390

Ich würd auf mei - nem Pfad_ mit Thränen oft hin_zum_fer - nen_ En - - de_

Sei du mein Trost   K. 391

Sei du __ mein Trost, ver-schwiegne Trau - - rig - keit

Verdankt sei es dem Glanz   K. 392

Verdankt sei es dem_ Glanz der Gro-ssen, dass er mein Nichts mir_deutlich zeigt,

Mia speranze adorata (recitative and concert aria)   K. 416

Ah, non_ sa - i, qual pe - - na si - a il ___ do - ver-ti,

No, no, che non sei capace (concert aria)   K. 419

No, no, no, che non sei ca-pa-ce di cor-te- sia, d'o-no- re,

Per pietà, non ricercate   K. 420

A
Per pie - tà, non ri-cer-ca-te la ca-gion_ del mio_tor - men.-to,

B
Ah, tra l'i-re_e tra gli sdegni del - la mia fu-ne-sta sor-te

Mass in C minor   K. 427

Ky - - ri-e e - lei - son, e - lei - - - - son. Ky - ri - e - leison

Glo - - ri - a in ex-cel - - - - - - - - - - - - - - - sis

Lau - da - - - - - - - - mus_ te, _ be-ne-di-ci-mus_ te,

Do- mi - ne De-us_ rex_coe - le-stis, rex_ coe - le-stis,

Qui tol - - lis pec - ca-ta mun - di qui tol-lis pec - ca-ta,

Quo - ni - am tu so - - - - - - - - - - - - lus sanc - - tus,

MOZART

Mass in C minor K. 427

Cum san----cto spi-ri-tu in glo--------------ri-a

Et in-car-na-tus est de spi--ri-tu san---cto

Et in Spi-ri-tum san-ctum, do-mi-num, et_ vi-vi--fi- cantem

Cre-do, Cre-do in u-nam sanctam ca-tho-li-cam et a-posto-li-cam

Et vi-tam ven-tu-ri sae-cu-li, a---------------- men,

Be-ne-di----ctus qui_ve-nit, Be-ne-di---ctus qui__ ve-nit

Cosi dunque tradisci K. 432

A-spri ri-mor-si_a-tro-ci, a-spri ri-mor-si_a-tro-ci

Warnung K. 433

Män-ner su-chen stets zu na-schen, lässt_man sie al-lein_

Gesellenreise (Masonic Song) K. 468

Die ihr ei-nem_neu-en_ Gra-de der Er-kennt-niss nun_euch_ naht_

Der Zauberer K. 472

Ihr Mäd-chen, flieht Damö-ten ja! als ich zum er-stenmal ihn sah,

Das Veilchen K. 476

Ein Veil-chen auf der Wie-se stand ge-bückt in sich und un-be-kannt;

Der Schauspieldirektor (The Impresario) (opera) K. 486 No. 1

Da schlägt die Ab-schieds-stun-de, um grau-sam uns zu trennen

Ein Herz, das so_ der Ab-schied krän-ket, dem ist kein Wan-kel-mut_

No. 2

Bes-ter Jüng-ling, mit Ent-zü-cken nehm' ich dei-ne Lie-be_ an

Le Nozze di Figaro (The Marriage of Figaro) (opera) K. 492 Act I

Cinque, dieci, venti, trenta, trenta se-i quaranta tre

O-ra si,_ ch' io_ son con--ten--ta

Se_a ca-so Ma-da-ma la not-te ti chia-ma

Se vuol bal-la--re, Signor con-ti-no, se vuol bal-ba--re,

La ven-detta Oh! la ven-det-ta è_un pia-cer ser-ba-to_ai saggi

MOZART

Le Nozze di Figaro (The Marriage of
Figaro) (opera) K. 492
Act I

A — Via re-sti ser-vi-ta, Ma-da--ma bril-lan-te!

B — Non so più co-sa son, co-sa fac-cio, or di fo-co o-ra sono di ghiaccio

C — Co-sa sento! Tosto an-da-te, e scac-ciate il se-du-tor

D — In mal punto son qui giunto, per-do-na-te, o mio Si-gnor

E — Gio--va-ni lie-te, fio--ri spar-ge-te

F — Non più an-drai far-fal-lo-ne a-mo-ro-so, notte e gior-no d'intor-no

Act II

G — Por-gi a-mor__ qual-che ri-sto-ro al mio duo--lo,

H — Voi che sa-pe-te, che co--sa è a-mor

I — Ve-ni-te in-gi-noc-chia-te-vi re-sta-te fer-mo lì

J — A-pri-te, presto a-pri-te, a-pri-te, è la Su-san-na, sor-ti-te,

Act III

K — Cru-del! per-chè fi-no-ra far----mi lan-guir co-sì?

L — Mi sen-to__ dal con-ten-to pie-no di gio-ja il cor,__

M — Ve-drò mentr'io so-spi-ro fe-li-ce un ser-vo mi-o?

N — Do-ve so-no i bei mo-men-ti di dol-cez-za e di pia-cer?__

O — Sull' a-ria! Che so-a--ve zef-fi-ret--to

P — Bi-ce-ve-te o pa-dron-ci-na, que-ste ro-se e que-sti fior

Q — A-man-ti co-stan-ti, se-gua-ci d'o-nor,

Act IV

R — L'ho per-du-ta, me me-schi-na! ah chi sa do-ve sa-rà!

S — Il ca-pro e la ca-pret-ta son sempre in a-mi-sta__

MOZART

Le Nozze di Figaro (The Marriage of Figaro) (opera) K. 492 Act IV

In quegli anni in cui val poco la mal pratica ragion,

A pre-te un po' quegli occhi uomini incauti e sciocchi!

Deh vieni non tardar o gioja bella!

Finale

Pian, pianin! la andrò più presso, tempo perso non sarà

Pace! pace! mio dolce tesoro! io conobbi la voce

Ch'io mi scordi di te (recitative and concert aria) K. 505

Non temer amato bene per te sempre

Alme belle, che vedete le mie pene in tal momento,

Alcandro, lo confesso (recitative) K. 512

Non so d'onde viene quel tenero affetto quel moto

Nel seno a destarmi sì fieri contrasti

Mentre ti lascio, o figlia K. 513

Men tre ti lascio, o figlia, o figlia,

Ti chiedo un sol momento, un sol momento

Die Alte K. 517

Zu meiner Zeit, zu meiner Zeit bestand noch Recht und Billigkeit

Die Verschweigung K. 518

So bald Damötas Cloen sieht, so sucht er mit beredten Blicken

Das Lied der Trennung K. 519

Die Engel Gottes weinen, wo Liebende sich trennen,

Als Luise die Briefe ihres ungetreuen Liebhabers verbrannte K. 520

Erzeugt von heisser Phantasie in einer schwärmerischen Stunde

Abendempfindung K. 523

Abend ist's, die Sonne ist verschwunden,

An Chloe K. 524

Wenn das Lieb' aus deinen blauen, hellen, offnen Augen sieht

Don Giovanni (Don Juan) (opera) K. 527 Act I

Notte e giorno faticar, per chi nulla sa gradir

Ah! chi mi dice mai quel barbaro dov' e?

MOZART

Don Giovanni (Don Juan) (opera)
K. 527

Act I Catalogue Song

Ma - da - mi - na! Il ca - to - lo - go è que - sto,

Nel - la __ bion - da e gli ha l'u - san - za

Gio - vi - net - te, che fa - te all'a - mo - re, che fa - te all'a - mo - re,

Ho ca - pi - to, Si - gnor, sì! Si - gnor, sì!

Là ci da - rem la ma - no, là mi di - rai di sì

An - diam, an - diam, mio be - ne, __ a ri - sto - rar le pe - ne __

Ah! fug - gi il tra - di - tor! Non lo las - ciar più dir;

Or sai, che l'o - no - re ra - pi - re a me vol - se

Dal - la sua pa - ce la mia di - pen - - - - - de,

Finch'han dal vi - no cal - da la tes - ta u - na gran fe - sta

Bat - ti, bat - ti o bel Ma - set - to, la tua po - ve - ra Zer - li - na:

Pa - ce, pa - ce, o vi - ta mi - a! pa - ce, pa - ce o vi - ta mi - a!

Act II

Eh via, buf - fo - ne, eh via, buf - fo - ne, non mi sec - car!

Serenade

Deh vie - ni al - la fi - ne - stra o mio __ te - so - ro,

Ve - drai, ca - ri - no, se sei buo - ni - no,

Ah, pie - tà! Si - gno - ri miei! Ah pie - tà, pie - tà, pie - tà, pie - tà

Il mio te - so - ro in - tan - - to an - da - te,

Per que - ste tu - e ma - ni - ne, Can - di - de e te - ne - rel - le,

Mi tra - dì quell' al - ma in - gra - ta, quell' al - ma in - gra - ta

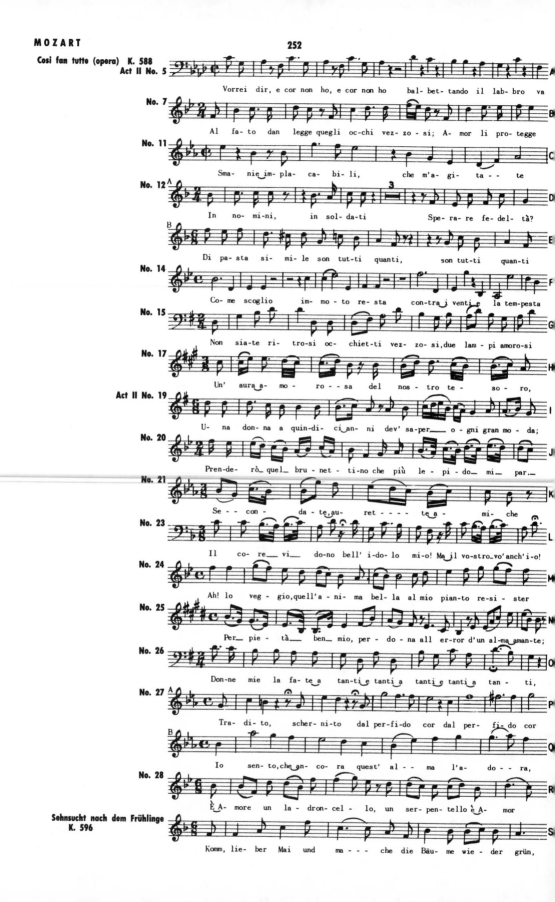

MOZART

Das Kinderspiel K. 598

Wir Kin-der, wir schmecken-der_ Freu-den_ recht_ viel,

Per questa bella mano K. 612

Per que-sta bel-la ma-no, per que-sti va-ghi ra-i

Vol-gi lie-ti o fie-ri sguar-di, dim-mi pur che m'odi o m'ami

Ave verum corpus K. 618

A-ve,_ a-ve, ve-rum_ cor-pus, na-tum de Ma-ri-a vir-gi-ne,

Die Zauberflöte (The Magic Flute)
(opera) K. 620
Act I No. 2

Der_ Vo-gel-fän-ger_ bin ich ja, stets lus-tig, hei-sa, hop-sa-sa!

No. 3

Dies Bild-niss ist be-zau-bernd schön, wie noch kein Au-ge je ge-seh'n!

No. 4

Zum Lei-den bin ich auser-ko-ren, denn mei-ne Toch-ter feh-let mir,_

Du, du du wirst_ sie_ zu be-frei-en ge - - - - - - hen,

No. 5 Quintet

Hm, Hm, Hm, Hm,_ Hm, Hm, Hm, Hm,_ Hm, Hm, Hm, Hm, Hm, Hm, Hm,_ Hm, Hm!

No. 7

Bei Män-nern, wel-che Lie-be fühlen, fehlt auch ein gu-tes Her-ze nicht

Finale

Wie_ stark ist_ nicht_ dein_ Zau - - ber - ton!

Schnelle Fü-sse, ra-scher Mut schützt vor Feindes-List und_ Wuth;

Das_ klinget so herr-lich das_ klin-get so schön!

Act II No. 10

O I-sis und O-si-ris,_ schenket der Weisheit Geist dem_ neuen Paar

No. 11

Bewah-ret euch vor Wei-ber-tü-cken, dies ist des Bun-des er-ste_ Pflicht!

No. 13

Al-les_ fühlt der Lie-be_ Freu-den, schnäbelt, tän-delt, herzt und küsst;

No. 14
Queen of the Night Aria

Der Höl-le Ra-che kocht in mei-nem Her-zen, Tod und Ver-zweiflung!

Cadenza

cadenza

No. 15

In die-sen heil'gen_ Hal-len kennt man die Ra-che_ nicht,_

MOZART

Die Zauberflöte (The Magic Flute)
(opera) K. 620
Act II No. 17

Ach, ich fühl's, es ist ver-schwun-den e - wig___ hin der Lie-be___ Glück,

No. 18

O I - - - sis und O - si - ris, wel - che Won - ne!

No. 20

Ein Mäd-chen o - der Weib - chen wünscht Pa-pa-ge - no___ sich,

Dann schmeckte mir Trinken und Es - sen, dann könnt ich mit Für-sten

Finale

Pa-pa-ge-na! Pa-pa-ge-na! Pa-pa-ge-na! Weib-chen! Täubchen,

Klin-get, Glöck-chen, klin-get, schafft mein Mäd-chen her

La Clemenza di Tito (Titus) (opera)
K. 621   Act I No. 2

Deh, se pia-cer mi - vuo - i deh, se pia-cer mi - vuo - i

Chi cie - ca-men-te cre-de, im-pe-gna a sen-bar fe-de

No. 6

Del più su - bli-me___ so - glio l'u-ni-co frut-to è que-sto

No. 8

Ah se fos-se in-torno al Tro-no o - - gni___ cor co-si sin-ce-ro

No. 9

Par-to, Par-to ma tu, ben mi - o me-co ri-torna in pa-ce

Act II No. 13

Tor - na di Ti-to a la-to, torna, torna, tor-na e l'error pas-sa-to

No. 16

Tardi s'av-vede d'un tra-di-men-to chi mai di fe-de man-car non sà

No. 17

Tu fo-sti tra-di-tor e de-gno di mor-te ma il cor-di Ti-to

No. 19

Deh par que-sto i-stan-te so - lo ti ri-cor-da il pri-mo a-mor

No. 20

Se all'im-pe-ro, a - mi-ci Dei! ne-ce-sa-rio è un cor

Se la fe - - de___ re - gni mie-i coll' a-mor non

No. 21

S'al-tro che la-cri-me per lui non___ ten - ti,

No. 23

Non più di fio-ri vaghe ca-te-ne discenda I-me - ne ad in-trec-ciar,

Laut verkünde uns're Freude (Masonic Cantata) — K. 623
Laut ver-kun-de uns'-re Freu-de fro-her In-strumen-ten-schall

Requiem K. 626

No. 1 — Re-qui-em ae-ter-nam, ae-ter-nam do-na e-is

Ky-ri-e e-le-i-son, e-le-i-son

No. 2 — Di-es i-rae di-es il-la sol-vet sae-chum in fa-vil-la,

No. 3 — Tu-ba mi-rum spargens so-num, tu-ba mi-rum

No. 4 — Rex! Rex! Rex! Rex tremen-dae ma-je-sta-tis

No. 5 — Re-cor-da-re Je-su pi-e,

No. 6 — Con-fu-ta-tis ma-le-di-ctis, flam-mis a-cribus ad-di-ctis,

No. 7 — La-cri-mo-sa di-es il-la qua re-sur-get

No. 8 — Do-mi-ne Je-su Chri-ste Rex glo-ri-ae, Rex glo-ri-ae!

No. 9 — Ho-sti-as et pre-ces ti-bi, Do-mi-ne ti-bi, Do-mi-ne,

quam o-lim A-bra-hae promi-si-sti et se-mi-ni e-jus,

No. 10 — San-ctus, San-ctus San-ctus Do-mi-nus De-us Sa-ba-oth!

O-sa-na in ex-cel-sis,

No. 11 — Be-ne-di-ctus, qui ve-nit in no-mi-ne Do-mini

No. 12 — Ag-nus De-i qui tol-lis pec-ca-ta mun-di,

MUDARRA, Alfonso (16th Cent.)

De la sangre de tus nobles
De la san-gre de tus no-bles

La mañana de Sant Juan
La ma-ña-na de Sant Juan, Al tie-po que albore-a-ba

Triste estaba el Rey David

Tris - - te es-ta- ba el rey Da- vid_____ **A**

MUSSORGSKY, Modeste (1839-1881)

Boris Godunov (opera)
Prologue Scene I Opening Chorus

Wilt thou_ leave us all un- pro- tect-ed, our_ fa- ther? **C**

Coronation Scene (chorus)

As re- splen-dent the sun_ fills the hea- ven with glo- ry, **D**

My soul is sad! I did not seek this charge_ **E**

Act I Scene I Pimen's Monologue

Yet one more tale the last of all these re- cords, **F**

Scene II Varlaam's Song

Here's the tale of what hap-pened at Ka- zan,_____ **G**

Drunken Scene

I'll hold my tongue_ I'll hold my tongue_ Reason got plen- -ty **H**

Act II Song of the Gnat

Once a gnat, as all gnats should, Did draw wa- ter, hew the wood **I**

Monologue

I have a- chieved the highest 'Tis now six years that I have reign'd with peace_ **J**

The hand of God, the aw- ful judge is on me, **K**

Song of the Parrot

Our cock-a- too was play- ing with the at- tend- ants_ **L**

Clock Scene

Ah! give me air! this suf- fo- cates my soul! **M**

Act III Scene II Polonaise

Your pro-fessed de - vo-tion, sir I trust not, All in vain your_ sol-emn oaths **N**

Oh! Tzar-e- vitch, I be- seech thee, do not curse me **O**

Act IV Scene I Revolutionary Chorus

Sirs,'tis time we got to work, what hinders? Sirs,_ your o- pin-ion first, **P**

Pimen's Tale A

A peace-ful her-mit of sim- ple mind, un- versed in worldly things **Q**

B

There came once at vesper hour a herds-man at my door a grey beard old and hoary **R**

Fare-well my son I am dy-ing From now thou wilt be-gin thy reign **S**

MUSSORGSKY

Boris Godunov (opera)
Act IV Scene I Farewell, my son (chorus)
Weep and mourn, ye mor-tal men,__ for his life is fled__

The Fair at Sorochinsk (opera)
Act I Revery of the Young Peasant
My heart,__ why weep-est thou? Why art__ thou__ pin-ing

Sor- row, for-sake thou me! De- spair, I bid thee go

Act II Song of Khivria
Who would not love me, such a charm-ing love-bird, Who would not gladly

Since the time when first I met my Bru-de-us, Bru-de-us,

Act III Parasha's Revery and Dance
Grieve nev-er, my be-lov-ed, Griev-ing nev-er ban-ish'd sor- row

Hi__ my young and black eyed lov- er Standing up so__straight and tall.

Khovantchina (opera)
Act II Divination by Water
Spi-rits of ne-ther worlds, Hid-den be-low the floods! Bound by a ma-gic spell,

In shame and disgrace I be-hold thee In exile a- lone in a dis-tant__ land

Act III Martha's Song
And by day and by night I fare O- ver mountain and mead - - ow

Shakiltor's Aria
Ah! mal-heu- reu se Rus-si- e, mon__ pa- ys cher!__

SONGS:
After the Battle
He met his death in for-eign land, in bit-ter fight-ing hand to hand,

By the River Don
By the Don__ a gar-den fair__ All a-bloom__ with ro- ses

A Child's Song
In the vale,,oh! in the val-ley Grows a lit- tle ber- ry,

The Country Feast
They had opened wide the might-y doors of oak; Some on horse and some in sleds

Cradle Song of the Poor
By-bye, by__ By-bye by- bye Lower than the hum- ble way-side flow'rs

Gathering Mushrooms
Mush- rooms brown and tall,__ mus-ter'd, Mush-rooms white and small__

The Goat
Through a field of flow'rs en -chanting, walked a maid, her beau-ty flaunting

Hebraic Song

Ich bin schön wie der Lenz, wie die Blu- me im___ Tal

Hopak (Gopak)

Hoi! for the gay Ho-pak! Once I loved a fine Cos-sack

King Saul

O, mein Heer! Wenn ein feind-li-cher Speer o- der Pfeil

Little Star So Bright

Lit- tle star so___ bright, where dost thou hide___ thy___ light?

Love-Song of the Idiot

O my Sa-vish- na, bright-eyed falcon mine, Give thy love to me, Tho' a fool I be!

The Magpie

Thro' my gar- den wick- et hop- ping, who comes chatt'ring bright and gay?

Night

Thy gra- cious im- age spreads up- on me its en- chant-ment,

The Nursery (song cycle)
1. With Nanny

All a- bout the Bo- gy- man, Nan-ny dar-ling, do tell me

2. In the Corner

Ah, you young ras-cal! My wool you've un-wound, My stitches are dropped

3. The Beetle

Nan- ny, Hark, Nan- ny, what has hap- pened, Nan-ny Darl - ing!

4. Dolly's Cradle Song

Dol-ly bye - bye,_ Dol-ly go to sleep,_ Time it is you went to sleep

5. Evening Prayer

Bless O Lord, I pray thee, Dad- dy and Mum- my,

6. The Hobby Horse

Hy! Trot, trot, trot Trot, trot, go a-long! Gee-up! Gee-up!

Accompaniment melody

7. Pussy Cat, or, The Cat and the Bird Cage

Oh, oh, oh, oh, Mum- my Oh, darling Mum-my, Mummy dear I went to look

On the River Dnieper

Dnie-per,_ ho!_ Dnie-per,_ hark!_ Dnieper, my broad riv-er_

To- day you are wait- ing, to- day you are wait- ing,

The Orphan-Girl

Oh, Mis-ter, please be good! Dear Mis-ter, please be kind! Please let me tell to you

Oriental Chant (Lamentation), from Cantata "Josua Navine"

Hear ye A- mo- re-a's daughters hear_ their lamen-ta-tion__ un - to Ca-naan,

MUSSORGSKY

Peasant Cradle Song
By - bye,_ by - - - bye sleep, my_ pret - ty_ boy   Sleep, lit-tle one

Seminarist
Pa-nis, pis-cis, cri-nis, fi-nis; ig-nis, la-pis, pul-vis, ci-nis, Oh these La - tin_words!

Silently floated a spirit
Si - lent-ly float-ed a   spir-it a-cross the high heav-ens

Song of the Flea (from Goethe's "Faust")
Reign-ing in roy-al splen-dor A King had raised a flea

Songs and Dances of Death:
I Death and the Peasant (Trepak) A
Snow-fields in si - lence, So cold is the night

B
Hey, poor old man with a head so light!_ Too much you drank

II Death's Lullaby
Faint-ly the child sighs, The lamp dim-ly flickers, Sheds but a phantom of light

III Death's Serenade A
Sweet-scent-ed breath of Night, soft and ca- ress-- ing,

B
Lone - ly and fet-ter'd, in_ dark - - ness of bond-age

IV Death the Commander (Field Marshal Death)
With crash of bat-tle, ar-mor gleam-ing, The can-nons bel-low forth their fire,

Sunless
No. 1 Within four Walls (In my attic)
Si - lent the lit - tle room   Calm it is, dear to me.

No. 2 The Throng (After years)
Thine eyes in the crowd now a- void me, No an-swer-ing glance now is there

No. 3 All past the Feast Days (Retrospect)
All past the feast days, joy has gone The calm of night now falls on na-ture:

No. 4 Alas! It is my lonely fate (Resignation)
A- las! It is my lone-ly fate_ O when is joy with-out a smart?

No. 5 Elegy A
In sha-dow black as night The moon's pale sil-ver rays give forth

b
And so 'tis with my heart, for thoughts and sights un- bid - den

No. 6 On the River (By the Water)
Pale shines the moon-light, Be- low in the wa-ter calm

Yeremushka's Cradle Song
Schlafe, schlaf'_ein   Tie-fer als im Feld ein Blü - me-lein,

MYLIUS, Wolfgang (17th Cent.)

Ein Mägdlein stund

Ein Mägd-lein stund, Wo stund es denn? Ein Mägd-lein stund

NÄGELI, Hans Georg (1773-1836)

Freut euch des Lebens

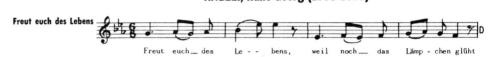

Freut euch__ des Le - - bens, weil noch__ das Lämp - chen glüht

NAGINSKI, Charles (1909-1940)

The Pasture
Copyright 1940, G. Schirmer, Inc.

I'm go-ing out to clean the pas- ture spring

Richard Cory
Copyright 1940, G. Schirmer, Inc.

When- ev- er Rich-ard Co- ry went down town

NANINI, Giovanni Maria (c.1545-1607)

Diffusa est gratia

Dif - - fu-sa est gra - - - - - - - - - - ti-a in la- bi-is,in la - - bi-is

NAPRAVNIK, Eduard (1839-1916)

Cradle Song, from Harold (opera)
Act V
Copyright 1906, G. Schirmer, Inc.

Hush thee, dear one, slumber well! Pain be gone,and grief's e- mo-tion,

NELSON, Sidney (1800-1862)

Mary of Argyle

I have heard the may is sing- ing, His love-song to the morn

NESSLER, Victor E. (1841-1900)

Behüt' dich Gott, from Der Trompeter
von Sakkingen (opera)

Das ist im Le- ben häss- lich ein ge- rich- tet,

Be- hüt' dich Gott!es wär'zu schön ge- we- sen, be- hüt dich Gott,

NEUMARK, Georg (1621-1681)

Gottestrost

Wer nur den lie- ben Gott lässt wal-ten und hof- fet

NEVIN, Ethelbert (1862-1901)

A Life Lesson

There, lit-tle girl, don't cry! They have bro-ken your doll, I know,

Little Boy Blue, Op. 12, No. 4

The lit-tle toy dog is cover'd with dust, But stur-dy and staunch he stands;

Might lak' a rose
Copyright by John Church Co.
Used by permission.

Sweetest li'-l' fel-ler, Ev'-ry bod-y knows; Dun-no what to call him,

Oh! that we two were maying, Op. 2, No. 8

Oh! that we two were may--ing Down the stream of the soft spring breeze

One Spring Morning

One spring morn-ing, bright and fair, Tra-la-la-la-la-la la

The Rosary

The hours I spent with thee, dear heart, are as a string of pearls to me

NICKERSON, Camille

Michieu Banjo (arr.)
Copyright by Boston Music Co.

Gar-dez pi-ti Mi-latte la, Mi-chieu Ban-jo,

NICOLAI, Karl (1810-1849)

The Merry Wives of Windsor (Die lustigen Weiber von Windsor) (opera)

Act I No. 3

Ver-füh - - - - - - - - - rer! Wa-rum stellt ihr so

Froh - sinn und Lau - ne wür - - - zen das Le - - - - ben

Act II No. 5

Als Büb-lein klein an der Mut-ter Brust, hopp hei-ssa bei Re-gen und Wind,

Act II No. 7b

Horch, die Ler-che singt im Hain, lau-sche, lausche Liebchen still,

Act III No. 11

So schweb' ich Dir Gelieb - - ter zu, so kennst Du mich, so na - hest Du,

O se - li - ge Träu - me, o sü - - - - - sses Glück

NIEDERMEYER, Abraham Louis (1802-1861)

Le Lac

Ain - si tou-jours pous-sés vers de nou-veaux ri-va-ges

Un soir t'en sou-vient-il? nous vo-guions en si-len-ce

NIELSEN, Carl (1865-1931)

Irmelin Rose
Copyright by Hansen, Copenhagen

Se, der var en Gang en Kon - - ge - man-gen Skat han kald - te sin

NIN, Joaquín (1879-1949)

Classiques espagnols du chant (arr.)
Alma, sintamos (Pablo Esteve, 1730?-1792?)
By permission Associated Music Publishers, Inc.

Al- ma, sin - ta- mos! O- jos, llo- rar!

Aria de Acis y Galatea (Antonio Literes, 1680?-1755)

Si de ra- ma en ra- ma si de flor en flor

Corazón que en prisión (José Marin, 1619-1699)

Co- ra- zon que en pri- sión de res- pe- tos cau- ti

Cloris Hermosa (Sebastian Duron, 1645?-1716?)

Gra- cio- sa mo- da e- sa que han da- do

Desengañémonos ya (José Marin, 1619-1699)

De- sen- ga- ñe- mo- nos ya; mal pa- ga- do pen-sa-mien - - to

El jilguerito con pico de oro (Blas de Laterna, 1751-1816)

El jil- que- ti - - to con pi- co de o - - ro

Minué cantado (José Bassa, 1670?-1730?)

Si de A- ma- ri- lis los o- jos dis- pa - - - - ran

Four Popular Spanish Songs
I Castellana (also No. 3 of Vingt chants populaires espagnols)
By permission Associated Music Publishers, Inc.

Yo me i- ba ma- dre a la ro- me- rí- a

So ell'en-ci-na en-ci- na So ell'en-ci- na Yo me i- ba mi madre,

II Catalana (also No. 16 of Vingt chants populaires espagnols)

Ei- xa nit es nit de vet- lla n'ha pa- rit u- na don- ze- lla

A- ni- rem al camp, po- mes a cu- llir, po- metes cu- lli- rem

III Gallega (also No. 12 of Vingt chants populaires espagnols)

Meu a- mor meu a- mo- ri- ño Ond'es- tás que no te ve- jo

IV Asturiana (also No. 14 of Vingt chants populaires espagnols)

Fuis- ti a la siega y Gol- vies- ti Fuis- ti a la siega y Gol-vies-ti

Vingt chants populaires espagnols
I Tonada de Valdovinos
By permission Associated Music Publishers, Inc.

Sos- pi- ras- te, val- do- vi- nos La co- sa que más que- rí- a

II Cantar

Quien a- mo- res ten a- fin- que los ben que non he vien-to

IV Montañesa

Se- ga- ba yo a- que- lla tar- de

OBRECHT, Jacob (1430-1505)

Missa super Maria Zart Et incarnatus est — A
Et in- car- na _____ tus est de_ Spiri- tu

Tsaat een meskin (No words in score) — B

OFFENBACH, Jacques (1819-1880)

La Belle Helene (opera) Act I No. 2 — D
A- mours di- vins ar- den- tes flam- mes! Ve- nus! A- do- nis!

No. 6 Le Jugement de Paris — E
Au_ mont I- da trois dé- es- ses se que- rel- laient dans un bois_

Act II No. 11 Invocation à Vénus — F
On me nomme Hé- lè- ne la blon- de, La blon- de fil- le de Lé- da

No. 15 Dream Duet — G
Oui! c'est un rê- ve, Oui, c'est un rê- ve, Oui! c'est un doux rê- ve_ d'a- mour

Couplets des fariniers, from La boulangère a des écus (opera) Act II No. 9 — H
Les fa- ri- niers, Les char- bon- niers Ont le mêm' sac

Duettino des époux, from Les Braconniers (opera) Act I — I
Que j'aime tes yeux e- veil- lés!_ Que j'aime ta no- ble tour- nu- re

Chanson de Fortunio, from La chanson de Fortunio (opera) No. 7 — J
Si vous cro- yez que je vais di- re Qui j'ose ai- mer

Les Contes d'Hoffmann (The Tales of Hoffmann) (opéra-comique) Act I — K
Il é- tait u- ne fois à la cour d'Ei- se- nach! À la cour d'Ei- se- nach!

Act II — L
Ah! vi- vre doux n'avoir qu' une même es- pé- ran- ce Un mê- me sou- ve- nir!

— M
J'ai des yeux,_ de vrais yeux, des yeux vi- vants, des yeux de flam - - - - me

— N
Les oi- seaux dans la char- mil - - - - - - - - le

Act III Barcarolle — O
Bel- le nuit, ô nuit d'a- mour, Sou- ris_ à nos i- vres- ses!

— P
Scin- til- le di- a- mant_ Mi- roir où se prend l'a- lou- et- te

— Q
O Dieu de quelle i- vresse em- bras- ses tu mon â- me

Act IV — R
Elle a fui, la tour- te- rel- le, Elle a fui loin de toi

— S
Jour et nuit je me mets en quatre, Au moin- dre si- gne je me tais,

Contes d'Hoffmann (The Tales of Hoffmann) (opera) Act IV

C'est u- ne chan-son d'a-mour qui s'en-vo- le Triste ou fol- le

J'ai le bon-heur___ dans l'â- me! De- main tu se-ras___ ma fem- me!

Chère en- fant! que___ j'ap-pel- le Comme au- tre- fois, C'est ta mè- re,___

Gendarmes' duet, from Geneviève de Brabant (opera) Act II, No. 14

Pro- te- ger le re- pos des vil - - - - les

Le Grande Duchesse de Gérolstein (opera) Act I Couplets de sabre

Voi- ci le sa-bre de mon pè- re Tu vas le mettre à ton_co- té

Voi- ci le sa- bre le sa- bre le sa- bre

Act II

Di- tes lui qu'on l'a re- mar- qué dis-tin-gué, Di- tes lui

Duo d'Alsace, from Lischen et Fritzchen (opera) No. 3

Je suis Al- sa- cien- ne, Je suis Al- sa- cien,

Juch- he! das Le- ben ist doch ei- ne Freu-de Juch- he!

Ronde des vignes, from Madame Favart (opera) Act I

Ma mère aux vi- gnes m'en voyait, Je n' sais com-ment ça s' dit___

La Périchole (opera) Act I

Ah! quel di- ner je viens de fai- re Et quel vin

No. 7 La lettre

O mon cher a- mant, je te ju- re, Que je t'aim- e de tout mon coeur;

Act II

Que veulent di-re ces co- lè- res Et ces ges-tes de mau-vais ton

Mon Dieu, mon Dieu, que les hom- mes sont bê- tes,

Act III No. 17b Couplets de l'aveu

Tu n'est pas beau tu n'est pas riche Tu man-ques tout

O'HARA, Geoffrey (1882-   )

Give a man a horse he can ride

Give a man a horse he can ride,___ Give a man a boat he can sail___

There is no death

OKEGHEM, Jean de (c. 1430-1493)

Ma Maitresse

Ma mai- tres- se____ et ma plus__ grant____ a my- - - - - - - B

OTHMAYR, Casper (1515-1553)

Brauns-Maidelein

Mir ist ein feins brauns Mai- de-lein ge- fal- len in mein Sinn D

PADILLA, José (Contemporary)

Princesita
Copyright by E. B. Marks Music Corp., N. Y.

Who'll Buy My Violets (La Violetera)
Copyright 1923, Harms, Inc.

Prin- ce- si- ta____ Prin- ce- si- ta la de o-jos a- zu- les F

Co-mo a ves pre-cur so- - ras de Pri-ma-ve - - - ra G

PAISIELLO, Giovanni (1740-1816)

Déserts écartés, from Proserpine (opera)

Nel cor più non mi sento, from La Molinara (opera)

De- serts é- car- tés som- bres lieux, Ca- chez mes sou- pirs, I

Nel cor più non mi sen- to bril-lar la____ gio- ven- tù J

PALADILHE, Emile (1884-1926)

Patrie (opera)
No. 4 Air du sonneur
Copyright by Choudens fils, Paris

No. 21 Cantabile de Rysor

No. 22 Air de Rysor

SONGS:
Psyché
Copyright 1911, G. Schirmer, Inc.

Le Roitelet
Copyright 1911, G. Schirmer, Inc.

Les Trois Prières

Ja- dis el- les chan-taient gaie- ment____ L

Pau- vre mar-tyr obs- cur,___ Hum-ble hé- ros d'une heu- re M

Fuir à ja- mais____ fuir en- sem- ble N

Je suis ja- loux, Psy- ché de tou- te la na- tu- re O

Ra- pi- de comme un rê- - ve, Vif comme un feu fol- let P

A l'heu- re où notre es-prit moins fier____ S'in- cli- ne comme un Roi Q

PALESTRINA, Giovanni Pierluigi da (1524-1594)

Hymns: I O crux ave

O crux____ a- - - ve,____ spes____ u- ni- ca,____ S

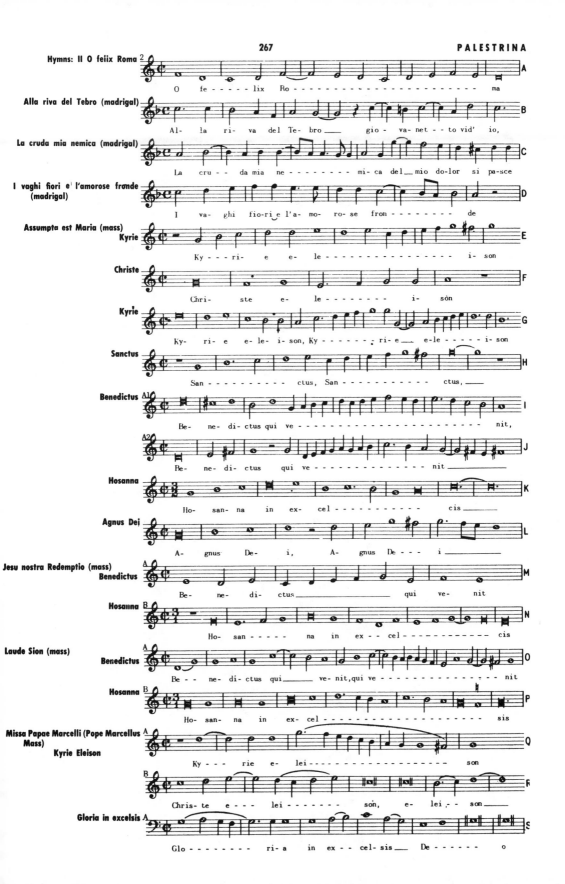

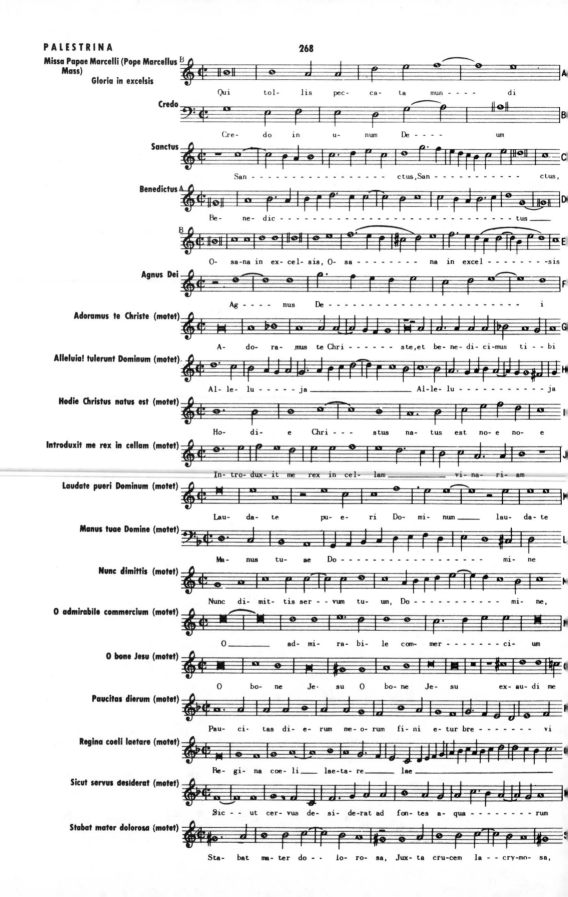

Tota pulchra es amica mea (motet) — To- ta pulchra es a- mi-ca me- - - - - - - - - - a_____ — A

Tribulationes civitatum (motet) 1 — Tri- bu- la- ti- o- - - - nes ci- - - - - vi- ta- - tum au- di- vi- mus — B

Peccavimus (motet) 2 — Pec- ca- vi- mus pec- - - - - ca- - - - - - vi- mus_____ — C

Vox dilecti mei (motet) — Vox vox di- le-cti me- - - - - - - - - i Vox___ di- le-cti — D

Vulnerasti cor meum (motet) — Vul- ne- ra-sti cor me- um vul- ne- ra-sti cor me- um, — E

Offertories:
Bonum est — Bo- - - - - num est con- fi- te- ri_____ — F

Exaltabo te, Domine — Ex- al- ta- bo- te _____ Do- - - - - - - - - - - - - - mi- ne — G

Improperium expectavit — Im- - - pro- pe- ri- um ex- pe- cta- vit___ cor me- - - - - - - - - um, — H

Laudate Dominum — Lau- - da- te Do- - - - - - mi- num, lau- da- - te Do- mi- num_____ — I

Super flumina Babylonis — Su- - - per flu- mi- na Ba- - by- lon- - - - - - - - - nis,___ — J

Alma redemptoris mater *(cantus firmus)* — Al- - - - - - - - - - ma Re- demp- to-ris ma- - - - - - ter — K

Ecce, quomodo moritur justus (response) — Ec- - ce quo- mo- do mo- - - - - ri- tur ju- stus, — L

Exultate Deo — Ex- ul- ta- - - - te De- o, ad- - ju- to- ri nos- - - - - - tro___ — M

Gloria Patri — Glo- ri- a Pa- tri Et Fi- li- o, Glo- ri- a Pa- tri — N

Incipit oratorio Jeremiae Prophetae (lamentation) — In- ci- pit O- ra- ti- o In- ci- pit O- ra- ti- o — O

Jubilate Deo (Psalm 99) — Ju- - bi- la- - - - - - - - - - - te De- - - - - - o — P

Pueri Hebraeorum (Antiphon) — Pu- - e- ri He- brae- o- rum, He- - - - - - brae- o- - - - - rum — Q

PALMGREN, Selim (1878-1951)

Finnish Lullaby
Lit- tle songs I'll sing thee, dear-est, Lit-tle tales I bring thee, dear-est — S

Summer Evening
Copyright by H. W. Gray Co.

The gol- den sun was sink- ing be- yond the__ hills of blue.

Summer Night (Läksin minä Kesäyönä Käymänn)

Sum- mer night__ in the north was glist-ning, For the day, in the

PAOLA DA FIRENZE, Don (14th Cent.)

Fra duri scogli senz' alcun governo

Fra du- - ri sco- gli senz' al- - cun__ go- - ver-no

PARADIES, Pietro Domenico (1707-1791)

M'ha preso alla sua ragna

M'ha pre- so al-la sua ra- - gna, m'ha pre-so al-la sua ra- - gna

Quel ruscelletto

Quel ru-scel- let- to Che l'on- de chia- re Or or col ma- - re__

PARKER, Horatio (1863-1919)

The Lark Now Leaves His Wat'ry Nest
Copyright by John Church Co.
Used by permission

The lark now leaves his wat- 'ry nest, And climb- ing, shakes

Love in May, Op. 51, No. 1
Copyright by John Church Co.
Used by permission

The green is on the grass a- gain, The blue is on the sea

PARRY, Sir Charles Herbert Hastings (1848-1918)

Armida's Garden
By permission Novello & Co., Ltd., London

I have been there be- fore thee, O__ my love! Each winding way I know

Jerusalem
Copyright 1916, C. H. H. Parry

And did those feet in an- cient__ time Walk up- on Englands' moun- tains

Love is a Bable
By permission Novello & Co., Ltd., London

Love is__ a ba- ble No man__ is__ a- ble To say 'tis this or 'tis that

The Maiden
By permission Novello & Co., Ltd., London

Who was this that came by the way, when the flowers were springing?

Under the Greenwood Tree
By permission Novello & Co., Ltd., London

Un- der the green - - - - - wood__ tree who loves to lie with me

A Welsh Lullaby
By permission Novello & Co., Ltd., London

Sleep, sleep, sleep,__ sleep! All na- ture now is sleep- ing

Whether I Live
By permission Novello & Co., Ltd., London

Whether I live, or whether I die, what-ev- er the worlds I see

Why So Pale and Wan
By permission Novello & Co., Ltd., London

Why so pale and wan, fond lov-er? Prythee, why so pale?

PEARSALL, R. L. (1795-1856)

In dulci jubiio

In dul-ci ju-bi- lo _____ Let us our hom-age

PEPUSCH, Johann Cristoph (1667-1752)

The Beggar's Opera (adapted by Gay; revised by Austin)

Act I   **No. 2 (Air: An old woman clothed in gray)**
Thro' all the employments of life Each neighbour a-bu-ses his brother,

No. 3 (Air: The Bonny Gray-eyed Morn)
'Tis wo-man that se-du-ces all man-kind, By her we first were taught_

No. 4 (Air: Cold and Raw)
If an-y wench Ve-nus' gir-dle wear, Though she be ne-ver so ug-ly

No. 5 (Air: Why is your faithful slave disdained)
If love the_____ vir-gin's heart in - - - - - vade,_____

No. 6 (Air: Of all the simple things we do)
A maid is like the gol-den ore, which hath guineas in-trin-si-cal in it

No. 8 (Air: Oh London is a fine town)
Our Pol- ly is a sad slut! Nor heeds what we have taught her

No. 9 (Air: Grim King of the Ghosts)
Can Love be con-trolled by ad-vice? Will Cu-pid our mo-thers o- bey

No. 10 (Air: O Jenny, where hast thou been?)
O Pol-ly, you might have toy'd and kiss'd. By keeping men off you keep them on

No. 11 (Air: Thomas, I cannot)
I, like_ a ship in storms was toss'd, yet a- fraid to put in-to land_

No. 12 (Air: A soldier and a sailor)
A fox_ may steal_your hens, sir, A wench_your heath_ and pence, sir,

No. 13 (Air: Now ponder well, ye parents dear)
O pon-der well! be not se- vere; so save a wretch-ed wife

No. 14 (Air: Pretty Parrot say)
Pretty Pol- ly, say, when_ I_ was_ a- way, Did your_fancy never stray

No. 15 (Air: Pray, fair one be kind)
My heart was so free, It roved like the bee, till Polly my passion re- quited,

No. 16 (Air: Over the hills and far away)
Were_ I_ laid_ on_ Greenland's coast and in_ my_ arms_ em - braced my lass;

No. 17 (Air: Gin thou wert my ain thing)
Oh! what pain it is to_ part! Can_ I_ leave_thee, Can_ I_ leave_thee?

Act II   **No. 18 (Air: Fill every glass)**
Fill ev'-ry glass for wine in- spires us and fires us with courage, love and joy

Beggar's Opera
Act II

Beggar's Opera Act III

No. 45 (Air: Come, sweet lass)
Come, sweet lass, Let's ba-nish sor-row till to-mor-row, Come, sweet lass,

No. 46 (Air: The last time I went o'er the moon)
Hi-ther, dear hus-band, turn your_ eyes, Be-stow one glance_ to cheer_ me.

No. 47 (Air: Tom Tinker's my true love)
Which way_ shall I turn me how can I de-cide

No. 48 (Air: Bonny Dundee)
The charge is pre-pared; the lawyers are met,_ the judges all ranged

No. 50 (Air: Happy Groves)
O cru-el, cru-el, cru-el case! Must I suf-fer this_ dis-grace?

(Air: Of all the girls)
Of_ all the friends in_ time of grief, when_ threat'ning death_ looks grimmer_

(Air: Did you ever hear of a gallant sailor)
But can I leave_ my pret-ty hussies, without one tear, or ten-der sigh?

(Air: Why are mine eyes still flowing)
Their eyes, their lips, their bus- - - - - - - - - - ses

No. 51 (Air: All you that must take a leap)
Would I might be hang'd! And I would so too! To be hang'd_ with you

No. 52 (Air: Lumps of pudding)
Thus I stand like the Turk, with his do-xies a- -round

PEREZ FREIRE, Osman

Ay, ay, ay

A só-ma te_a la ven-ta-na Ay, Ay Ay pa-lo-ma del al-ma mi - - a

PERGOLESI, Giovanni (1710-1736)

Ogni pena più spietata
O-gni_ pe-na_ più spie-ta-ta,_ più spie-ta-ta

Se tu m'ami
Se tu m'a-mi, se tu so-spi-ri sol_ per me,_

La Serva Padrona (opera) 1.
A-spet-ta- - re e non ve-ni-re, sta-re_a let-to e non dor-mi-re

2.
Sem-pre_in con-tra-sti con te si sta_ con te si sta,

3.
Stiz-zo-so mio_ stiz-zo-so voi fa-te_il bo- -ri-o-so

4.
Lo co-no-sco, lo co-no-sco_a que-gli_och-chietti a que-gli_oc-chietti

PERGOLESI

La Serva Padrona (opera)

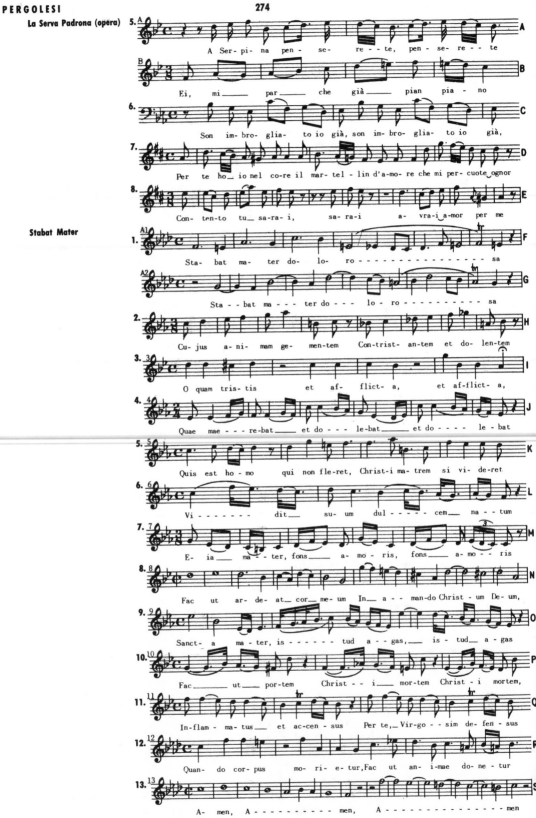

5. A Serpina penserete, penserete

B Ei, mi par che già pian pia-no

6. Son imbroglia-to io già, son imbroglia-to io già,

7. Per te ho io nel co-re il mar-tel-lin d'a-mo-re che mi per-cuote ognor

8. Con-tento tu sa-ra-i, sa-ra-i a-vra i-a-mor per me

Stabat Mater

1. A1 Sta-bat ma-ter do-lo-ro — — — — — sa

2. A2 Sta-bat ma-ter do-lo-ro — — — — sa

2. Cu-jus a-ni-mam ge-men-tem Con-trist-an-tem et do-len-tem

3. O quam tris-tis et af-flict-a, et af-flict-a,

4. Quae mae-re-bat et do-le-bat et do-le-bat

5. Quis est ho-mo qui non fle-ret, Christ-i ma-trem si vi-de-ret

6. Vi-dit su-um dul-cem na-tum

7. E-ia ma-ter, fons a-mo-ris, fons a-mo-ris

8. Fac ut ar-de-at cor me-um In a-man-do Christ-um De-um,

9. Sanct-a ma-ter, is-tud a-gas, is-tud a-gas

10. Fac ut por-tem Christ-i mor-tem Christ-i mortem,

11. In-flam-ma-tus et ac-cen-sus Per te, Vir-go sim de-fen-sus

12. Quan-do cor-pus mo-ri-e-tur, Fac ut an-i-mae do-ne-tur

13. A-men, A-men, A-men

PERI, Jacopo (1561-1633)

Euridice (opera)

Gio- i-te al can-to mio sel- ve fron-do-se; gio-i-te a-ma-ti col-li

Nel pu-ro ar-dor del___ la più bel- la stel-la Au- rea fa- cel- la

PESSARD, Emile (1843-1917)

L'Adieu du Matin

Le ma- tin, dès que je te quit-te, Son-geant aux longs en- nuis

Requiem du Coeur

Mon coeur est mort! De- dans la biè- re ce___ ma- tin

PESTALOZZA, Alberto (1851-1934)

Ciribiribin

I am wait- ing here for you,_ love,_ as the eve- ning bree-zes blow

Ci- ri- bi- ri- bin, more love than mine for thee

PFITZNER, Hans Eric (1869-1949)

Ist der Himmel darum im Lenz so blau? Op. 2, No. 2

Ist der Him- mel da-rum im Lenz so blau, weil er ü- ber die blu- mi-ge

Der Einsame, Op. 9, No. 2

Wär's dun-kel, ich läg im Wal- - de   Im Wal-de rauscht's

Gretel, Op. 11, No. 5

Vor der Tür im Son- nen-schei- ne wo das Kätz- chen. sonst. liegt_

Nachts, Op. 26, No. 2

Ich ste- he in Wal- des-schatten wie_ an des Le- bens Hand,

PIERNÉ, Gabriel (1863-1937)

L'Adieu Suprême

Lais- se- moi ché- rir ton fan- tô- me,_ Mais ne re- viens pas

Complainte des Arches de Noé

Dans la fo- rêt les me- nui-siers, taillez les ar- ches

En Barque

Pestons en- cor, Mi- gnon- ne! Ma barque est douce et bon- ne;

Ils étaient trois petits chats blancs

Ils é- taient trois pe-tits chats blancs Tou- jours pom-pon- nés

Les Marionettes
By permission Heugel & Cie, Paris, copyright owners

Les ma- ri- on- net- tes de bois ont des ro- bes de pa- pier

Le Moulin
Copyright by Boston Music Co.

Tour- ne, tour- ne, tour- ne, mon mou- lin

Le Petit Rentier
By permission J. Hamelle Music Publishers, Paris

Il s'en est al- lé par la rou- te le pauvre homme

Serenade

Au sein des nuits tout dort L'é- toi- le brille en- cor

PIETRI, Giuseppi (1886-)

Maristella (opera)

Act I

Io co- no- sco un giar- di- no a tut- ti sco- no- sciu- to

Act II

U- no stra- no sen- so ar- ca- no pren- de il cuor!

Qui di- nan- zi all'al- ta- re giu- ro che quest' ac- cu- sa è u- na men- zogna!

PILKINGTON, Francis (d. 1638)

Care for thy Soul

Care for thy soul, care for thy soul care for thy soul

Diaphenia

Di- a- phe- ni- a like the daff- down- dil- ly, white as the sun,

Down a down

Down a down, down a down, thus Phyllis sung, By fan- cy ones op- press- ed;

Rest, sweet nymphs

Rest, sweet nymphs, let gol- den sleep Charm your star- bright- er eyes

Underneath a cypress shade

Un- der- neath a cy- press shade the Queen of love sat mourn- ing

PINSUTI, Ciro (1829-1888)

The Arrow and the Song

I shot an ar- row in- to the air, It fell to earth

Bedouin Love Song A

From the des- ert I come to thee on my A- - rab shod with fire

B

Till the sun grows cold and the stars grow old

I fear no foe

I fear no foe in shin- ing ar- mour, Tho' his lance be swift

PISADOR, Diego (c. 1508-1557)

A las armas moriscote

A las ar- mas mo- ris- co- te Si las has en vo- lun- tad

PIZZETTI, Ildebrando (1880-1968)

I Pastori

Set- tem- - bre, an- dia- - mo. È tem- po di mi- gra- re

O- ra in ter- ra d'A- bruz- zi i miei pa- sto- ri

La madre al figlio lontano

O fi- glio, fi- glio____ in che mon- do ti tro- vi?

POLDOWSKI, (Lady Dean Paul) (1880-1932)

Columbine

My permission J. & W. Chester, Ltd., London, copyright owners

Le- an- dre le sot Pier- rot qui d'un saut de pu- ce

Dansons la gigue

By permission J. & W. Chester, Ltd., London, copyright owners

Dan- sons la gi- gue! j'ai- mais sur- tout ses jo- lis yeux

L'Heure Exquise

y permission J. & W. Chester, Ltd., London, copyright owners

La lu- ne blan- che Luit dans les bois; de cha- que bran- che

Mandoline

My permission J. & W. Chester, Ltd., London, copyright owners

Les don- neurs de sé- ré- na- des Et les bel- les é- cou- teu- ses

PONCE, M. M. (1882-1948)

Estrellita

Es- tre- lli- ta del le- ja- no cie- lo Que mi- ras mi do- lor

PONCHIELLI, Amilcare (1834-1886)

La Gioconda (opera)

Act I

Fes- te! Pa- ne! fes- te! fes- - ste e pa- ne! fes- te e pa- ne!

Trio

Fi- glia che reg- gi il tre- mu- lo piè che all'a- vel___ già pie- ga

Vo- ce di don- na o d'an- ge- lo le mi- e ca- te- ne ha sciol- to;

A te que- sto ro- sa- rio che le pre- ghie- re a- du- na,

O gri- do di que- st'a- ni- ma___ scoppia dal gon- fio co- re

PONCHIELLI

278

La Gioconda (opera)

Act I — A
O mo- nu- men- - - - to! re- gia e bol- gia do- ga- le!

B
O cuor! do-no fu- ne- sto!— re- tag-gio di— do- lo- - re.

Act II — A — C
Ho! he! ho! he! Fis-sa il ti-mo- ne! Ho! he! ho! he! Fis sa

D
Siam nel fon- do più— pro- fon- do del- la na- ve del- la ca- la,

E
Pes- ca- tor,— af- fon- da l'es- ca, a te l'on- da- sia fe- del,—

F
Cie- lo e mar! l'e- te- res— ve- lo splen-de co-me un santo altar

Duet — A — G
Deh! non tur- ba- re— con ree pa- u- ra— di que- sti i-stan- ti

B — H
Lag- giù— nel- le neb- bie re- mo- - te,— lag- giù —

I
Stel- la del ma- ri- nar! Ver- gi- ne San-ta, tu mi di- fen- di

J
L'a- mo co- - me il ful-gor del cre- a- to, co- me l'au- - ra che av- vi- va

Act III — A — K
Là tur- bi- ni_e far- ne- ti- chi, la ga- ja— ba- ra- on- da

B — L
Là del— pa- tri- - - - zio ve- - - - - - ne- to—

Già ti veg- go im- mo- ta e smor- - - ta

Duet — A
Bel- la co- sì ma- don- na, io non v'ho mai ve- du- ta

B
È trop- po, è trop-po or- ri- bi- le! a- ver di- nan- zi,

La ga- - ia can- zo- - ne, fa l'e- - - co lan- guir—

Act IV
Sui- ci- dio! In que-sti fie- ri mo- men- ti—

La Gioconda (opera) Act IV

Eb- brez- za!___ de- li- rio!___ So- gna- ta- mia gio- ia!

Raccogli e calma, from Il Figliol Prodigo (opera) Act III

Rac- cog- lie cal- ma sot- to al- la pi- a a la dol- cis- si- ma

POULENC, Francis (1899-1963)

Airs Chantés

No. 1 Air Romantique
Copyright by Salabert, Paris, N. Y.

J'al- lais dans la cam- pagne a- vec le___ vent d'o- ra- ge

No. 2 Air Champêtre

Bel- le sour- ce bel- le source, je veux me rap- pe- ler sans ces- se

No. 3 Air Grave

Ah! fuy- ez à pré- sent, mal- heu- reu- ses pen- sées! O co- lère, o! re- mords!

No. 4 Air Vif

Le tré- sor___ du ver- ger, et le jar- din en fête,

A sa guitarre
By permission Durand & Cie, Paris; Elkan-Vogel Co., Inc., Phila., copyright owners

Ma gui- ta- re, je te chan- te, Par qui seu- le je dé- çois

Banalités

No. 1 Chanson d'Orkenise
By permission Associated Music Publishers, Inc.

Par les por- tes d'Or- ke- ni- se veut en- trer un char- re- tier___

No. 2 Hotel

Ma chambre a la for- me d'u- ne ca- ge

No. 3 Fagnes de Wallonie

Tant___ de tris- tes- - ses___ plé- - ni- - è- res

No. 4 Voyage à Paris

Ah!___ la char- man- te cho- se Quit- ter un pa- ys

No. 5 Sanglots

Notre a- mour est rè- glé par les cal- mes é- - toi- les

Le Bestiaire

No. 1 Le Dromadaire
Copyright by Ed. de la Sirene, Paris

A- vec ses qua- tre dro- ma- daires___ Don Pe- dro d'Al- fa- rou- bei- ra

No. 2 Le Chèvre du Thibet

Les poils de cet- te chè- vre et mê- - me Ceux d'or

No. 3 La Sauterelle

Voi- ci la fi- ne sau- te- rel- le La nour- ri- ture___ de Saint Jean

No. 4 Le Dauphin

Dau- phins, vous jouez dans le mer Mais le flot est tou- jours a- mer

No. 5 L'Écrevisse

In- cer- ti- tude, O! mes___ de- - lices Vous et moi nous nous en al- lons

No. 6 Le Carpe

Dans vos vi- viers dans vos e- tangs Car- pes que vous vi- vez long- temps!

Bleuet

Jeune hom- me de vingt ans___ qui as vu des choses si af-freu- ses___

C

J'ai tra-ver-sé les ponts de C C'est là que tout a com- men-cé

Chansons Gaillardes
La belle jeunesse

Il faut s'ai- mer tou- jours, et ne s'é- pou- ser guè- re

Invocation aux parques

Il jure tant que je vi-vrai de vous ai- mer, Syl- vi- e

Chanson à boire

Les Rois d'E- gyp- te et de Sy- ri- e, vou-laient qu'on em-bau- mât

Chansons Villageoises
I Chansons du clair tamis

Où le be-deau a pas- se Dans les pa-pa- ve-ra- cé- es

II Les gars qui vont à la fête

Les gars qui vont à la fête Ont mis la fleur au cha-peau___

III C'est le joli printemps

C'est le jo- li prin-temps qui fait sor- tir les fil- les

IV Le mendiant

Jean Mar- tin prit sa be- sa- ce Vi- ve le pas- sant

V Chanson de la fille frivole

Oh dit la fil- le fri- vo- le Que le vent y vire,

VI Le retour du sergent

Le ser- gent s'en re- vient de guer- re Les pieds gon- flés

Les Chemins de l'Amour

Che- mins de mon a- mour___ Je vous cherche tou-jours___

Dans le jardin d'Anna

Cer- tes, si nous a- vions vé- cu en l'an dix-sept cent soi- xan-te

Fêtes Galantes

On voit des mar-quis sur des bi- cy-clet-tes On voit des mar- lous

Fiançailles pour rire
No. 1. La dame d'André

An- dré ne con- nait pas la da- me Qu'il prend au-jour-d'hui par la main

No. 2. Dans l'herbe

Je ne peux plus rien di- re Ni rien fai- re pour lui

No. 3. Il vole

En al- lant se cou-cher le soleil___ Se re-flète au vernis de ma ta-ble

No. 4. Mon cadavre est doux comme un gant

Mon ca-davre est doux comme un gant___ Doux comme un gant de peau gla-cé- e

No. 5. Le Violon

Couple a- mou- reux___ aux ac- cents mé- con- nus___

POULENC

Fiançailles pour rire
No. 6. Fleurs

Fleur pro- mi- ses, fleurs te-nues dans tes bras,__ Fleurs sor- ti-es__

Hier

Hi-er,__ c'est ce cha-peau fa- né__ Que j'ai long-temps trai-né.

Hyde Park

Les Fai- seurs de re- li-gions Pré-chaient dans le brouillard

Hymne

Som- bre nuit, a- veu-gles té- né- bres, Fu- yez;

Métamorphoses
I Reine des mouettes

Rei- ne des mouet-tes, mon orphé-li-ne Je t'ai vue ro-se, je m'en souviens

II C'est ainsi que tu es

Ta chair, d'â- me mê- lé- e Che- ve-lure em-mê- lé- e

III Paganini

Vio- lon,__ hip-po-campe et si-rè- ne Ber- ceau des coeurs

Montparnasse

O por- te de l'ho- tel__ a- vec deux plan-tes ver-tes

Nous voulons une petite soeur

Ma- dame Eus- tache a dix- sept fil- les ce n'est pas trop

Ce n'est pas ça que nous vou- lons__ Nous vou-lons u- ne pe-ti-te soeur

Petites voix (children's choruses)
I La Petite Fille Sage

Le pe-ti-te fil-le sa-ge est ren- trée__ de l'é-co-le a-vec son panier

II Le chien perdu

Qui est-tu, in-con-nu? qui es- tu, chien per- du? Tu rêves,tu som-meil-les;

III En rentrant de l'école

En ren-trant de l'é-co- le par un che- min per- du

IV Le petit garçon malade

Le pe- tit gar-con ma- la- de__ Ne veut plus re-gar-der les i- ma-ges__

V Le hérisson

Quand pa-pa trouve un hé- risson il l'ap-porte à la mai-son.

Poèmes de Ronsard
I Attributs

Les é- pis__ sont à Cé- rès, aux Dieux bou-quins les fo- rêts,

II Le Tombeau

Quand le ciel et mon heu- re ju- ge-ront que je meu-re

III Ballet

Le soir qu'A- mour vous fit en la sal- le des- cen- dre

IV Je n'ai plus que les os

Je n'ai plus que les os, un squelet-te je sem- ble,__

Poèmes de Ronsard
V À son page

Fais ra-frai-chir mon vin de sor-te qu'il passe en froi-deur un gla-çon

Tel Jour, telle Nuit No. 1.
By permission Durand & Cie, Paris;
Elkan-Vogel Co., Inc., Phila.,
copyright owners

Eon-ne jour-né---e j'ai re-vu qui je n'ou-blie pas

No. 2.

U-ne rui-ne co-quil-le vi-de pleu-re dans son ta-bli-er

No. 3.

Le front comme un drapeau per-du Je te traî-ne quand je suis seul

No. 4.

U-ne rou-lot-te couverte en tui-les Le che-val mort un en-fant maître

No. 5.

A tou-tes bri-des toi dont la fan-tô-me

No. 6.

Une her-be pau-vre Sau-va-ge App-a-rut dans la nei-ge

No. 7.

Je n'ai en-vie que de t'ai-mer Un o-rage em-plit la val-lé

No. 8.

Fi-gu-re de for-ce brûlante et fa-rou-che Che-veux noirs

No. 9.

Nous a-vons fait la nuit je tiens ta main, je veil-le

PRAETORIUS, Michael (1571-1621)

Es ist ein Ross entsprungen (D'un
arbre séculaire)

D'un ar-bre sé-cu lai-re Du vieux tronc d'I-sa i

Lobet den Herren

Lo-bet den Her-ren, al-le Hei-den, prei-set sei-nen Na-men

PRESSEL, Gustav (1827-1890)

Ich sah den Wald sich färben

Ich sah den Wald sich fär-ben, die Luft war grau und stumm,

PROCH, Heinrich (1809-1878)

Air and Variations, Op. 164

Deh tor-no mio be- ne mio te-ne- ro a-mor

PROKOFIEFF, Serge (1891-1953)

Alexander Nevsky, Op. 78
Part II Song about Alexander
Nevsky
Copyright 1945, Leeds Music Corp., N. Y.
Used by permission.

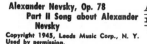

Yes, 'twas on the Riv-er Ne-va it oc-curred

Alexander Nevsky, Op. 78
Part II Song about Alexander Nevsky

Ah! how we did fight,___ how we rout-ed them **A**

Part IV Arise, ye Russian people

A-rise to arms, ye_ Rus-sian folk, in bat-tle just, in_ fight to death **B**

In our Rus-sia great, in our na-tive Rus-sia no foe shall live___ **C**

Part VI Field of the Dead

I shall go___ a-cross the snowclad field. I shall fly a-bove the field_of_death **D**

Snowdrops

Snow-drops grow on___ yon-der hill,___ Snow-drops blos-som___ **E**

Snowflakes

O-ver field and plain___ come steal - - - - ing **F**

PUCCINI, Giacomo (1858-1924)

La Bohême (opera)
Act I
Copyright by G. Ricordi & Co., Inc.

Nei cie-li bi-gi guar-do fu-mar dai mil-le co-mi-gno-li Pa-ri-gi **H**

Che ge-li-aa ma-ni-na, se la la-sci ri-scal-dar. Cer-car **I**

Ta-lor dal mio for-zie-re___ ru-ban tut-ti_i gio-iel--li **J**

Si Mi chia-ma-no Mi-mi, ma_il mio no-me_è Lu-ci-a___ **K**

Mi piaccion quel-le co-se che_han si dol-ce ma-lì-a **L**

Duet

O so-a-ve fan-ciul-la,___ O dol-ce vi-so **M**

Act II Quartet

Questa è Mi-mi, ga-ia fio-ra-ia. Il suo ve-nir com-ple-ta **N**

U-na cuf-fietta a piz-zi, tut-ta ro-sa, ri-ca-ma-ta **O**

Musetta's Waltz

Quan-do me'n vo'___ quan-do me'n vo so-let-ta per la via **P**

Act III Mimi's Farewell

Don-de lie-ta u-scì al tuo gri-do d'a-mo-re **Q**

A-scol-ta, a-scol-ta. Le po-che ro-be_a-du-na che la-sciai spar-se **R**

Quartet

Ad-di-o dol-ce sve-glia-re Al-la___ mat-ti-na___ **S**

La Bohême (opera)
Act IV

O Mi- mi tu più non tor- ni o gior- ni_ bel- li,

Colline's Song

Vec-chia zi- mar- ra, sen- ti, io re-sto al pian, tu a- scen-de-re il

So-no_an-da-ti? fin-ge- vo di dor-mi-re_ per-chè vol-li con te so-la

La Fanciulla del West (The Girl of the Golden West) (opera) Act I
Copyright by G. Ricordi & Co., Inc.

Min- nie, dal-la mia ca- sa son par- ti- to che è là dai mon- ti

Lag- giù___ nel So- le- dad, e- ro pi- ci- na

Act II

Io non son che u- na po- ve- ra fan- ci- ulla___

Oh, se sa- pe- ste co- me il vi- ve-re è al-le- gro!

Or son sei me- si_ che mio pa-dre mo- rì E tutto ap-pre-si

Act III

Ch'el-la mi cre- da li- be-ro_e lon-ta- na, so-vra u-na nuo- va via

Gianni Schicchi (opera)
Copyright by G. Ricordi & Co., Inc.

Fi- ren-ze è come un al- be-ro fio- ri- to___ che in piaz-za dei Si-gnori

Oh, mio bab-bi- no ca- ro, mi pia-ce è bel- lo, bel- lo;

Mes- ser no- ta-io, pre-sto, Via da l:uo-so Do- na- ti!

In___ te- sta la cap-pel- li- na! Al vi- so la pez-zo-li-na!

Madama Butterfly (opera) Act I
Copyright by G. Ricordi & Co., Inc.

Do-vun-que al mondo lo Yan-kee va-ga-bon- do si go-de_e traf-fi-ca

A- mo- re o gril- lo,_ dir non sa- pre- i. Cer- to co-ste- i

Spi-ra sul ma-re_e sul-la ter-ra un pri-ma- ve-ril sof-fio gio-con- do

Io se- guo il mio de- sti - - no e pie- na d'u-mil- tà

Bim- ba da-gli occhi pie- ni di ma-lì- a o-ra sei tut-ta mi-a

Dam- mi ch'io ba- ci le tue ma- ni ca- re___

PUCCINI

adama Butterfly (opera) Act I
A
Oh__ quan-ti oc-chi fi-si, at-ten-ti   d'o-gni par-te a ri-guar-dar!__

Act II Scene 1
B
Un__ bel dì, ve-dre-mo   le-var-si un fil di fu-mo

Flower duet
C
Scuo-ti quel-la fron-da di ci-lie-gio e m'in-non-da di fior__

D
Tut-ti i fior? Tut-ti i fior__   Tut-ti-tut-ti. Pe-sco, vio-la

Humming Chorus
E
Hum throughout _____

Act II Scene 2
F
Ad-di-o, fio-ri-to a-sil di le-ti-zia e d'a-mor

G
Tu? Tu?   pic-co-lo Id-di-o! A-mo-re amo-re mi-o,

H
Lo   so che al-sue pe-ne non ci so-no con-for-ti

I
Che tua ma-dre do-vrà pren-der-ti in brac-cio

Manon Lescaut (opera)
Copyright by G. Ricordi & Co., Inc.
Act I
J
Tra voi, bel-le, bru-ne e bion-de si na-scon-de gio-vi-net-ta

K
Don-na non vi-di ma-i   si-mi-le a que-sta!

Act II
L
In quel-le tri-ne mor-bi-de nell'al-co-va do-ra-ta

M
L'o-ra, o Tir-si, e va-ga e bel-la, Ri-de il gior-no, ri-de in-tor-no

A
N
Tu,   tu a-mo-re? Tu? Ah__ mio im-men-so a-mo-re?

B
O
O ten-ta-tri-ce!__   O ten-ta-tri-ce!

P
Ah! Ma-non__   mi tra-di-sce il tuo fol-le pen-sier

Act III
Q
Guar-da-te, paz-zo son, guar-da-te, co-m'io pian-go e im-plo-ro

Act IV
R
Ve-di, ve-di, son io che pian-go   io che im-plo-ro

S
So-la, per-du-ta, ab-ban-do-na-ta,__   per-du-ta,

La Rondine (opera) Act I
Copyright by Sonzogno, Milan

Chi bel so- gno di Do- ret- ta po- tè in- do- vi- nar

A

O- re dol- ci e di- vi- ne di lie- ta ba- ra- on- da

B

Fan- ciul- - - la, è sboc- cia- to l'a- mo- re!___ Di- fendi, di- fen- di

Senza mamma, from Suor Angelica
(opera)
Copyright by G. Ricordi & Co., Inc.

Sen- za mam- ma, o bim- bo, tu sei mor- to Le tue lab- bra

Il Tabarro (opera)
Copyright by G. Ricordi & Co., Inc.

Se tu sa- pes- - si gli og- get- ti___ stra- ni

Hai ben ra- gio- ne; me- glio non pen- sa- re pie- ga- re il ca- po

Tosca (opera)
Act I
Copyright by G. Ricordi & Co., Inc.

Re- con- di- ta ar- mo- ni- a di bel- lez- ze di- ver- se!

Non la so- spi- ri la no- stra ca- set- ta

Duet

Qua- l'oc- chio al mon- - - - do può star di pa- ro

Duet

Mia ge- lo- sa! Si, lo sen- to___ ti tor- men- to sen- za pò- sa

Te De- um Glo- ri- a Vi- va il Re! Si fe- steg- gi la vit- to- ria!

Act II

Già!___ Mi di- con ve- nal___ mi di- con ve- nal,

A

Vis- si d'ar- te, vis- si d'a- mo- re, non fe- ci mai ma- le

B

Sem- pre___ con fe___ sin- ce- ra la mia pre- ghie- ra

Cantata A

Sa- le a- scen- de___ l'u- man___ can- - - - - - ti- co

B

A te___ que- st'in- no di glo- ria vo- li a te

Act III

E lucevan le stelle
(Not beginning of aria,
but most salient
phrase.)

Oh! dol- ci ba- cio lan- gui- di ca- rez- ze, mentr' io fre- men- te

O dol- ci ma- ni man- su- e- te e pu- re, o ma- nie le- te

A- ma- ro sol per te m'era il mo- re- re, Da te la vi- ta

Turandot (opera)
Copyright by G. Ricordi & Co., Inc.
Act I

Si-gno-re a-scol-ta! Ah si-gno-re a-scol-ta! Liù non reg-ge più!　　A

Non pian-ge-re, Liù___ Se in un lon-ta-no gior-no io t'ho sor-ri-so　　B

Trio (Ping, Pang and Pong)

Fer-mo! che fai T'ar-re-sta! Chi sei, che fai,　　C

Non v'è in Chi-na per no-stra for-tu-na'　　D

Act II Turandot's Air

In que-sta Reg-gio, or son mil-l'an-ni e mil-le___　　E

O prin-ci-pi, che a lun-ghe ca-ro-va-ne d'o-gni par-te del mon-do　　F

Trio (Ping, Pang and Pong)

Ad-dio, a-mo-re ad-dio,___ raz-za! Ad-dio___　　G

Act III

Nes-sun dor-ma! nes-sun dor-ma! Tu pu-re o Prin-ci-pes-sa　　H

Tan-to a-mo-re se-gre-to e in-con-fes-sa-to,　　I

Death of Liu

Tu che di gel sei cin-to___ da tan-to fiam-ma vin-ta　　J

Le Villi (opera)
Copyright by G. Ricordi & Co., Inc.
Act I

If I were but like you,___ my frail for-get-me nots fair of a-zure hue___　　K

Act II

O pure and sim-ple soul of her that was my daugh-ter,___　　L

Back to the van-ished years,___ My sor-row-ful thoughts re-turn___　　M

PURCELL, Henry (c. 1659-1695)

Ah! how sweet it is to love, from Tyrannic Love　Act IV

Ah!___ how sweet, Ah!___ how sweet, how sweet it is to love,　　O

Celia has a thousand charms, from The Rival Sisters　Act II

Ce-lia has a thousand, thousand, thou - - - - - - - - - - - - - -sand charms,　　P

From Rosy Bowers, from Don Quixote (opera) Part III Act V

From ro-sy bowers, where sleeps___ the God___ of Love　　Q

Or if more in-flu-en-cing, Is___ to be brisk_ and ai_ ry,　　R

Hence with your trifling deity, from Timon of Athens (masque) No. 5

Hence! Hence! Hence with your trif-ling dei-ty A great - - - -er,　　S

Music for a while, from Oedipus

Music, mu - - sic for a __ while shall all your__ cares be - guile,

Nymphs and Shepherds, from The Libertine (opera)

Nymphs and shep - herds, come __ a - way, come a - way,

Retir'd from any mortal's sight, from King Richard II Act IV

Re - tir'd __ from a - ny mor - tal's sight The pen - sive Da - - - - mon lay

Dido and Aeneas (opera)

Act I

Shake _____ the cloud from __ off your brow,

B

Ban - ish sor - row, ban - ish care, Grief should ne'er __ ap - proach __ the __ fair,

Fear no dan - ger __ to en - sue, The he - ro loves as well as you

Cu - pid on - ly throws the __ dart that's dread - ful, dread - ful, dread - ful

To the hills and the vales, to the rocks and the moun - tains

Harm's our de - light and mis - - - chief __ all __ our __ skill,

But ere we this __ per - form, We'll con - jure for a storm __

(echo)

In our deep vault - ed cell - ed cell the __ charm we'll pre - pare

Ah! Ah! __ Ah! Be - lin - da, I __ am prest __ with __ tor - ment

Act II

Thanks to these lone - some, __ lone-some vales, These de - sert, de - - sert

Oft she vis - its this __ lone __ moun - tain, Oft she bathes her

Haste, haste to town, haste, haste, haste, haste haste __ to town

Act III

Come a - way, fel - low sai - lors, come a - way, Your an - chors

Our next mo - tion must be to storm __

De - struc - tion's our __ de - light, De - light our great - est sor - row

Great minds a - gainst them - selves con - spire, great minds

Dido and Aeneas (opera)

Act III — A — When I am laid, am laid in earth.

B — With droop - - - - - ing wings, ye Cu - pids, come

Dioclesian (opera)

C — What shall I do to show how much I love her?

D — Let us dance, let us sing, let us sing

The Fairy Queen (opera)

Act III — E — When I have of-ten heard young maids com - plain - ing

Act IV — F — Next, win-ter comes slow-ly, pale, mea-ger and old,

Act V — G — Hark! Hark! the ech'-ing air a tri - - - - umph sings

The Indian Queen (opera)

H — I at-tempt from Love's sick-ness to fly - - - - in vain

Act III — A — I — Ye twice ten hun-dred de - i-ties, to whom, to whom

B — J — By the croak-ing of the toad, In their caves that make a-bode

K — We the spir-its of the air That of hu-man things take care,

King Arthur (opera)

Act II — L — How blest are shep-herds, how hap-py their lass - es,

M — Shep-herd, shep-herd, leave de - cry-ing: Pipes are sweet on sum-mer's day

Act V — N — Fair-est Isle all Isles ex-cell-ing, Seat of plea - sures and of loves.

The Tempest (opera)

Act II — O — A-rise, a-rise, ye sub - - - - ter-ranean

Act III — P — Come un-to these yel - - - - low sands and there take hands

Q — Full fa-thom five thy fa - ther lies; Of his bones are co - - - rals made

R — Dry those eyes which are o'er - flow - - - ing

S — Kind fortune smiles and she has yet in store for thee

The Tempest (opera)
Act V
See, see the hea----vens smile with clouds no more o'er cast — A

Songs:
Ah! how pleasant 'tis to love
Ah! how pleasant 'tis to love, Ev--ry mo-ment does im-prove: — B

Ah what pains
Ah what pains Ah what pains — C

Anacreon's defeat
This po-et sings the Tro--jan wars — D

Ask me to love no more
Ask me to love no more, no more, no more, no more, no more, no more, — E

Bess of Bedlam (Mad Bess)
From si-lent shades, and the E-lys-ian groves, — F
Bright Cyn-thia kept her re--vels late, while Mab, the Fai-ry Queen — G

The Blessed Virgin's Expostulation
(realization by Benj. Britten)
Tell me, tell me, some, some Pi----ty-ing An-gel, tell, quick-ly — H
Me Ju-dah's daughters once car-ess'd — I
How, how how shall my soul its Mo-------------tions guide? — J

Cease, O my sad soul
Cease O my sad soul, cease to mourn I see my love and faith are paid — K

Evening Hymn
Now, now that the sun hath veil'd his light, — L

Fly swift, ye hours
Fly swift, ye hours, make haste, make haste, fly — M

How delightful's the life
How de-light---ful's the life of an in-no-cent swain, — N

I envy not a monarch's fate
I en--vy not a mon-----arch's fate, — O

I fain would be free
I fain would be free and to sev-er all kind, But the dev-il, — P

If music be the food of love (2nd setting)
If mu--sic be the food of love, Sing on, sing on, sing on, sing on, — Q

I gave her cakes (round)
I gave her cakes and I gave her ale, and I gave her sack and sher-ry — R

I'll sail upon the Dog-star
I'll sail up-on the Dog-star, and then pur-sue the morn-ing — S

PURCELL

I love and I must
I love and I must, I love and I must And yet I would fain

In Cloris, all soft charms agree
In Clor-is, all soft charms a-gree, en-chant - ing hu-mor pow'r-ful wit,

I saw that you were grown so high
I saw that you were grown so high, You forc'd me from your com-pa-ny

I see she flies me A
I see, I see she flies me, she flies me

B
Were she but kind, kind, Were she but kind

The Knotting Song
Hears not my Phyl-lis how the birds their fea-ther'd mates sa-lute!

Let each gallant heart
Let each gal-lant heart, Un-touch'd with love's dart, Pre-pare

Let the dreadful engines A
Let the dread-ful en-gines of e-ter-nal will,

B
Can noth-ing, can no - - - - thing warm me? Can no-thing

C
Where, where are now, where are now, where are now

D
When a wo-man love pre-tends, 'tis but till she gains her ends

Lilliburlero
Ho! brod-er Teague, dost hear de de-cree? Lil-li-bur-'le-ro

May her blest example
May her blest es-am - - ple chose Vice in troops

More love or more disdain I crave
More love or more dis-dain I crave, Sweet, be not still in-dif-fer-ent

My heart, whenever you appear
My heart, when-ev-er you ap-pear, Does something so de-light - - - ful find

Not all my torments
Not all, all, not all my tor - - - - - - - - - - - ments

No watch, dear Celia
No watch, dear Ce - - - - - - lia just is found

Ode on St. Cecelia's Day
No. 4.
'Tis Na-ture's voice, 'tis Na-ture's voice, thro'all the mo - - - - - - - - - -

No. 6.
Thou tun'st this world, this world be-low the spheres a-bove

PURCELL

292

PURCELL

Ode on St. Cecelia's Day

No. 8. — Won-drous, won-drous, won-drous won---drous ma---chine,— A

No. 9. — The ai----ry, ai-----ry vi-o-lin and lof---ty Viol B

No. 11. — The fife, the fife and all,all,all,all,all the har--------mo ny C

An Ode to Cynthia walking on Richmond Hill
On the brow— of Rich-mond—Hill,Which Europe scarce can par-al-lel, D

Ode to Queen Mary 167 (Come ye Sons of Art)
Sound _____ the trum-pet, Sound the trum-pet E

Phillis, I can ne'er forgive it
Phil-lis, I can ne'er for-give it, Nor, I think,shall e'er out-live it, F

The Queen's Epicedium A
In-cas-sum, in-cas---------sum,— Les-bia, G

B
En------nym---phas en pas-to----res! H

Rejoice in the Lord alway (anthem)
Re-joice in the Lord al-ways and a-gain I say re-joice I

Silvia, now your scorn give over
Sil-via, now—your scorn give o-ver,— Lest you— lose a— faithful lov-er— J

Solitude
O sol-i-tude my sweet--------est choice! K

The Storm
Fare-well, ye rocks,ye seas and sands,Green Nep-tune— I ____ des-pise L

Stript of their green our groves appear
Stript— of their green our— groves— ap-pear, Our vales— lie— bur-ied— M

Sweet, be no longer sad
Sweet, be no lon-ger sad, Pri-thee be wise, Recall that quick-ness N

Sweet tyranness
Sweet ty-ran-ness, I now re-sign my heart,for ev-er-more 'tis thine O

To thee and a lass (round)
To thee, to thee,and to a lass, that kind-ly will— fill— up P

Turn, turn then thine eyes
Turn,— turn— then— thine eyes, Turn,—turn— then—thine eyes,turn,—turn,—turn Q

When I a lover pale do see
When I a lo-ver pale do see Rea-dy to faint and sick-ish be, R

When the cock begins to crow
When the cock be-gins to crow, the cock be-gins to crow S

The Yorkshire Feast Song No. 6   A

The pale and the pur--ple Rose that af--ter cost so ma--ny blows,

PURCELL-COCKRANE, E. (Edward C. Purcell) (-1932)

Passing By   C
Copyright 1932, G. Schirmer, Inc.

There is a la--dy sweet and kind, Was nev-er face so pleas'd my mind

QUILTER, Roger (1877-1953)

Love's Philosophy, Op. 3, No. 1   E
By permission Boosey & Hawkes, Inc.,
copyright owners

The fountains min-gle with the riv-er And the riv--ers with the o-cean;

Come away, death, Op. 6, No. 1   F
By permission Boosey & Hawkes, Inc.,
copyright owners

Come a-way, come a-way death, And in sad cy--press

O mistress mine, No. 2   G

O mis-tress mine, where are you roam-ing? O stay and hear

Blow, blow, thou winter wind, No. 3   H

Blow, blow, thou win-ter wind, Thou art not so un-kind

To Daisies, Op. 8, No. 3   I
By permission Boosey & Hawkes, Inc.,
copyright owners

Shut not so soon: The dull-eyed night has not as yet be-gun

Weep you no more, Op. 12, No. 1   J
By permission Boosey & Hawkes, Inc.,
copyright owners

Weep you no more, sad foun-tains; What need you flow so fast?

Fair House of Joy, No. 7   K

Fain would I change that note to which fond Love hath charm'd me.

Autumn Evening, Op. 14, No. 1   L
By permission Boosey & Hawkes, Inc.,
copyright owners

The yel-low pop-lar leaves have strown Thy qui-et mound

Song of the Blackbird, No. 4   M

The Night-in-gale has a lyre of gold, The Lark's is a cla-rion call

I will go with my father a-ploughing,   N
Op. 22, No. 1
By permission of Galaxy Music Corporation,
N. Y., copyright by Elkin & Co., Ltd.

I will go with my fa-ther a-plough-ing, To the green field

Fear no more the heat o' the sun,   O
Op. 23, No. 1
By permission Boosey & Hawkes, Inc.,
copyright owners

Fear no more the heat o' the sun, Nor the fur-ious win-ter's

It was a lover and his lass, No. 3   P

It was a lov-er and his lass, with a hey and a ho,

Take, O take those lips away, No. 4   Q

Take, O take those lips a-way, That so sweet-ly were for-sworn;

Hey, ho, the Wind and the Rain, No. 5   R

When that I was and a lit-tle ti-ny boy, With hey, ho,

Go, Lovely Rose, Op. 24, No. 3

The Fuchsia Tree, Op. 25, No. 2
By permission Boosey & Hawkes, Inc., copyright owners

O what if the fowl-er my black-bird has tak-en?   A

Who is Silvia? Op. 30, No. 1
By permission Boosey & Hawkes, Inc., copyright owners

Who is Sil-via? What is she, that all our swains com-mend her?   B

Now sleeps the crimson petal
By permission Boosey & Hawkes, Inc., copyright owners

Now sleeps the crimson petal, Now the white;__ Nor waves the cypress   C

Over the Mountains
Copyright by Boston Music Co.

Ov-er the__ moun-tains and__ ov-er the waves   D

RABAUD, Henri (1873-1949)

Mârouf (opera)
Act I
Copyright by Choudens fils, Paris

Il est des Mu-sul-mans _____   F

Act II La Caravane

A tra-vers le dé-sert, mil-le cha-meaux char-gés__ d'é-tof-fes   G

Act III

Ô__ mar-chand si ri-che ou si pau-vre   H

Act IV

Dans le jar--din fleu-ri de fleurs, moi, je suis le jet d'eau   I

Act IV

Viens, ô mon é-pou-se fleu-ri-e   J

RABEY, René (Contemporary)

Tes Yeux!
By permission Durand & Cie, Paris;
Elkan-Vogel Co., Inc., Phila.,
copyright owners

Tes yeux,__ tes jo-lis yeux __ aux longs regards si doux __   L

RACHMANINOFF, Sergei (1873-1943)

Romance of the Young Gypsy, from Aleko (opera)

See __ how beneath the dis-tant sky__ dome __ There wanders air-i-ly   N

Oh stay, my love, Op. 4, No. 1
By permission Boosey & Hawkes, Inc., copyright owners

Oh stay, my love, forsake me not __ The great-est grief   O

In the silent night, No. 3
Copyright 1943, G. Schirmer, Inc.

Oh, in the si-lent night I see your vi-sion near-ing,   P

The Songs of Grusia (O, cease thy singing, maiden fair) No. 4
Copyright 1923, G. Schirmer, Inc.

O cease thy sing-ing maid-en fair, The old Gru-se-nian songs   Q

O thou billowy harvest field, No. 5
Copyright 1911, G. Schirmer, Inc.

O thou bil-low-y har-vest field of__ grain!   R

The Soldier's Bride, Op. 8, No. 4
By permission Boosey & Hawkes, Inc., copyright owners

To my sor-row I fell__ in love with him__ with a poor or-phan,   S

The Island, Op. 14, No. 2
Copyright 1936, G. Schirmer, Inc.

A

Far out at sea an is-land lies with gentle slopes and flow'ring masses,

Floods of Spring, No. 11
By permission Boosey & Hawkes, Inc., copyright owners

B

While yet the fields are wrapp'd in snow The waters hear the call of spring

Fate, Op. 21, No. 1

C

With pil-grim's staff with wear- y gait, With gloom- y brows

The Answer, No. 4

D

They won-der'd a while: Shall our ves-sel so light____

Lilacs, No. 5
Copyright 1910, G. Schirmer, Inc.

E

Morn-ing skies are a- glow where the li- lac trees blow,

How sweet the place, No. 7

F

How sweet the place! Far dis - - tant gleams the riv-er in the sun;

Sorrow in Spring, No. 12

G

How__ my heart aches! yet fain would I live now that spring__

Christ is risen, Op. 26, No. 6
By permission Galaxy Music Corporation, N. Y.

H

The Christ is ris'n__ The choirs are singing My soul is sad,

To the Children, No. 7
By permission Boosey & Hawkes, Inc., copyright owners

I

How oft-en at midnight in days long since fled, Dear children

Before my window, No. 10
By permission Boosey & Hawkes, Inc., copyright owners

J

Be-fore my win-dow stands a flow'ring cher- ry tree,__

When yesterday we met, No. 13
By permission Boosey & Hawkes, Inc., copyright owners

K

When yes-ter- day we met, her words and glances fal-ter'd;

All things depart, No. 15
By permission Boosey & Hawkes, Inc., copyright owners

L

All things de-part,__ no single thing return- eth. Life hur-ries on,__

Vocalise, Op. 34, No. 14 (wordless song)
By permission Boosey & Hawkes, Inc., copyright owners

M

Daisies, Op. 38, No. 3
By permission Boosey & Hawkes, Inc., copyright owners

N

Behold, my friend, the dai - - sies sweet and ten-der Wher-e'er I go,

Dreams, No. 5

O

Say, oh whi- ther art bound, rare en- chant-ment of dreams,

RADECKE, Robert (1829-1893)

Aus der Jugendzeit

Q

Aus der Ju- gend- zeit, aus der Ju- gend- zeit klingt__ ein Lied

RAFF, Joseph Joachim (1822-1882)

Sei still

S

Ach, was ist Le- ben doch so schwer, wenn was du lieb__ hast

RAMEAU, Jean Philippe (1683-1764)

Air Tendre, from Diane et Acteon (cantata)
Quand le si- lence et le mys-tè- re Dans vos feux

L'Impatience (cantata)
I Air gai
Ce n'est plus le poids de ma chaî - - - - - - - - - - - ne

II Air tendre
Pour- quoi leur en- vi- er leur jus- te ré- com- pen- se?

III Air léger
Tu te plais, en- fant de Cy- - the- re, A faire a- che- ter

Musette, from La Musette (cantata)
L'ai- ma- ble Li- set- te for- me ces con- certs, Et sur la mu- set- te

Les Indes Galantes (opera ballet)
Ra- ni- mez vos flam- beaux, rem- plis- sez vos car- quois

Il faut- que_ l'a- mour_ s'en- vo- - - - - - - - - - le

Per- met- tez,_ as- tre du jour, Qu'en chantant_ vos feux

A- mour,_ A- mour, quand du des- tin j'é-prou- ve la ri- gueur

Pa- pil- lon in- cons- tant, vo- le dans ce bo- ca- ge,

Laboravi (motet)
La- bo- ra- - - - - - - - - vi cla- - - - - - - - - mans

Beati qui habitant, from Quam dilecta (motet)
Be- a- ti, be- a- ti qui ha- - bi- tant_ in do- mo tu- a,

Chassons de nos plaisirs, from Acanthe et Céphise (opera)
Chas- sons De nos plaisirs tran- quil- les Les plaintes i- nu- ti- - les

Tristes apprêts, from Castor et Pollux (opera) Act I
Tris- tes ap- prêts pâ- les flam- beaux, Jour plus af- freux

Rossignols amoureux
Ros- si- gnols a- mou- reux, ré- pon- dez à nos voix

RASBACH, Oscar (1888-)

Trees
I think that I shall never see a po- em love- ly as a tree.

RASI, Francesco (c. 1580-c. 1650)

Dove, misero, mai

Do- ve mi- se- ro ma- i Spe- rar deg-gio con-for- to

Filli mia

Fil- li mi- a, Fil- li, Fil- li___ mia dol- ce,

Filli, tu vuoi partire

Fil- li tu vuoi par- ti- re E non vuoi___ch'io so- spi-ri

Occhi sempre sereni

Oc- chi sem- pre se- re- ni Per cui vi- vo con- ten- to,

RAVEL, Maurice (1875-1937)

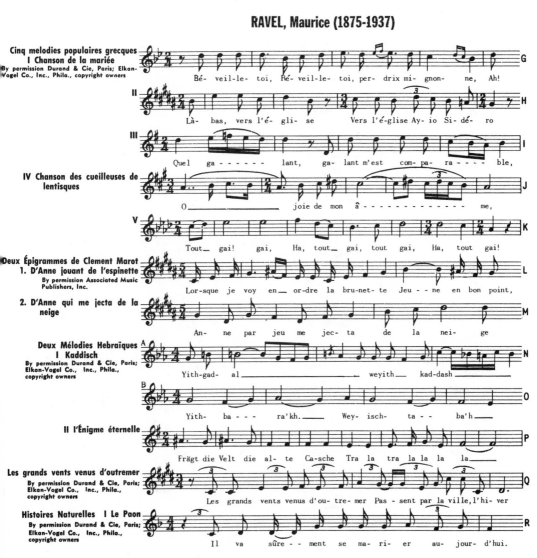

Cinq melodies populaires grecques
I Chanson de la mariée
By permission Durand & Cie, Paris; Elkan-Vogel Co., Inc., Phila., copyright owners

Bé- veil-le- toi, Ré- veil-le- toi, per- drix mi- gnon- ne, Ah!

II

Là- bas, vers l'é- gli- se Vers l'é-glise Ay- io Si- dé- ro

III

Quel ga- lant, ga- lant m'est com- pa- ra- ble,

IV Chanson des cueilleuses de lentisques

O___ joie de mon â- me,

V

Tout_ gai! gai, Ha, tout_ gai, tout gai, Ha, tout gai!

Deux Épigrammes de Clement Marot
1. D'Anne jouant de l'espinette
By permission Associated Music Publishers, Inc.

Lor-sque je voy en_ or-dre la bru-net- te Jeu - ne en bon point,

2. D'Anne qui me jecta de la neige

An- ne par jeu me jec- ta de la nei- ge

Deux Mélodies Hebraïques
I Kaddisch
By permission Durand & Cie, Paris; Elkan-Vogel Co., Inc., Phila., copyright owners

Yith-gad- al___ weyith___ kad-dash___

B

Yith- ba- ra'kh.___ Wey- isch- ta- ba'h___

II l'Énigme éternelle

Frägt die Velt die al- te Ca-sche Tra la tra la la la la___

Les grands vents venus d'outremer
By permission Durand & Cie, Paris; Elkan-Vogel Co., Inc., Phila., copyright owners

Les grands vents venus d'ou-tre-mer Pas- sent par la ville, l'hi- ver

Histoires Naturelles I Le Paon
By permission Durand & Cie, Paris; Elkan-Vogel Co., Inc., Phila., copyright owners

Il va sûre - ment se ma- ri- er au- jour- d'hui.

RAVEL

Sainte

A la fe- nê-tre re-cé- lant Le san-tal vieux qui se dé-do-re

Sur l'Herbe

L'abbé di-vague Et toi, marquis, Tu mets de travers ta peruque

Chansons Madécasses

I

Na-han-do - - ve, o bel-le Na-han- do- - ve! l'oiseau noc-turne

II A

Aoua! _____ Aoua! _____ Me- fi-ez- vous des blancs,

B

Du temps de nos pè-res, des blancs descen- dirent dans cette î- le,

III Repos

Il est doux de_ se cou-cher du-rant la chaleur sous un ar-bre touf-fu, _____

Don Quichotte à Dulcinée
I Chanson Romantique

Si vous me di-siez que la ter- re A tant_ tour-ner _____

II Chanson Épique

Bon Saint Mi- chel_ qui me don-nez loi-sir _____ de voir ma Da- - me

III Chanson à boire

Foin du bâ- tard, il- lus- tre Da- me, _____ qui pour me perdre

L'Enfant et les Sortilèges (opera-ballet)
Song of the clock

Ding, ding, ding, ding; et encor ding, ding, ding et en-cor ding

Song of the cup

Keng-ça-fou, Mah jong, _ Keng- ça- fou, _____ Puis'kong, kong, panpa, Ça-oh- rã,

Song of the fire

Je ré- chauf-fe les bons, Je ré- chauf-fe les bons,

Lullaby

Toi, le coeur de la ro- se Toi, le par-fum du lys blanc_

Song of the little old man

Deux ro- bi- nets cou- lent dans un ré- ser- voir!

L'Heure Espagnole (comédie-musicale)
Scene IX Inigo's Air

Tant pis, ma foi, si je dé- roge! Je con-çois à l'ins-tant

Scene XV Gonzalve's Air

En dé- pit de cette in- hu- maine_ Je ne veux pas quit- ter

Scene XVII Concepción's Air

Oh! la pi- toy- able a- ven- tu- re!

Trois Chansons I Nicolette

Ni- co- lette, à la ves- prée, S'al- lait pro- me- ner au pré,

II Trois beaux oiseaux du Paradis

Trois beaux oi- seaux du Pa- ra- dis, (Mon a- mi z-il est à la guer- re

Trois chansons III Ronde
N'al-lez pas au bois d'Or-mon-de, Jeu-nes fil-les, n'al-lez pas au bois:

Trois poèmes de Mallarmé
By permission Durand & Cie, Paris;
Elkan-Vogel Co., Inc., Phila.,
copyright owners
I Soupir
Mon â-me vers ton front___ où rêve, ô cal-me soeur,

II Placet futile
Princesse!___ à jalou-ser le des-tin d'une Hé-bé___

III Surgi de la croupe et du bond
'Sur-gi de la croupe et du bond d'une verre-rie é-phé-me-re___

REGER, Max (1873-1916)

Volkslied, Op. 37, No. 2
By permission Associated Music
Publishers, Inc.
Ein Vög-lein___ singt im Wald, singt Lieb' und Lei-den,

Darum, Op. 75, No. 5
Hab'___ Sin-gen für mein Le-ben gern, hallt's___ froh___ durch Feld___ und Tann;

Aeolsharfe, No. 11
Ge-heim-nis-vol-ler Klang, für Gei-ster der Luft___ be-sai-tet

Waldeinsamkeit, Op. 76, No. 3
By permission Associated Music
Publishers, Inc.
Ge-stern A-bend in der stil-len Ruh' sah ich im Wald___

Herzentausch, No. 5
Du___ sagst, mein lie - - - bes Müt-ter-lein

Beim Schneewetter, No. 6
Die___ Eng-lein ha-ben's Bett___ ge-macht, di___ Fe-dern fliegen 'run-ter,

Einen Brief soll ich schreiben, No. 8
Ei-nen Brief soll ich schrei-ben mei-nem Schatz in der Fern

Am Brünnele, No. 9
An dem Brün-ne-le an dem Brün-ne-le hab' ich oft___ ge-lauscht,

Mit Rosen bestreut, No. 12
Ich ha-be mein Kind-lein in Schlaf___ ge-wiegt

Es blüht ein Blümlein rosenrot, No. 20
Es blüht___ ein Blüm-lein ro-sen-rot und müsst___ doch ster-ben

Des Kindes Gebet, No. 22
Wenn die kleinen Kin-der be-ten hö - -ren all die Stern-lein zu

Friede, No. 25
Tief im Tal-grund ü-berm Bach sich die Wei - - - - - den nei-gen

Schelmendiedchen, No. 36
Wenn hell die lie-be Son-ne lacht, dann blei-be ich

Maria Wiegenlied (Virgin's Slumber
Song) No. 52 (Same tune as
Brahms' "Geistliches Wiegen-
lied" and "Joseph, lieber
Joseph")
Ma-ri-a sitzt am Ro-sen-hag und wiegt ihr Je - - sus-kind,

Zum Schlafen, Op. 76, No. 59

O- ben in den Bir- nen- baum sitzt ein Vög- lein

Das Dorf, Op. 97, No. 1
By permission Associated Music Publishers, Inc.

Wie ist die Nacht voll hol- der Heim- lich- kei- ten!

An die Hoffnung, Op. 124
Copyright by C. F. Peters Corp. Music Publishers

O Hoff-nung hol-de! hol-de! gü- tig ge-schäf- ti-ge

Im grü- nen Ta- le dort, wo die fri- sche Quell

Morgengesang, Op. 137, No. 8
Copyright by C. F. Peters Corp. Music Publishers

Steht auf, ihr lie- ben Kin- der- lein! Der Mor- gen- stern

Traum durch die Dämmerung
By permission Associated Music Publishers, Inc.

Wei- te wie- sen im Däm- mer- grau; die Son- ne

REICHART, (1778-1825)

Hoffnung

Wenn die Ro- sen blü- hen, hof- fe, lie- bes Herz,

REIMANN, Heinrich (1850-1906)

Wiegenlied der Hirten

Schlaf wohl, du Him- mels- kna- be du, Schlaf wohl,

RESINARIUS, Baltasar (d. 1546)

Gelobet seist du, Jesu Christ

Ge- lo- bet seist du, Je- su Christ

RESPIGHI, Ottorino (1879-1936)

Abbandono
Copyright by F. Bongiovanni, Bologna

Io so- no tan- to stan- ca di lot- ta- re, Dam- mi la pa- ce

Au milieu du jardin
Copyright by F. Bongiovanni, Bologna

Non so qual io mi vo- glia O vi- ver o mo- rir

Canto Funèbre
Copyright by G. Ricordi & Co., Inc.

Ru- de ven- to, che dif- fon- di in suon di pian- to

Cinque canti all' antica
Copyright by F. Bongiovanni, Bologna

L'u- dir tal- vol- ta no- mi- na- re il lo- co Do- ve di- mo- ri,

Ma co- me po- trei io mai sof- fri- re Di par- tir- mi di te

Cinque canti all' antica III Ballata

A — Non so qual io mi vo- glia, o vi- ver o mo- rir,

IV

B — Bel- la por- ta di ru- bi- ni Ch'a-pri-il var-co a' dol-ci ac- cen- ti

V Canzone
di re Enzo

C — A- mor mi fa so- ven- te Lo me- o co- re pe- na- re

E se un giorno tornasse
Copyright by G. Ricordi & Co., Inc.

D — E se un gior- no tor- nas- se che do- vrei dir- gli

Invito alla danza
Copyright by F. Bongiovanni, Bologna

E — Ma- don- na, d'un brac-cio so- a- ve ch'i-o cin- ga

In alto mare
Copyright by F. Bongiovanni, Bologna

F — E sdru- sci-to il na- vil l'i- ra del flot- te tre-gua non da.

Mattinata
Copyright by F. Bongiovanni, Bologna

G — Span- do- no le cam- pa- ne a la pri-m'al- ba l'a-ve

Nebbie

H — Sof-fro, lon-tan lon- ta- no Le neb-bie son-no-len-te Sal-go-no

Nevicata
Copyright by F. Bongiovanni, Bologna

I — Sui cam-pi e su le stra- de Si- len- zi- o- sa e lie- ve

Notte
Copyright by F. Bongiovanni, Bologna

J — Sul giar- di- no fan- ta- sti- co Pro- fu-ma-to di ro- sa

Pioggia
Copyright by F. Bongiovanni, Bologna

K — Pio-ye- a per le fi- ne-stra spa- lan-ca- te

Scherzo
Copyright by F. Bongiovanni, Bologna

L — U- na not-te al da- van- za- le, e-ro so-la o pur non e- ro?

Stornellatrice
Copyright by F. Bongiovanni, Bologna

M — Che mi gio- va can- tar: "Fior di be- tul- la:

Il Tramonto
Copyright by G. Ricordi & Co., Inc.

N — Oh! quan- ta te- ne- ra gio- ia, che gli fè il re-spi-ro

O — Ne- ri gli oc- chi ma non ful- gi- de più

REYER, Ernest (1823-1909)

Air des colombes, from Salammbo
(opera)
Copyright by Choudens fils, Paris

Q — Oh! qui me don-ne- ra comme à la co- lombe des ailes, pour fuir

Sigurd (opera) Act II
By permission Heugel & Cie, Paris,
copyright owners

R — Et toi, Fré- ïa, dé- es- se de l'A-mour Belle é- pou-se

Sigurd (opera) Act II

J'ai gar-dé mon âme in-gé-nue— A la fi-an-cée in-con-nue—

Es- prits,— gar-diens de ces lieux vé-né- rés,   sa-chez quel nom,

Sa- lut!— splen-deur— du jour!   Sa-lut! astre au front pur,—

Act IV

O pa- lais ra-di- eux— de la voûte é - -toi-lé- e!

RHEINBERGER, Josef (1839-1901)

In Heaven the Stars now are shining

In Heav'n the stars now are shin- ing, The o- cean waves flash—

RHENÉ-BATON (1879-1940)

Berceuse
By permission Durand & Cie, Paris;
Elkan-Vogel Co., Inc., Phila.,
copyright owners

Quand l'en-fant s'en-dort dans son ber-ceau blanc, son an- ge gar-dien

Il pleut des petales de fleurs, Op. 14, No. 6
By permission Durand & Cie, Paris;
Elkan-Vogel Co., Inc., Phila.,
copyright owners

Il pleut— des pe- ta- les de fleurs La flam- me

Tendresse, Op. 16, No. 5
By permission Durand & Cie, Paris;
Elkan-Vogel Co., Inc., Phila.,
copyright owners

Mets ta main sur mes yeux Je ne veux plus rien voir

RICHARD, Coeur de Lion (1157-1199)

Ja nun hons pris

Ja nun hons pris ne di- ra- sa rai- son

RICHARDSON, T. (Contemporary)

Mary

Kind, kind and gen- tle is she, Kind is my Ma- ry

RIEGO, Teresa del (1876-1968)

Homing

O Dry Those Tears!

O dry those tears, and calm those fears, Life is not made— for sor- row;

RIISAGE, Knudage (1897-)

Mor Danmark
Copyright by Hansen, Copenhagen

Der er et Land, som daar-lig kan bli' me- get min- dre

RIMSKY-KORSAKOFF, Nicolai (1844-1908)

The Czar's Bride (opera) Lykow's Aria — So anders sind die Leute und das Land.

Ssobakin's Aria — Wer hätt das ah - - - - - - - nen kön - - - nen

Grjasnoy's Aria — Du Ü - - - ber-muth wo- hin bist du ent-schwun-den

Martha's Aria — Deut- lich liegt vor mir der grü - ne Gar-ten / Die Ver-wand - - ten all wenn sie sa - - hen uns

Hymn to the sun, from Le Coq d'Or (opera) Act II — Sa-lut à toi, so-leil de flam-me! Nous re-viens-tu de l'O-ri-ent

May Night (opera) Act I Levko's Song — L'om-bre dis- crè-te La nuit mu-et-te, Viens, je t'at-tends

Song to the Village Mayor — Hé gar-cons, le sa-vez vous? No-tre mai-re perd les jam-bes, Hey!

Act II Slumber Song — Dors, ma dou-ce cré-a-tu-re, dors en paix

Sadko (opera) Scene I — Mes na-vi-res ra-pi-des aux flancs ver-meils

Scene II Forest Song — Qu-vre-toi, fo-rêt im-pé-ne-trable! Lais-se-moi fray-er

Scene IV Song of the Viking Guest — Les va-gues en hur-lant as-sie-gent nos ri-va-ges

Song of India — Les di-a-mants chez nous sont in-nom-bra-bles, / Dans un de nos si - - - - - - - tes

Song of the Venetian Guest — Planche et tout en mar-bre an-cien jo-yaux / Vil-le su-per-be, bel-le Ve-ni-se, Rei-ne du mon-de

Scene VII Berceuse — Sur la ri-ve er-rait le Rêve, sur le pré le Som-meil.

Snégourotchka (The Snow Maiden) (opera) Act I Air of Snégourotchka — Al - - ler au bois, cueil-ler la fram-boise

Snégourotchka (The Snow Maiden) (opera) — Act I Air of Snégourotchka — **A**
Le soir, le soir je chan-te-rai

Arietta of Snégourotchka — **B**
Je con-nais, je con-nais, ma mè----re,

Carnival Chorus — **C**
Les coqs chant-ent de-puis l'au-ro----re

Act III Song of the shepherd, Lehl — **D**
Said the thun-der to the cloud passing by, Rum-ble, grum-ble,

Songs,
The Nightingale and the Rose, Op. 2, No. 2 — **E**
The rose has charm'd the night-in-gale, By day and night

The Cloud and the Mountain, Op. 3, No. 3 — **F**
Thro' the night a gol-den cloudlet rest-ed On a lof-ty moun-tain

A Southern Night, Op. 3, No. 6 — **G**
O'er yon moun-tain-ous height Rides the Queen of the Night,

On the Georgian Hills, Op. 3, No. 8 — **H**
The mists are hang-ing low a-bove the Geor-gian hills

Gonets, Op. 4 — **I**
De-bout, mon gars! Sur ton che-val! Tra-ver-se bois et champs

Chanson Hébraïque, Op. 7 — **J**
I sleep; my heart at break of day can nev-er sleep

Oh, if you could, Op. 39, No. 1 — **K**
Hé-las! si tu pou-vais, ne fût-se qu'un in-stant,

It is not the wind blowing from the height, Op. 43, No. 2 — **L**
The wind's not blow-ing from the height, Qui-et the evening,

The Prophet, Op. 49, No. 2 — **M**
Le vrai, d'un coeur, ar-dent, cher-chant j'er-rais dans le dé-sert

The Maid and the Sun, Op. 50, No. 1 — **N**
Far a-way be-yond three o-ceans

ROBERTON, Sir Hugh S. (1874-1952)

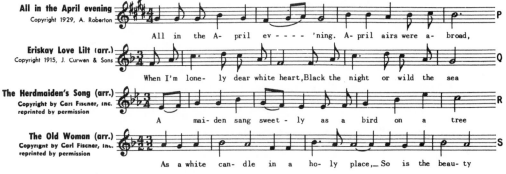

All in the April evening
Copyright 1929, A. Roberton — **P**
All in the A-pril ev----'ning. A-pril airs were a-broad,

Eriskay Love Lilt (arr.)
Copyright 1915, J. Curwen & Sons — **Q**
When I'm lone-ly dear white heart, Black the night or wild the sea

The Herdmaiden's Song (arr.)
Copyright by Carl Fischer, inc.
reprinted by permission — **R**
A mai-den sang sweet-ly as a bird on a tree

The Old Woman (arr.)
Copyright by Carl Fischer, inc.
reprinted by permission — **S**
As a white can-dle in a ho-ly place, So is the beau-ty

ROBINSON, Earl (1911-   )

Ballad for Americans
Copyright by Robbins Music Corp., N. Y.

In sev-en-ty six the sky was red   Thun-der rum-bling o-ver-head

No-bod-y ___ who was a-ny-bod-y ___ be-lieved it

The House I Live In

ROGERS, James H. (1857-1940)

At Parting

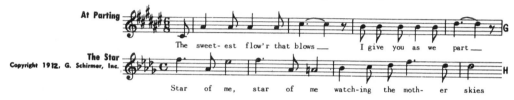

The sweet-est flow'r that blows ___   I give you as we part ___

The Star
Copyright 1912, G. Schirmer, Inc.

Star of me, star of me watch-ing the moth-er skies

RONALD, Sir Landon (1873-1938)

Down in the Forest, from A Cycle of Life, No. 2
By permission Boosey & Hawkes, Inc., copyright owners

Down in the for-est some-thing stirred So faint that I scarce-ly heard:

ROOT, George F. (1820-1895)

Just before the Battle, Mother

Just be-fore the bat-tle, mo-ther   I am think-ing most of you

The Vacant Chair

We shall meet but we shall miss him, There will be one va-cant chair

ROPARTZ, J. Guy (1864-1955)

Berceuse
Copyright by Salabert, Paris, N. Y.

O pe-tits en-fants; Voi-ci l'heure où tout bruit cesse

La Mer
Copyright by Salabert, Paris, N. Y.

Le flot, mi-roir mou-vant des cieux, S'é-veille au so-leil

ROSA, Salvator (1615-1673)

Star vicino al bell' Idol

Star vi-ci-no al bell' I-dol che s'a-ma,

Vado ben spesso

Va-do ben spes-so can-gian-do ___ lo - - - co

ROSSETER, Philip (c. 1575-1623)

If she forsake me

If she for-sake me, I must die; Shall I tell her so?

ROSSI, Francesco (17th Cent.)

Ah! rendimi quel core, from Mitrane (opera)

Ah ren-di-mi quel co - - - - re, Ren-di-mi quel'a-mo - - - - re!

Il tuo fu il mi-o pen-sie - - re Tuo sempre il mi-o vo-le - - - re

ROSSINI, Gioacchino (1792-1868)

La Danza (Tarantella Napoletana)

Già la luna è in mez - - zo al ma - - re, mam - ma mia

La la ra la ra_____ la ra la_ la ra la

The Barber of Seville (opera)
Act I

Pia - no, pia-ni-si-mo sen-za par-lar! Tut-ti con me veni-te quà,

Ec-co ri-den-te il cie - - - - - - lo spun-ta la bel-la au-ro - - - ra

Serenata

Se il mio no - me sa - per voi bra - - - - - - - - te,

Lar - - - go al fac- to- tum della cit- tà; lar - go!

All' i- dea di quel me- tal-lo por-ten-to-so on-ni-pos-sen-te

U- na vo-ce po- co fa qui nel cor mi- ri- suo-no,

Io so - - no___ do-ci- le, son ri-spet-to - - sa,

La ca- lum-nia è un ven-ti- cel - - lo, un' au-ret-ta

duet

Dun-que io son? tu non m'in-gan-ni? dun-que io son la for-tu-na-ta?

Ah! tu so - - - - - lo, a-mor,_____ tu se - - - - - - - - - i,

A un Dot- tor della mia sor-te que- ste scu- se, Si- gno-ri- na

The Barber of Séville (opera)
Act I Finale

A Ah! ve- - -nisse_ il_ ca- ro_og- get- to

B Mi_ par_ d'es- - - ser_ col- - -la te- - -sta

Act II

C Qui mi man-ca un mez-zo fo-glio e le di-ta pien d'in-chiostro,

D Quan-do mi sei vi-ci- - - - -na, a- ma-bi-le Ro- si- - - - -na

E Buo- na se- - -ra, mio Si- gno- - re! Buo-na_ se- ra, buo-na_ se- ra!

F Il vec-chiotto cer- ca mo- glie, vuol ma- ri- to la ra- gaz- za

Trio

G Zit-ti, zit-ti, pia-no, pia- - -no, non fac-ciam più con-fu- sio- - -ne

La Cenerentola (opera) No. 5

H Si- gnor_ u-na pa-ro-lo_u-na pa- ro-la Si-gnor_

No. 15 Air and Rondo

Air

I Nac- qui all'af-fa-no al pian- - - - - - - - - - -to

Rondo

J Non più me-sta_ac-can-to_al fo- co sta-ro so- la_agor- gheg- - giar

Di tanti palpití, from Tancredi (opera)

K Di tan-ti pal- pi-ti di- - - - - - -tan-te pe- - - - - -ne

La Gazza Ladra (opera) Act I

A
L Di pia-cer_ mi balza il cor, ah bra-mar_ di_ più non so

B
M Tut- to_ sor- ri-de- re mi veg-go_in-tor- - - - -no

N Il mio pia-no_è pre-pa- ra- - -to e fal-li-re_e fal-li- re

Act II

O Deh! tu reg- - -gi in tal mo- men- - -to il mio_ cor

L'Italiana in Algeri (opera) Act I

A
P Lan- guir per u- na bel- - - - -la, e star_ lon-tar.

B
Q Con- ten- - -ta quest'al- - -ma in mez- -zo_al- le pe- ne

R Cru- da sor-te! a-mor ti-ran- - -no!questo è il premio_

duet

S Oh! che mu-so che_ fi- gu- ra qua-li_oc- chia-te!

ROSSINI

L'Italiana in Algeri (opera) Act II

A — Per lui che a- do- ro ch'è il mio te- so- ro, più bel- la__ ren- di- mi,

B — Pen- sa al- la pat- ria e in- tre- pi- do e in- tre- pi- do

C — Qual pia - - - cer! fra pochi i- stan- ti fra pochi i- stan- ti

Mosè in Egitto (opera)

Invocazione

D — E- ter- no! Im- men- so! in- com- pren- si- bil Di- o!

Prayer

E — Dal tuo stel- la- to so- glio, Si- gnor ti vol- gi a noi

Que ton âme si noble, from Robert Bruce (opera)

F — Que ton â- me si no- ble, si bon- ne, Fil- le chè- re

Semiramide (opera)

Act I

G — Ah! quel gior- no o o- gnor ram- men - - - - - - - - - - - to,

H — Ah co- me__ da quel__ dì, tut- to, tut- to per me can- gio

I — Bel rag - - - gio lu- sin - - - - - - - - - - - gher

J — Dol- ce pen- sie - - - - - - - ro, di quell'i- stan - - - - - te

Act II

K — In si bar- ba - - ra scia - gu - - - - - - - - ra,

William Tell (opera) Act I

L — Ah! Ma- thil- de, i- do - - - le de mon â - - me,

Bridal Chorus

M — Ciel, qui du mon - - de est la pa- ru - - re

Act II

N — Som- bre__ for- êt, dé- sert triste et sau- va- ge

Act III Tyrolean

O — Toi que l'oi- seau ne suivrait pas__

P — Sois im- mo- bi- le, et vers la ter- re in- cline un ge- nou

Act IV

Q — A- sile hé- re- di- tai- re, ou mes yeux s'ou- vri- rent au jour,

Stabat Mater No. 2

R — Cu- jus__ a- ni- mam ge- men- tem, con- tris- tan- tem,

No. 3

S — Quis est ho- mo qui non fle- ret, Christi ma- trem si vi- de- ret,

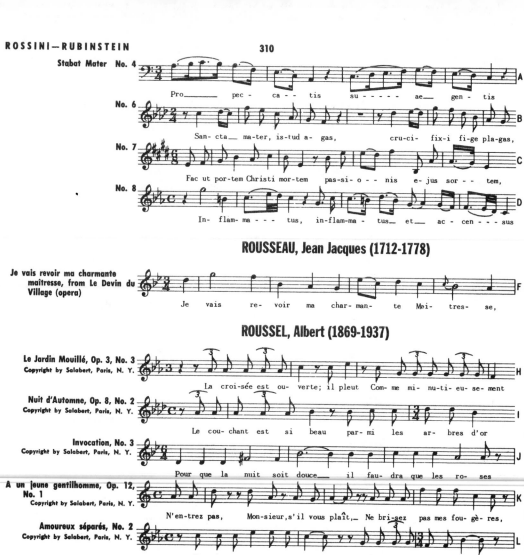

Stabat Mater No. 4
Pro_____ pec - ca - tis su ----- ae_ gen - tis

No. 6
San - cta__ ma-ter, is-tud a - gas, cru-ci - fix-i fi-ge pla-gas,

No. 7
Fac ut por-tem Christi mor-tem pas-si-o - - nis e - jus sor - - tem,

No. 8
In - flam-ma - - - tus, in-flam-ma-tus_ et_ ac - cen - - - sus

ROUSSEAU, Jean Jacques (1712-1778)

Je vais revoir ma charmante maîtresse, from Le Devin du Village (opera)
Je vais re - voir ma char-man - te Maî-tres - se,

ROUSSEL, Albert (1869-1937)

Le Jardin Mouillé, Op. 3, No. 3
Copyright by Salabert, Paris, N. Y.
La croi-sée est ou - verte; il pleut Com - me mi - nu-ti-eu - se - ment

Nuit d'Automne, Op. 8, No. 2
Copyright by Salabert, Paris, N. Y.
Le cou - chant est si beau par - mi les ar - bres d'or

Invocation, No. 3
Copyright by Salabert, Paris, N. Y.
Pour que la nuit soit douce__ il fau - dra que les ro - ses

A un jeune gentilhomme, Op. 12, No. 1
Copyright by Salabert, Paris, N. Y.
N'en-trez pas, Mon-sieur,s'il vous plaît,_ Ne bri-sez pas mes fou-gè-res,

Amoureux séparés, No. 2
Copyright by Salabert, Paris, N. Y.
Dans le roy-au-me de Yen__ un jeune ga-lant ré-si-de

Light, Op. 19, No. 1
By permission Durand & Cie, Paris; Elkan-Vogel Co., Inc., Phila., copyright owners
Des lar-mes ont cou-lé_____ D'un coeur se-cret et ten-dre

Sarabande, Op. 20, No. 2
By permission Durand & Cie, Paris; Elkan-Vogel Co., Inc., Phila., copyright owners
Les jets d'eau dan - sent des sa - ra - ban - des

Réponse d'une épouse sage, Op. 35, No. 2
By permission Durand & Cie, Paris; Elkan-Vogel Co., Inc., Phila., copyright owners
Con - nais-sant, sei - gneur,_ mon é - tat d'é - pou - se

Jazz dans la nuit, Op. 38
By permission Durand & Cie, Paris; Elkan-Vogel Co., Inc., Phila., copyright owners
Le bal, sur le parc in-cen-dié__ jet - te ses feux

Coeur en Peril, Op. 50, No. 2
By permission Durand & Cie, Paris; Elkan-Vogel Co., Inc., Phila., copyright owners
Que m'im-por - te que l'in-fan-te de Por-tu-gal__

RUBINSTEIN, Anton (1829-1894)

Der Traum, Op. 8, No. 1
Am Wie - sen-hü - gel schlum-mert ich dem brei - ten Weg

RUBINSTEIN

Sehnsucht, Op. 8, No. 5
Gönnt mir gold-ne Ta-ges-hel-le, öff-net mir des Ker-kers Schloss — A

bist wie eine Blume, Op. 32, No. 5
Du bist wie ei-ne Blu-me so hold, und schön und rein — B

Frühlingslied, Op. 32, No. 2
Die blau-en Früh-lings-au-gen schau'n aus dem Gras her-vor — C

Lied (The Page), Op. 32, No. 4
Es war ein al-ter Kö-nig, sein Herz war schwer, sein Haupt war grau — D

Persian Songs, Op. 34, No. 1
Nicht mit En - geln im blau-en Himmels-zelt, — E

No. 2
Mein Herz schmückt sich mit dir wie sich der Him-mel mit der Son-ne — F

No. 3
Seh' ich dei-ne Zar-ten Füss-chen an, so be-greif' ich nicht, — G

No. 4 Die Rose
Es hat die Ro - - - se sich be-klagt, dass gar — zu schnell — H

No. 9
Gelb rollt mir zu Füs-sen der brau-sen-de Kur — I.

Der Engel, Op. 48
Es schweb-te ein En-gel den Him-mel ent-lang — J

Nun die Schatten dunkeln, Op. 57, No. 2
Nun die Schat-ten dun-keln, Stern an Stern er-wacht — K

Clärchen's Lied, No. 4
Freud-voll und leid voll, ge-dan - - - - - - - - ken-voll sein — L

Es blinkt der Thau, Op. 72, No. 1
Es blinkt der Thau — in den Grä-sern der Nacht, der Mond zieht vor-ü-ber — M

The Prisoner, Op. 78, No. 6
Im Ker-ker ge-fan-gen ver-schmacht' ich da-hier — N

Der Asra
Täg-lich ging die wun-der-schö-ne Sul-tans-toch-ter auf und nie-der — O

Die Lerche (The Lark)
Ler-che stei-get im Ge-sang, zieht hin-auf zu blau-en Räu-men, — P

Sang das Vögelein
Sang wohl, sang das Vö-ge-lein, und ver-stumm-te — Q

Wanderers Nachtlied
Al-ler Ber-ge Gi-pfel ruh'n in dunk-ler Nacht, — R

RUSSELL, Henry (1871-1937)

Woodman, spare that tree

Wood- man, spare that tree! Touch not a sin- gle— bough!

SADERO, Geni (1891-   )

Amuri, Amuri

A- mu- ri,a- mu- ri___ che m'ai fat- tu

Fa la nana, bambin

Fà la na- na bam- bin, Fà la na- na bel bam- bin

In mezo al Mar

In me- zo al mar ghe xe un ca- min che fu- ma___

SAINT-SAËNS, Camille (1835-1921)

O beaux rêves évanouis, from Étienne Marcel (opera) Act II
By permission Durand & Cie, Paris; Elkan-Vogel Co., Inc., Phila., copyright owners

O beaux rê- ves é- va- nouis___ Es- pé- ran- ces tant ca- res- sé- es!

Qui donc commande, from Henry VIII (opera) Act I
By permission Durand & Cie, Paris; Elkan-Vogel Co., Inc., Phila., copyright owners

Qui donc com- man- de quand il ai- me Et quel em- pi- re

Samson et Dalila, Op. 47 (opera) Act I
By permission Durand & Cie, Paris; Elkan-Vogel Co., Inc., Phila., copyright owners

Ar- rê- tez ô mes frè- res! Et bé- nis- sez le nom de Dieu saint

Ce Dieu que vo- tre voix im- plo- re Est de- meu- ré sourd

Mau- di- te à ja- mais soit la ra- ce des en- fants d'Is- ra- ël!

Voi- ci le prin- temps nous por- tant des fleurs

Je viens cé- lé- brer la vic- toi- re De ce- lui qui regne en mon coeur

Prin- temps qui com- men- ce Por- tant l'és- pe- ran- ce

Act II

A- mour! viens ai- der ma fai- bles- se Ver- se le poi- son

A

Mon coeur s'ouvre à ta voix, com- me s'ou- vrent les fleurs

B

Ah!___ ré- ponds à ma ten- dres- se

Act III

Vois ma mi- sère, hé- las vois ma dé- tres- se! Pi- tié! Sei- gneur!

Samson et Dalila, Op. 47 (opera)
Act III

A — Gloire à Da- gon vain-queur! Gloire à Da- gon vain-queur! Il ai-dait

Oratorio de Noël (Christmas Oratorio)
Op. 12 No. 2
By permission Durand & Cie, Paris;
Elkan-Vogel Co., Inc., Phila.,
copyright owners

B — Glo- ri- a in al- ti- si- mis De- o

No. 4

C — Do- mi- ne e- go cre- di- di e- go cre- di- di

No. 5

D — Be- ne- dic- tus, be- ne- dic- tus, be- ne- dic - - - - tus

No. 7

E — Te - - cum prin-ci-pi- um te-cum prin-ci- pi- um in di- e vir - tu-tis

No. 8

F — A- le- lu- ia, Al- le - - lu- ia, Al- le- lu- ia

No. 10

G — Tol- li- te hos-ti- as, et a- do- ra- te Do- mi-num in a tri- o

Aimons-nous
By permission Durand & Cie, Paris;
Elkan-Vogel Co., Inc., Phila.,
copyright owners

H — Ai- mons nous et dor-mons___ Sans son- ger au res-te du mon- de

L'Attente
By permission Durand & Cie, Paris;
Elkan-Vogel Co., Inc., Phila.,
copyright owners

I — Monte, é- cu- reuil.___ monte au grand chê- ne, sur la bran-che des cieux

Ave Verum
By permission Durand & Cie, Paris;
Elkan-Vogel Co., Inc., Phila.,
copyright owners

J — A- ve A- ve ver - - rum Cor- pus natum de Ma- ri- a Vir- gi- ne

Le bonheur est chose légère
By permission Durand & Cie, Paris;
Elkan-Vogel Co., Inc., Phila.,
copyright owners

K — Le bon-heur est cho- se lé- gè- re, Pas- sa- gè - - - - - - - re

La Cloche
By permission Durand & Cie, Paris;
Elkan-Vogel Co., Inc., Phila.,
copyright owners

L — Seule___ en ta som- bre tour___ aux fai- tes den-te- lés

Danse Macabre

M — Zig et zig et zig, La mort en ca- den-ce Frap-pant u- ne tombe

N — Le vent d'hi-ver souffle, et la nuit est som- bre

Guitares et Mandolines
By permission Durand & Cie, Paris;
Elkan-Vogel Co., Inc., Phila.,
copyright owners

O — Gui- ta- res et man-do-li- nes Ont des sons qui font_ ai- mer___

Mai
By permission Durand & Cie, Paris;
Elkan-Vogel Co., Inc., Phila.,
copyright owners

P — Mai! les ar-bres du ver- ger Sont pou-drés de nei- ge ro- se

Mélodies Persanes, Op. 26:
Au cimetière
By permission Durand & Cie, Paris;
Elkan-Vogel Co., Inc., Phila.,
copyright owners

Q — As- sis sur cet-te blanche tom- be Ouvrons___ no - tre coeur

La Solitaire

R — Ô fier___ jeune___ homme, ô___ tu - eur___ de ga- zel - les

The Nightingale and the Rose
(wordless song), from incidental
music to Parysatis
By permission Durand & Cie, Paris; Elkan-
Vogel Co., Inc., Phila., copyright owners

S

Le Pas d'armes du Roi Jean
By permission Durand & Cie, Paris; Elkan-Vogel Co., Inc., Phila., copyright owners

Par saint Gil - les, Viens nous en, Mon a - gi - le A - le - zan

Los aux da - mes! au roi los! Vois les flammes Des champs clos

Tournoiement
By permission Durand & Cie, Paris; Elkan-Vogel Co., Inc., copyright owners

Sans que nul - le part je sé - jour - ne Sur la poin - te du gros or - teil

SALTER, Mary Turner (1856-1938)

The Cry of Rachel
Copyright 1905, G. Schirmer, Inc.

I stand in the dark, I beat on the door: Death, let me in

The Pine-Tree
Copyright 1904, G. Schirmer, Inc.

O pine-tree lone-ly stand-ing, Out-lined a-gainst the blue

SANDERSON, James (1769-1841)

Hail to the Chief

Hail to the Chief, who in tri - umph ad - van - ces,

Heav'n send it hap-py dew, Earth lend it sap a-new

SANDERSON, Wilfrid

Until
By permission Boosey & Hawkes, Inc., copyright owners

No rose in all the world un - til you came,

SARTI, Guiseppe (1729-1802)

Lungi dal caro bene

Lun-gi dal ca-ro be - ne, Vi-ve-re non pos-s'i-o

SARTORIUS, Thomas (1577-1637)

Wohlauf, ihr lieben Gäste

Wohl-auf wohl-auf, ihr lie-ben Gä - - - - - ste

SATIE, Erik (1866-1925)

Le Chapelier
Copyright by Salabert, Paris, N. Y.

Le cha-pe-lier s'é-ton - - ne de con-sta-ter que sa mon - - tre

Daphénéo
Copyright by Salabert, Paris, N. Y.

Dis - moi, Da - phé - né - o, quel est donc cet ar - bre

Je te veux
Copyright by Salabert, Paris, N. Y.

J'ai com-pris ta dé tres - se, cher a - mou - reux

Je n'ai pas de re - grets et je n'ai qu'u - ne en - vi e

La Statue de Bronze
Copyright by Salabert, Paris, N. Y.

A — La gre- nou- ille du jeu de tonneau S'en- nu- – ie le soir

SCANDELLI, Antonio (1517-1580)

Ein Hennlein weiss

C — Ein Henn- lein- weiss ein Henn-lein weiss mit gan- zen Fleiss

SCARLATTI, Alessandro (1659-1725)

Chi vuole innamorarsi

E — Chi vuo-le_in-na- mo- rar- si, Chi vuo-le_in-na-ma- rar-si,

Già il sole dal Gange

F — Già il so- le_ dal_ Gan- ge, già il so- le dal Gan- ge più chia-ro,

O cessate di piagarmi

G — O ces- sa- te di_ pia-gar- mi, o las- cia- te-mi mo- rir

nbre opache, from Correa nel peno amato (cantata)

H — Om- bre o- pa- che che il chia-ro- re del- la lu- ce

Povera pellegrina (cantata)

I — Po- – – ve- ra pel- le- gri- na_ Son io cor mio per te_

Rugiadose, odorose

J — Ru- gia- do-se, o- do- ro- se, Vi- o- let- te gra- zi- o- se,

Se Florindo è fedele

K — Se Flo- rin-do_è fe- – de- le io m'in-na- mo- re- – – rò,

Sento nel core

L — Sen- to nel co- re cer-to do- lo- re, cer-to do- lo- re,

Se tu della mia morte

M — Se tu_ del-la mia mor- te a que-sta de-stra for- – te

Son tutta duolo

N — Son tut-ta duo- lo, non ho che affan-ni e mi da mor- te

Su, venite a consiglio

O — Su, su su, ve- ni-te_a con-si-glio, ve- ni-te_a con-siglio

SCARLATTI, Domenico (1685-1757)

Consolati e spera

Q — Con-so- la- ti!_ e spe- ra!_ po-trai d'altro ogget- – to

Qual farfalletta amante

R — Qual far-fal-let-ta_a- man- – – te in vo- lo_a quel- la fiam- ma

SCHEIN, Johann Hermann (1586-1630)

Wenn Filli ihre Liebesstrahl

Wenn Fil-le ih-re Lie-bes-strahl wirft in mein Herz

SCHILLINGS, Max von (1868-1933)

Wie wundersam, Op. 2, No. 3
By permission Associated Music Publishers, Inc.

Wie wun - - - der-sam ist dies Verlo-ren-geh'n in Lie-bes-tie-fen

SCHÖNBERG, Arnold (1874-1951)

Erhebung, Op. 2, No. 3

Gieb mir dei-ne Hand, nur den Fin-ger, dann__ seh ich

Warnung, Op. 3, No. 3

Mein Hund, du,__ hat dich bloss be-knurrt und__ ich hab ihn

Hochzeitslied, No. 4

So voll und reich wand noch das Le-ben nim-mer euch sei-nen Kranz,

Geübtes Herz, No. 5

Wei-se nicht von dir mein schlichtes Herz,weil es schon so viel ge-lieb-et!

Mädchenlied, Op. 6, No. 3

Ach,wenn es nun die Mut-ter wüsst, wie du so wild mich hast ge-küsst,

Verlassen, No. 4

Im Mor-gen-grau-en schritt ich fort Ne-bel lag in den Gas-sen

Ghasel, No. 5

Ich hal-te dich in mei-nem Arm, du__ hältst die Ro-se zart__

Das Buch der hängenden Gärten, Op. 15, No. 5
By permission Associated Music Publishers, Inc.

Sa - - get mir, auf wel-chem Pfa-de heu - te sie vor-ü-ber schrei-te,

No. 12

Wenn sich bei heil-ger Ruh in tie-fen Mat-ten

Gurrelieder, Op. 35
Waldemar's Song
By permission Associated Music Publishers, Inc.

So tan-zen die En-gel vor Got-tes Thron nicht, wie die Welt__

Tove's Song

Nun sag ich dir zum er-sten Mal:"Kö-nig Vol-mer, ich lie-be dich!"

Waldemar's Song

Du wun-der-li-che To-ve! So reich durch dich nun bin ich

Waldtaube's Song

Tau-ben von Gur-re Sor - - ge qualt__ mich,vom Weg

Weit__ flog ich, Kla-ge sucht' ich fand gar viel!

SCHUBERT, Franz (1797-1828)

Die schöne Müllerin, Op. 25 (song cycle) No. 16 Die liebe Farbe

In Grün will ich mich klei-den, in grü-ne Trä-nen-wei-den:

No. 17 Die böse Farbe

Ich möch-te ziehn in die Welt hin-aus, hin-aus in die wei-te_ Welt;

No. 18 Trockne Blumen

Ihr Blüm-lein al-le, die sie_ mir gab, euch soll man le-gen

No. 19 Der Müller und der Bach

Wo ein treu-es Her - - - ze in Lie - - - ' be ver-geht,

No. 20 Des Baches Wiegenlied

Gu-te Ruh, gu-te Ruh! tu die Au-gen zu!

Schwanengesang (14 Lieder) No. 1 Liebesbotschaft

Rau-schen-des Bäch-lein, so sil-bern und hell, eilst zur Geliebten

No. 2 Kriegers Ahnung

In tie-fer Ruh liegt um mich her der Waf-fen-bru-der Kreis;

Nc. 3 Frühlingssehnsucht

Säu-seln-de Lüf-te we-hend so mild, blu-mi-ger Düf-te

No. 4 Ständchen (Serenade)

Lei - se flie-hen mei-ne Lie-der durch die Nacht_zu Dir

No. 5 Aufenthalt

Rau-schen-der Strom, Brau-sen-der Wald, Star-ren-der Fels

No. 6 In der Ferne

We-he dem Flie-hen-den Welt hin-aus zie-hen-den!

No. 7 Abschied

A-de! du mun-tre, du fröh-li-che Stadt, A-de!_

No. 8 Der Atlas

Ich un-glück-sel-ger At-las, ich un-glück-sel-ger At-las!

No. 9 Ihr Bild

Ich stand in dun-keln Träu-men und starrt' ihr Bild-nis an

No. 10 Das Fischermädchen

Du schö-nes Fi-scher-mäd-chen, trei-be den Kahn ans Land;_

No. 11 Die Stadt

Am fer-nen Ho-ri-zon-te er-scheint wie ein Ne-bel-bild,

No. 12 Am Meer

Das Meer er-glänz-te_ weit hin-aus im letz-ten A-bend-schei-ne

No. 13 Der Doppelgänger

Still ist die Nacht, es ru-hen die Gas-sen, in die - -sem Hau-se

No. 14 Die Taubenpost

Ich hab ei-ne Brief-taub in mei-nem Sold, die ist gar er-ge-ben

SCHUBERT

Die Winterreise, Op. 89 (song cycle)
No. 1 Gute Nacht

Fremd bin ich ein-ge-zo - - gen, fremd zieh ich wie-der aus   A

No. 2 Die Wetterfahne

Der Wind spielt mit der Wet - - ter-fah - ne   B

No. 3 Gefrorne Tränen

Ge-fror-ne Trop-fen fal-len von mei-nen Wan-gen ab: C

No. 4 Erstarrung

Ich such im Schnee ver-ge-bens nach ih-rer Tritt-te Spur,   D

No. 5 Der Lindenbaum

Am Brun-nen vor dem To - re da steht ein Lin-den-baum;   E

No. 6 Wasserflut

Man-che Trän' aus mei-nen Au-gen ist ge-fal-len in den Schnee: F

No. 7 Auf dem Flusse

Der du so lus-tig rauschtest, du hel-ler, wil-der Fluss,   G

No. 8 Rückblick

Es brennt mir un-ter bei-den Soh-len, tret ich auch schon auf Eis und Schnee   H

No. 9 Irrlicht

In die tief-sten Fel-sen grün-de lock-te mich ein Irr-licht hin: I

No. 10 Rast

Nun merk ich erst,wie müd ich bin, da ich zur Ruh mich le-ge   J

No. 11 Frühlingstraum

Ich träum-te von bun-ten Blu-men, so wie sie wohl blü-hen im Mai,   K

No. 12 Einsamkeit

Wie ei-ne trü-be Wol-ke durch hei-tre Lüf-te geht,   L

No. 13 Die Post

Von der Stra-sse her ein Post-horn klingt.   Was hat es,   M

No. 14 Der greise Kopf

Der Reif hat ei-nen weiss-en Schein mir ü - - - bers Haar ge-streu-et   N

No. 15 Die Krähe

Ei-ne Krä-he war mit mir aus der Stadt ge-zo - - gen,   O

No. 16 Letzte Hoffnung

Hie un da ist an den Bäu-men man-ches bun-te Blatt zu sehn,   P

No. 17 Im Dorfe

Es bel-len die Hun-de, es ras-seln die Ket-ten;   Q

No. 18 Der stürmische Morgen

Wie hat der Sturm zer-ris-sen des Him-mels grau-es Kleid!   R

No. 19 Täuschung

Ein Licht tanzt freundlich vor mir her, ich folg ihm   S

SCHUBERT

Die Winterreise, Op. 89 (song cycle)
No. 20 Der Wegweiser

Was ver-meid ich denn die We-ge, wo die An-dern Wand-rer gehn,

No. 21 Das Wirtshaus

Auf ei-nen To-ten-ak-ker hat mich mein Weg ge-bracht

No. 22 Mut!

Fliegt der Schnee mir ins Ge-sicht, schüttl ich ihn her-un-ter

No. 23 Die Nebensonnen

Drei Son-nen sah ich am Him-mel stehn, hab lang und fest sie an-gesehn;

No. 24 Der Leiermann

Drü-ben hin-term Dor-fe steht ein Lei-er-mann,

Gretchen am Spinnrade, Op. 2

Mei-ne Ruh ist hin, mein Herz ist schwer; ich fin-de,

Meeres Stille, Op. 3, No. 2

Tie-fe Stil-le herrscht im Was-ser, oh-ne Re-gung ruht das Meer,

Heidenröslein, No. 3

Sah ein Knab ein Rös-lein stehn, Rös-lein auf der Hei-den,

Jägers Abendlied, No. 4

Im Fel-de schleich' ich still und wild ge--spannt

Der Wanderer, Op. 4, No. 1

Ich kom-me vom Ge-bir-ge her Es dampft das Tal

Wo bist Du, wo bist Du, mein ge-lieb-tes Land?

Wanderers Nachtlied, No. 3

Der du von dem Him-mel bist, al-les Leid und Schmerzen stillst,

Rastlose Liebe, Op. 5, No. 1

Dem Schnee, dem Re-gen, dem Wind ent-ge-gen, in Dampf der Klüf-te,

Nähe des Geliebten, No. 2

Ich den--ke dein, wenn mir der Son---ne Schimmer vom Mee--re strahlt

Das König in Thule, No. 5

Es war ein König in Thu-le, gar treu bis an das Grab,

Memnon, Op. 6, No. 1

Den Tag hin-durch nur ein-mal mag ich spre-chen,

Am Grabe Anselmos, No. 3

Dass ich dich ver-lo--ren ha-be, Dass du nicht mehr bist,

Der Tod und das Mädchen, Op. 7, No. 3

Vor-ü-ber, ach, vor-ü-ber! geh, wil-der Kno-chen-mann

Erlafsee, Op. 8. No. 3

Mir ist so wohl, so weh' am stil-len Er-laf-see;

SCHUBERT

Am Strome, Op. 8, No. 4

Ist mir's doch, als sei mein Le-ben an den schö-nen Strom ge-bun-den;

Die Nachtigall, Op. 11, No. 2 (men's chorus)

Be- schei-den ver-bor-gen im bu-schich-ten Gang

So Freun-de, ver-hall-te manch' himm-li-sches Lied

Gesänge des Harfners, Op. 12, No. 1

Wer sich der Ein-sam-keit er-gibt, ach! der ist bald al-lein,

No. 2

Wer nie sein Brot mit Trä-nen ass, wer nie die kum-mer-vol-len Näch-te

No. 3

An die Tü-ren will ich schlei-chen, still und sitt-sam

Lob der Tränen, Op. 13, No. 2

Lau-e Lüf-te, Blu-men-düf-te, al-le Lenz und Ju-gend-lust;

Der Alpenjäger, No. 3

Auf ho-hem Ber-ges-rü-cken, wo fri-scher al-les grünt,

Suleika I, Op. 14, No. 1

Was be-deu-tet die Be-we-gung? Bringt der Ost mir fro-he Kun-de?

Ach, die wah-re Her-zens-kun-de, Lie-bes-hauch

Geheimes, No. 2

Ü- ber mei-nes Lieb-chens Äu-geln stehn ver-wun-dert al-le Leu-te;

Die Nacht, Op. 17, No. 4 (men's voices)

Wie schön bist Du, freundliche Stil-le, himm-li-sche Ruh'!

An Schwager Kronos, Op. 19, No. 1

Spu-te dich, Kro-nos! fort den rasseln-den Trott!

Ganymed, No. 3

Wie im Mor-gen-glan-ze du rings mich an-glüh'st

Sei mir gegrüsst! Op. 20, No. 1

O du Ent-riss-ne mir und mei-nem Küs-se, sei mir ge-grüsst,

Frühlingsglaube, No. 2

Die lin-den Lüf-te sind er-wacht, sie säu-seln und we-hen

Der Schiffer, Op. 21, No. 2

Im Win-de, im Stur-me be-fahr ich den Fluss,

Der Zwerg, Op. 22, No. 1

Im trü-ben Licht ver-schwin-den schon die Ber-ge, es schwebt das Schiff

Wehmuth, No. 2

Wenn ich durch Wald und Flu-ren geh', es wird mir dann so wohl und weh,

Im Haine, Op. 56, No. 3   A
Son- nen- strah- len durch die Tan - - - nen, wie sie fal- len

Der Schmetterling, Op. 57, No. 1   B
Wie soll ich nicht tan - - zen? es macht kei- ne Mü- he

An den Mond, No. 3   C
Geuss, lie - - - - - ber Mond, geuss dei- ne Sil- ber- flim- mer

es Mädchens Klage, Op. 58, No. 3   D
Der Eich- wald braust, die Wol - - ken ziehn, das Mägd - - lein sitzt

u liebst mich nicht, Op. 59, No. 1   E
Mein Herz ist zer- ris - - sen, du liebst mich nicht!

Dass sie hier gewesen! No. 2   F
Dass der Ost- wind Düf- te hau - - - chet in die Lüf - - te,

Du bist die Ruh, No. 3   G
Du bist die Ruh, der Frie- de mild, die Sehn- sucht du,

Lachen und Weinen, No. 4   H
La - - chen und wei - - nen zu jeg - li- cher Stun- de

Dithyrambe, Op. 60, No. 2   I
Nim- mer, das glaubt mir, er- schei- nen die Göt- ter, nim- mer al- lein,

Lied der Mignon I, Op. 62, No. 1   J
Heiss mich nicht re- den, heiss mich schwei- gen denn mein Ge- heim- niss

Lied der Mignon II, No. 2   K
So lasst mich schei- nen bis ich wer- de;

Lied der Mignon III, No. 3   L
So lasst mich schei- nen bis ich wer- de zieht mir das wei- sse

Lied der Mignon IV, No. 4   M
Nur wer die Sehn- sucht kennt, weiss, was ich lei- de,

ed eines Schiffers an die Dioskuren, Op. 65, No. 1   N
Di- os- ku- ren, Zwil- lings- sterne, die ihr leuch- tet mei- nen Na- chen,

Aus "Heliopolis" I, No. 3   O
Im kal- ten, rau- hen Nor- den ist Kun- de mir ge wor- den

Der Wachtelschlag, Op. 68   P
Ach! mir schallt's dor- ten so lieb- lich her- vor: fürch- te Gott!

Auf dem Wasser zu singen, Op. 72   Q
Mit- ten im Schimmer der spie- geln- den Wel- len gleitet, wie Schwäne,

Die Rose, Op. 73   R
Es lock- te schö- ne Wär- me mich an das Licht zu wa- gen,

   S
Was soll der mil- de A- bend? muss ich nun trau- rig fra- gen;

SCHUBERT

Über Wildemann, Op. 108, No. 1 — A
Die Win- de sau- sen am Tan- nen- hang, die Quel- len brau- sen

Todesmusik, No. 2 — B
In des To- des Fei- er- stun- de wenn ich einst von hin- nen schei- de,

Das Lied im Grünen, Op. 115, No. 1 — C
Ins Grü- ne, ins Grü- ne, da lockt uns der Früh- ling,

Sprache der Liebe, No. 3 — D
Lass dich mit ge- lin- den Schlägen rüh- ren mei- ne zar- te Lau- te!

An die Sonne, Op. 118, No. 5 — E
Sin- ke, liebe Son- ne, sin- ke, en- de dei- nen trü- ben Lauf

Die Spinnerin, No. 6 — F
Als ich still und ru- hig spann, oh- ne nur zu sto- cken

Der Hirt auf dem Felsen, Op. 129 (for soprano, clarinet and piano)
A — G
Wenn auf dem hoch- sten Fels ich steh',

B — H
Der Früh- ling will kom- men, der Früh- ling mei- ne Freud',

Das Echo, Op. 130 — I
Herz- lie- be, gu- te Mut- ter, O grol- le nicht mit mir,

Psalm, Op. 132, No. 23 — J
Gott ist mein Hirt, mir wird nichts man- geln Gott ist mein Hirt,

Nachthelle, Op. 134 (men's chorus) — K
Die Nacht ist hei- ter und ist rein, Die Nacht ist hei- ter und ist rein

Ständchen, Op. 135 — L
Zo- gernd lei- se, Zo- gernd lei- se in des Dun- kels

Miriams Siegesgesang, Op. 136
A — M
Rührt die Cym- bel, schlagt die Sai- ten, lasst den Hall

B — N
Aus E- gyp- ten vor dem Vol- ke

Nachtgesang im Walde, Op. 139b (men's chorus) — O
Sei uns stets ge- grüsst, O Nacht! a- ber dop- pelt hier im Wald,

— P
Es regt in den Lau- ben des Wal- des sich schon,

Das Bild, Op. 165, No. 3 — Q
Ein Mäd- chen ist's, das früh und spät mir vor der See- le schwe- bet,

An die Nachtigall, Op. 172, No. 3 — R
Geuss nicht so laut der lieb- ent- flamm- ten Lie- der ton- reichen Schall

Abendbilder — S
Still be- ginnt's im Hain zu thau- en, ru- hig webt der Dämm'- rung Grau- en

Abendstern
Was weilst du ein- sam an dem Him- mel, o schö- ner Stern?

Abschied (Lebewohl)
Le- - be wohl,__ le- be wohl, du__ lie- ber Freund

Als ich sie erröthen sah
All'__ mein Wir- - ken, all'__ mein Le- ben

Am Bach im Frühling
Du brachst sie nun, die kal- te Rin- de und rie- selst froh

Am Flusse
Ver- flie- sset, viel ge- lieb- te Lie- - der, zum Mee- - - - re

Am See
In des See- es Wo- gen- spie- le fal- len durch den Son- nen- schein

An den Mond
Fül- lest wie- der Busch und Tal__ still mit Ne- bel- glanz,

An den Tod
Tod, du Schre- cken der Na- tur, im- mer rie- selt dei- ne Uhr;

An die Entfernte
So hab' ich wirk- lich dich ver- lo- ren? Bist du, o Schö- ne mir ent- floh'n,

An die Freunde
Im Wald, im Wald da grabt__ mich ein, ganz stil- le oh- ne Kreuz

An die Sonne
Kö- nig- li- che Mor- gen- son- ne, sei__ ge- - grüsst

An mein Clavier
Sanf- tes Cla- vier, sanf- tes Cla- vier! wel- che Ent- zü__ ckung- en

Arietta, from Claudine von Villabella No. 3 (operetta)
Hin und wie- - - - der flie- gen die Pfei- le, A- mors leich- - - te

Auflösung
Ver- birg dich, Son- ne, denn die Glu- ten der Won- ne__ ver- ven- - gen

Aus "Heliopolis" II
Fels auf Fel- sen hin- ge- wäl- zet, fe- ster Grund und treu- er Halt;

Blumenlied
Es ist ein hal- bes Him- mel- reich, wenn, Pa- ra- die- ses- blu- men_ gleich,

Der Entfernten
Wohl denk'__ ich all- ent- hal- - - ben, O du Ent- fern- te, dein

Erlkönig
Wer rei- tet so spät durch Nacht und Wind? Es ist der Va- ter

Du lie- bes Kind, komm, geh mit mir! Gar schö- ne Spie- le

SCHUBERT

Erster Verlust — Ach, wer bringt die schö---nen Ta-ge, je-ne Ta-ge — A

Fahrt zum Hades — Der Na-chen dröhnt, Cy-pres-sen flü--stern,horch, Gei-ster re-den — B

Des Fischers Liebesglück — Dort blin-ket durch Wei-den und win-ket ein Schim-mer — C

Fragment aus dem Aeschylus — So wird der Mann, der son-der Zwang ge-recht ist,nicht un-glück-lich_ sein — D

Freiwilliges Versinken — Wo-hin? O He-li-os! wo-hin? — E

Ich neh-me_ nicht, ich pfle-ge nur zu ge-ben — F

Frühlingslied — Die Luft ist blau, das Thal ist grün, die klei-nen Mai-en-glo-cken blühn, — G

Gebet während der Schlacht — Va-ter,ich ru-fe dich! Brül-lend um-wölkt mich der Dampf — H

Va-ter, du füh-re mich!Führ' mich zum Sie-ge, führ mich zum To-de — I

Gondelfahrer — Es tan-zen Mond_ und Ster-ne den flücht'_gen Gei--ster-reih'n_ — J

Gott im Frühlinge — In sei-nem schim-mern-den Ge-wand hast du den Früh-ling — K

Grenzen der Menschheit — Wenn der ur-al-te hei-li-ge Va-ter mit ge-las-se-ner_Hand — L

Gretchen (from Goethe's "Faust") — Ach, nei--ge, du Schmer-zen-rei----che, dein Ant-litz — M

Ihr Grab — Dort ist ihr Grab, die einst im Schmelz der Ju-gend_glüh--te — N

Im Abendrot — O, wie schön ist dei--ne Welt, Va-ter,wenn sie gol-den strah-let! — O

Im Frühling — Still sitz' ich an des Hü-gels Hang, der Him-mel ist_ so_ klar, — P

Der Jüngling am Bache — An der Quel-le sass der Kna-be, Blu-men_ wand er sich_ zum_ Kranz, — Q

Der Jüngling an der Quelle — Lei--se, rie-seln-der Quell! ihr wal-len-den,flispern-den Pop-peln! — R

Der Jüngling auf dem Hügel — Ein_ Jüng-ling auf dem Hü-gel mit_ sei-nem Kum-mer sass___ — S

Der Jüngling und der Tod — A
Die Son-ne sinkt_ o könnt ich, o könnt ich mit ihr schei-den,

Der Knabe — B
Wenn ich nur ein Vög-lein_ wä-re, ach, wie wollt' ich lu-stig_flie-gen

Der Kreuzzug — C
Ein Mü-nich steht in sei-ner Zell' am Fen-ster-git-ter_ grau

Die Liebe — D
Freud-voll und leid-voll, ge-dan---ken-voll sein

Die Liebe — E
Wo weht der Lie-be ho-her Geist?_ Er weht in Blum' und_ Baum

Liebhaber in allen Gestalten — F
Ich wollt' ich wär' ein Fisch, so hur-tig und frisch;

Der liebliche Stern — G
Ihr Stern-lein, still in der Hö-he, ihr Stern-lein, spie-lend im Meer,_

Liebe schwärmt auf allen Wegen,
from Claudine von Villabella
(operetta) Act I No. 6 — H
Lie-be schwärmt auf al-len We-gen: Treu-e wohnt_für sich al-lein

Liebeslauschen — I
Hier un-ten steht ein Rit-ter in hel-len Mon-den-strahl,

Lied der Mignon (Nur wer die
Sehnsucht kennt) (two
different settings) — J
Nur wer die Sehn-sucht kennt weiss_ was_ ich lei-de!

— K
Nur wer die Sehn-sucht kennt weiss was_ ich lei-de!

Litanei auf das Fest "Aller Seelen" — L
Ruh'n in Frie-den al----le See----len,

Das Mädchen — M
Wie_ so in-nig, möcht'_ich sa-gen, sich_ der Mei-ne mir er-giebt

Die Männer sind méchant — N
Du sag-test mir es, Mut-ter: Er ist ein Spring ins feld

Minnelied — O
Hol-der klingt_ der Vo-gel-sang, wenn die En-gel-rei-ne,

Die Nacht — P
Du_ ver-störst uns nicht, o Nacht! Sieh, wir trin-ken

Nachtgesang — Q
O_gieb vom wei-chen Pfüh-le träu-mend, ein halb_ Ge-hör

Nachtviolen — R
Nacht-vi-o-len, Nacht-vi-o-len! dun-kle Au-gen, see-len-vol-le,

Wiederschein
Tom lehnt har- rend auf der Brü- cke, die Ge- lieb- te säumt,

Der Winterabend
Es ist so still, so heim- lich um mich, die Sonn' ist un- ter,

Der zürnende Barde
Wer wagt's, wer wagt's, wer wagt's, wer will mir die Lei- er zer- bre- chen,

SCHULTZ, Johann Abraham Peter (1747-1800)

Am Sylvester-Abend
Des Jah- res letz- te Stun- de er- tönt mit ern- stem Schlag

SCHUMANN, Clara (1819-1896)

Liebst du um Schönheit, Op. 37, No. 4
Liebst du um Schön- heit O nicht mich lie- be!

SCHUMANN, Robert (1810-1856)

Der Contrabandiste (Spanish Songs)
Ich bin der Con- tra- ban- di- ste, Weiss wohl Respect mir zu schaffen,

Morgens steh ich auf und frage, Op. 24, No. 1
Mor- gens steh' ich auf und fra- ge: Kommt fein's Lieb- chen heut'?

Es treibt mich hin, No. 2
Es treibt mich hin, es treibt mich her! Noch we- ni- ge Stun- den,

Ich wandelte unter den Bäumen, No. 3
Ich wan- del- te un- ter den Bäu- men mit mei- nem Gram al- lein

Lieb' Liebchen, No. 4
Lieb' Lieb- chen, leg's Händ- chen auf's Her- ze mein;

Schöne Wiege meiner Leiden, No. 5
Schö- ne Wie- ge mei- ner Lei- den, schö- nes Grab- mal -

Mit Myrthen und Rosen, No. 9
Mit Myr- then und Ro- sen, lieb- lich und hold,

Myrthen, Op. 25, No. 1 Widmung
Du mei- ne See- le, du mein Herz, du mei- ne Wonn' o du mein Schmerz,

Du bist die Ruh', du bist der Frie- den, du bist vom Him- mel

No. 2 Freisinn
Lasst mich nur auf mei- nem Sat- tel gel - - ten!

No. 3 Der Nussbaum
Es grü- net ein Nuss- baum vor dem Haus, duf- tig, luf- tig brei- tet

SCHUMANN

Myrthen, Op. 25, No. 4 Jemand — A
Mein Herz ist be- trübt, ich sag' es nicht, mein__ Herz ist be- trübt__

No. 7 Die Lotosblume — B
Die Lo- tos- blu- me äng- stigt sich vor der Son- ne Pracht,

No. 8 Talismane — C
Got- tes ist der O- ri- ent! Got- tes ist der Oc- ci- dent!

No. 9 Lied der Suleika — D
Wie, mit in- nig- stem Be- ha- gen, Lied, em- pfind' ich dei- nen Sinn!

No. 11 Lieder der Braut — E
Mut- ter,__ Mut- ter! Glau- be nicht, weil ich ihn lieb' al____ so sehr,

No. 12 — F
Lass mich ihm am Bu- sen han- gen, Mut- ter, Mut- ter!

No. 14 Hoch- ländisches Wiegenlied — G
Schla- fe, sü- - - - sser klei- ner Do- - - - - - nald;

No. 15 Aus den hebräischen Gesängen — H
Mein Herz ist schwer Auf! von der Wand die Lau- te,

No. 17 Zwei Venetianische Lieder — I
Leis' ru- dern hier, mein Gon- - - - do- lier, leis', leis'!

No. 18 — J
Wenn durch die Pi- a- zet- - ta die A- bend- luft weht,

No. 21 Was will die einsame Thräne? — K
Was will die ein- sa- me Thrä- ne? sie trübt mir ja__ den Blick.

No. 23 Im Westen — L
Ich schau ü- ber Forth, hin- ü- ber nach Nord: was hel- fen mir Nord

No. 24 Du bist wie eine Blume — M
Du bist__ wie ei- ne Blu- me, so hold und schön__ und rein;

No. 25 Aus den östlichen Rosen — N
Ich sen- de ei- - nen Gruss wie Duft der Ro- sen,

No. 26 Zum Schluss — O
Hier in die- sen erd be- klomm- nen Lüf- ten, wo__ die Weh- mut taut,

Was soll ich sagen! Op. 27, No. 3 — P
Mein Aug' ist trüb', mein Mund ist stumm, du heissest mich re- den,

Jasminenstrauch, No. 4 — Q
Grün ist der Jas- mi- nen- strauch A- bends ein- ge- schla- fen.

Der Page, Op. 30, No. 2 — R
Da ich nun ent- sa- gen müs- sen Al- lem, was mein Herz

Der Hidalgo, No. 3 — S
Es ist so süss zu scher- zen mit Lie- dern und mit Her- zen

Der Hidalgo, Op. 30, No. 3 — Die Schö- nen von Se- vil- la, mit Fä- cher-und Man- til- la,

Die Kartenlegerin, Op. 31, No. 2 — Schlief die Mut- ter end- lich ein ü- ber ih- rer Haus- po-stil- le?

Liebesgarten, Op. 34, No. 1 — Die Lie- be ist ein Ro- - sen-strauch, wo blüht er, wo blüht er?

Unter'm Fenster, No. 3 — Wer ist vor mei- ner Kam- mer-thür? Ich bin es, ich bin es!

Familien-Gemälde, No. 4 — Gross- va- ter und Gross- mut- ter, die sas- sen im Gar- ten-hag,

Lust der Sturmnacht, Op. 35, No. 1 — Wenn durch Berg' und Tha- - le drau- ssen Re- gen schau- ert,

Stirb, Lieb' und Freud, No. 2 — Zu Augs- burg steht ein ho- - - - - hes Haus

Wanderlied, No. 3 — Wohl- auf! noch ge-trun- ken den fun- kelnden Wein! A- de nun, ihr Lie- ben,

Erstes Grün, No. 4 — Du jun- ges Grün, du fri-sches Gras, wie man-ches Herz durch_ dich ge- nas,

Auf das Trinkglas eines verstorbenen Freundes, No. 6 — Du herr- lich Glas, nun stehst du leer, Glas, das er oft

Wanderung, No. 7 — Wohl- auf und frisch ge-wan- dert in's un- be-kann- te Land!

Stille Liebe, No. 8 — Könnt'ich dich in Lie- dern prei- sen, säng ich dir das läng- ste Lied,

Frage, No. 9 — Wärst du nicht, heil' ger A- bend-schein! wärst du nicht,

Stille Thränen, No. 10 — Du bist_ vom Schlaf_ er- stan-den und wan- delst durch_die Au'_

Wer machte dich so krank? No. 11 — Dass du so krank_ ge- wor-den, wer hat es denn ge- macht?

Alte Laute, No. 12 — Hörst du den Vo- gel sin- gen? Siehst du den Plü-then-baum?

Sonntags am Rhein, Op. 36, No. 1 — Des Sonn- tags in der Mor- gen-stund' wie wan-dert's sich so schön

Ständchen, No. 2 — Lieb- chen, was zö- gerst Du? Lieb- chen, was zö- gerst Du?

An den Sonnenschein, No. 4 — O Son- nen-schein, o Son- nen-schein! wie_ scheinst du mir in's Herz hinein,

SCHUMANN

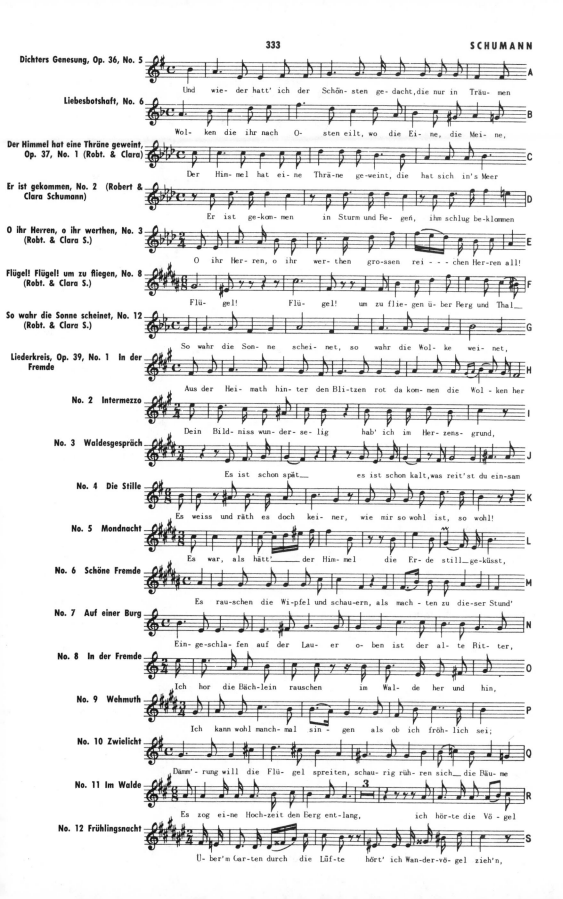

Dichters Genesung, Op. 36, No. 5 — A
Und wie-der hatt' ich der Schön-sten ge-dacht,die nur in Träu-men

Liebesbotshaft, No. 6 — B
Wol-ken die ihr nach O-sten eilt, wo die Ei-ne, die Mei-ne,

Der Himmel hat eine Thräne geweint, Op. 37, No. 1 (Robt. & Clara) — C
Der Him-mel hat ei-ne Thrä-ne ge-weint, die hat sich in's Meer

Er ist gekommen, No. 2 (Robert & Clara Schumann) — D
Er ist ge-kom-men in Sturm und Re-gen, ihm schlug be-klommen

O ihr Herren, o ihr werthen, No. 3 (Robt. & Clara S.) — E
O ihr Her-ren, o ihr wer-then gros-sen rei - - - chen Her-ren all!

Flügel! Flügel! um zu fliegen, No. 8 (Robt. & Clara S.) — F
Flü-gel! Flü-gel! um zu flie-gen ü-ber Berg und Thal

So wahr die Sonne scheinet, No. 12 (Robt. & Clara S.) — G
So wahr die Son-ne schei-net, so wahr die Wol-ke wei-net,

Liederkreis, Op. 39, No. 1 In der Fremde — H
Aus der Hei-math hin-ter den Bli-tzen rot da kom-men die Wol-ken her

No. 2 Intermezzo — I
Dein Bild-niss wun-der-se-lig hab' ich im Her-zens-grund,

No. 3 Waldesgespräch — J
Es ist schon spät es ist schon kalt,was reit'st du ein-sam

No. 4 Die Stille — K
Es weiss und räth es doch kei-ner, wie mir so wohl ist, so wohl!

No. 5 Mondnacht — L
Es war, als hätt' der Him-mel die Er-de still ge-küsst,

No. 6 Schöne Fremde — M
Es rau-schen die Wi-pfel und schau-ern, als mach-ten zu die-ser Stund'

No. 7 Auf einer Burg — N
Ein-ge-schla-fen auf der Lau-er o-ben ist der al-te Rit-ter,

No. 8 In der Fremde — O
Ich hor die Bäch-lein rauschen im Wal-de her und hin,

No. 9 Wehmuth — P
Ich kann wohl manch-mal sin-gen als ob ich fröh-lich sei;

No. 10 Zwielicht — Q
Dämm'-rung will die Flü-gel spreiten, schau-rig rüh-ren sich die Bäu-me

No. 11 Im Walde — R
Es zog ei-ne Hoch-zeit den Berg ent-lang, ich hör-te die Vö-gel

No. 12 Frühlingsnacht — S
Ü-ber'm Gar-ten durch die Lüf-te hört' ich Wan-der-vö-gel zieh'n,

Märzveilchen, Op. 40, No. 1

Der Him- mel wölbt sich rein und blau, der Reif stellt Blu- men

A

Muttertraum, No. 2

Die Mut- ter be- tet her- zig, und schaut ent- zückt

B

Der Soldat, No. 3

Es geht bei ge-däm- pfter Trom-meln Klang. Wie weit noch die Stät- te,

C

Frauenliebe und Leben (cycle), Op. 42, No. 1

Seit ich ihn ge- se- hen, glaub ich blind zu sein,

D

No. 2

Er, der herr-lich-ste von al- len, wie so mil- de, wie__ so gut

E

No. 3

Ich kann's nicht fassen,nicht glau-ben, es hat ein Traum mich be-rückt,__

F

No. 4

Du Ring an mei-nem Fin - - ger, mein__ gol-de-nes Rin-ge- lein,

G

No. 5

Helft mir,ihr Schwes-tern freundlich mich schmücken, dient__ der Glück-li-chen

H

No. 6

Sü - - - sser Freund, du bli-ckest mich ver-wun- dert an

I

No. 7

An mei-nem Her- zen, an mei- ner Brust, du mei- ne Won- ne,

J

No. 8

Nun hast du mir den er-sten Schmerz ge- tan, der a- ber traf

K

Der Schatzgräber, Op. 45, No. 1

Wenn al- le Wäl- der schlie-fen, er an zu gra-ben hub.

L

Frühlingsfahrt, No. 2

Es zo-gen zwei rüst-'ge Ge-sel-len zum__ er-sten mal__ von Haus,

M

Dichterliebe (cycle), Op. 48, No. 1

Im wun-der schö-nen Mo-nat Mai, als al- le Knos- - pen spran-gen

N

No. 2

Aus mei nen Thrä-nen sprie-ssen viel blü-hen-de Blu-men her- vor,

O

No. 3

Die Ro- se, die Li- lie, die Tau- be, die Son- ne,

P

No. 4

Wenn ich in dei- ne Au-gen seh' so schwin-det all' mein Leid

Q

No. 5

Ich will mei-ne See- le tau-chen in den Kelch der Li-lie hin- ein;

R

No. 6

Im Rhein, im hei-li-gen Stro-me, de spie-gelt sich in den Well'n,

S

Belsatzar, Op. 57 — Die Mit-ter-nacht zog nä-her schon; in stum-mer Ruh' lag Ba-by-lon — A

Die Soldatenbraut, Op. 64, No. 1 — Ach, wenn's nur der Kö-nig auch wüsst', wie wa-cker mein Schätze-lein ist! — B

Das verlassne Mägdelein, No. 2 — Früh wann die Häh-ne krah'n eh' die Stern-lein schwin-den, — C

Tragödie, No. 3 1 — Ent-flieh' mit mir und sei mein Weib und ruh' an mei-nem Her-zen aus! — D

2 — Es fiel ein Reif in der Früh-lings-nacht, er fiel auf die zar - - - ten Blau — E

Die Rose stand im Thau, Op. 65, No.1 (male chorus) — Die Ro-se stand im Thau, es wa-ren Per-len grau. — F

Melancholie, Op. 74, No. 6 — Wann, wann er-scheint der Mor-gen, wann denn, wann denn! — G

Geständniss, No. 7 — Al-so lieb' ich euch, Ge-lieb-te, dass mein Herz es nicht mag wa-gen, — H

Im Walde, Op. 75, No. 2 (chorus) — Es zog ei-ne Hoch-zeit den Berg ent-lang, den Berg ent-lang — I

Geisternähe, Op. 77, No. 3 — Was weht um mei-ne Schlä-fe wie lau-e Früh-ling-luft, — J

Stiller Vorwurf, No. 4 — In ein-sa-men Stun-den drängt Weh-muth sich auf, — K

Aufträge, No. 5 — Nicht so schnel-le, nicht so schnelle! wart' ein wenig, kleine Wel-le! — L

Er und Sie, Op. 78, No. 2 — Seh' ich in das stil-le Thal, wo im Son-nen-schei-ne — M

Ich denke dein, No. 3 — Ich den-ke dein, wenn mir der Son-ne Schim-mer vom Mee-re strahlt; — N

Wiegenlied, No. 4 — Schlaf', Kind-lein, schlaf, wie du schläfst, so bist du brav! — O

Liederalbum für die Jugend, Op. 79, No. 1 Der Abendstern — Du lieb-li-cher Stern, du leuch-test so fern, — P

No. 4 Frühlingsgruss — So sei ge-grüsst viel tau-send-mal, hol-der, hol-der Früh-ling! — Q

No. 7a Zigeunerliedchen — Un-ter die Sol-da-ten ist ein Zi-geu-ner-bub' ge-gan-gen, — R

No. 7b Jeden Morgen — Je-den Mor-gen, in der Frü-he, wenn mich weckt das Ta-ges-licht, — S

SCHUMANN

338

Drei Gesänge (Hebrew Melodies) Op. 95, No. 1 Die Tochter Jephtas

Da die Hei-math, o Va-ter, da Gott von der Toch-ter

No. 2 An den Mond

Schlaf-lo-ser Son-ne, me-lan-chol-scher Stern! Dein thrän-en-voller Strahl

No. 3 Dem Helden

Dein Tag ist aus, dein Ruhm fing an, es preist des Volks Ge-sang

Nachtlied, Op. 96, No. 1

Ü-ber al-len Gipfeln ist Ruh', in al-len Wi-pfeln spü-rest du

Schneeglöckchen, No. 2

Die Son-ne sah die Er-de an, es ging ein mil-der Wind

Ihre Stimme, No. 3

Lass' tief in dir mich le-sen, ver-hehl auch dies mir nicht,

Himmel und Erde, No. 5

Wie der Bäu-me küh-ne Wip-fel zu des Lich-tes Hö-hen

Nur wer die Sehnsucht kennt, Op. 98a, No. 3

Nur wer die Sehn-sucht kennt, weiss was ich lei-de,

Wer nie sein Brot mit Thränen ass, No. 4

Wer nie sein Brot mit Thränen ass, wer nie die kum-mer-vol-len Näch-te

Heiss' mich nicht reden, No. 5

Heiss' mich nicht re-den, heiss' mich schweigen denn mein Ge-heim-nis

Wer sich der Einsamkeit ergiebt, No. 6

Wer sich der Ein-sam-keit er-giebt ach! der ist bald al-lein;

So lasst mich scheinen, No. 9

So lasst mich scheinen bis ich wer-de, zieht mir das weisse Kleid nicht aus!

An die Türen will ich schleichen, No. 8

An die Tü-ren will ich schlei-chen, still und sittsam will ich stehn,

Liebster, deine Worte stehlen, Op. 101, No. 2

Lieb-ster, dei-ne Wor-te steh-len aus dem Bu-sen mir das Herz

Mein schöner Stern, ich bitte dich, No. 4

Mein schö-ner Stern! ich bit-te dich, o las-se du dein heitres Licht

O Freund, mein Schirm, mein Schutz, No. 6

O Freund, mein Schirm, mein Schutz! o Freund mein Schmuck, mein Putz!

An den Abendstern, Op. 103, No. 4

Schweb' em-por am Him-mel, schö - - ner A-bend-stern

Viel Glück zur Reise, Schwalben, Op. 104, No. 2

Viel Glück zur Rei-se, Schwalben! ihr eilt, ein lan-ger Zug,

Der Zeisig, No. 4

Wir sind ja, Kind, im Mai-e, wirf Buch und Heft von dir

SCHUMANN

Die Spinnerin, Op. 107, No. 4 — A
Auf dem Dorf' in den Spinn stu-ben sind lus - - tig die Mäd-chen.

Nänie, Op. 114 (women's chorus) — B
Un - ter den ro-ten Blu - men schlum-me - re, schlum- me - re,

— C
Senkt die Nacht den sanf-ten Fit - tig nie-der tönt der Zi - ther

— D
O bli-cke, wenn den Sinn dir will die Welt_____ ver-wir-ren

Der Husar, tra-ra! Op. 117, No. 1 — E
Der Hu-sar, Tra- ra! was ist die Ge- fahr? Sein herz-lieb-ster Schatz

Da liegt der Feinde gestreckte Schaar, No. 4 — F
Da liegt_ der Feinde ge-stre-ckte Schaar, sie liegt in ihrem blutroten Blut

Frühlingslust, Op. 125, No. 2 — G
Nun ste-hen die Ro-sen in Blü- the, da wirft die Lie - be ein Netz-lein aus,

Die Meerfee, No. 3 — H
Hel - - le Sil-ber-glöck-lein klin-gen aus der Luft vom Meer;

Jung Volkers Lied, No. 4 — I
Und die mich trug im Mut-ter-arm, und die mich schwang_ in Kis-sen,

Dein Angesicht, Op. 127, No. 2 — J
Dein An- ge-sicht, so lieb und schön, das hab' ich jungst im Traum ge-seh'n,

Es leuchtet meine Liebe, No. 3 — K
Es leuch-tet mei - ne Lie - be in ih - rer dun - keln Pracht,

Tief im Herzen trag' ich Pein, Op. 138, No. 2 — L
Tief_____ im Her - zen trag' ich Pein, muss nach aus-sen stille sein,

O wie lieblich ist das Mädchen, No. 3 — M
O wie lieb-lich ist das Mäd-chen wie so schön und voll An- muth_____

Romanze, No. 5 — N
Flu - - ten rei-cher Eb- ro, blü - - - hen-der U- fer,

Weh, wie zornig ist das Mädchen, No. 7 — O
Weh, wie zor - nig ist das Mädchen, weh, wie zornig, weh, weh!

Hoch, hoch sind die Berge, No. 8 — P
Hoch, hoch sind die Ber- ge und steil ist der Pfad,

Provenzalisches Lied, Op. 139, No. 4 — Q
In dem Ta- len der Pro- ven-ce ist_____ der Min-ne-sang entsprossen,

SCHÜTZ, Heinrich (1585-1672)

Bringt her dem Herren — S
Bringt her dem Her- ren, bringt her dem Her- ren, bringt her dem Her - - ren

Geistliche Konzerte (Psalm 40)
Ei- le mich, Gott, zu er- ret- ten Herr, mir zu hel- fen — A

Erhöre mich
Er- hö- re mich, er- hö- re mich, wenn ich ru- fe, — B

Die Furcht des Herren
Die Furcht des Her- ren Ist der Weis-heit An- fang, — C

O lieber Herre Gott
O lie- ber Hee- re Gott we-cke uns auf,__ dass wir be-reit sein, — D

Schaffe, in mir, Gott
Schaf-fe in mir, Gott, ein rei- nes Herz und gieb mir einen neu-en, — E

Ich danke dem Herrn
Ich dan- ke dem Herrn von ganzem Her- zen im Rath der From- men — F

Ich liege und schlafe
Ich lie- ge und schla-------- fe — G

Psalm 20
Der Herr er- hör dich in der Not, Sein Nam' dich wohl be- hü- te, — H

Psalm 74
Wie sehr lieb- lich und schö-ne, Sind doch die Woh- nung dein! — I

Psalm 97
Der Herr ist Kö---nig ü- ber all, Das Erd-reich sich__ des fre- ue — J

Psalm 121
Ich heb mein Aug- en sehn-lich auf und seh die Ber- ge — K

Selig sind die Toten
Se- lig sind die To- ten Se- lig sind, se-lig sind, — L

Symphonie Sacrae Part I
Ich wer- de, ich wer- de, ich wer- de nicht ster----- ben, — M

Part II
Herr, un-ser Herr-scher, Herr, un-ser Herr-scher,wie herrlich ist dein Nam, — N

SCOTT, Lady John (Alicia Ann Scott) (1810-1900)

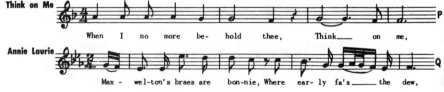

Think on Me
When I no more be- hold thee, Think__ on me, — P

Annie Laurie
Max- wel-ton's braes are bon-nie, Where ear- ly fa's__ the dew, — Q

SCOTT, Cyril (1879-1970)

Blackbird's Song, Op. 52, No. 3
By permission of Galaxy Music Corporation, N. Y., copyright by Elkin & Co., Ltd.
Sweet- heart, I ne'er may know,__ Nev- er may see__ — R

Lullaby, Op. 57, No. 3
Copyright by G. Ricordi & Co., Inc.

Lul- la- by,   oh   Lul- la- by,   Flow'rs are closed and lambs_are_sleep-ing

The Unforeseen, Op. 74, No. 3
By permission of Galaxy Music Corporation, N. Y., copyright by Elkin & Co., Ltd.

How could I   dream a   day would ev - - er___ dawn___

SCUDERI, Salvatore

Dormi Pure

Dor- mi   pu- re dor-mi fe- li - - ce dell' a- mor mi- o

SECCHI, Antonio (1761-1833)

Love Me or Not

Love me   or   not,___   Love her I   must   or   die,___

Lungi dal caro bene

Lun- gi dal ca- ro   be- ne   Vi- ve-re non___ poss'_ i - - o

SENFL, Ludwig (c. 1492-c. 1555)

Kling, Klang

Kommt her,   Leu- te all',   und helft uns ein- mal;   Kommt her, Kommt her

SERMISY, Claudin de (16th Cent.)

Au joly bois (madrigal)

Au   jo- ly   bois en   l'om- bre d'ung sou- cy   My fault al- ler

En entrant en ung jardin

En en- trant en   ung jar- din   j'ay trou- vé Guil- lot Mar- tin

SEVERAC, Déodat de (1873-1921)

À l'aube dans la montagne
Copyright by Salabert, Paris, N. Y.

La long du ciel gre- nat,   d'un gre- nat d'i- ris   et   roux,

Aubade
Copyright by Salabert, Paris, N. Y.

Voi- ci ton   Jean, ton Jean,   ô!___ Mar- gue- ri - - te

Chanson de la nuit durable
Copyright by Salabert, Paris, N. Y.

Oh!   ma pe- ti- te prin- ces- se   de   clar- té

Chanson pour le petit cheval
Copyright by Salabert, Paris, N. Y.

Pe- tit che- val, qui m'est si   cher___   va_ promp-te- ment___

Le ciel est par-dessus le toit (In Prison)
Copyright by Salabert, Paris, N. Y.

Le ciel est, par dessus le toit   si bleu si cal - - - - me,

Les Hiboux

Sous les ifs noir qui les a- bri-tent Les hi-boux se tien-nent ran-gés

Ma poupée chérie

Copyright by Salabert, Paris, N. Y.

Ma pou-pée ché-rie ne veut pas___ dor- -mir!

SHOSTAKOVICH, Dmitri (1906-1975)

United Nations
Copyright 1946
Leeds Music Corp., N. Y.
Used by permission.

The sun and the stars are all ring-ing___ with song ris-ing strong

SIBELIUS, Jean (1865-1957)

Våren Flyktar Hastigt (Spring is Fleeting), Op. 13, No. 4
Copyright by Oliver Ditson Co.
Used by permission

Swift the spring-time pass-es yet more swift the sum-mer,

Vilse (Astray) (Verirrt), Op. 17, No. 4
By permission Associated Music Publishers, Inc.

Wir lie-fen wohl ir-re den an-dern vor-an,

Lastu lainehilla (Driftwood), No. 7
By permission Associated Music Publishers, Inc.

Span, wo- her auf Wel-len spu-ren? Ru-ne auf der Wo-ge Rük-ken?

Svarta rosor (Black Roses), Op. 36, No. 1
By permission Associated Music Publishers, Inc.

Tell me what grief o-ver-comes you to-day, You that ev-er are

Säf, säf, susa (Schilfrohr, säus'le!), No. 4
By permission Associated Music Publishers, Inc.

Schilf-rohr, säus- le, Wel- le, flieh', doch sagt, wo ist jung In-ga-lill,

Den första Kyssen (The First Kiss), Op. 37, No. 1
By permission Associated Music Publishers, Inc.

Zum A- bend-stern am Sil-ber-wol-ken ran-de

Var det en dröm? (Was it a dream?), No. 4
By permission Associated Music Publishers, Inc.

War___ es ein Traum___ dass Zei-ten lang Dein___ Her-zens freund_ich war?

Tuol Laulaa Neitonen (A Maiden Yonder Sings), Op. 50, No. 3
Copyright by Oliver Ditson Co.
Used by permission

A mai-den yon-der___ sings Per-chance is___ dead___ her___ lov-er,

O wert thou here (Aus banger Brust), No. 4
By permission Associated Music Publishers, Inc.

The ro-ses___ blos-som as last year, Soft_ breezes thro' the fol-iage_sigh

The Silent Town (Die stille Stadt), No. 5
By permission Associated Music Publishers, Inc.

A town lies in the val-ley, The pal-lid gloam-ing___ dies;

Kom nu hit, död (Come away, Death), Op. 60, No. 1 (Shakespeare)
By permission Associated Music Publishers, Inc.

Komm her-bei, komm her-bei, Tod! Ver-senk in Cy-pres-sen den Leib,

Vår förnimmelser (Coming of Spring), Op. 86, No. 1
Copyright by Hansen, Copenhagen

Öf-ver drif-vans is-kri-stall blän-der so-len vär-ligt.

Blåseppan (The Anemone), Op. 88, No. 1
Copyright by Hansen, Copenhagen

Wie in der Luft du Ler-chen-schlag So willst auch Du im grü-nen_Hag,

Norden (From the North), Op. 90, No. 1
Copyright by Hansen, Copenhagen

Welk___ sind die Blät- - ter,_ Eis___ deckt die Se- - -en

SIBELLA, Gabriele

La Girometta (arr.)
Copyright 1919, G. Schirmer, Inc.

A: Chi t'ha fat- to quel- le scar- pet- te che ti stan si ben

B: Me l'ha fat- te lo mio A- mo- re,___ me l'ha fat- te lo mio A- mo- re

SIECZYNSKI, Dr. Rudolf

Wien, du Stadt meiner Träume

A: Mein Herz und mein Sinn schwärmt stets nur für Wien

B: Wien, Wien, nur du al- lein sollst stets die Stadt meiner Träu- me

SILCHER, Friedrich (1789-1860)

Aennchen von Tharau

Die Lorelei

Aenn- chen von Tha- rau ist, die mir ge- fällt, sie ist mein Le- ben,

Ich weiss nicht was soll es be- deu- ten dass ich so trau- rig bin___

SINDING, Christian (1856-1941)

Moderen Synger (The mother sings)

Der Skreg un Fugl (There cried a bird)

Sylvelin, Op. 55, No. 1
Copyright 1912, G. Schirmer, Inc.

Gret- chen lies in her gloom- y bed in the wet, wet mold

There cried___ a bird in its lone - - - - - some flight

O Syl- ve- lin, God's own blessing be on you the whole day through!

SJÖBERG, C.

Tonerna

Tan- ke, hvars stri- der blott nat- ten ser___ To- ner,___

SJÖGREN, Emil (1853-1918)

Lehn' deine Wang', Op. 16, No. 5

Lehn' die- ne Wang' an mei- ne Wang' dann fliessen die Thrä- nen

SMETANA, Bedrich (1824-1884)

OPERAS

The Bartered Bride   Act I
Opening Chorus

Seht am Strauch die Knos-- pen___ sprin- gen!__ Hört die mun- tern Vö- gel

The Bartered Bride Act I

A: Gern ja will ich dir ver- trau- en, gläu- big bli- cken auf zu dir,

Duet A

B: Mit der Mut- ter sank zu Gra- be mein gan- zes jun- ges Glück

B: O Du gu- ter, ar- mer Kna- be, wie klang_ ich_ um Dein Ge- schick

D: Nun in Lust_ und_ Lei- - de, nun in Schmerz und Freu- de sind vereint

E: Al- les ist so gut wie rich- tig, das Fi- ne ist nur wich- tig

F: Ge- kom- men_ wär' er mit mir wie_ ger- ne doch zar- te Rück- sicht,

Polka (Finale) A

G: Durch die Reih- en hin zu flie- gen! Sich zu Zwei- en an- zu- schmie- gen!

B

H: Ging es, wie es uns ge- fällt tanz- - - te mit die gan- ze Welt

Act II Drinking Chorus

I: Wie schäumst du in den Glä- sern, ed- ler Ger- sten- saft,

Sextet

J: Noch ein Weil- chen, Ma- rie, be- denk' es Dir

Stuttering Song

K: Theu- - - -theu- - - - - - - - -theu- theu- ren Sohn, spra- - -spra- - - - -sprach Müt- ter- lein,

L: Ich weiss Euch ei- nen lie- ben Schatz den man- cher schon be- gehrt,

Duet A

M: Komm, mein Söhn- chen, auf ein Wort! Will dir was ver- trau- - en

B

N: Wer in Lieb' entbrannt, hält aus Un- ver- stand Wei- ber für En- gel,

O: Weiss ich doch Ei- ne, die hat Du- ka- ten, hat Du- ka- ten

P: Es muss ge- lin- gen! Al- les soll nach Wunsch und Wil- len ge- hen

Act III Duet

Q: Al- les geht am Schnür- chen, da man Dich nicht quält

R: Wie fremd und todt ist Al- les um- her,

S: Mein lie- ber Schatz, nun_ auf- ge- passt! Ich geb' Dir was zu hö- ren,

SMETANA

The Bartered Bride Act III — A
Ge- seg- net, ge- seg- net, wer liebt und auch ver- traut!

Finale — B
Kom- men wir ger- ne, so kom- men wir gleich, gleich, gleich,

— C
So ist's recht, es freut uns Al- le, so ist's recht,

Dalibor Act II Love duet — D
Ta du- še ta tou- ha, to srd- ce, ten čar tot' lás- ky mé

Duet — E
Ó nev- ý- slov- né š tě- sti lá- sky

The Devil's Wall (Certova Sténa) Act I — F
Stast- ná vím on přijde dnes přec mě vsr- déč- ku cos trá- nu

— G
Ciž poz- by- la jsi ve mne ví- ry? A kdy- by můj byl kraj ten sí- rý

— H
Tak věč- ně k to- bě ïnout rtem na rtu spo- či nout

— I
Jen je- di- na- mě ze- ny krá- sna tvář tak do- ja- la

Act II — J
Kam prch- nout, kam prch- nout před je- jím tak sladkym o- brazem?

— K
Ach, žie se to- mu při- vy- ka Mně se to zvot- lo s nejkrásně jším

Act III — L
Ti- se krad- me pře- po- zor- ně špe- hům chy- trým pro- ne- snáz,

— M
O Bo- že lá- sky V té- to hrů- zné chvi- li mi ro- stou kří- dla

The Kiss Act I Duet — N
Für e- wig ver- eint treu in Lie- be ist un- ser heisses flehen

Cradle Song — O
Schla- fe mein Kind- lein, schlaf' ein, schla- fe ein,

— P
Wie hell am Him- mel die Ster- ne auch steh'n, wie sanft im Mond- licht

Act II Smugglers' Chorus — Q
Lei- se, auf- ge- passt oh- ne Ruh noch Rast; lauscht im Mor- gen- wind

If I knew how to wipe out my fault — R
Zu süh- nen mei- ne gro- sse Schuld, will ich die Ge- lieb- te

Duet — S
Ach, ar- mer Freund, früh starb dein Gluck, schwer kehrt, was man ver- lor, zu- rück!

The Kiss Act II Duet

Wir su-chen sie wir fin-den sie, du rufst die ganze Nach-bar-schaft

Trio

Ach! Ste-fan schel-tet mei- ne Thor-heit nur! Längst nagt am Her- zen mir

Lark Song

Lass   dein Lied er- schal - - len dass der Mor- gen neu er- wacht!

Libusa Act I

Bo-ho-vé věč-ní ta- mo nad o-bla-ky   v mi-lo-sti shlí- žejte

Act II Scene I

A toz,   když v bla-hé tou- ze lá- sky   on   plal

Za- po- li to- va- ni tě___ pro- sim,   za je- di- ný,

Scene III

Již pla- ne slun- ce   bla-hý mí-ru sen se vzná-si

A- no, mar-ně vzdo-ru-ji tvé mo- ci lá- - sko sva-tá

Ó vy lí-py, o vy lí-py! pra-ot-cův ru- ká vsa-di- la vás

Act III Scene V

Hoj! tvr-dý Vy- šehrad   bud stokrát ví - - - - tan!

Bo- - - - - ho- vé moc-ní!___ Za ten-to šta-stný den dik bu-diž vám!

Love Duet from The Brandenburgers
in Bohemia Act II

Ó jak bla-há krás-ná ta-to chir- - le   ó jak stast-né to

The Secret (Tajemství) Act I

O slyš to pře-da-le-ký svě-te,   jak v ob-ci ka-li-na nám kve-te!

Act II

Nač o tom dá- le bá-dat? též ra-dost' a bla-ho chci znát!

Ven, ven, ven! ven z po-dze-mi ven! ó zla-tá ré-vo, chme- li!

Duet

Vše- cko je tvo-je, Vše-cko je tvo-je ze sr-dce tvé-ho

Kdy sly-ším jen tvé-ho ro-hu pě-ni,   tvé pu-šký jen rá-nu,

Ó, kdy- by on mé tak byl me-lo-val, tak kdy-by on byl

Jsem vo-ják, jsem vo-ják stál jsem v bi-tvách pro-ti Pru-su

SMETANA

The Secret — Act III — A
Coz ta vo-da s vý-še strá-ní pa-dá,___ pa-da, pa-da___

The Two Widows (Dvé Vdovy) Act I — B
Ji-tro krás-né, ne-be jas-né, ky-ne nám,

C
Sa-mo-stat-né vlád-nu já___ vše-mi stat-ky svý-mi

Quartet — D
O ja-kou tí--sen mé srd-ce cí-tí, jej mám zde zří-ti,

E
Aj, viz-te lov-ce tam, jak blou-di sám a sám,

Act II — F
Kdy za-vi-tá máj, lás-ky čas, tu ob-živ-ne háj

G
Roz-hod-nu-to, u-za-vře-no, za-mit-nu-to po-stou-pe-no!

H
Ach, jak kru-tě sou-zi chlad-ný od-por ten srd-ce mé,___

I
Aj, ja-ký to kras-ny den, k ra-dos-ti jen u-stvo-řen

J
Necht' co-ko-liv mne, co-ko-liv mne zlo-bi svě-tě,

Trio — K
Co to, hol-ka, co-to, nač ta pý-cha pan-ská? vzdyt' se tan-ci pro-to

Evening Songs (Vecerni Pisne) I — L
Who's mas-ter of the gol-den strings, him you should more than hon-our,

II — M
Don't throw a-gainst the pro-phets stones! Like birds they par-don ne-ver,

III — N
I fan-cied once "pain has grown old, not to out-live to-mor-row

IV — O
Hey! what a joy-ful plea-sure to clasp a girl in danc-ing

V — P
Out of my songs___ I build_for thee a throne as po-ets of-ten feign

First Songs 1. Milenciny oči (My dear eyes) — Q
Nichts kann mir so ge-nü-gen, wie mei-nes Lieb-chens Blick,

2. S bohem (Goodbye) — R
Nun, wohl-an es muss ja sein le-be wohl du En-gel mein

3. Smutek Opuštěné (Sorrow of de-parture) — S
Oft am Ran-de stil-ler Flu-ten sitz' ich ein-sam_ da,

First Songs 4. Vyzvání (Invitation) — A

Pojď mil- ko, Pojď mil- ko! Hle sklá-ni se les k tobě néž

5. Jaro lásky — B

Die - ses Sai-ten-spiel der Brust, das___ du hast so reich be- sai- tet

SMITH, John Christopher (1712-1795)

No more dams I'll make for fish — D

No more dams___ I'll make___ for fish; Nor fetch fir - ing

SPEAKS, Oley (1876-1948)

Morning A
Copyright 1910, G. Schirmer, Inc. — F

Nev- er star was in the sky, Win- ter winds went wail-ing by,

B — G

Morn- ing on the ho- ly hills, Mead- ows that en- fold the rills

On the Road to Mandalay A1
Copyright 1907, G. Schirmer, Inc. — H

By the old Moul-mein Pa- go- da, look- in' east- ward___ to the sea

A2 — I

Come you back to Man- da- lay, Where the old Flo-til- la lay

Sylvia
Copyright 1914, G. Schirmer, Inc. — J

Syl- via's hair is like the night, Touched with glancing star- ry beams

To You — K

Some- where, I know, from the blue of the sky

SPILMAN, James E.

Flow gently, sweet Afton — M

Flow gen- tly, sweet___ Af- ton, a- mang thy green braes

SPOHR, Ludwig (1784-1859)

As pants the Hart — O

As pants the Hart for cool- ing streams When heat- ed in the chase,

The Last Judgment Part I No. 12 — P

Lord God of Heav'n and Earth, we a- dore_____ thee

Part II No. 19 — Q

Blest are the de- part- ed Who in the Lord are sleep - - ing

Rose, softly blooming — R

Rose soft- ly bloom- ing formed___ to___ al- - lure

SPONTINI, Gasparo (1774-1851)

La Vestale (opera) Act I

Dans le sein d'un a-mi fi-dè---le

L'a-mour est__ un__ mon-stre,est un__ mons-tre bar-ba-re

O__ ma__ fil-le, ma fil---le, ton coeur__ s'é-ga-re

Act II

Toi__ que j'im-plo-re a-vec__ ef-froi re-dou-ta--ble dé-es-- se

O Nu-- me-- tu-te--lar degl'__ in-fe-li-- ci,

Act III

Toi__ que je lais-se sur la__ ter---re, mor-tel

STANFORD, C. Villers (1852-1924)

A Carol of Bells

Ring,__ Christ-mas bells of Lon-don, Swing__ wild-ly with a will

"Greet-ings to all!" Boom the Bells of St. Paul;

Cavalier Songs No. 1

Kent-ish Sir Byng stood for his King, bid-ding the crop-head-ed

No. 2

King Charles! and who'll do him right now! King Charles!

No. 3

Boot, sad-dle, to horse and a-way! Res-cue my Cas-tle

Coelos ascendit hodie, Op. 38
By permission Boosey & Hawkes, Inc.,
copyright owners

Coe-los as-cen--dit ho-di-e Je-sus Christus Rex__ glo-ri-ae

Father O'Flynn

Of priests we can of-fer a charm-in' va-ri-e-ty

Oh! Breathe not his Name (Air, the Brown Maid)

Oh__ breathe__ not his name,__ let it sleep__ in the shade,

A Soft Day, Op. 140, No. 3
Copyright by Stainer & Bell, Ltd., London;
Galaxy Music Corporation, N. Y.,
U. S. agents

A soft day, thank God! A wind from the south with a hon-ey'd mouth

Songs of the Fleet, No. 5. Fare Well
Copyright by Stainer & Bell, Ltd., London;
Galaxy Music Corporation, N. Y.,
U. S. agents

Mo-ther, with un-bowed head Hear thou a-cross the sea

STANGE, Max (1856-1932)

Die Bekehrte, Op. 13, No. 1

Bei dem Glanz der A-- bend- rö- the ging___ ich still

STAUB, Victor (Contemporary)

L'Heure Silencieuse

By permission Durand & Cie, Paris; Elkan-Vogel Co., Inc., Phila., copyright owners

C'est l'heu-re dis-crête__ et tran-quil-le Qu'at-tend__ pour ren-trer___

STEFFANI, Agostino (1654-1728)

Sei si caro, from Marco Aurelio
(opera)

Sei si ca- ro, si vez-zo- so Hai nel vol-to un cer - - to__ che,

STEVENS, Richard J. S. (1757-1837)

Sigh no more, ladies

Sigh no more, la- dies, la- dies, sigh no more___

STORACE, Stephen (1763-1796)

The Pretty Creature

Oh! the pret-ty, pret-ty crea-ture___ When I next do__ meet her,

STRADELLA, Alessandro (c. 1645-1682)

Pietà, Signore (aria di chiesa)

Pie- tà, Si- gno- re, di, me do-len- te Si- gnor, pie- tà!___

STRAUS, Oskar (1870-1954)

OPERETTAS
The Chocolate Soldier
Copyright 1908, Ludwig Doblinger
(Bernard Herzmansky)
Copyright 1909, M. Witmark & Sons
Act I My Hero

Sympathy

Waltz Dream Act. I Waltz

Come! Come! I love you on- ly, My heart is true___

Oh you lit-tle cho-co-late sol- dier man, You're__ far too sweet

My life is sweet, I hold it dear; All death is grue-some, dark and drear,

Ti- ra- la-la! Ti-ra-la-la! Tell no one! All men sus-pi-cious are,

For- give, for- give, for-give,___ Why was I there? I wished to live___

The soft sum- mer twi-light is fad- ing, I sat in the gar- den a-lone

STRAUSS, Johann (1825-1899)

OPERETTAS
Die Fledermaus Op. 56
Act II No. 11 Finale

Mar- ian- ka, komm und tanz' me' hier! Heut ist's schon schetzko jedno mir!

Ha, welch ein Fest, wel- che Nacht voll Freud! Lie- be und wein

Act III No. 14

Spiel' ich die Un- schuld vom Lan- de, na- tür- lich im kur- zen Ge- wan- de

Wenn Sie das ge- sehn, müs- sen Sie ge- steh'n, es wär der Scha- den

Al- les mach'n voll Ehr- furcht mir Spa- lier; lauscht den Tö- nen

Spiel' ich 'ne Da- me von Pa- ris, ach, ach,

No. 15

Ein selt- sam A- ben- teu- er ist ge- stern mir pas- siert

Ja, ich bins, den Ihr be- tro- gen, ja, ich bins den Ihr be- tro- gen

No. 16

O Fle- der- maus, o Fle- der- maus, lass end- lich jetzt dein O- pfer aus;

Die ganze Nacht durchschwärmt,
from Waldmeister

Die gan- ze Nacht durch schwärmt ge- - trun- ken und ge- lärmt

Eine Nacht in Venedig (A night in
Venice) Act I

Dein Lied von Lieb und Treu- e hat ei- nen fal- schen Ton

Pel- le- gri- na ron- di- nel- la, ron- di- nel- la pel- le- gri- na

Al- le mas- kirt, Al- le mas- kirt, cos- pet- to! wie a- mu- sant

Sei mir ge- grüsst du hol- des Ve- ne- - - tia,

Komm' in die Gon- del, mein Lieb- chen, o stei- ge doch ein,

Act II

Treu sein, das liegt mir nicht, weil ich leicht den Kopf ver- lier,

Act III Lagunen
Walzer

Ach, wie so herr- lich zu schau'n sind all' die lieb- li- chen Frau'n

Wie sie schmei- cheln, Lie- be heu- cheln, uns durch Thrä- nen

Nature, from Der Lustige Krieg (The
Merry War)

Na- - ture loved she fair to see and so free, She'd be roam- ing

STRAUSS, Richard (1864-1949)

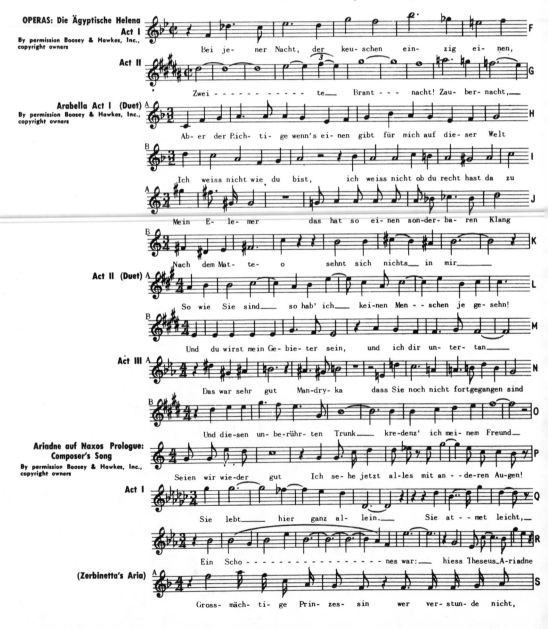

Ariadne auf Naxos (Zerbinetta's Aria)

Noch glaub' ich dem ei- nen ganz mich ge- hö- rend,

Als ein Gott kam je- der ge- gan-gen und sein Schritt schon

Capriccio, Op. 85
By permission Boosey & Hawkes, Inc., copyright owners

Kein An- dres, das mir so im Her- zen loht, nein, Schö- ne.

Ih- re Lie- be schlägt mir ent-ge- gen, zart- ge- wo- ben

Du Spie- gel- bild- der ver- lieb- ten Made- leine,

Daphne, Op. 82
By permission Boosey & Hawkes, Inc., copyright owners

O wie ger- ne blieb ich bei dir

Göt- ter! Bru- der im ho- hen O- lym- pos!

Wind- spie- le mit mir! Se- li- ge Vö- gel woh-net in mir

Der Rosenkavalier, Op. 59
Act I Italian Serenade
By permission Boosey & Hawkes, Inc., copyright owners

Di- ri- go- ri ar- ma-to il se- no con-tro a-mor mi ri- bel- lai

Da geht er hin, der auf- ge-blas-ne, schlech- te Kerl

Kann mich auch an ein Mä- del er- in-nern, die frisch aus dem Klos-ter

Die Zeit, die ist ein son-der-bar Ding, Wenn man so hin-lebt

Act II Presentation of the Rose

Mir ist die Eh- re wi- der fah-ren dass ich der hoch

Hat ei- nen star- ken Ge- ruch wie Ro- sen,

Ich kenn ihn schon recht wohl, mon Cou- sin!

Mit Ih- ren Au- gen voll Trä- nen kommt Sie zu mir

Herr Ca- va- lier Den mor- gi- gen A- bend hätt' i frei.

Act III Trio

Hab' mir's ge- lobt, ihn lieb zu haben in der rich-ti-gen Weis',

Duet

Ist ein Traum, kann nicht wirk- lich sein dass wir zwei bei ei- nan-der sein,

STRAUSS

Songs, Op. 10, No. 1 Zueignung
By permission Associated Music Publishers, Inc.

Ja, du weisst es, theu- re See- le, dass ich fern von dir ___ mich quä- le,

No. 3 Die Nacht

Aus dem Wal - - - de tritt die Nacht, aus den Bäu-men schleicht sie lei- se

No. 4 Die Georgine

Wa- rum so spät erst, Ge- or- gi- ne? Das Ro- sen-mär-chen ist er-zahlt

No. 5 Geduld

Ge- duld, sagst du und zeigt mit weis-sem Fin- ger

No. 6 Die Ver-schwiegenen

Ich ha- be wohl, es sei hier laut vor al- ler Welt ver- kün-digt,

No. 7 Die Zeitlose

Auf frisch ge- mäh- tem Wei- de-platz steht ein- sam die Zeit- lo- se,

No. 8 Allerseelen

Stell' auf den Tisch die duf- ten- den Re- se- den,

Op. 15, No. 1 Madrigal

In's Joch beug' ich den Nak- ken de- mut- voll, beug' lä- chelnd

No. 2 Winternacht

Mit Re- gen und Sturm- ge- brau- se sei mir will-kom- - men,

No. 5 Heimkehr

Lei- ser schwan- ken die Ä - - - - ste, der Kahn fliegt u- fer-wärts,

Op. 17, No. 1 Seitdem dein Aug' in meines schaute

Seit-dem dein Aug' in mei- nes schau- te und Lie- be wie von Him-mel

No. 2 Ständchen (Serenade)

Mach' auf, ___ mach' auf, ___ doch lei- se, mein Kind ___ um Kei- nen vom Schlummer

No. 3 Das Geheimnis

Du frag'st mich, Mäd- chen, was ___ flüs-ternd der West

No. 6 Barkarole

Um der fal - - len-den Ru- der Spi-tzen zit-tert und leuch- tet

Op. 19, No. 1 Wozu noch, Mädchen
By permission Associated Music Publishers, Inc.

Wo- zu noch, Mäd- chen, soll es from- men, dass du vor mir

No. 2 Breit über mein Haupt

Breit' ü- ber mein Haupt dein schwarzes Haar, heig' zu mir dein An- ge- sicht,

No. 4 Wie sollten wir geheim sie halten

Wie soll- ten wir ge- heim sie hal- ten, die Se- lig-keit

No. 6 Mein Herz ist stumm

Mein Herz ist stumm, mein Herz ist Kalt, er-starrt ___ in des Win-ters Ei-se

Op. 21, No. 1 All mein Gedanken
By permission Associated Music Publishers, Inc.

All mein Ge- dan- ken, mein Herz und mein Sinn da, wo die Lieb- ste ist,

STRAUSS

Songs, Op. 21, No. 2 **Du meines Herzens Krönelein** — Du mei-nes Her - - zens Krö - ne-lein, du bist von lau-trem Gol-de A

No. 3 **Ach Lieb, ich muss nun scheiden** — Ach, Lieb, ich muss nun schei - den, geh'n ü - ber Berg und Thal, B

Op. 26, No. 1 **Frühlingsgedränge**
By permission Boosey & Hawkes, Inc., copyright owners — Früh - lings - kin - der im bun - ten Ge - drän - ge; flatternde Blü - ten, C

Op. 27, No. 1 **Ruhe, meine Seele**
By permission Associated Music Publishers, Inc. — Nicht ein Lüft-chen regt sich lei-se, sanft ent-schlummert ruht der Hain; D

Ru - he, ru - he, mei - ne See - le dei - ne Stür - me gin - gen wild E

No. 2 **Cäcilie** — Wenn du es wüss - test was träu - men heisst von bren-nen-den Küs - sen F

No. 3 **Heimliche Aufforderung** — Auf, he - be die fun - keln-de Schaa - le em - por zum Mund, G

No. 4 **Morgen** — Und mor - gen wird die Son - ne wie - - der schei - nen H

Op. 29, No. 1 **Traum durch die Dämmerung**
By permission Associated Music Publishers, Inc. — Wei - te Wie - sen im Däm - mer-grau; die Son - ne ver - glomm, I

No. 2 **Schlagende Herzen** — Ü - ber Wie - sen und Fel - der ein Kna - be ging; kling, klang J

No. 3 **Nachtgang** — Wir gin - gen durch die stil - le mil - de Nacht, dein Arm in mei - nem, K

Op. 31, No. 1 **Blauer Sommer**
By permission Boosey & Hawkes, Inc. copyright owners — Ein blau - er Som - mer glanz und glu - ten-schwer geht ü - ber Wie - sen, L

No. 3 **Weisser Jasmin** — Blei - che Blü - te, Blü - te der Lie - be, leuch - te ü - ber dem Lau - ben-dach M

Op. 32, No. 1 **Ich trage meine Minne vor Wonne stumm**
By permission Associated Music Publishers, Inc. — Ich tra - ge mei - ne Min - ne vor Won - ne stumm im Her - zen N

No. 2 **Sehnsucht** — Ich ging den Weg ent - lang, der ein - sam lag den stets allein O

No. 3 **Liebeshymnus** — Heil je - nem Tag, der dich ge - bo - ren, Heil ihm, P

No. 4 **O süsser Mai** — O süs - ser Mai, o ha - be du Er - bar - men, o süs - ser Mai, Q

Op. 33, No. 4 **Pilgers Morgenlied**
By permission Associated Music Publishers, Inc. — Mor - gen - ne - bel Li - la, hül - len dei - nen Thurm ein. R

Op. 36, No. 2 **Für fünfzehn Pfennige**
By permission Boosey & Hawkes, Inc., copyright owners — Das Mägd - lein will ein' Frei - er habn, und sollt sie'n aus der Er - de grabn, S

Songs, Op. 36, No. 3 Hat gesagt, bleibt's nicht dabei

Mein Va-ter hat ge-sagt__ ich soll das Kindlein wie - gen, wie - - - gen,

Op. 37, No. 1 Glückes genug
By permission Boosey & Hawkes, Inc., copyright owners

Wenn sanft__ du__ mir im Ar - - me__ schliefst,

No. 2 Ich liebe dich

Vier ad - li - ge Ros - se vo - ran un - serm Wa - gen,

No. 3 Meinem Kinde

Du schläfst und sach - te neig' ich mich ü - ber dein Bett - chen

No. 4 Mein Auge

Du bist mein Au - ge! Du__ durch-dringst mich ganz

Op. 39, No. 4 Befreit
By permission Boosey & Hawkes, Inc., copyright owners

Du wirst nicht wei - nen Lei - se, lei - - se wirst du lä - cheln

No. 5 Lied an meinem Sohn

Der Sturm__ be - horcht__ mein Va - ter - haus, mein Herz

Op. 41a, No. 1 Wiegenlied
By permission Associated Music Publishers, Inc.

Träu - - - - - me, träu - - me du, mein sü - sses Le - - ben

No. 3 Am Ufer

Die Welt__ ver-stummt,__ dein Blut__ er-klingt__ in seinem hel-len Ab-grund

No. 5 Leise Lieder

Lei - se Lie - der sing' ich dir bei Nacht, Lie - - der, die kein sterb - lich Ohr

Op. 43, No. 2 Muttertändelei
By permission Boosey & Hawkes, Inc., copyright owners

Seht mir doch mein schö - - nes Kind, mit den gold' - - nen Zot - - tel -

Op. 46, No. 4 Morgenrot
By permission Boosey & Hawkes, Inc., copyright owners

Dort wo der Mor - gen-stern her - geht__ und wo der Mor - gen-wind herweht,

Op. 47, No. 2 Des Dichters Abendgang

Er - gehst du dich im A - bend - licht (das ist die Zeit)

Op. 48, No. 1 Freundliche Vision
By permission Boosey & Hawkes, Inc., copyright owners

Nicht im Schla - fe hab ich das ge-träumt__ hell am Ta - ge sah__ ich's

No. 2 Ich schwebe

Ich schwe - be wie auf En - gels-schwin - gen, die Er - de kaum be - rührt

No. 3 Kling

Kling! Mei - ne See - le gibt rei - - nen Ton. Und ich wähn - te die Ar - me

No. 4 Winterweihe

In die - sen Win - ter - ta - gen, nun sich das Licht ver - hüllt,__

No. 5 Winterliebe

Der Son - ne ent - ge - gen in Lie - bes - glu - ten wand'r__ ich

No. 7 Wer lieben will, muss leiden

Wer lie - ben will, muss lei - - den ohn Lei - den, ohn Lei - den liebt man nicht,

Songs, Op. 49, No. 1 Waldseligkeit
By permission Boosey & Hawkes, Inc., copyright owners

Der Wald be-ginnt zu rau--schen,den Bäu-men naht die Nacht: A

No. 3 Wiegenliedchen

Bien-chen, Bien-chen, wiegt sich im Son-nen-schein   B

Op. 51, No. 2 Der Einsame
By permission Boosey & Hawkes, Inc., copyright owners

Wo ich bin, mich rings um-dun-kelt Fin-ster-nis   C

Op. 56, No. 1 Gefunden
By permission Associated Music Publishers, Inc.

Ich ging im Wal-de so für mich hin, und nichts zu su-chen,   D

No. 2 Blindenklage

Wenn ich dich fra-ge, dem das Le---ben blüht: E

No. 3 Im Spätboot

Aus der Schiffs-bank mach' ich mei-nen Pfühl, end---lich wird   F

No. 4 Mit deinen blauen Augen

Mit dei-nen blau---en Au-gen siehst du mich lieb-lich an,   G

No. 5 Frühlingsfeier

Das ist des Früh-lings trau-ri-ge Lust! Die blü--hen-den Mäd-chen   H

No. 6 Die heiligen drei Könige aus Morgenland

Die heil'-gen drei Kön'-ge aus Mor-gen-land, sie fru-gen   I

Op. 68, No. 4 Als mir dein Lied erklang

Dein Lied er-klang! ich ha--be es ge-hört,   J

No. 5 Amor

An dem Feu----------er sass das Kind A-mor   K

Op. 69, No. 3 Einerlei
By permission Boosey & Hawkes, Inc., copyright owners

Ihr Mund ist stets der-sel-----------be,   L

No. 5 Schlechtes Wetter

Das ist ein schlech-tes Wet-ter, es reg---------net und stürmt   M

Olympische Hymne

Völ---ker! Seid des Vol-kes Gä-ste, kommt durch's off-ne Tor her-ein   N

STRAVINSKY, Igor (1882-1971)

Symphonie de Psaumes No. 1
By permission Boosey & Hawkes, Inc., copyright owners

E--xau-di o--ra-ti-o-nem me-am, Do--mi--ne,   P

Quo-ni-am ad-ve-na e-go sum a------pud te   Q

No. 2

Ex-pec---tans ex-pec-ta-----vi Do-mi-num   R

Et im-mi-sit in os me-um can-ti-cum nov-um   S

Symphonie de Psaumes No. 3

Lau- da- te, Lau- da- te, Lau- da- te Do- mi- num

Lau- da- te___ E- um in___ tim- pa- no et cho- ro

Lau- da- te E- - um in cym- ba- lis be- ne___ so- nan- ti- bus

Les Noces

Tableau I Chez la mariée

By permission J. & W. Chester, Ltd., London, copyright owners

Tres- se, tres- - - se, ma- - - ma tres- se à moi,

On___ tresse on tres- sera la tresse à Nas- ta- sie

Con- so- le toi con- so- le toi___ pe- tit oi- seau

Dai- gne, dai- - - gne très ai- - ma- ble mè- re

Tableau II Chez le marié

Dai- gne ai- ma- ble mère, daigne en- trer dans la chau- mière,

A- vec quoi qu'on pei- gne- ra les bou- cles de Fé- é- é- tis?___

Hier soir___ Hier soir en- co- re___ Fe- tis é- tait

Et vous père et___ mè- re___ be- nis- sez votre en- fant

Tableau IV Le Repas de Noces

Ya deux fleurs sur___ la branche u- - ne rouge une___ blan- che

J'é- tais___ loin___ sur la mer, j'é- tais loin sur la___ mer im- mense

Sou- laud, vieux___ sa- laud___ Père de Nas- - - - ta- sie___

Le beau lit bien fait, le beau lit___ car- ré!

Pulcinella, (ballet) (music after Pergolesi) I

By permission J. & W. Chester, Ltd., London, copyright owners

Men- - - - tre l'er- bet- - ta___ pas- ce l'a- guel- la

II

Con- ten- to for- se vi- ve- re nel mi- o___ mar- tir po- trei

III

Con que- ste___ pa- ro- - - li- ne,___ pa- ro- - - li- ne

IV

Sen- to di- re no'___ nce pa- ce sen- to di- re

Pulcinella IV
Chi di----se ca la fem-me-na

V
U-na te fa-lanz em-pre-ce ed è ed è

VI
Pu-pil-let-te fiam-met-te d'a--mo---re

Four Russian Peasant Songs
I On Saints' Days at Chigisakh
By permission J. & W. Chester, Ltd., London, copyright owners
On, on Saints' Days on Saints' Days in Chi-gi-sakh

II Ovsen
Ov-sen, ov-sen, ov-sen I'm a hunt-ing the grouse,

III The Pike
Once a pike swam out of Nov-go-rod Glo-ry!

IV Master Portly
Mas-ter Port-ly tramp'-d thro' the big tur-nip field

Pastorale (without words)
By permission Associated Music Publishers, Inc.
A a-ou A-ou A A-ou

Trois Histoires pour Enfants
I Tilimbom
By permission J. & W. Chester, Ltd., London, copyright owners
Ti-lim-bom, ti-lim-bom, c'est la cloche du feu qui sonne

II Les canards, les cynges, les oies
Les ca-nards, les cy-gnes, les oies qui sont ve-nus de Sa-voie

III Chanson de l'ours
Grin-ce, grin-ce, grin-ce patte en bou-leau De-dans, de-hors

STRICKLAND, Lily (1887-   )

Mah Lindy Lou
Copyright 1920, G. Schirmer, Inc.
Hon-ey did you heah dat mock-in-bird sing las' night

My Lover is a Fisherman
Oh, my lov-er is a fish-er-man, and he sails on the big

STROZZI, Barbara (c. 1644-1664)

Amor dormiglione
A-mor, a-mor, mon dor-mir più! Su, su, su, su, Sveg-lia-te,

STULTS, R. M. (1861-1923)

The Sweetest Story Ever Told
Copyright by Oliver Ditson Co.
Used by permission
Oh, an-swer me a ques-tion, love, I pray,
Tell me, do you love me? Tell me soft-ly, sweet-ly, as of old,

SULLIVAN, Sir Arthur (1842-1900)

OPERAS
The Gondoliers Act I, No. 1

List and learn, list and learn, List and learn ye dain-ty ro-ses,

We're called gon-do- lier- i, but that's a va- ga- ry,

Thank you, gal-lant gon-do- lier- i: In a set and for-mal mea-sure

Gay and gal-lant gon-do- lier- i Take us both and hold us tight-ly

No. 3 In en-ter-prise of mar-tial kind, when there was an-y fight-ing

No. 6 I stole the Prince and brought him here, and left him gai-ly pratt-ling

No. 8 Try we life long, we can nev-er, Straighten out life's tan-gled skein,

No. 9 When a mer-ry mai-den mar-ries, Sor-row goes and plea-sure tar-ries,

No. 10 Finale Kind sir, you can-not have the heart our lives to part

Oh, 'tis a glo-rious thing, I ween to be a regu-lar Roy-al Queen

Then a-way they go to an is-land fair That lies in a Southern sea:

Act II, No. 1 Of hap-pi-ness the ve-ry pith In Ba-ra-ta-ria you may see:

No. 3 Take a pair of spark-ling eyes, Hid-den ev-er and a-non,

No. 5 Dance a-ca- chu-cha, fan-dan-go, bo-le-ro,

Old Xe-res we'll drink Man-za-nil-la, Mon-te-ro,

No. 6 There lived a King, as I've been told, In the won-der-work-ing days of old

No. 7 In a con-tem-pla-tive fa-shion, And a tran-quil frame of mind

No. 9 On the day when I was wed-ded to your ad-mi-ra-ble sire,

OPERAS
The Gondoliers Act II, No. 10

A — Small ti-tles and or-ders for Mayors and Re-cor-ders

No. 11

B — I__ am a cour-tier grave and se-rious Who__ is a-bout to kiss your hand,

No. 12
Finale

C — Here is a fix un- pre- ce-den-ted! Here are a King and Queen ill-starr'd!

H. M. S. Pinafore Act I, No. 1

D — We__ sail the o- cean blue, and our sau- cy ship's a beau-ty;

No. 2

E — I'm called lit-tle But-ter-cup, dear lit-tle But- ter-cup, though I could never tell why

No. 3

F — A maid-en fair to see, the pearl of min-strel-sy, A bud of blush-ing beau-ty,

No. 4

G — I am the cap-tain of the Pin- a- fore,__ and a right__ good__ cap-tain too

No. 4 B

H — Then give three cheers, and one cheer more, For the har- dy cap-tain

No. 5 A

I — Sor-ry her lot__ who loves__ too well, Hea- vy the heart__ that hopes

No. 5 B

J — Hea- vy the sor-row that bows__ the head, When love is a- live__

No. 8

K — I am the mon- arch of the sea, The ru-ler of the Queen's Na- vee,

No. 9

L — When I was a lad I serv'd a term as of- fice boy__

No. 11 A

M — Re- frain, au- da- cious tar, Your suit__ from__ press- ing

No. 11 B

N — I'd laugh my rank to scorn, in u- - nion__ ho- ly,

No. 13

O — Fair moon to thee__ I__ sing! Bright re-gent of the hea- vens

No. 14 A

P — Things are sel- dom what they seem, Skim milk mas- que- rades as cream,

No. 14 B

Q — Stern con- vic-tion's o'er__ him__ steal-ing, That the mys-tic la- dy's__ deal-ing

No. 15

R — A sim- ple sail- or, low- ly born, un- let-ter'd and un- known,

No. 16

S — Nev-er mind the why and where- fore, Love can lev- el ranks

OPERAS

H. M. S. Pinafore Act II, No. 17

Kind Cap-tain, I've im- por-tant in- for-ma- tion Sing hey,

No. 18

Care- ful- ly on tip- toe steal- ing, breathing gently as we may

No. 18A

For___ he him-self has said___ it, and it's great-ly to his cred- it,

No. 19

Fare- well, my own, Light of my life, fare- well! For crime un-known I go

No. 20

A ma- ny years a- go, when I was young and charm- ing,

No. 21

Oh joy, oh rap-ture un- for-seen, The cloud-ed sky is now se- rene

Iolanthe Act I, No. 1

Trip- ping hi- ther, trip-ping thi- ther, No- bo- dy knows why or whi-ther

No. 3

We are dain- ty lit- tle fai- ries E- ver sing-ing e- ver danc-ing

Good mor- row, good mo-ther___ Good mo- ther, good mor-row___

No. 5

None shall part us from each o- ther, One in life and death are we:

No. 6

Bow, bow, ye low- er mid-dle class- es, Bow, bow, ye trades-men,

We are___ peers of___ high-est___ sta- tion,

No. 7

The Law is the true em- bo- di-ment of ev'- ry-thing that's ex- cel-lent

No. 8

Of all the young la-dies I know,___ This pret-ty young la-dy's the fair-est,

No. 10

Spurn not the no- bly born With love___ af - - fect- ed!

No. 12

When I went to the bar as a ve- ry young man,

No. 13 Finale

When dark- ly looms the day, and all is dull and grey,

Go a- way, ma- dam; I should say, ma- dam, You dis-play, ma- dam,

Act II, No. 2

Stre-phon's a Mem-ber of Par- lia-ment! car-ries ev-'ry Bill___ he choos- es

OPERAS

The Mikado Act I, No. 11 Finale

For__ he's go-ing to mar-ry Yum-Yum, Yum-Yum! Your an-ger pray bu-ry,

We do not heed their dis-mal_ sound, For joy reigns ev'ry-where__

Act II, No. 1

Braid the ra-ven hair,__ Weave the sup - - - - - - ple tress,__

No. 2

The sun, whose rays are all a-blaze with e-ver liv-ing glo-ry

I mean to rule the earth,__ as he the sky, we real-ly know our worth__

No. 3

Bright-ly dawns our wed-ding day; Joy-ous__ hour, we give the greet-ing!

No. 4

Here's a how-de-do! If I mar-ry you, when your time has come to perish,

No. 5

Mi-ya sa-ma, mi-ya sa-ma, On n'ma-ma no ma-ye ni

From ev-'ry kind of man O-be-dience I__ ex-pect

No. 6

My ob-ject all sub-lime__ I shall a-chieve in time,

No. 7

The cri-mi-nal cried, as he dropp'd him down, In a state_of wild a-larm

Oh, never shall I for-get the cry, or the shriek_that shriek-ed he,__

No. 8

See how the Fates their gifts al-lot, For A is hap-py B is not

No. 9

The flow-ers that bloom in the spring, Tra-la Breathe pro-mise

No. 10

Oh liv-ing I come, tell_me_ why, when hope is gone, Dost thou stay on?

No. 11

On a tree by a riv-er a lit-tle tom-tit Sang_ "Wil-low,

No. 12

There is beau-ty in the bel-low of the blast,

If that is so, Sing der-ry down der-ry! It's e-vi-dent ve-ry,

Patience Act I, No. 1

Twen-ty love-sick mai-dens we,__ Love-sick all a-gainst our will.__

Patience Act I, No. 2

I can-not tell what this love may be That com-eth to all

No. 4

In a dole-ful train two and two we walk all day for we love in vain!

Through my book I seem to scan In a rapt ec-sta-tic way

No. 5

When I first put this u-ni-form on, I said, as I looked in the glass

No. 6

If you're anx-ious for to shine— in the high aes-the-tic line—

And ev-ery one will say As you walk your mys-tic way,

No. 8

Pri-thee, pret-ty mai-den pri-thee, tell me true (Hey, but I'm dole-ful,

No. 9 Finale

Let the mer-ry cym-bals sound, Gai-ly pipe Pan-dae-an plea-sure

Now tell us, we pray you, Why thus they ar-ray you, Oh po-et,

List Re-gi-nald, while I con-fess a love that's all un-sel-fish-ness

Act II, No. 2

Sil-vered is the ra- - ven—hair, Spread-ing is the part-ing_straight,

No. 3

Turn, oh turn in this di-rec-tion, Shed, oh shed a gen-tle smile

No. 4

A mag-net hung in a hard-ware shop And all a-round was a lov-ing crop

No. 5

Love is a plain-tive song. Sung by a suf-fering maid

Love that no wrong can cure, Love that is al-ways new,

No. 6

So go to him and say to him, with com-pli-ment i-ron-i-cal

Sing "Hey to you good-day to you" Sing "Lah to you ha! ha! to you"

No. 7

You hold your-self like this, You hold your-self like that, By hook and crook

No. 8

If Sa-phir I choose to mar-ry, I shall be fixed up for life;

OPERAS
Patience Act II, No. 8

B

In that case un-pre-ce-dent-ed, Sin-gle he will live and die,

No. 9

When I go out of door of da-mo-zels a score All sighing and burning,

The Pirates of Penzance
Act I, No. 1

Pour, O King, the pi-rate sher-ry, Fill, O King, the pi-rate glass!

No. 2

When Fred'ric was a— lit-tle lad He— proved so brave and da-ring,

No. 3 A

Oh bet-ter far to live— and die Un-der the brave black flag I fly

B

For— I am a Pi-rate King!— And it is, it is, a glo-rious thi

No. 5 A

Climb-ing o-ver—rock-y moun-tain, Skip-ping ri- -vu-let and fountain,

B

Let us gai-ly tread—the mea-sure, Make the most of fleet-ing—pleas-ure

No. 7

Oh, is there not one mai-den breast which does not feel the mo-ral beau-ty

No. 8 A

Poor wan-d'ring one— Tho' thou hast surely strayed,—Take heart of grace,

B

Take heart, no dan-ger lowers, Take a-ny heart— but ours

No. 10 A

How beau-ti-ful-ly blue the sky, The grass is ris-ing ve-ry high

B

Did e-ver mai-den wake from dream—of home- -ly du-ty

No. 11

Now here's a first rate op-por-tu-ni-ty To get mar-ried

No. 13

I am the ve-ry pat-tern of a mo-dern Ma-jor Ge-ne-ral

Finale A

These chil-dren whom you see are all that I can call my own.

B

I'm tell-ing a ter-ri-ble sto-ry, but it does-n't di-min-ish

Act II, No. 1

Oh, dry the glis-t'ning tear that dews— that mar-tial cheek!—

No. 3 A

When the foe-man bares his steel, Ta-ran- ta-ra, ta-ran- ta-ra

SULLIVAN

OPERAS
The Pirates of Penzance
Act II, No. 3

Go___ ye he-roes, go___ to glo-ry Though___ ye die in com-bat go - -ry

No. 5

When you had left our pi-rate fold, we tried to raise our spi-rits faint.

No. 6

A pa-ra-dox, a pa-ra-dox, a most in-ge-nious pa-ra-dox

No. 8

A-way, a- way___ my heart's on fire!___ I burn this base de-cep-tion

No. 10

Ah, leave me not to pine a-lone and de-so-late

Oh, here is love, and here is truth, and here is food for joy- ous___ laugh-ter

No. 12

When a fe-lon's not en-gaged in his em-ploy-ment, his em-ploy-ment,

With cat like tread up-on our prey we steal; In si-lence dread

No. 14 Finale

Come, friends, who plough the sea, truce to na-vi-ga-tion,

Soft-ly sigh-ing to the ri- - ver, Comes the lone-ly breeze___

Princess Ida Act I, No. 1

We tri-umph now for well___ we trow Your___mor-tal ca-reer's cut___short

No. 2

Search through-out the pa-no-ra-ma, For a sign of roy-al Ga-ma

No. 3

Now heark-en to my strict com-mand On ev'-ry hand, on ev'-ry hand

No. 5

I- da was a twelve-month old twen- ty years a- go

No. 6

We are war-riors three,___ Songs of Ga-ma Rex,___ Like most sons are we___

Bold___ and fierce and strong, ha, ha! For___ a war we burn

No. 7 Finale

If you give me your at- ten- tion, I will tell you what I am:

P'raps if you ad- dress the la- dy most po-lite-ly, most po-lite-ly

Ex- press ive glan-ces shall be our lan-ces and pops of Sil- le- ry

OPERAS

Princess Ida Act I, No. 7 Finale

For a month to dwell in a dun-geon cell, grow-ing thin and wi-zen

Act II, No. 8

To-wards the em-py-re-an heights___ of ev'-ry kind of love,

No. 9

Migh-ty mai-den with a mis-sion, Pa-ra-gon of com-mon sense

No. 10

Oh, god-dess wise that lov--est___ light En-dow with___ sight

No. 11

Come might-y Must! In-e-vi-ta-ble Shall! In Thee I trust.

No. 13

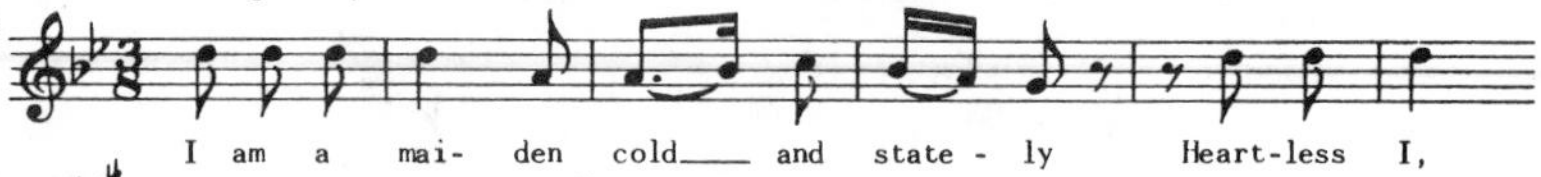

I am a mai-den cold___ and state-ly Heart-less I,

No. 14

The world is but a bro-ken toy, Its plea-sures hol-low false its joy,

No. 15

A La-dy fair, of___ lin-eage high, When loved by an Ape

No. 16

The wo-man of the wis-est wit may some-times be mis-ta-ken, O!

No. 19

Would___ you know the kind___ of maid Sets___my heart a-flame___ a?

No. 22 A

When-e'er I spoke sar-cas-tic joke Re-plete with mal-ice spite-ful,

B

Oh, don't the days seem lank and long When all goes right

No. 23

I built up-on a rock, But ere De-struc-tion's hand

No. 24

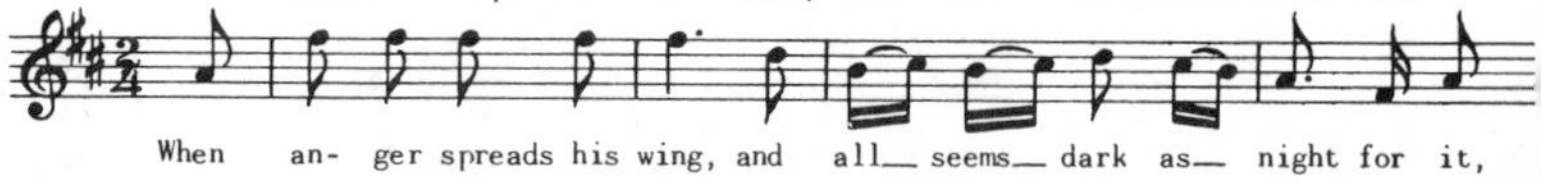

When an-ger spreads his wing, and all___ seems___ dark as___ night for it,

No. 25

This hel-met, I sup-pose was meant to ward off blows, It's ve-ry hot

Ruddigore Act I, No. 1

Fair___ is Rose as bright May day, Soft___ is Rose as warm west wind,

No. 2 A

Sir Ru-pert Mur-ga-troyd His lei-sure and___ his rich-es

B

This sport___ he much en-joy'd,___ Did Ru-pert Mur-ga-troyd___

No. 3 A

If some-bo-dy there chanced to be Who loved me in a man-ner true

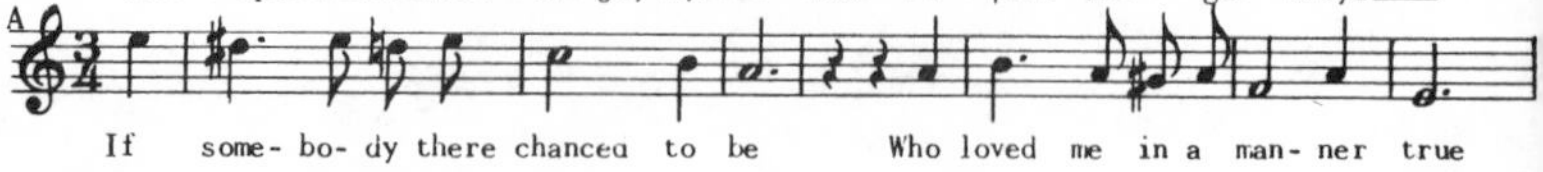

Ruddigore Act II, No. 8

My eyes are ful-ly o-pen to my aw-ful sit-u-a-tion,

No. 10

There grew a lit-tle flow-er 'Neath a great oak tree

Sing____ hey, lack-a-day, let the tears fall free

The Sorcerer Act I, No. 1

Ring forth, ye bells, with cla-rion sound, For-get your knells,

For to-day young A-lex-is, Young A-lex-is Point-dex-tre

No. 2 A

When he is here I sigh with plea-sure, When he is gone I sigh with grief

No. 3 A

Time was, when love and I were well ac-quain-ted,

No. 5

With heart and with voice Let us wel-come this ma-ting to the youth

No. 6 A

Oh, hap-py young heart____ Comes thy young lord a-woo-ing

No. 8

With heart and with voice let us wel-come this mat-ing

No. 9

Wel-come joy! a-dieu to sad-ness! As Au-ro-ra gilds the day

No. 10

All is pre-pared for seal-ing and for sign-ing, The contract has been drafted

No. 11

Love feeds on ma-ny kinds of food, I know; Some love for rank,

No. 12

My name is John Well-ing-ton Wells__ I'm a deal-er in ma-gic and spells__

No. 13 (Incantation)

Sprites of earth and air! Fiends of flame and fire! Demon souls, come

No. 14 Finale A

Eat, drink and be gay, Ba-nish all wor-ry and sor-row

Oh love, true love! un-world-ly, a-bid-ing, Source of all pleasure

Act II; No. 15

Hap-py are we in our lov-ing fri-vol-i-ty Hap-py and jol-ly

No. 16 A

Dear friends, take pi-ty on my lot, My cup is not of nec-tar

OPERAS
The Sorcerer Act II, No. 16

Oh, bit- ter joy! No words can tell How my poor heart is blight-ed

No. 19

The fear- ful deed is done, My love is near, I go to meet my own

No. 20

Thank you for your kind- ly prof- fer, Good your heart and full your cof- fer,

Trial by Jury No. 1

Hark, the hour of ten is sound- ing; hearts with anx-ious fears are bounding

No. 2

When first my old, old love I knew, My bo-som well'd with joy

No. 4

When I, good friends, was call'd to the bar, I'd an appe- tite fresh

No. 6

Comes the bro- ken flow- er, comes the cheat- ed maid,

No. 8

With a sense of deep e- mo-tion, I ap-proach this pain-ful case

He de- ceiv'd a girl con-fid-ing, Vows, et ce- te- ra, de- rid- ing

No. 10

Oh, gen- tle-men, lis- ten, I pray, Tho I own that my heart

No. 13

I love him, I love him, with fer- vour un- ceas- ing,

No. 14 Finale

Oh, joy un-bound- ed, with wealth sur - round-ed, The knell is sound- ed

The Yeomen of the Guard
Act I, No. 1

When maid- en loves, she sits and sighs, She wan- ders to and fro;

No. 2

Tow- er war- ders, un- der or- ders, Gal- lant pike- men,

No. 3

This the au-tumn of our life This the eve-ning of our day,

No. 5

"The screw may twist and the rack may turn, And men may bleed

No. 7

Is life a boon? If so, it must be-fall that Death when-e'er he call

I have a song to sing, O! Sing me your song, O

It is sung to the moon By a love- lorn loon,

OPERAS

The Yeomen of the Guard
Act I, No. 9

I've wis- dom from the East and from the West,

No. 10

Though tear and long drawn sigh ill fit a bride__ no sad-der wife than I

No. 11

Were I thy bride, then all the world be- side were not too wide

Act II, No. 1

Night__ has spread her pall once more, and__ the pris- 'ner still is free

No. 2

Oh! a pri- vate buf- foon is a light heart- ed loon,

No. 3

Here- up- on we're both a- greed, all that we two Do a- gree to

No. 4

Far from his fet-ters grim Free to de- part;__ Free both in life and limb

No. 5

Strange ad- ven- ture!Mai-den wed- ded To a__ groom she'd nev-er__ seen!

No. 7

If he's made the best use of his time,__ His twig he'll so care-ful-ly lime__

No. 8

Oh, the hap- py days of do- ing! Oh, the sigh-ing and the su-ing

No. 9

Rap- ture, rap- ture, when love's vo- ta- ry;Flushed with cap-ture,

God shall wipe away all tears, from
The Light of the World (oratorio)

God shall wipe a- way all tears from their eyes,There shall be no more death

The Golden Legend Evening Hymn

O glad- some Light of the Fa- ther im- mor - - - - - tal,

The Night is calm

The night is calm and cloud-less, And still as still__ can be

How many hired servants, from The
Prodigal Son

How ma- ny hi- red ser-vants of my fa-ther's have bread e-nough

Songs: Birds in the Night

Birds__ in the night__ that soft - - ly__ call

Ho, Jolly Jenkin, from Ivanhoe
(grand opera)

Then ho, jol- ly Jen- kin I spy a knave in drink- in

The Long Day Closes

No star is o'er the lake, Its pale watch keep- ing,

The Lost Chord

Seat- ed one day at the or- gan, I was wea- ry and ill at ease

Songs: Onward Christian Soldiers (hymn)
On- ward, Chris-tian sol - - - diers Mar- ching as to war, — A

Orpheus with his Lute
Or - - - - - pheus with his lute, with his lute made__ trees B

SUPPÉ, Franz von (1819-1895)

Boccaccio (operetta) No. 3
Hol- de Schö-ne, hör' die-se Tö-ne, hör' mein zärt-li-ches Lie-ber-ge-stöh-ne! D

No. 6
Hab' ich nur dei-ne Lie-be, die Treu-e brauch'_ich nicht, E

No. 18
Flo- renz hat schö- ne Frau- en,__ die Schön- -ste bist du F

SWEELINCK, Jan Pieterzoon (1562-1621)

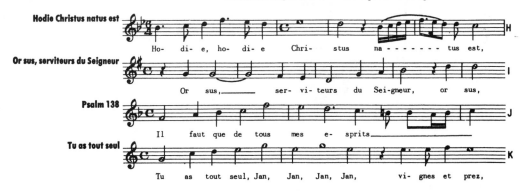

Hodie Christus natus est
Ho- di- e, ho- di- e Chri- stus na - - - - - - - tus est, H

Or sus, serviteurs du Seigneur
Or sus, — ser- vi-teurs du Sei-gneur, or sus, I

Psalm 138
Il faut que de tous mes e- sprits_____ J

Tu as tout seul
Tu as tout seul, Jan, Jan, Jan, Jan, vi- gnes et prez, K

SZULC, Joseph (1874-1935)

Clair de Lune, Op. 83, No. 1
Copyright 1920, G. Schirmer, Inc.
Votre âme est un pa- y- sa- ge choi- si Que vont char- mant M

La Lune Blanche No. 8
Copyright by Salabert, Paris, N. Y.
La lu- ne blan- che luit dans le bois, de cha-que bran- che N

En Sourdine No. 9
Cal- mes dans le de-mi jour, Que les bran-ches hau- tes font, O

Mandoline No. 10
Les don-neurs de sé-ré- na-des et les bel-les e-cou- teu - - - - ses P

TAUBERT, Wilhelm (1811-1891)

rdling, why sing in the forest wide
Bird- ling why sing in the for - - est wide? Say, why? R

TAVERNER, John (c. 1495-1545)

Audivi

Au- di - vi:

TAYLOR, Deems (1885-1966)

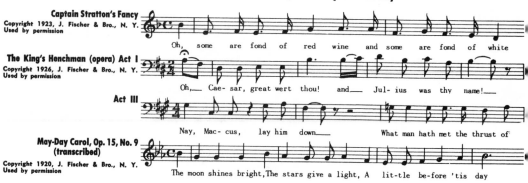

Captain Stratton's Fancy
Copyright 1923, J. Fischer & Bro., N. Y.
Used by permission

Oh, some are fond of red wine and some are fond of white

The King's Henchman (opera) Act I
Copyright 1926, J. Fischer & Bro., N. Y.
Used by permission

Oh,— Cae- sar, great wert thou! and— Jul- ius was thy name!

Act III

Nay, Mac- cus, lay him down— What man hath met the thrust of

May-Day Carol, Op. 15, No. 9 (transcribed)
Copyright 1920, J. Fischer & Bro., N. Y.
Used by permission

The moon shines bright, The stars give a light, A lit-tle be-fore 'tis day

TCHAIKOVSKY, Peter Ilyich (1840-1893)

Moscow (cantata) Arioso No. 2

Ist ein Him- mels-licht, das so strahlt und blinkt durch die fin- stre Nacht.

Arioso No. 5

Wird mir, Herr mein Gott, nicht zu schwer das Kreuz, das mir auf-er- legt

OPERAS
Adieu, forêts, from Jeanne d'Arc

A- dieu, fo- rêts, a- dieu, près fleur-is champs d'or

Eugene Onegin, Op. 24 Act I, No. 1

Did'st thou not hear? how like the night- in- gale One sang by night

No. 6 Lenski's Aria

Yes, I love you, yes, I love you, Ol- ga fierce and hot,

No. 9 Letter scene A

Tho' I should die for it I've sworn now I first shall live—

B

No, ne- ver a- ny oth- er, For any oth- er I had loathed!

No. 11

Come, ye maid-ens all, and dance, Run while yet ye have a chance

No. 12 Onegin's Aria

If in this world a kind-ly for-tune for house-hold cares had destined me

Act II, No. 13 Waltz

Re- gale you all! Hail, hail to all beau- ty

(Instrumental acc. to waltz)

Instrumental accompaniment to Waltz

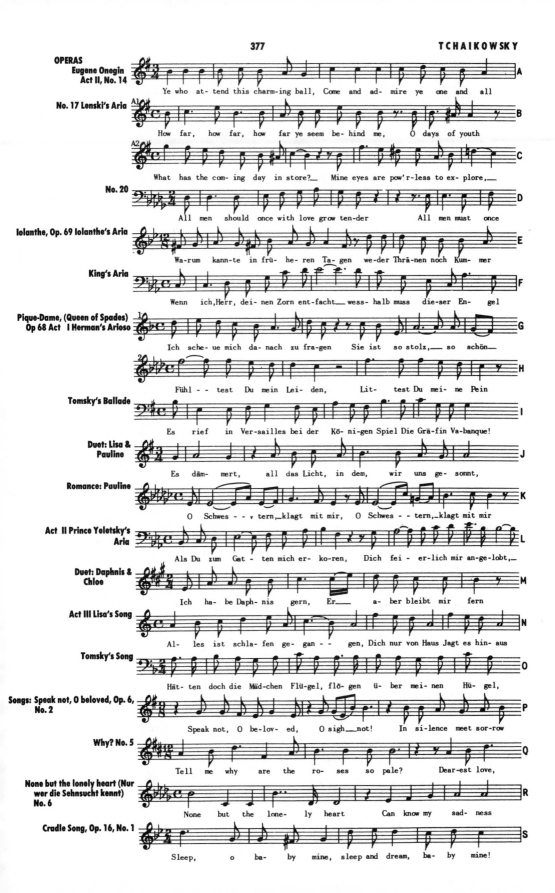

OPERAS
Eugene Onegin
Act II, No. 14
Ye who at-tend this charm-ing ball, Come and ad-mire ye one and all A

No. 17 Lenski's Aria
How far, how far, how far ye seem be-hind me, O days of youth B

What has the com-ing day in store?__ Mine eyes are pow'r-less to ex-plore,__ C

No. 20
All men should once with love grow ten-der All men must once D

Iolanthe, Op. 69 Iolanthe's Aria
Wa-rum kann-te in frü-he-ren Ta-gen we-der Thrä-nen noch Kum-mer E

King's Aria
Wenn ich,Herr, dei-nen Zorn ent-facht__ wess-halb muss die-ser En-gel F

Pique-Dame, (Queen of Spades)
Op 68 Act I Herman's Arioso
Ich scheu-ue mich da-nach zu fra-gen Sie ist so stolz,__ so schön__ G

Fühl - - test Du mein Lei-den, Lit-test Du mei-ne Pein H

Tomsky's Ballade
Es rief in Ver-sailles bei der Kö-ni-gen Spiel Die Grä-fin Va-banque! I

Duet: Lisa & Pauline
Es däm-mert, all das Licht, in dem, wir uns ge-sonnt, J

Romance: Pauline
O Schwes - - r tern,__klagt mit mir, O Schwes - -tern,klagt mit mir K

Act II Prince Yeletsky's Aria
Als Du zum Gat - ten mich er-ko-ren, Dich fei-er-lich mir an-ge-lobt,__ L

Duet: Daphnis & Chloe
Ich ha-be Daph-nis gern, Er__ a-ber bleibt mir fern M

Act III Lisa's Song
Al- les ist schla-fen ge-gan - - gen, Dich nur von Haus Jagt es hin-aus N

Tomsky's Song
Hät-ten doch die Mäd-chen Flü-gel, flö-gen ü-ber mei-nen Hü-gel, O

Songs: Speak not, O beloved, Op. 6, No. 2
Speak not, O be-lov-ed, O sigh__not! In si-lence meet sor-row P

Why? No. 5
Tell me why are the ro-ses so pale? Dear-est love, Q

None but the lonely heart (Nur wer die Sehnsucht kennt) No. 6
None but the lone-ly heart Can know my sad-ness R

Cradle Song, Op. 16, No. 1
Sleep, o ba-by mine, sleep and dream, ba-by mine! S

Songs: Linger yet, Op. 16, No. 2
Lin-ger yet! Thought of part-ing O ban-ish! Like an ar - - - row

Wherefore? Op. 28, No. 3
Why did you come in dreams to me, My ab-sent love, I ne'er for-get

Er liebt mich so sehr! No. 4
Nein, nim-mer lieb-te ich! Und doch sah ich ihn kom-men,

Kein Wort von dir, No. 5
Kein Wort von dir, der Freu-de o-der Kla-ge,

One small word, No. 6
Small head droop-ing, here you stand be-fore me

Don Juan's Serenade, Op. 38, No. 1
All Gra-na-da li - - -eth qui-et In thy bal-co-ny ap-pear

It was in days of early spring, No. 2
It was in days of ear-ly spring, when ten-der grass was grow-ing

At the Ball, No. 3
I know not how love-ly your face is, For that,when I met you

Oh, but to hear thy voice (I wish) No. 4
Oh would but Heav'n in pi-ty grant a boon to me!

Pimpinella (Florentine Song) No. 6
Non con-tras-tar cogl' uo - -mi - ni, fal-lo per ca-ri-ta!

Whether Day Dawns, Op. 47, No. 3
Whe-ther day dawns or night sha-dows are fall-ing Whe-ther I dream

Pilgrim's Song (Benediction) No. 5
My bless-ing rest on ye, o woods, o val-leys moun-tains

Toujours à toi, No. 6 (confused with Toi seul, Op. 57, No. 6)
Que le jour bril - -le ou que l'om-bre nous cou-vre

Was I not a blade of grass in meadow green, No. 7
A
Was I not a blade of grass in mead-ow green

B
Ah. my heart, how hard is life to bear! Ah! my heart,

Songs for Young People, Op. 54, No. 5 Legend
Child Je-sus in his gar-den fair Some sweet red ro-ses once had grown

No. 8 The Cuckoo
From out the ci-ty thou hast flown: Now prith-ee, what word

No. 14 Autumn
De broui-llards mo-ro-ses Les cieux sont cou-verts;

The Nightingale, Op. 57, No. 1
O Sprich wo-von die Nach-ti-gall wenn rings die Welt ver-sank

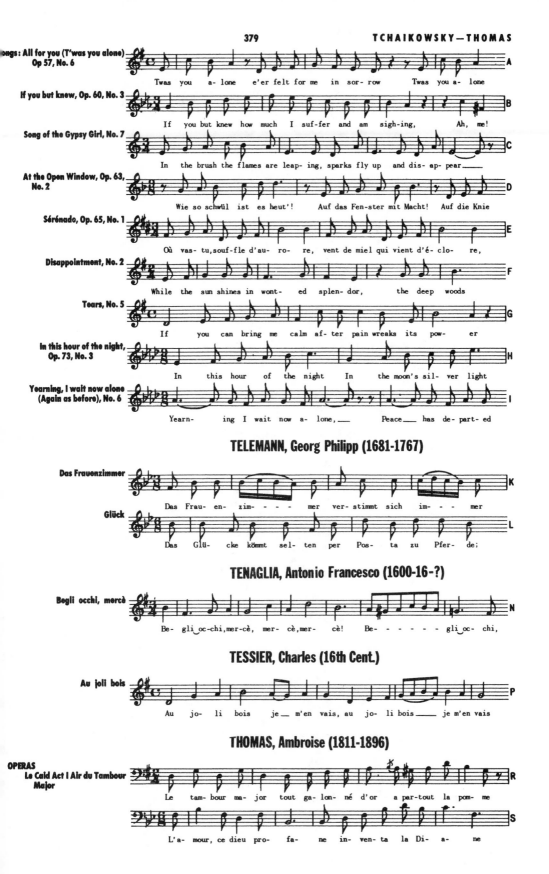

Songs: All for you (T'was you alone) Op 57, No. 6
Twas you a-lone e'er felt for me in sor-row Twas you a-lone

If you but knew, Op. 60, No. 3
If you but knew how much I suf-fer and am sigh-ing, Ah, me!

Song of the Gypsy Girl, No. 7
In the brush the flames are leap-ing, sparks fly up and dis-ap-pear

At the Open Window, Op. 63, No. 2
Wie so schwül ist es heut'! Auf das Fen-ster mit Macht! Auf die Knie

Sérénade, Op. 65, No. 1
Où vas-tu, souf-fle d'au-ro-re, vent de miel qui vient d'é-clo-re,

Disappointment, No. 2
While the sun shines in wont-ed splen-dor, the deep woods

Tears, No. 5
If you can bring me calm af-ter pain wreaks its pow-er

In this hour of the night, Op. 73, No. 3
In this hour of the night In the moon's sil-ver light

Yearning, I wait now alone (Again as before), No. 6
Yearn-ing I wait now a-lone, Peace has de-part-ed

TELEMANN, Georg Philipp (1681-1767)

Das Frauenzimmer
Das Frau-en-zim-mer ver-stimmt sich im-mer

Glück
Das Glü-cke kömmt sel-ten per Pos-ta zu Pfer-de;

TENAGLIA, Antonio Francesco (1600-16-?)

Begli occhi, mercè
Be-gli oc-chi, mer-cè, mer-cè, mer-cè! Be-gli oc-chi,

TESSIER, Charles (16th Cent.)

Au joli bois
Au jo-li bois je m'en vais, au jo-li bois je m'en vais

THOMAS, Ambroise (1811-1896)

OPERAS
Le Caid Act I Air du Tambour Major
Le tam-bour ma-jor tout ga-lon-né d'or a par-tout la pom-me
L'a-mour, ce dieu pro-fa-ne in-ven-ta la Di-a-ne

OPERAS

Hamlet, Act I, Scene I

Dou- te de la lu- miè- re   Dou- te du so- leil et du jour,

Pour mon pa- ys,___ en ser- vi- teur fi- dè- le

Scene II

Spectre in- fer- nal!   I- ma- - ge vé- né- ré- e!

Act II

A- dieu, dit il, a- yez foi!___   Mon coeur vous aime, ai- mez moi!

Les ser- ments_ont des ai- les! Dans le coeur des in- fi- dè- - les___

Dans son re- gard plus som- - bre,___ J'ai vu passer___ comme un é- clair!

Ô vin dis- si- pe la tris- tes- - - - se Qui pè- se sur mon coeur___

Act III

Ê- - tre_ou ne pas ê- tre! ô mys- tè- re! Mou- rir! dor- mir! dor- mir!___

Je___ t'im- plo- re Ô___ mon frè- re! Si tu m'en- tends,___

Act IV

Pâle et blon- de dort sous l'eau pro- fon- de Les wil- lis au re- gard de feu!

Act V

Comme u- ne pâ- le fleur É- close au souf- fle de la tom- be

Mignon Act I

Bons bour- geois et no- ta- bles, as- sis au- tour des ta- bles,

Fu- gi- tif et trem- blant,___ je vais de_porte en por- te,

A

Oui, je veux, par___ le mon- - - de pro- me- ner li- bre- ment

B

Si l'a- mour___ sur ma rou- te Ce soir m'é- tend la main,

A1

Con- nais- tu le pays où fleu- rit l'o- ran- ger

A2

C'est là que je vou- drais vi- - vre, Ai- mer, ai- mer et mou- rir,___

Lé- gè- - - res hi- ron- del- les, Oi- seaux bé- nis de Dieu,

Act II Madrigal

Belle, a- yez pi- tié de___ nous, Belle a- yez pi- tié de___ nous

THOMAS, Christopher J. (1894-   )

THOMÉ, Francis (1850-1909)

THOMPSON, Randall (1899-   )

THOMSON, Virgil (1896-)

Four Saints in Three Acts
Prologue
Copyright by Arrow Music Press, N. Y.

To know to know to love her so___ Four saints pre-pare for saints

Act I

There are a great man-y per-sons___ and pla-ces near___ to- geth-er

She can have no one no one can have an- y- one___

A scene and with-ers Scene three and scene two. How can a sis-ter

Could they grow and tell it so if it was left to be to go

There can be no peace on earth with calm with calm___

They nev- er knew a- bout it green and they nev- er knew a- bout it

Act II

Can an- y- one feel an- y one mov-ing and in mov-ing can

How man- y saints are there in it There are ver- y man- y man- y saints

There are as man- y saints as there are in it.

Act III

Pi-geons on the grass a- las. Pi-geons on the grass a- las.

He asked for a dis-tant mag - pie as if they make a dif- fer-ence

There are ver- y sweet- ly ver- y sweet- ly Hen- ry

Once in a while and where and where a- round a- round

Let-ting pin in let-ting let in let in in in in in let

Variant

With wed led said with led dead said with dead led said

Act IV

Be-gin to trace be-gin to race be-gin to place be-gin and in

The Mother of Us All
Act I Scene I
Copyright by Arrow Music Press, N. Y.

Yes I was, said Su- san. You mean you are, said Anne

OPERAS
The Mother of Us All
Act I, Scene I

They be-gan to trav-el, not to trav-el you know but to go

Men are so__ con-ser-va-tive, so sel-fish so bore-some,

Do come Su-san B. An-tho-ny, do come no-bod-y no-bod-y

Scene II

Pit- y the poor__ per - se-cu-tor If mon- ey is mon-ey,

He digged a pit, he digged it deep, he digged it for his bro-ther.

Dan- iel was his fa-ther's name, fa- ther's name, fa- ther's name

Not an- y more   I am not a mar- tyr an- y- more__

Hush, I hush, you hush, they hush, we hush, Hush, we hush,

Scene III

I be- lieve in pub- lic school ed- u- ca- tion

Dear Miss Con- stance Fle-tcher, it is a great plea- sure

Scene IV

If I be- lieve__ that I am right and I am__ right if they be-lieve__

We are the cho-rus of the V. I. P. Ve- ry im-por-tant per-sons

Scene V

Will they re-mem- ber that it is true that neither they, that neither you,

So beau- ti- ful. It is so beau- ti-ful to meet you here,

Act II, Scene II

I have just con-vert- ed Lil- li- an Rus- sell to the cause

Dear friends, it is so beau- ti-ful__ to meet__ you all__

That so long that the gor- geous en-sign of the re- pub- lic

Scene III

The vote, wo- men have the vote. They have it each and ev'ry one

THRANE, Waldemar (1790-1828)

Kom Kjyra (Norwegian Echo Song)

Kom Kjy- ra! Kom Kjy- ra mi! kom kjy- - - ra!

TIERSOT, Julien (1857-1936)

Noel Provençal I (arr.)
By permission Heugel & Cie, Paris,
copyright owners

Un flam- beau,— Jean- nette, I- sa- bel- le! Un flam- beau—

Noel Provençal II (arr.)

Guil- laume, An- toi- ne, Pier- re, Clau- de, Jac- ques, Ni- co- las—

Noel Provençal III (arr.)

Ah! quand re- vien- dra- t-il le temps, ber- ge- re? Ah!

Le Pauvre Laboreur (arr.)
By permission Heugel & Cie, Paris,
copyright owners

Le pau- vre la- - - bou- reur, Il——— a bien du mal- heur

Le Retour du Marin (chanson Poitevine)
By permission Heugel & Cie, Paris,
copyright owners

Quand le ma- rin re- vint de guer- re, Tout doux

TOMKINS, Thomas (1573-1656)

(madrigals)

Oyez! Has any found a lad

O- yez has a- ny found a lad, has a- ny found,

See, see, the shepherds Queen

See, see, see, the shep- herds' Queen, fair Phyl- lis all— in green

When David heard

When, When Da- - - - vid heard that Ab- sa- lom was slain

TORELLI, Giuseppe (1650-1708)

Tu lo sai

Tu lo— sa- i Quan-to t'a- ma- i, Tu lo— sa- i,

TOSELLI, Enrico (1883-1926)

Serenade (Rimpianto)
By permission Heugel & Cie, Paris,
copyright owners

Co- me un so- gno d'or scol- pi- to è nel co- re

Ma fu mol- to bre- ve in me la dol- cez- za di quel ben

TOSTI, F. Paolo (1846-1916)

L'Alba separa dalla luce l'ombra
By permission Heugel & Cie, Paris,
copyright owners

L'al- ba se- pà- ra dal- la lu- ce l'om- bra—

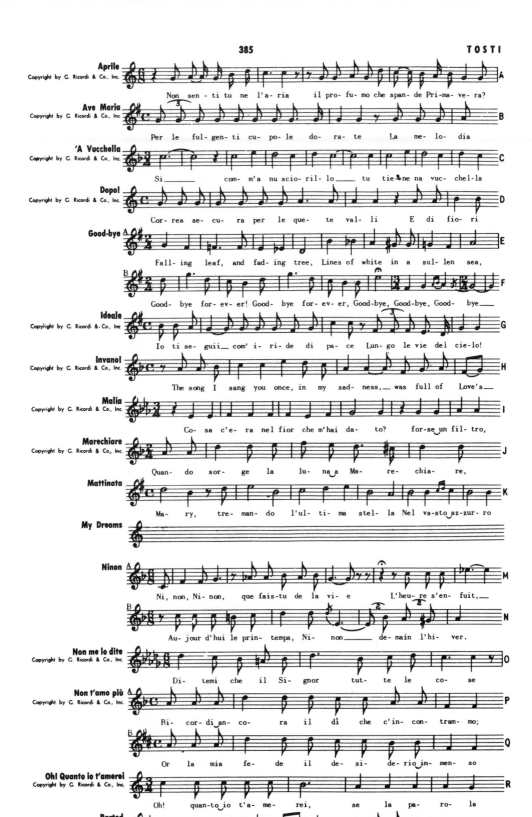

385   TOSTI

Aprile
Copyright by G. Ricordi & Co., Inc.   A
Non sen- ti tu ne l'a- ria il pro- fu- mo che span- de Pri- ma- ve- ra?

Ave Maria
Copyright by G. Ricordi & Co., Inc.   B
Per le ful- gen- ti cu- po- le do- ra- te La me- lo- dia

'A Vucchella
Copyright by G. Ricordi & Co., Inc.   C
Si_____ com'a nu scio- ril- lo_____ tu tie- ne na vuc- chel- la

Dopo!
Copyright by G. Ricordi & Co., Inc.   D
Cor- rea se- cu- ra per le que- te val- li E di fio- ri

Good-bye   A   E
Fall- ing leaf, and fad- ing tree, Lines of white in a sul- len sea,

B   F
Good- bye for- ev- er! Good- bye for- ev- er, Good- bye, Good- bye, Good- bye_____

Ideale
Copyright by G. Ricordi & Co., Inc.   G
Io ti se- guii__ com' i- ri- de di pa- ce Lun- go le vie dei cie- lo!

Invano!
Copyright by G. Ricordi & Co., Inc.   H
The song I sang you once, in my sad- ness,__ was full of Love's__

Malia
Copyright by G. Ricordi & Co., Inc.   I
Co- sa c'e- ra nel fior che m'hai da- to? for- se un fil- tro,

Marechiare
Copyright by G. Ricordi & Co., Inc.   J
Quan- do sor- ge la lu- na a Ma- re- chia- re,

Mattinata
Copyright by G. Ricordi & Co., Inc.   K
Ma- ry, tre- man- do l'ul- ti- ma stel- la Nel va- sto az- zur- ro

My Dreams

Ninon   A   M
Ni, non, Ni- non, que fais- tu de la vi- e L'heu- re s'en- fuit,__

B   N
Au- jour d'hui le prin- temps, Ni- non_____ de- main l'hi- ver.

Non me lo dite
Copyright by G. Ricordi & Co., Inc.   O
Di- temi che il Si- gnor tut- te le co- se

Non t'amo più   A
Copyright by G. Ricordi & Co., Inc.   P
Ri- cor- di an- co- ra il dì che c'in- con- tram- mo;

B   Q
Or la mia fe- de il de- si- de- rio im- men- so

Oh! Quanto io t'amerei   R
Copyright by G. Ricordi & Co., Inc.
Oh! quan- to io t'a- me- rei, se la pa- ro- la

Parted   S
Copyright by G. Ricordi & Co., Inc.
Dear- est, our day is__ o- ver, End- ed the day di- vine

Pensol
Copyright by G. Ricordi & Co., Inc.

Pen- so al- la pri- ma vol- ta in cui vol- ge- sti　A

Ridonami la calma
Copyright by G. Ricordi & Co., Inc.

A- ve Ma- ri- a, per l'a- ria va il suon d'u- na cam- pa- na　B

La Serenata

Vo- la, o se- re- na- ta: La mia di- let- ta è so- la,　C

Sogno
Copyright by G. Ricordi & Co., Inc.

Ho so- gna- to che sta- vi a gi- noc- chi Co- me un san- to　D

L'Ultimo Canzone (The Last Song) A
Copyright by G. Ricordi & Co., Inc.

M'han det- to che do- ma- ni, Ni- na, vi fa- te spo- sa　E

B

Fo- glia di ro- sa, O fio- re d'a- ma- ran- to　F

Vorrei (Could I) A
Copyright by G. Ricordi & Co., Inc.

Vor- rei al- lor che tu pal- li- do e mu- to pie- ghi la fron- te　G

B

Vor- rei per in- can- te- si- mi d'a- mo- re pia- na- men- te　H

Vorrei morir A
Copyright by G. Ricordi & Co., Inc.

Vor- rei mo- rir ne la sta- gion del l'an- no,　I

B

Vor- rei mo- rir, vor- rei mo- rir quan- do tra- mon- ta il so- le　J

TOURS, Frank E. (1877-　　)

Mother o' Mine!

TOYE, Francis (1883-1964)

The Inn
Copyright 1925, F. Toye

Do you re- mem- ber an inn, Mi- ran- da?　N

TRADITIONAL

Barbara Allen

In Scar- let town, where I was born, There was a fair maid dwel- lin'　P

Early one morning

Ear- ly one morn- - - ing just as the sun was ris- ing　Q

The Holly and the Ivy

The hol- ly and the i- vy Now both are full well grown,　R

The Lincolnshire Poacher

When I was bound ap- pren- - tice, in fam- ous Lin- coln- shire,　S

O Can Ye Sew Cushions

O can ye sew cush- ions and can ye sew sheets,

TROTERÉ, Henry (1855-1912)

In Old Madrid

Long years a- go in old Mad- rid where soft- ly sighs

TURINA, Joaquin (1882-1950)

Cantares
Copyright by Unión Musical Española

Ay!

Mas 'cer- ca de mi te sien- to cuan- do mas hu- yo de tí

Las locas por amor
Copyright by Unión Musical Española

Te a- ma- re dio- sa Ve - - - - - - - - - - nus

Rima
By permission Associated Music Publishers, Inc.

Yo soy ar- den- te yo soy mo- re- na

eta en forma de Salve a la Virgen de la Esperanza

Dios te sal- ve, Ma- ca- re - - - - na ma- dre de los se- vi- lla - - nos

Triptico I. Farruca
Copyright by Unión Musical Española

Es- tá tu i- ma- gen que ad- mi- ro, tan pe- ga- da a mi de- se- o

II. Cantilena

Por un a- le- gre pra- do de flo- res es- mal- ta - - - - - - to

III. Madrigal

Tus o- jos, o- jos no son, ni- ña si- no dos na- va- jos

VALDERRABANO, Enriquez de (16th Cent.)

A monte sale (Soneto)

A mon- te sa- le- el a- mor de la Is- la muy nom- bra- da

Señora, si te olvidaré

Se- ño- ra, si te ol- vi- da- ré La mi dies- tra ol vi- de à mi

VALVERDE, Joaquin (1846-1910)

Clavelitos (Carnations)
right by E. B. Marks Music Corp., N. Y.

Cla- ve- li- tos a quien le doy cla- ve - - les!

VANDERPOOL, Frederick W. (1877-1947)

Values (Another Hour with Thee)
Copyright 1918, M. Witmark & Sons

Ah, love, could I but take the hours That once I spent with thee

VARNEY, Louis (1844-1908)

Valse du Colibri, from L'Amour Mouillé (comic-opera)
Copyright by Choudens fils, Paris

P'tit fi!   P'tit mi-gnon!   gen-til   com-pag-non

VAUGHAN WILLIAMS, Ralph (1872-1958)

Bushes and Briars
Copyright by Novelli & Co., Ltd., London

Through bush-es and through bri-ars I late-ly took my way

A farmer's son so sweet
Copyright by Stainer & Bell, Ltd., London; Galaxy Music Corporation, N. Y., U. S. Agents

A far-mer's son so sweet was keep-ing of his sheep

The House of Life 1. Love-Sight
Copyright by Edwin Ashdown, London

When do I see thee most, be-lov-ed one

2. Silent Noon

Your hands lie o-pen in the long fresh grass

3. Love's Minstrels

One flame-winged brought a white winged harp play-er

4. Heart's Haven

Some-times she is a child with-in my arms

5. Death in Life

There came an im-age in Life's ret-in-ue

6. Love's Last Gift

Love to his sin-ger held a glis-ten-ing leaf,

How can the tree but wither
By permission Oxford Univ. Press, London, copyright owners

How can the tree but waste and wi-ther a-way

Linden Lea
By permission Boosey & Hawkes, Inc., copyright owners

With-in the wood-lands, flow'r-y glad-ed, by the oak-trees moss-y moot,

Mass in G Minor I. Kyrie
Copyright 1922, J. Curwen

ky - - - - - ri e e lei - - - - - - - son

II. Gloria in excelsis

Et in ter-ra pax ho-mi-ni-bus bo-nae vo-lun-ta-tis

III. Credo

Pa-trem o-mni-pot-en-tem, fac-to-rem cae-li

IV. A. Sanctus

San - - - - - - - - - - - - - - - ctus

The Twilight People
By permission Oxford Univ. Press, London, copyright owners

It is a whis-per a-mong the ha--zel bush--es;

The Water Mill
By permission Oxford Univ. Press, London, copyright owners

There is a mill, an an-cient one, Brown with rain and dry with sun,

The Winter is gone
Copyright by Novello & Co., Ltd., London

The win-ter is gone and the sum-mer is come

Arrangements: Ca' the yowes
Copyright 1922, J. Curwen

Ca' the yowes, tae the knowes, Ca' them whar the hea-ther grows

The Dark Eyed Sailor
Copyright by Stainer & Bell, Ltd., London; Galaxy Music Corporation, N. Y., U. S. agents

It was a come-ly young la--dy fair, Was walk-ing out

Down in yon forest
Copyright by Stainer & Bell, Ltd., London; Galaxy Music Corporation, N. Y., U. S. agents

Down in yon for-est there stands a hall, The bells of Par-a-dise

Just as the tide was flowing
Copyright by Stainer & Bell, Ltd., London; Galaxy Music Corporation, N. Y., U. S. agents

One mor-ning in the month of May, Down by some roll-ing ri-ver

Loch Lomond
Copyright by Stainer & Bell, Ltd., London; Galaxy Music Corporation, N. Y., U. S. agents

By yon bon-ny banks and yon bon-ny braes, where the sun shines

The Springtime of the year
Copyright by Stainer & Bell, Ltd., London; Galaxy Music Corporation, N. Y., U. S. agents

As I walked out one morn-ing, in the spring-time of the year

The Turtle Dove
Copyright 1919, J. Curwen

Fare you well my dear, I must be gone, and leave you

Wassail Song
Copyright by Stainer & Bell, Ltd., London; Galaxy Music Corporation, N. Y., U. S. agents

Was-sail, Was-sail all o-ver the town

Wassail Song
Copyright by Stainer & Bell, Ltd., London; Galaxy Music Corporation, N. Y., U. S. agents

We've been a-while a-wan-der-ing A-mongst the leaves

VECCHI, Orazio (1550-1603)

Il bianco e dolce cigno

Il bian--co e dol-ce cig-no can-tan---do mo-re

Can-tan-----------do, can-tan------do

VEHANEN, (1887-   )

Tuku, tuku, lampaitani (arr.) (Finnish folk tune)
By permission Galaxy Music Corporation, N. Y.

Tu-ku, tu-ku, lam-pai-ta-ni, ki- li, ki- li, ki- li- a- ni

VERACINI, Francesco (1690-1750)

Pastoral, from Rosalinda (opera)

Me- co ver-rai su quel-la, A- me-na col-li- net-ta

VERDI, Giuseppe (1813-1901)

OPERAS
Aida Act I — Ce- le- ste A- i- da, for- ma di- vi- na, mi- sti- co ser- to — B

Su! del Ni- lo al sa- cro li- do ac- cor- re- te E- gi- zii e- rir, — C

Ri- tor- na vin- ci- tor! E dal mio lab- bro u- sci l'em- pia pa- ro- la! — D

L'in- sa- na pa- ro- la O nu- mi sper- de- te! — E

I sa- cri no- mi di pa- dre d'a- man- te — F

Nu- mi, pie- tà del mio sof- frir! Spe- me non v'ha — G

Finale — Pos- sen- te, pos- sen- te Ftha — H

Nu- me, cu- sto- de e vin- di- ce di que- sta sa- cra ter- ra — I

Act II, Scene I Introduction — Chi mai chi mai fra gl'inni e i plau- si er- ge al- la glo- ria il vol — J

Vie- ni: sul crin ti pio- va- no, Vie- ni sul crin ti pio- va- no — K

Ah! vie- ni, vie- ni a- mor mio, m'i- neb- bria, — L

Duet — A- mo- re a- mo- re! gau- dio tor- men- to so a- ve eb- brez- za — M

A tut- ti bar- ba- ra non si mo- stro la sor- te — N

Scene II — Gloria al E- git- to, ad I- si- de che il sa- cro suol pro- teg- ge! — O

S'in- trec- ci il lo- to al lau- ro sul crin dei vin- ci- to- ri — P

Gra- zie a- gli De- i ren- de- te, — Q

Ma tu, Re, tu si- gno- re pos- sen- te, a co- sto- ro ti vol- gi — R

Act III Nile Song — Oh pat- ria mia, mai più, mai più ti ri- ve- drò! — S

OPERAS

Aida Act III (Nile Song)

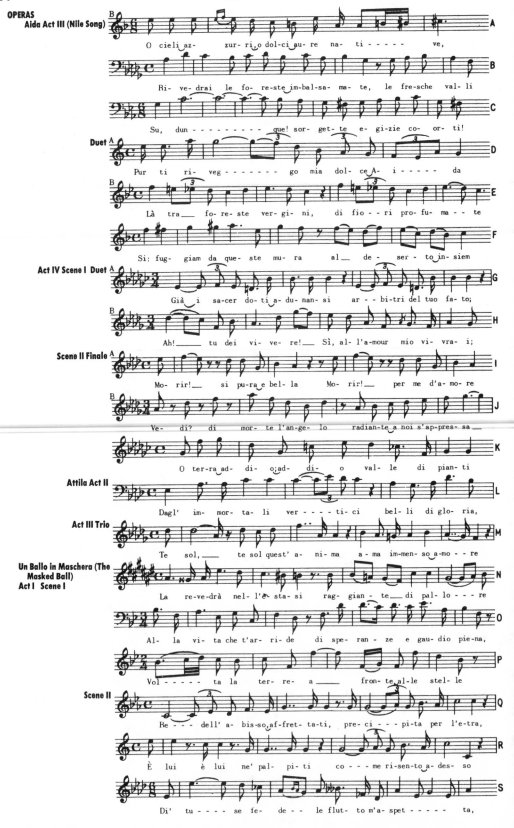

O cieli az- zur-ri o dol-ci au- re na- ti - - - - ve,

Ri- ve-drai le fo- re-ste im-bal-sa- ma-te, le fre-sche val- li

Su, dun - - - - - - - que! sor- get- te e- gi-zie co- or- ti!

Duet

Pur ti ri- veg - - - - - - go mia dol- ce A- i - - - - da

Là tra_ fo- re- ste ver- gi- ni, di fio - - ri pro- fu- ma - - te

Si: fug- giam da que- ste mu- ra al_ de- ser- to in- siem

Act IV Scene I Duet

Già i sa-cer do- ti a- du-nan- si ar - - bi-tri del tuo fa- to;

Ah!_ tu dei vi- ve- re! Sì, al- l'a-mour mio vi- vra- i;

Scene II Finale

Mo- rir!_ si pu-ra e bel- la Mo- rir!_ per me d'a- mo- re

Ve- di? di mor- te l'an-ge- lo radian-te a noi s'ap-pres-sa_

O ter-ra ad- di- o; ad- di- o val- le di pian- ti

Attila Act II

Dagl' im- mor-ta- li ver - - - ti- ci bel- li di glo- ria,

Act III Trio

Te sol,_ te sol quest' a- ni- ma a- ma im-men-so a-mo - - re

Un Ballo in Maschera (The Masked Ball)
Act I Scene I

La re-ve-drà nel- l'è- sta- si rag- gian- te_ di pal- lo - - re

Al- la vi- ta che t'ar- ri- de di spe- ran- ze e gau-dio pie- na,

Vol - - - - ta la ter- re- a_ fron-te al-le stel- le

Scene II

Re - - - dell' a- bis-so af-fret- ta-ti, pre-ci - - - pi-ta per l'e-tra,

È lui è lui ne' pal- pi- ti co - - me ri-sen-to a- des- so

Di' tu - - - se fe- de - - le flut- to m'a-spet - - - - ta,

VERDI

OPERAS
Un Ballo in Maschera (The
Masked Ball)
Act I Scene II

È scher- zo od è fol- li - - a si f-fatta pro-fe- zi - a

Act II

Ma dal-l'a- ri- do stelo di-vul- sa co-me a-vrò di mia ma-no

Love duet

Non sai tu che se l'a- ni- ma mi- a - - il ri- mor- so

Oh qual so- a- ve bri- vi- do l'ac- ce- so pet-to ir-ro- ra!

Ve' se di not- te qui col-la spo- sa l'in-na-mo- ra- - to

Act III

Mor- rò, ma pri-ma in gra - - zia deh! mi con-sen-ti_al-me- no

E- ri tu che mac-chia- ve quel-l'a - - -ni-ma, la de-li- zia

Ma se m'è for- za per- der ti per sem-pre_o lu- ce mi - a

(Air of the page)

Sa- per vor-re- ste di che si ves- te, quan-do l'è co- sa

Don Carlos Act I

Io la vi-di_e_al su - - - - o sor- ri- so scin-til- lar,_

Act II

Dio,_ che nell' al- ma in- fon - - - - de- re a- mor_

Nel giar-din del bel- lo_ sa- ra-cin o-stel- lo,_

Non_ pian- ger, mia com- pa - - gna, non pian- ger no,

Act IV

Dor- mi- rò sol nel man-to mio re-gal, quan-do la mia gior-na- ta

O don fa- ta- le, o don cru- del che in suo fu- ror_

O_ mia Re- gi- na, io t'im- - mo- - - la- i

Per me giun- to_è il dì su- pre-mo, no, mai più ci ri- - ve- drem;

Io mor- rò, ma lie-to in co- re, chè po- tei co-si_ ser-bar

Act V

Tu che le va- ni- tà co- no- sce- sti del mon- do

OPERAS

Don Carlos Act V

S'an-cor si pian-ge in cie — — lo pian-gi sul mio do- lo — — — re,

I Due Foscari Act I

Dal più re- mo- to e- si- glio, sull'a- li del — de- si — o

Tu al ciu squardo onni- pos- sen — — — te tut- to e- sul- ta o

O vec-chio cor che bat — — — — — ti come a' prim' an- ni in se — — — no

Act II

Non ma- le- dir- mi, o pro — — de se son del Do- ge fi — — glio;

Act III

Al- l'in — fe- li- ce ve- glio con- for — — ta tu il do- lo — — re,

Que- sta dun- que è l'i- ni- qua mer- ce- de, che ser- ba- ste

Ernani Act I

Co- me ru- gia- da al co- spi- te d'un ap- pas- si- to fio — — — re

Ev- vi — — va! be- viam! be- viam! Nel vi- no cer- chiam

Er- na- ni! Er- na — — ni in- vo- la- mi all' ab- bor- ri — to am- ples — so

Tut- to — sprez- zo — che d'Er- na — ni non — fa — vel- la

Da quel dì — che t'ho ve- du- ta bel- la co- me un pri mo a —

In- fe- li- ce! e tu cre- de- vi si bel ci- glio

Act II

Lo ve- dre — mo, o ve- gli au- da — — ce se re- si- ster- mi

Vie- ni me- co, sol di ro — — se in- trec-ciar ti vo' la vi — ta,

Act III

Oh de' verd' an — — — ni — mie — — — i so gui e bugiar de — lar — — ve

Si ri- des- ti, il Le- on di — Ca- sti — — glia, e d'I- be — — ria

O som- mo Car- lo, più del tuo no- me le tue vir- tu — di —

Act IV

So- lin- go, er- ran- te e mi- se- ro, Fin da prim' an- ni mie- i

OPERAS
Falstaff Act I

So __ che se an-diam, la not- te, di ta- ver - - - na in ta-ver- na

M'ar- de- a l'e-stro ama- to- rio nel cor. La Dea vi- bra- va

L'O- no- re! La- dri! Voi state ligi all'onor vostro, voi!

De- vo tal or da un la- to por- re il ti- mor di Di- o

Quel- l'o- tre! quel ti- no! Quel Re del- le pan- cie,

Lab- bra di fo- co! Lab-bra di fio- re! Che il va- go gio- co

Act II Scene I

Pri- ma di tut- to, sen- za com- pli- men- ti,

È so- gno? o re- al- tà Due ra-mi enor-mi crescon

Scene II

Giun- ta all' Al- ber- go del- la Giar- ret- tie- - - ra

Ga- je co- ma- ri di Vind- sor! e l'o- - - - - - ra

Quand e- ro pag- gio del Du- ca di Nor-folck, e- ro sot- ti- le,

Act III

Dal lab- bro il can- to e- sta- si- a- to vo- la

Sul fil d'un sof- fio e- te- si- o Scor- re- te a- gi- li lar- - - ve,

La Forza del Destino
Act I

Me pel- le- gri- na ed or- fa- na lun- gi dal pa-trio ni- - do

Ah, per sem- pre o mio bel l'an- giol, ne con- giun- ge il cie- lo

Act II Scene I

Al suon del tam- bu- ro al brio del cor- sie- ro,

Son Pe- re- - da, son ric- co d'o- no- re bac- cel- - lie- - re

Scene II

Ma- dre, Ma- dre, pie- to- sa Ver- gi- ne, per- do- na

OPERAS
La Forza del Destino
Act II Scene II

Act III Tarantella

Act IV

Deh! non m'ab-ban-do-nar, pie-tà, pie-tà di me, Si-gno-re.

Il san-to no-me di Di-o Si-gno-re sia be-ne-det-to.

Ma-le-di-zio-ne, ma-le-di-zio-ne, ma-le-di-zion!

La Ver-gi-ne de-gli an-ge-li mi co-pra del suo man-to,

Nel-la guer-ra e la _____ fol-li-a

So-len-ne in que-st'o-ra giu-rar-mi do-ve-te

Or muo-io tran-quil-lo, Vi strin-go al cor mi-o

Oh, tu che in se-no a-gli an-ge-li e-ter-na-men-te pu-ra,

Toh, toh! Pof-fa-re il mon-do! oh che tem-po-ne

Ur-na fa-ta-le del mio de-sti-no, va,t'al-lon-ta-na,

E-gli è sal - - - vo! oh gioja im-men-sa che m'in-non - - - di

(chorus)

Com-pa-gni, so-stia-mo, il cam-po e-splo-ria-mo;

Sle-a-le! Il se-gre-to fu dun-que vio-la-to?

(chorus)

No,d'un i-me-ne il vin-co-lo strin-ga fra noi la spe - - - me;

(soprano & chorus)

Lor - - chè _ pif - - fe - - ri_ l tam - - - bu-ri

Ra-ta-plan, ra-ta-plan, del-la glo-ria pel sol-da-to

Le me-nac-cie,fie-ri ac-cen-ti por-tin se-co in pre-da i ven-ti,

Pa-ce, pa-ce, pa-ce, mio Di-o, pa-ce mio Di-o!

(Trio)

Non im-pre-ca-re, u-mi-lia-ti a Lui che è giu-sto

OPERAS
La Forza del Destino
Act IV

Del mon- do i __ di- sin ___ gan- ni,

I Lombardi alla Prima Crociata
Act I

Te, ver- gin san- ta in- vo- co Sal- ve Ma- ri- a!

Act II

La mi ___ a le- ti- zia in- fon- de- re

A

O ma- dre, dal cie- lo soc- cor- ri al mio pian- to

B

Se va- no se va- no è il pre- ga ___ re,

Act III

Qual vo- lut- tà __ tra- sco- re- re sen- to di ve- na in- ve- na

Act IV Polonaise

Non fu so ___ gno In __ fon- do 'all' al ___ ma

Chorus of Pilgrims

O si- gno- re, dal tet- to na- ti- o ci chia- ma- sti

Luisa Miller Act I

Lo vi- di, e'l pri- mo pal- pi- to il cor __ sen- ti d'a- mo- re

Sa- cra la scel- ta è d'un con- sor- te, es- ser ap- pie ___ no

Il mio san- gue, la vi- ta da- re- i per ve- der- lo fe- li- ce,

Act II

Tu pu- ni- sci- mi o Si- gno ___ re, se t'of- fe- si,

Quan- do le se- re al pla- ci- do chia- ror d'un ciel stel- la ___ to

Macbeth Act II

Co- me dal ciel pre- ci- pi- ta l'om- bra più sem- pre o- scu- ra!

Act IV Coro di Profughi
Scozzesi

Pa- tria op- pres- sa! il dol- ce no- me no, di ma- dre a- ver

Ah, la pa- ter- na ma- no non vi fu scu- do o ca- ri

U- na mac- chia è qui tutt' o- ra via ti di- co,

Pie- tà, ri- spet- to, a- mo ___ re con- for- to a' dì ca- den ___ ti

Nabucodonosor
Act I Sperate, O figli

D'E- git- to là sui lì ___ di E- gli a Mo- sè diè vi- ta

OPERAS

Nabucodonosor
Act I Sperate, O figli

Co - me not - te a sol ful - gen - to, co - me pol - ve

Tre - min gl' in - sa - ni del mio__ del mi - o fu - ro - re

Act II

Tu sul lab - bro de' veg - gen - - - - ti ful - mi - na - sti,

Coro di Leviti

Il ma - le - det - to non ha fra - tel - li non v'ha mor - ta - le

Per a - mor del Dio vi - ven - te dall' a - na - te - ma ces - sa - te

Chi mi to - glie il re - gio scet - tro? Qual m'in - cal - za or - ren - do

Act III

Va, pen - sie - ro sull' a - li do - ra - - - - te;

Del fu - tu - ro nel bu - jo__ di - scer - no

Act IV

Di - o di__ Giu - da! l'a - - - - ra, il tem - - pio

Otello Act I (chorus)

Dio ful - gor del - la bu - fe - ra! Dio sor - ri - so del - la du - na!

Ar - de la pal - ma__ col si - co - mo - ro

Brindisi

I - naf - fia__ l'u - go__ la!__ trin - ca, tra - can - na

Chi all' e - sca ha mor - so del di - ti - ram - bo spa - val - do

Già nel - la not - te den - sa s'e - stin - gue ogni cla - mor

(Duet)

Quan - do nar - ra - vi l'e - su - le tua vi - ta

E tu m'a - ma - vi per le mie sven - tu - re

Act II

Cre - - - do in un Dio cru - del che m'ha cre - a - to si - mi - le a sè,

Cre - - - do con fer - mo cuor sic - co - me cre - de la ve - do - vel - la

Do - ve guar - di splen - do - no rag - gi, av - vam - pan cuo - re,

OPERAS
Othello Act II

VERDI

A te le por-po-re, le per-le e gli o-stri

O- ra e per sem-pre Addio san-te me-mo-rie, ad dio

The Dream

E- ra la not-te, Cas-sio dor-mi-a, gli sta-va ac-can-to

Si, pel ciel mar-mo-reo giu-ro! Per le at-tor-te fol-go-ri!

Te-sti-mon è il Sol ch'io mi-ro, che m'ir-ra-dia

Act III

Dio ti gio-con-di o spo-sa del-l'al-ma mi-a so-vra - - - - no

Ma o pian-to o duol! m'han ra-pi-to il mi-rag-gio

(Trio)

Vie- ni; l'au-la è de-ser-ta. T'i nol-tra,

Questa è una ra - gna do-ve il tuo cuor ca-sca,

A ter-ra sì nel li-vi-do fan-go, per-cos-sa

E un di sul mio sor-ri-so fio-ria la spe - - - me

Act IV Willow Song

Pian-gea can-tan-do nel-l'er-ma lan-da

Prayer

Pre- ga per chi a-do-ran-do a te, si pro - - - - stra,

Death of Othello

E tu co-me sei pal-li-da! e stan-ca, e mu-ta, e bel - - la

Rigoletto Prologue

Questo o quel-la per me pa-ri so-no a quan-t'al - - - tre

Par- ti-te? Cru-de-e-le! Se-gui-re lo spo - - so

Tut-to è fe-sta, tut-to è gio-ia, tut-to è fe-sta;

Act I (Duet)

Si-gnor, Va non ho nien-te Nè il chie-si A voi pre-sen-te un uom

Pa- ri sia-mo io la lin-gua, egli ha il pu-gna-le;

OPERAS
Rigoletto Act I (Duet)

A — Fi- glia! Mio pa- dre! A te d'ap- pres- so

B — Deh non par-la-re al mi- se- ro del suo per-du-to be- - - ne

C — Ve-glia o don- na, que- sto fio- re che a te pu- ro con-fi-da- - i;

D — È il sol del- l'a- ni- ma, la vi-ta è a- mo- - re

E — Ad- di- o, ad- di- o, spe- ran- za ed a- ni- ma

F — Ca- ro no- me che il mio cor fe-sti pri- mo pal- pi- tar

(Final chorus)
G — Zit- ti, zit-ti mo- via-mo a ven-det- ta, ne sia col- to

Act II
H — Par- mi ve-der le la- gri- me scor-ren- ti da quel ci-glio,

(chorus)
I — Scor- ren- do u- ni- - - ti re- mo- ta vi- - - a

J — Pos- sen- te a- mor mi chia- - - ma, vo- lar io deg- gio a le- i;

K — La rà, la rà, la la, la rà, la rà la rà, la rà,

A
L — Cor- ti- gia- ni, vil raz- za dan- na- ta,

B
M — Miei si- gno- ri per-do- - no, pie- ta- - - - - te

N — Tut- te le fe-ste al tem- pio men-tre pre-ga- va Id-di- o,

A
O — So- lo per me l'in-fa- - - mia a te chie-de- va o Di- o

B
P — Pian- gi, pian- gi, fan-ciul- - - la, fan-ciul- la, pian- gi.

Q — Si, ven- - - det- ta, tre- men- da ven-det- - ta

Act III
R — La don-na è mo- bi- le qual piu-ma al ven- - to,

(Quartet) A
S — Un dì, se ben ram-men-to-mi o bel- la, t'in-con-tra- i

OPERAS
Rigoletto Act III (Quartet)

Simon Boccanegra Prologue

Act I

Act II

La Traviata Act I   Brindisi

(Part 2 of Ah fors'e lui)

Act II Scene I

Bel- la fi-glia del-l'a- mo- re, schia-vo son de'vez-zi tuoi; — i;

Ah! ah! ri- do ben di co- re chè tai ba- ie co-stan po-co

In- fe- li- ce co- re,cor tra-di- to,per an- go- scia non

V'ho in-gan-na- to col-pe-vo- le fu- i l'a- mai trop-po

Las- su in cie- - - lo, vi- ci- na al la ma-dre

Il la- ce-ra- to spi- ri- to del me-sto ge-ni- to- re

Co- me in que-st'o- ra bru- na sor- ri- - -!- don gli a- stri

Fig- lia a tal no- me io pal- pi- to qual se m'a-pris-se i cie- li

Ple- be! Pa-tri-zi! Po- po- lo dal- la fe-ro- ce sto- ria

Pian- go su voi sul pla- - ci-do— rag-gio del vo-stro cli- vo

Sen- to av-vam-par nel l'a-ni- ma fu- ren- te— ge- lo- si- - a

Cie- lo pie-to- so, ren- di- la ren- di- la a que-do co- re

Li- bia- - - - mo, li- bia- mo ne' lie- - - ti ca- - - li- ci,

Un dì fe- li- ce, e- te- re- a, mi ba- le- na-ste in-nan- - - - te

Ah, for- s'e lui che l'a- ni- ma so-lin-ga ne' tu- mul- - ti,

A quel l'a- mor, quel l'a- mor— ch'e pal- pi- to,

Sem- pre li- be- ra— deg- g'i- o fol- leg- gia- re

De miei bol-len- ti spi- ri- ti il gio-va-ni-le ar-do- re

O— mio ri- mor- so!oh in- fa- mia! io— vis- si

OPERAS

La Traviata Act II Scene I

Non sa- pe- te qua- le af- fet- to vi- vo im- men- so___ A

Pu- ra sic- co- me un an- ge- lo, Id- dio mi diè u- na fi- - glia B

Di- te al- la gio- - - vi- ne si bel- la e pu- - - ra, C

A- ma- mi Al- fre- - do, a- ma- mi quan-t'io t'a- - - mo D

Di Pro- ven- za il mar, il suol chi dal cor ti can-cel- lo E

No, non u- drai rim- pro- ve- ri, co- priam d'o- blio il pas- sa- to;___ F

Scene II Chorus of Gypsies

Noi sia- mo zin- ga- rel- le ve- nu- te da lon- ta- no; G

Se___ con- sul- tiam le stel- le nul- l'av- vi a noi d'o- scur, H

Chorus of Matadors

È___ Pi- quil- lo un bel ga- gliar- do bi- - sca- gli- no ma- - ta- dor; I

Cin- que to- ri in un sol gior- no vo' ve- der- ti ad at- ter- rar, J

Act III

Ad- di- o del pas- sa- to, bei___ so- gni ri- - - - den- ti K

Pa- ri- gi o ca- - - - - ra, noi la- sce- re- mo, L

Pren- di quest' è l'im- ma- gi- ne de miei pas- sa- ti gior- ni M

Il Trovatore Act I

Ab- biet- ta- zin- ga- ra, fos- - - ca ve- gliar- da! N

Ta- cea la not- te pla- ci- da e bel- la in ciel se- re- - no; O

Di ta- le a- mor, che dir___ si mal può dal- la pa- ro- - - - la, P

De- - - - ser- to sul___ la ter- - - - - - ra Q

Di ge- - lo- - so a- mor sprez- za- - - - - to R

Act II

Ve- di! le fo- sche not- tur- ne___ spo- lie___ dè cie- li sve- ste S

Stri - de la vam - - - - - pa, la _____ fol - la in - do - - - - mi - ta   A

Chi del gi - ta - - no i gior - - ni ab- bel - la?   B

Con - dot - ta el - l'era in cep - pi al su - o de - stin tre - men - do   C

Mal reg - - gen - do all' a - - - - spro as - sal - to,   D

Pe - ri gliar - ti an - cor lan - guen - - te per cam - min sel - vag - gio   E

Il ba - len del suo sor - ri - so d'u - - na ___ stel - la   F

Per me o - ra fa - ta - - le, i tuoi mo - men - ti af - fret - ta   G

Finale

E deg - gio e pos - so cre - der - lo? Ti veg - go a me_ d'ac - can - to!   H

**Act III Soldiers'
Chorus**

Or co da - di, ma fra po - co gio - che - rem ben_ al - tro gio - co!   I

Squil - li e cheg - gi la trom - ba guer - rie - ra, chia - mi all' ar - mi   J

Ah si, ben mio coll' es - se - re io tuo, tu mia con - sor - te,   K

Di quel - la pi - - - - - ra l'or - ren - do fo - - - - - - co   L

All' ar - mi! All' ar - mi all' ar - mi all' ar - - - mi!   M

Gior - ni po - ve - ri vi - ve - - a, pur con - ten - ta   N

Act IV Scene I

D'a - mor sull' a - - li ro - se - e van - ne, so - spir_ do - len - - te;   O

Miserere

Quel son, quel - le pre - - - ci so - len - ni, fu - ne - - ste   P

Ah _____ che la morte o- gno - - ra è _ tar - da nel ve - nir   Q

Tu ve - drai che a - more in ter - ra mai del mio non fa più for - te   R

Mi - ra, di a - cer - be la - gri - me spar - go al tuo piedi un ri - o!   S

OPERAS
Il Trovatore Act IV Scene II

Si, la stan-chez-za m'op-prime, o fi - - glio

I Vespri Siciliani Act II

Ai nos-tri mon - ti ri-tor-ne-re - - mo, l'an-ti-ca pa - ce

Vi - vra! Con-ten-de il giu-bi - lo i det-ti a me, Sig-no-re

I Vespri Siciliani Act II

O tu, Pa-ler-mo, ter-ra a-do-ra-ta, a - - me si ca - - ro___

Act III

In bra-ccio alle do-vi - - zie, nel se-no___ de-gli o-nor,

Quan-do al mio sen per te par - la-va pie-tà sin - ce - ra

Act IV

Gior-no di pian - to, di fier do - lo - re! Men-tre l'a-mo - re

Act V Siciliana

Mer - - cè, di-let-te a-mi - - che___ di_ quoi leg-gia-dri fior;

La brez-za a-leg-gia in-tor-no a car-ez-zar-mi_il vi - so e

Sacred Music:
Ave Maria (scala enigmatica)

A - ve___ Ma-ri - - - a, gra-ti-a ple-na,

Requiem I   Requiem and Kyrie

Re-qui-em   Re-qui-em   Re-qui-em ae-ter-nam do-na, do-na e-is,

Te de-cet hym-mus, De - - - - - - us, in Si - on,

Ky-ri-e e-le - - - - - - - - - - - i-son

II Dies Irae

Di-es i-rae, Di-es i - - - - - - - - - - - - - - - - - rae,

Tu - ba mi - - - - rum___ spar - - gens___ so-num

Quid sum, mi - - - - - ser! tunc - - dic-tur-us

Rex tre-men-dae maj-es-ta - - - tis___

Re - - - cor-da - re, Je - - - su_pi - e Quod sum_cau-sa

In-ge-mi - - sco tam-quam re - us, Cul-pa ru-bet vul-tus me-us:

Requiem II Dies Irae
Qui _____ Ma - ri - am ab-sol vis - - - - - - - ti,

O- ro sup-plex et ac-cli-nis, Cor con-tri-tum qua-si ci-nis,

La- cry - mo - sa di - es___ il-la! Qua re-surg-et ex fa-vil-la

III Domine Jesu
Do - - - mi - ne   Do - - - mi - ne Je - su Chris-te,

li - be - ra a - - - - - ni - - - - - mas

Quam o - lim A - bra-hae, quam o - lim Ab - - ra-hae,

Ho - - - - - sti - as   et pre - - - - - ces - ti - bi, Do - - mi - ne

IV Sanctus (fugue for two choirs)
San- ctus,san-ctus, san - ctus, Do - mi-nus De - - us___ Sa-ba- oth,

San- ctus,_san-ctus, san - ctus___ Do - - - mi - nus De - us___ Sa - ba - oth

V Agnus Dei
Ag - nus De - i, A - - - gnus De - i, qui___ tol - lis pecca-ta mun-di,

VI Lux aeternam
Lux ae - ter - na lu - ce - at e - is Do - - mi - ne

Re - qui - em ae - ter - - nam do na e - - - - - - - - - - is,

et ___ lux___ per - pe - tu - a lu - - - ce - at e - is

VII Libera me
Li - be - ra me, Do - mi - ne, de mor - te ae - ter - na,___

VIDAL, Paul (1863-1931)

Ariette
Si j'é - tais ray - on, j'i - rais, jeu - ne fil - le

Le Fidèle Coeur
Copyright 1898, G. Schirmer, Inc.
Je se - rai ta dou-ceur pro - fon - de Ta der-niè - re joie

VIDE, Jacques (15th Cent.)

Las! j'ay perdu mon espincel
Las! j'ay per - - du mon es - pin - - - - cel

Vit encore ce faux Dangier

Vit en-co- re ce faux Dan-gier _____

VILLA-LOBOS, Heitor (1887-1959)

Bachianas Brasileiras No. 5
By permission Associated Music
Publishers, Inc.

Ah _____

Tar- de u- ma nu- vem ro- sea len- ta e tran-spa-ren- te

Canção de Saudade

Ah _____

Mi- nha mae que- ri- da Tu es meu pen- sa- men- to

Estrella é lua nova (Brazilian folk song) (arr.)
By permission Associated Music
Publishers, Inc.

Es- trel- la do céo é lu- a no- va cra-ve- ja- da

Nozani - ná (Brazilian folk song) (arr.)
By permission Associated Music
Publishers, Inc.

No- za- ri ná ô- re ku- á ku- á,___ Ka- za ê- tê

Serestas No. 1 Pobre Céga

Po-bre cé- ga, por-que cho-ram as-sim tan-to esses teus o - - -lhos

No. 2 O anjo da guarda

Quan- do min-ha ir-mã mor- reu (De- via ter si-do as- sim

No. 3 Canção de folha morta

Fol- ha ca- his-te ao meu la- do La-gri- ma ver-de dos ra- mos!

No. 4 Saudades da minha vida

Sau- da- de- do tem- po, Do tem-po_pas- sa- do,

No. 6 No paz do outono

Na paz do ou- to- no, Gra- ve, pro- fun- da___

No. 7 Cantiguo do viuvo

A noi-te ca- in na minha al- ma, Fi-quel tris- te sem que- rer

No. 8 Canção do carreiro

Na, na! na na na na na na na na na na na na na na na

No. 9 Abril

De- pols da chu- va- ra- da su- bi- ta que i- num- dou

No. 10 Desejo

Pe- la- ja- nel-la a- ber-ta eu ve- ja a lu- a pen- du- ra- da

No. 11 Redondilha

A vi- da Fin- gi da Me cha- ma Me bei- ja Me fo- go

No. 12 Realejo

Be- a- le- jo é co- mo os ou- tros são, que vao e vem___

VITTORIA, Tomas Luis de (c. 1535-1611)

VIVALDI, Antonio (c. 1676-77-1741)

Stabat Mater II Recitative

Cu- jus a- ni- ma ge- men- tem con- tri- stan- tem

III Andante

Pro- pec ca- - - - tis su- - - e gen- ti

IV Largo

E- ja, Ma- - - ter fons a- mo- - - - - - - ris,

V Lento

Fac ut ar- de at cor me- - - um in a- man- do

VUILLERMOZ, Emile (1878-1960)

Jardin d'amour
Copyright by Salabert, Paris, N. Y.

Quand je vais au___ jar- din, jar- din d'a- mour

WAGNER, Richard (1813-1883)

OPERAS

Der fliegende Holländer (The Flying Dutchman)
Act I Sailor's song

Mit Ge- wit- ter und Sturm aus fer- nem Meer, mein Mä- del, bin dir nah'!

Wie oft in Mee- res tief- sten Schlund stürzt' ich voll Sehn- sucht mich hin- ab,

Dich fra- ge ich, ge- pries'ner En- gel Got- - - tes

Durch Sturm und bö- sen Wind ver- schla- gen, irr' auf den Was- sern ich

Act II Spinning Chorus

Summ'___ und___ brumm', du___ gu- tes Räd- - - - - - - - - chen

Senta's Ballad

Jo- ho- hoe! Jo- ho- ho- hoe! Ho- ho- hoe! Jo- - - - - hoe

Traft ihr das Schiff im Mee- re an; blut- rot die Se- gel,

Doch kann dem blei- chen Man- ne Er- lö- sung ein- stens noch wer- - den

Mein Herz voll Treu- e bis___ zum Ster- ben,

Erik's dream

Auf ho- hem Fel- sen lag' ich träu- mend, sah un- ter mir des Mee- res Flut;

Daland's Aria

Mögst du, mein Kind, den frem- den Mann will- kom- men heis- sen;

Wie aus der Fer- ne längst ver- gang' ner Zei- ten

Der fliegende Holländer (The Flying Dutchman)
Act II

Love Duet

Wohl hub auch ich voll Sehn-sucht mei-ne Bli-cke

Wirst du des Va-ters Wahl nicht schel-ten? was er ver-sprach,

Ach! könn-test das Ge-schick du ah-nen, dem dann mit mir

Ver-sank ich jetzt in wun-der-ba-res Träu-men?

Act III Sailor Chorus

Steu-er-mann! Lass die Wacht! Steu-er-mann! Her zu uns

Willst je-nes Tag's du nicht dich mehr ent-sin-nen

Lohengrin Act I Elsa's Dream

Ein-sam in trü-ben Ta-gen hab' ich zu Gott ge-fleht,

Ge-grüsst du gott-ge-san-dter Held! Sei ge-grüsst, sei ge-grüsst,

Nun sei be-dankt, mein lie-ber Schwann! Zieh' durch die wei-te Flut zurück

Wenn ich im Kam-pfe für dich sie-ge willst du dass ich dein Gat-te sei?

Mein Herr und Gott, nun ruf' ich dich, dass du dem Kampf

Du kun-dest nun dein wahr Ge-richt; mein Gott und Herr,

Des rei-nen Arm gieb Hel-den-kraft; des Fal-schen Stär-ke

O fänd ich Ju-bel-wei-sen dei-nem Ruh-me gleich,

Dank, Kö-nig dir, dass du zu rich-ten kamst

Act II

Durch dich musst' ich ver-lie-ren mein Ehr',all' mein-en Ruhm

Euch Lüf-ten,die mein Kla-gen so trau-rig oft er-füllt,

Ent-weih - - - - te Got-ter Helft jetzt mei-ner Ra-che

OPERAS
Lohengrin Act II

Ge- seg- net soll sie schreiten die lang' in De- muth litt

Du Ärm- ste kannst wohl nie er- mes- sen wie zwei- fel- los

Act III Bridal Chorus

Treu- lich ge- führt zie- het da- hin wo euch der Se- gen

Das sü- sse Lied ver- hallt; wir sind al- lein, zum er- sten Mal al- lein,

Ath- mest Du nicht mit mir die sü- ssen Düf- te O wie so hold

Lohengrin's narration

In fer- nem Land un- nah- bar eu- ren Schrit- ten liegt eine Burg,

Mein lie- ber Schwan! Ach, die- se let- zte traur'- ge Fahrt

Kommt er dann heim, wenn ich ihm fern im Le- ben, dies Horn, dies Schwert,

Die Meistersinger von Nürnberg
Act I Scene I

Da zu dir der Hei- - - land kam wil- lig dei- ne Tau- fe nahm,

Scene II Chorus of Apprentices

Schuh- ma- che- rei und Po- e- te- rei die lern ich da all- ei- ner- lei

Al- ler End' ist doch Da- vid der al- - ler ge- scheit'st

Das Blu- men- kränz- lein aus Sei- den fein, wird das dem Herrn Rit- ter

Scene III

Das schö- ne Fest, Jo- han- nis- tag, ihr wisst, be- geh'n wir mor- gen

Am stillen Herd in Win- ters zeit wann Burg und Hof mir ein- ge- schneit.

So rief der Lenz in den Wald, dass laut es ihn durch- hallt

Scene V

Ja, ihr seid es; nein! Du bist es Al- les sag' ich

"Ein Meis- ter- - sin- ger muss es sein; nur wen ihr krönt

Act II Scene I

Jo- han- nis- tag! Jo- han- nis- tag! Blu- men und Bän- - der

Scene III Sachs's Monologue

Was duf- tet doch der Flie- - der so mild, so stark und voll

OPERAS
Die Meistersinger von Nürnberg
Act II Scene III Sach's
Monologue

Len- zes Ge- bot, die_ sü- sse Noth

Dem Vo- gel, der heut' sang, dem war der Schna-bel hoch ge- wach-sen

Scene V Nightwatch-
man's Song

Hört, ihr Leut' und lasst euch sa-gen die Glock' hat zehn_ ge-schla-gen

Scene VI Cobbler's
Song

Je- rum! Je- rum Hal- la hal- lo he! O- ho!

Als E- va aus dem_ Pa- ra- dies vom Gott dem Herrn ver-stos-sen,

Beckmes-
ser's Song

"Den Tag seh' ich er- schei- nen, der mir_ wohl ge- fall'n thut

Act III Scene I David's Song

Am Jor- dan Sankt_ Jo- han-nes stand all_ Volk der Welt_ zu- tau-fen

Wahn! Wahn Ü- ber-all Wahn! wo- hin ich for-schend blick'

Scene II Prize Song

Mor- gen-lich leuch-tend_ in_ ro- si-gem Schein von Blüth und Duft

Sei euch ver- traut, welch'_ heh- res Wun- der mir ge- scheh'n_

Scene III

Die ich mir aus er- ko- ren, die ganz für mich ge- bo- ren,

Scene IV

O Sachs!_ mein Freund! du theu- rer_ Mann! Wie ich dir Ed- - lem

Die Zeu gen sind_ da, Ge- vat- ter zur_ Hand

Steh' auf Ge- sell und denk_ an_ den_ Streich

Quintet

Se - - - lig wie_ die_ Son- ne mei- nes_ Glü- ckes lacht;_

Scene V

Sankt kris- pin, lo- - bet ihn! War gar ein hei- lig Mann,

Wach' auf! es na- - het gen_ den Tag: ich hör'_ sin-gen im grü-nen Hag

Euch_ macht ihr's leicht, mir macht ihr's schwer gebt ihr mir Armen

Ge-schmückt mit König Da-vid's Bild, nehm ich euch auf in der Meis-ter Gild?

OPERAS

Die Meistersinger von Nürnberg
Act III Scene V

A. Ver- ach- tet mir die Meis- ter nicht, und ehrt mir ih- re Kunst!

B. Fhrt eu- re deut-schen Meis- ter, Dann bannt ihr gu- te Geis - - - ter

Parsifal Act I   Guileless fool motive

C. „durch Mit- leid wis- send, der rei- ne Tor, har- re sein', den ich er- kor"

D. Des Hai- nes Tie- re nah- ten dir nicht zahm; grüssten dich freund-lich

E. Vom Ba- de kehrt der Kö- nig heim; hoch steht die Son- ne

F. Zum letz- ten Lie- bes- mah- - le ge- rüs- tet Tag für Tag

G. Weh - - vol-les Er- be, dem ich ver- fal- len, ich__ einz'- ger Sün- der

H. Der Glau- be lebt; die Tau- be schwebt des Hei - - - lands hol - - der Bo- te:

I. „Neh- met hin mei- nen Leib, neh- met hin mein__ Blut__

Act II Flower Maidens' Waltz

A.

J. Komm'! __ Komm'! __ Hol- der Kna- be! Komm'! __ Oh hol- der Kna- be

B.

K. Im Lenz __ pflückt uns der Mei- ster! Wir wach - - - - - sen __ hier __

L. Ihr kin- di-schen Buh- len, wei-chet von Ihm __ früh_ wel - ken- de Blu- men

M. Ich sah das Kind an sei- ner Mut - - ter Brust

N. Am- for- tas! Die Wun- de! Die Wun- de!

Act III

O. Wie dünkt mich doch die Au- e heut' so schön __

Amfortas' Prayer

P. Mein Va- ter Hoch- ge- seg - - - - ne- ter der__ Hei- den

Q. Nur ei- ne Waf- fe taugt: __ die Wun- de schliesst_ der Speer

R. Höch- sten Hei- les Wun- der!

Rienzi Act I

S. Die Frei- heit Rom's sei dies Ge-setz, ihn un- ter-than sei je- der Rö- mer,

OPERAS
Rienzi Act II

A — Ich sah__ die Stä-dte, sah__ das Land, ich zog__ ent--lang

Act III

B — In sei-ner Blü-the bleicht__ mein Le-ben, da-hin da--hin

Act V Rienzi's Prayer

C — All-mäch't' ger Va-ter, blick her-ab! Hör' mich im Stau-be

Der Ring des Nibelungen
Das Rheingold
Scene I Woglinde's Song

D — Wei- a! Wa-ga! Wo-ge, du Wel-le, wal-le zur Wie-ge!

Scene II

E — Im-mer ist Un-dank Lo-ge's Lohn! Für dich nur be-sorgt__

F — So weit Le-ben und We-ben im Was-ser, Erd' und Luft,

G — Ü-ber Stock und Stein zu Thal stap-fen sie hin

Scene IV Erda's Warning

H — Wei- che, Wo-tan, wei-che! Fleih' des Rin-ges Fluch!

Entrance of the Gods into Valhalla

I — Zur Burg führt die Brü-cke leicht, doch fest eu-rem Fuss:

Wotan's Song on entrance to Valhalla

J — A- bend-lich strahlt der Son-ne Au-ge; in präch-ti-ger Gluth

Song of the Rhinemaidens

K — Rhein- gold! Rhein-gold! rei - - - - - - - nes Gold!__

Die Walküre
Act I Scene III

L — Ein Schwert verhiess mir der Va-ter, ich fänd' es in höch-ster Noth

M — Der Män-ner Sip-pe sass hier im Saal, von Hun-ding zur Hoch-zeit

Finale: Love Duet

N — Win- ter-stür- me wi-chen dem Won- ne-mond,__

O — Du bist der Lenz nach dem ich ver-lang-te

P — O süs-ses-te Won- ne! se-lig-stes Weib!

Q — Sieg-mund heiss' ich und Sieg-mund bin ich be-zeug, es diess Schwert

Act II Scene I Call of the Walküre

R — Ho-jo-to-ho! Ho-jo-to-ho!__ hei-a-ha! hei-a-ha!__

Fricka-Wotan Duet

S — Der al-te Sturm, die al-te Müh'! Doch Stand muss ich hier-hal-ten

WAGNER
OPERAS
Der Ring des Nibelungen
Die Walküre
Act II Scene I Fricka-Wotan Duet

So ist es denn aus mit den e- wi- gen Göt- tern,

O _____ was ___ klag' ich um E- he und Eid,

Dei- ner ew- gen Gat- tin hei- li- ge Eh- re be- schir- me heut'

Scene IV

Sieg- mund! Sieh' auf mich! Ich bin's der bald du folg'st

Act III Scene I

Fort ___ denn ei- le nach O- - - sten ge- wandt!

Scene II

Nicht send' ich dich mehr aus ___ Wal- hall; nicht weis' ich dir mehr

Scene III Brunnhilde's pleading

War es so schmäh- lich, was ich ver- brach, dass mein Ver- bre- chen

Wotan's farewell

Leb' wohl, du Küh- nes, herr- li- ches Kind! Du mei- nes Her- zens

Der Au- gen leuch- ten- des Paar das oft ich lä- chelnd ge- kos't,

Siegfried Act I Scene I

Zwang- vol- le Pla- ge! Müh' oh- ne Zweck! Das bes- te Schwert,

Da hast du die Stü- cken, schänd- li- cher Stüm- per

Als zul- len- des Kind zog ich dich auf wärm- te mit Klei- den

Es san- gen die Vög- lein so se- lig im Lenz

Aus dem Wald fort in die Welt zieh'n! ___ nim- mer kehr' ich zu- rück!

Scene II

Auf wol- ki- gen Höh'n woh- nen die Göt- ter Wal- hall heisst ___ ihr Saal

Scene III

No- thung! No- thung! Neid- li- ches Schwert! Was muss- test du

Zu Spreu nun schuf ich die schar- fe Pracht, im Ti- gel

Schmie- de, mein Ham- mer, ein har- tes Schwert! Ho- ho! Ha- hei!

Act II Scene II

Du hol- des Vög- lein, dich hört' ich noch nie:

OPERAS
Der Ring des Nibelungen
Siegfried Act II Scene III
Voice of
Forest Bird

Act III Scene I

Scene III

Scene III

Götterdämmerung
"Twilight of the Gods"
Prologue: Brünnhilde & Siegfried

Act I Scene I Hagen's Watch

Scene III Waltraute's
Narrative

Act II Scene III Hagen's Call

(Chorus)

Scene IV

Act III Scene I Song of the
Rhinemaidens

Scene II Siegfried's
Narration

OPERAS Der Ring des Niebelungen
Götterdämmerung
Act III Scene II Siegfried's
Narration

In Leid____ zu dem Wi-pfel lausch ich hin-ein____

Scene III Brünnhilde's
Immolation

Star-ke Schei-te schichtet mir dort am Ran-de des Rhein's zu Hauf'!

Wie Son-ne lau-ter strahlt mir sein Licht!

Oh ihr, der Ei-de e-wi-ge Hü-ter

Tannhäuser
Act I Scene I Baccanale
(Chorus of Sirens)

Naht euch dem Lan - - - - de! Wo in den Ar - - - - men glü-hender Lie-be____

Scene II

Dir tö - - ne____ Lob! Die Wun-der sei'n ge-prie - - - sen,

Ge-lieb-ter, komm! Sieh' dort die Grot-te von ros'gen Düf-ten mild

Scene III Shepherd Song

Frau Hol-de kam aus dem Berg____ her-vor zu zieh'n durch Flu-ren

Scene IV

Als du im küh-nem San-ge uns be-strit-test,

War's Zau-ber, war es rei-ne Macht, durch die solch' Wun-der

Act II Scene I

Dich, teu-re Hal - - - le, grüss' ich wie-der, froh grüss' ich dich,

Ver-zeihe, wenn ich nicht weiss, was ich be-gin-ne!

Der Sän-ger Klu-gen Wei - - - sen lausch ich____ sonst

Der Un-glück-sel'-ge, den ge-fan-gen ein furcht-bar mächt' ger

Scene II Elizabeth &
Tannhäuser
Duet

Ge-prie - - sen sei____ die Stun-de, ge-prie-sen sei____ die Macht!

Scene III

Noch blei-be denn un-aus-ge-spro-chen dein süss Ge-heim-niss

Scene IV Entrance of the
Guests

Freu-dig be-grü - - - ssen wir die ed-le Hal-le

Freu-dig____ be - -grü - - - ssen wir die ed-le____ Hal-le

Wo____ lan-ge noch der Ru-fer-schal-le, Wo lan-ge noch der Ru-fer-schalle

OPERAS

Tannhäuser
Act II Scene IV Landgrave's Welcome

A — Gar viel und schön ward hier in die-ser Hal- le

B — Blick' ich um- her in die- sem ed- len Krei- se,

C — Auch ich darf mich so glück-lich nen-nen, zu schau'n, was, Wolf-ram, du geschaut!

D — O Him- mel! Lass' dich jetzt er-fle-hen! Gieb mei- nem Lied der wei- he

E — Dir, ho- he Lie- be, tö- - ne be- geis-tert mein Ge- sang

Act III Scene I

F — Wohl wusst' ich hier sie im Ge- bet zu fin- den,

Pilgrims' Chorus

G — Be- glückt darf nun dich, o Hei- math, ich schau- en

Elizabeth's Prayer

H — All- mächt' ge Jung- frau, hör' mein Fle-hen! Zu dir, Ge-pries' ne,

Scene II Song to the Evening Star

I — Wie To- des- ah- nung Dämm' rung deckt die Lan- de,

J — O du mein hol- der A- - bend- stern, wohl grüsst' ich im- - mer

Scene III Rome Narrative

K — In- brunst im Her- zen wie kein Bü- sser noch sie je- - ge- fühlt,

L — Nach Rom ge- langt' ich so zur heil'- gen Stel- le,

Tristan und Isolde
Act I Scene I Sailor's Song

M — West- wärts schweift der Blick, ost- wärts streicht das Schiff.

Scene II

N — Herr Mo- rold zog zu Mee- re- her, in Korn-wall- Zins- zu- ha- ben,

Act II Scene II Love Duet

O — O sink' her- nie- der, Nacht, O sink'- her- nie- der Nacht- der Lie- be

Brangäne's Warning

P — Ein- - - - - sam wa- - chend in- der Nacht,- wem- der Traum

Scene III

Q — Wo- hin nun Tris- tan- schei- det willst du, I- sol- de fol- gen?

Act III Scene I

R — Wie sie se- lig, hehr und- mil- de- wan- delt durch des Meer's Ge- fil- de?

Scene III Liebestod

S — Mild und lei- se wie er lä- chelt, wie das Au- ge hold er öff- net,

Songs: L'Attente

Monte, é- cu-reuil monte au grand chê- ne, Sur la bran-che des cieux

Les Deux Grenadiers

Long- temps cap- tifs chez le Rus- se loin- tain

Peut- ê- tre bien qu'en ce choc meur- tri- er,

Five Wesendonck Songs
1. Der Engel

In der Kind-heit frü- hen Ta- gen hört' ich oft von En -- geln sa- gen,

2. Stehe still!

Sau- sen-des, brau-sen-des Rad der Zeit, Mes- ser du der E- wig-keit;

3. Im Treibhaus

Hoch- ge-wölb- te Blät- ter-kro- nen, Bal- da-chi- ne von Sma- ragd,

4. Schmerzen

Son- ne, wei- nest je- den A- bend dir die schö-nen Au- gen roth;

5. Träume

Sag', welch' wun-der-ba- re Träu-me hal- ten mei- nen Sinn um- fan-gen

Mignonne

Mi- gnon -ne, al-lons voir si la Ro-se qui ce ma-tin

Schlaf', holdes Kind

Schlaf hol- des Kind, ich wieg' dich in Schlum- mer,

Der Tannenbaum

Der Tan- nen-baum steht schwei-gend ein- sam auf grau- er Höh';

WALLACE, William Vincent (1812-1865)

Maritana (opera) Act I No. 4

An- gels that a-round us ho- ver, Guard us till the close of day

Act II No. 13

Yes! let me like a Sol- dier fall up- on some o- pen plain

No. 14

In hap- py mo-ments day by day, The sands of life may pass,

No. 19

There is a flow'r that bloom- eth when au- tumn leaves are shed,

Act III No. 22

Scenes that are bright- est, May charm a --- while

WALTHER von der Vogelweide (12th-13th Cent.)

Kreuzfahrlied (Crusader's Song)
(also called Palästinalied)

Al- ler erst lebe ich mir wer- de, sit mie sün- dic

WALTON, William (1902-   )

Belshazzar's Feast (choral work)
By permission Oxford Univ. Press, London, copyright owners

By the wa - - - - - - ters of Ba - by-lon There___ we sat down

Sing us one of the songs of Zi - on

How___ shall we sing___ the Lord's song, the Lord's___ song

If___ I for-get thee,___ for-get___ thee

In Ba - - - - - by-lon Belshazzar the King made a great___ feast

Bring ye the cor - - - - - - - - - - - - net

Praise___ ye the___ god of sil- ver

Praise___ ye praise___ ye

Then sing___ a-loud to God___ our strength

Then sing, sing a-loud___ to God our strength: Make a joy-ful noise

Then___ sing,___ sing a-loud,___ Sing_ a-loud_

Al- le- lu- ja Al- le- lu - - - ja, al- le- lu- ja

WARD, John (16th-17th Cents.)

Hope of my heart

Hope___ of___ my heart, Hope of my___ heart O where- fore

Out from the vale

Out from___ the vale___ of deep de - - - spair, of deep de- spair

Upon a bank of roses

Up- on a bank with Ros- es set a- bout, up- on a bank

WARE, Harriet   (Contemporary)

Boat Song
Copyright by John Church Co.
Used by permission

Where will you take___ me lit- tle boat, All on a sum- mer's day___

WARLOCK, Peter (1894-1930) (Philip Heseltine)

As ever I saw
By permission Boosey & Hawkes, Inc.,
copyright owners
She is gen- tle and al - - so wise; of all ___ o- thers

Captain Stratton's Fancy
By permission of Augener, Ltd., London
Oh, some are fond of red wine and some are fond of white,

Chop Cherry
By permission J. & W. Chester, Ltd., London,
copyright owners
When as the rye reach ___ to the chin, and chop- cher- ry,

Corpus Christi (old English carol) (arr.)
Copyright 1921, J. Curwen
Lul- ly, lul- lay, lul- ly, lul- lay, The fau- con hath borne my make- a- way

Fair and True
By permission Oxford Univ. Press, London,
copyright owners
Love- ly kind, and kind- ly lov- ing, Such a mind were worth the mov- ing;

The Fox
By permission Oxford Univ. Press, London,
copyright owners
At 'The Fox Inn' the tat- ter'd ears, the fox'- s grin

Good Ale
By permission of Augener, Ltd., London
Bring us in no brown bread ___ for ___ that is made of bran,

Jillian of Berry
By permission Oxford Univ. Press, London,
copyright owners
For Jil- lian of Ber- ry she dwells on a hill, And she hath good beer

Passing by
By permission Oxford Univ. Press, London,
copyright owners
There is a la- dy sweet and kind, Was nev- er face so pleased my mind

The Passionate Shepherd
By permission of Galaxy Music Corporation,
N. Y., copyright by Elkin & Co., Ltd.
Come live with me, and ___ be my love, And we will all

Piggesnie
By permission of Augener, Ltd., London
She is so pro- per and so pure, Full stead- fast, sta- ble and de- mure

Pretty Ring Time
By permission Oxford Univ. Press, London,
copyright owners
It wa- a lov- er and his lass, With a hey and a ho

Rest, sweet Nymphs
By permission Oxford Univ. Press, London,
copyright owners
Rest, sweet nymphs, let gold- en sleep Charm your star- bright- er eyes, ___

Sigh no more, Ladies
By permission Oxford Univ. Press, London,
copyright owners
Sigh no more, la- dies, sigh no more; ___ Men were de- cei- vers ev- er.

Sleep
By permission Oxford Univ. Press, London,
copyright owners
Come, sleep, and with thy sweet de- ceiv- ing Lock me in de- light a- while;

Take, O take those lips away
By permission Boosey & Hawkes, Inc.,
copyright owners
Take, O take ___ those lips a- way that so sweet - - ly

Williow, willow (arr.)
By permission Oxford Univ. Press, London,
copyright owners
The poor soul sat sigh- ing By a sy- ca- more tree

WEAVER, Powell (1890-1951)

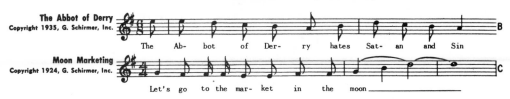

The Abbot of Derry
Copyright 1935, G. Schirmer, Inc.

The Ab- bot of Der- ry hates Sat- an and Sin

Moon Marketing
Copyright 1924, G. Schirmer, Inc.

Let's go to the mar- ket in the moon

WEBER, Carl Maria von (1786-1826)

OPERAS
Abu Hassan No. 2

Ich ge- be_ Gas- ter- ei- en, Mit Lied- ern_ und mit Tän- zen,

O Fa- ti- me, mei- ne Trau- te, die so zärt - - lich zu_ mir_ spricht,

No. 5

Wird Phi- lo- me - - le trau- ern, dem Kä- fig kaum_ ent- schlüpft,

Euryanthe Act I

Un- ter blüh'nden Man- del- bäu- men, an der Loi- re grü- nem Strand,

O mein Leid ist un- er- mes- sen, du kannst mir_ dein_ Herz_ ent- zieh'n

Act II

Schweigt glüh'nden Sehn- ens wil- de Trie- be, ihr Au- ge sucht

We- hen mir Lüf- te Ruh, strö- men mir Düf- te zu,

O Se- lig- keit, dich fass' ich kaum, O Se- lig- keit, dich fass' ich kaum

Act III

Hier dicht am Quell wo Wei- den steh'n, die Ster- ne hell durchschau- en,

Jaegerchor

Die Tha- le damp- fen die Hö- hen glühn!

Der Freischütz Act I

Durch die Wäl- der, durch die Au- en zog ich leich- ten_ Sinns_ da - hin!

Jetzt ist wohl ihr Fen- ster of- fen und sie horcht auf mei- nen Tritt,

Hier im ird' schen_ Jam- mer- thal war doch nichts als_ Plack und_ Qual

Schweig'! schweig'! da- mit dich Nie- mand warnt, schwei- ge!

Der Höl- le Netz hat dich __ um - - garnt,

OPERAS
Der Freischütz Act I

Tri- umph! ____ die Ra- che ge- lingt!

Act II Brides-maids' Chorus

Wir win- den dir den Jung-fern-kranz mit veil-chen-blau-er_ Sei- de

Kommt ein schlan- ker Bursch ge- gan- gen, blond_ von_ Lo- cken_ o-der braun

Lei- se, lei- se, from- me_ Wei- se, schwing'dich auf zum Ster- nen-krei- se

Al- les pflegt schon längst_ der_ Ruh'! Trau- ter Freund, wo wei-lest_ du?

Act III

Und ob die Wol- ke sie_ ver- hül- le, die Son- ne bleibt

Romanze and Aria

Einst träum- te mein- er sel'- gen Ba- se, die Kam-mer-thür er- öff- ne sich,

Trü- be Au- gen, Lieb- chen_ tau- gen ei- nem_ hol- den Bräut-chen_ nicht,

Hunting Chorus

Was gleicht wohl_ auf_ Er- den dem Jä- ger- ver- gnü- - gen

Oberon Act I No. 5

Von Ju- gend auf in dem Kampf- ge- fild, die Lan- - - - ze_ hoch

Jetzt giesst ____ sich aus ein sanft'- - rer Glanz

No. 6

Ja o Herr! mein Heil,_ mein_ Le- ben Re- zia ist_ für_ e- - wig_ dein!

Act II No. 11 Prayer

Va- ter! Hör' mich fleh'n zu dir Va- ter Hör' mich fleh'n zu dir!

No. 12 Ocean, thou mighty monster

O- ze- an Du Un- ge- heu- er! schlan-gen-gleich hältst du um- schlun- gen

Noch seh ich die Wel- len to- ben durch ____ die_ Nacht ____

Wol- ken- los strahlt jetzt die Son- ne auf die Pur- pur- wel- len nie- der

O Won- - - - - - ne! Mein Hü- - on! Zum U- - fer her- bei!

No. 14

A- ra- bi-en, mein Hei- mat-land, du Land so teu- er mir

No. 17 Cavatina

Trau- - re, mein_ Herz, um ver- schwun- de- nes Glück!

Der kleine Fritz an seine jungen Freunde

Ach, wenn ich nur ein Lieb - - - chen hät- te, so gross wie ich   A

**Leyer und Schwert, Op. 42, No. 2
No. 2 Lützows wilde Jagd**

Was glänzt dort vom Wal- de im Son- nen-schein? Hör's nä- her   B

No. 6 Schwertlied

Du Schwert an mei- ner Lin- ken, was soll dein heit- res ___ Blin- ken?   C

Schwertlied (variant)

Du Schwert an mei- ner Lin- ken, was soll dein hei- tres Blin- ken?   D

No. 7 Gebet vor der Schlacht

Hör uns, All- mäch- ti- ger! Hör uns, All- gü- ti- ger   E

Wiegenlied, Op. 13, No. 3

Schlaf, Herz- ens- söhn- chen, mein Lieb- ling bist du!   F

WECKERLIN, Jean Baptiste (1821-1910)

Bergerettes (arrangements)

Aminte

Viens dans ce bo- ca- ge, belle A- min- te, Sans con- train- te   H

L'Amour s'envole

L'a- mour est un en- fant ti- mi- de, La sé- vé- ri- té   I

Bergère Légère

Ber- gè- re Lé- gè- re, Je crains tes ap- pas; ___   J

Chantons les amours de Jean

Chan- tons, chan- tons les a- mours de Jean- ne, chan- tons, chan- tons   K

Chaque chose a son temps

Cha- que chose a son temps, Fil- let- te, Cha- que chose a son temps   L

Je connais un berger discret

Je con- nais un ber- ger dis- cret, qui se plaint __ et sou- pi- re,   M

Jeunes fillettes A

Jeu- ne fil- le- te, pro- fi- tez du temps, La vi- o- let- te   N

B

Cet- te fleu- ret- te Passe en peu de temps Toute a- mou- ret- te passe   O

Lisette

En me- nant pai- tre mon trou- peau Je vis dans un bo- ca - - - - - ge   P

Maman, dites-moi

Ma- man, di- tes- moi ce qu'on sent quand on ai- me,   Q

Menuet d'Exaudet

Cet é- tang Qui s'e- tend dans la plai- ne, Ré- pète, au sein de ses eaux,   R

La mère Bontemps

La mè- re Bon- temps s'en al- lait dis- ant aux fil- let- tes: S

Bergerettes (arrangements) Nanette

E- loi- gné de Na- net- te, Le beau ber- ger Tir- cis

Non, je ne crois pas

Non, je ne crois pas ce que Co- lin m'a dit tout bas, tout bas

Non, je n'irai plus au bois

Non, je n'i-rai plus au bois, Non, non, je n'i-rai plus seu- let- te,

O ma tendre musette

O ma ten- dre mu- set- te, mu- set- te mes a- mours

Par un matin

Par un ma- tin Li- set- te se- le- va, Par un ma- .tin

Philis plus avare que tendre

Phi- lis, plus a- va- re que ten- dre, ne ga-gnant rien à re- fu- ser

Que ne suis-je la fougère

Que ne suis- je la- fou- gè- re, Où, sur la fin d'un beau jour,

Trop amable Sylvie

Trop ai- ma- ble Syl- vi- e, Plus con- tent d'ê- tre sous ta loi

Venez, agréable printemps

Ve- nez a- gré- a- ble prin- temps, Ra- nim- er tou- te la na- tu- - re,

Lison dormait (arr.)

Li- son dor- mait dans un bo- ca- ge, Un bras i- ci,

Margoton va-t-à l'eau

Mar- go- ton va-t- á l'iau a- vec- que son cru- chon

Mignonette

Si j'é-tais fleur des bois, Pa- que- ret- - te

WEELKES, Thomas (c. 1575-1623)

(madrigals)
As Vesta was descending

As Ves- ta was from Lat- mos hill de- scend- ing, From Lat- mos hill,

Hark, all ye lonely saints (madrigal)

Hark, all ye love- ly saints a- bove, Di- an- a hath a- greed with love

Hence, Care, Thou Art Too Cruel

Hence Care; thou art too cru- - - - el,

Lady, the birds right fairly

La- dy the birds right fair- ly, La- dy the birds right fair- - - - - ly

O Care, thou wilt despatch me

O Care, thou wilt des- - - - patch me, if Mu- sic do

On the Plains

On the plains Fai- ry trains were a- tread- ing meas- ures,

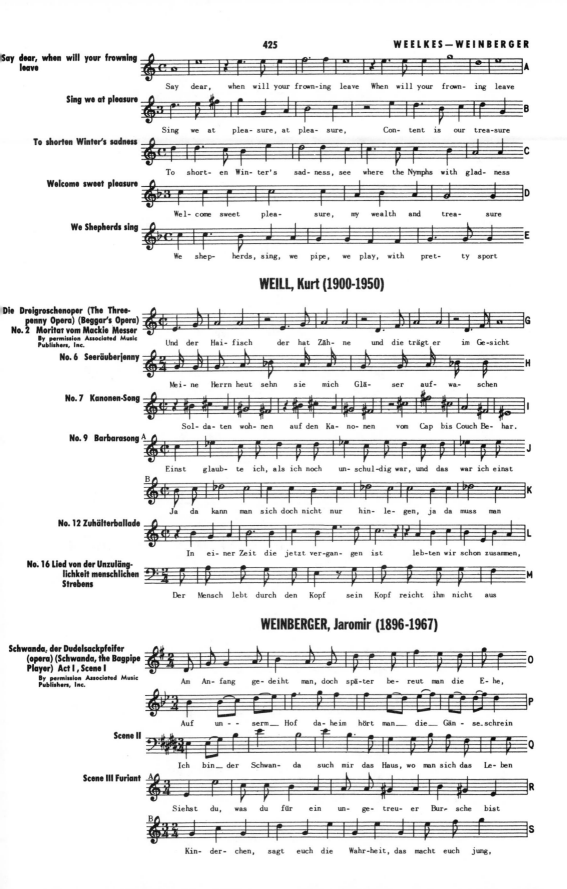

Say dear, when will your frowning leave

Say dear, when will your frown-ing leave When will your frown- ing leave   A

Sing we at pleasure

Sing we at plea-sure, at plea-sure, Con-tent is our trea-sure   B

To shorten Winter's sadness

To short- en Win-ter's sad-ness, see where the Nymphs with glad- ness   C

Welcome sweet pleasure

Wel-come sweet plea- sure, my wealth and trea- sure   D

We Shepherds sing

We shep- herds, sing, we pipe, we play, with pret- ty sport   E

WEILL, Kurt (1900-1950)

Die Dreigroschenoper (The Three-penny Opera) (Beggar's Opera) No. 2 Moritat vom Mackie Messer
By permission Associated Music Publishers, Inc.

Und der Hai-fisch der hat Zäh- ne und die trägt er im Ge-sicht   G

No. 6 Seeräuberjenny

Mei- ne Herrn heut sehn sie mich Glä- ser auf-wa- schen   H

No. 7 Kanonen-Song

Sol- da-ten woh- nen auf den Ka- no-nen vom Cap bis Couch Be- har.   I

No. 9 Barbarasong

A Einst glaub- te ich, als ich noch un-schul-dig war, und das war ich einst   J

B Ja da kann man sich doch nicht nur hin- le- gen, ja da muss man   K

No. 12 Zuhälterballade

In ei- ner Zeit die jetzt ver-gan- gen ist leb-ten wir schon zusammen,   L

No. 16 Lied von der Unzuläng-lichkeit menschlichen Strebens

Der Mensch lebt durch den Kopf sein Kopf reicht ihm nicht aus   M

WEINBERGER, Jaromir (1896-1967)

Schwanda, der Dudelsackpfeifer (opera) (Schwanda, the Bagpipe Player) Act I, Scene I
By permission Associated Music Publishers, Inc.

Am An- fang ge-deiht man, doch spä-ter be- reut man die E- he,   O

Auf un- - serm Hof da-heim hört man die Gän- se schrein   P

Scene II

Ich bin der Schwan- da such mir das Haus, wo man sich das Le- ben   Q

Scene III Furiant

A Siehst du, was du für ein un- ge-treu- er Bur-sche bist   R

B Kin- der- chen, sagt euch die Wahr-heit, das macht euch jung,   S

Schwanda, der Dudelsackpfeifer (opera) (Schwanda, the Bagpipe Player) Act II, Scene IV

Wie kann ich denn ver- ges- sen, was mein Lieb- stes war,

WEINGARTNER, Felix (1863-1942)

Du bist ein Kind, Op. 28, No. 12
By permission Associated Music Publishers, Inc.

Du bist ein Kind und sollst es e- wig blei- ben;

Liebesfeier, Op. 16, No. 2

An ih- rem bun- ten Lie- derin Klet- tert die Ler- che

WERNER, H.

Haidenröslein

Sah ein Knab' ein Rös- lein stehn, Rös- lein auf der Hai- den

WERT, Giaches de (1536-1596)

Ah dolente partita (madrigal)

Ah do- len- te par- ti - - - ta! Ah fin del- la mia vi- ta

Un jour je m'en allai

Un jour je m'en al- lai, cueil- lant de vi- o- let- tes,

WESTENDORF, Thomas (Contemporary)

I'll take you home again, Kathleen

I'll take you home a- gain, Kath- leen A- cross the o- cean wild and wide

WEYSE, Christoph Ernst Friedrich (1774-1842)

De klare Bolger rulled, from Sovedrikken (opera)

De Kla- re Bol- ger rul- led mod dunk- le Af- ten lund

Gud skee Tak og Lov

Gud skee tak og Lov! vi saa dei- lig sov:

Han gik til Ludlams Hule, from Ludlams Hule (opera)

Han gik til Lud- lams Hu- le i mör- ke Mi- die- nat

I Osten stiger Solen op

I O- sten sti- ger So- len op: den spre- der Guld paa Sky

Lysets Engel gaar med Glands

Ly- sets En- gel gaaer med Glands gjen- nem Him- mel- por- te

Nu ringer alle Klokker mod sky

Nu rin- ger al- le klok- ker mod sky, det Ki- mier

Nu vaagne alle Guds Fugle smaa

Nu vaag- ne al- le Guds Fug- le smaa, de fly- ve fra Re- de

Teklas Sang (from Schiller's Wallenstein)

Der Eich-wald brau-set, die Wol- ken ziehn, das Mägd- lein wan- delt — A

WIDOR, Charles Marie (1845-1937)

L'Aurore, Op. 22, No. 2
By permission J. Hamelle Music Publishers Paris

L'au- ro- re s'al- lu- me, L'ombre__ é- pais- se fuit — C

Je ne veux pas autre chose, Op. 43, No. 1
By permission J. Hamelle Music Publishers Paris

Je ne veux pas au- tre cho- se que ton sou- rire et ta voix — D

Mon bras pressait, Op. 43, No. 3
By permission J. Hamelle Music Publishers Paris

Mon bras pres- sait ta tail- le, frêle et sou-ple com- me le ro- seau, — E

Non Credo
By permission Durand & Cie, Paris; Elkan-Vogel Co., Inc., Phila., copyright owners

Je ne crois pas que le Sa- veur soit né Je ne crois pas, — F

Nuit d'Étoiles, Op. 14, No. 1
By permission J. Hamelle Music Publishers, Paris

Nuit d'é- toi- les, sous tes voi- les, sous ta bri- se et tes par- fums, — G

Le Plongeur, Op. 43, No. 4
By permission J. Hamelle Music Publishers, Paris

Le plon- geur, sur qui la va- gue dé- fer- le, m'a cri- é du fond — H

WILBYE, John (1574-1638)

Madrigals: Adieu, sweet Amaryllis (4-voice)

A- dieu, a- dieu, a- dieu, sweet A- ma- ril- lis! A- dieu, — J

Draw on Sweet Night

Draw ____ on sweet night,____ draw,____ draw on sweet night — K

Flora gave me fairest flowers (5-voice)

Flo- ra gave me fair- est flow- ers, Flo- ra gave me fair- est flow- ers, — L

Lady, when I behold

La- dy, when I be- hold the ros- es sprout- ing — M

Stay, Corydon thou Swain A1

Stay, Stay__ Co- ry- don ____ thou swain, talk not so soon__ of dy - - - ing, — N

A2

Stay ____ Co- ry- don thou swain, talk not so soon__ of dy- ing — O

Sweet honey-sucking bees (5-voice)

Sweet ho- ney- suck- ing bees, Sweet ho- ney- suck- ing bees, — P

WILLAERT, Adrian (c. 1480-1562)

Con lagrime e sospir

Con la- gri- me e so- spir ne- gan- do por- ge — R

WILSON, H. Lane (1870-1915)

Carmena

Dance and song ___ make glad ___ the night ___

Ah! now ___ rings a voice I know ___ from ev'-ry voice a-part

WOLF, Hugo (1860-1903)

Abschied

Un- an- ge- klopft ein Herr tritt a- bends bei mir ein:

Der glei-chen hab' ich nie ge-sehn, all' mein Leb- ta- ge_ nicht ge-sehn,

Ach, des Knaben Augen

Ach, des Kna - -ben Au-gen sind mir so schön und klar er- schie-nen,

Ach, im Maien war's

Ach, im Mai- en war's, ___ im Mai _- en

Agnes

Ro- sen- zeit! wie schnell vor-bei, schnell vor-bei, bist du doch _ ge-gan-gen!

Alle gingen, Herz, zur Ruh

Al- le gin- gen, Herz, zur Ruh, al- le schla- fen, nur nicht du.

Alles endet, was entstehet

Al- les en- det, was ent-ste-het, Al- les, al- les rings ver- geh- et

Als ich auf dem Euphrat schiffte

Als ich auf dem Eu - - phrat ___ schiff- te

Anakreons Grab

Wo die Ro- se hier blüht, __ wo Re- ben um Lor-beer sich schlin-gen,

Andenken

Ich den - - ke dein ___ wenn durch_ den Hain ___

An den Schlaf

Schlaf! __ su- sser Schlaf! ob-wohl dem Tod, wie du, nichts gleicht, _

An die Geliebte

Wenn ich, von dei- nem An-schaun tief ge-stillt, mich stumm ___

An eine Aeolsharfe

An- ge-lehnt an die E- pheu- wand die-ser al- ten Ter- ras- se

Auch kleine Dinge

Auch klei- ne Din- ge kön- nen uns ent- zü- cken,

Auf dm grünen Balkon

Auf dem grü- nen Bal- kon mein Mäd- chen schaut, nach mir durchs Git-ter-lein,

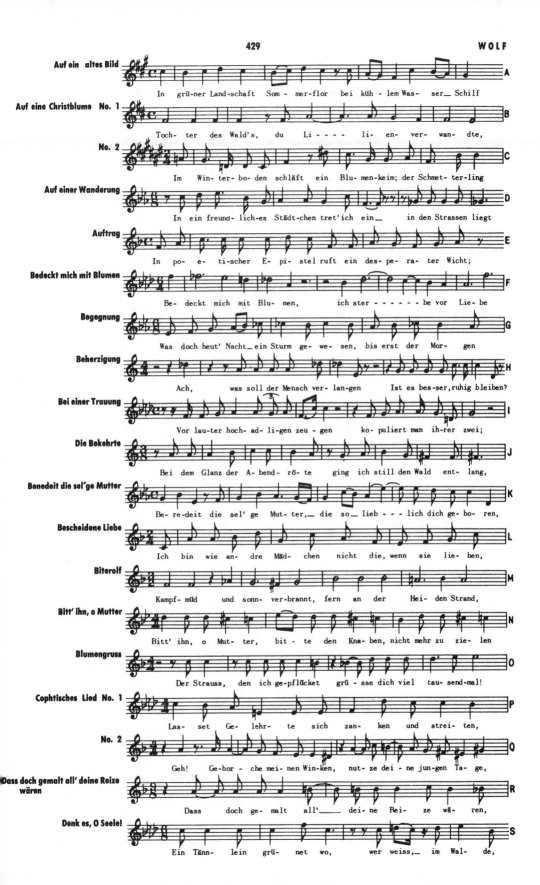

Auf ein altes Bild — In grü-ner Land-schaft Som-mer-flor bei küh-lem Was- ser_ Schilf A

Auf eine Christblume No. 1 — Toch- ter des Wald's, du Li - - - - li- en- ver- wan-dte, B

No. 2 — Im Win-ter-bo-den schläft ein Blu-men-keim; der Schmet-ter-ling C

Auf einer Wanderung — In ein freund- lich-es Städt-chen tret'ich ein_ in den Strassen liegt D

Auftrag — In po- e- ti-scher E- pi-stel ruft ein des-pe- ra- ter Wicht; E

Bedeckt mich mit Blumen — Be- deckt mich mit Blu- men, ich ster - - - - - - be vor Lie- be F

Begegnung — Was doch heut' Nacht_ ein Sturm ge- we- sen, bis erst der Mor- gen G

Beherzigung — Ach, was soll der Mensch ver- lan-gen Ist es bes-ser,ruhig bleiben? H

Bei einer Trauung — Vor lau-ter hoch- ad- li-gen zeu- gen ko- puliert man ih-rer zwei; I

Die Bekehrte — Bei dem Glanz der A- bend- rö- te ging ich still den Wald ent- lang, J

Benedeit die sel'ge Mutter — Be- re-deit die sel' ge Mut- ter,_ die so_ lieb - - - lich dich ge-bo- ren, K

Bescheidene Liebe — Ich bin wie an- dre Mäd- chen nicht die, wenn sie lie- ben, L

Biterolf — Kampf- müd und sonn- ver-brannt, fern an der Hei- den Strand, M

Bitt' ihn, o Mutter — Bitt' ihn, o Mut- ter, bit- te den Kna- ben, nicht mehr zu zie- len N

Blumengruss — Der Strauss, den ich ge-pflücket grü - sse dich viel tau- send-mal! O

Cophtisches Lied No. 1 — Las- set Ge- lehr- te sich zan- ken und strei- ten, P

No. 2 — Geh! Ge-hor- che mei-nen Win-ken, nut-ze dei- ne jun-gen Ta- ge, Q

Dass doch gemalt all' deine Reize wären — Dass doch ge- malt all'_ dei- ne Rei- ze wä- ren, R

Denk es, O Seele! — Ein Tänn- lein grü- net wo, wer weiss,_ im Wal- de, S

WOLF

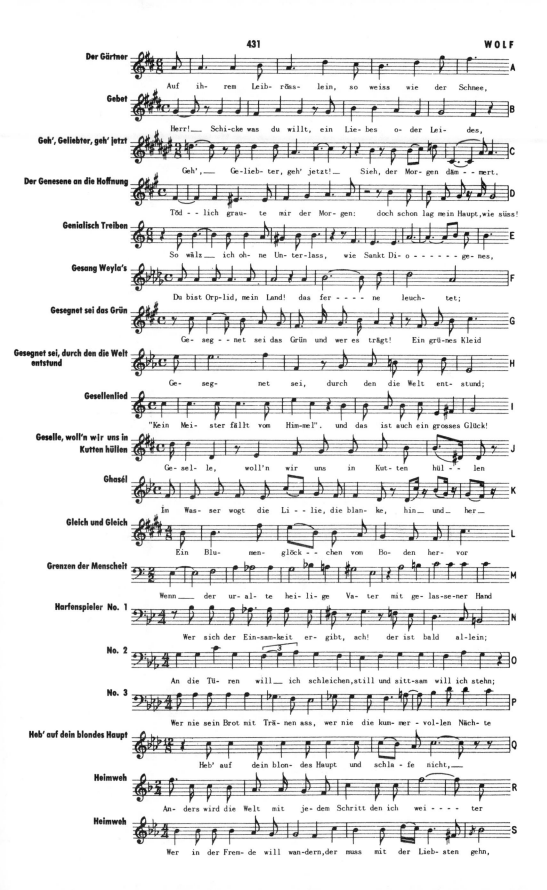

Der Gärtner — Auf ih-rem Leib-röss-lein, so weiss wie der Schnee, — A

Gebet — Herr!__ Schi-cke was du willt, ein Lie-bes o-der Lei-des, — B

Geh', Geliebter, geh' jetzt — Geh',__ Ge-lieb-ter, geh' jetzt!__ Sieh, der Mor-gen däm--mert. — C

Der Genesene an die Hoffnung — Töd--lich grau-te mir der Mor-gen: doch schon lag mein Haupt,wie süss! — D

Genialisch Treiben — So wälz__ ich oh-ne Un-ter-lass, wie Sankt Di-o------ge-nes, — E

Gesang Weyla's — Du bist Orp-lid, mein Land! das fer----ne leuch-tet; — F

Gesegnet sei das Grün — Ge-seg--net sei das Grün und wer es trägt! Ein grü-nes Kleid — G

Gesegnet sei, durch den die Welt entstund — Ge-seg--net sei, durch den die Welt ent-stund; — H

Gesellenlied — "Kein Mei-ster fällt vom Him-mel". und das ist auch ein grosses Glück! — I

Geselle, woll'n wir uns in Kutten hülien — Ge-sel-le, woll'n wir uns in Kut-ten hül--len — J

Ghasél — Im Was-ser wogt die Li--lie, die blan-ke, hin__ und__ her__ — K

Gleich und Gleich — Ein Blu-men--glöck--chen vom Bo-den her-vor — L

Grenzen der Menscheit — Wenn__ der ur-al-te hei-li-ge Va-ter mit ge-las-se-ner Hand — M

Harfenspieler No. 1 — Wer sich der Ein-sam-keit er-gibt, ach! der ist bald al-lein; — N

No. 2 — An die Tü-ren will__ ich schleichen,still und sitt-sam will ich stehn; — O

No. 3 — Wer nie sein Brot mit Trä-nen ass, wer nie die kum-mer-vol-len Näch-te — P

Heb' auf dein blondes Haupt — Heb' auf dein blon-des Haupt und schla-fe nicht,__ — Q

Heimweh — An-ders wird die Welt mit je-dem Schritt den ich wei----ter — R

Heimweh — Wer in der Frem-de will wan-dern,der muss mit der Lieb-sten gehn, — S

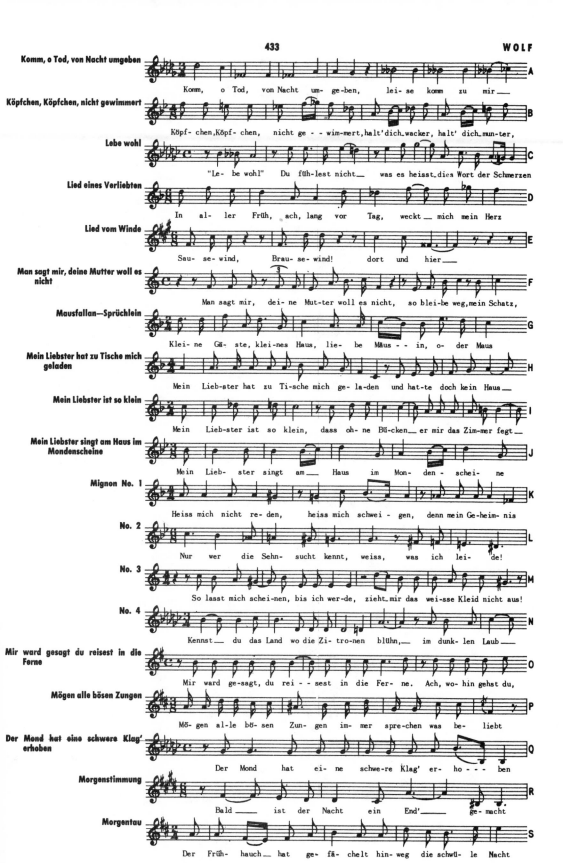

Mühvoll komm' ich
Müh - - voll komm' ich und be- la - - - - den, nimm mich an, — A

Der Musikant
Wan- dern lieb' ich für mein Le- ben, le- be e- ben, wie ich kann, — B

Nachtzauber
Hörst du nicht die Quel-len ge- hen zwi-schen Stein und Blu-men weit. — C

Nein, junger Herr
Nein, jun - - ger Herr, so treibt man's nicht, für- wahr; — D

Neue Liebe
Kann auch ein Mensch des an- dern auf der Er- de ganz, — E

Nimmersatte Liebe
So ist die Lieb'! So ist die Lieb'! Mit Küs-sen nicht zu stil- len: — F

Nixe Binsefuss
Des Was- ser- manns sein Töch-ter- lein tanzt auf dem Eis im Voll-mond — G

Nun lass uns Frieden schliessen
Nun lass uns Frie-den schlie - - ssen, lieb-stes Le - - ben — H

Nun wandre Maria
Nun wan- dre, Ma- ri - - a, nun wan- dre nur fort, — I

O wär dein Haus durchsichtig wie ein Glas
O wär dein Haus durch-sich-tig wie ein Glas, mein Hol- der — J

Peregrina I
Der Spie- gel die- ser treu- en brau- nen Au- - gen — K

II
Wa- rum Ge-lieb- te, denk' ich dein auf ein - - mal — L

Phänomen
Wenn zu der Re- gen- wand Phö- bus sich gat- tet, — M

Philine
Sin- get nicht in Trau - - er- tö- nen von der Ein- sam- keit — N

Prometheus
Be- dek- ke dei- nen Him- mel, Zeus, mit Wol- ken- dunst — O

Rat einer Alten
Ein jung ge- we- sen, kann auch mit re- den, und alt ge- wor- den, — P

Der Rattenfänger
Ich bin der wohl- be- kann-te Sän- ger, der viel ge- rei - - ste — Q

Schlafendes Jesuskind
Sohn der Jung-frau, Him- mels-kind! am Bo- den auf dem Holz der Schmerzen — R

Der Scholar
Bei dem an- ge- nehm - - sten Wet- ter sin- gen — S

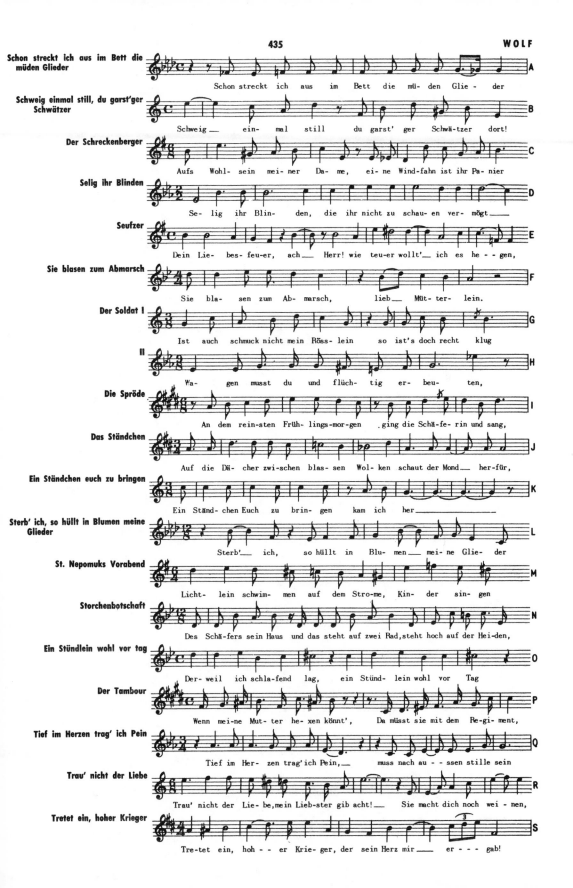

Schon streckt ich aus im Bett die müden Glieder
Schon streckt ich aus im Bett die mü-den Glie-der   A

Schweig einmal still, du garst'ger Schwätzer
Schweig ein-mal still du garst' ger Schwä-tzer dort!   B

Der Schreckenberger
Aufs Wohl-sein mei-ner Da-me, ei-ne Wind-fahn ist ihr Pa-nier   C

Selig ihr Blinden
Se-lig ihr Blin-den, die ihr nicht zu schau-en ver-mögt   D

Seufzer
Dein Lie-bes-feu-er, ach Herr! wie teu-er wollt' ich es he-gen,   E

Sie blasen zum Abmarsch
Sie bla-sen zum Ab-marsch, lieb Müt-ter-lein.   F

Der Soldat I
Ist auch schmuck nicht mein Röss-lein so ist's doch recht klug   G

II
Wa-gen musst du und flüch-tig er-beu-ten,   H

Die Spröde
An dem rein-sten Früh-lings-mor-gen ging die Schä-fe-rin und sang,   I

Das Ständchen
Auf die Dä-cher zwi-schen blas-sen Wol-ken schaut der Mond her-für,   J

Ein Ständchen euch zu bringen
Ein Ständ-chen Euch zu brin-gen kam ich her   K

Sterb' ich, so hüllt in Blumen meine Glieder
Sterb' ich, so hüllt in Blu-men mei-ne Glie-der   L

St. Nepomuks Vorabend
Licht-lein schwim-men auf dem Stro-me, Kin-der sin-gen   M

Storchenbotschaft
Des Schä-fers sein Haus und das steht auf zwei Rad, steht hoch auf der Hei-den,   N

Ein Stündlein wohl vor tag
Der-weil ich schla-fend lag, ein Stünd-lein wohl vor Tag   O

Der Tambour
Wenn mei-ne Mut-ter he-xen könnt', Da müsst sie mit dem Re-gi-ment,   P

Tief im Herzen trag' ich Pein
Tief im Her-zen trag'ich Pein, muss nach au - - ssen stille sein   Q

Trau' nicht der Liebe
Trau' nicht der Lie-be, mein Lieb-ster gib acht! Sie macht dich noch wei-nen,   R

Tretet ein, hoher Krieger
Tre-tet ein, hoh - er Krie-ger, der sein Herz mir er - - gab!   S

Treibe nur mit lieben Spott

Trei- be nur mit Lie- ben Spott, Ge- lieb- te___ mein;

Über Nacht

Ü- ber Nacht, ü- ber Nacht kommt still das Leid, und bist du er- wacht,

Um Mitternacht

Ge- las- sen stieg die Nacht___ ans Land,___ lehnt träu- mend

Und steht Ihr früh am Morgen auf

Und steht ihr früh am Mor- gen auf vom Bet- te,

Und willst du deinen Liebsten sterben sehen

Und willst du deinen Liebsten ster- ben se- hen so tra- ge nicht dein Haar

Unfall

Ich ging bei Nacht einst ü- - - ber Land, ein Bürsch- lein traf ich

Verborgenheit

Lass, o Welt, O lass mich sein! lo- cket nicht mit Lie- bes- ga- ben

Das Verlassene Mägdlein

Früh wann die Häh- ne krähn, eh' die Stern- lein schwin- den,

Verschling' der Abgrund

Ver- schling' der Ab- - - grund mei- - nes Lieb- sten Hüt- te,

Verschwiegene Liebe

Ü- ber Wip- fel und Saa- ten in den Glanz___ hin- ein___

Der verzweifelte Liebhaber

Stu- die- ren will nichts brin- gen, mein Rock hält kei- nen Stich

Wanderers Nachtlied

Der du von dem Him- mel bist, al- les Leid___ und Schmer- zen stillest,

Was für ein Lied soll dir gesungen werden

Was___ für ein Lied soll dir ge- sun- gen wer- den,

Was soll der Zorn, mein Schatz

Was soll der Zorn, mein Schatz, der dich er- hitzt?

Wenn Du, mein Liebster, steigst zum Himmel auf

Wenn Du, mein Lieb- ster, steigst zum Him- mel auf,

Wenn du mich mit den Augen streifst

Wenn du mich mit den Au- gen streifst und lachst,

Wenn du zu den Blumen gehst

Wenn du zu den Blu- - men___ gehst, pflü- cke die schön- sten,

Wer rief dich denn?

Wer rief dich denn? Wer hat dich her- be- stellt? Wer hiess dich kom- men

Wer sein holdes Lieb verloren

Wer sein hol- des Lieb ver- lo- ren, weil er Lie- be nicht ver- steht,

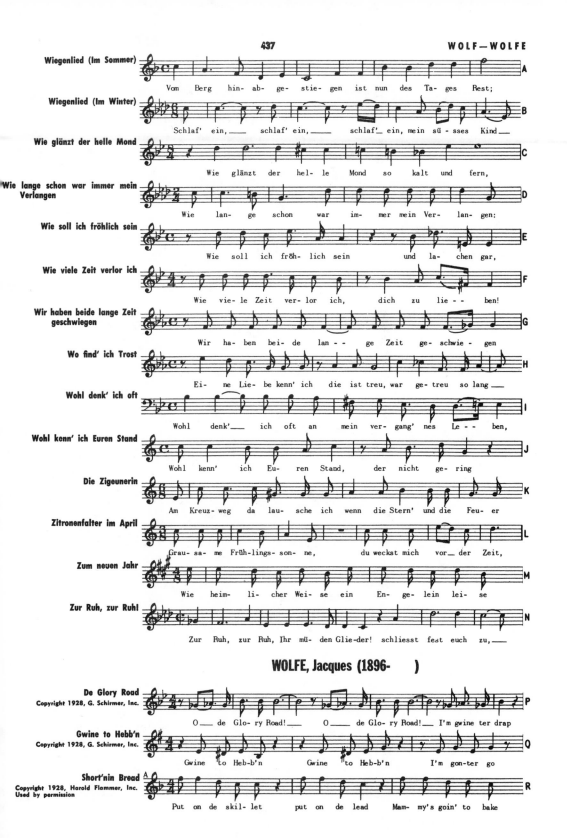

Wiegenlied (Im Sommer) A
Vom Berg hin- ab- ge- stie- gen ist nun des Ta- ges Rest;

Wiegenlied (Im Winter) B
Schlaf' ein,___ schlaf' ein,___ schlaf' ein, mein sü- sses Kind___

Wie glänzt der helle Mond C
Wie glänzt der hel- le Mond so kalt und fern,

Wie lange schon war immer mein Verlangen D
Wie lan- ge schon war im- mer mein Ver- lan- gen;

Wie soll ich fröhlich sein E
Wie soll ich fröh- lich sein und la- chen gar,

Wie viele Zeit verlor ich F
Wie vie- le Zeit ver- lor ich, dich zu lie- - ben!

Wir haben beide lange Zeit geschwiegen G
Wir ha- ben bei- de lan- - ge Zeit ge- schwie- gen

Wo find' ich Trost H
Ei- ne Lie- be kenn' ich die ist treu, war ge- treu so lang___

Wohl denk' ich oft I
Wohl denk'___ ich oft an mein ver- gang' nes Le- - ben,

Wohl kenn' ich Euren Stand J
Wohl kenn' ich Eu- ren Stand, der nicht ge- ring

Die Zigeunerin K
Am Kreuz- weg da lau- sche ich wenn die Stern' und die Feu- er

Zitronenfalter im April L
Grau- sa- me Früh- lings- son- ne, du weckst mich vor___ der Zeit,

Zum neuen Jahr M
Wie heim- li- cher Wei- se ein En- ge- lein lei- se

Zur Ruh, zur Ruh! N
Zur Ruh, zur Ruh, Ihr mü- den Glie- der! schliesst fest euch zu,___

WOLFE, Jacques (1896-)

De Glory Road P
O___ de Glo- ry Road!___ O___ de Glo- ry Road! I'm gwine ter drap

Gwine to Hebb'n Q
Gwine to Heb- b'n Gwine to Heb- b'n I'm gon- ter go

Short'nin Bread R
Put on de skil- let put on de lead Mam- my's goin' to bake

Short'nin Bread

Mam- my's lit- tle ba- by loves short'- nin', short'- nin'

WOLFF, Erich (1874-1913)

Alle Dinge haben Sprache

Al- le Din- ge ha- ben Spra- che, seit du da bist,

Aus der Ferne in die Nacht, Op. 12, No. 5

Wenn im brau- nen Ha- fen al- le Schif- fe schla- fen,

Entzücket dich ein Wunderhauch?
By permission Associated Music Publishers, Inc.

Ent- zück- et dich ein Wun- der-hauch, der ein- zig ist

Es werde Licht!
By permission Associated Music Publishers, Inc.

Es wer- de Licht!_____ so tö- ne- te____ der Ruf Got- tes

Fäden, Op. 13, No. 1

Vie- le Fä- - - den glei- ten zwi- schen mir____ und dir,____

Friede
By permission Associated Music Publishers, Inc.

A- bend- ru- - - - he liegt ü- ber dem Land

Horch, hörst du nicht
By permission Associated Music Publishers, Inc.

Horch hörst du nicht____ von Him- mel her____

Ich bin eine Harfe, Op. 13, No. 6

Ich bin ei- ne Har- fe mit gol- de- nen Sai- ten auf einsamen Gip-fel

Im Entschlafen
By permission Associated Music Publishers, Inc.

Blas- se Blü- - ten nei- gen ih- re duf- - ten- de Pracht,

Immer wieder, Op. 8, No. 3

Eh' wir uns tren- nen konn- ten, o wie hielt mich dein_ Ge-sicht

Knabe und Veilchen, Op. 9, No. 4

Blü- he, blü- he lie- bes Veil-chen, das so lieb- - lich roch,___

Märchen
By permission Associated Music Publishers, Inc.

Glaub' es mir ju- beln- de Kin- der-schar, all die schö- nen Mär-chen

Maria und der Schiffer
By permission Associated Music Publishers, Inc.

Ma- ri- a wollt' zur Kir- - - che gehn, da kam sie

Marienruf
By permission Associated Music Publishers, Inc.

Ma- ri- a, du zar- te! Du bist ein Ro- sen-gar- te,

Meine Lebenszeit verstreicht
By permission Associated Music Publishers, Inc.

Mei- ne Le- bens-zeit ver-streicht, stünd- lich eil' ich hin

Recht wie ein Leichnam
By permission Associated Music Publishers, Inc.

Recht wie ein Leich- nam wand- le ich um- her nachts zu sei- ner Tür

Soll ich denn sterben
By permission Associated Music Publishers, Inc.

Soll ich denn ster- ben, bin noch so jung? Wenn das mein Va- ter wüsst;

Ein Sonntag, Op. 17, No. 5
By permission Associated Music Publishers, Inc.

Von Me- lo- di- en die mich um- flie-hen bin ich im Raum um-ringt, A

Spaziergang, Op. 12, No. 1

Ü- ber wei-te Wie- sen schweif ich wo's__ aus tau- send Kei- men bricht,__ B

Der süsse Schlaf
By permission Associated Music Publishers, Inc.

Der sü- sse Schlaf, der sonst stillt al- les wohl, C

Täuscht euch, ihr Augen, nicht
By permission Associated Music Publishers, Inc.

Tauscht__ euch, ihr Au- gen, nicht, die Zeit ver- ge- het, D

Der Trauende
By permission Associated Music Publishers, Inc.

Mein Mu- ter mag mi net, und kein Schatz han i net, E

Viel bin ich umhergewandert
By permission Associated Music Publishers, Inc.

Viel bin ich um- her- ge- wan- dert, um zum Hei- le zu ge- lan- gen F

Wer hat's Lieben erdacht?
By permission Associated Music Publishers, Inc.

Zum Ster- ben bin__ i ver- lie- bet in di, G

Wüsst' ich nur
By permission Associated Music Publishers, Inc.

In der See- le ein Wach- sen und Kei- men, so viel H

WOLF-FERRARI, Ermano (1876-1948)

OPERAS
Le Donne Curiose Act II
Copyright 1911, G. Schirmer, Inc.

Ah_____ tut- ta per te, mio be - - - - ne J

Il cor, il cor nel con- ten- to im- prov- vi- so K

I Gioielli della Madonna (The Jewels of the Madonna) Act I
Copyright 1911, G. Schirmer, Inc.

Ma- don- na con so- spi - - ri, in lun-ghe ve-glie ar-den- di L

Be- ne- di- ci- mi tu__ Ma- dre mia buo - - - na__ M

Act II Serenata

A- pri- la, bel- la, la___ fe- ne- strel- la a__ pri- la por- ta, N

Lucieta e un bel nome, from I Quattro Rusteghi

Lu- cie- ta, Lu- cie- ta, Lu- cie- ta xe un bel no- me O

Non sono buffone, from Sly
Copyright by Sonzogno, Milan

Non so - - no buf- fo- ne, io so - - - no un po-ver uo - - mo__ P

The Secret of Suzanne
Copyright 1911, G. Schirmer, Inc.

Oh tell me, be- lov- ed, Do you re-mem- ber Those blissful moments Q

No, I can not let you leave me I've been weep- ing, lone-ly, lone- ly R

Oh, joy to be mus- ing with half closed eyes, to fol- low the va-pour S

The Secret of Suzanne

All the world is but smoke and vapor and a puff of wind   **A**

WOOD, Haydn (1882-1959)

A Brown Bird Singing

Roses of Picardy

WOODFORDE-FINDEN, Amy (d. 1919)

Indian Love Lyrics 1. The Temple Bells
By permission Boosey & Hawkes, Inc., copyright owners

The Temple bells are ringing, the young green corn is springing,   **F**

2. Less than the Dust

Less than the dust beneath thy chariot wheel   **G**

3. Kashmiri Song

Pale hands I loved beside the Shalimar, Where are you now?   **H**

4. Till I Wake

When I am dying, lean over me,   **I**

A Lover in Damascus
By permission Boosey & Hawkes, Inc., copyright owners
1. Far across the desert sands

Far, far across the desert sands I hear the camel bells   **J**

2. Where the Abana flows

Through the old city's silence Where the Abana flows   **K**

3. Beloved in your absence

Beloved, in your absence, I have told   **L**

4. How many a lonely caravan

How many a lonely caravan sets out   **M**

5. If in the great bazaars

If in the great bazaars They sold the golden stars   **N**

6. Allah be with us

Ah, when the dark on many a heart descends   **O**

WOODMAN, A. Huntington

A Birthday
Copyright 1909, G. Schirmer, Inc.

My heart is like a singing bird Whose nest is in a watered shoot   **Q**

I am thy harp
Copyright 1907, G. Schirmer, Inc.

I am thy harp, that all unknown thou sweepest,   **R**

YOUNG, Anthony (late 17th Cent.-early 18th Cent.)

Phillis has such charming graces

Phil - - - - lis has such charm - ing gra - ces

YRADIER, Sebastian (1809-1865)

El Areglito
(Bizet admitted using this for the Habanera in Carmen)

Chi-ni-ta mi-a ven por a- qui que tu ya sa-bes que mue-ro por tí

si tu me quie-res di-lo que di-to y en-se-gni-di-ta

La Calesera

Ya sue-nan las cam-pa-ni-les Mi ca-le-se-ro ha lle-ga-o

La Paloma

Cuan- do - - - - - sa-li de la Ha-ba-na val-ga-me Dios

ZONDONAI, Riccardo (1883-   )

OPERAS
Giuliano Prologue
Copyright by G. Ricordi & Co., Inc.

Non toc-che-rò mai più ar-co e sa-et-ta_ più il fo-co-la-re

Act I Love Duet

Re- i-na bel-la! Mi do-na-ste pa-ce il dì che ven-ni

Si Qua-le vuoi,_ sa-rò. Om-bra lon-ta-no

Oc-chi so-a-vi come in sul-la se-ra

Act II

Dal-la gai- - ba fug-gi-to è il lu-si-gno-lo_____

Giulietta, son io, from Giulietta e Romeo
Copyright by G. Ricordi & Co., Inc.

Giu-liet-ta! Son i- o! I- o, non mi ve-di Io che non pian-go più_

Paolo, datemi pace, from Francesca da Rimini
Copyright by G. Ricordi & Co., Inc.

Pa-o-lo, da-te-mi pa-ce È dol-ce co-sa vi-ve-re

ZELLER, Karl (1842-1898)

OPERETTAS
Der Obersteiger

Wo_ sie war die Mül-ler-in; Zog_ es auch den Fi-scher hin

Sei nicht bös', es kann_____ nicht sein,_ Sei nicht bös',

Der Vogelhändler Act I

Schenkt man sich Ro-sen in Ti-rol, Schenkt man das Herz

When my sire was twen-ty years__ and a poach-er with-out fears__

Sing a-gain,sing a-gain nightin- gale,__ that sweet strain,__ sing a- gain__

HOW TO USE
THE NOTATION INDEX*

To identify a given theme, play it in the key of C (C major for major themes, C minor for minor themes) and look it up under its note sequence using the following alphabet as a guide:

A Ab A♯ B B♭ B♯ C C♭ C♯ D D♭ D♯
E E♭ E♯ F F♭ F♯ G G♭ G♯

Double flats follow flats; double sharps follow sharps.

The number and letter to the right of the definition indicate the page and listing where the theme may be found in its correct key with the name of the composition and the composer. For example, 32B signifies page 32, theme B.

Trills, turns, grace notes, and embellishments are not taken into consideration here. However, it must be remembered that the appoggiatura is a regular note. In some cases the grace note may be of such nature as to give the aural impression of being a regular note, in which case the theme is indexed both with and without the grace note.

Keys are, in the main, determined by the harmonic structure of the opening bars, not by the cadence. The phrase that. begins in C and goes to G is considered to be in C. Themes that may be analyzed in two keys are listed under both keys.

There are themes that defy key definition. However, if the melodic line carries a key implication of its own, if only for the first few notes, that key is used. If the theme carries no such implication, then, for the sake of convenience, the first note is assumed to be C and the rest transposed accordingly.

Each definition is carried to six places except in the case of duplication. Duplicates are continued to a point of difference. When a note is repeated many times, for space conservation an exponent is used; i.e., GGGGGGG = G⁷.

H. B.

* Publisher's Note: The Notation Index was conceived by Harold Barlow.

NOTATION INDEX

Notation	Ref	Notation	Ref	Notation	Ref
A A A A A D	284D	A C D C D D	239F	A G G B A A	222P
A A A A B C♯	333L	A C D E F G	108O	A G G C D B	66O
A A A A F G	277K	A C D G E G	219G	A G G C E F	96K
A A A B B C	412E	A C E C B A	410L	A G G C G G	118G
A A A C C C A A	218R	A C E G G F	177R	A G G E E G	313S
A A A C C C A E	310L	A C G A D C	51S	A♭ A♭ A A B♭ B	404N
A A A G F E	410D	A C G A D C	52A	A♭ A♭ A♭ A A♭ A♭	316R
A A B C G G	35K	A C G G B A	222D	A♭ A♭ A♭ A♭ A♭ A♭	88F
A A C C G G	216G	A C♯ F E D F	340C	A♭ A♭ A♭ A♭ A♭ C	310H
A A C E A D	433G	A D C B A G	80O	A♭ A♭ A♭ A♭ A♭ C	433F
A A D D D C♯	143M	A D C B C D	337N	A♭ A♭ A♭ A♭ E G	431C
A A D D F E	89B	A D D E F G E	337F	A♭ A♭ A♭ G F A♭	435Q
A A D E G F	414M	A D D E F G F	55N	A♭ A♭ A♭ G F E♭ E♭	243Q
A A D♯ D♯ G B	301B	A D D G G D	410R	A♭ A♭ A♭ G F E♭ G	43C
A A E E E E	367Q	A D E F A G	51D	A♭ A♭ A♭ G G	23K
A A F D A B	63J	A D E F C B	32G	A♭ A♭ A♭ G G F♯	286F
A A F F F F	186A	A D F E D A	184B	A♭ A♭ A♭ G G G A♭	224J
A A G E A A	185S	A D F F G A	316Q	A♭ A♭ A♭ G G G C	220Q
A A G F D G	409N	A E G A E G	222M	A♭ A♭ B♭ B♭ C♭ C♭	430J
A A G F E D	184K	A E G E F G	173B	A♭ A♭ F E♭ D E♭	428I
A A G F F E A	377H	A F E D G A	379A	A♭ A♭ G C E♭ G	404P
A A G F F E D	410K	A F G E D C	218B	A♭ A♭ G D D D	66A
A A G F F F	356G	A F♯ D G G G	333F	A♭ A♭ G F E♭ F	185K
A A G G E E	296R	A G A B C A G	117B	A♭ A♭ G G F G	177M
A A G G F E	288K	A G A B C A C	440D	A♭ A♭ G G G A♭	224J
A A G G F F	104I	A G A E D B	179R	A♭ B C D E♭ F	432D
A A♭ G C C D	432L	A G A E E D	298E	A♭ B C G E♭ D	33B
A A♭ G D C B	338N	A G A G A C	413K	A♭ B♭ A♭ C C C	437P
A A♭ G F D B	80C	A G A G A G A	114I	A♭ B♭ A♭ G F E♭	337Q
A A♭ G F♯ F C	429F	A G A G A G D	402P	A♭ B♭ A♭ G G C	256Q
A B A B C B	146N	A G B C F E	361S	A♭ B♭ B♭ C C D	41G
A B A G F E	377G	A G C A G C	295E	A♭ B♭ C C G F♯	396C
A B B A C C	377R	A G C B B B	211A	A♭ B♭ C D E♭ E♭	435I
A B C B C D	395J	A G C F E C	395F	A♭ B♭ C E♭ E♭ D	120G
A B C C C C	272D	A G C G F E	121K	A♭ D E♭ D E♭ F	376D
A B C C E G	133A	A G D C F E	277O	A♭ D G G C C	439D
A B C D C D	374F	A G D C♯ E D	372C	A♭ E A♭ C A♭ E	413R
A B C D D D	395L	A G D D F E	381D	A♭ F A♭ F D F♯	319P
A B C D E F	391K	A G D D F F	129M	A♭ F A♭ F E♭ C	69M
A B C E B D	430I	A G D E A G	80L	A♭ F D A♭ A♭ F	422O
A B C E C B	75Q	A G D G C B	66N	A♭ F D A♭ A♭ G	259H
A B C G A B	339Q	A G E A G E	254D	A♭ F G C A♭ F	256I
A B C G E F	429D	A G E C C G	399Q	A♭ F G C G E♭	171E
A B C G G A	420B	A G E C D E	354I	A♭ F♯ G E♭ F♯ G	234O
A B D C C B	354A	A G E C E G	225G	A♭ G A A A A	435A
A B D C G A	339Q	A G E D C G	413D	A♭ G A♭ F A♭ G	219N
A B G A B D	284E	A G E D D C	90R	A♭ G A♭ F G A♭	55F
A B G♯ A A B	236E	A G E D F D	400C	A♭ G A♭ G B♭ A♭	59M
A B♭ C B♭ C D	194N	A G E F D E	357S	A♭ G A♭ G B♭ B♭	61K
A C A B B A	276D	A G E F E D	115J	A♭ G A♭ G C B	63E
A C A C C F	41S	A G F E D C E	329H	A♭ G B♭ B♭ A♭ B♭	91L
A C A G E F	270K	A G F E D C G	146Q	A♭ G C C A♭ G	315Q
A C B A G A	196M	A G F E D E C A	308E	A♭ G D D F E♭	336K
A C B B G G	386J	A G F E D E C G	180D	A♭ G D E♭ E F	316G
A C C C C B	286G	A G F E E D	286L	A♭ G E C B C	259L
A C C E D C	246H	A G F F E E	410B	A♭ G E♭ C C A♭	401O
A C C♯ C♯ E C♯	300D	A G G A G E	371D	A♭ G E♭ C D C	87H

Notes	Ref	Notes	Ref	Notes	Ref
Ab G F Ab G F	78K	B C D E F E	27C	C A D E F G	411M
Ab G F Ab G G	395C	B C D E F G A	430E	C A D G C F	11B
Ab G F C F G	278M	B C D E F G Ab	179B	C A D G F F	33S
Ab G F E F B	15R	B C D Eb D Eb	263C	C A F D C C	56N
Ab G F Eb D C	414G	B C D Eb F G G C	215Q	C A F D G E	169I
Ab G F Eb D Db	428K	B C D Eb F G G G	22I	C A A F# F# F#	441O
Ab G F Eb D Eb	414F	B C D F Eb G	50J	C A G B D D	29M
Ab G F Eb F F#	432K	B C D F G E	10J	C A G C D E F G A	185I
Ab G F F Eb F	258S	B C D G D G	94R	C A G C D E F G F	269I
Ab G F G Ab G	391Q	B C E G D E	219C	C A G E C E	36J
Ab G F# F F B	124L	B C Eb G Bb A	316F	C A G E D C	91A
Ab G F# G C C	187Q	B C G G F E	286P	C A G E E E	409O
Ab G F# G D E	338B	B D C B E E	386L	C A G E F G	172G
Ab G F# G D Eb	79G	B D C E A C	215M	C A G F E F	13E
Ab G G Eb G F	279O	B D C G E C	278O	C A G F E G	54G
Ab G G F# F F	179Q	B D D D D Eb	387J	C A G G A G	242I
Ab G G G G F	104Q	B D G A C E	222J	C A G G F E D	158I
B A A A A A	333M	B E G C G C	413Q	C A G G F E F	158Q
B A A G A G	47P	B Eb Eb B B Eb	411P	C A G G G G	40C
B A B A C B	92H	B F D D C# D	299O	C A G# F# C G	316N
B A B C B A	51P	B G F# F E D	302N	C Ab Ab Ab G F	18H
B A B G F F	11Q	B G# A A C B	413P	C Ab Ab G F Eb	334B
B A G B G E	80H	Bb A Bb A A A	415N	C Ab Ab G G D	42A
B A G C G E	225D	Bb A B C G F	31H	C Ab Bb Bb G G	166F
B A G F# G A	186D	Bb A C G G G	437N	C Ab C G C F	42E
B A G# C E F#	316I	Bb A G G G G	193M	C Ab F B B C	25O
B Ab G E Bb A	139O	Bb Ab Ab G G F	432B	C Ab F B D F	436N
B A# A# Bb Bb C	259O	Bb Ab D G F Eb	24L	C Ab G Ab D Eb	11M
B A# B C B C	66F	Bb Bb A A Ab B	232B	C Ab G C Ab G	26C
B B A A D E	268A	Bb Bb A G F D	194M	C Ab G C C Ab	336S
B^{17}	87S	Bb Bb Bb Ab Ab Ab	87M	C Ab G E F B	417M
B^9 C	89S	Bb Bb Bb B G Bb	358F	C Ab G Eb C Ab	404Q
B B B B B D	87P	Bb Bb Bb Bb A Bb	432A	C Ab G F Bb C	379A
B B B Bb A A	281E	Bb Bb Bb C G A	147Q	C Ab G F Eb D C B	203B
B B B C B A	268I	Bb Bb Bb C G G	438F	C Ab G F Eb D C G	16O
B B B C C G	126J	Bb Bb Bb G G A	406I	C Ab G F Eb D F Bb	18S
B B B D D D	298S	Bb Bb C D Eb D	415R	C Ab G F Eb D F Eb	312K
B B Bb C# B Bb	88E	Bb Bb G F Bb Bb	31L	C Ab G F Eb F D	290C
B B C B A# B	405D	Bb C Bb Bb C Bb	298G	C Ab G F Eb F G	27I
B B C C C C	263O	Bb C Bb C Bb C	194J	C Ab G F F Eb	19E
B B C C C D#	280M	Bb C C Eb D G	430C	C Ab G G Eb D	151L
B B D D D E	87A	Bb C C Eb Eb F	389K	C Ab G G F Eb	164I
B B Eb D C B	323F	Bb D D Bb C D	89Q	C Ab G G G G	151F
B B F# C B A	415P	Bb G A F Bb G	195N	C B A A C D	66D
B B G G B B	281C	Bb Gb Gb F F C	42A	C B A A G A	275E
B Bb Bb Bb Bb C	259O	C A A A G F	335P	C B A A G D	56K
B C A B G A	121F	C A A F# F# F#	441O	C B A A G G F	78Q
B C B C A G A	402F	C A A G G A	347O	C B A A G G G	151P
B C B C B C	161D	C A B A G C	143A	C B A Ab G C	428L
B C C C G G	417L	C A B B B C	5B	C B A Ab G F#	312R
B C C D D D	268E	C A B C C D	344O	C B A B A G A	212Q
B C C E D C	354O	C A B C C E	168E	C B A B A G E	401P
B C D A B C	67A	C A B C C F	123D	C B A B C A	62Q
B C D C B Eb	377E	C A B C D C	263Q	C B A B C B	360C
B C D C Eb G	106K	C A B C E G	418M	C B A B C C	188H
B C D D D D D	277B	C A B G A C	82A	C B A B C D D	184O
B C D D D D F	329K	C A B G C D	117E	C B A B C D E	268C
B C D D Eb D	268S	C A B G E D	66E	C B A B C D G	136B
B C D D G G	381E	C A C A A B	299D	C B A B C E	405A
B C D E C C	256J	C A C A B B	285B	C B A B C G	199Q
B C D E D E	5H	C A C A G A	204L	C B A B G A	219J

Notation	Ref.	Notation	Ref.	Notation	Ref.
C B A B G C	427O	C B A G G B	96R	C B C C E D	117J
C B A B G F#	90I	C B A G G E	234J	C B C D B C Bb	117L
C B A C A B	206M	C B A G G F	227A	C B C D B C D	133G
C B A C B A B	236C	C B A G# A G	391L	C B C D B G	251B
C B A C B A C	102L	C B A G# B A	57E	C B C D C B A A	441F
C B A C B A G	224I	C B Ab C B Bb	198J	C B C D C B A G	13K
C B A C F E	5Q	C B Ab G C B	8N	C B C D C C	69L
C B A D B B	105S	C B A# E D# D	316L	C B C D C D Eb	72D
C B A D E D	63L	C B B A A A	321G	C B C D C D Eb	198G
C B A D G C	277J	C B B A A G	396O	C B C D E A	154H
C B A E A G	212S	C B B A C B A A	374D	C B C D E D	267N
C B A E D C	198K	C B B A C B A B	420Q	C B C D E E	376G
C B A E E E	348I	C B B A C B B	196K	C B C D E F E D	213S
C B A E G A	51H	C B B A G F E D	23A	C B C D E F E E	149R
C B A F E E	439P	C B B A G F E F	325D	C B C D E F G F E	156I
C B A F G F	68P	C B B B A A	421C	C B C D E F G F G	248E
C B A F# G E	393P	C B B B A G	49P	C B C D E F G G	265B
C B A G A A	384N	C B B B Bb G	51O	C B C D Eb Ab	398R
C B A G A B A	285L	C B B B D C	201R	C B C D Eb D G G F C	194O
C B A G A B B B	66C	C B B Bb A A	289F	C B C D Eb D G G F G	194I
C B A G A B B C	202C	C B B C C# C#	234L	C B C D G C	69N
C B A G A B C B	50B	C B B C D G	222O	C B C D G D	216H
C B A G A B C B	50B	C B B C G A	133N	C B C D G F	19Q
C B A G A B C C	52E	C B B F G A	316M	C B C D G G	118S
C B A G A B C E	345B	C B Bb A A D	11R	C B C Db G D	355H
C B A G A B C G	197A	C B Bb A Ab G	198J	C B C E Ab D	300H
C B A G A F E	203L	C B Bb Bb A Ab G E C	77S	C B C E C G	246C
C B A G A F F	245E	C B Bb Bb A Ab G E Eb	385E	C B C E D C D	322S
C B A G A G A	237C	C B Bb Bb Bb A	46F	C B C E D C E	140Q
C B A G A G F	125R	C B Bb E Eb D	316L	C B C E F G	20L
C B A G B A G B	441R	C B C A A G	12F	C B C E G# D	300H
C B A G B A G E	278A	C B C A B A#	393R	C B C Eb C G	397N
C B A G C D E C	133Q	C B C A B C D C B	169B	C B C Eb D C B C Bb	157F
C B A G C D E D	4R	C B C A B C D CC	213N	C B C Eb D C B C Eb	225Q
C B A G C E	221M	C B C A B C D E	29Q	C B C Eb D C F	59E
C B A G D C	12B	C B C A G A F	12F	C B C Eb D Eb	62S
C B A G D E	10K	C B C A G A G	62M	C B C Eb F Eb	8M
C B A G E C	142D	C B C A G C	159G	C B C Eb F Eb	8O
C B A G E F B	1G	C B C A G E	128C	C B C Eb G B	316J
C B A G E F G	94D	C B C A G G	202R	C B C F G A	226D
C B A G E G A	295B	C B C A G# A	252E	C B C G A G	55A
C B A G EGFEDCB	222N	C B C Ab Ab G	79O	C B C G B A	428C
C B A G EGFEDCD	36S	C B C Ab C B	402Q	C B C G Bb Ab	319O
C B A G EGFEDCD	349P	C B C B A A A	365L	C B C G C B	437Q
C B A G F D	402D	C B C B A A B	364K	C B C G C F	11F
C B A G F E A A	26O	C B C B A B A	1H	C B C G C F#	392K
C B A G F E A F	326I	C B C B A B C	90O	C B C G D C	23C
C B A G F E A G	98O	C B C B A E	219S	C B C G E D C#	115E
C B A G F E D B	400F	C B C B A G A	203S	C B C G E D E	20Q
C B A G F E D CA	158N	C B C B A G C	416S	C B C G E G C	330A
C B A G F E D CG	150H	C B C B Ab G	311H	C B C G E G G	323I
C B A G F E D D	376R	C B C B B A	206F	C B C G F Ab	292F
C B A G F E E	108E	C B C B B B	415N	C B C G F E	181F
C B A G F E F G A	167J	C B C B C G	353J	C B D C A B	285A
C B A G F E F G E	105R	C B C B G B	220J	C B D C B B	221C
C B A G F# G C	368K	C B C Bb Ab G	179H	C B D C B C B	70C
C B A G F# G G#	378I	C B C Bb G E	14R	C B D C B C C	397G
C B A G G A B	163L	C B C C C Bb	54S	C B D C B G	75L
C B A G G A C	152B	C B C C C D	19H	C B D C E B	400Q
C B A G G A F	86M	C B C C C Db	269L	C B D C E G B	179J
C B A G G A G	99N	C B C C D C	441F	C B D C E G E	94L

Notation	Code	Notation	Code	Notation	Code
C B D C F E D	167F	C Bb Ab G F Eb D Eb F Eb	290M	C C Ab Ab C C	281C
C B D C F E E	234D	C Bb Ab G F Eb D Eb F F	194A	C C Ab C B C	175I
C B D C G Bb	84H	C Bb Ab G F F	95A	C C Ab F C D	63J
C B D F A B	118H	C Bb Ab G F G Ab Bb	268L	C C Ab F D B	405N
C B D F E B	62B	C Bb Ab G F G Ab G	302O	C C Ab G G G	255F
C B D G C B D G C B	380N	C Bb Ab G G Eb	28Q	C C B A A A	370E
C B D G C B D G C D	395O	C Bb Ab G G F#	256M	C C B A A B	141P
C B D G F F	43D	C Bb Bb A A G	25D	C C B A A G	329N
C B E A G C	392H	C Bb Bb Ab Bb G	302Q	C C B A B A G A	137H
C B E D E C	151K	C Bb Bb Bb C Bb	31N	C C B A B A G E	138K
C B E D F E	335O	C Bb Bb Bb C C	89H	C C B A B C	175G
C B E D G F	42M	C Bb Bb Bb G A	15S	C C B A B G	257O
C B E F G A	104G	C Bb Bb C Bb G	360J	C C B A C B	436M
C B E G A G	74K	C Bb Bb C D Eb	189S	C C B A D D	79H
C B Eb D G F	274F	C Bb Bb C Eb C	279N	C C B A G Bb	143L
C B Eb Eb Eb G	433A	C Bb Bb Eb Eb F	125D	C C B A G C D D	11O
C B Eb G G G	206H	C Bb Bb G G Eb	110C	C C B A G C D E E	52M
C B F A A A	413O	C Bb C A Bb C	267F	C C B A G C D E G	375J
C B F E C B	234A	C Bb C Ab Bb C	378O	C C B A G F E D C A	213H
C B F E C G	255N	C Bb C Ab G F	388N	C C B A G F E D C C	382E
C B F E D A	255G	C Bb C Bb Ab Ab	440M	C C B A G F E D F	28M
C B G A A C	142E	C Bb C Bb Ab Bb	293F	C C B Ab Ab D	412N
C B G A B A E A	220E	C Bb C Bb Ab G	234C	C C B B A A B	365E
C B G A B A E D	136F	C Bb C Bb C G	176K	C C B B A A G	90P
C B G A B A G	264L	C Bb C Bb G Bb	360D	C C B B A C	437J
C B G A B C	36C	C Bb C Bb G C	360J	C C B B A E	348G
C B G A B G	85O	C Bb C D Eb D	288M	C C B B A G	417I
C B G A C B	232I	C Bb C Eb D Bb	91D	C C B B A# C#	232B
C B G A E E	185H	C Bb C Eb F Eb	376B	C C B B B B	173L
C B G A F D	54F	C Bb C G F G	100A	C C B B B Bb	313H
C B G A F G	7M	C Bb C G G G	259D	C C B B Bb Bb	49Q
C B G A G E	126S	C Bb Eb F D D	187B	C C B B C A	164D
C B G B A A	143N	C Bb G Bb C Bb	140J	C C B B C C	289J
C B G C A B	285N	C Bb G Bb C C	276B	C C B B C D E	171J
C B G D C G	335H	C Bb G Bb C Db	30M	C C B B C D Eb D	255B
C B G E D C	389O	C Bb G Bb G C	294R	C C B B C D Eb Eb	431D
C B G F A G	233J	C Bb G C D B	36P	C C B B C Eb	58C
C B G G A B	173D	C Bb G F C Bb	286M	C C B B G G	147D
C B G G B G	353K	C Bb G F Eb Bb	291M	C C B Bb A G	13R
C B G G F D	439S	C Bb G F G F	428B	C C B Bb Bb Bb	441D
C Bb A A A C#	333S	C Bb G G Bb G	299F	C C B Bb E E	159O
C B# A A G G	186B	C Bb G G C Bb	123K	C C B C A A	281M
C Bb A Bb C A	16C	C Bb G G G Bb	285R	C C B C C E	327J
C Bb A Bb C Bb	189F	C Bb G G G G	369P	C C B C C G	153D
C Bb A G A C	226F	C C A A A G F	64N	C C B C D A	105A
C Bb Ab Ab G G	410B	C C A A A G G	303J	C C B C D B	29B
C Bb Ab Bb C Ab	69G	C C A A B A	236B	C C B C D E D	307O
C Bb Ab Bb G F	78G	C C A A G A	179G	C C B C D E F	349N
C Bb Ab Db	404J	C C A A G C	66B	C C B C D Eb	168C
C Bb Ab G Ab F	26L	C C A A G G	438A	C C B C F D	260B
C Bb Ab G Ab G Ab	202M	C C A B C E	398B	C C B C G A	10O
C Bb Ab G Ab G B	10D	C C A Bb C Bb	10L	C C B C G Eb	156J
C Bb Ab G Ab G F	15I	C C A C C C	389S	C C B D C C	88E
C Bb Ab G Bb Bb	239N	C C A F A D	45G	C C B D C C	375R
C Bb Ab G Bb C	258P	C C A F G F	45L	C C B D C F E A	332C
C Bb Ab G C Bb	102E	C C A G E C	314I	C C B D C F E E	264D
C Bb Ab G C C	189K	C C A G F E	346M	C C B D F E	279A
C Bb Ab G Eb C	286E	C C A G G C	437R	C C B E C C	197I
C Bb Ab G Eb D	99A	C C A G G F E	159C	C C B E E D	161C
C Bb Ab G Eb F	138L	C C A G G F F	43H	C C B Eb Eb Eb	288L
C Bb Ab G F Eb Ab	353H	C C Ab Ab Ab G	211Q	C C B G A A B	351E

Notation	Ref.
C C B G A A G	38F
C C B G F F	243F
C C B G G B	73K
C C Bb A Ab G	225O
C C Bb A C C	93A
C C Bb A D G	105B
C C Bb A G G	354Q
C C Bb Ab Ab Cb	42S
C C Bb Ab Bb C D	175J
C C Bb Ab Bb C F	175H
C C Bb Ab C C	220S
C C Bb Ab G Ab	305H
C C Bb Ab G Bb	84G
C C Bb Ab G F Eb D C	262B
C C Bb Ab G F Eb D Eb	22G
C C Bb Ab G F Eb Eb	296I
C C Bb Ab G F G Bb	421B
C C Bb Ab G F G G	184K
C C Bb Ab G G	163D
C C Bb Bb A Ab	78D
C C Bb Bb Ab Ab	110D
C C Bb Bb G G	89C
C C Bb C	279R
C C Bb Eb D Bb	4P
C C Bb Eb F G	378P
C C Bb F Bb Bb	194S
C C Bb G C C Bb	420E
C C Bb G C C C	185S
C C C	33K
C C C A A F	33K
C C C A C E	23H
C C C A F F	393E
C C C A F G	230F
C C C A G G	366H
C C C Ab F F	413S
C C C B A B A	188J
C C C B A B C G C	366S
C C C B A B C G G	384J
C G C B A D	285K
C C C B A G A A A	96S
C C C B A G A A G	242B
C C C B A G C	26R
C C C B A G E D	399E
C C C B A G E E	412F
C C C B A G G A A	221G
C C C B A G G A B	194E
C C C B B A A A	374R
C C C B B A A C	196L
C C C B B A B	306D
C C C B B A G	280H
C C C B B B	395K
C C C B C C	364F
C C C B C D D B	187J
C C C B C D D D	9F
C C C B C D E	168Q
C C C B C D F	22C
C C C B C G	287P
C C C B D C	295O
C C C B D D	26F
C C C B D F	166I
C C C B F F	67F
C C C B G Ab	398P
C C C B G C D Eb Bb	291C
C C C B G C D Eb Eb	25Q
C C C B G C D Eb Eb	27S
C C C B G Eb	339B
C C C Bb Ab Bb	178S
C C C Bb Ab G Ab	421Q
C C C Bb Ab G F	426H
C C C Bb Bb Bb Bb	88R
C C C Bb Bb Bb G	386N
C C C Bb Bb C	189G
C C C Bb C C Bb	196B
C C C Bb C C C	360H
C C C Bb G Bb	190L
C C C Bb G G	190M
C C C C A A	221I
C C C C A G	386R
C C C C A# A#	407A
C C C C B A	45E
C C C C B B D	365N
C C C C B B F	255L
C C C C B C C	289I
C C C C B C D C D E C	247R
C C C C B C D C D E E	209K
C C C C B C D E	169A
C C C C B C D Eb	334R
C C C C Bb Ab	407H
C C C C Bb Bb Ab	407A
C C C C Bb Bb Bb A	194D
C C C C Bb Bb Bb Ab	93B
C C C C Bb Bb Bb Bb	194D
C C C C Bb C C	76K
C C C C Bb C D	262Q
C C C C Bb D	298H
C C C C C Ab	210S
C C C C C B A A A	385R
C C C C C B A A F	312H
C C C C C B A G	22B
C C C C B C C C C B	340A
C C C C C B C C C C Eb	112Q
C C C C C B C C Eb	112P
C C C C C B C D	197S
C C C C C B C Eb	378F
C C C C C Bb Bb	31K
C C C C C Bb G	190M
C C C C C C A	20N
C C C C C C B A	406J
C C C C C C B A#	265N
C C C C C C B B	237M
C C C C C C Bb	154D
C^7 A A	238S
C^7 A B	435K
C^7 Ab	322C
C^7 B	245J
C^7 Bb A	434A
C^7 Bb Bb	240I
C^8 B	403M
C^8 Bb	239M
C^9 B	168P
C^{10}	206R
C^{11} A	111P
C^{11} B	211G
C^{12} A	236H
C^{17} D	148F
C^{14} D	385B
C^{13} D	374S
C^{13} G	199D
C^{12} G	434O
C^{11} D	214L
C^{10} Eb	282I
C^9 D	398Q
C^8 D	145S
C^8 E	175E
C^8 Eb C	282E
C^8 Eb D	396I
C^7 D D	238M
C^7 D E	85D
C^7 Eb	75E
C C C C C C C#	395H
C C C C C C D C	295C
C C C C C C D D	398N
C C C C C C D Eb	65K
C C C C C C Db	36A
C C C C C C E	370A
C C C C C C Eb	280K
C C C C C C F	406K
C C C C C C G F	45O
C C C C C C G G A	322P
C C C C C C G G Ab	242C
C C C C C C G G C	280G
C C C C C D B	140M
C C C C C D C B	378F
C C C C C D C C	323E
C C C C C D D	310I
C C C C C D E A	175K
C C C C C D E C	196R
C C C C C D E D C	333R
C C C C C D E D D	320L
C C C C C D E F	178O
C C C C C D F	167Q
C C C C C Db	78H
C C C C C E C B	431I
C C C C C E C C	346D
C C C C C E C D	359I
C C C C C E C G	422N
C C C C C E D C C	70Q
C C C C C E D C F	354M
C C C C C E E	373S
C C C C C Eb C	143P
C C C C C Eb D C C	155I
C C C C C Eb D C G	309P
C C C C C Eb Eb D D	306C
C C C C C Eb Eb D Eb	441K
C C C C C Eb Eb Eb	320P
C C C C C F Ab	71D
C C C C C F C	256F
C C C C C G E	114E
C C C C C G F	161K
C C C C C G G	50R
C C C C C# C# D	340I
C C C C C# D	254F
C C C C C# E	330B

Notation	Ref
C C C C D Ab	22M
C C C C D B	103J
C C C C D C B B	116R
C C C C D C B C C	324J
C C C C D C B C F	394P
C C C C D C C C	311J
C C C C D C C G	412B
C C C C D D C	381I
C C C C D D D	383I
C C C C D D E	172L
C C C C D D Eb	12L
C C C C D E C C	5O
C C C C D E C D	365R
C C C C D E D	250O
C C C C D E E	288P
C C C C D E F E	49N
C C C C D E F G C C	153E
C C C C D E F G C D	158L
C C C C D Eb	281O
C C C C Db Bb	175F
C C C C Db Db	231S
C C C C Db F	65E
C C C C Db G	280I
C C C C E C C C	45P
C C C C E C C D	332B
C C C C E D C B	303L
C C C C E D C G E	359N
C C C C E D C G G	273P
C C C C E D D	130K
C C C C E E	253I
C C C C E G D	36K
C C C C E G G	386Q
C C C C Eb C C C C	371R
C C C C Eb C C C D	104N
C C C C Eb D	164L
C C C C Eb Eb	371J
C C C C Eb F	389I
C C C C Eb G	246O
C C C C F C	299N
C C C C F D	311N
C C C C F E D C	34A
C C C C F E D E	360S
C C C C F E E	394P
C C C C F F	196D
C C C C F G	95N
C C C C G C	413M
C C C C G E E	250M
C C C C G E G	299J
C C C C G F E F	307H
C C C C G F E G	36H
C C C C G G G C	24S
C C C C G G G G	408Q
C C C C Gb Gb	48L
C C C C# D Eb	438R
C C C D Ab Ab	399J
C C C D Bb Bb	193S
C C C D Bb G	196H
C C C D C B A	391C
C C C D C B B	202L
C C C D C G	193Q
C C C D D D D	418C
C C C D D D E A	324A
C C C D D D E E	35Q
C C C D D D Eb	334S
C C C D D D F	423R
C C C D D D G G E	148H
C C C D D D G G G	307I
C C C D D E C	390N
C C C D D E D	347L
C C C D D E E C	241J
C C C D D E E E	110R
C C C D D E F	85G
C C C D D E G E	427M
C C C D D E G G	275B
C C C D D Eb C	126B
C C C D D Eb D	287M
C C C D D Eb Eb	216K
C C C D D Eb F	180E
C C C D E A	165J
C C C D E B	283M
C C C D E D C C	256P
C C C D E D C E	211N
C C C D E D G	381R
C C C D E E E	160B
C C C D E E F	137B
C C C D E F E A	24M
C C C D E F E D F	266D
C C C D E F E D G	269Q
C C C D E F E F	4K
C C C D E F F C	41K
C C C D E F F G	431J
C C C D E F G A	43J
C C C D E F G Bb	345G
C C C D E F G G E	281K
C C C D E F G G G	40E
C C C D E G	37S
C C C D Eb Bb	257A
C C C D Eb C C C C	100L
C C C D Eb C C C D	207O
C C C D Eb C D	223C
C C C D Eb D C C	258Q
C C C D Eb D C G Ab	390Q
C C C D Eb D C G Eb	282D
C C C D Eb D D	425H
C C C D Eb Eb	429J
C C C D Eb F	185L
C C C D Eb G	139S
C C C D F F	157R
C C C D G F	99M
C C C D G G	149B
C C C Db D Eb	438R
C C C E B A	284K
C C C E B B	117O
C C C E C C A	102G
C C C E C C C	67Q
C C C E C C F	11K
C C C E C C G	250J
C C C E C F	38I
C C C E C G	144M
C C C E D C B B	250O
C C C E D C B D	318Q
C C C E D C D	345P
C C C E D C G	152D
C C C E Db Db	415E
C C C E E E E E	417B
C C C E E E E F	441J
C C C E E F	94A
C C C E E G E	130O
C C C E E G G	244M
C C C E F F	33K
C C C E F G A G C	21M
C C C E F G A G G	271B
C C C E G G	68A
C C C Eb D C Bb Ab	189O
C C C Eb D C Bb Bb	241I
C C C Eb D C E	389O
C C C Eb D D	240G
C C C Eb Eb C	401F
C C C Eb Eb D C	130C
C C C Eb Eb D D	420G
C C C Eb Eb E	73D
C C C Eb Eb Eb	320O
C C C Eb Eb G	255J
C C C Eb F G	125P
C C C Eb G C	404O
C C C Eb G F	72B
C C C F A G	92O
C C C F Ab Bb	177M
C C C F Bb Bb	295H
C C C F E C	305L
C C C F Eb D	107H
C C C F F Bb	295H
C C C F F E	348P
C C C F F F	296O
C C C F G Ab	29D
C C C G A B C B	21L
C C C G A B C B	234B
C C C G A B C	212P
C C C G A C	313B
C C C G A G C	422C
C C C G A G F	195O
C C C G Ab G	99O
C C C G B A	82G
C C C G Bb Ab	340K
C C C G C C C C	321R
C C C G C C C G	341R
C C C G C D C	69B
C C C G C D F	399S
C C C G C D G	99K
C C C G C E	243I
C C C G C F	338C
C C C G D E	241E
C C C G D Eb C	439F
C C C G D Eb D	318J
C C C G E D	398C
C C C G E E E C A	101L
C C C G E E C G	254E
C C C G Eb Eb	181R
C C C G F E	194G
C C C G F F	111S
C C C G F G D	89M
C C C G F G Eb	184L
C C C G F G#	356C

Notation	Ref	Notation	Ref	Notation	Ref
C C G G A	26Q	C C D D E♭ E♭ F	77Q	C C D E♭ D C C D	70N
C C G G B♭	65F	C C D D F C	298C	C C D E♭ D D	389F
C C G G C C C	335J	C C D D F E	313J	C C D E♭ D E♭	40D
C C G G C C G C	117B	C C D D F F	56E	C C D E♭ D♭ C	53N
C C G G C C G E	260F	C C D D G G	307P	C C D E♭ E♭ D	429I
C C G G C D	321S	C C D E B B	176R	C C D E♭ E♭ F E♭	277E
C C G G F	111S	C C D E C A	250E	C C D E♭ E♭ F F	295L
C C G G G E	64O	C C D E C A♭	259M	C C D E♭ F D	140C
C C G G G G	244H	C C D E C C B	409D	C C D E♭ F E♭	408D
C C♭ B♭ B♭ B♭	441D	C C D E C C C E	182D	C C D E♭ F G A♭ A♭	436C
C C# C# C# C	236O	C C D E C C C D	275C	C C D E♭ F G A♭ G D	440F
C C# D C B	247I	C C D E C C F	187I	C C D E♭ F G A♭ G F	420P
C D A♭ G F	159F	C C D E C D C	190P	C C D E♭ F G A♭ G G	169D
C D B A G	380K	C C D E C D E D	126C	C C D E♭ F G B♭	438I
C D B C C	273I	C C D E C D E F E	148O	C C D E♭ F G D	235Q
C D B C D	323L	C C D E C D E F G	251Q	C C D E♭ F G G G C	319G
C C B G A	121I	C C D E C F	407I	C C D E♭ F G G G G	25G
C D B♭ B♭ C	45H	C C D E C♭ C♭	176R	C C D E♭ G A♭	403P
C D B♭ C A♭	213P	C C D E D C A	51A	C C D E♭ G C	377F
C D C B A A	329N	C C D E D C B	10B	C C D F E D	54K
C D C B A B	250Q	C C D E D C D C	185N	C C D F E F	401N
C D C B C D	114G	C C D E D C D E	27K	C C D F E♭ E♭	329O
C D C B C G D	2S	C C D E D C E	136E	C C D G C B♭	162A
C D C B C G G	230O	C C D E D D D	251N	C C D G C C	66G
C D C B♭ B♭	193O	C C D E D D E	274J	C C D♭ C B♭ C	281D
C D C B♭ C	341S	C C D E D E	114R	C C D♭ D♭ D♭ C	236O
C D C C B	124P	C C D E D F	72A	C C D♭ D♭ D♭ E	280M
C D C C B♭	341O	C C D E E D C	160A	C C D# E F E	321O
C D C C C	327C	C C D E E D D	436L	C C E A A G	179L
C D C C D C	366N	C C D E E E E F A	205N	C C E A G C	182L
C D C C D D	384L	C C D E E E E F E	146M	C C E C C C	117C
C D C C D E	23I	C C D E E E E G	368N	C C E C G A	247N
C D C C D♭	243N	C C D E E E F D	400D	C C E C G F	129Q
C D C C E	110F	C C D E E E F E	345I	C C E C G G	247S
C D C D E	374A	C C D E E E F	203P	C C E D C G	327L
C D C D E♭	319R	C C D E E F E D C E	327D	C C E D E F F	111M
C D C E D	119I	C C D E E G F E D C G	284I	C C E D E F G	269P
C D C E F	267P	C C D E E F G A B	108B	C C E E C C C	49K
C D C E♭ F	179P	G C D E E F G A F#	7K	C C E E C C E	52J
C D C G C	268R	C C D E E F G A G	32K	C C E E E G F	411L
C D C G D	41P	C C D E E F G F	361C	C C E E E G G	251L
C D D C B	201M	C C D E F E	94N	C C E E G G	227J
C D D D D	385I	C C D E F G A B A	271H	C C E F E D	44R
C D D D E♭ E♭ E♭ E♭	242J	C C D E F G A B C	12O	C C E F G D	84B
C D D D E♭ E♭ E♭ F	285I	C C D E F G A B♭	9H	C C E G A A	36M
C D D D E♭ F	302F	C C D E F G A G E	213E	C C E G A G	56C
C D D D F	235N	C C D E F G A G G	425P	C C E G B B	253A
C D D D G G G D	190C	C C D E F G A♭	320J	C C E G C B A G F E E	365K
C D D D G G G F	73E	C C D E F G E	389R	C C E G C B A G F E F	405H
C D D D♭ E♭	77M	C C D E F G F E A	132C	C C E G C C B	29E
C D D E C	195G	C C D E F G F E D	114Q	C C E G C C G	134Q
C D D E E D C	194Q	C C D E F G G C	280C	C C E G C G C	425Q
C D D E E D D	110N	C C D E F G G G	33N	C C E G C G E	252S
C D D E E F	344A	C C D E G E	389H	C C E G D E	112D
C D D E E G G C	411K	C C D E G F	185Q	C C E G G C	168G
C D D E E G G F	264B	C C D E♭ A♭ G	409C	C C E G G F	110H
C D D E F G E	85G	C C D E♭ C C	282H	C C E♭ C C C	258H
C D D E F G G	152K	C C D E♭ C G	156L	C C E♭ C C G	419C
C D D E F G#	431H	C C D E♭ D B♭	294A	C C E♭ C E♭ F	389M
C D D E G	190K	C C D E♭ D C C B	262D	C C E♭ C G G	86K
C D D E♭ E♭ E♭	430J	C C D E♭ D C C C	192J	C C E♭ D B C	386A

Notation	Ref
C C Eb D B G	380M
C C Eb D C B	318N
C C Eb D C Bb	340J
C C Eb D C C	48J
C C Eb D C D Eb D	47H
C C Eb D C D Eb F	120N
C C Eb D C Eb	214N
C C Eb D C# D	429M
C C Eb Eb C C	415F
C C Eb Eb C D	225I
C C Eb Eb D C	418S
C C Eb Eb Eb B	231O
C C Eb Eb Eb Eb	298Q
C C Eb Eb F Ab	344C
C C Eb Eb F Eb	297Q
C C Eb Eb F F	201L
C C Eb Eb G Eb	310O
C C Eb Eb G G C Ab	231L
C C Eb Eb G G C C	292A
C C Eb F Eb D	283D
C C Eb F G Eb	322L
C C Eb F G G	269A
C C Eb F# G C	372O
C C Eb G Ab G	319N
C C Eb G C Eb	246N
C C Eb G G Eb	57B
C C Eb G G F	52K
C C F C C Ab	258C
C C F C D Eb	377K
C C F E D E	339M
C C F F D D	299R
C C F F D G	170C
C C F F E D	109C
C C F F Eb C	193P
C C F F Eb Eb	188R
C C F F G G	67N
C C F G G G	195H
C C F# G G G	42O
C C G A B C	240O
C C G A B G	404M
C C G A Bb Bb	279I
C C G A C C	116A
C C G A F C	6P
C C G A F E	157I
C C G A G F	200D
C C G Ab G F	281P
C C G Bb Bb G	108S
C C G C B C	392M
C C G C C G	379L
C C G C D Eb	403C
C C G C D F	389D
C C G C G C	102R
C C G Db C Bb	415P
C C G E C A	134D
C C G E D C	29O
C C G E E C G E	309D
C C G E E C G G	252R
C C G E E D	397E
C C G E F A	308G
C C G Eb Eb Eb	394S
C C G Eb Eb F	239I
C C G Eb F G C	424K
C C G Eb F G G	206K
C C G F A G	106G
C C G F Ab F	381A
C C G F D C	169K
C C G F Eb D	101B
C C G F Eb Eb	310N
C C G F F F	165E
C C G F G F	41H
C C G G A A B	109Q
C C G G A A G	2A
C C G G A F	167M
C C G G A G F E D C	26H
C C G G A G F E D E	272H
C C G G Ab G Ab	104L
C C G G Ab G F	288A
C C G G B C	156B
C C G G C C A	181J
C C G G C C D	194L
C C G G C G	192M
C C G G D D A	207N
C C G G D D F	222H
C C G G E C	321Q
C C G G Eb D	192O
C C G G F Ab	319I
C C G G F E D E F G	16J
C C G G F E D E F E	27M
C C G G F Eb	390L
C C G G F F	110M
C C G G F G	51C
C C G G G D	276L
C C G G G E	332H
C C G G G F	320N
C C G G G G C	344E
C C G G G G G C	88P
C C G G G G G F	256G
C C G G G# A	209L
C Cb Cb F G A	316M
C C# D D# E B	392F
C C# D E F G	357H
C C# D G G G	104J
C C# F E D C#	323F
C D A Bb C D	193N
C D A C C D	284G
C D A C G B	287I
C D Ab G F G	157K
C D B A D C	221D
C D B C A B	197D
C D B C C D	236G
C D B C D B C D B C E	307L
C D B C D B C D B C G	253P
C D B C D E D E	5K
C D B C D E D F	153H
C D B C D E E	424F
C D B C D E F E	84E
C D B C D E F G	18B
C D B C E G	15G
C D B C Eb D	296B
C D B C Eb F	27A
C D B C G G	243E
C D B G A B C B	139E
C D B G A B C G	35(
C D B G C D	309)
C D Bb C D Bb	360.
C D Bb C D Eb	238)
C D C A B B	241
C D C A B G	7:
C D C B A B A	40(
C D C B A B C	232
C D C B A G E E	231N
C D C B A G E F	131(
C D C B A G G	386
C D C B B A	37:
C D C B B B	302.
C D C B B D	402)
C D C B C D C	92
C D C B C D G	11
C D C B C E E	248)
C D C B C E F	244(
C D C B C F Ab	17
C D C B C F E	13
C D C B D C	71
C D C B E D	156O
C D C B G C	235)
C D C B G G	392O
C D C Bb Ab G	222O
C D C Bb C D	390
C D C Bb C G	194I
C D C C B A	151N
C D C C C D	21)
C D C C C G	151.
C D C D C D	65)
C D C D C Eb	63
C D C D C G	59
C D C D D Eb	54
C D C D E D	161
C D C D E F D	377
C D C D E F E D	268O
C D C D E F E F	289
C D C D E F F	26
C D C D E F G A G A	179
C D C D E F G A G E	7O
C D C D E G	3O
C D C D Eb C	299
C D C D F E	310N
C D C D G Eb	16O
C D C E E D	291
C D C Eb Eb G	424I
C D C Eb G F	271.
C D C G A B	224
C D C G Eb C	157.
C D C G F E	194.
C D C G G G F Eb D C Eb	256O
C D C G G G F Eb D C G	194I
C D D C D D	361
C D D C D E	162I
C D D D D D	407
C D D D D Eb	292
C D D E C D	354
C D D E C G	313.
C D D E D C	22
C D D E E A	75)

C D D E E C	311E	C D E D E F E D	263E	C D E F E D C A C	383K
C D D E E G G C	374P	C D E D E F E F A	97F	C D E F E D C A G	25I
C D D E E G G E	217G	C D E D E F E F G	226E	C D E F E D C C	177E
C D D E F E	164C	C D E D E F G A D	297C	C D E F E D C D	44E
C D D E F G	162N	C D E D E F G A G	161H	C D E F E D C E	154F
C D D Eb D Eb	71F	C D E D E F G F	129N	C D E F E D C G	228D
C D D Eb Eb D	323M	C D E D E G	234Q	C D E F E D D C	309M
C D D Eb F B	172A	C D E D F E D B	171H	C D E F E D D E D	343S
C D D Eb G G	77I	C D E D F E D C	18C	C D E F E D D E F	34J
C D D G A B	161P	C D E D G E	290E	C D E F E D E C E	120R
C D D# E C A	123S	C D E E C C	417A	C D E F E D E C E F E	22S
C D D# E F F	101I	C D E E C D	382G	C D E F E D E C F E	24A
C D E A A C	264G	C D E E D C B	2C	C D E F E D E C F G	20E
C D E A B C	225N	C D E E D C D	35G	C D E F E D E D	1N
C D E A G E	79E	C D E E D C E	327H	C D E F E D G C	207D
C D E A G G	132I	C D E E D C G	124F	C D E F E D G E	243J
C D E C A G C	340R	C D E E D D	72L	C D E F E E D C B	7A
C D E C A G E	134R	C D E E D E C C	372E	C D E F E E D C C	215F
C D E C B A	113K	C D E E D E C E	333J	C D E F E G A	160P
C D E C C C	207B	C D E E E D E	72M	C D E F E G F E D	165L
C D E C C D	245S	C D E E E D G	137G	C D E F E G F E F	44B
C D E C C G E	207B	C D E E E E C	64M	C D E F E G G	421H
C D E C C G F	189E	C D E E E E E	135J	C D E F F E	148J
C D E C D D	195D	C D E E E E E F	335Q	C D E F F F	204I
C D E C D E F	200P	C D E E E F E D G#	407J	C D E F F G	272N
C D E C D E G	119G	C D E E E F E D D	20S	C D E F G A B C F	43J
C D E C D F	220D	C D E E E F E D E	143O	C D E F G A B C G	236P
C D E C D G	175L	C D E E E F G A B	264N	C D E F G A B Bb	27D
C D E C F D	307N	C D E E E F G A E	350O	C D E F G A C	127N
C D E C G E	420O	C D E E E F#	336L	C D E F G A D	241F
C D E C G F D	309F	C D E E E G	436Q	C D E F G A F E	21B
C D E C G F E C	36Q	C D E E F A	62E	C D E F G A F G	179A
C D E C G F E D	155E	C D E E F D	37N	C D E F G A G A F G F E C	244E
C D E D C A	155H	C D E E F E D D	321A	C D E F G A G A F G F E F	158P
C D E D C B A	404L	C D E E F E D G	47L	C D E F G A G A G	161N
C D E D C B C	384S	C D E E F E E	325B	C D E F G A G C	112H
C D E D C C B	34G	C D E E F E F	109N	C D E F G A G F	382N
C D E D C D C	285E	C D E E F F B	249H	C D E F G A G G	137N
C D E D C D D	292M	C D E E F F G	147K	C D E F G Ab	391D
C D E D C D E C	267R	C D E E F G	181A	C D E F G C C Bb	121S
C D E D C D E D	271Q	C D E E G A	208K	C D E F G C C C	242A
C D E D C D E F	13S	C D E E G E C A	325C	C D E F G C D	186Q
C D E D C D E F# D	107K	C D E E G E C C	362R	C D E F G D	164G
C D E D C D E F# E	297J	C D E E G E D	305R	C D E F G E A	150J
C D E D C D E G A	64R	C D E E G F	48C	C D E F G E C C	378Q
C D E D C D E G C	366D	C D E E G G	192A	C D E F G E C F	234H
C D E D C D G	392P	C D E F A C	58N	C D E F G E D	200Q
C D E D C E A	300Q	C D E F A G E	45N	C D E F G F E A G A	214C
C D E D C E D	364G	C D E F A G F	51B	C D E F G F E A G F	304L
C D E D C E F G A	157M	C D E F B C	405I	C D E F G F E D C	197B
C D E D C E F G G	288B	C D E F D E D C	22H	C D E F G F E D E	23M
C D E D C F A	237L	C D E F D E D E	262O	C D E F G F E D G	315J
C D E D C F E	159I	C D E F D E F	46E	C D E F G G A	262L
C D E D C G A	21K	C D E F D F	259Q	C D E F G G C	239C
C D E D C G E	346L	C D E F D G	72I	C D E F G G F	42Q
C D E D C G F	439H	C D E F E A	93J	C D E F# F# F#	89F
C D E D C G G	145H	C D E F E C C B	3D	C D E F# G B	79C
C D E D D E	414N	C D E F E C C D	325M	C D E F# G E	200Q
C D E D E C C	424H	C D E F E C D	72J	C D E G A B	134L
C D E D E C D	105P	C D E F E D A	382C	C D E G A G	51J
C D E D E F E D	28J	C D E F E D C A Bb	290N	C D E G C B	306L

Notation	Ref
C D E G C D E C	203K
C D E G C D E D	120E
C D E G C D E F	355D
C D E G C E	229C
C D E G D B	242N
C D E G E C	37M
C D E G E C	387A
C D E G E D E D	266G
C D E G E D E F	351M
C D E G E G A E	294N
C D E G E G A G	42J
C D E G F A	310C
C D E G F E D C C	223A
C D E G F E D C D E F	72Q
C D E G F E D C D E G	195L
C D E G F E D C G	315K
C D E G F E D E	278L
C D E G F E D F	369G
C D E G F E F E	375H
C D E G F E F G	4S
C D E G F# E	177S
C D E G G A G E	116F
C D E G G A G F	399O
C D E G G C A	200S
C D E G G C C	376S
C D E G G C D	384Q
C D E G G E	162K
C D E G G F	244J
C D E G# G# G#	434M
C D Eb B C B	340D
C D Eb B C Eb	321F
C D Eb B C F	408B
C D Eb B C G	71M
C D Eb C Ab F	257E
C D Eb C Ab G D	307K
C D Eb C Ab G Eb	151D
C D Eb C Ab G F	279K
C D Eb C C Bb	75P
C D Eb C C C C	364R
C D Eb C C C D C	139I
C D Eb C C C D D	346O
C D Eb C C D Eb C	382Q
C D Eb C C D Eb D	301P
C D Eb C D D	80K
C D Eb C D Eb	404A
C D Eb C D G G C	163R
C D Eb C D G G G	138B
C D Eb C Eb D	220R
C D Eb C Eb F	397K
C D Eb C Eb G	61I
C D Eb C F D	216S
C D Eb C F Eb C	390I
C D Eb C F Eb D	305F
C D Eb C G C	155G
C D Eb D B C	129P
C D Eb D B G	367N
C D Eb D Bb Bb	293L
C D Eb D Bb C	202I
C D Eb D C Ab	310A
C D Eb D C B C C	169F
C D Eb D C B C D Eb C	279H
C D Eb D C B C D Eb F	61P
C D Eb D C Bb	314A
C D Eb D C C C	273J
C D Eb D C C D C	360G
C D Eb D C C D Eb	402A
C D Eb D C C G	28L
C D Eb D C D Eb D	196I
C D Eb D C D Eb F	101M
C D Eb D C D Eb Gb	178L
C D Eb D C D G	134M
C D Eb D C Eb D C B	150C
C D Eb D C Eb D C Eb	56R
C D Eb D C Eb F	188O
C D Eb D C Eb G	390J
C D Eb D C G D D	296K
C D Eb D C G D Eb	157O
C D Eb D C G G A	296G
C D Eb D C G G C	61Q
C D Eb D D F	262J
C D Eb D Eb C D C	47Q
C D Eb D Eb C D Eb	146R
C D Eb D Eb D C D Eb D Eb C	148P
C D Eb D Eb F	282C
C D Eb D F D	10N
C D Eb D G C	29A
C D Eb Eb C C	277D
C D Eb Eb D C Bb	293O
C D Eb Eb D C D	199F
C D Eb Eb D C Eb	86O
C D Eb Eb D E	289A
C D Eb Eb D Eb	382P
C D Eb Eb D F B	338J
C D Eb Eb D F Eb	215B
C D Eb Eb Eb D C	333H
C D Eb Eb Eb D Eb	379F
C D Eb Eb Eb Eb Eb C D Eb Eb	215R
C D Eb Eb Eb Eb Eb C D Eb F	320A
C D Eb Eb Eb Eb Eb Eb D C	86A
C D Eb Eb Eb Eb Eb Eb D Eb	272D
C D Eb Eb Eb F#	134N
C D Eb Eb Eb G C	288E
C D Eb Eb Eb G G	117D
C D Eb Eb F D	167P
C D Eb Eb F Eb	336E
C D Eb Eb F G A	212L
C D Eb Eb F G G	96J
C D Eb Eb G G F	375M
C D Eb Eb G G G	87R
C D Eb F Ab C	56I
C D Eb F Ab G	59G
C D Eb F C Eb	189L
C D Eb F D C	239S
C D Eb F D D	87K
C D Eb F D Eb	43G
C D Eb F D G	221E
C D Eb F Db Eb	100P
C D Eb F Eb D	202H
C D Eb F Eb F	72F
C D Eb F F Eb	124R
C D Eb F F F Eb	404F
C D Eb F F F G	312I
C D Eb F F G	96
C D Eb F F# G	96
C D Eb F G A B	26
C D Eb F G A F	176
C D Eb F G A G	81
C D Eb F G Ab Ab F	282
C D Eb F G Ab Ab G	402
C D Eb F G Ab B C Bb	274
C D Eb F G Ab B C D	391
C D Eb F G Ab D	307
C D Eb F G Ab Eb	403
C D Eb F G Ab G C Bb	152
C D Eb F G Ab G C D	199N
C D Eb F G C B C	6N
C D Eb F G C B D	135
C D Eb F G C C	262
C D Eb F G C D	420
C D Eb F G C Db	21
C D Eb F G C Eb	377
C D Eb F G D	156
C D Eb F G Eb D	332
C D Eb F G Eb G	85
C D Eb F G F D	255
C D Eb F G F Eb C	341
C D Eb F G F Eb D	343
C D Eb F G F Eb Eb	177
C D Eb F G F F	263
C D Eb F G G C	24
C D Eb F G G G	101
C D Eb G Ab F	61
C D Eb G C C	276
C D Eb G D C Eb	85
C D Eb G D C Eb	423
C D Eb G Eb D	213
C D Eb G F D	44
C D Eb G F Eb D	276
C D Eb G F Eb F	378
C D Eb G F# A	217
C D Eb G G Ab	5
C D Eb G G C	369
C D Eb G G F	232
C D F A C A	200
C D F Ab C B	39
C D F E D C	424
C D F E E E	16
C D F Eb D D	17
C D F Eb Eb F	342
C D F F E C	33
C D F F E D	26
C D F F Eb D	106
C D F G A B	35
C D F G F G	12
C D G A G F	22
C D G C E F	15
C D G C E G	25
C D G C Gb Db	29
C D G F G C	17
C D G G C B	23
C D G G G B	16
C Db B C Bb Ab	39
C Db B C D C	2

Notation	Ref	Notation	Ref	Notation	Ref
C Db C C Db C	65C	C E D C G G G A	296M	C E F G A E	267K
C Db Db C C F	208R	C E D C G G G G	291H	C E F G A F E D	69E
C Db Db Db Db Db	418K	C E D D A A	42R	C E F G A F E E	158O
C Db Db Eb C B	140O	C E D D C E	302I	C E F G A F G	267H
C Db E F G Ab	127H	C E D D D E	158H	C E F G A G C	271L
C D# E A G C	417E	C E D D D F	149J	C E F G A G D	103S
C D# E G C E	416F	C E D D E F	20M	C E F G A G E	90C
C E A C F E	34K	C E D D F E	244B	C E F G A G G F	45F
C E A G E D	52G	C E D E C C	51R	C E F G A G G G	269K
C E A G F A	119J	C E D E F E D	161N	C E F G B A	30E
C E A G F# G	369L	C E D E F E F	292J	C E F G C B A G#	375J
C E A G G B	314P	C E D E F G A	274B	C E F G C B A G G	180B
C E B A G F	233R	C E D E F G F	103M	C E F G C B C	45J
C E B C C D	336N	C E D F B G	18J	C E F G C Bb	165F
C E B D C E	258N	C E D F E D D	19A	C E F G C C	143D
C E C A A C	236A	C E D F E D E	152M	C E F G C D	97S
C E C A G A	41A	C E D F E G A	169G	C E F G C E G A A	357Q
C E C B B C	129H	C E D F E G F	19L	C E F G C E G A G E	1L
C E C B C E	328R	C E D F E G G	100C	C E F G C E G A G F	210R
C E C C G G	168J	C E D G A B	152R	C E F G C F	227L
C E C E C C C	186H	C E D G B A	353I	C E F G E A B	153R
C E C E C C E	142O	C E E D C B	8I	C E F G E A G	28N
C E C E C D	222F	C E E D C E	70F	C E F G E C Ab	97O
C E C E C E C	249B	C E E D D C	43K	C E F G E C C	309R
C E C E C E F	372Q	C E E E D C A	37Q	C E F G E C D	202K
C E C E F F	250H	C E E E D C F	272Q	C E F G E E	18K
C E C E G E C	159E	C E E E E F	171K	C E F G E F A	420M
C E C E G E G	15A	C E E E E F	171L	C E F G E F D	152C
C E C F D G	248S	C E E E F G A	320S	C E F G E G	160C
C E C G A B A	321L	C E E E F G G	230O	C E F G F E D C D E C	241N
C E C G A B C	245D	C E E E F# G	212D	C E F G F E D C D E G	386P
C E C G A G	290D	C E E F F G	345K	C E F G F E F	162I
C E C G B A	308O	C E E F G A	212K	C E F G F G	341P
C E C G C E	16L	C E E F G G	130L	C E F G G A A C	143H
C E C G E A	160R	C E E G A A	412I	C E F G G A A G	165N
C E C G E C	168J	C E E G A G	183G	C E F G G A B	99I
C E C G E D	354S	C E E G C E	300G	C E F G G A Bb	272S
C E C G E F	403I	C E E G C F	391O	C E F G G A C	267L
C E C G E G	419G	C E E G C G	164B	C E F G G A G A	267E
C E C G G C	242H	C E E G G A	313Q	C E F G G A G F	239O
C E C G G G	22E	C E E G G C	55C	C E F G G F E D C B	152E
C E D B G G	399H	C E E G G E C C	49A	C E F G G F E D C G	107B
C E D C A A	336P	C E E G G E C D	289O	C E F G G F E D D	241G
C E D C B C	126P	C E F C E F	53M	C E F G G G A	116G
C E D C C A	109R	C E F D B C B	273H	C E F G G G C	390S
C E D C C B A B	406E	C E F D B C D	172B	C E F G G G G G A	265D
C E D C C B A F	130I	C E F D B G	246M	C E F G G G G G G	122I
C E D C C B B A A G G A	131H	C E F D C C	227H	C E F G G# A	41B
C E D C C B B A A G G F#	251C	C E F D C D	131A	C E F# G C D	282B
C E D C C C B	43O	C E F D E D	398S	C E F# G G G	407P
C E D C C C G	22F	C E F D G F	169P	C E G A A G	60F
C E D C C E D	151A	C E F E D C	291G	C E G A B C C B	362N
C E D C C E G	383N	C E F F D D	252F	C E G A B C C C B	153G
C E D C D C	138F	C E F F G B	279E	C E G A B C C C F	380L
C E D C E D	157B	C E F F G G	45N	C E G A Bb A	124D
C E D C E G F	228R	C E F F# G B	352F	C E G A C A	270M
C E D C E G G	114M	C E F G A A	341H	C E G A C C C	124H
C E D C G A	19D	C C F G A C A	83J	C E G A C C E	59D
C E D C G C	163O	C E F G A C D	53S	C E G A F D	169S
C E D C G G A	18O	C E F G A C F	53R	C E G A F G	21S
C E D C G G C	18O	C E F G A D	290F	C E G A G A	232E

Notation	Ref	Notation	Ref	Notation	Ref
C E G A G C C	230J	C E G G G C	243G	C Eb D D D Eb	189P
C E G A G C G	229B	C E G G G E	315O	C Eb D D Eb D	289R
C E G A G E C A	368C	C E G G G G A A	115N	C Eb D D F Bb	299C
C E G A G E C C E	190I	C E G G G G A F	184N	C Eb D D G F	188N
C E G A G E C C F	311R	C E G G G G A G A	72S	C Eb D Eb F G	179S
C E G A G E C B	363D	C E G G G G A G C	429E	C Eb D Eb G F#	90M
C E G A G E C C	305Q	C E G G G G A G G	17K	C Eb D F Eb C	262E
C E G A G E G	400H	C E G G G G A G G	17M	C Eb D F Eb D	235I
C E G A G F	204P	C E G G G G C	103E	C Eb D F Eb G G Ab	130M
C E G A G G C	208H	C E G G G G D	9B	C Eb D F Eb G G G	392Q
C E G A G G F#	247M	C E G G G G E C	167D	C Eb D G Eb C	136A
C E G B A B	294P	C E G G G G G E G	311P	C Eb D G Eb D	19C
C E G B B C	251K	C E G G G G G A B C B	460	C Eb D G F D	407S
C E G B C D	11H	C E G G G G G G A B C G	366F	C Eb D G G Ab	350F
C E G Bb A A	18L	C E G G G G G G G E	249E	C Eb Db C Bb C	42G
C E G C A G	128B	C E G G G G G G G G	362F	C Eb Eb C B D	202J
C E G C B A	225R	C E G# A A D	62R	C Eb Eb C C Bb C	123R
C E G C B D	308L	C Eb C B C G	154R	C Eb Eb C C Bb Eb	208G
C E G C C E	163P	C Eb C C B D	240H	C E Eb D C B	286O
C E G C C G B	161I	C Eb C C C Bb	118J	C Eb Eb D Eb C	329E
C E G C C G E	415O	C Eb C C C Eb C C	87O	C Eb Eb Db Db C	44G
C E G C D E	288O	C Eb C C C Eb C Eb	388J	C Eb Eb Eb C C	60I
C E G C E D C B A	74Q	C Eb C C Eb D	361F	C Eb Eb Eb D C	81Q
C E G C E D C B D	383G	C Eb C D C Bb	182F	C Eb Eb Eb D D	239H
C E G C E E	235B	C Eb C D Eb C	192K	C Eb Eb Eb Eb C	35O
C E G C E G	9M	C Eb C D Eb D	313M	C Eb Eb Eb Eb Eb Eb Eb D C	238I
C E G C F E	384K	C Eb C D Eb F	131C	C Eb Eb Eb Eb Eb Eb Eb D Eb	47N
C E G D E F	128P	C Eb C Eb C B	33H	C Eb Eb Eb Eb F	7H
C E G E A G	59N	C Eb C Eb C G	355L	C Eb Eb F F G	281H
C E G E C A	246K	C Eb C Eb D C	425J	C Eb Eb F G Ab	389A
C E G E C E F	309K	C Eb C Eb D F	326A	C Eb Eb F G D	240L
C E G E C E G E C	308B	C Eb C Eb Eb Eb	294O	C Eb Eb F G G F#	202B
C E G E C E G E E	164K	C Eb C F C G	157H	C Eb Eb F G G G	239L
C E G E C E G E F#	171D	C Eb C F Eb C	45C	C Eb Eb F# F# B	298O
C E G E C G	163K	C Eb C G B D	249N	C Eb F Ab F G	269F
C E G E D E	290B	C Eb C G C B	154E	C Eb F C Bb Eb	193L
C E G E F A	44L	C Eb C G G Ab	158M	C Eb F Eb D C	258A
C E G E F E	255A	C Eb C G G C	292P	C Eb F Eb F G	213I
C E G E F G	241S	C Eb D B C G	171A	C Eb F G A B	84L
C E G E F# E	315A	C Eb D Bb C D	121P	C Eb F G A F	297L
C E G E G F	102N	C Eb D C B C	28B	C Eb F G Ab Eb	185C
C E G F E D	254G	C Eb D C B G	274P	C Eb F G Ab F	189J
C E G F E E	253H	C Eb D C Bb G	189B	C Eb F G Ab G	5D
C E G F E F	166H	C Eb D C C B	262D	C Eb F G C Bb	210O
C E G F G A	179E	C Eb D C C Bb	135A	C Eb F G C C	202E
C E G F# E D	177N	C Eb D C C C	360P	C Eb F G C Eb	54M
C E G G A A	53E	C Eb D C C D	195Q	C Eb F G Eb F	231H
C E G G A G A	270G	C Eb D C C Eb	217D	C Eb F G F G A	99J
C E G G A G E C D	382S	C Eb D C D D	274K	C Eb F G G C Eb F G Ab	148C
C E G G A G E C E	143C	C Eb D C D E	407M	C Eb F G G C Eb F G Bb	340B
C E G G B C	243P	C Eb D C D Eb	3I	C Eb F G G Eb	124A
C E G G C B A	183B	C Eb D C Eb F Eb	178Q	C Eb F G F G F	42I
C E G G C B G	281A	C Eb D C Eb F G	140N	C Eb F# G C Eb	117S
C E G G F E D A C	220B	C Eb D C Eb G Ab	154C	C Eb F# G Eb F#	82R
C E G G F E D A E	219K	C Eb D C Eb G D	57Q	C Eb F# G Eb Gb	82R
C E G G F E D C	162F	C Eb D C Eb G F	249L	C Eb G Ab G Ab	403N
C E G G F E D E	50L	C Eb D C G G C B	433D	C Eb G Ab G C	326O
C E G G F E E	230L	C Eb D C G G C Bb	164E	C Eb G Ab G Eb	311O
C E G G F E G	183Q	C Eb D C G G Cb	433D	C Eb G Ab G F	60N
C E G G F# E	217H	C Eb D D C C	93M	C Eb G B D Eb	380J
C E G G G B	135S	C Eb D D D D	434P	C Eb G C Ab Ab	408A

Notation	Ref	Notation	Ref	Notation	Ref
C Eb G C B A	26P	C G A Bb F F	34B	C G C C# E C#	42D
C Eb G C Bb Ab G F Eb D	152A	C G A C B C	16Q	C G C D C B	287S
C Eb G C Bb Ab G F Eb G	151B	C G A D B G	54N	C G C D D E	143I
C Eb G C C Eb	161F	C G A E A G F	289Q	C G C D E C D	135K
C Eb G C D Eb	152O	C G A E A G G	247D	C G C D E C E	30S
C Eb G C E F	10S	C G A E C F	292R	C G C D E D C B	194P
C Eb G C Eb G	403O	C G A E F E D	56M	C G C D E D C D E	22P
C Eb G C G Eb	319F	C G A E F E F	216M	C G C D E D C D G	149M
C Eb G D Eb D	43N	C G A E G C	384P	C G C D E D E F E D	160Q
C Eb G F Eb C	68E	C G A F E D	71I	C G C D E D E F E E	149S
C Eb G F Eb D	44N	C G A F G C	25F	C G C D E D F	68I
C Eb G G A A	76I	C G A F G E	426N	C G C D E F E	295I
C Eb G G Eb Ab	144D	C G A G C E	292D	C G C D E F G	215P
C Eb G G F Eb	150N	C G A G C G A G C B	362H	C G C D Eb C	320E
C Eb G G G Ab	79R	C G A G C G A G C C	163S	C G C D Eb F Eb D C	101H
C Eb G G G Bb	389N	C G A G E C D	196S	C G C D Eb F Eb D Eb	285P
C Eb G G G Eb	390A	C G A G E C F	290G	C G C D Eb F G	71Q
C Eb G G G G Bb	29H	C G A G F E C	309B	C G C Db E Db	42D
C Eb G G G G C	365C	C G A G F E D C C	283E	C G C E A G	159B
C Eb G G G G G	172J	C G A G F E D C G	51M	C G C E C G	289D
C F D C B C	242D	C G A G F G F E	371O	C G C E E A	90E
C F D C C B	344F	C G A G F G F G	419J	C G C E E G	278F
C F D E A D	324L	C G A G# A C	261N	C G C E F G	81G
C F D E A D	324L	C G Ab Bb C G	105J	C G C Eb C C	32R
C F D G E C	292S	C G Ab E F G	70I	C G C Eb D B	347A
C F D G F E D	361K	C G Ab F Eb D	14A	C G C Eb D C	328K
C F E A G F	247A	C G Ab F Eb F	153F	C G C Eb F G	160S
C F E D C B	57N	C G Ab G C Ab	129S	C G C F E C	359B
C F E D C C	110G	C G Ab G Eb D	347S	C G C F E D#	393J
C F E D C# D	33R	C G Ab G F Ab	264M	C G C G C A	279Q
C F E D E C	395P	C G Ab G F Eb	281R	C G C G C Bb	281Q
C F E D E G	106F	C G Ab G G Ab	168L	C G C G C C	132D
C F E D G C	192C	C G Ab G G C	280E	C G C G C E	383C
C F Eb Eb D C	414H	C G B A E G	396K	C G C G C G	249R
C F F Ab Ab Ab	336J	C G B Ab C G	4D	C G C G E C	326H
C F F F Ab G	340G	C G B C A F	150K	C G C G F A	351L
C F F F F F	179N	C G B C C G	162B	C G C G G G	70S
C F G Ab Eb D	32G	C G B C G B	67I	C G D C# G# D#	175Q
C F G Ab F C	347J	C G B C G B	306S	C G D E A B	205S
C F G E F D	248I	C G B F A D	392O	C G D E F G	213B
C F G E G C	409L	C G Bb A Bb G	87F	C G D Eb C G	74D
C F# G A G E	418N	C G Bb F Eb F	258J	C G D G C E	254K
C F# G G D F	8F	C G C Ab F F	163J	C G D G D G	255D
C G A A A F	269J	C G C B A F	303Q	C G D G E C	255M
C G A A B C	189D	C G C B A G A	222B	C G D G E D	346C
C G A A E F	407F	C G C B A G C	164O	C G D G Eb D	278D
C G A B A A	440H	C G C B A G G	8G	C G D G G F	156H
C G A B A G	364O	C G C B B C	150A	C G E A A C#	358E
C G A B C B	269G	C G C B C C D	20G	C G E A A F	251G
C G A B C D C B	400P	C G C B C C E	84J	C G E A D E	289L
C G A B C D C D	11L	C G C B C D	274O	C G E A G E	273A
C G A B C D E C	329A	C G C Bb Ab G F Eb D C	154J	C G E C A A	134G
C G A B C D E D	151C	C G C Bb Ab G F Eb D Eb	153S	C G E C A G	183S
C G A B C D E F	410I	C G C Bb G Bb	297M	C G E C C C	309B
C G A B C D E G E A	283A	C G C C C C	149N	C G E C C G	254P
C G A B C D E G E D	348B	C G C C D D Eb Eb	171N	C G E C D E	25N
C G A B C G	271G	C G C C D D Eb F	21N	C G E C E G C C	331C
C G A B D F	23D	C G C C D E D	234N	C G E C E G C D D	122C
C G A B E G	301F	C G C C D E F	13F	C G E C E G C D E	11C
C G A Bb A G	294F	C G C C D E G	256D	C G E C E G E	382O
C G A Bb Bb G	110A	C G C C G B	164F	C G E C F D B	272O

Notation	Code
C G E C F D G	249A
C G E C F G	326K
C G E C G A	18Q
C G E C G E C D	321C
C G E C G E C E	255E
C G E C G E C G A	152I
C G E C G E C G E E	94M
C G E C G E C G E F	234T
C G E C G E G	165I
C G E C G F E	156F
C G E C G F F	229H
C G E D B G E C A	289E
C G E D B G E C G	402S
C G E D C B A	254J
C G E D C B C D E	171G
C G E D C B C D G	150B
C G E D C C A	245Q
C G E D C C D	165C
C G E D C D E	227S
C G E D C D G	158B
C G E D C F	161A
C G E D G F	403J
C G E D# E F	39H
C G E D# F# C	41Q
C G E E C B	400A
C G E E F G Bb	203I
C G E E F G C	251I
C G E E F G E	33I
C G E E G E	217F
C G E F A A	247K
C G E F A G E C C	176L
C G E F A G E C D	170G
C G E F D C	154O
C G E F D D	254M
C G E F G A	23E
C G E F G B	120H
C G E F G C E	116C
C G E F G C G	165G
C G E F G E	188Q
C G E F G G#	233K
C G E G A F	7B
C G E G C C	6N
C G E G C D	33A
C G E G C E	358C
C G E G C G	347K
C G E G F D B	286C
C G E G F D C	254O
C G E G G A	244P
C G E G G F	251D
C G Eb C Ab G	215G
C G Eb C C Ab	162C
C G Eb C C D	23J
C G Eb C D Eb F D	169J
C G Eb C D Eb f G	402R
C G Eb C D G	255H
C G Eb C Eb G	321M
C G Eb C G C	273N
C G Eb C G G Eb	427A
C G Eb C G G G	87C
C G Eb D Ab G	247J
C G Eb D B C	287R
C G Eb D C B C	153L
C G Eb D C B G C	290J
C G Eb D C B G F	151Q
C G Eb D C Bb	58B
C G Eb D C Eb	149L
C G Eb D C G	408C
C G Eb D Eb C	52B
C G Eb Eb C C	162H
C G Eb F Ab G	393S
C G Eb F G C	279F
C G Eb G C C	102O
C G F D Eb D	91E
C G F D G G	381M
C G F E A C	246P
C G F E A G	54J
C G F E C D	273R
C G F E C E	5C
C G F E D C B C D G E	6L
C G F E D C B C D G G	161O
C G F E D C D D	129M
C G F E D C D E	303S
C G F E D C F	155N
C G F E D C G B	159P
C G F E D C G G	172H
C G F E D E D	201K
C G F E D E E	242Q
C G F E E B	164M
C G F E E D	314N
C G F E F D	292I
C G F E F G A A	245N
C G F E F G A Bb	20R
C G F E F G A D	27R
C G F E F G A G	361H
C G F E G C	25B
C G F E G G	103B
C G F Eb C D	88S
C G F Eb D Bb	192N
C G F Eb D C Bb	304E
C G F Eb D C Eb	111R
C G F Eb D Eb	6R
C G F Eb D G	48B
C G F Eb F C	280D
C G F Eb F D	176P
C G F F E C	180M
C G F F F C	89K
C G F# F E Eb	417J
C G F G Ab Bb Ab	85M
C G F G Ab Bb Eb	44P
C G F G Bb Ab	41F
C G F G Eb C	3M
C G F G Eb D	78S
C G F G F Eb	407C
C G F G F G	48A
C G F# C F E	124E
C G F# F# C D	82Q
C G F# G D Eb	363P
C G G A A A	111F
C G G A A C	8E
C G G A B A	223I(A)
C G G A B C B	125F
C G G A B C C	26K
C G G A B C D	325E
C G G A B G	386C
C G G A G A	230R
C G G A G G	303D
C G G Ab Ab Ab	315M
C G G Ab C Ab	152Q
C G G Ab Fb Cb	110B
C G G Ab G C	79D
C G G Bb F F	222G
C G G Bb G F	175D
C G G C Ab Ab	433E
C G G C B A A	235G
C G G C B A G	46D
C G G C B C D	165H
C G G C B C G	380A
C G G C Bb Ab	141L
C G G C C B	165M
C G G C C Bb Ab	289M
C G G C C Bb Bb	189M
C G G C D E	70E
C G G C E A	20B
C G G C E D	413N
C G G C E E	37G
C G G C E G	150M
C G G C Eb F	271O
C G G C G G	232D
C G G D D G	212E
C G G D G E	248H
C G G E A Bb	327N
C G G E C B A B	188P
C G G E C B A G	224M
C G G E C D	289G
C G G E D C	252C
C G G E D D	386B
C G G E E C	38B
C G G E G A	322N
C G G E G C	113F
C G G Eb C D	408N
C G G Eb Eb C	235E
C G G Eb Eb F	110J
C G G Eb G F	83N
C G G F Ab Ab	109E
C G G F C Bb	16I
C G G F E E D	431R
C G G F E E G	226Q
C G G F Eb C	189Q
C G G F Eb D C C	428Q
C G G F Eb D C D	270B
C G G F Eb F C	280D
C G G F Eb F G	68L
C G G F Eb G	172F
C G G F F E	349D
C G G F G C	423I
C G G F# G E	418I
C G G G A A	435D
C G G G A B	128S
C G G G A E	237S
C G G G A F	179M
C G G G A G F E D	223R
C G G G A G F E G	217I
C G G G A G G	337M

Notes	Ref	Notes	Ref	Notes	Ref
C G G G Ab Ab	79Q	D C C B A G	249D	D D F F F G Ab	56L
C G G G Ab Bb	77A	D C C D E F	263A	D D G D Bb Ab	48N
C G G G Ab G	347E	D C D D D C	275Q	D D G D D B	329M
C G G G C C	247L	D C D D E D	275Q	D D G D D C#	299P
C G G G C D	84I	D C D E F Eb	196A	D D G E E G	70R
C G G G C F F A	212J	D C D E F G	196A	D D G F E D	268F
C G G G C F F E	338E	D C E D B C	127A	D D G G A B	112C
C G G G C G	23Q	D C F Eb Ab G	274G	D D G G G D	356M
C G G G D Eb	427J	D C G C D E	136G	D D G G G Eb	347N
C G G G E C	422M	D C G C E C	197O	D D G G G G	331R
C G G G E E	17R	D C G F B B	352P	D Db C C C C	360E
C G G G E G	109L	D D A Eb D C	415P	D E A G E G	390D
C G G G F D	251J	D D A F C A	438Q	D E C C D E	250D
C G G G F Eb D	139P	D D A G A F	51K	D E C D E D	213R
C G G G F Eb G	262I	D D B F D E	324P	D E C E E F	291I
C G G G F F	118N	D D C C F Eb	172M	D E C G D E	326S
C G G G F G	282M	D D C D E G	175M	D E C G E G	355R
C G G G F# F	359R	D D D C B C	100O	D E D C C G	197J
C G G G G A	276C	D D D C C G	53H	D E D C D E D	271N
C G G G G Ab	425A	D D D C D Eb	91J	D E D C D E F	170B
C G G G G Bb	419D	D D D C Eb D	240M	D E D E A D	257N
C G G G G C	62I	D D D D B B	28D	D E D E D E D	55D
C G G G G E	248J	D D D D C D	239B	D E D E D E G	412J
C G G G G Eb	103G	D D D D D C	416L	D E E F D	250F
C G G G G G A	154S	D D D D D D Bb	322C	D E E D D C	38N
C G G G G G Ab	339F	D^{10} Eb	437G	D E E E E	232M
C G G G G G C	35S	D D D D D D D Eb	89N	D E E F E	320B
C G G G G G E	3B	D D D D D Eb	225K	D E E F F E	22Q
C G G G G G G Ab	324Q	D D D D D F	178C	D E F A F E	265A
C G G G G G G E	246E	D D D D D G	132G	D E F D F A	222I
C G G G G G G G	235S	D D D D E E	279J	D E F D G F E D	8C
C G Gb C F Fb	124E	D D D D Eb D	268P	D E F D G F E F	139M
C G# A D B F#	60O	D D D D F F	88L	D E F E D A	120M
C G# C G C F	42E	D D D D G E	224A	D E F E D E F	19R
C G# G# A A E	428E	D D D E C A	360N	D E F E D E F#	51N
C# D D E E E	327E	D D D E C D	258E	D E F E D G A	287K
C# D E F E F	316P	D D D E D C	236N	D E F E D G E	395D
D A B Eb D Eb	417Q	D D D E F# G	414O	D E F F A A	87R
D A C D A C	361I	D D D E G F	240J	D E F F F E	257C
D A G A A B	435L	D D D E G G	190H	D E F G A A	96F
D A G F D A	419L	D D D Eb B C	259G	D E F G A A	379D
D B A B G A	192Q	D D D Eb Eb G	131H	D E F G A B	183I
D B B D G G	414R	D D D F F A	177O	D E F G A G	328E
D B C B B C	258M	D D D G B B	427F	D E F G Ab D	283K
D B C C A C	286D	D D D G Db Bb	356E	D E F G D D	357F
D B C D Ab G	354K	D D D G F E D C	267Q	D E F G E B	208E
D B C D E D	178F	D D D G F E D F	276K	D E F G E G	63D
D B C D F Eb	387F	D D D G G Eb	277I	D E F G G D	293P
D B Eb C D G	33M	D D Db E D Db	88E	D E F G G G	106L
D B F A F E	411R	D D E A C B	337L	D E F# A C D	44F
D B G A B C	58S	D D E C A A	96E	D E F# G D A	435P
D C A G F D	415A	D D E D E D	102S	D E G A C B	173S
D C Ab F Ab C	179K	D D E D G E	23G	D E G A G E	293E
D C B A G A	268H	D D E E E G	355K	D E G C D C	64K
D C B A G C C	13G	D D E F G A	375O	D E G C D E D	347Q
D C B A G C G	183E	D D E F G D	185O	D E G C D E G	178J
D C B C C F	218M	D D E G E D	270L	D E G D D E	200J
D C B C D F	323K	D D F D C D	243A	D E G G D E	340S
D C Bb Ab G F	418G	D D F F Ab G	180F	D E G G G A	220M
D C Bb G D C	91Q	D D F F E D	145O	D Eb B C D G	331H
D C C B A E	220I	D D F F F G A	77J	D Eb B C F# G	127D

Notation	Code
D Eb Bb D Eb B	360A
D Eb C Bb Ab Ab	61H
D Eb C C C E	378A
D Eb C G C Eb	37O
D Eb D C B B	268O
D Eb D C B C	272J
D Eb D C D D	326R
D Eb D C D Eb	301Q
D Eb D C G Bb	438S
D Eb D C G D	405S
D Eb D D G F	269C
D Eb D Eb B C	77E
D Eb D Eb D Eb	263N
D Eb D Eb D G	55O
D Eb D Eb F G	426I
D Eb D G F D	263R
D Eb Eb D C Bb	283B
D Eb Eb F# G B	209B
D Eb F Eb D C	231K
D Eb F G Ab Bb	179B
D Eb F G G C	104H
D Eb F G G D	77H
D Eb G D Eb G	55J
D Eb G F# G C	259P
D F A E D F	283N
D F A F E D	410L
D F B C D E	416A
D F C Eb B B	221A
D F D Eb D G	54D
D F E F E D	87J
D F E F F E	22N
D F E G F A	223N
D F E G F D	381H
D F Eb D Eb D	113N
D F F F F Ab	88J
D F G A A F	144G
D F G Ab F Eb	34H
D G C Bb Ab F	54L
D G C D B C	345H
D G D D D E	91K
D G D D F F	89R
D G D E D D	159R
D G D Eb F G	208D
D G E A C F	412R
D G E C F D	247O
D G E C G D	381C
D G E E F E	76P
D G F E C G	186S
D G F E D C	125K
D G F F E F	212M
D G G A E G	47J
D G G D D E	357E
D G G D Eb C	376F
D G G G Ab Bb	106E
D G G G F G	106D
Db A A A A Db	429H
Db Db C C B	316K
Db 7	434A
D# D# D# D# E E	209S
D# D# F E E G	44C
D# E A D E G	112B
D# E E E E E E D#	303I
D# E E E E E E G	92A
D# E F G A G	375N
D# E G C G E	415J
D# E G D# E G	84O
D# G E G G A	438E
E A Ab Ab G C	82I
E A B C B A	354N
E A C# D E F	435C
E A E D B E	351B
E A E D D E	84N
E A E E E A	417N
E A E F E E	337G
E A E F G C	132P
E A F C C D	60L
E A F G E D	301E
E A G A C D	176C
E A G C B A	55B
E A G C B E	113M
E A G C D E	238F
E A G C E D	136R
E A G D C B	396E
E A G D C# D	208N
E A G E A G	104B
E A G E C A	222A
E A G E F E	51F
E A G E G C	193G
E A G E G E	352J
E A G F D B A	136J
E A G F D B G	440L
E A G F E D	137S
E A G G C F	133E
E A G G E A	187O
E A G G G F	323H
E A G G G G	370D
E B A E D C	338O
E B C C D E	322M
E B C C E B	415G
E B C D E D	265G
E B C D G E	331E
E B C E B C E	265M
E B C E B C F	174B
E B C E D E	411I
E B C F E D	367O
E B C G E D	380O
E B D A B G	58G
E B D C B A	348K
E B D C E A	136N
E B D C F# A	97B
E C A A B D	300C
E C A A E C	236R
E C A E C A	351S
E C A F D B	65A
E C A G C D	199H
E C A G F E	86E
E C A G G F#	353O
E C A G G G	400G
E C B A G F	107R
E C B C D E	114F
E C B D D C	321J
E C C B C A	324S
E C C B D F	60D
E C C C A A	115S
E C C C C C	358P
E C C C C D	276H
E C C C D C	101R
E C C C F E	337J
E C C D E C	194C
E C C D E E	294H
E C C D E F E	199A
E C C D E F F E	345L
E C C D E F F F	130J
E C C F F E	209H
E C C G A B	397B
E C C G F D	373N
E C C# D A B	348J
E C D B A G	66Q
E C D B D C	283F
E C D C A B	224D
E C D C E G	37R
E C D E A B	290P
E C D E C B	357G
E C D E C D	440C
E C D E E D	201B
E C D E E E	388I
E C D E E F	185M
E C D E E G	339S
E C D E F E E	308D
E C D E F E F	18I
E C D E F G A	105Q
E C D E F G E	145J
E C D E F G F E E F	27B
E C D E F G F E E F	27O
E C D E F G F E E G	26B
E C D E G A	439N
E C D G A B	270O
E C D G E C	382F
E C E A G F#	143E
E C E B A A	208M
E C E B A G	415H
E C E C C A	68F
E C E C E C	383D
E C E C E D	75K
E C E C E E	173M
E C E C F Db	258F
E C E C F E	411D
E C E C G E	150L
E C E D G C	291F
E C E Eb Cb Cb	280S
E C E F E C	404R
E C E F G D	294D
E C E F G F	290I
E C E G C# C#	328D
E C E G E E	383Q
E C E G G F	335L
E C E G G G C	126E
E C E G G G F	317O
E C F D A G	422L
E C F D G E A B	115K
E C F D G E A G	203D
E C F G C E	149A
E C Fb Eb Cb Cb	280S

Notation	Ref	Notation	Ref	Notation	Ref
E C G A B C D C	328H	E D C B C C	162S	E D C E E F E	40O
E C G A B C D E	108L	E D C B C C#	374L	E D C E E F G	342I
E C G A G A	419H	E D C B C D A	260K	E D C E F F	440R
E C G A G F	351R	E D C B C D C D	210D	E D C E F G	171Q
E C G C D C	404B	E D C B C D C E	376Q	E D C E G A	75O
E C G C E G	61N	E D C B C D D	223C	E D C F D C	158R
E C G D C B	184A	E D C B C D E D	203R	E D C F D E	239R
E C G D G G	219A	E D C B C D E F	14D	E D C F E D C D	155K
E C G E A A	338R	E D C B C D E G	90G	E D C F E D C E	119P
E C G E C B	180L	E D C B C E	21A	E D C F E D D	174J
E C G E C E	360B	E D C B C G F	371B	E D C F E D E	357P
E C G E C G	233T	E D C B C G G	10Q	E D C F E D F	231J
E C G E D# E	46R	E D C B E D	57P	E D C F E D G A	35P
E C G E G C	60I	E D C B G G	137F	E D C F E D G F E A A	348Q
E C G E E E	402B	E D C C B A A	82J	E D C F E D G F E A G	166G
E C G F E A	162L	E D C C B A G	342L	E D C F E E	337D
E C G F E E	346K	E D C C B B A A F	409Q	E D C F F E A	293K
E C G F# B C	65H	E D C C B B A A G	131L	E D C F F E D#	372F
E C G G C B	16E	E D C C B B A A G#	410B	E D C F F F	335A
E C G G C E	137E	E D C C B C	427L	E D C G A G G	229F
E C G G E C C	311L	E D C C B D	130N	E D C G C D C	150S
E C G G E C G	235A	E D C C C B	341C	E D C G C D E D	144S
E C G G G E	434B	E D C C C C	67S	E D C G C D E E	62D
E C G G G G E	188L	E D C C C D	282S	E D C G D E	289H
E C G G G G G Eb	51Q	E D C C C G	53C	E D C G E D C B	365B
E C G G G G G F#	325L	E D C C D C B A	422E	E D C G E D C D	420N
E D A A B B	333A	E D C C D C B C	253E	E D C G E F	370J
E D A B A G	331K	E D C C D C D	115H	E D C G F E A	224K
E D A B C C	309C	E D C C D E D	273B	E D C G F E C B	85I
E D A B D C	293I	E D C C D E F G B	308R	E D C G F E C G	364S
E D A C B G	279B	E D C C D E F G F	325N	E D C G F E D A	365D
E D A G E E	141S	E D C C E G	307D	E D C G F E D B	157J
E D Ab Ab E D	434F	E D C C F E	153M	E D C G F E D C D	160E
E D B C G E	380E	E D C C F F	109O	E D C G F E D C E A	270P
E D B C G F	317Q	E D C C G C C	226J	E D C G F E D C E D	328M
E D B G E D	346A	E D C C G C E	408O	E D C G F# A	149C
E D Bb D E E	218N	E D C C G E	332M	E D C G G A A	370P
E D C A C E	53F	E D C C G F E E A	343Q	E D C G G A G	236K
E D C A G E D C	144L	E D C C G F E E D	33F	E D C G G A G#	401H
E D C A G E D E	115M	E D C C G G	169H	E D C G G C	46P
E D C A G F	169E	E D C D A C	67L	E D C G G E D C G B	337P
E D C A G G	136C	E D C D C A	116P	E D C G G E D C G G	357I
E D C Ab Eb Ab	259C	E D C D C B	324R	E D C G G F	345F
E D C B A A	324R	E D C D C D	170F	E D C G G G E	398G
E D C B A B C B	204F	E D C D E C	46A	E D C G G G F	398A
E D C B A B C E	120K	E D C D E E	405G	E D C G# E D	316S
E D C B A B C F	432O	E D C D E F D	246L	E D C G# G# B	434E
E D C B A C	99D	E D C D E F E	405J	E D C G# G# G#	429P
E D C B A F E D C B A	341G	E D C D E F F	107N	E D C# D E C	166K
E D C B A F E D C B G	346P	E D C D E F G A G A	79B	E D C# D E F	365O
E D C B A D	83R	E D C D E F G A G F	26D	E D D C B C D D	318H
E D C B A G A B C D D#	167L	E D C D E F G F	75M	E D D C B C D E	331I
E D C B A G A B C D E	154A	E D C D G C	28P	E D D C C B B A A G A	173I
E D C B A G A G	128R	E D C E C A	383H	E D D C C B B A A G G	398E
E D C B A G C	390G	E D C E D C C A	116K	E D D C C B C	113O
E D C B A G E	96L	E D C E D C C F	345A	E D D C C Bb	19N
E D C B A G F	55H	E D C E D C D	421F	E D D C D C B C	113O
E D C B A G G	250P	E D C E D C F	409E	E D D C D C B F	47G
E D C B B C B A	80R	E D C E D E	342B	E D D C D E	226M
E D C B B C B C	187H	E D C E E D C C	368J	E D D C E A	442A
E D C B Bb Bb	428J	E D C E E D C E	349K	E D D C E F	130A

Notation	Ref	Notation	Ref	Notation	Ref
E D D C F E	364J	E D G E E F	288S	E E C G A C	147G
E D D C G F	233E	E D G F E D C	299S	E E C G E E	278B
E D D D C C	240B	E D G F E D E	296F	E E C G G A E	410N
E D D D D D	91C	E D G G D E	68O	E E C G G A G	319S
E D D D D D F#	110P	E D# D# G E D	110E	E E C G G E C	250R
E D D E C G	344R	E D# E A D F	265K	E E C G G E E	348A
E D D E D E	331M	E D# E B A G	392N	E E C G G F	84F
E D D E F G	50I	E D# E C E F	35H	E E C G G G A	78F
E D D F E E	330R	E D# E C G F	309A	E E C G G G E	409H
E D D F F E	399P	E D# E C G F#	309S	E E C G G G F#	319S
E D D F F G	73C	E D# E C G G	98I	E E D Ab E E	208F
E D E Ab G Bb	428O	E D# E E D# E E C	94K	E E D B G G	373G
E D E C B B	267G	E D# E E D# E E F	364L	E E D C A F	349R
E D E C B D	30P	E D# E E F E	94K	E E D C A G	373B
E D E C D E E	5N	E D# E E F E A	83E	E E D C B A	431G
E D E C D E F G A	439K	E D# E F E D C	264I	E E D C C C C	385G
E D E C D E F G E	267M	E D# E F E D E	397I	E E D C C C D	328C
E D E C D E G	373R	E D# E F E E D	233B	E E D C C D E E D	396L
E D E C E G	236J	E D# E F E E E	198C	E E D C C D E E E	204L
E D E C G A	393I	E Db E F F F	260O	E E D C C E	340N
E D E C G C	380B	E D# E F G A	79F	E E D C D C A	74L
E D E C G E	423P	E D# E G D G	353F	E E D C D C B	358Q
E D E C G G	237I	E D# E G E D#	265O	E E D C D C D	185B
E D E D C A B	223I (B)	E D# E G F D#	373M	E G D C D D	187D
E D E D C A C	183N	E D# E G F F	217L	E E D C D E F	372L
E D E D C D C	121H	E D# E G F# F	277S	E E D C D E G	329D
E D E D C D E	204E	E D# E G G C	372R	E E D C E C	115C
E D E D C G	188F	E E A A A C	58L	E E D C E G	97D
E D E E D E	20A	E E A A A F	63J	E E D C F F	156Q
E D E E E D	62O	E E A A E E	310K	E E D C G A	434R
E D E F A F	203N	E E A A G E	167H	E E D C G E	234F
E D E F A G E C	270N	E E A Ab G A	83D	E E D C G G G G F E	371I
E D E F A G E D	68M	E E A C D E	356H	E E D C G G G G F F	218E
E D E F B C	171S	E E A D C# D	208B	E E D D C A	303N
E D E F B G	421K	E E A D D E	357C	E E D D C C C	110L
E D E F E C	305S	E E A D E E	63A	E E D D C C E	118D
E D E F E D D	70D	E E A E G E	213C	E E D D C C F	349G
E D E F E D E C	330Q	E E A G E C	426A	E E D D C C G C	221H
E D E F E D E F	90N	E E A G E E	235J	E E D D C C G F	332L
E D E F E D G	149P	E E A G F D	392D	E E D D C G	369I
E D E F F E	228B	E E A G G A	1J	E E D D D D	210H
E D E F G F E D A	200K	E E A G G C	31B	E E D D D E	320D
E D E F G F E D F	152N	E E A# B C C#	281B	E E D D F A	334N
E D E G A G	144O	E E B B C C#	347H	E E D E D C	142J
E D E G B A	215J	E E B B C G	103F	E E D E D E D	366I
E D E G C A	175P	E E C A A G	211I	E E D E D E E	154L
E D E G E D	260P	E E C A G E	134J	E E D E E E	166L
E D E G E E	347P	E E C B A B	385S	E E D E F B	1B
E D E G F E D	308I	E E C C E E	103H	E E D E F E D C	72R
E D E G F E F	295S	E E C C G G Bb	358J	E E D E F E D E	312L
E D F E A B	171I	E E C C G G G	392R	E E D E F G C	304H
E D F E C B	119O	E E C D C E	109P	E E D E F G D	337A
E D F E D C	154I	E E C D E E D	201B	E E D E F G E	91I
E D F E D D	243K	E E C D E E E	351D	E E D E G A	299L
E D F E D G	148L	E E C D E G E	364I	E E D E G D	101J
E D F E E D	228H	E E C E C F	432P	E E D E G E	48G
E D F G A A	349B	E E C E E C	349M	E E D E G F E D	120F
E D G A C E	218H	E E C E F G	1K	E E D E G F E E	47E
E D G A G D	135D	E E C E G D	53O	E E D F E G F	302R
E D G C B A	240L	E E C F E E	141H	E E D F E G G	33E
E D G E E D	339C	E E C F F E	111I	E E D F F E C	231D

E E D F F E G	53L	E E E D E F G	174L	E^7 F D	255R
E E D G C C	211R	E E E D F E	431B	E^7 F E D D	428P
E E D G C E	296J	E E E D F F	326L	E^7 F E D G	137O
E E D G C E	47S	E E E D G E	293C	E^7 F#	159S
E E D G F E	120F	E E E D G G F	136H	E^7 G C	50K
E E D G F F	72C	E E E D G G G	41J	E^7 G D C	78C
E E D G G E	86Q	E E E D# E F	95H	E^7 G D D	201F
E E D# E D# E	372B	E E E D# E G	278H	E^7 G E	85E
E E D# E E D	364D	E E E E A A	399G	E^7 G F	137M
E E D# E E D#	333K	E E E E A G E	357A	E E E E E F E D	433H
E E D# E G C	352N	E E E E A G F E D	397F	E E E E E F E E	400O
E E D# E G D	66L	E E E E A G F E G	191C	E E E E E F E G	436E
E E D# E G F D	397C	E E E E A G G	374E	E E E E E F F	433O
E E D# E G F E	397D	E E E E C D E E D	277K	E E E E E F G A	7Q
E E D# E G G	372I	E E E E C D E E E	103Q	E E E E E F G E A	440K
E E D# F E E	413B	E E E E D C A	403B	E E E E E F G E D	335N
E E E A A G E	167H	E E E E D C B	198S	E E E E E F G F	362M
E E E A A G G	193F	E E E E D C C	148Q	E E E E E G G	3P
E E E A E E	258G	E E E E D C E D	239J	E E E E E Eb	341A
E E E A E# D	301N	E E E E D C E E	85K	E E E E E F E	334O
E E E A F F	345D	E E E E D C G E	410O	E E E E E F F E D C	113G
E E E A G E	101K	E E E E D C G F	371G	E E E E E F F E D G	388K
E E E A G F#	337C	E E E E D D C	340P	E E E E E F F E E	363Q
E E E B B C	110K	E E E E D D D C D	303H	E E E E E F F F	104P
E E E B D C	137C	E E E E D D D C E	145C	E E E E E F G A	346F
E E E C C Ab	102K	E E E E D E F	360K	E E E E E F G Ab	88B
E E E C C G	401J	E E E E D E E G	416H	E E E E E G A	87P
E E E C D E F E C	374M	E E E E D E F D	35D	E E E E E G C E	120P
E E E C D E F E F	115P	E E E E D E F F	265C	E E E E E G C G	324F
E E E C E E	250A	E E E E D E F G	308K	E E E E E G E E C	334Q
E E E C E F	323N	E E E E D G	134S	E E E E E G E E E	426D
E E E C G E	414C	E E E E D# D	433K	E E E E E G F	139G
E E E D C B A	126N	E E E E D# E	148N	E E E E E G G A	220G
E E E D C B B	144P	E E E E E C	342H	E E E E E G G F	429B
E E E D C C B	86J	E E E E E D C B	430Q	E E E E E Eb D	433K
E E E D C C Eb	117Q	E E E E E D C D	118C	E E E E F D	258L
E E E D C C F	324O	E E E E E D C E	138N	E E E E F C#	331Q
E E E D C C G	413C	E E E E E D C G G C A	114J	E E E E F E D C	377A
E E E D C D A	4H	E E E E E D C G G C C	344P	E E E E F E D E F F	327O
E E E D C D D	32E	E E E E E D E F	397M	E E E E F E D E F G	223B
E E E D C E	2L	E E E E E D E G	211E	E E E E F E E C	331O
E E E D C F	436P	E E E E E E A	421P	E E E E F E E E	383J
E E E D C G	312B	E E E E E E B	112N	E E E E F E F	403L
E E E D D A	224S	E E E E E E C D D	134C	E E E E F F E	369J
E E E D D C A	345C	E E E E E E C D E	122K	E E E E F F F	5S
E E E D D C C	211H	E E E E E E D C C	145L	E E E E F G E	288R
E E E D D D D C B	4F	E E E E E E D C G	365Q	E E E E F G F E D	327O
E E E D D D D C C	63F	E E E E E E D D	374B	E E E E F G F E E	204R
E E E D D E C	110S	E E E E E E D#	146L	E E E E F G G	46I
E E E D D E D	63B	E E E E E A	330S	E E E E F# F#	429R
E E E D D E E	80S	E^7 D	217A	E E E E G D	306J
E E E D D F	138A	E^8 D C E	431Q	E E E E G F C#	95P
E E E D D G	138G	E^8 D C G	428S	E E E E G F E C	231B
E E E D E D D C	80J	E^9 D	50E	E E E E G F E D C	301H
E E E D E D D D	344K	E^{12} D	72H	E E E E G F E D E	355S
E E E D E E F F	333C	E^{13} G	52R	E E E E G F E E	275K
E E E D E E F G	79N	E^{10} F	344N	E E E E G F E F	243O
E E E D E F D	333G	E^9 F	439O	E E E E G F F D	116O
E E E D E F E	350N	E^8 F	436D	E E E E G F F E	320H
E E E D E F F E E A	230I	E^8 F#	405K	E E E E G G B	311B
E E E D E F F E E D	346R	E^3 G	407O		

Notation	Ref
E E E E G G C A	356P
E E E E G G C C	430S
E E E E G G D	174R
E E E E G G E	320G
E E E E G G G	318S
E E E F B C	80I
E E E F E A	395I
E E E F E D A	427C
E E E F E D C	76D
E E E F E D E E	139C
E E E F E D E F	268I
E E E F E D G	329P
E E E F E D#	39K
E E E F E E D C	261E
E E E F E E D D	313C
E E E F E E E	148M
E E E F E E G	399B
E E E F E F	402C
E E E F F D	155F
E E E F F E	148D
E E E F F F	382D
E E E F F G	5F
E E E F G A A	224N
E E E F G A B	170N
E E E F G C	98M
E E E F G E C	369E
E E E F G E E	231P
E E E F# B B	266O
E E E F# F# A	60Q
E E E G A G	1D
E E E G Ab A	112E
E E E G B A	56J
E E E G C B	124M
E E E G C C	330P
E E E G C D	218C
E E E G D E E	91P
E E E G D E F	305L
E E E G D# E	204H
E E E G E D	305P
E E E G E E E	147M
E E E G E E F	137Q
E E E G E E G	272R
E E E G E F	331G
E E E G E G	201E
E E E G F D D	400R
E E E G F D E	407E
E E E G F E C	282O
E E E G F E D	269O
E E E G F F	345M
E E E G G A	346Q
E E E G G C D	209R
E E E G G C E	175B
E E E G G D D	208C
E E E G G D E	266M
E E E G G E C	210J
E E E G G E E	314F
E E E G G F A	426C
E E E G G F F	187P
E E E G G F#	246B
E E E G G G A	293R
E E E G G G E	298S
E E E G G G F#	261G
E E E G G G G	311M
E E E G G G Gb	261G
E E E G G# A	112E
E E E G# F F	415E
E E E G# G# C	310J
E E Eb D C# D	264J
E E Eb D G F	428R
E E F A G F	160I
E E F B C E G C	326F
E E F B C E G E	426Q
E E F C# D D	365M
E E F D B A	317N
E E F D C B	331D
E E F D C D	300O
E E F D C E	98A
E E F D D E	393K
E E F E A G	228E
E E F E C D	134O
E E F E D B	127Q
E E F E D C A	48E
E E F E D C B A	128A
E E F E D C B B	308F
E E F E D C G	134I
E E F E D E C	275M
E E F E D E F	304P
E E F E D E G	377O
E E F E D G G B	256N
E E F E D G G E	86Q
E E F E E E	397Q
E E F E F E	174K
E E F E G E	353E
E E F E G F	437B
E E F E G G	433N
E E F F D G	205R
E E F F E D	435F
E E F F E E	197G
E E F F E F	6Q
E E F F F D	117R
E E F F F F E	166E
E E F F F F G	147O
E E F F F# E#	357M
E E F F G G	302B
E E F F# G D	347D
E E F F# G E	408P
E E F F# G G	363N
E E F G A A	306P
E E F G A B	396N
E E F G A F	330J
E E F G A G	76J
E E F G B D	362B
E E F G E D C B	150F
E E F G E D C D	177B
E E F G E G	356S
E E F G F E D C B	327G
E E F G F E D C E	382J
E E F G G A E	237D
E E F G G A G	45A
E E F G G B	385H
E E F G G C C B	314L
E E F G G C C E	284L
E E F G G C#	367A
E E F G G D	40J
E E F G G F E D C	38E
E E F G G F E D E	35M
E E F G G F#	49H
E E F G G G F	241E
E E F G G G G	324I
E E F# F# C C	101Q
E E F# F# E E	89I
E E G A C G	300P
E E G A F E	423M
E E G C C C Bb	130P
E E G C C C E	347B
E E G C C D	271M
E E G C D E D	5G
E E G C D E E	346J
E E G C D E F	400B
E E G C E A	334A
E E G C E D C	351K
E E G C E D D	261S
E E G D E E	147H
E E G D E F	328E
E E G E C C D	330N
E E G E C C G	413F
E E G E D C C	204G
E E G E D C E	371K
E E G E D E	311K
E E G E E A	442B
E E G E E D	372K
E E G E E E G	57J
E E G E E G G	184N
E E G F E D C	136O
E E G F E D D D	426F
E E G F E D D E	367J
E E G F E E	321P
E E G F F F#	38D
E E G G A A B	430K
E E G G A A C	30I
E E G G A B	199N
E E G G A E	104O
E E G G A G	134P
E E G G C B	322J
E E G G C C C B	53C
E E G G C C C C	65O
E E G G C C G	109F
E E G G C E	58K
E E G G D# D#	70P
E E G G D# F	434I
E E G G F E E D	35A
E E G G F E E F	252H
E E G G F F	171M
E E G G G A A	73M
E E G G G A E	112K
E E G G G A E G	409I
E E G G G B	352A
E E G G G E	174G
E E G G G F	174G
E E G G G F#	428M
E E G G G G B	394C
E E G G G G C C C D E D	332S
E E G G G G C C C D E G	7S

Notes	Ref	Notes	Ref	Notes	Ref
E Eb A B C C	65B	E F E G D E	362J	E F G A GFEDEC	326M
E Eb C A F# Eb	282A	E F E G G G	132M	E F G A G F E F	211C
E Eb D A A A	433O	E F F A G G	45R	E F G A G G A	272B
E Eb D C G G	412L	E F F C# D A	124J	E F G A G G F	104F
E F A A B G	314S	E F F E D E	78E	E F G Ab G Bb	132O
E F A D E F	336H	E F F E E D E	146S	E F G Ab G F	196F
E F A D# E A	338L	E F F E E D F	264O	E F G B A G	173H
E F A F C C	419K	E F F E E F	359P	E F G B C D	12G
E F A F# A G	39P	E F F E E	59R	E F G Bb C A	10J
E F A G E C	113I	E F F G D E	137P	E F G C A B	66S
E F A G F E D C	401Q	E F F G E E	318F	E F G C A G	122P
E F A G F E D E	90Q	E F F G G A	131S	E F G C B A G A G A	21R
E F A G F E D#	79L	E F F G G G	327E	E F G C B A G A G E	96Q
E F A G G F	398I	E F F# A G E D C C	237F	E F G C B A G C	141O
E F B B B D	329J	E F F# A G E D C E	101S	E F G C B A G D	399F
E F B C D G	34F	E F F# G A B	438C	E F G C B A G F	35C
E F B G C E	412C	E F F# G A D	188E	E F G C B A G G	157G
E F D A B C	338K	E F F# G C B	421O	E F G C B D	55E
E F D A B G C	338F	E F F# G C C	409F	E F G C C B	39D
E F D A B G E	79A	E F F# G C E	1Q	E F G C C C B	97R
E F D B C C	170H	E F F# G E C	253K	E F G C C C E	327Q
E F D C D E	273G	E F F# G F# G	233O	E F G C C F	309G
E F D D C E	63O	E F F# G G E C	230B	E F G C D B	150E
E F D D G A	300K	E F F# G G E D	234G	E F G C D E A A D	135C
E F D E C G	363B	E F G A A D	127G	E F G C D E A A E	379E
E F D E D C	233G	E F G A B A	148K	E F G C D E A B	136P
E F D G E C	246J	E F G A B C A A	126L	E F G C D E B	117K
E F E A G E C B A	310B	E F G A B C A G	333B	EFGCDEFEDCDC	67H
E F E A G E C B C	47R	E F G A B C B A B	286S	EFGCDEFEDCDE	274A
E F E A G F	321K	E F G A B C B A G D	146D	E F G C E D C B A	1E
E F E A G G	333P	E F G A B C B A G E	108I	E F G C E D C B C	237T
E F E C E F	402L	E F G A B C C B	256K	E F G C E D F	222E
E F E D A G	332Q	E F G A B C C C	93K	E F G C E F G A	21E
E F E D B G	205K	E F G A B C D E B	39O	E F G C E F G C	273S
E F E D C A	382L	E F G A B C D E D	345R	E F G C E F G G#	38Q
E F E D C B C B	214H	E F G A B C D E E	146P	E F G C F E	420F
E F E D C B C D	10M	E F G A B C G D F	408H	E F G C G A	68J
E F E D C B D	352O	E F G A B C G E	365I	E F G D D C B	221Q
E F E D C C	14K	E F G A B C G G	356B	E F G D D C D	285O
E F E D C D B	313K	E F G A B D	381O	E F G D D D	176A
E F E D C D C	244F	E F G A B F	41R	E F G D E C A	161G
E F E D C D F	439M	E F G A Bb A	27C	E F G D E C C	276F
E F E D C E	355I	E F G A C B	148E	E F G D E F	306R
E F E D C F	151J	E F G A D G	7D	E F G D# D# E	387H
E F E D C G	441Q	E F G A E G A	6B	E F G E A B	199S
E F E D D C	312O	E F G A E G F	138M	E F G E A F	251R
E F E D D G	295Q	E F G A F D D	380P	E F G E A G E	312E
E F E D E C G A	24B	E F G A F D E	421M	E F G E A G F	343B
E F E D E C G C	411B	E F G A F E	30L	E F G E C A	422H
E F E D E C G E	423L	E F G A F G	24D	E F G E C B B	317G
E F E D E G F E D C#	308I	E F G A F# G	393C	E F G E C B C	270S
E F E D E G F E D D	38L	E F G A G A	152J	E F G E C C A	13O
E F E D G G	79J	E F G A G B	144A	E F G E C C D E C	92J
E F E E D C	210P	E F G A G C A	105H	E F G E C C D E F	249F
E F E E D D	414S	E F G A G C C	27H	E F G E C D	170J
E F E F C# E	391N	E F G A G C E	359K	E F G E C E	8B
E F E F D E	395A	E F G A G E	294C	E F G E C F D	247C
E F E F E F	344D	E F G A G F C	280B	E F G E C F G	118E
E F E F G C	260D	E F G A GFEDCB	152F	E F G E C G	325G
E F E G C A	126M	E F G A GFEDCD	276A	E F G E D C A	260M
E F E G D D	314J	E F G A GFEDEA	92A	E F G E D C B C A B	156N

E F G E D C B C A E	119S	E F G G F E E	183R	E G C B A G D	112M
E F G E D C C	229N	E F G G G A A	263H	E G C B A G E	54C
E F G E D C D	285C	E F G G G A F	253C	E G C B C D	254S
E F G E D C G	16R	E F G G G A G	440A	E G C B D C	364H
E F G E D D	98H	E F G G G B	176I	E G C B F F	363J
E F G E D E	180N	E F G G G C C	131O	E G C B G C	172R
E F G E D# E	221K	E F G G G C D	272A	E G C B G F	103I
E F G E E D	104M	E F G G G E D C C	146K	E G C C A A	129K
E F G E E E E	32C	E F G G G E D C D	146K	E G C C A G	128L
E F G E E E F	288I	E F G G G E D C G	367B	E G C C B A	199K
E F G E E F	94O	E F G G G F#	115I	E G C C C A	102F
E F G E F E	337O	E F G G G G C	94B	E G C C C C	191R
E F G E F F	38G	E F G G G G E	190R	E G C C D D	412Q
E F G E F G A	155R	E F G G G G F	209I	E G C C D D#	233S
E F G E F G E F G A	115R	E F G G G G G C	249Q	E G C C D E	198O
E F G E F G E F G D	147B	E F G G G G G E	317E	E G C C G A	127P
E F G E F G E F G E	250C	E F G G G G G F	371M	E G C D E C	347C
E F G E F G F E	121G	E F# F# F# E E	88C	E G C D E D	8R
E F G E F G F G	63R	E F# F# G D D	421J	E G C D E F A	355C
E F G E F G G	318E	E F# G A F# G	300A	E G C D E F F	399M
E F G E G A	356N	E F# G A G A	417R	E G C D E F G	107O
E F G E G F	151I	E F# G A G F	428H	E G C D E G C	376P
E F G F A G	354G	E F# G B A F#	44H	E G C D E G F E C	102Q
E F G F E A	294B	E F# G C E G	135B	E G C D E G F E D	429K
E F G F E D C B	151E	E F# G F E	432F	E G C D F G	108N
E F G F E D C C	254L	E G A A A A	422P	E G C E A G	207R
E F G F E D C D	51E	E G A A C E	423K	E G C E D B	181D
E F G F E D C F	350H	E G A A E D	434N	E G C E D C	155O
E F G F E D C G	13M	E G A A E G	425G	E G C E E A	221S
E F G F E D E C	94G	E G A A G E	203J	E G C E F G	74J
E F G F E D E D	82O	E G A B A A	148I	E G C E G A B	96O
E F G F E D G	158E	E G A B C D C B	379B	E G C E G A G	29S
E F G F E E	141D	E G A B C D C E	438H	E G C E G B	391R
E F G F E F E	223O	E G A B C E	362D	E G C F E C	49R
E F G F E F G	351Q	E G A B G C	76Q	E G C F E D C	61F
E F G F E G	74R	E G A B G E	144K	E G C F E D E	257K
E F G F# G C	38O	E G A B C A	101O	E G C F E G	206S
E F G G A B C	10I	E G A B C C	269B	E G C G A F	285J
E F G G A C	227I	E G A C B A	379C	E G C G A G A B	289N
E F G G A F E	297K	E G A C B E	380I	E G C G A G A Bb	289N
E F G G A F G	142I	E G A C B F	148A	E G C G E C	246I
E F G G A G C	311G	E G A C D E	68B	E G C G F F	198A
E F G G A G F	98P	E G A D E F	283S	E G C G F G	285M
E F G G A G G	95M	E G A G A A	239F	E G C G G C	286R
E F G G Ab G	196F	E G A G C C B B	325I	E G D A E B	439E
E F G G B C D E	378L	E G A G C C B C	12N	E G D C A C	376M
E F G G B C D F	223Q	E G A G E D	439B	E G D C D E	203J
E F G G B C E	327I	E G A G E G	113Q	E G D C E B	314R
E F G G B C F	296P	E G A G F A B	296N	E G D C F E	98Q
E F G G C A	350B	E G A G F A G	422D	E G D D D D	353S
E F G G C B	343C	E G A G F E	438G	E G D D D E	301Q
E F G G C D	68S	E G A G F G	76M	E G D D D G	106P
E F G G C G	221P	E G A G F# A	91H	E G D E C G	287C
E F G G E A	199S	E G B A E G	295F	E G D E F A	93N
E F G G E F G E F G C	214R	E G B B G B	186C	E G D E F E E	324M
E F G G E F G E F G E	180S	E G B C D E	394B	E G D E F E F	366O
E F G G F D	122S	E G B C G C	381J	E G D E G D	345N
E F G G F E D C	37E	E G B D C E	61O	E G D E G G#	306H
E F G G F E D D E F G E	18A	E G C A C B	278J	E G D F A C	278E
E F G G F E D D E F G F	27Q	E G C B A C	362E	E G D G C A	57A
E F G G F E D E	324K	E G C B A G A	119H	E G D G C C	205H

Notation	Ref	Notation	Ref	Notation	Ref
E G D G C D	174N	E G F E E F	95Q	Eb C D Eb F G Eb	182J
E G D# G E G	173F	E G F E F E	213O	Eb C D G Ab F	224H
E G E A E G	354B	E G F E F G C	171O	Eb C Eb B Eb Eb	257P
E G E C B C	324C	E G F E F G E	250B	Eb C Eb B Eb Eb	259R
E G E C D C	382K	E G F E G F	95Q	Eb C Eb C Db Eb	294G
E G E C D E	229J	E G F F D# E	92B	Eb C Eb C Eb C	281S
E G E C E G	300S	E G F F E D	112F	Eb C Eb Cb Eb Eb	259R
E G E C G A	164P	E G F# E B A	399K	Eb C Eb D B Eb	359H
E G E C G C	326N	E G F# F D E	277Q	Eb C Eb D Bb G	69M
E G E C G G	422Q	E G F# G A F#	55M	Eb C Eb Eb Eb D	421R
E G E D A C	337E	E G G A A C C B	88M	Eb C Eb Eb Eb Eb	395R
E G E D C C D C	227C	E G G A A C C C	387K	Eb C Eb F Eb Ab	357C
E G E D C C D D	78O	E G G A B C	206E	Eb C Eb G G B	258I
E G E D C D E	288F	E G G A G G G C	181E	Eb C F Eb D D	22D
E G E D C D G F C	136L	E G G A G G G G	41M	Eb C G Ab G F	25L
E G E D C D G F E	141E	E G G Ab G G	43F	Eb C G C Eb D	415D
E G E D C E	59H	E G G C B C	229A	Eb C G F E F	211K
E G E D D E	89G	E G G C C E	322O	Eb C G F Eb D	383B
E G E D E F	290R	E G G C E G	358D	Eb C G F G F	258D
E G E D E G	244A	E G G C G C	291R	Eb C G G D Eb	212C
E G E D F A	331P	E G G C G G	153I	Eb D Ab Ab G C	429C
E G E E D C	375E	E G G E A A	205P	Eb D Ab G F G	411H
E G E E D D	304N	E G G E C C	177K	Eb D B Ab G G	144R
E G E E D E	230M	E G G E C F	191S	Eb D C Ab G F	262M
E G E E E G	334A	E G G E D C	102H	Eb D C Ab G G	338H
E G E E F A	81S	E G G E D C	102C	Eb D C B C Ab	150R
E G E E F D	294L	E G G E F D	86G	Eb D C B C C	195I
E G E E G E	198D	E G G E G G	131D	Eb D C B C D B	234S
E G E Eb G Eb	208A	E G G Eb Eb Eb	438N	Eb D C B C D C	339L
E G E F E D	100M	E G G F F E	270A	Eb D C B C Eb	385O
E G E F G B	132H	E G G G G Ab	387J	Eb D C B C F	11I
E G E F G E	427N	E G G G G C E	78A	Eb D C B C G Ab Ab	84K
E G E G E D C	167G	E G G G G C G	3K	Eb D C B C G Ab G	155M
E G E G E D G	237A	E G G G G D	322G	Eb D C B C G G	149E
E G E G E D#	103O	E G G G G G	261B	Eb D C B D C B	73H
E G E G E F C#	367K	E G G G G# G#	310P	Eb D C B D C Bb	57E
E G E G E F G	183K	E G# G# A Bb B	430L	Eb D C B D G	433M
E G E G E G E D	374K	Eb Ab Ab F G Eb	297H	Eb D C Bb A Ab	414J
E G E G E G E G	216Q	Eb Ab Ab G Eb Eb	256E	Eb D C Bb Ab C G Eb	215H
E G E G F D	45D	Eb Ab Eb D D D	191E	Eb D C Bb Ab C G G	293H
E G E G F E D	328B	Eb Ab F# G F B	339O	Eb D C Bb Ab F#	299Q
E G E G F E F	401L	Eb B B C C G	428E	Eb D C Bb Ab G	377C
E G E G F F	264H	Eb B B C D G	140R	Eb D C Bb C Ab	102M
E G E G G G	285D	Eb B B D C D	127J	Eb D C Bb Eb F	305D
E G F A G F	42H	Eb B C C C# D	240D	Eb D C Bb G F	176N
E G F C B D	61L	Eb B C G G G	74O	Eb D C C B C	193H
E G F D C A	57M	Eb B D C C F	386D	Eb D C C Bb C	391S
E G F D C G	344Q	Eb B D G D F	87E	Eb D C C C G	266N
E G F D D C	244Q	Eb B Eb G Eb B	413R	Eb D C C D B	290K
E G F D E C	439G	Eb C B C C D	130D	Eb D C C Eb D	118O
E G F D F A	352L	Eb C B C C D	8Q	Eb D C C Eb Eb	329Q
E G F D F E	348D	Eb C Bb C Eb D	267A	E D C C# D D	326C
E G F E A G	406R	Eb C C C C C	86F	Eb D C D B D	288D
E G F E D C B	59C	Eb C C C C G	298L	Eb D C D C D	121C
E G F E D C D	405B	Eb C C D Eb F	277P	Eb D C D D D	297B
E G F E D C F	345E	Eb C C Eb Eb Eb	161B	Eb D C D D Eb	181P
E G F E D E C	128D	Eb C D B D C	289C	Eb D C D Eb Bb	58O
E G F E D E F	211F	Eb C D Bb Eb C	195N	Eb D C D G C D	326B
E G F E D F A A	245K	Eb C D Eb Eb D	5B	Eb D C D G C Eb	323J
E G F E D F A G	374H	Eb C D Eb Eb F	344O	Eb D C D G G	292H
E G F E E D	244R	Eb C D Eb F G C	37K	Eb D C Eb Ab G	5Q

Notation	Page
E♭ D C E♭ C C	258R
E♭ D C E♭ D C C	178H
E♭ D C E♭ D C E♭	379I
E♭ D C E♭ D G A	3G
E♭ D C E♭ D G A♭	3G
E♭ D C E♭ D G F	23R
E♭ D C E♭ F G A♭	272F
E♭ D C E♭ F G G E♭	69S
E♭ D C E♭ F G G G	100Q
E♭ D C E♭ G D	436O
E♭ D C E♭ G G F	424G
E♭ D C E♭ G G G	353Q
E♭ D C F C D	337H
E♭ D C F D B	157E
E♭ D C F E♭ D G A♭ C	155P
E♭ D C F E♭ D G A♭ G	328J
E♭ D C G A♭ C	95L
E♭ D C G C D	153J
E♭ D C G E♭ D	319A
E♭ D C G F E♭	99C
E♭ D C G G A♭ G A♭	234I
E♭ D C G G A♭ G F	125E
E♭ D C G G G A♭	437H
E♭ D C G G G C	400N
E♭ D C G G G F	157N
E♭ D C♭ A♭ G G	144R
E♭ D D B♭ D C	279O
E♭ D D C B D	400L
E♭ D D C C B♭	299A
E♭ D D C E♭ D C	420Q
E♭ D D C E♭ D G	126R
E♭ D D D A B	240F
E♭ D D E♭ D E♭	275L
E♭ D D♭ A♭ B♭ A♭	415C
E♭ D E♭ C B A	271D
E♭ D E♭ C C C	336O
E♭ D E♭ C D C	232P
E♭ D E♭ C D E♭	295M
E♭ D E♭ D C C B♭ A♭	63N
E♭ D E♭ D C C B♭ B♭	424B
E♭ D E♭ D C D	176F
E♭ D E♭ D C♯ D	399I
E♭ D E♭ D E♭ F	239K
E♭ D E♭ E♭ E♭ C	201Q
E♭ D E♭ F E♭ D	188S
E♭ D G B D C	391I
E♭ D G C B A	215K
E♭ D G D E♭ E♭	212F
E♭ E E E E E	303I
E♭ E F A♭ G F	43I
E♭ E♭ B B G G	142P
E♭ E♭ D B C E♭ E♭	80E
E♭ E♭ C C E♭ C	314C
E♭ E♭ D A D♭ A♭	348F
E♭ E♭ D B C E♭ G	83H
E♭ E♭ D C A D♭	77L
E♭ E♭ D C C B	59O
E♭ E♭ D C C C	417K
E♭ E♭ D C D D	79M
E♭ E♭ D C E♭ C	377P
E♭ E♭ D C F♯ G	349F
E♭ E♭ D C G G	327M
E♭ E♭ D D C B	416N
E♭ E♭ D D C C	223G
E♭ E♭ D D E♭ E♭	60B
E♭ E♭ D D♭ D♭ D♭	431N
E♭ E♭ D E♭ C B	229P
E♭ E♭ D E♭ F F	335M
E♭ E♭ D F E♭ G	55P
E♭ E♭ D F F D	14Q
E♭ E♭ D G E♭ E♭	197I
E♭ E♭ D G G F	187G
E♭ E♭ E♭ A B♭ A	333Q
E♭ E♭ E♭ B♭ A♭ B	356C
E♭ E♭ E♭ C E♭ E♭	406N
E♭ E♭ E♭ C F G	256H
E♭ E♭ E♭ D C C	24O
E♭ E♭ E♭ D C D	347M
E♭ E♭ E♭ D C G G A♭	138S
E♭ E♭ E♭ D C G G G	278I
E♭ E♭ E♭ D D C B♭	280H
E♭ E♭ E♭ D D C C	335D
E♭ E♭ E♭ D D D	131G
E♭ E♭ E♭ D D F	336F
E♭ E♭ E♭ D D G	138H
E♭ E♭ E♭ D E♭ D C C B	430P
E♭ E♭ E♭ D E♭ D C C C	200C
E♭ E♭ E♭ D E♭ E♭ E♭	124C
E♭ E♭ E♭ D E♭ E♭ F	103C
E♭ E♭ E♭ D E♭ F D	55K
E♭ E♭ E♭ D E♭ F G	281N
E♭ E♭ E♭ D G F	394R
E♭ E♭ E♭ E E F	340I
E♭ E♭ E♭ E♭ C C	71A
E♭ E♭ E♭ E♭ C E♭	180C
E♭ E♭ E♭ E♭ D B	437I
E♭ E♭ E♭ E♭ D C B	342P
E♭ E♭ E♭ E♭ D C G	437L
E♭ E♭ E♭ E♭ D E♭	414P
E♭ E♭ E♭ E♭ E♭ D D D C	128G
E♭ E♭ E♭ E♭ E♭ D D D D	432N
E♭ E♭ E♭ E♭ E♭ D D D F	181O
E♭ E♭ E♭ E♭ E♭ D D D G	413E
E♭ E♭ E♭ E♭ E♭ D♭	431P
E♭ E♭ E♭ E♭ E♭ E♭ C	138O
E♭ E♭ E♭ E♭ E♭ E♭ D	136Q
E♭ E♭ E♭ E♭ E♭ E♭ D♭	236L
E♭⁻ E	238N
E♭ 14	383E
E♭ˣ F	433Q
E♭ˣ G	175E
E♭ E♭ E♭ E♭ E♭ F E♭	423C
E♭ E♭ E♭ E♭ E♭ F E♭	423D
E♭ E♭ E♭ E♭ E♭ F G	433J
E♭ E♭ E♭ E♭ E♭ F♯	48K
E♭ E♭ E♭ E♭ E♭ F G	138Q
E♭ E♭ E♭ F A♭ A♭	78B
E♭ E♭ E♭ F C D	414I
E♭ E♭ E♭ F E♭ D D	305I
E♭ E♭ E♭ F E♭ D E♭	285S
E♭ E♭ E♭ F F F	140L
E♭ E♭ E♭ F F G	85B
E♭ E♭ F D C B♭	57I
E♭ E♭ F D D G	212G
E♭ E♭ F F A♭ E♭	298C
E♭ E♭ F F G G	194Q
E♭ E♭ F F♯ G G	133B
E♭ E♭ F G A♭ D	135G
E♭ E♭ F G E♭ E♭	295K
E♯ E♯ F G F B♭	264A
E♭ E♭ F G F E♭	51A
E♭ E♭ F G G F	121R
E♭ E♭ G A♭ G A♭	359S
E♭ E♭ G G C B	127K
E♭ E♭ G G C C	238E
E♭ E♭ G G E♭ C	207L
E♭ E♭ G G G F♯	435R
E♭ F A♭ G A C	54I
E♭ F A♭ G E♭ D	58N
E♭ F D B♭ C D	139J
E♭ F D E♭ C D	53C
E♭ F D E♭ C G	311Q
E♭ F D G A♭ E♭	238G
E♭ F E♭ D C B	131E
E♭ F E♭ D C G B	17G
E♭ F E♭ D C G G	287O
E♭ F F A♭ F G	338P
E♭ F F E♭ F F	361E
E♭ F G A♭ G F	383K
E♭ F G A♭ G F♯	335R
E♭ F G A♭ G G F	215F
E♭ F G A♭ G G G	320P
E♭ F G B B C	315I
E♭ F G B D C	339A
E♭ F G C C B♭	150P
E♭ F G C C D	182G
E♭ F G D E♭ D	108R
E♭ F G E♭ D C	22A
E♭ F G E♭ D D	402N
E♭ F G F E♭ D C B B♭	28H
E♭ F G F E♭ D C B C	22A
E♭ F G F E♭ D C D	20K
E♭ F G F E♭ D E♭	85C
E♭ F G F E♭ F	136D
E♭ F G F G B♭	323C
E♭ F G F G C	175O
E♭ F G F♯ G A♭	436S
E♭ F G G A♭ B♭	421I
E♭ F G G A♭ F	230H
E♭ F G G C C	70J
E♭ F G G E♭ D	292O
E♭ F G G G B♭	100E
E♭ F G G G E♭	118K
E♭ F G G G G B♭	327S
E♭ G G G G E♭	31O
E♭ F G G G G G C B♭	348G
E♭ F G G G G G C E♭	156A
E♭ F G♭ F F F	192H
E♭ F♯ F♯ G E♭ G	143R
E♭ F♯ G C B D	408J
E♭ F♯ G F♯ E♭ A	178D
E♭ G A♭ A♭ A♭ G	201P
E♭ G C B C E♭	315N

Notation	Ref.
Eb G C Bb Ab G	228L
Eb G C Bb C D	192P
Eb G C C Eb G	209M
Eb G C Eb G G	176G
Eb G D D G D	291J
Eb G D F Ab G	281F
Eb G Eb D Eb C	380D
Eb G Eb G Eb D	230A
Eb G F Eb F Ab	406C
Eb G G C C F	240E
Eb G G G A A	6D
Eb G G G G G Eb	256R
Eb G G G G G G	263D
F A B B A F	285G
F A D D D F	339D
F A F D F A	61C
F A G F E E	91M
F Ab Ab D Ab Ab	51G
F Ab Ab F F Eb	208G
F Ab Bb C D E	88H
F Ab C B G Eb	127B
F Ab G Eb C Bb	68N
F Ab G Eb D F	434S
F Bb G A D G	324L
F C C Bb Ab Bb	294J
F C C Bb F Bb	194S
F C D D A Bb	407F
F C D Eb D C	294F
F C G F# C# G#	175Q
F C# C# D E F	411A
F D A C D A	415K
F D B C E G	380F
F D C B B D	414E
F D C E D E	33G
F D C Eb F D	441M
F D D D F E	410J
F D D F Bb Bb	414R
F D F D F G	30O
F E A B A E	300M
F E A C D E	287G
F E C E F F	88N
F E C G G E	101P
F E D A D E	278M
F E D C B C	119D
F E D C E G	184P
F E D C G A	20H
F E D C G C	271S
F E D C G F	424E
F E D C# D D	410P
F E D D F E	342J
F E D E C C	68Q
F E D E D D	5A
F E D E F B	136M
F E D E F G A	223K
F E D E F G G	253R
F E D G C C	423A
F E D# E E D	278G
F E E D C B	87N
F E E D D C	225E
F E F D C C	63H
F E F G A G	267N
F E G C G E	293G
F Eb D C B D	180A
F Eb D C D Eb	195E
F Eb D D C Ab	433R
F Eb Db D C# C	433L
F Eb Db D Db C	433L
F Eb F Ab F Eb	88A
F Eb F Eb D C	195M
F Eb F G F F	270D
F Eb G F Eb F	213Q
F Eb Gb F F F	186N
F F Bb Bb C D	195C
F F C Ab Eb C	438Q
F F E C C C	396M
F F E D D C	263F
F F E E D D D C	197H
F F E E D D D D	269S
F F E E D D D E	197H
F F E E Eb Eb	280J
F F E G F E	337S
F F Eb D Eb F	59P
F F Eb D G C	105B
F F Eb Eb Eb D	80M
F F F Ab Ab Ab	104R
F F F Ab G G	415M
F F F C F G	99K
F F F D D	436I
F F F E D E	331F
F F F E E	286F
F F F F E D	258K
F F F F E D	76R
F F F F Eb F	80G
F F F F F A	310H
F F F F F Ab	358G
F F F F F Eb	430B
F F F F F F B	410S
F F F F F F F Eb	434A
F F F F F F F F	76O
F F F F G Eb	175F
F F F F# F F	316Q
F F F G Ab Bb	302K
F F G A A F	89O
F F G F Eb F	341S
F F G G F F F Ab	289N
F F G G F F F G	110O
F G Ab G Ab Bb	179P
F G Ab G Eb Eb	378C
F G Ab G F G	404S
F G Ab G G G	425K
F G Bb Bb Bb C	220M
F G C C C Bb	167R
F G C C F G A	185F
F G Eb F D D	201S
F G F D E E	241K
F G F E D C	337Q
F G F Eb F G	31Q
F G F G Ab Bb	106R
F G G F D G	390B
F G G G F E	252D
F G G G F F	196N
F G G G G G#	99Q
F Gb F F F Gb	186N
F# A G B D C D E	401S
F# A G B D C D F	403H
F# Bb A G F# Eb	432M
F# Eb D B F E	139O
F# Eb F# Eb D D	297P
F# F# F# G E E	149D
F# F# F# G G C	295N
F# F# F# G G G	224R
F# F# G B F# F#	192E
F# G A Ab Ab	100H
F# G A E A E	92C
F# G A F D E	329S
F# G A G A G	363H
F# G A G F# G	363S
F# G A G G G	328Q
F# G Ab Ab G G	432I
F# G B C D Eb	305B
F# G C B F# B	42B
F# G C Cb Gb Cb	42B
F# G D D C B	286P
Fb G D F Ab F	13P
F# G D# E C B	351J
F# G E F# G D	76F
F# G Eb D C F#	425I
Fb G F# Eb C G	123Q
F# G F# G Bb A	123P
F# G F# G Eb C	63C
F# G F# G G Ab	38R
F# G G# A D A	352D
G A A A A B	225A
G A A A C C	90A
G A A A G G	34M
G A A B B C A	100N
G A A B B C C	51L
G A A B C G	126F
G A A Bb Bb A	22Q
G A A C C B	64B
G A A C C D	370C
G A A C C Eb	417O
G A A D D D	297R
G A A E D E	219R
G A A E F D	276R
G A A E G G	353R
G A A G A D	273L
G A A G B B	300B
G A A G E C	84R
G A A G E G	144J
G A A G F D	326G
G A A G F E E D	393Q
G A A G F E E E	242R
G A A G F E F	269D
G A A G G A A G G A A B	373F
G A A G G A A G G A A D	87I
G A A G G A B	424N
G A A G G C	58I
G A A G G E	425M
G A B A B C B	83B
G A B A B C D	268D
G A B A C B	205J
G A B A G A B A	92Q

Notes	Code	Notes	Code	Notes	Code
G A B A G A B G	4B	G A B C D C E D	225J	G A Bb C Bb A	106B
G A B A G A G	67R	G A B C D C Eb	202F	G A Bb C C C	299H
G A B A G D	203H	G A B C D E B	379H	G A Bb C D Bb	287J
G A B A G E D	82L	G A B C D E C	384H	G A Bb C D Eb	39Q
G A B A G E E	219Q	G A B C D E D C B	286I	G A Bb C G F	167O
G A B A G F	352C	G A B C D E D C C	328P	G A Bb G Bb A	220R
G A B A G G	226B	G A B C D E E D	332R	G A Bb G G A	139I
G A B B A G	427G	G A B C D E E E D C	412A	G A C A B A	2D
G A B B B D	298A	G A B C D E E E D G	440O	G A C A B G	237N
G A B B C C	83F	G A B C D E F D	358L	G A C A C A	362I
G A B B C G A	147F	G A B C D E F E C	20I	G A C A D C	191B
G A B B C G C	340F	G A B C D E F E D C#	378J	G A C A D G	419I
G A B B C G G	76S	G A B C D E F E D E	10F	G A C A G C	186A
G A B C A C	284A	G A B C D E F G D	377L	G A C A G E	103P
G A B C A D	219O	G A B C D E F G E A	283O	G A C B A B	190B
G A B C A G	114O	G A B C D E F G E G	439J	G A C B A G	376I
G A B C B A F	351O	G A B C D E G	222K	G A C B B C	269H
G A B C B A G A B C D	412D	G A B C D Eb C C	220H	G A C B C E	312M
G A B C B A G A B C E	224P	G A B C D Eb C D	17J	G A C B D C	420L
G A B C B A G A B C#	376O	G A B C D Eb D	416I	G A C B G A C	350Q
G A B C B A G A G	314H	G A B C D Eb Eb D C	216N	G A C B G A E	406H
G A B C B A G B	99H	G A B C D Eb Eb D Eb	429G	G A C B G B	352S
G A B C B A G E	16A	G A B C D Eb Eb Eb	391D	G A C B G E	293Q
G A B C B A G F	12H	G A B C D Eb F	313I	G A C C B F	50N
G A B C B A G#	214I	G A B C D G G A	391B	G A C C C B	293N
G A B C B C B	246Q	G A B C D G G F	121S	G A C C C C C	365F
G A B C B C D C	420I	G A B C E B	224E	G A C C C C D	268M
G A B C B C D D	182H	G A B C E C	339N	G A C C C D C A	67B
G A B C B C D E D	75F	G A B C E D B	17I	G A C C C D C B	66H
G A B C B C D E F	93F	G A B C E D C	278P	G A C C E F	147S
G A B C B D	395G	G A B C E D E	184M	G A C D C D	30J
G A B C C B A	109M	G A B C E E	394O	G A C D E G A	405Q
G A B C C B B	267D	G A B C E F F# G F#	94E	G A C D E G Ab	105K
G A B C C B D	307J	G A B C E F F# G G	93S	G A C D E G C	220K
G A B C C C B	113P	G A B C E G D	277M	G A C D E G E	178G
G A B C C C C C B A	246D	G A B C E G F	331S	G A C D F E	88K
G A B C C C C C B C	161R	G A B C F B	173P	G A C D G A	73F
G A B C C C C G	363K	G A B C G A A	40L	G A C E A G	121J
G A B C C C C F	37A	G A B C G A C	44J	G A C E B C#	206G
G A B C C C E	184Q	G A B C G A G G F	335I	G A C E C G	376N
G A B C C D D C	159D	G A B C G A G G F#	315C	G A C E E E	370L
G A B C C D D E	226K	G A B C G D B	435P	G A C E E G	181N
G A B C C D E F A	425B	G A B C G D D	42N	G A C E F F	214G
G A B C C D E F G	276P	G A B C G E C A	34P	G A C E G A	377Q
G A B C C D F	123F	G A B C G E C D	38C	G A C E G E	200H
G A B C C E	410E	G A B C G E D	420J	G A C E G G	261D
G A B C C F	9J	G A B C G F E	374N	G A C F B B	217N
G A B C C G	267J	G A B C G F F	225F	G A C G F G	415Q
G A B C C# E	223D	G A B C G G A B C G E	329R	G A D E F G E	69D
G A B C D B C D	158K	G A B C G G A B C G G	135R	G A D E F G G	66J
G A B C D B C E D C	146O	G A B D C B A	423O	G A D G Db Ab	299B
G A B C D B C E D E	187K	G A B D C B D	133H	G A E C G A	197E
G A B C D B F	379G	G A B D C E	147R	G A E F G A	374G
G A B C D B G	54B	G A B D C G	60A	G A E F G G	77P
G A B C D C A	438K	G A B F F F	30C	G A E F# G E	151G
G A B C D C B A E	224G	G A B G A B	362P	G A E G G A E	188D
G A B C D C B A G	286H	G A B G C G	246A	G A E G G A G	410G
G A B C D C B C	308A	G A B G D C	24E	G A E G G C	176B
G A B C D C C	133F	G A Bb A G A	268J	G A F D C C	212N
G A B C D C D	72P	G A Bb A G G	297I	G A F D C D	245B
G A B C D C E B	198E			G A F D G F	352R

G A F E D C	141N	
G A F F E F	7J	
G A F G A A	34D	
G A F G A G	48R	
G A F# G E D	97C	
G A G A B A G A	204M	
G A G A B A G E	204J	
G A G A B C C#	344J	
G A G A B C D	161Q	
G A G A C A	15J	
G A G A G A B	408L	
G A G A G A G	194J	
G A G A G C	399C	
G A G A G D	67K	
G A G A G E	203E	
G A G A G F E	37C	
G A G A G F F	389J	
G A G A G G	63M	
G A G B D C	385A	
G A G C B A G A E	295A	
G A G C B A G A G	141M	
G A G C B B	98F	
G A G C C C	214Q	
G A G C C C#	355F	
G A G C D C	167E	
G A G C D E A B	347G	
G A G C D E A G	201G	
G A G C E	64I	
G A G C E D C A	363C	
G A G C E D C C	404D	
G A G C E D#	206A	
G A G C E F	416K	
G A G C F F	247E	
G A G C G A	229L	
G A G C G F	121K	
G A G D C A	405E	
G A G E B C	128I	
G A G E C E	389P	
G A G E D C C	115O	
G A G E D C E	204D	
G A G E D G	352G	
G A G E D E	299K	
G A G E E D	341E	
G A G E E E C	406M	
G A G E E E D	46N	
G A G E F G C	46Q	
G A G E F G F	103A	
G A G E G A F	206O	
G A G E G A G	145J	
G A G E G C	216A	
G A G E G F	167B	
G A G F E D C B A B	214A	
G A G F E D C B A G	432J	
G A G F E D C B D	286B	
G A G F E D C D	182R	
G A G F E D C E D	224C	
G A G F E D C E F	329H	
G A G F E D C E G	140B	
G A G F E D D E C	168B	
G A G F E D D E D	138I	
G A G F E E D D	199B	
G A G F E E D E	147C	
G A G F E E E	182P	
G A G F E F D	41C	
G A G F E F E	423H	
G A G F E F G D E F	383F	
G A G F E F G D E F#	24H	
G A G F E F G G A	73O	
G A G F E F G G A	142M	
G A G F F B	392I	
G A G F G	109B	
G A G F G A	262K	
G A G F G E	112J	
G A G F G F	91B	
G A G F G G E	427R	
G A G F G G	267S	
G A G F# A G A	313R	
G A G F# A G E	373K	
G A G F# D E	122B	
G A G F# D F	378B	
G A G F# F E	435M	
G A G F# G A	133D	
G A G F# G C	369R	
G A G F# G D	308M	
G A G Fb G E E E	366C	
G A G F# G E E F	428N	
G A G F# G E G	39C	
G A G G A G	398K	
G A G G B B	358S	
G A G G B C	158A	
G A G G B Cb	358S	
G A G G C C D E D	343H	
G A G G C C D E F	94J	
G A G G C D	230D	
G A G G D F	222R	
G A G G E E	373L	
G A G G F E D C	273E	
G A G G F E D D	150I	
G A G G F F	59F	
G A G G F# A	227O	
G Ab A G F# E	424P	
G Ab Ab Ab Ab Ab	138J	
G Ab Ab Ab A D	436K	
G Ab Ab Ab G F F	75I	
G Ab Ab Ab G F G	154B	
G Ab Ab Ab G G	333D	
G Ab Ab Bb Ab Bb	88Q	
G Ab Ab Bb Ab G	305K	
G Ab Ab E F C	124J	
G Ab Ab F F F#	280P	
G Ab Ab G C C	23N	
G Ab Ab G Eb D	157Q	
G Ab Ab G F# F	435R	
G Ab Ab G G Ab	359P	
G Ab Ab G G C	18N	
G Ab B C D Eb	127H	
G Ab B C D F	13Q	
G Ab B C F Eb	106S	
G Ab B C F# Eb	9G	
G Ab B C G F	24Q	
G Ab B F D G	14F	
G Ab Bb Ab G Ab	375P	
G Ab Bb Ab G B	9E	
G Ab Bb Ab G F D	15Q	
G Ab Bb Ab G F Eb	54R	
G Ab Bb C Ab D	342F	
G Ab Bb C Bb Ab G Ab	192D	
G Ab Bb C Bb Ab G F	387E	
G Ab Bb C D Ab	41R	
G Ab Bb C D G	378H	
G Ab C B B Bb	431M	
G Ab C B C Bb	154G	
G Ab C C B Ab	14S	
G Ab C Cb Cb Bb	431M	
G Ab C F# G C	338L	
G Ab C G G C	282G	
G Ab C G G F	377B	
G Ab D Bb Eb G	412C	
G Ab D D Eb F	210F	
G Ab D Eb F G	86C	
G Ab Eb Eb D D	239A	
G Ab Eb F G Ab	336R	
G Ab F B B C	16G	
G Ab F C B G	76C	
G Ab F C D Bb	79A	
G Ab F E D C	84P	
G Ab F Eb D Eb	14H	
G Ab F F F F	78F	
G Ab F F G Eb	273O	
G Ab F G B C	12I	
G Ab F G C D	122Q	
G Ab F G Eb C	257F	
G Ab F G Eb D	13C	
G Ab F G F Eb	10E	
G Ab F G G Eb	239P	
G Ab G Ab Ab G G Ab	260G	
G Ab G Ab Ab G G F	267C	
G Ab G Ab G G	43M	
G Ab G Bb Ab G	178K	
G Ab G C A G	54Q	
G Ab G C B D	55L	
G Ab G C B E	408S	
G Ab G C B Eb	155L	
G Ab G C C C	199L	
G Ab G C D Eb	376L	
G Ab G C F Eb	17P	
G Ab G C G Ab	60K	
G Ab G C G Eb	225L	
G Ab G C G F	318I	
G Ab G D D Eb	17Q	
G Ab G Eb C C	401K	
G Ab G Eb C D	313D	
G Ab G Eb F D	274N	
G Ab G F C D	127R	
G Ab G F Eb D Eb C	304C	
G Ab G F Eb D Eb F G F	290Q	
G Ab G F Eb D Eb F G G	195S	
G Ab G F Eb D F	239E	
G Ab G F Eb D G	414L	
G Ab G F Eb F C	280O	
G Ab G F Eb F Eb D	274S	
G Ab G F Eb F Eb F F	263S	

Notation	Index	Notation	Index	Notation	Index
G Ab G F Eb F Eb F G	199J	G Bb Ab G F Eb	235F	G C B A E F	213D
G Ab G F Eb F G	183A	G Bb Ab G F# G	57O	G C B A F D	188B
G Ab G F Eb G	168R	G Bb Ab G G G	246G	G C B A F E	132F
G Ab G F F Eb	424R	G Bb Bb A G F	194M	G C B A G A B	412H
G Ab G F F G	19G	G Bb Bb C A G Eb	89E	G C B A G A C	371A
G Ab G F G C F D	200O	G Bb Bb C A G Eb	89P	G C B A G C B A G E	18D
G Ab G F G C F Eb	24R	G Bb Bb Eb D Eb	202D	G C B A G C B A G F	28E
G Ab G F G Eb C	25E	G Bb C Bb Bb A	259A	G C B A G C D	288Q
G Ab G F G Eb D	238J	G Bb C D Eb C	189J	G C B A G E A	225C
G Ab G F G F	292Q	G Bb C D Eb Eb	269B	G C B A G E F	168H
G Ab G F G G	380H	G Bb C G C G	70A	G C B A G F E D C B	228A
G Ab G F# F G	26S	G Bb C G F Bb	193L	G C B A G F E D C D	12H
G Ab G F# G B	404H	G Bb D C G Bb	295F	G C B A G F E D C#	308H
G Ab G F# G Eb	141I	G Bb Eb G C C	102J	G C B A G F E D E	199F
G Ab G F# G F#	46H	G Bb G Ab G Bb	201O	G C B A G F E F E E	19F
G Ab G G C Bb	269C	G C A A B B	301D	G C B A G F E F E G	165K
G Ab G G C C	414K	G C A A B G	40N	G C B A G F# A G F	95J
G Ab G G C G	323Q	G C A B A G	6E	G C B A G F# A G G	368I
G Ab G G G B	9K	G C A B B G	144H	G C B A G F# F	405F
G Ab G G G Bb	320R	G C A B G A	257Q	G C B A G F# G A	261K
G Ab G G G F	276J	G C A B G C	98K	G C B A G F# G G	274D
G B A A D D	207S	G C A B D C	435G	G C B A G G E	186F
G B A F E E	123B	G C A C A C	177I	G C B A G G G	81F
G B A F# C B	197F	G C A C D A	70K	G C B A G G#	349F
G B A G D G	78R	G C A C G G	231E	G C B Ab G F#	173F
G B B D C Eb	30Q	G C A F D A	422A	G C B B A A C#	337
G B B G A B	89Q	G C A F G A	254Q	G C B B A A F#	366F
G B B G F G	297N	G C A G A F	275S	G C B B A B	334F
G B C A B B	262R	G C A G C A	371P	G C B B A D	148S
G B C Ab F# G	193B	G C A G E C	366R	G C B B A F	135F
G B C Bb Ab G	240R	G C A G E F	154H	G C B B A G A G B	222S
G B C C C D	325S	G C A G F E D	304S	G C B B A G A G F	52S
G B C C D E	390H	G C A G F E F C	127M	G C B B A G#	104F
G B C C E F	226P	G C A G F E F E	353D	G C B B Ab Ab	20F
G B C C F F	244I	G C A G F# F	264Q	G C B B F Ab	245M
G B C C# D Eb	219D	G C A G G C	163H	G C B B G G Ab	69
G B C D D E	267E	G C Ab Ab Ab Ab	313O	G C B B G G E	254F
G B C D D G	128E	G C Ab F D C	60H	G C B B G G F#	109C
G B C D E F	160O	G C Ab F G C	47B	G C B C B A	12
G B C D G F	165F	G C Ab G Ab B	6J	G C B C B C A	366
G B C Db C B	312D	G C Ab G F Eb C	315L	G C B C B C B A	375J
G B C Db D Eb	219D	G C Ab G F Eb F	165Q	G C B C B C B C	362C
G B C E E D	321N	G C Ab G F Eb G	400K	G C B C B C Bb	364A
G B C Eb D C	310D	G C B A A G	99B	G C B C B C D E Eb B	162C
G B C Eb D F	29I	G C B A B C A	392B	G C B C B C D E Eb D	164F
G B C Eb Eb D	29I	G C B A B C B	367P	G C B C B C G	243S
G B C F F E	61E	G C B A B C C	405M	G C B C B E	365C
G B C G Ab G B	157L	G C B A B C D	353B	G C B C Bb Ab Ab	24
G B C G Ab G F	157S	G C B A B C E D	332G	G C B C Bb Ab G	164C
G B C G E D	129F	G C B A B C E G	368I	G C B C Bb Bb	419F
G B D C B A	132L	G C B A B C G Bb	14B	G C B C C A	363A
G B D C C E	170E	G C B A B C G G	81C	G C B C C B	129F
G B D C F E	401C	G C B A B D	106F	G C B C C D	426
G B D C G A	173K	G C B A B G E	358H	G C B C C E	169F
G B D F D D	205M	G C B A B G G	395P	G C B C D B C B	397A
G B D F E D	19M	G C B A C B A G D	283J	G C B C D B C C	195M
G B D F Eb D	299I	G C B A C B A G G	354D	G C B C D B C E	313
G Bb A A Ab G	284M	G C B A C C	406G	G C B C D C D E D D	21C
G Bb A Bb Bb A	22N	G C B A C F	56G	G C B C D C D E D G	272C
G Bb Ab C G G	224B	G C B A D A	336B	G C B C D D	22
G Bb Ab G Eb Eb	294Q	G C B A E E	3S	G C B C D E B	342C

G C B C D E D B — 158D
G C B C D E D E — 362G
G C B C D E D G — 245H
G C B C D E F D — 241P
G C B C D E F G C — 315F
G C B C D E F G F — 169L
G C B C D E G — 422B
G C B C D Eb B — 107J
G C B C D Eb D C Bb — 157C
G C B C D Eb D C C — 170M
G C B C D Eb D C G — 62L
G C B C D Eb D Eb C B — 156R
G C B C D Eb D Eb C C — 248K
G C B C D Eb F D — 330K
G C B C D Eb F G — 422G
G C B C D F — 271E
G C B C D G — 63G
G C B C E C — 290S
G C B C E C# — 317I
G C B C E D C B — 44M
G C B C E D C D — 37J
G C B C E D F — 24F
G C B C E G F# — 2M
G C B C E F — 153K
G C B C E G G D — 367R
G C B C E G G E — 7L
G C B C Eb D — 271J
G C B C F# G — 81I
G C B C G A B — 373Q
G C B C G A G — 35E
G C B C G Bb — 365S
G C B C G C B C B — 351K
G C B C G C B C G — 152P
G C B C G E — 9A
G C B D C Ab — 131F
G C B D C B — 375F
G C B D C E A — 135P
G C B D C E D — 94P
G C B D C E F — 163E
G C B D C G — 404I
G C B D G C — 393A
G C B G A E — 399A
G C B G A G — 144E
G C B G C C — 9N
G C B G C G — 341J
G C B G D F — 286A
G C B G Eb D — 252P
G C B G F A — 147E
G C B G G Ab — 69J
G C Bb A A F — 242P
G C Bb A G A — 184H
G C Bb Ab Ab G — 313E
G C Bb Ab Bb Ab — 305E
G C Bb Ab Bb G — 54P
G C Bb Ab G Ab — 274L
G C Bb Ab G Eb — 128J
G C Bb Ab G F F — 108M
G C Bb Ab G F G — 27E
G C Bb Ab G F# — 392C
G C Bb Bb Ab Bb — 305G
G C Bb Bb Bb C — 201N

G C Bb C Eb G — 256L
G C Bb Eb Bb C — 387N
G C Bb Eb D C — 310F
G C Bb G Bb C — 126H
G C Bb G Eb Ab — 102I
G C Bb G Eb F — 233D
G C Bb G F Eb — 213J
G C C A A E — 350R
G C C A A G — 291B
G C C A B C — 361K
G C C A F E — 239D
G C C Ab F D — 317B
G C C Ab G Ab — 153C
G C C Ab G F — 407Q
G C C B A G A D — 166D
G C C B A G A G — 289P
G C C B A G E D — 349C
G C C B A G E E — 368R
G C C B A G F E — 242F
G C C B A G F G — 411G
G C C B B A A A — 402E
G C C B B A A B — 302C
G C C B B A E — 298B
G C C B B A G — 243D
G C C B B B A — 250L
G C C B B B C — 131N
G C C B B G — 92G
G C C B Bb C — 417S
G C C B C A — 266P
G C C B C Ab — 13A
G C C B C D B — 317J
G C C B C D E D — 140D
G C C B C D E F — 384D
G C C B C D Eb C — 338M
G C C B C D Eb D — 106I
G C C B C D G D — 157D
G C C B C D G G — 93I
G C C B C E E — 230E
G C C B C E G — 230G
G C C B C Eb — 274R
G C C B C G Ab — 377S
G C C B C G C — 101E
G C C B D F — 98E
G C C B E D — 229G
G C C B Eb D — 82C
G C C B Eb D — 205O
G C C B G A — 33O
G C C B G B — 248G
G C C B G D — 373O
G C C Bb Ab G — 157P
G C C Bb Bb Ab Ab — 108H
G C C Bb Bb Ab G — 109I
G C C Bb Bb Bb Ab — 414Q
G C C Bb Bb Bb G — 232C
G C C Bb F C — 220N
G C C Bb G C — 125J
G C C C A E — 143G
G C C C A E — 102F
G C C C B A B B — 367M
G C C C B A B G — 24G
G C C C B A C — 369H

G C C C B A D — 119Q
G C C C B A G E — 203O
G C C C B A G F — 386S
G C C C B B — 128K
G C C C B C A — 244G
G C C C B C D C — 439Q
G C C C B C D D — 330L
G C C C B C D F — 156K
G C C C B C D G — 5L
G C C C B C D G — 156C
G C C C B C D E — 232J
G C C C B D C — 312J
G C C C B D F — 55S
G C C C B E — 226H
G C C C B G — 36I
G C C C Bb Bb Bb A — 313N
G C C C Bb Bb Bb Ab — 328A
G C C C Bb Bb Bb C — 48P
G C C C C B A G C — 152L
G C C C C B A G G — 209E
G C C C B B B A A B — 2H
G C C C B B B A A C — 328I
G C C C C B C C — 154N
G C C C C B C D — 398M
G C C C C B D D — 172C
G C C C C B D G — 216F
G C C C C Bb — 298I
G C C C C C B A B A — 373E
G C C C C C B A B C — 430G
G C C C C C B B — 363L
G C C C C C B D Ab — 95E
G C C C C C B D C — 322F
G C C C C C Bb Ab — 219E
G C C C C C Bb C Bb — 287Q
G C C C C C Bb C G — 178I
G C C C C C B C B — 211D
G C C C C C C B G — 34Q
G C C C C C C B A — 7P
G C C C C C C B C — 370Q
G C C C C C C C — 35N
G C C C C C C D — 334K
G C C C C C C E — 71H
G C C C C C C Eb — 278Q
G C C C C C C G — 394I
G C C C C C D Eb — 432S
G C C C C C D F — 209A
G C C C C C E C — 270F
G C C C C C E D — 183J
G C C C C C Eb — 315R
G C C C C C G C — 20J
G C C C C C G G — 315E
G C C C C D C B — 217P
G C C C C D C D — 170P
G C C C C D D D — 420C
G C C C C D D G D — 328F
G C C C C D D G F — 72N
G C C C D E F F E C — 426O
G C C C D E F F E D — 336D
G C C C C D E F G — 210O
G C C C C D Eb D — 37D
G C C C C D Eb Eb Eb — 333N

Notation	Ref	Notation	Ref	Notation	Ref
G C C C C D Eb Eb F	185E	G C C D C F	267O	G C C E F G F E D	230M
G C C C C D G	256O	G C C D D Bb	384E	G C C E F G F E F	272M
G C C C C E C	145R	G C C D D C	76B	G C C E G G	183M
G C C C C E D A	322Q	G C C D D E E D C	107G	G C C Eb C C	366R
G C C C C E D C	170P	G C C D D E E D D	371E	G C C Eb D C B	292C
G C C C C E E	346I	G C C D D E E D E	90L	G C C Eb D C D	285C
G C C C C E F G F	180J	G C C D D E E G	377M	C C C Eb Eb D Ab	327M
G C C C C E F G G	52O	G C C D D E F D	170L	G C C Eb Eb D D	434C
G C C C C Eb	131M	G C C D D E F E	254C	G C C Eb Eb Eb	392M
G C C C C G C	388L	G C C D D E G	118M	G C C F Eb Ab	339J
G C C C C G E	147L	G C C D D Eb D	298K	G C C F Eb D	125E
G C C C C# D	168K	G C C D D Eb Eb	330C	G C C F F F	162M
G C C C D B A	62N	G C C D E C C B	189C	G C C G A A A	87C
G C C C D B B	285H	G C C D E C C G	264P	G C C G A A C	149R
G C C C D C B A	62J	G C C D E D C C	128O	G C C G Ab F	376M
G C C C D C B C	379K	G C C D E D C D	390H	G C C G Ab G	288C
G C C C D C Bb	37L	G C C D E D C G G A	425O	G C C G Bb G	301C
G C- C C D D D E	169O	G C C D E D C G G C	64Q	G C C G C Bb	122J
G C C C D D D Eb	329L	G C C D E F E D A	382M	G C C G C C C	337R
G C C C D D E	147N	G C C D E F E D D	202Q	G C C G C C G	408M
G C C C D D D Eb	343M	G C C D E F E D G	306B	G C C G C D	422J
G C C C D E C D	359A	G C C D E F E G	235T	G C C G C G	358A
G C C C D E C G	102B	G C C D E F F	332J	G C C G D G	197J
G C C C D E E E	44Q	G C C D E F G F G	411Q	G C C G E C	13J
G C C C D E E G	352Q	G C C D E F G G	160D	G C C G F E	62J
G C C C D E F E	390K	G C C D E G F E D	108P	G C C G G A	7F
G C C C D E F G	6O	G C C D E G F E E	136I	G C C G G C Bb	438C
G C C C D E G G A	118A	G C C D Eb Bb	280A	G C C G G C C	112J
G C C C D E G G D	225M	G C C D Eb C	36L	G C C G G D	318A
G C C C D Eb	165P	G C C D Eb D C B	25H	G C C G G Eb	146M
G C C C D F	74P	G C C D Eb D C F	377I	G C C G G F	195J
G C C C E C B	335G	G C C D Eb D C G	177A	G C C G G F#	361F
G C C C E C C	184R	G C C D Eb D Eb	275P	G C C G G G Bb	83M
G C C C E D C C	141B	G C C D Eb Eb Eb	335K	G C C G G G G	324F
G C C C E D C D	37J	G C C D Eb Eb F	385M	G C D B C D E F E	162E
G C C C E D C E	399R	G C C D Eb F Eb D	107S	G C D B C D E F G	93C
G C C C E E E A	64L	G C C D Eb F Eb G	304R	G C D B C D F	165E
G C C C E E E D	346S	G C C D Eb F G Ab	17A	G C D B C Eb C	10C
G C C C E E F#	434C	G C C D Eb F G Bb	409B	G C D B C Eb D	233H
G C C C Eb B	318M	G C C D Eb F G G	14I	G C D B C F	28J
G C C C Eb C C	245A	G C C E A A	324E	G C D B C G Ab	162M
G C C C Eb C G	413L	G C C E A C	324E	G C D B C G C	291A
G C C C Eb F#	278K	G C C E C C	74H	G C D B C G G	248C
G C C C F Eb	356I	G C C E C D	272L	G C D B G B	130P
G C C C G D	410C	G C C E C G A G F E C	113D	G C D B G C	13J
G C C C G E C	383R	G C C E C G A G F E G	326P	G C D B G D	387C
G C C C G E D	417H	G C C E C G A G G	170A	G C D B G E	250C
G C C C G G C	265R	G C C E D C B	271R	G C D C B A B	52J
G C C C G G G	170R	G C C E D C C B	130E	G C D C B A C	92K
G C C D A A	218O	G C C E D C C G	182N	G C D C B C D	170D
G C C D A B	263J	G C C E D C C G	348M	G C D C B C E	309H
G C C D B C G	183D	G C C E D F	49O	G C D C B C Eb	21C
G C C D B C G G C	183H	G C C E E C	322H	G C D C Bb C	390C
G C C D B C G G G	251A	G C C E E E	262S	G C D C C B	272M
G C C D B G	285F	G C C E E G D	292C	G C D C C C	271F
G C C D C Bb Bb	177F	G C C E E G E	186O	G C D C C D E A	411F
G C C D C Bb C	388F	G C C E E G F E C	276G	G C D C C D E G	36C
G C C D C C	384L	G C C E E G F E D	40F	G C D C D C	370C
G C C D C D C	180P	G C C E E G G A A G D	403S	G C D C D E F	139F
G C C D C D E	124B	G C C E E G G A A G G	265J	G C D C D E G D	304J
G C C D C D Eb	330I	G C C E E G G G	118F	G C D C D E G F	57C

Notation	Page
G C D C G A	1O
G C D C G C	59A
G C D C G D	9C
G C D D E D G D E E F	21F
G C D D E D G D E E G	252B
G C D D E E	115L
G C D D E F	143J
G C D D D Eb B	17B
G C D D D Eb C	163I
G C D D D Eb Eb	44K
G C D D D Eb F F	330M
G C D D D Eb F G	120A
G C D D D F E	184S
G C D D D# E F#	412K
G C D E C A	169Q
G C D E C B	206P
G C D E C D C	206P
G C D E C D E A	237G
G C D E C D E F D	349J
G C D E C D E F F	234P
G C D E C E A	54O
G C D E C E E	144F
G C D E C E F E	1M
G C D E C E F G	309O
G C D E C G	122D
G C D E D B	61D
G C D E D C B A	308P
G C D E D C B C A	114D
G C D E D C B C D	55I
G C D E D C D C	379P
G C D E D C D D	332K
G C D E D C D E C	372D
G C D E D C D E F E	153N
G C D E D C D E F G	171F
G C D E D C D E G	384G
G C D E D C E	292B
G C D E D C G A G A	163C
G C D E D C G A G F	146H
G C D E D D E F E D	15E
G C D E D D E F E G	9I
G C D E D E C	205A
G C D E D E F	10H
G C D E D F E D C B	19F
G C D E D F E D C D	168O
G C D E D G F	57F
G C D E D G G	18M
G C D E E C	418A
G C D E E D C B	383M
G C D E E D C D	253O
G C D E E D C G	164S
G C D E E D E	47M
G C D E E E D	354H
G C D E E E F	39G
G C D E E F D	37B
G C D E E F E	327D
G C D E E F F	217R
G C D E E F G A	17D
G C D E E F G E	264E
G C D E E F G G A	12K
G C D E E F G G E	321H
G C D E E G C	441E
G C D E E G F	218D
G C D E E G G	313L
G C D E F D C	15F
G C D E F D E	242S
G C D E F E D C B	6K
G C D E F E D C C	389B
G C D E F E D C D	382R
G C D E F E D E C	14N
G C D E F E D E D	311I
G C D E F E D E F	23L
G C D E F F F#	233Q
G C D E F G A F	183F
G C D E F G A G C B	214P
G C D E F G A G C G	38A
G C D E F G A G E C	215I
G C D E F G A G E D	284J
G C D E F G Ab	46K
G C D E F G C	16S
G C D E F G E C A	241Q
G C D E F G E C B	26A
G C D E F G E C D	144Q
G C D E F G E D	180Q
G C D E F G F	15K
G C D E F G F	15N
G C D E F G G A	62K
G C D E F G G F	424J
G C D E F G G G	122G
G C D E F F# G	220O
G C D E G A B	204B
G C D E G A C G E	61J
G C D E G A C G G	90J
G C D E G A G	388O
G C D E G C D E B	356Q
G C D E G C D E F	204C
G C D E G C D E G C	369F
G C D E G C D E G G	228C
G C D E G E B	103K
G C D E G E D C	46G
G C D E G E D G	57R
G C D E G E G	375K
G C D E G F E A	56H
G C D E G F E F	93P
G C D E G G D	82N
G C D E G G E	366E
G C D E G G F	38J
G C D E G G F#	340H
G C D E G G G	12Q
G C D Eb Bb Ab	142R
G C D Eb C B	78M
G C D Eb C Bb	2Q
G C D Eb C C	172E
G C D Eb C D	62G
G C D Eb C Eb	213L
G C D Eb C F#	226R
G C D Eb C G C	398D
G C D Eb C G Eb	151H
G C D Eb D B	231F
G C D Eb D C Ab	304F
G C D Eb D C B C Bb	184G
G C D Eb D C B C C	26M
G C DEb D C B C D Eb D	158C
G C DEb DCBCDEb F	11G
G C D Eb D C B C G Ab	159L
G C D Eb D C B C G B	15L
G C D Eb D C B C G C	207C
G C D Eb D C B C G D	272K
G C D Eb D C Bb Ab	20F
G C D Eb D C Bb Bb	334L
G C D Eb D C Bb C	438D
G C D Eb D C D B A	21Q
G C D Eb D C D B G	260R
G C D Eb D C D D	342M
G C D Eb D C D G C	228F
G C D Eb D C D G D	320C
G C D Eb D C Eb	107P
G C D Eb D C F	13N
G C D Eb D C G Bb	89A
G C D Eb D C G F	304M
G C D Eb D D C	325A
G C D Eb D D D Eb	9R
G C D Eb D Eb C Bb	75H
G C D Eb D Eb C D	398L
G C D Eb D Eb C G	27F
G C D Eb D Eb F	106Q
G C D Eb D Eb F#	257L
G C D Eb D F Eb C	391J
G C D Eb D F Eb G	114N
G C D Eb E F	36D
G C D Eb E F#	412K
G C D Eb Eb D C Bb	13B
G C D Eb Eb D C D	405C
G C D Eb Eb D D	208S
G C D Eb Eb D Eb	343L
G C D Eb Eb D G	378R
G C D Eb Eb G	26G
G C D Eb F D	162O
G C D Eb F Eb C	195F
G C D Eb F Eb D	293A
G C D Eb F F	314E
G C D Eb F F#	309E
G C D Eb F G A Bb	419Q
G C D Eb F G A G	72O
G C D Eb F G Ab Ab G G B	96B
G C D Eb F G Ab Ab G G Eb	142L
G C D Eb F G Ab Bb	60G
G C D Eb F G Ab G	349F
G C D Eb F G Bb	90K
G C D Eb F G C B	263K
G C D Eb F G C D	15B
G C D Eb F G C G Ab	311D
G C D Eb F G C G C	415I
G C D Eb F G C G G	46L
G C D Eb F G G	163M
G C D Eb G C C	292L
G C D Eb G C D	365P
G C D Eb G F Eb D C	291O
G C D Eb G F Eb D Eb	55R
G C D Eb G F Eb F	166C
G C D Eb G F#	281I
G C D F E D C B	298J
G C D F E D C E	36R
G C D F Eb D	342S

Notation	Code	Notation	Code	Notation	Code
G C D G D G	214J	G C E E E F F	35B	G C Eb D B C Eb D	25J
G C D G G A	231I	G C E E F A	417C	G C Eb D B C Eb G	404E
G C D G G C	338I	G C E E F B	98D	G C Eb D C B C C	361G
G C D G G G	439E	G C E E F E D D	62C	G C Eb D C B C D Ab	135I
G C Db F Db C	242M	G C E E F E D G	261M	G C Eb D C B C D G	166A
G C E A A B	409K	G C E E F G	265I	G C Eb D C Bb Ab	386E
G C E A B D	206J	G C E E G C E E	49F	G C Eb D C Bb G	370R
G C E A F C	411N	G C E E G C E E F	266F	G C Eb D C C G C C	327F
G C E A G D	422F	G C E E G G	39R	G C Eb D C C G C G	350L
G C E A G E	96D	G C E F B E	128H	G C Eb D C Eb D	98J
G C E A G F E	120D	G C E F E D	17C	G C Eb D C Eb G	317R
G C E A G F F	358K	G C E F E F	105I	G C Eb D C G Ab	376J
G C E B A B	173R	G C E F F E	217K	G C Eb D C G F	120J
G C E B A G	382B	G C E F F F	34N	G C Eb D C G G	214L
G C E B C G	394N	G C E F G A B	137A	G C Eb D Eb B	25A
G C E B D C	`97E	G C E F G A G D	174H	G C Eb D Eb C	108L
G C E B D B	213G	G C E F G A G G	397R	G C Eb D Eb D	399N
G C E C B C	231A	G C E F G C A A	351H	G C Eb D F G	414D
G C E C B D	210M	G C E F G C A G	180R	G C Eb D G Ab	323O
G C E C D Eb	200I	G C E F G C E	141C	G C Eb D G C D	159A
G C E C G C	194H	G C E G A A	225S	G C Eb D G C Eb	434G
G C E C G E	145E	G C E G A B	411J	G C Eb Eb Ab C	227Q
G C E C G G	182S	G C E G A G	144B	G C Eb Eb D C	184J
G C E D B C	93H	G C E G B A	142G	G C Eb Eb D D	59K
G C E D C A F D	336Q	G C E G B B	303C	G C Eb Eb D F	257I
G C E D C A F E	164A	G C E G B D	394A	G C Eb Eb F D	215C
G C E D C B A G	134H	G C E G C A	58P	G C Eb Eb G G	291G
G C E D C B A G#	308N	G C E G C C C	359J	G C Eb F D B	337B
G C E D C B B A	418H	G C E G C C G	413I	G C Eb F# Eb D	140A
G C E D C B B G#	364B	G C E G C E D	327R	G C Eb F# G F	12A
G C E D C B C	15H	G C E G C E G B	324N	G C Eb G Ab F	57H
G C E D C C	415B	G C E G C E G C	404C	G C Eb G Ab G	144I
G C E D C E	300Q	G C E G D E	41D	G C Eb G C Eb D	320Q
G C E D C F B	119M	G C E G E A	76N	G C Eb G C Eb G C Eb	62H
G C E D C F E	357J	G C E G E C A	392J	G C Eb G C Eb G C G	136K
G C E D C F G	184D	G C E G E C B	171P	G C Eb G F Eb	321D
G C E D C G A B C D	21I	G C E G E C C	64H	G C Eb G G G	235R
G C E D C G A B C G	159Q	G C E G E D C	17H	G C F E A G	336I
G C E D C G E	10A	G C E G E D E	190Q	G C F E C D	266L
G C E D D G	388G	G C E G E G	131P	G C F E D C B	406A
G C E D E C	28K	G C E G F D	234E	G C F E D C D	360M
G C E D E G	15O	G C E G F E C	137J	G C F G A B	410Q
G C E D F E C	241R	G C E G F E D C B	284O	G C F G Ab Bb	32M
G C E D F E D C B	236F	G C E G F E D C D	14O	G C G A B C B	160L
G C E D F E D C G	156E	G C E G F E D E	215L	G C G A B C D	422J
G C E D F E F	296D	G C E G F E G F E C	131B	G C G A B C G	15C
G C E D G E	420D	G C E G F E G F E G	160K	G C G A B G	277R
G C E E A A	416O	G C E G F# F	253D	G C G A C B	290A
G C E E C E	136S	G C E G G A	917M	G C G A C C	349Q
G C E E D C B A	411E	G C E G G D	57K	G C G A D D	297D
G C E E D C B C	363G	G C E G G F E	242K	G C G A E D	205Q
G C E E D C B D	355B	G C E G G F F	283H	G C G A E F E	270J
G C E E D C D	135E	G C E G G G A	34E	G C G A E F G	349L
G C E E D C E	150D	G C E G G G F	330E	G C G A F E	81B
G C E E D D C	68D	G C E G G G F#	1P	G C G A G A	284N
G C E E D D D	423E	G C E G G G G	252G	G C G A G C	230K
G C E E D E	318L	G C Eb A G Eb	178E	G C G A G F E E	137R
G C E E E D	68G	G C Eb Ab Eb Ab	413Q	G C G A G F E F	227M
G C E E E E E	370L	G C Eb B D C	233F	G C G A G G	159R
G C E E E E F	371C	G C Eb C D D	200L	G C G Ab Ab G	326E
G C E E E F Ab	212A	G C Eb D A B	119K	G C G Ab C Bb	401I

Notation	Code	Notation	Code	Notation	Code
G C G Ab F G	279D	G C G F E D C B	345O	G D E F E D	221B
G C G Ab G C	58A	G C G F E D C D	47F	G D E F G A	284S
G C G Ab G Eb	65P	G C G F E D F	347F	G D Eb B C D	292N
G C G Ab G F Eb	395B	G C G F E E	237R	G D Eb C C Bb	79K
G C G Ab G F G C C	153Q	G C G F E F D	360R	G D Eb C C G	73S
G C G Ab G F G C G	14L	G C G F E F E	223P	G D Eb C D B	108Q
G C G Ab G G	262G	G C G F E F G	334M	G D Eb C G D	252A
G C G B A G	226A	G C G F E G	385F	G D Eb C G G	193C
G C G Bb G D	301C	G C G F Eb D	337R	G D Eb F Eb Ab	379N
G C G C B C	324G	G C G F# Eb F#	440I	G D Eb F Eb B	27L
G C G C B D	95F	G C G F# F# F	376K	G D Eb F G F	286Q
G C G C C A	18G	G C G G A A	32N	G D Eb G F Eb	336G
G C G C C C	91S	G C G G A B	21D	G D F C D Bb	58G
G C G C D D	81R	G C G G Ab Ab	407K	G D F Eb D C	277F
G C G C D E A	174M	G C G G B A	235C	G D F Eb F Ab	10G
G C G C D E C E	218K	G C G G B C	365A	G D G Ab B Ab	42D
G C G C D E C G	338S	G C G G B E	388D	G D G D B B	278C
G C G C D Eb	150Q	G C G G C B	410A	G D G E G D	91G
G C G C D G	94Q	G C G G D G	8P	G D G F# E D	282F
G C G C E C	320I	G C G G E C	347Q	G D G G# B G#	42D
G C G C E G	234M	G C G G E G G A	325P	G D# B Db A F	41O
G C G C G A	160H	G C G G E G G C	57G	G D# E C C C	334I
G C G C G C C	408M	G C G G Eb C	363M	G E A D B B	160G
G C G C G C E	369M	G C G G Eb D	378D	G E A D E F	134F
G C G C G E	251M	G C G G F E D	174O	G E A F F D	266B
G C G C G G	379R	G C G G F E E	358B	G E A F G E	35I
G C G D E D	380S	G C G G F Eb	170O	G E A G B C	11J
G C G D G C	426R	G C G G F G	90S	G E A G C F	401G
G C G D G E C	163A	G C G G G C Bb	417N	G E A G E A	94I
G C G D G E F	253N	G C G G G C D	336A	G E A G E C	114A
G C G D G E G	425S	G C G G G E D C B	309L	G E A G F E	74B
G C G D G Eb	209Q	G C G G G E D C C	2I	G E A G G E A	391G
G C G E A A	138R	G C G G G F E E	183L	G E A G G E D	252K
G C G E A F	249I	G C G G G F E F	246K	G E B C B C	421L
G C G E C D	118B	G C G G G G A	12R	G E B C D E	409A
G C G E C E E	36B	G C G G G G Ab	9D	G E B D C C	332A
G C G E C E G C C	130G	G C G# G# A F	438M	G E B D C C	83P
G C G E C E G C D	349O	G C# D E F F#	411O	G E B D C E A E	179I
G C G E C F	409R	G D A B B C	357D	G E B D C E A G	410M
G C G E C G A	96H	G D C B C E	233P	G E C A A C C	112I
G C G E C G E	11D	G D C C C B	417D	G E C A A C G	370H
G C G E C G F#	309I	G D C E E E	306E	G E C A B C E	87G
G C G E C G G	17F	G D C G D E	264R	G E C A B C G	203Q
G C G E D C A	160M	G D C G F Eb	338O	G E C A B G	437A
G C G E D C B B	248L	G D C G G E	223F	G E C A C B A A	438P
G C G E D C B C	5J	G D D B D G	113F	G E C A C B A G	227D
G C G E E C	228P	G D D D D E D	219H	G E C A D E	274C
G C G E E D	339I	G D D D D E F	100F	G E C A F D	52P
G C G E E F	417G	G D D D E C	116J	G E C A F F	250I
G C G E E G	261O	G D D D Eb D	75A	G E C A G A	273Q
G C G E F D B	245O	G D D E D C	133P	G E C B A G C C	174S
G C G E F D F	254N	G D D E F G A	290L	G E C B A G C D	426S
G C G E F G	232A	G D D E F G E	336M	G E C B C A	153B
G C G E G C C	379S	G D D E F G G	279L	G E C B C D C C	45K
G C G E G C E C	324H	G D D Eb D C	387L	G E C B C D C E	10P
G C G E G C E D	12E	G D D Eb F C	139K	G E C B C D E D	165O
G C G E G C E E	380G	G D D F Eb D	193R	G E C B C D E F E	168M
G C G E G C E G	318B	G D E B C G	163Q	G E C B C D E F G	93L
G C G Eb G C Eb	421S	G D E D B G	293M	G E C B C E	229Q
G C G Eb G C G	227N	G D E D C E	56P	G E C B D C F	170K
G C G Eb G Eb	27J	G D E F E C	75D	G E C B B C G	137I

Notation	Ref.
G E C B G F	424L
G E C Bb Bb A	230S
G E C C A F	170S
G E C C A G	201C
G E C C B A	38P
G E C C B D	58D
G E C C C C C	40R
G E C C C C E	307S
G E C C D C A	116E
G E C C D C B	416Q
G E C C D D A	376E
G E C C D D D	129A
G E C C D D E	245R
G E C C D E	248O
G E C C E A	202N
G E C C E G	379S
G E C C F F	155B
G E C C G F	416Q
G E C D A B	64C
G E C D B C	391I
G E C D C B	171R
G E C D E C	16B
G E C D E D	119B
G E C D E E	98G
G E C D E F	14P
G E C D E G	300I
G E C D G E	86H
G E C E D D	276N
G E C E F G	206L
G E C E G A G E	60E
G E C E G A G G	49C
G E C E G C C B	30D
G E C E G C C D	334E
G E C F D F	251E
G E C F D G A	83I
G E C F D G C	253B
G E C F# E F#	214B
G E C G A A	34I
G E C G A B B	88G
G E C G A B C	60R
G E C G A G F	64S
G E C G A G G	11P
G E C G C C C B	129L
G E C G C C C F	60M
G E C G C E	393D
G E C G E C B	45M
G E C G E C E	396P
G E C G E C G	14G
G E C G E D	384B
G E C G E G	418Q
G E C G F E D C	71N
G E C G F E D D	65D
G E C G F E G	355N
G E C G F G	11P
G E C G F# A	98B
G E C G G A	344H
G E C G G E	208J
G E C G G G A	242G
G E C G G G F	371H
G E C G G G G	80D
G E D A A G	338Q
G E D A G F#	356O
G E D B C D C	309J
G E D B C D E	54A
G E D B C E	255O
G E D B G G	143Q
G E D C A B	155A
G E D C A G	30G
G E D C B A B	308P
G E D C B A G A	312N
G E D C B A G C	204S
G E D C B A G D	183O
G E D C B A G F	253F
G E D C B A G G A	339H
G E D C B A G G F	97Q
G E D C B B	226O
G E D C B C A	275H
G E D C B C D	421N
G E D C B C G C	59Q
G E D C B C G G	15D
G E D C B D	317K
G E D C B G#	1R
G E D C C A A	95O
G E D C C A B	156S
G E D C C B A G E	28R
G E D C C B A G A	228I
G E D C C B A G G	156S
G E D C C B C D C	366P
G E D C C B C D G	36E
G E D C C C C C A	19I
G E D C C C C C D	271I
G E D C C D E D	6G
G E D C C D E F D	170Q
G E D C C D E F E	316H
G E D C C E	308S
G E D C C G	366G
G E D C D C B	12M
G E D C D C F	4Q
G E D C D D	69C
G E D C D E F G A	229R
G E D C D E F G E	344I
G E D C D E G	419S
G E D C D G A	70M
G E D C D G F	203M
G E D C E C	313F
G E D C E F D	60C
G E D C E F E	161S
G E D C E F G A	401E
G E D C E F G E	323P
G E D C E G	378K
G E D C E G	378M
G E D C F A	174P
G E D C F E	424I
G E D C G A B	13D
G E D C G A C	366M
G E D C G A G	28O
G E D C G C	388M
G E D C G E F	380Q
G E D C G E G	388B
G E D C G F	164O
G E D C G G A	17E
G E D C G G F	96G
G E D C# D E	300J
G E D D C A	350D
G E D D D C A	413A
G E D D D C C B	81J
G E D D D C C F	104D
G E D D D C G	375D
G E D E C B C	371S
G E D E C B G	245F
G E D E C D	192Q
G E D E C G	2O
G E D E D C	173O
G E D E E C	301O
G E D E F E	314Q
G E D E F G A	237J
G E D E F G E	223S
G E D E G F	210Q
G E D E G G	182E
G E D F E D C B	45Q
G E D F E D C D	359D
G E D F E D F	204A
G E D G E E	218J
G E D# E B D C E	236T
G E D# E B D C G	370G
G E D# E D# E E	364Q
G E D# E D# E F	363F
G E D# E G E	94C
G E E A G C	418O
G E E B A F	32I
G E E B C D	96M
G E E C A F	24C
G E E C C A	232H
G E E C C B	368H
G E E C C C	355G
G E E C C G	252N
G E E C D# E	1S
G E E C E G	58Q
G E E C G C	430H
G E E C G G	207H
G E E D A F	208P
G E E D C D	115B
G E E D D C	358R
G E E D D C	225B
G E E D D D	266J
G E E D E F E E D E	127C
G E E D E F E E D F	4A
G E E E D E F E F	23O
G E E E D# D# E	386H
G E E E C D E D	390E
G E E E C D E E	354C
G E E E C F	249J
G E E E C G	368B
G E E E D B	318O
G E E E D C A	412S
G E E E D C G G C	394H
G E E E D C G G G	416E
G E E E D D	251O
G E E E D E	430R
G E E E D# E	368M
G E E E E D#	372N
G E E E E E C	370N
G E E E E E D	30B

G E E E E E E	371F
G E E E E E E F	208O
G E E E E E E F#	370B
G E E E E F	'97M
G E E E E G E C	329I
G E E E E G E G	198Q
G E E E E F D	421G
G E E E F E	94H
G E E E F F	116Q
G E E E F G C	301J
G E E E F G G	228O
G E E E G F E D	359J
G E E E G F E E	376G
G E E F A D	429L
G E E F D A	426K
G E E F D C	229O
G E E F F# G	330O
G E E F G A	205E
G E E F G G	383P
G E E G A E	50O
G E E G C E	348O
G E E G D E	56S
G E E G E E	340M
G E E G G F	374C
G E Eb C Eb D	178A
G E F A G G	254R
G E F B C A	261L
G E F D C C	18P
G E F D C D	171B
G E F D E C	97K
G E F D G E	345S
G E F E D G A A	268B
G E F E D G A A Bb	23F
G E F E D G A A G	208I
G E F E F D E	9Q
G E F E F D F	304K
G E F E F E	403R
G E F E F G	319P
G E F F D C	381B
G E F F E A	56O
G E F F G G	17N
G E F F# G A	232R
G E F F# G C	261P
G E F F# G D	31F
G E F G A A	242L
G E F G A B B	113B
G E F G A B C A	441G
G E F G A B C B	24N
G E F G A B C C	327K
G E F G A Bb	16N
G E F G A F	54H
G E F G A G C	397J
G E F G A G F E D C	179C
G E F G A G F E D D	382I
G E F G B A	228N
G E F G Bb Ab	220F
G E F G C B A B	304Q
G E F G C B A G F	352E
G E F G C B A G G	187R
G E F G C B C	129C
G E F G C C	246F
G E F G C D E E	116B
G E F G C D E F	162G
G E F G C G A	211L
G E F G C G E	150O
G E F G D C	423F
G E F G E C	156M
G E F G F E D C	10R
G E F G F E D E	193D
G E F G F E F	326D
G E F G G C	120B
G E F G G E F D	133R
G E F G G E F G	360Q
G E F G G G A A	427K
G E F G G G A G	215A
G E G A A D	57D
G E G A C E F	300R
G E G A C E G	366L
G E G A E F	385K
G E G A E G B	353C
G E G A E G E	323R
G E G A G A	341Q
G E G A G E F D	67D
G E G A G E F E	401R
G E G A G G	64E
G E G B A G	39J
G E G C A C	237E
G E G C A G	439J
G E G C C G	212B
G E G C D E A	43P
G E G C D E C	113J
G E G C E A	64P
G E G C G C	265F
G E G C G F	7C
G E G D B C	312P
G E G D C F	416C
G E G D E C	344M
G E G D G D	280L
G E G D G E C	329C
G E G D G E G C	373D
G E G D G E G D	209F
G E G E A B	184C
G E G E A E	63K
G E G E A G	81M
G E G E C B	37H
G E G E C G	32S
G E G E D C	438L
G E G E D E	361D
G E G E E F G	401M
G E G E F E	352M
G E G E F G A	228M
G E G E F G E	248P
G E G E G A E	232Q
G E G E G A G	145N
G E G E G E	323B
G E G E G G	56A
G E G F A G	141G
G E G F D F	249M
G E G F E D C	37P
G E G F E D D	107E
G E G F E E	353A
G E G F E F	123M
G E G F G E	140S
G E G G E A	284Q
G E G G E D C	101N
G E G G E D E	215D
G E G G E G A	360F
G E G G E G G	116H
G E G G F G	186L
G E G G G D	270I
G E G G G G	369C
G E G G# E G#	42C
G Eb Ab B C D	163G
G Eb Ab G Eb B	408K
G Eb Ab G F B	18E
G Eb Abb Gb Ebb Ebb	280S
G Eb B B C C Ab	9O
G Eb B B C C D	171E
G Eb B C D Eb	317S
G Eb B D C Bb	393O
G Eb B D C Eb	221N
G Eb B G C Bb	155C
G Eb C Ab A C	61S
G Eb C Ab C Bb	159M
G Eb C Ab F D	418E
G Eb C B B C D	227E
G Eb C B B C Eb	165A
G Eb C B D F	412G
G Eb C Bb Ab G	422S
G Eb C C B G	255I
G Eb C C Bb C	361N
G Eb C C C Ab	23B
G Eb C C C C	151N
G Eb C C D Eb	108A
G Eb C D B C	19B
G Eb C D B G	74E
G Eb C D E C	201J
G Eb C D E Eb Eb	56B
G Eb C Eb F G	288J
G Eb C F Ab D	435B
G Eb C F Ab G	61A
G Eb C G A D	55G
G Eb C G Bb Eb	416D
G Eb C G C C	153P
G Eb C G C D	189I
G Eb C G Eb C	234K
G Eb C G Eb D Bb	257B
G Eb C G Eb D C	61R
G Eb C G Eb Eb	192L
G Eb C G Eb G	177C
G Eb D B A G	158F
G Eb D B C Ab	149Q
G Eb D B C F	12D
G Eb D C Ab Ab	165S
G Eb D C Ab G Eb	422R
G Eb D C Ab G F	8S
G Eb D C B B C	249O
G Eb D C B B D	17L
G Eb D C B C C	27P
G Eb D C B C D	274M
G Eb D C B C G Ab	25C
G Eb D C B C G F	20C
G Eb D C B D	319B

Notation	Ref	Notation	Ref	Notation	Ref
G Eb D C Bb Ab	227R	G Eb G B C F	28C	G F E D C D G E	154K
G Eb D C C Ab	120I	G Eb G B D D	386G	G F E D C D G F	258O
G Eb D C C B	163N	G Eb G B D F	149O	G F E D C E G	25K
G Eb D C C G C	164R	G Eb G C C D	158S	G F E D C E G#	434D
G Eb D C C G Eb	14J	G Eb G Db F C	359M	G F E D C F	29K
G Eb D C D Bb	177D	G Eb G Eb G A	104E	G F E D C G C	287R
G Eb D C D Eb	396Q	G Eb G F Eb Eb	227B	G F E D C G F	148B
G Eb D C F G	8S	G Eb G F Eb F	123O	G F E D C# D	228G
G Eb D C G Ab	43A	G Eb G F G Ab	27G	G F E D C# E	333I
G Eb D C G Eb	58H	G Eb G F# D D	280S	G F E D D C A	135O
G Eb D C G G C	16M	G F A G F D	431K	G F E D D C B	283R
G Eb D C G G G	16H	G F Ab C B C	432C	G F E D D C C	105N
G Eb D C# B# B#	359C	G F Ab G Eb F	87L	G F E D E C	305N
G Eb D D C Bb	97G	G F Ab G F Eb	61G	G F E D E D	139L
G Eb D D C C	402N	G F Ab G G F	9P	G F E D E F	292E
G Eb D D C G	331A	G F B C D G	60P	G F E D E G F	209D
G Eb D Db C C	359C	G F B D G C	206C	G F E D F E	132K
G Eb D Eb Ab Ab	15P	G F Bb A G F	388P	G F E D G G	74M
G Eb D Eb C Ab	16K	G F Bb Ab G F	31J	G F E D# E F	367E
G Eb D Eb C G	156D	G F Bb G F Bb	196C	G F E E C B	229D
G Eb D Eb D C	60S	G F C B G F	259I	G F E E D C A A	345J
G Eb D Eb Eb D	239Q	G F D C A G	420K	G F E E D C A G	248B
G Eb D Eb G Ab	109A	G F D C C D	170I	G F E E D C C	33Q
G Eb D F E A	354F	G F D C D D	251P	G F E E D C G	190F
G Eb D F# D F	281G	G F D C E D	113S	G F E E D D C	252O
G Eb D G Db C	229K	G F D C G F	182Q	G F E E D D E	206D
G Eb Db C B C	11S	G F D Eb Eb D	23S	G F E E D D F	132B
G Eb Eb C C C	413H	G F D Eb F G	291Q	G F E E D D G	186B
G Eb Eb C D Eb	402K	G F D Eb F G	291S	G F E E D E	141F
G Eb Eb D B C	328N	G F E A B C	6S	G F E E E A	70L
G Eb Eb D C Ab	218P	G F E B C D	154P	G F E E E D C C A	248D
G Eb Eb D C C	322E	G F E C B B	39I	G F E E E D C C C	210A
G Eb Eb D C F	160F	G F E C C B	240P	G F E E E E D	71J
G Eb Eb D D A	42A	G F E C C D	241C	G F E E E E D#	366A
G Eb Eb D D C C	65I	G F E C D E C	99L	G F E E E E E F D	247H
G Eb Eb D D C D	146G	G F E C D E G	162J	G F E E E E E F E	417F
G Eb Eb D D C G	364E	G F E C D F	364C	G F E E E F E	4L
G Eb Eb D D Eb	67M	G F E C E C	308J	G F E E E F F	253M
G Eb Eb Db C C	77K	G F E C F E	81F	G F E E E F G A	33C
G Eb Eb Eb B B	437K	G F E C# D A	174A	G F E E E F G G	253C
G Eb Eb Eb D C	214K	G F E C# D F	352B	G F E E E G	1C
G Eb Eb Eb D D	36N	G F E D C A	6I	G F E E F G	130F
G Eb Eb Eb Eb D	393M	G F E D C B A	252Q	G F E E G A	165R
G Eb Eb Eb Eb G	306G	G F E D C B B	129J	G F E F D C B	130R
G Eb Eb Eb Eb Eb	322A	G F E D C B C D C	131I	G F E F D C F	16P
G Eb Eb G B C	74F	G F E D C B C D G	276S	G F E F D E D	73Q
G Eb Eb G Eb D	129D	G F E D C B D C C	153A	G F E F D E D	273F
G Eb Eb G Eb Eb	117G	G F E D C B D C G	120L	G F E F D G	67G
G Eb F G A F	240A	G F E D C B E	109S	G F E F E D C	151R
G Eb F G Ab Bb	24K	G F E D C C B	152H	G F E F E D E D	249K
G Eb F G C Ab	13H	G F E D C C C	20D	G F E F E D E F	223H
G Eb F G Eb C C	201I	G F E D C C D	73J	G F E F E D F	40G
G Eb F G Eb C D	154Q	G F E D C D A	126D	G F E F F A	46S
G Eb F G Eb F G Ab	47A	G F E D C D B	127O	G F E F F# G	113R
G Eb F G Eb F G C	294S	G F E D C D C B C	296C	G F E F G A B	28G
G Eb F G F Ab G C	231C	G F E D C D C B F	250K	G F E F G A G	390O
G Eb F G F Eb	299K	G F E D C D C D	268H	G F E F G E	16C
G Eb F G G Ab	425L	G F E D C D D	99E	G F E F G F E E	189F
G Eb F G G B	28F	G F E D C D E F E	117N	G F E F G F E F	25M
G Eb F G G G	230C	G F E D C D E F G	52D	G F E F G F F	127S
G Eb G Ab Eb G	323S	G F E D C D G C	165D	G F E F G G	360Q

Notation	Ref	Notation	Ref	Notation	Ref
G F E G C F	291K	G F F E F E	33L	G F♯ F♯ G F♯ G	440G
G F E G D F	380R	G F F F E♭ G F	238R	G F♯ G A A G	116L
G F E G E F	235L	G F F F D E	15S	G F♯ G A B C B	213S
G F E G F E	224Q	G F F F F D E	47C	G F♯ G A B C C	416R
G F E G F G	33P	G F F F F E♭ D	260I	G F♯ G A B D	47D
G F E G G B	275R	G F F F F F E♭	138D	G F♯ G A G C	394K
G F E G G E	235L	G F F F F F F	373P	G F♯ G A G E C	197L
G F E G G F A	264S	G F F G B♭ G	279N	G F♯ G A G E F	403Q
G F E G G F E	243B	G F F G E♭ D	99F	G F♯ G A G E G	369S
G F E♭ B C G	27N	G F G A A A	105O	G F♯ G A G F♯ G A	142Q
G F E♭ C C D	129R	G F G A B A	19S	G F♯ G A G F♯ G F	7R
G F E♭ C E♭ D	172K	G F G A♭ A♭ A♭	342O	G F♯ G A♭ A♭ A♭	260O
G F E♭ C E♭ E♭	295G	G F G A♭ G A	69P	G F♯ G A♭ G C	233L
G F E♭ D C A♭ B♭	155Q	G F G A♭ G A♭	297O	G F♯ G B A G	403Q
G F E♭ D C A♭ F	155D	G F G A♭ G F F	70D	G F♯ G B♭ A♭ G	119A
G F E♭ D C A♭ G	325R	G F G A♭ G F G	429A	G F♯ G B♭ C B♭	8M
G F E♭ D C B C A♭	424C	G F G A♭ G G B♭ A	70B	G F♯ G C C G	369A
G F E♭ D C B C C	14M	G F G A♭ G G B♭ C	69Q	G F♯ G C D C	369B
G F E♭ D C B C D E♭ D C	18R	G F G B♭ A F	91D	G F♯ G C E A	281J
G F E♭ D C B C D E♭ D G	384F	G F G C B♭ G	298M	G F♯ G C E♭ D	119R
G F E♭ D C B C G	296I	G F G C C D	191A	G F♯ G C G F♯	97I
G F E♭ D C C B	29C	G F G E F D	248M	G F♯ G D E♭	344S
G F E♭ D C C C	254A	G F G E F G	267F	G F♯ G E C C	39M
G F E♭ D C D B♭	107Q	G F G E G D	257M	G F♯ G E E D♯	97L
G F E♭ D C D E♭ D	296E	G F G E♭ C C	291N	G F♯ G E F G	135Q
G F E♭ D C D E♭ F F♯	59B	G F G F A♭ G	281L	G F♯ G E G C	267I
G F E♭ D C D E♭ F G	419O	G F G F E D	388S	G F♯ G E♭ C D	344B
G F E♭ D C E♭	108C	G F G F E G	380R	G F♯ G E♭ D C B	396S
G F E♭ D C G C D	289B	G F G F E♭ D	125N	G F♯ G E♭ D C G	258B
G F E♭ D C G C E♭	63I	G F G F E♭ F	69O	G F♯ G F E F	214O
G F E♭ D D F	363I	G F G F G F	298R	G F♯ G F E♭ D C	258B
G F E♭ D D G	28S	G F G G E D	241D	G F♯ G F E♭ D E♭ D	325F
G F E♭ D E♭ C	25S	G F G G F D	145P	G F♯ G F E♭ D E♭ D♭	179H
G F E♭ D E♭ D	14E	G F G G G A♭	259N	G F♯ G F G E♭ D	370S
G F E♭ D F E♭ B	434J	G F G G G♭ A♭	354J	G F♯ G F G E♭ G	370K
G F E♭ D F E♭ D C	206I	G F♯ A A B C	83C	G F♯ G F♯ E♭ D	207P
G F E♭ D F E♭ D E♭ D	301R	G F♯ A G B D	210N	G F♯ G F♯ G C	373C
G F E♭ D F E♭ D E♭ F	71R	G F♯ A G C B	400I	G F♯ G F♯ G F	46M
G F E♭ D F E♭ D♭	12C	G F♯ A G C C	236S	G F♯ G G F♯ G	222Q
G F E♭ D F E♭ E♭	336C	G F♯ A G E C	134K	G F♯ G G♯ A G♯	46C
G F E♭ D G G	401D	G F♯ A G E E	369N	G G A A A A	87B
G F E♭ E♭ D C♯	146I	G F♯ A G E G	94S	G G A A A B B	48M
G F E♭ E♭ D E♭	103D	G F♯ C D E♭ D	364N	G G A A A B C	302H
G F E♭ E♭ D F	312S	G F♯ C D E♭ G	61B	G G A A A E	356J
G F E♭ E♭ E♭ F♯	100J	G F♯ D E G F♯	232I	G G A A B B C C B	372S
G F E♭ F E♭ D B	163F	G F♯ D F E♭ A	257C	G G A A B B C C D	80Q
G F E♭ F E♭ D E♭ D C C	291E	G F♯ E♭ D G F♯	8N	G G A A B B C G	224O
G F E♭ F E♭ D E♭ D C D	307G	G F♯ E♭ F♯ G F♯	298P	G G A A B C	112O
G F E♭ F G A♭ A♭	107N	G F♯ F D F E♭	414B	G G A A C B♭	77R
G F E♭ F G A♭ B♭	47K	G F♯ F D G A	436G	G G A A C D D	348J
G F E♭ F G E♭	241B	G F♯ F E C D	357L	G G A A E♭ E♭	101Q
G F E♭ F G F	140P	G F♯ F E D E	392E	G G A A G A	147P
G F E♭ F G G	215O	G F♯ F E E C	396R	G G A A G D	183M
G F E♭ G F E♭	43L	G F♯ F E E G	228K	G G A A G E	215E
G F F E D C B B	77O	G F♯ F E E♭ E♭	430A	G G A A G F E	247B
G F F E D C B C	252J	G F♯ F E F D	50A	G G A A G F G	387O
G F F E D C D	243C	G F♯ F E G E	275I	G G A A G F♯	201M
G F F E D E G C	114C	G F♯ F E G F	304O	G G A A G G A	427H
G F F E D E G F	247P	G F♯ F♯ F F E♭	432E	G G A A G G E	264F
G F F E E F E	243L	G F♯ F♯ F♯ C B	339G	G G A A G G F	304G
G F F E E F G	283P	G F♯ F♯ F♯ G B♭	143F	G G A A G G G	346G

Notation	Page
G G A A# B G	124G
G G A B C A D	86P
G G A B C A G	125G
G G A B C B A E	415R
G G A B C B A G A	187S
G G A B C B A G F	84D
G G A B C C C	188A
G G A B C C E	93R
G G A B C D B	421E
G G A B C D C	303F
G G A B C D E D	147A
G G A B C D E E A	229E
G G A B C D E E G#	112R
G G A B C D E F E B	164J
G G A B C D E F E D E C D E	119N
G G A B C D E F E D E C D G	161J
G G A B C D E F G	372H
G G A B C D E G C	62A
G G A B C D E G G	325H
G G A B C D Eb	320J
G G A B C D G	357O
G G A B C E D	418P
G G A B C E E	295D
G G A B C E G E	350S
G G A B C E G G	49I
G G A B C G E	130S
G G A B C G G	308Q
G G A B Eb D	25P
G G A B G C	273C
G G A Bb A A B	15M
G G A Bb A A G	389F
G G A Bb A G	185J
G G A Bb B G	124G
G G A C A C	374J
G G A C B A	363E
G G A C B D	18F
G C A C D E	145D
G G A C D G	388R
G G A C E G	343E
G G A C G E	223M
G G A C G F	338D
G G A D C B	172O
G G A E E D	206B
G G A F E A	122H
G G A F G E D	115Q
G G A F G E E	40H
G G A G A B C G E	214E
G G A G A B C G G	314B
G G A G A G A	368O
G G A G A G C	362O
G G A G C A G E D	167I
G G A G C A G E D#	361M
G G A G C B	343I
G G A G C C	394M
G G A G C G C	355A
G G A G C G G	316O
G G A G E C A	2K
G G A G E C C	186J
G G A G E C D	95S
G G A G E D C B	182C
G G A G E D C D	99S
G G A G E E D C	319K
G G A G E E D D	287A
G G A G E E F	172N
G G A G E F G C#	218F
G G A G E F G F	198H
G G A G F D	139N
G G A G F E D B	266I
G G A G F E D C	342D
G G A G F E D F	107D
G G A G F E D#	97H
G G A G F E E D C B	252M
G G A G F E E D C E	397L
G G A G F E F G A	328O
G G A G F E F G E	236D
G G A G F E G	340L
G G A G F F	343F
G G A G F G	111C
G G A G F# F	137D
G G A G G A	50H
G G A G G F	211P
G G A G G G C A	334D
G G A G G G C D	419M
G G A G G G F	179D
G G A G G G G	242E
G G Ab Ab A G#	357M
G G Ab Ab Ab C	228Q
G G Ab Ab Ab F	117R
G G Ab Ab C G	418F
G G Ab Ab Eb Eb	142B
G G Ab Ab F F	86L
G G Ab Ab G C	100I
G G Ab Ab G F	435F
G G Ab B Ab B	305J
G G Ab Bb Ab Bb	263M
G G Ab Bb Bb G	406F
G G Ab Bb C C	50D
G G Ab Bb G G	80F
G G Ab C B C	124N
G G Ab Ab Ab G	236O
G G Ab C B D	59I
G G Ab C Bb Ab	149F
G G Ab C D Eb	108F
G G Ab D D G	338G
G G Ab D Eb F	216O
G G Ab Eb C Ab	419E
G G Ab Eb F F# F# F#	432R
G G Ab Eb F F# F# G	435O
G G Ab F Eb D	211O
G G Ab F Eb	146E
G G Ab G A G	433I
G G Ab G Ab G	319L
G G Ab G F Ab	398J
G G Ab G F C	233N
G G Ab G F D	351N
G G Ab G F Eb D C	195B
G G Ab G F Eb D D	398F
G G Ab G F Eb Eb Eb	405F
G G Ab G F Eb Eb F	233I
G G Ab G F F	246R
G G Ab G F G Ab	281D
G G Ab G F G G	56D
G G Ab G F# G	370M
G G Ab G G Ab Bb	216D
G G Ab G G Ab C	192G
G G Ab G G Ab G	329G
G G Ab G G B	255P
G G Ab G G Bb	319J
G G Ab G G D F D	203F
G G Ab G G D F F	338A
G G Ab G G F Eb	29G
G G Ab G G F G	9L
G G Ab G G G A	98R
G G Ab G G G F D	259F
G G Ab G G G F Eb	268G
G G Ab G G G F	26N
G G Ab G G G G G	407N
G G B A G A	385C
G G B A E E D	89D
G G B A E E G	223J
G G B A G F#	353P
G G B B B C	331J
G G B B Bb A	406S
G G B C A G	86I
G G B C B C	359S
G G B C D Eb	319H
G G B C G Ab	207Q
G G B C G F	408R
G G B C G G	408R
G G B E D C	396A
G G B G G B	53I
G G B G G G B	353L
G G B G G G G	416B
G G Bb Ab F Ab	92M
G G Bb Ab G Ab	28A
G G Bb B B Bb	89J
G G Bb Bb A G	88D
G G Bb Bb Ab Eb	89L
G G Bb C C F	180H
G G Bb C D C	207F
G G Bb F G Ab	269E
G G Bb G F F	126O
G G C A B C	436F
G G C A B G	381K
G G C A C E	300L
G G C A G C	362C
G G C A G F	306O
G G C A G G A	181M
G G C A G G G	213A
G G C Ab Bb C	19K
G G C Ab G F	347R
G G C Ab G G	31S
G G C B A A	128F
G G C B A B C G G E D	196P
G G C B A B C G G E G	119L
G G C B A E	109J
G G C B A G D	100R
G G C B A G F	402J
G G C B B A A	108K
G G C B B A G	70G
G G C B C B C B C B	16F
G G C B C B C B C E	366Q
G G C B C D C	296L

Notation	Ref	Notation	Ref	Notation	Ref
G G C B C D D C	227K	G G C C C G E	111A	G G C E C E	95B
G G C B C D D E	116I	G G C C C G G C C	365J	G G C E D C A	307Q
G G C B C D E E	394L	G G C C C G G C G	185G	G G C E D C B	272I
G G C B C D E F	160N	G G C C D B	106H	G G C E D C E	358O
G G C B C D G	116D	G G C C D Bb	176Q	G G C E E D	282Q
G G C B C F	71E	G G C C D C	68C	G G C E E F	265I
G G C B C G	48H	G G C C D D B	262P	G G C E E G	245M
G G C B F E	317D	G G C C D D C	244O	G G C E F A	224F
G G C B G B	30A	G G C C D D E E	344M	G G C E F E	396G
G G C Bb Ab Bb	132J	G G C C D D E E F	333E	G G C E F G A D A	96K
G G C Bb Ab G Bb	257K	G G C C D D E F	198M	G G C E F G A D E	95R
G G C Bb Ab G F	304D	G G C C D E C	33J	G G C E F G A G	403G
G G C Bb Ab G G	122O	G G C C D E E	112C	G G C E F G E	242O
G G C Bb Ab G G	244D	G G C C D Eb D C B	385J	G G C E F# G	422K
G G C Bb C C	200B	G G C C D Eb D C C	288N	G G C E G C C	249C
G G C Bb C D	263G	G G C C D Eb D Eb	85S	G G C E G C E	141J
G G C Bb G Eb	412P	G G C C D Eb Eb D	333O	G G C E G D	205T
G G C C A A	307M	G G C C D Eb Eb G Ab	290H	G G C E G F	244N
G G C C A B	387Q	G G C C D Eb Eb G Bb	284F	G G C E G F#	422K
G G C C B A B	311A	G G C C E A	430F	G G C E G G	411S
G G C C B A G A	34S	G G C C E C C	91O	G G C Eb Ab C	220L
G G C C B A G E	373H	G G C C E C F	34R	G G C Eb G Bb	55Q
G G C C B A G F	156P	G G C C E D	356A	G G C Eb G F	34L
G G C C B B B	2J	G G C C E E D	332E	G G C Eb G F	144C
G G C C B B C	130Q	G G C C E E D#	367J	G G C F E E	158G
G G C C B B F	83Q	G G C C E E E	339E	G G C F F E	111N
G G C C B B G#	433P	G G C C E G Bb	387G	G G C G A E	286J
G G C C B C C	62F	G G C C E G C	383O	G G C G Ab G	439L
G G C C B C F	37I	G G C C Eb D	100K	G G C G Bb G	213C
G G C C B C F	73P	G G C C Eb Eb	177P	G G C G C D	374I
G G C C B D	196E	G G C C F E	113L	G G C G C G	400J
G G C C B G G C	95K	G G C C G Bb	389G	G G C G E A	251H
G G C C B G G Eb	323D	G G C C G C	209N	G G C G E C	245G
G G C C Bb Bb	155S	G G C C G G D	321B	G G C G E D	346H
G G C C C Ab	246S	G G C C G G E	367C	G G C G E E	214M
G G C C C Ab	63J	G G C C G G G	367S	G G C G E F E	290O
G G C C C B A	250N	G G C D B C	279G	G G C G E F G	230Q
G G C C C B Bb	435J	G G C D B C B	424Q	G G C G E G	383A
G G C C C B C D	288H	G G C D C C	420R	G G C G Eb C Eb	398H
G G C C C B C E	371L	G G C D C D	272E	G G C G Eb C G	214S
G G C C C B D	245I	G G C D C Eb	150G	G G C G Eb Eb	268K
G G C C C B E	96N	G G C D D Eb	288C	G G C G F G	431O
G G C C C Bb	244L	G G C D D G	192S	G G C G F# F#	66M
G G C C C C B	95D	G G C D E A	159H	G G C G G E A	132S
G G C C C C C A	436R	G G C D E C B	146A	G G C G G E E	356D
G G C C C C C B	312F	G G C D E C G	49J	G G C G G Eb	436B
G G C C C C C C	197N	G G C D E F G E	269M	G G C G G F E	265Q
G G C C C C E	394Q	G G C D E F G G	39E	G G C G G F C	280F
G G C C C C Eb	209P	G G C D E G A	209O	G G C G G F#	299P
G G C C C D	284C	G G C D E G F	176D	G G C G G G C F	65S
G G C C C E	308C	G G C D E G G	301A	G G C G G G C G G G C C	344G
G G C C C G	245L	G G C D Eb C	159N	G G C G G G C G G G C G	183C
G G C C C D B	81D	G G C D Eb D B	393H	G G C G G G E	95J
G G C C C D C B C D B	81D	G G C D Eb D G	423S	G G D C D C	41H
G G C C C D C B C D F	180K	G G C D Eb Eb	142H	G G D C G G	431L
G G C C C D C Bb	182B	G G C D F Eb	303A	G G D D D D	88P
G G C C C D E D	209J	G G C D G G	40M	G G D D E E	417P
G G C C C D E E	95G	G G C E A G E	356K	G G D D Eb D	107L
G G C C C D G	209C	G G C E A G G	135F	G G D D G G	142F
G G C C C Eb C	251F	G G C E C B	168N	G G D E C G	6P
G G C C C Eb D	273D	G G C E C D	137K	G G D Eb D C	234R

Notation	Code
G G D Eb D G	212H
G G D Eb F Eb	14C
G G D Eb G C	291D
G G D F Eb D	74A
G G E A A G	237B
G G E A E G	46J
G G E A F D	340E
G G E A G F E D	303B
G G E A G F E F	254I
G G E A G G	132R
G G E Ab Ab G	178R
G G E B A D	439A
G G E B C A	173Q
G G E Bb G A	324P
G G E C A B	111K
G G E C A F	178M
G G E C A G G C	202G
G G E C A G G E	211B
G G E C B A	265L
G G E C B C	426M
G G E C C A B	207J
G G E C C A G	320K
G G E C C B B	317F
G G E C C B F	19J
G G E C C C C	198N
G G E C C C D E	275F
G G E C C C D F	34O
G G E C C D	218Q
G G E C C E	220P
G G E C C G E	210E
G G E C C G F	355O
G G E C D E F	219M
G G E C D E G	116M
G G E C E A	45G
G G E C E C	409M
G G E C E D	317P
G G E C E G C	67F
G G E C E G F	325Q
G G E C E G G	43B
G G E C F C	249P
G G E C F E	305A
G G E C F F E	190A
G G E C F F F	331L
G G E C G C	317M
G G E C G D	381C
G G E C G E D	58J
G G E C G E F	254H
G G E C G G	322D
G G E D C B A	362L
G G E D C C A	327P
G G E D C C B B	153O
G G E D C C B C	366P
G G E D C D E	368S
G G E D C D G	325O
G G E D C E	138E
G G E D C G A	98C
G G E D C G G	354P
G G E D C# A	112S
G G E D D	287D
G G E D E F	395Q
G G E D E G	433S
G G E D F E D	329F
G G E D F E G	283L
G G E D G G	31L
G G E D# F# B	71B
G G E D# G G	143B
G G E E C A	190O
G G E E C F	69A
G G E E C G	212I
G G E E D D	365H
G G E E D G	286K
G G E E E C B	140G
G G E E E C C B	253J
G G E E E C C C	367I
G G E E E D	416P
G G E E E D#	394J
G G E E E E C C C	372G
G G E E E E C C D	319E
G G E E E E D	322K
G G E E E E E D	128M
G G E E E E E E	362S
G G E E E E E E G	367D
G G E E E E E E G	359F
G G E E E E F	248C
G G E E E F	111B
G G E E E G	232G
G G E E F Ab	87D
G G E E F E	409G
G G E E G F	409G
G G E E G G C	37F
G G E E G G D	335E
G G E E G G E	373A
G G E E G G Eb	381F
G G E E G G F	195K
G G E F A A	346N
G G E F A G	368P
G G E F D E	237P
G G E F E D C	177H
G G E F E G D	31D
G G E F E G F	3E
G G E F G A B C A	441G
G G E F G A B C B A G D	11A
G G E F G A B C B A G F	371N
G G E F G A B C D	210B
G G E F G A C	214F
G G E F G A G C E	38M
G G E F G A G C F	159J
G G E F G C B	12S
G G E F G C C	74G
G G E F G C D	274E
G G E F G E C D E	109K
G G E F G E C D F	231G
G G E F G E D C	271K
G G E F G E D D	32B
G G E F G F	10L
G G E F G G E	219B
G G E F G G G	221L
G G E G B A	229S
G G E G C B	142C
G G E G C C B	323A
G G E G C C G G B	174I
G G E G C C G G D	403F
G G E G C D	96C
G G E G C F	205F
G G E G C G F	354R
G G E G C G G	367F
G G E G F G	140S
G G E G G E G C	251S
G G E G G E G G	248F
G G E G G F	195P
G G E G G G	59S
G G Eb Ab B B	255C
G G Eb C C C Bb	368E
G G Eb C C C D	407B
G G Eb C C D	335S
G G Eb C D Eb	332I
G G Eb C F Ab	69F
G G Eb C G G	105D
G G Eb D C B	317H
G G Eb D C C C	322R
G G Eb D C C D	50C
G G Eb D D D	284H
G G Eb D Eb D	229M
G G Eb D Eb G	435N
G G Eb D F F	380C
G G Eb D G Ab	200F
G G Eb Eb D C	425R
G G Eb Eb Eb Eb C	186A
G G Eb Eb Eb Eb D	393B
G G Eb Eb Eb Eb Eb	256S
G G Eb F G Ab	215S
G G Eb F G C	173C
G G Eb F G Eb	21P
G G Eb F G G Bb	53Q
G G Eb F G G G	287B
G G Eb G Ab G	126K
G G Eb G C Eb	359E
G G Eb G Eb C C	402F
G G Eb G Eb C G	130H
G G Eb G Eb G	403K
G G Eb G F D	243H
G G Eb G G Eb	231R
G G Eb G G F	83M
G G F Ab D D	437E
G G F Ab G G	423Q
G G F C C G	302J
G G F C D E	359L
G G F D A G	177J
G G F E A A	134B
G G F E A G	425C
G G F E C B	372P
G G F E C D	283C
G G F E C E	267B
G G F E D C C	42K
G G F E D C F	346M
G G F E D C G	163B
G G F E D D	93G
G G F E D E C	300F
G G F E D G	106N
G G F E E G	245C
G G F E E D C C	40B
G G F E E D C D	274Q
G G F E E D C F	326Q

G G F E E D D C	425E	
G G F E E D D F	108G	
G G F E E D E	193E	
G G F E E D F	129E	
G G F E E E	369K	
G G F E E F	181Q	
G G F E F D C	155J	
G G F E F D G	437M	
G G F E F D	187M	
G G F E F E	42P	
G G F E F E	243R	
G G F E F F	244S	
G G F E F G C	167K	
G G F E F G E A	252L	
G G F E F G E C	158J	
G G F E F G G	181K	
G G F E G C	381G	
G G F E G E	117H	
G G F Eb C B	392S	
G G F Eb D C Bb	107I	
G G F Eb D C C	402O	
G G F Eb D C G	24I	
G G F Eb D Db	409P	
G G F Eb D Eb C G F#	272G	
G G F Eb D Eb C G G	56Q	
G G F Eb D Eb F C	226S	
G G F Eb D F G	21J	
G G F Eb D F Eb D C B	229I	
G G F Eb D F Eb D C Db	414L	
G G F Eb D G D	318D	
G G F Eb D G F	357B	
G G F Eb D G G	435E	
G G F Eb Eb D C	129O	
G G F Eb Eb D Eb	319C	
G G F Eb Eb D G F	436J	
G G F Eb Eb D G G	427P	
G G F Eb Eb Eb	253G	
G G F Eb F D	139Q	
G G F Eb F Eb	121B	
G G F Eb F F	391F	
G G F Eb F G Ab	47K	
G G F Eb F G F	25R	
G G F Eb F G G Bb	294I	
G G F Eb F G G C	65N	
G G F Eb F G G G	40P	
G G F Eb G C	131R	
G G F F C C	137L	
G G F F D C	321E	
G G F F E D	35J	
G G F F E D#	331B	
G G F F E E	351A	
G G F F E E E	169C	
G G F F Eb D	215N	
G G F F Eb Eb D C B	261F	
G G F F Eb Eb D C C	335B	
G G F G Ab Ab	79I	
G G F G Ab Bb	359Q	
G G F G Ab G C	69R	
G G F G Ab G G	342N	
G G F G B B	124K	
G G F G C Eb	190J	
G G F G C G	166B	
G G F G E F	307R	
G G F G F E	72K	
G G F G F Eb	6A	
G G F G G G A	178P	
G G F G G G Ab	178B	
G G F# A G E	309Q	
G G F# A G G	413B	
G G F# D Ab Ab	437D	
G G F# D E G	88I	
G G F# Eb G G	218I	
G G F# F E D C	71L	
G G F# F E D Db	434K	
G G F# F E Eb	418J	
G G F# F E F	316D	
G G F# F# E# G#	232B	
G G F# F# F Ab	232B	
G G F# F# F G	433B	
G G F# G A B	401B	
G G F# G A G C	372M	
G G F# G A G F	373J	
G G F# G C B B	353M	
G G F# G C B F	352I	
G G F# G E C	191Q	
G G F# G F E	97J	
G G F# G F F	274I	
G G F# G F# G A	372A	
G G F# G F# G C	46H	
G G F# G G Ab	239G	
G G G A A A A G E	227G	
G G G A A A G G	265E	
G G G A A B B B C	204N	
G G G A A B B B E	219F	
G G G A A B B C C	398O	
G G G A A B B C D	225H	
G G G A A Bb	279M	
G G G A A C A C	40S	
G G G A A C A G	100G	
G G G A A C B C D	304G	
G G G A A C B C G	323G	
G G G A A D	58M	
G G G A A F	76G	
G G G A A G D E	424S	
G G G A A G D G	310S	
G G G A A G G F	168D	
G G G A A G G G	192R	
G G G A B A A	312Q	
G G G A B A G	142N	
G G G A B B B	49E	
G G G A B B C	109E	
G G G A B C A	121D	
G G G A B C B	343O	
G G G A B C C Db	357K	
G G G A B C C E	35F	
G G G A B C D B	249G	
G G G A B C D C	377D	
G G G A B C D E	414O	
G G G A B C D G	388H	
G G G A C B A G B	186R	
G G G A C B A G F	187A	
G G G A C C B	190D	
G G G A C C C	8K
G G G A C D	295J
G G G A C E	80B
G G G A D G	148G
G G G A E D	59J
G G G A E E D C	218G
G G G A E E D D	73B
G G G A E E E	410H
G G G A E G	138P
G G G A F C	135N
G G G A F E	378E
G G G A F G E	140K
G G G A F G G	307B
G G G A G A	77D
G G G A G C A B	301L
G G G A G C A G	65R
G G G A G C B	431A
G G G A G E D	190N
G G G A G E F	325K
G G G A G E F#	424O
G G G A G E G C	311C
G G G A G E G E	145B
G G G A G F E D	325J
G G G A G F E E	97A
G G G A G G C	324D
G G G A G G D	102A
G G G A G G E	282L
G G G A G G F E D#	39N
G G G A G G F E G	269N
G G G A G G F#	428G
G G G A G G G A	238B
G G G A G G G C	432H
G G G A G G G F	268N
G G G A G G G G	334H
G G G Ab Ab Ab Ab	386I
G G G Ab Ab Ab G	111G
G G G Ab Ab B	311F
G G G Ab Ab Bb	109H
G G G Ab Ab G E	430M
G G G Ab Ab G F	394E
G G G Ab Ab G G Db	322I
G G G Ab Ab G G F	262F
G G G Ab Ab G G G A	441L
G G G Ab Ab G G G C	397O
G G G Ab Bb C Bb	219P
G G G Ab Bb C D	205L
G G G Ab Bb G	393F
G G G Ab C C	77N
G G G Ab C G	326J
G G G Ab D G	394C
G G G Ab Eb Ab	259E
G G G Ab Eb D	419B
G G G Ab Eb Eb A	259K
G G G Ab Eb Eb Eb	145A
G G G Ab F Eb	110I
G G G Ab G Ab Ab	30N
G G G Ab G Ab F	151O
G G G Ab G Ab G	105L
G G G Ab G C Bb	76L
G G G Ab G C G	209G
G G G Ab G F E	262H

Notation	Ref
G G G Ab G F Eb	47I
G G G Ab G G G C	320M
G G G Ab G G G G	248R
G G G B D C	104K
G G G Bb A Bb	404G
G G G Bb A G	241I
G G G Bb Ab G	269O
G G G Bb Bb Bb	189R
G G G Bb G F	316B
G G G Bb G G	272R
G G G C A B	133L
G G G C A C	298D
G G G C Ab Bb	94F
G G G C B A A	216J
G G G C B A G F	44O
G G G C B A G G	35L
G G G C B B	247Q
G G G C B D	39B
G G G C B G A	305M
G G G C B G G	198R
G G G C Bb Ab	261R
G G G C Bb F	57S
G G G C C A	133J
G G G C C B A	187E
G G G C C B B	362K
G G G C C B G	284P
G G G C C Bb	106C
G G G C C C B A E	389L
G G G C C C B A G	35R
G G G C C C B B	385Q
G G G C C C B D	39A
G G G C C C Bb	385P
G G G C C C C A	332O
G G G C C C C A	332P
G G G C C C C B	236G
G G G C C C C C	36G
G G G C C C C D	401A
G G G C C C C E	174F
G G G C C C E C A	355Q
G G G C C C E C G	401A
G G G C C C Eb D Eb	318C
G G G C C C Eb D G	335C
G G G C C C F	436H
G G G C C D D B	334J
G G G C C D D D	169M
G G G C C D E E F	227P
G G G C C D E E G	39F
G G G C C D Eb	397P
G G G C C E A	5E
G G G C C E D	363R
G G G C C E E D	410F
G G G C C E E F	243M
G G G C C Eb D Bb	125M
G G G C C Eb D Eb	322B
G G G C C Eb Eb D	125B
G G G C C Eb Eb Eb	345Q
G G G C D B	142K
G G G C D C	416J
G G G C D D	169N
G G G C D E C	38K
G G G C D E E	297E
G G G C D E F G A B	22L
G G G C D E F G A F	22K
G G G C D E G	257J
G G G C D F	357N
G G G C E D C A	227F
G G G C E D C B	250S
G G G C E D C C B	39L
G G G C E D C C D	181B
G G G C E D C G	97N
G G G C E F	32P
G G G C Eb D C	17O
G G G C Eb D D	221R
G G G C F# G	416G
G G G C G Ab	11N
G G G C G B	355J
G G G C G C B	330G
G G G C G C D	259J
G G G C G D	141K
G G G C G Eb D	318G
G G G C G Eb Eb	253Q
G G G C G Eb G	408I
G G G C G F E	300N
G G G C G F G	218S
G G G C G G A A	36F
G G G C G G A G F	313G
G G G C G G A G F#	98S
G G G C G G F	416M
G G G C G G G B	42L
G G G C G G G C C	356R
G G C G G G C G G A	190S
G G C G G G C G G G	369D
G G G C G G G E	270Q
G G G C G G G F	180G
G G G C G G G G	45S
G G G D B G	238O
G G G D C D	179O
G G G D C E	358I
G G G D D C	77G
G G G D E F E	194F
G G G D E F G	126Q
G G G D G G	199P
G G G E C Ab	3L
G G G E C C B	111H
G G G E C C C	75B
G G G E C D	352K
G G G E C G A	216B
G G G E C G E	5I
G G G E D C C	95C
G G G E D C G	317L
G G G E E C	329B
G G G E E D C	131J
G G G E E D F	226L
G G G E E E A	23P
G G G E E E D	187C
G G G E E E E C	368A
G G G E E E E E	396B
G G G E E E E G	67O
G G G E E E F	122M
G G G E E E G	369Q
G G G E E F	375D
G G G E E F F	181L
G G G E F G A E	120C
G G G E F G A G	152G
G G G E G A D	378S
G G G E G A G	115F
G G G E G B	23H
G G G E G C	346E
G G G E G G A	116N
G G G E G G G	231Q
G G G Eb Ab Ab Ab	105F
G G G Eb Ab Ab F	129I
G G G Eb C Ab	43E
G G G Eb C C Ab	74C
G G G Eb C C C	189H
G G G Eb D C C	396H
G G G Eb D C G	210L
G G G Eb D D	240C
G G G Eb D Eb	58F
G G G Eb D G	192F
G G G Eb F F	256A
G G G Eb F G Ab	120O
G G G Eb F G G	293I
G G G Eb G G	257H
G G G F Ab C	58E
G G G F Ab G	240M
G G G F C G	360O
G G G F D G	139D
G G G F E A	115G
G G G F E C A	351F
G G G F E C C	138C
G G F E D C A C D E C	178N
G G F E D C A C D E G	305C
G G G F E D C#	432J
G G G F E D E	193F
G G G F E D F	266Q
G G G F E D G	16D
G G G F E E	252I
G G G F E G	134E
G G G F Eb D D Bb	241L
G G G F Eb D D C	144P
G G G F Eb D D C#	429Q
G G G F Eb D Eb	139F
G G G F Eb Db	119C
G G G F Eb F Eb	149H
G G G F Eb F G	368D
G G G F Eb G	407G
G G G F F Eb Eb D	432G
G G G F F Eb Eb F	80P
G G G F F F E	131K
G G G F F F Eb D	235O
G G G F F F Eb Eb	208L
G G G F G A F	176O
G G G F G A G	175N
G G G F G Ab Bb Ab	91F
G G G F G Ab Bb G	304I
G G G F G D	342K
G G G F G E D C	236I
G G G F G E D D	361G
G G G F G G	381Q
G G G F# A G	356F
G G G F# E F#	108J
G G G F# F Ab	429N

Notation	Index	Notation	Index	Notation	Index
G G G F♯ F E	441I	G G G G C B B	249S	G G G G F F F F G	194D
G G G F♯ F♯ F E	437C	G G G G C B C D	400S	G G G G F F F F G	196G
G G G F♯ F♯ F F	279P	G G G G C B C E♭	30F	G G G G F G A	140F
G G G F♯ F♯ G	364M	G G G G C B C G	367H	G G G G F G C	127E
G G G F♯ G A A	385N	G G G G C B♭ A♭ B♭	387I	G G G G F G F	3N
G G G F♯ G A B	397H	G G G G C B♭ A♭ G	77C	G G G G F♯ F	436A
G G G F♯ G A G	368G	G G G G C B♭ C	234C	G G G G F♯ G B♭	403A
G G G F♯ G C	193J	G G G G C C B B	50G	G G G G F♯ G C	228S
G G G F♯ G E	202A	G G G G C C B C	441N	G G G G A A A B	283Q
G G G A A A A	351G	G G G G C C C A A	317C	G G G G A A A E	219L
G G G A A A B B C	135M	G G G G C C C A B♭	91R	G G G G A A A F	396D
G G G A A A B B G	280N	G G G G C C C B	441N	G G G G A A B	347I
G G G A B A	302E	G G G G C C C D	315H	G G G G A A C	147J
G G G A A E	114K	G G G G C C E	430O	G G G G A A D	339J
G G G A B C C A	363O	G G G G C C E♭	413G	G G G G A B C C	210C
G G G A B C C C	255K	G G G G C C G	82K	G G G G A B C D	400M
G G G A B C G	418D	G G G G C E	228J	G G G G A B C E	200A
G G G A C	115D	G G G G C E♭ D C B	319D	G G G G A B G	350P
G G G A E	342R	G G G G C E♭ D C B♭	119F	G G G G A B♭	419F
G G G A F	253S	G G G G C G A	211S	G G G G A F	50P
G G G A G E D	190N	G G G G C G B♭	299N	G G G G A G C A	238K
G G G A G E E	364P	G G G G C G G	429S	G G G G A G C C	230P
G G G A G F E F E D	408F	G G G G D C C C D	210G	G G G G A G D	375A
G G G A G F E F E E	360L	G G G G D C C C G	236M	G G G G A G E	342Q
G G G A G F E G	141Q	G G G G D D	370F	G G G G A G F	284R
G G G A G F♯	388Q	G G G G D E	31I	G G G G A G G F E	360I
G G G A G G C	306M	G G G G E C B	441S	G G G G A G G F G	166N
G G G A G G G A	331N	G G G G E C B♭	34C	G G G G A♭ B♭	287F
G G G A G G G F	434H	G G G G E C C	93D	G G G G A♭ G C	432Q
G G G A G G G G G C	241H	G G G G E D	332D	G G G G A♭ G E♭ E♭	335F
G G G A G G G G G G	275N	G G G G E E E	319Q	G G G G A♭ G E♭ F	132A
G G G A A♭ A♭ A♭ A♭ B♭	415L	G G G G E E G	319M	G G G G A♭ G F E♭	187F
G G G A A♭ A♭ A♭ F♯	414A	G G G G E F D	355P	G G G G A♭ G F F	43S
G G G A A♭ A♭ A♭ G	231S	G G G G E F G	195A	G G G G A♭ G G A	175S
G G G A♭ A♭ A♭ B	133I	G G G G E G C D	395E	G G G G A♭ G G F	318P
G G G A♭ A♭ A♭ B♭	220C	G G G G E G C E	225P	G G G A♭ G G G B♭	371Q
G G G A♭ A♭ A♭ G A♭	315G	G G G G E G G	49S	G G G A♭ G G G F	334F
G G G A♭ A♭ A♭ G G	78I	G G G G E♭ C	247G	G G G G B A	430N
G G G A♭ A♭ G	233M	G G G G E♭ E♭	277H	G G G G B G	77B
G G G A♭ B♭ A♭	315G	G G G G E♭ F G A♭	297G	G G G G B♭ E♭	120P
G G G A♭ B♭ B♭	280R	G G G G E♭ F G G F F	277K	G G G G B♭ G	406O
G G G A♭ B♭ C	188C	G G G G F♭ F G G F G	71P	G G G G C B A	197Q
G G G A♭ G F E♭	392A	G G G G F C	192I	G G G G C B B	128Q
G G G A♭ G F G	118I	G G G G F E A A	286N	G G G G C B♭	57J
G G G A♭ G G E♭	396F	G G G G F E A C	181H	G G G G C C B	56F
G G G A♭ G G F	268P	G G G G F E A G	328G	G G G G C C C C B	370I
G G G A♭ G G G	318K	G G G G F E D D C	102P	G G G G C C C C B	48O
G G G B B	39S	G G G G F E D D G	238H	G G G G C C C C D♭	40K
G G G B C C	65J	G G G G F E D E	3Q	G G G G C C C D	396C
G G G B C D	12P	G G G G F E E	431S	G G G G C C C G	280Q
G G G B D	106M	G G G G F E G F	382H	G G G G C C E	97P
G G G B♭ A	341L	G G G G F E G G D♭	431E	G G G G C D C	278N
G G G B♭ B♭	298F	G G G G F E G G G	389E	G G G G C D E	101G
G G G B♭ C	389I	G G G G F E♭ C	202O	G G G G C E F	356L
G G G B♭ F	327A	G G G G F E♭ D C	247F	G G G G C E G	372J
G G G B♭ G G F	110Q	G G G G F E♭ D E♭	26E	G G G G C G G D	358M
G G G B♭ G G G	140I	G G G G F E♭ D G	392A	G G G G C G G E	412O
G G G C A	238Q	G G G G F F E E E D	261I	G G G G D B	440Q
G G G C A♭	118Q	G G G G F F E E E E	69I	G G G G D G	406L
G G G C B A	223E	G G G G F F F E♭	437F	G G G G E D	427E
		G G G G F F F F A	96A	G G G G E F	425D

Notation	Ref
G G G G G E G G C	423B
G G G G G E G G F	248A
G G G G G Eb	302D
G G G G G F D	413J
G G G G G F E A	4I
G G G G G F E C	368F
G G G G G F E D D	393L
G G G G G F E D F	430D
G G G G G F Eb D	78J
G G G G G F Eb F F	118C
G G G G G F Eb F G	405L
G G G G G F Eb G	434I
G G G G G F F E	361J
G G G G G F F Eb D	263L
G G G G G F F Eb Eb	439R
G G G G G F F F	86S
G G G G G F G	299G
G G G G G F#	133M
G G G G G A A	4N
G G G G G A G	263I
G G G G G G Ab Ab Ab Ab Bb	433O
G G G G G G Ab Ab Ab Ab G	119E
G G G G G G Ab G C	189N
G G G G G G Ab G Eb	206N
G G G G G G Ab G F	287E
G G G G G G Ab G Gb	50F
G G G G G G Bb	38S
G G G G G G C B	198P
G G G G G G C Bb Ab	114B
G G G G G G C Bb Bb	393G
G G G G G G C Bb C	194R
G G G G G G C Bb G	102D
G G G G G G C C C A	409J
G G G G G G C C C C	418B
G G G G G G C C C C	40K
G G G G G G C E G A	302M
G G G G G G C E G G	358N
G G G G G G C G G Ab	334F
G G G G G G C G G C	321I
G G G G G G C G G G G	395M
G G G G G G E C C D	200E
G G G G G G E C C E	411C
G G G G G G G E E	362B
G G G G G G G E F	222L
G G G G G G G Eb C	318R
G G G G G G G Eb Eb	244K
G G G G G G G F Ab	139B
G G G G G G G F E	236L
G G G G G G G F F	105E
G G G G G G G F G Ab	389C
G G G G G G G F G D#	279S
G G G G G G G F G F	106J
G G G G G G G F# F	429O
G G G G G G G F# F#	146L
G G G G G G G F# G	394G
G^7 A A	385D
G^7 A C	431F
G^7 A G	33D
G^7 Ab	393N
G^7 C C	126G
G^7 C E C	383L
G^7 C E G	146B
G^7 E	406P
G^7 Eb Eb	302G
G^7 Eb G	322C
G^7 F E	31R
G^7 F F	406Q
G^8 A A	64J
G^8 A B	284B
G^8 A C	88O
G^8 Ab G Ab	361B
G^8 Ab G F	111E
G^8 C	126I
G^8 D	240N
G^8 F F F F F F	216C
G^8 F F F F F G	238P
G^9 A A A A	398Q
G^9 A A A G	111J
G^9 A B B	43Q
G^9 A B C	427D
G^9 Ab	259B
G^9 D D C	283I
G^9 D D D	202P
G^{10} A	261C
G^{10} B	147I
G^{10} F D	355M
G^{10} F F	74S
G^{11} C	44D
G^{11} E	374O
G^{12} C	404K
G^{12} F E	287H
G^{12} F G	299M
G^{13} A	399D
G^{14} Ab	395N
G^{14} C	402M
G^{14} F	406D
G^{19}	238L
G^{80}	83G
G^{16} G#	3R
G^7 G#	368Q
G^9 G#	51I
G G G G G G#	143K
G G G G# A B	353G
G G G G# E D	332N
G G G G# E G	358F
G G G G# G# A	172P
G G G# A Ab G	53J
G G G# A B C	353G
G G G# A C B	353N
G G G# A A	302L
G G G# G# A	236O
G G# A B A E	391M
G G# A B C B	173S
G G# A B C D	435S
G G# A C C B	352H
G G# A C# D A	173G
G G# A E Eb D	173J
G G# B B A E	142A
G G# G# A A B	49M
G# A B D C A	412M
G# A C E G F#	316F
G# A C F# G C	351I
G# A G F B C	428F
G# B A D E F	378G
G# C C G# G# C	411P
G# G F# F F B	124L

A

A, B, C, D, 210 R
A casa, a casa, amici, 220 C
A ce joly moys, 186 Q
A ce matin, 201 I
A chaque saison ramenée, 87 D
A che più debb' io mai l'intensa, 65 I
A Chloris, 146 K
A consolar mi affretisi, 96 R
A des oiseaux, 181 J
A deux pas de la mer, 148 E
A dissonance, 51 O
A fosco cielo, 39 N
A gyulai kert alatt, 31 H
A hipp og hoppe, 144 H
A la fenêtre, 299 A
A la fleur du bel âge, 174 M
A la fontaine, 226 D
A la Kaila fut battue, 51 I
A la lueur de leurs torches, 234 L
A la pêche des moules, 184 O
A la 'Santé,' 177 M
A la voix d'un amant fidèle, 47 I
A las armas moriscote, 277 B
A l'aube dans la montagne, 341 O
A l'autel j'allais rayonnant, 200 E
A l'heure accoutumée, 90 L
A l'heure où notre esprit, 266 Q
A mes pas le plus doux chemin, 110 M
A moi les plaisirs, 134 J
A monte sale, 387 N
A morire, 73 S
A mules, 76 I
A noite cain na minha, alma, 406 N
A notte cupa, 50 J
A nous les amours et les roses, 224 F
A quell' amor, 401 P
A questo seno deh vieni, K.374, 245 G
A sa guitarre, 279 H
A Serpina penserete, 274 A
A solis ortu cardine, 45 C
A soma te a la ventana, 273 L
A son page, 282 A
A suoi piedi padre, 157 L
A tanto amor, 95 P
A te le porpore, 399 A
A te, o cara, amor talora, 39 B
A te quest' inno di gloria, 286 P
A te queto rosario, 277 N
A terra si nel livido fango, 399 J
A toi mon âme, je suis ta femme, 136 C
A toi, mon Dieu, mon coeur monte, 133 Q
A toutes brides, 282 F
A toz, kdyz v blahé touze lásky, 346 E
A travers le désert, 294 G
A tutti barbara, 391 N
A un dottor della mia sorte, 307 S
A un jeune gentilhomme, 310 K

A Vesta, portez vos offrandes, 136 O
A vida Fingi da Me chama, 406 R
'A Vucchella, 385 C
Abbandono, 301 N
Abbé divague, L', 299 B
Abbietta zingara, 402 N
Abbondono, L', 39 S
Abbot of Derry, The, 421 B
Abduction from the Seraglio, The, K.384, 245 H
Abécédé, Rajtam kezdé, 194 G
Abencerages, Les, 78 M
Abend ist still und dunkel, Der 105 K
Abend ist's, die Sonne ist verschwunden, 249 P
Abend wie milde, 143 I
Abendbilder, 325 S
Abendempfindung, 249 P
Abendlich schon rauscht der Wald, 119 R
Abendlich strahlt der Sonne Auge, 413 J
Abendlied, 35 A, 231 G, 337 I
Abendruhe liegt über dem Land, 438 H
Abends, 119 R
Abendstern, Der, 326 A, 336 P
Aber der Richtige, 354 H
Aber sie steigt aus dem Meer, 54 O
Abri, L', 48 L
Abril, 406 P
Abroad as I was walking, 177 A
Abscheulicher, wo eilst du hin, 33 C
Abschied, 37 G, 119 M, 215 N, 318 L, 326 B, 428 E
Abschied vom Wald, 229 Q
Abschiedslied der Zugvögel, 230 A
Absence, L', 42 L
Absent, 233 B
Absent, L', 107 M
Acanthe et Céphise, 296 N
Ach, armer Freund, 345 S, 346 A
Ach Bruder ich kann dir nicht tragen, 215 D
Ach, das Leid hab ich ertragen, 83 C
Ach, des Knaben Augen, 428 G
Ach, die wahre Herzenskunde, 321 J
Ach, Elslein, liebes Elslein mein, 120 N
Ach es schmeckt doch gar zu gut, 21 A
Ach Herr, lass dein Lieb, 26 O
Ach Herr, mich armen Sünder, 17 I
Ach Herr Schösser, 21 B
Ach Herr! was ist ein Menschenkind, 16 K
Ach herzigs Herz, 113 B
Ach, ich fühl's, 254 A
Ach ich liebte, war so glücklich, 245 L
Ach, in Maien war's, 428 H

Ach, jak krutě souzi, 347 H
Ach könnt' ich vergessen sie, 55 S
Ach! Könntest das Geschick du Ahnen, 409 C
Ach, lege das Sodom der sündlichen Glieder, 11 J
Ach, Lieb, ich muss nun scheiden, 357 B
Ach, lieber Christen, seid getrost, 16 N
Ach, lieber Herre Jesu Christ, 62 Q
Ach, mein Sinn, 26 C
Ach mir fehlt, nicht ist da, 58 N
Ach! mir schallt's dorten, 323 P
Ach, neige, du Schmerzenreiche, 327 M
Ach nun ist mein Jesus hin, 27 L
Ach, schläfrige Seele, wie? 16 O
Ach, schlage doch bald, 15 G
Ach! Stefan scheltet meine Thorheit nur, 346 B
Ach, treuer Gott, Herr Jesu Christ, 118 Q
Ach, um deine feuchten Schwingen, 228 Q, 322 G
Ach, und du mein kühles Wasser!, 59 P
Ach, was ist Leben, 295 S
Ach, was soll der Mensch verlangen, 429 H
Ach, wende diesen Blick, 570
Ach, wenn es nun die Mutter wüsst', 316 J
Ach, wenn ich nur ein Liebchen hätte, 423 A
Ach, wenn's nur der König auch wüsst', 336 B
Ach, wer bringt die schönen Tage, 327 A
Ach, wer heilet die Schmerzen, 54 I
Ach, wer nimmt von meiner Seele, 60 B
Ach wie flüchtig, ach wie nichtig, 10 C
Ach, wie ist möglich dann, 199 H
Ach, wie so bald verhallet der Reigen, 230 C
Ach, wie so herrlich zu schau'n, 352 Q
Ach zie se tomu privyka, 345 K
Achieved is the glorious work, 170 B
Achzen und erbärmlich weinen, 9 G
Acis and Galatea, 158 J
Acis y Galatea, 262 E
Adam muss in uns verwesen, 10 J
Adamastor, roi des vagues, 233 I
Addio a Napoli, 83 P
Addio, addio, 400 E
Addio al mamma, 200 F
Addio, amore!, 287 G
Addio del passato, 402 K
Addio dolce svegliare, 283 S
Addio, fiorito asil, 285 F
Addio, o miei sospiri, 131 B

Ade. du muntre, du fröhlche Stadt, 318 L
Adelaide, 35 B
Adieu, 108 G, 177 Q, 185 C
Adieu, chère Louise! 237 R
Adieu, conservez dans votre âme, 130 F
Adieu de l'hôtesse arabe, 47 Q
Adieu des Bergers, L', 42 H
Adieu, dit il, ayez foi, 380 D
Adieu donc, vains objets, 222 P
Adieu du matin, L', 275 E
Adieu fière cité, 43 B
Adieu, forêt profonde, 66 J
Adieu, forêts, adieu, 376 K
Adieu m'amour, 99 H
Adieu, Mignon, Courage, 381 D
Adieu, mon doux rivage, 233 D
Adieu, notre petite table, 223 L
Adieu suprême, L', 275 P
Adieu, sweet Amaryllis, 427 J
Adieux, va, mon homme, 298 I
Adina, credimi, 95 A
Adios Tortosa, 263 E
Admeto, 150 O
Adolescentulus sum, 84 H
Adoramus te, Christe, 122 O, 268 G
Adoramus te Jesu Christe, 166 K
Adoramus te, K.327, 244 D
Adriana Lecouvreur, 80 B
Adriano in Seria, 122 G
Aennchen von Tharau, 343 H
Aeolsharfe, 300 H
Aetherische ferne Stimmen, 59 C
Affanni del pensier, 154 B
Afraid, am I afraid?, 232 G
Africaine, L', 233 D
Aftenstimmung, 193 B
After night has gone comes the day, 91 O
After the battle, 257 L
After years, 259 L
Again as before, 379 I
Again my Lyre, 38 A
Agathe, 1 E
Agnes, 58 F, 428 I
Agnes la jouvencelle, 7 M
Agnus dei, 23 S, 34 H, 43 Q, 47 R, 66 G, 70 B, 109 D, 134 B, 169 H, 202 J, 208 L, 213 R, 243 N, 244 C, 255 P, 267 L, 268 F, 317 B, 389 C, 405 J
Agrippina, 151 A
Agyptische Helena, Die, 354 F
Ah! Alga di mare, 80 R
Ah beaux faiseurs de systèmes, 90 P
Ah! Belinda, 288 L
Ah! bello a me ritorna, 38 M
Ah! ce n'est pas encore, 99 Q
Ah! ce soir là vraiment, 180 G
Ah! c'est l'amour endormi, 91 I
Ah! c'est toi que j'embrasse, 51 M
Ah! che a voi perdoni Iddio, 113 R
Ah! chi mi dice mai, 249 S
Ah come da quel di, 309 H
Ah come, weary one, 51 R
Ah, dear heart, why do you rise?, 125 D
Ah! del Tebro al giogo, 38 Q
Ah dit la fille frivole, 280 J
Ah, divinités implacables, 129 E

Ah, do not wreathe, 127 J
Ah dolente partita!, 426 H
Ah! dov' è il perfido?, 251 G
Ah! faut-il me venger, 212 N
Ah! fors'e lui, 401 O
Ah! fuggi il traditor, 250 G
Ah! fuyez à présent, 279 F
Ah! fuyez, douce image, 224 D
Ah! give me air, 256 M
Ah! how pleasant 'tis to love, 290 B
Ah! how sweet it is to love, 287 O
Ah! how we did fight, 283 A
Ah! jarniqué, 221 I
Ah! Je ris de me voir si belle en ce miroir, 135 E
Ah! la charmante chose, 279 L
Ah, la paterna mano, 397 P
Ah, leave me not to pine alone, 369 L
Ah! lève-toi, soleil, 137 F
Ah. lo previdi, K. 272, 243 Q
Ah! lo veggio, quell' anima bella, 252 M
Ah, Love, But a Day, 32 M
Ah, love, could I but take the hours, 388 B
Ah, mai non cessate, 93 F
Ah, malgré moi mon faible coeur partage, 129 A
Ah! malheureuse Russie, 257 K
Ah! Manon mi tradisce, 285 P
Ah! Mathilde, idole de mon âme, 309 L
Ah! may the red rose live alway, 115 B
Ah! mio bene, 95 J
Ah! mio cor, 151 F
Ah! mon ami, j'implore ta pitié, 130 N
Ah! mon fils, sois béni!, 234 O
Ah! mon remords te venge, 233 Q
Ah Monsieur Florestan! 232 Q
Ah, moon of my delight, 204 R
Ah, my heart, how hard is life to bear, 378 O
Ah! my heart is back in Napoli, 173 K
Ah! non credea mirarti, 39 Q
Ah! non giunge, 39 R
Ah, non sai, qual pena sia, 24F J
Ah! non son io che parlo, 245 E
Ah! nôw rings a voice I know, 428 Y
Ah! per sempre, 39 A
Ah per sempre, o mio bell' angiol, 395 O
Ah! Perfido, 35 C
Ah, pietà! signori miei, 250 P
Ah! quale incognito, 131 G
Ah! quand reviendra-t-il le temps, 384 F
Ah! quanto è verro, 75 H
Ah! quel diner, 265 K
Ah! quel giorno, 309 G
Ah, quel plaisir, 49 H
Ah, quel tourment, 141 N
Ah! qu'il est loin mon pays!, 224 J
Ah rendimi quel core, 307 D
Ah! responds à ma tendresse, 312 R
Ah! rido ben di core, 401 B
Ah, ritorna età, 230 S

Ah! ritrovarla, 221 B
Ah, se fosse intorno al trono, 254 J
Ah. se intorno a quest' urna, 130 Q
Ah si, ben mio coll' essere, 403 K
Ah! si fa core e abbraccia mi, 38 N
Ah, si j'avais des ailes de colombe, 178 Q
Ah! si j'avais souffert, 200 C
Ah! si je redevenais belle, 136 J
Ah, si la liberté, 129 J, 212 D
Ah sieh da, ein herrlich Frauenbild, 353 G
Ah s'il est dan votre village, 85 G, 132 K
Ah! spietato, 151 L
Ah, stay with me, my lovely boy, 6 E
Ah! sweet mystery of life, 173 I
Ah, t'in vola agl' occhi, 243 Q
Ah, tra l'ire e tra gli sdegni, 246 M
Ah! tu dei vivere, 392 H
Ah! tu non sai, 154 C
Ah! tu solo, amor, 307 R
Ah, tutta per te, mio bene, 439 J
Ah, twine no blossoms, 127 J
Ah, un foco in solito, 93 S
Ah! venisse il caro oggetto, 308 A
Ah! vieni, vieni amor mio, 391 L
Ah! viens, ah! viens! responds au tendre appel, 51 F
Ah! Viens dans la forêt profonde, 91 K
Ah! vivre doux, 264 L
Ah! vous dirais-je maman, 2 A
Ah what pains, 290 C
Ah, when the dark on many a heart descends, 440 O
Ah, who once wore a fine bonnet, 172 J
Ah, you young rascal, 258 I
Ah—che la morte ognora, 403 Q
Ahi ca so acerbo, 240 E
Ahi sventurato amente, 240 I
Ahi troppo è duro, 238 G
Ai nostri monti, 404 B
Aïda, 391 B
Aillte, 190 H
Aimable Lisette forme ces concerts, L', 296 F
Aimons-nous, 137 M, 313 H
Ainsi que la brise legère, 134 P
Ainsi toujours poussés, 261 R
Aio dè rotso, L', 72 I
Air and Variations, 282 Q
Air champêtre, 279 E
Air, L', 146 L
Air de Roses, 42 N
Air des colombes, 302 Q
Air du Rossignol, 221 L
Air est embaumé, L', 225 Q
Air est léger, L', 40 O
Air from County Derry, 5 H
Air gai, 296 C
Air grave, 279 F
Air léger, 296 E
Air of Venus, 75 H
Air romantique, 279 D
Air serieux, 84 D
Air tendre, 296 B
Air vif, 279 G
Airs chantés, 279 D
Airy violin, The, 292 B

Aj, jaky to krásny den, 347 I
Aj, vizte lovce tam, 347 E
Ajo lovas katonának, 194 D
Ak, hvem der Havde en Hue, 172 J
Ak, kjaereste, Hr. Guldsmed, 122 D
Akkor szép az erdö, 194 O
Al fato dan legge, 252 B
Al paño fino en la tienda, 106 I
Al sen ti stringo e parto, 151 K
Al suon del tamburo, 395 P
Al veurer despuntar, 263 K
Alas, alas, 101 M
Alas! It is my lonely fate, 259 N
Alas! my love you do me wrong, 5 D
Alas! that spring should vanish with the rose, 204 S
Alba separa dalla luce l'ombra, L', 384 S
Albatros, L', 199 D
Alcandro, lo confesso, 249 H
Alceste, 128 O, 211 O
Alcina, 151 F
Alcools, 177 M
Aleko, 294 N
Alessandro, 153 N
Alessandro Stradella, 114 B
Alexander Balus, 158 O
Alexander Nevsky, 283 A
Alexander's Feast, 149 S
Alfin son tua, 98 A
Alinde, 324 C
All' abend bevor ich zur Ruhe, 1 C
All about the Bogyman, 258 H
All' armi!, 403 M
All blessings that our God hath given, 5 B
All creatures now, 41 J
All danger disdaining, 159 E
All day on the prairie, 145 R
All for you, 379 A
All Granada lieth quiet, 378 F
All Hussars are splendid fellows, 196 G
All' idea di quel metallo, 307 M
All in a misty morning, 272 O
All in the April evening, 305 P
All in the April morning, 177 K
All in the downs, 272 L
All in the Downs the fleet was moor'd, 207 C
All' infelice veglio, 394 F
All is prepared for sealing and for signing, 372 L
All mein Gedanken, 356 S
All' mein Wirken, 326 C
All men should once with love grow tender, 377 D
All my days are clouded, 196 A
All our homes, 195 L
All past the feast days, 259 M
All the hemp, 196 H
All the things you are, 191 E
All the world is but smoke, 440 A
All things depart, 295 L
All things here remind me, 86 K
All through the day, 191 F
All through the night, 440 C
All we like sheep have gone astray, 163 H
All you that must take a leap, 273 I

Allá arribita, 263 D
Alla riva del Tebro, 267 B
Alla vita che t'arride, 392 O
Allah, 75 O
Allah be with us, 440 O
Alle de duggvaate blomster har sennt, 29 O
Alle Dinge haben Sprache, 438 C
Alle gingen, Herz, zur Ruh, 428 R
Alle maskirt, 352 M
Alle Tage klopfen, 168 J
Alle Winde schlafen, 56 D
Allégez moy, 189 B
Allegro, L', 150 B
Allein zu dir, Herr Jesu Christ, 10 L
Alleluia, 4 Q, 4 R, 179 F, 313 F, 381 Q
Alleluia! tulerunt Dominum, 268 H
Alleluja! 159 I, 242 N, 242 R, 419 M
Aller au bois, 304 S
Aller Berge Gipfel ruh'n, 311 R
Aller End' ist doch David, 410 K
Aller erst lebe ich mir werde, 418 S
Allerseelen, 201 E, 356 F
Alles, Alles, Alles was Odem hat, 229 H
Alles endet, was entstehet, 428 K
Alles fühlt der Liebe Freuden, 253 P
Alles geht am Schnürchen, 344 Q
Alles ist schlafen gegangen, 377 N
Alles ist so gut wie richtig, 344 E
Alles mach'n voll Ehrfurcht mir Spalier, 352 E
Alles nur nach Gottes Willen, 13 G
Alles pflegt schon längst der Ruh'!, 422 E
Alles theile unser Glück, 114 C
Alles, was denn hat, 24 E
Allez remplir ma place, 212 B
Allmacht, Die, 324 A
Allmächt'ge Jungfrau, 417 H
Allmächt'ger Vater, blick herab! 413 C
Allnächtlich im Traume, 335 H
Allons gaiment recevons leur homage, 49 K
Allons, gay, gay, gay Bergéres, 83 M
Allons! jeunes gens, 137 E
Allorchè sorge astro lucenti, 156 C
Alma mia, 153 B
Alma redemptoris mater, 99 I, 269 K
Alma, sintamos, 262 D
Alme belle, che vedete, 249 G
Alme belle innamorate, 243 C
Almira, 158 I
Alouette, L', 186 R
Alpenjäger, Der, 321 H
Als Büblein klein, 261 M
Als der Frühling sich vom Herzen, 329 O
Als die alte Mutter, 102 L
Als du im kühnem Sange, 416 I
Als du zum Gatten mich erkoren, 377 L
Als ein Gott, 355 B
Als Eva aus dem Paradies, 411 E
Als flotter Geist doch früh, 353 D

Als ich auf dem Euphrat schiffte, 428 L
Als ich das erste Veilchen blickt, 228 K
Als ich sie erröthen sah, 326 C
Als ich still und ruhig spann, 325 F
Als Luise die Briefe ihres ungetreuen Liebhabers verbrannte, 249 O
Als mir dein Lied erklang, 359 J
Als zullendes Kind, 414 L
Also hat Gott die Welt geliebt, 12 S
Also ihr lebt noch, 192 D
Also lieb' ich euch, 336 H
Altal mennék én a Tiszán, 31 I
Altdeutsches Lied, 229 L
Alte, Die, 249 L
Alte Herr, Der, 139 E
Alte Laute, 332 P
Alte Liebe, 59 I
Alte Sturm, die alte Müh', Der, 413 S
Alten, bösen Lieder, Die, 335 J
Altes Minnelied, 62 P
Altra notte, L', 50 D
Am Abend aber desselbigen Sabbaths, 11 B
Am Abend da es kühle war, 28 F
Am Anfang gedeiht man, 425 O
Am Bach im Frühling, 326 D
Am Bach viel kleine Blumen stehn, 317 M
Am Brünnele, 300 M
Am Brunner vor dem Tore, 319 E
Am Donaustrande, 63 G
Am Feierabend, 317 H
Am Fenster, 324 P
Am fernen Horizonte, 318 P
Am Flusse, 326 E
Am frisch geschnitt'nen Wandestab, 430 R
Am Gesteine rauscht die Flut, 62 S
Am Grabe Anselmos, 320 Q
Am Jordan Sankt Johannes stand, 411 G
Am jüngsten Tag ich aufersteh, 60 O
Am Kreuzweg da lausche ich, 437 K
Am leuchtenden Sommermorgen, 119 N, 335 F
Am Meer, 318 Q
Am Neckar, am Rhein, 1 B
Am Rhein, 184 D
Am schönsten Sommerabend war's, 142 R
Am See, 326 F
Am Sonntag Morgen zierlich angetan, 57 J
Am stillen Herd, 410 N
Am Strande, 112 L
Am Strome, 321 A
Am Sylvester-Abend, 330 E
Am Ufer, 358 I
Am Ufer des Flusses, des Manzanares, 187 S
Am Wiesenhügel, 310 S
Amadigi, 151 L
Amadis, 211 Q
Amami, Alfredo, 402 D
Amant Jaloux, L', 141 L
Amanti costanti, 248 Q

A-many years ago, when I was young and charming, 364 E
Amarilli mia bella, 70 I
Amaro sol per te, 286 S
Ambo nati in questa valle, 96 N
Ame d'une flûte, L', 110 I
Ame évaporée et souffrante, L', 88 L
Amelette Ronsardelette, 298 N
Amen, 274 S
Amen Chorus, 164 G
Amerò, saro costante, L', 243 E
Amfortas! Die Wunde! 412 N
Amfortas' Prayer, Parsifal, 412 P
Amico Fritz, L', 218 M
Aminte, 423 H
Amis, la matinée est belle, 7 Q
Amo, Amas, I love a Lass, 7 F
Amo come il fulgor del creato, L', 278 J
Amor, 238 D, 359 K
Amor, amor che langue il cor, 69 J
Amor, amor, non dormir più, 361 P
Amor Brujo, El, 106 B
Amor commanda, 153 C
Amor dice amor, 238 D
Amor dormiglione, 361 P
Amor mi fa sovente, 302 C
Amor, nel mio penar, 152 Q
Amor, Summa injuria, 3 K
Amor ti vieta, 126 P
Amor y odio, 139 K
Amore, amore! gaudio tormento, 391 M
Amore dei tre re, L', 238 B
Amore! Misterio celeste profondo!, 50 H
Amore o grillo, 284 O
Amorosi miei giorni, 93 G
Amour auquel tout invite, L', 179 L
Amour, ce dieu profane, L', 379 S
Amour d'antan, 77 G
Amour de Moi, L', 5 E
Amour, donne moy payx, 201 J
Amour en soit béni, 44 F
Amour est un enfant Bohême, L', 46 G
Amour est un enfant timide, L', 423 I
Amour est un monstre, L', 349 C
Amour est un oiseau rebelle, L', 46 F
Amour est une vertu rare, L', 224 Q
Amour Mouillé, L', 388 D
Amour, quand du destin, 296 J
Amour, que veux-tu de moi?, 211 S
Amour qui meurs, 147 C
Amour, ranime mon courage, 137 K
Amour sacré de la patrie, 7 R
Amour s'envole, L', 423 I
Amour toujours l'amour, L', 121 F
Amour! viens aider, 312 P
Amour, vois quels maux, 212 F
Amoureux séparés, 310 L
Amours divins, 264 D
Amuri, amuri, 312 D

An Celia's Baum in stiller Nacht, 231 E
An Chloe, 249 Q
An dem Brünnele, 300 M
An dem Feuer sass das Kind Amor, 359 K
An dem reinsten Frühlingsmorgen, 435 I
An den Abendstern, 338 Q
An den Mond, 59 E, 323 C, 326 G, 338 B
An den Rhein, 231 M
An den Schlaf, 420 O
An den Sonnenschein, 332 S
An den Tod, 326 H
An der Quelle sass der Knabe, 327 Q
An die Entfernte, 230 G, 326 I
An die ferne Geliebte, 35 F
An die Freunde, 326 J
An die Geliebte, 35 L, 428 P
An die Hoffnung, 35 M, 301 C
An die Laute, 324 D
An die Leier, 322 P
An die Musik, 324 E
An die Nachtigall, 57 D, 324 L, 325 R
An die Sonne, 325 E, 326 K
An die Tauben, 58 K
An die Türen will ich schleichen, 321 F, 338 M, 431 O
An dir allein, 36 D
An eine Aeolsharfe, 56 B, 428 Q
An einem Bache, 143 G
An einen Boten, 199 J
An ihrem bunten Liederin, 426 D
An irdische Schätze, 10 C
An jenem Tag, 217 K
An mein Clavier, 326 L
An meinem Herzen, 334 J
An Schwager Kronos, 321 M
An Silvia, 324 S
Anacreon's defeat, 290 D
Anakreons Grab, 428 M
Anathema, 112 P
Anch' io vorrei dormir cosi, 80 K
And by day and by night, 257 J
And did those feet in ancient time, 270 N
And every one will say, 367 F
And he came by her cabin, 81 L
And he shall purify, 162 O
And how are you? And how is John?, 232 I
And it's will ye quaff with me, 197 N
And so 'tis my heart, 259 P
And the brass will crash, 365 J
And the glory to the Lord, 162 L
And with His stripes we are healed, 163 G
And you should gaze deep down in my eyes, 198 A
Andaluza, 263 C
Andenken, 35 E, 428 N
Anders wird die Welt, 431 R
Andiam, andiam, mio bene, 250 F
André ne connait pas la dame, 280 O
Andrea Chenier, 126 B
Ane blanc, L', 181 K
Anemone, The, 342 R
Anèmone et l'ancolie, L', 177 N
Ange adorable, 137 D

Ange est venu, Un, 40 J
Ange Guardien, L', 117 N
Angelehnt an die Epheuwand, 56 B, 428 Q
Angelina Baker, 115 C
Angels ever bright and fair, 166 D
Angel's Serenade, 52 R
Angels that around us hover, 418 M
Angélus, Les, 87 M
Angelus de la Mer, L', 133 L
Anges du paradis, 136 H
Anges purs, anges radieux, 135 N
Angiol caro, soave, beato, 95 H
Anima ho stanca, L', 80 E
Animam meam, 407 E
Anirem al camp, 262 N
Anklänge, 55 P
Ann Street, 185 S
Anna Magdalena Bach Notebook, 28 I
Anneau d'argent, L', 76 B
Anne par jeu me jecta, 297 M
Année en vain, L', 87 C
Annie Laurie, 341 C
Ano, marně, 346 H
Another good cow-puncher has gone, 186 A
Another hour with thee, 388 B
Answer, The, 295 D
Antiphon, 269 Q
Antoine, L', 72 L
Antonius zur Predigt die Kirche findt ledig, 214 N
Antouèno, L', 72 L
Anzoletta sang: Komm mia bella, 237 E
Aoua, 299 D
Apaisement, 77 H
Aperite mihi portas justitiae, 68 S
Apothecary, The, 168 J
Appalachia, 91 O
Apple Blossoms, 198 D
Après un rêve, 107 P
Apri la tua finestra! 220 J
April is in my mistress' face, 241 B
Aprila, bella, 439 N
Aprile, 385 A
Aprite, presto aprite, 248 J
Aprite tutte le finestra, 80 O
Apró alma lehulott, 194 P
Aquarelles, 87 R
Arabella, 354 H
Arabien, mein Heimatland, 422 R
Arapete fenesta, 73 H
Arboles de Aranjuez, Los, 263 F
Archibald Douglas, 209 S
Arde la palma, 398 K
Ardo, 238 E
Ardo si ma non t'amo, 238 F
Areglito, El, 441 D
Arge dich, o Seele, nicht, 19 E
Argwohn Josephs, 175 O
Aria de Acis y Galatea, 262 E
Ariadne auf Naxos, 354 P
Ariane et Barbe-Bleue, 99 Q
Ariette, 405 P
Ariettes oubliées, 87 N
Ariodante, 151 K, 226 M
Arioso, 90 I, 92 M
Arise to arms, 283 B
Arise, ye Russian people, 283 B

Arise, ye subterranean winds, 289 O
Arlesiana, 80 I
Arm, arm ye brave, 161 I
Arme Jonathan, Der, 237 G
Arme Peter, Der, 335 Q
Arme Peter wankt vorbei, Der, 335 S
Armellin vita non cura, L', 152 R
Armen will der Herr umarmen, Die, 19 E
Armez vous d'un noble courage, 129 Q
Armida's garden, 270 L
Armide, 129 G, 212 B
Arminio, 158 H
Armorer's Song, 197 Q
Arnes Sang, 172 K
Arpège, 110 I
Arrêtez ò mes frères! 312 J
Arról alúl, 194 K
Arrow and the song, The, 276 P
As a spirit didst thou pass before me, 104 I
As a white candle in a holy place, 305 S
As ever I saw, 420 B
As I walked out one morning, 390 I
As I was goin' to Ballynure, 182 B
As pants the hart, 348 O
As resplendent the sun fills the heaven, 256 D
As someday it may happen, 365 M
As the gloaming shadows creep, 213 I
As torrents in summer, 104 B
As Vesta was from Latmos hill descending, 424 N
As when the dove laments her love, 158 J
As with rose steps the morn, 166 E
Ascolta, ascolta, 283 R
Ash Grove, The, 64 H
Asie, 298 O
Asile héréditaire, 309 Q
Ask if yon damask rose, 165 P
Ask me to love no more, 290 E
Aspettare e non venire, 273 P
Aspri rimorsi atroci, 247 G
Asra, Der, 311 O
Assis sur cette blanche tombe, 313 Q
Assumpta est Maria, 267 E
Astray, 342 G
Astres étincelants, 222 N
As-tu souffert, 381 F
Asturiana, 106 K, 262 P
Aszszony, Aszszony, 194 L
Aszszonyok, Aszszonyok, 31 J
At dawning, 70 P
At parting, 197 L, 306 G
At the ball, 378 H
At the Brookside, 143 G
At the cry of the first bird, 145 S
At The Fox Inn the tatter'd ears, 420 G
At the open window, 379 D
At the tree I shall suffer, 272 E
At the well, 146 D
Atalanta, 151 Q
Athalia, 158 R
Athmest du nicht, 410 E
Atlas, der, 318 M

Attaque du Moulin, L', 66 J
Attente, L', 313 I
Attila, 392 L
Attributs, 281 P
Atys, 212 H
Au beau milieu de l'ile verte, 236 A
Au bord de l'eau, 107 R
Au bord du chemin, 221 L
Au bruit de la guerre, 96 D
Au bruit des lourds marteaux, 136 K
Au ciel sept chérubins, 236 L
Au cimetière, 109 H, 313 Q
Au clair de la lune, 211 N
Au fleuve le ruisseau, 137 M
Au fond du lac silencieux, 47 O
Au fond du temple saint, 47 J
Au joli bois, 379 P
Au joly bois, 341 L
Au joly jeu, 186 S
Au loin c'est l'Angelus, 133 L
Au loin dans la mer, 184 S
Au milieu du jardin, 301 O
Au mont Ida trois déesses, 264 E
Au pays, 176 K
Au pays où se fait la guerre, 100 E
Au, peu m'importe à moi!, 51 D
Au premier jour du joly moys de may, 187 A
Au Printemps, 137 N
Au Rossignol, 137 O
Au sein des nuits tout dort, 276 D
Saint Esprit, 73 D
Au soleil brilliant glorie, 51 A
Au verd boys, 187 B
Au village sur la rivière, 127 O
Aubade, 200 D, 341 P
Aubry's Cent Motets, 4 S
Auch das Schöne muss sterben, 54 N
Auch ich dart mich so glücklich nennen, 417 C
Auch ich war ein Jüngling, 210 Q
Auch kleine Dinge, 428 R
Auch mit gedämpften schwachen Stimmen, 10 Q
Audivi, 376 B
Auf! Auf! Ergreifet der Verräther, 34 Q
Auf, Auf, Gläubige, 17 H
Auf, auf mit hellem Schall, 17 C
Auf, auf zu Gottes Lob, 118 M
Auf Christi Himmelfahrt allein, 17 C
Auf das Trinkglas eines verstorbenen Freundes, 332 J
Auf dem Dorf' in den Spinnstubn, 339 A
Auf dem Flusse, 319 G
Auf dem grünen Balkon, 428 S
Auf dem Hügel sitz' ich, 35 F
Auf dem Kirchhofe, 61 H
Auf dem Meers, 119 C
Auf dem Schiffe, 61 C
Auf dem See, 58 D
Auf dem Teich, dem regungslosen, 230 H
Auf dem Wasser zu singen, 323 Q
Auf der Bruck, 324 H
Auf der Heide weht der Wind, 59 G
Auf der Messe, 209 N

Auf der Reise zur Heimat, 143 H
Auf der Treppe sitzen meine Ohrchen, 175 E
Auf die Dächer zwischen blassen Wolken, 435 J
Auf die Nacht in den Spinnstubn, 61 P
Auf ein altes Bild, 429 A
Auf eine Christblume, 429 B
Auf einem verfallenen Kirchof, 192 L
Auf einen Totenakker, 320 B
Auf einer Burg, 333 N
Auf einer Wanderung, 429 D
Auf Flügeln des Gesanges, 228 O
Auf frisch genähtem Weideplatz, 356 F
Auf geheimen Waldespflade, 41 P
Auf, Gesellen, greift zur Axt, 211 C
Auf, hebe die funkelnde Schaale empor zum Mund, 357 G
Auf hohem Bergesrücken, 321 H
Auf hohem Felsen lag' ich träumend, 408 Q
Auf ihrem Leibrösslein, 431 A
Auf olkigen Höh'n, 414 O
Auf unserm Hof, 425 P
Aufenthalt, 318 J
Auferzesteh'n, ja aufersteh'n, 216 A
Auflösung, 326 N
Aufs Wohlsein meiner Dame, 435 C
Auftrag, 429 F
Aufträge, 336 L
Augen leuchtendes Paar, Der, 414 I
Aujourd'hui le printemps, 385 N
Auld Lang Syne, 37 J
Auprès de cette grotte sombre, 89 E, 89 P
Aura amorosa, Un', 252 H
Aurore, 108 L, 235 Q
Aurore s'allume, L', 427 C
Aus alten Märchen winkt es, 335 I
Aus banger Brust, 342 N
Aus dem Wald fort in die Welt, 414 N
Aus dem Walde tritte die Nacht, 356 B
Aus den hebräischen Gesängen, 331 H
Aus den Himmelsaugen droben, 119 C
Aus den östlichen Rosen, 331 N
Aus der Ferne in die Nacht, 438 D
Aus der Heimat hinter den Blitzen, 55 K, 333 H
Aus der Jugendzeit, 295 Q
Aus der Schiffsbank mach' ich meinen Pfühl, 359 F
Aus des Nachbars Haus trat mein Lieb, 105 H
Aus Egypten vor dem Volke, 325 N
Aus Goethe's Faust, 35 N
Aus "Heliopolis", 323 O, 326 O
Aus Liebe, 28 A
Aus meinen grossen Schmerzen, 119 A

Aus meinen Thränen spriessen, 334 O
Aus tiefer Not, 65 P
Ausfahrt, 142 C
Aussi nombreux, 234 P
Automne, 108 D, 177 O
Autour de la Sainte Vierge, 179 P
Autour d'elle des amants, 87 A
Autrefois un roi de Thulé, 42 O
Autumn, 170 L, 201 B, 378 R
Autumn evening, 293 L
Autumn Storm, 142 H
Aux voiles, aux cordages, 233 J
Avvezzo al contento, 131 N
Avant de quitter ces lieux, 134 L
Avant que tu ne t'en ailles, 110 D
Ave Maria, 5 N, 65 R, 83 B, 99 J, 137 P, 189 C, 189 D, 190 F, 220 B, 231 A, 251 P, 322 S, 385 B, 386 B, 404 J, 407 F
Ave Signor, 49 M
Ave verum, 70 C, 189 E, 253 D, 313 J
Avec la garde montante, 46 D
Avec quoi qu'on peignera les boucles, 360 I
Avec sa belle prestance, 179 I
Avec ses quatre dromadaires, 279 N
Avoir tant adorée, L', 233 M
Avril est de retour, 107 N
Awake, sweet love, 98 O
Awake the harp, the lyre awake, 169 N
Awake the trumpet's lofty sound, 164 K
Away, away, my heart's on fire, 369 D
Awful pleasing Being, say, 160 O
Ay, Ay, Ay, 273 L
Ay majo de mi vida, 139 P
Aymer est ma vie, 82 C
Azaël! Pourquoi m'as tu quittée, 87 E
Azok, Azok, 92 S

B

Babes in Toyland, 173 B
Baccanale (Chorus of Sirens), Tannhäuser, 416 E
Bacchanal, 79 B
Bacchus ever fair and young, 149 S
Bäche von gesalznen Zähren, 9 P
Bachianas Brasileiras No. 5, 406 C
Bacio, Il, 5 S
Bacio di mano, Un, 251 N
Bächlein, lass dein Rauschen, 317 O
Back to the vanished years, 287 M
Bada, Santuzza schiavo, 219 P
Baigne d'eau, 224 S
Baigne d'eau, 224 S
Bail. re, 72 H
Baisers de Dorinde, Les, 44 H
Bal, sur le parc incendié, Le, 310 P
Balcon, Le, 88 G
Bald gras ich am Nekkar, 214 Q
Bald ist der Nacht, 433 R
Ballad for Americans, 306 B
Ballad of Annie Miller, 195 N
Ballad of Stephen Kadar, 195 H
Ballad of trees and the Master, A, 75 P

Ballade à la lune, 199 P
Ballade de Villon à s'amye, 89 L
Ballade des femmes de Paris, 89 N
Ballade des gros Dindons, 75 K
Ballade of Queen Mab, 137 B
Ballade que Villon fait à la requeste de sa mère pour prier Nostre-Dame, 89 M
Ballato, 302 A
Ballet, 281 R
Balletto della Ingrate, Il, 238 G
Ballo in maschera, Un, 392 N
Ballynure ballad, A, 182 B
Banalités, 279 I
Banish sorrow, banish care, 288 E
Banjo song, A, 177 I
Banks of Allan Water, The, 181 D
Bannis la crainte, 128 S
Barbara Allen, 386 P
Barbarasong, 425 J
Barbare, non, sans toi, 129 D
Barber of Seville, The, 307 I
Barbier von Bagdad, Der, 83 C
Barcarolle, 7 M, 7 Q, 107 Q, 138 I, 264 O, 278 E, 392 S
Barcheta, La, 146 M
Barkarole, 356 N
Bartered bride, The, 343 S
Basies moy, 189 F
Bastien and Bastienne, 241 P
Bat, The, 351 D
Bataille de Marignan, La, 187 C
Batti, batti, o bel Masetto, 250 K
Battle's roar is over, The, 371 E
Be glad then America, 44 N
Be not afraid, 227 D
Be not extreme, O Lord, 104 H
Be now gracious O kind heaven, 170 H
Be silent despair of affection, 128 G
Be thou faithful unto death, 228 D
Beati mortui, 231 D
Beati qui habitant, 296 M
Beatitudes, Les, '117 O
Beato chi può, 75 D
Beau ciel, tu m'apparais, 3 I
Beau lit bien fait, Le, 360 O
Beau monstre de nature, 44 G
Beau soir, 88 B
Beautiful dreamer, 115 E
Beautiful morning is breaking, A, 206 P
Because, 166 P
Because you're you, 173 P
Bedecke deinen Himmel, 329 E
Bedeckt mich mit Blumen, 429 F
Bedekke deinen Himmel, Zeus, 434 O
Bedouin love song, 276 Q
Been a-lis'nin' all de night long, 67 O
Beet, schon lokkert sich in die Höh, Das, 430 O
Beetle, The, 258 J
Before my window, 295 J
Before the barndoor crowing, 272 D
Befraget mich ein zartes Kind, 241 R
Befreit, 358 F
Begegnung, 429 G
Beggar student, The, 236 R

Beggar's Opera, 271 D, 425 G
Beggar's song, The, 207 B
Begin to trace, 382 N
Begli occhi, mercè, 379 N
Begl'occhi del mio ben, 156 D
Begluckt darf nun dich, 417 G
Beglückte Heerde, 16 B
Beherzigung, 429 H
Behold and see, 163 J
Behold, my friend, the daisies, 295 N
Behold, o weak and foolish man, 170 Q
Behold the lamb of God, 163 D
Behold the Lord High Executioner!, 365 K
Behold the wide extended meads, 170 M
Behüt' dich Gott, 260 O
Bei dem angenehmsten Wetter singen, 434 S
Bei dem Glanz der Abend, 429 J
Bei dem Glanz der Abendröthe, 350 B
Bei dem Waldessaum, 105 I
Bei der Wiege, 229 F
Bei dir sind meine Gedanken, 60 L
Bei einer Trauung, 429 I
Bei jener Nacht, 354 F
Bei Männern, welche Liebe fühlen, 253 J
Bei Nacht im Dorf der Wachter rief, 430 E
Bei raggi lucenti, 95 I
Beiden Grenadiere, Die, 335 K
Beim Schneewetter, 300 K
Bekehrte, Die, 350 B, 429 J
Bel piacere, 150 A
Bel raggio lusinghier, 309 I
Bell Chorus from Pagliacci, 205 S
Bell song, 91 E
Bella Asteria, 157 M
Bella Colombetta, 69 I
Bella così madonna, 278 N
Bella figlio dell' amore, 401 A
Bella mia fiamma, addio, 251 J
Bella porta di rubini, 105 N, 302 B
Bella siccome un angelo, 93R
Belle au Bois Dormant, La, 88 C, 117 A
Belle, ayez pitié de nous, 380 S
Belle esclave more, La, 44 G
Belle est au jardin d'amour, La, 64 I
Belle Hélène, La, 263 D
Belle Hermione, 212 G
Belle Inès fait florès, La, 7 K
Belle jeunesse, La, 280 C
Belle nuit, ô nuit d'amour, 264 O
Belle source, 279 E
Bells of Saint Mary's, The, 2 F
Bells of San Marco, The, 185 E
Beloved, in your absence, 440 L
Belsatzar, 336 A
Belshazzar, 159 B
Belshazzar's Feast, 419 B
Ben' io sento l'ingrata, 151 Q
Benche ora piova, 200 P
Beneath a weeping willow's shade, 180 P
Beneath the cypress gloomy shade, 165 Q

Benedeit die sel'ge Mutter, 429 K
Benedicimi tu, madre, 439 M
Benediction, 378 L
Benedictus, 23 R, 34 G, 66 F, 69 A, 70 A, 121 R, 134 C, 201 I, 208 K, 243 M, 247 F, 255 O, 267 I, 267 M, 267 O, 268 U, 313 D, 389 B
Benedictus, qui venit, 69 A
Bens of Jura, The, 190 J
Benvenuto Cellini, 92 M
Berceaux, Les, 108 L
Berceuse, 72 R, 77 A, 106 M, 132 G, 140 K, 177 S, 235 R, 303 H, 304 R, 306 O, 381 H
Berceuse de la Sirène, 177 S
Beredsamkeit, Die, 171 G
Bereite dich, Zion, 25 A
Berenice, 152 G
Berg op Zoom, 198 G
Bergère Légère, 423 J
Bergerettes, 423 H
Bescheiden verborgen im buschichten Gang, 321 B
Bescheidene Liebe, 429 L
Bess of Bedlam, 290 F
Bess, you is my woman now, 124 D
Bester Jüngling, 247 N
Bestiaire, Le, 279 N
Bettelstudent, Der, 236 R
Bewahret euch vor Weifertücken, 253 O
Bewundert, o Menschen, 12 H
Bheir mi oro bhan, 190 I
Bianco e dolce cigno, Il, 5 0, 390 N
Biblical songs, 101 Q
Bid me discourse, 45 J
Bien aimé, prends ma main, 179 B
Bien aimé s'accoudant, Le, 206 S
Bien des jeunes gens, 146 O
Bienchen, Bienchen, 359 B
Bientôt, nous plogerons, 107 L
Bild, Das, 325 Q
Bill, 191 H
Bimba dagli occhi, 284 R
Bin eben angelangt, 195 P
Bin ich gleich von dir gewichen, 28 Q
Bin jung gewessen, 434 P
Bionda, bionda Clori, 68 I
Bird of the wilderness, The, 181 H
Bird songs at eventide, 82 E
Birdling why sing in the forest wide, 375 R
Birds in the night, 374 P
Birds of the forest are calling, The, 175 C
Birthday, A, 440 O
Birthday Cantata, 20 L
Bisher habt ihr nichts gebeten in meinem Namen, 14 Q
Bist du bei mir, 28 I
Biterolf, 429 M
Bitt' ihn, o Mutter, 429 N
Bitte, 119 H
Bitten, 29 G, 35 R
Bitteres zu sagen denkst du, 56 J
Bittersweet, 84 N
Blabaer-Li, 144 E
Black roses, 342 I
Black swan song, 232 C
Blackbird's song, 340 R
Black-ey'd Susan, 207 C
Blanche Dourga, 90 M
Blanche et tout en marbre, 304 P

Blasen nu alla, 40 B
Blasippan, 342 R
Blasse Blütten neigen ihre duftende Pracht, 438 K
Blauen Frühlingsaugen, Die, 120 D, 311 C
Blauer Himmel, blaue Wogen, 58 D
Blauer Sommer, Ein, 357 L
Bleib' bei uns, 8 Q
Bleiche Blüte, Blüte der Liebe, 357 M
Bless O Lord, 258 L
Bless the Lord, O my soul, 185 B
Bless this house, 53 E
Blessed are the men who fear him, 226 P
Blessed Virgin's expostulation, The, 290 H
Blest are the departed, 348 Q
Bleuet, 280 A
Blick' ich umher, 417 B
Blick von deinen Augen in die meinen, Ein, 230 O
Blicke mir nicht in die Lieder!, 214 E
Blind ploughman, The, 81 O
Blinde Kuh, 57 Q
Blindenklage, 359 E
Blondels Lied, 335 O
Bloom is on the Rye, The, 45 Q
Blow, blow thou winter wind, 6 I, 293 H
Blow one and all, 40 B
Bloweth the West Wind, 190 K
Blue Bell, The, 213 A
Blühe, blühe, liebes Veilchen, 438 M
Blümelein sie schlafen, Die, 55 I
Blümelein weiss am Wiegesrand, 101 N
Blumen Kränzlein, Das, 410 L
Blumengartenstrauss, Der, 229 E
Blumenglöckchen, Ein, 431 L
Blumengruss, 429 O
Blumenkranz, Der, 231 E
Blumenlied, 326 P
Blümlein im Garten, 119 B
Blute nur, 27 A
Boat on the waves is rocking, A, 144 K
Boat Song, 419 S
Bocca Vaga, La, 151 G
Boccaccio, 375 D
Boheme, La, 205 J, 293 H
Bohemian Girl, 29 S
Bohové mocní, 346 K
Bohové věcní, 346 D
Bois chers aux ramiers, 77 S
Bois épais redouble ton ombre, 211 R
Bois frissonant, 77 N
Bold and fierce and strong, ah, ha!, 369 P
Bolero, 90 K
Bon jour, bon jour, 201 K
Bon jour, bon mois, 99 K
Bon Saint Michel, 299 H
Bonheur est chose légère, Le, . 313 K
Bonjour, bonjour les fauvettes, 181 J
Bonjour, Suzon, 90 J
Bonne chanson, La, 109 R
Bonne journée, 282 B

Bonny Dundee, 273 D
Bonny Earl o' Moray, The, 64 J
Bonny gray-eyed moon, The, 271 E
Bonny laddie, Highland laddie, 37 N
Bons bourgeois et notables, 380 L
Bonum est, 269 F
Boot, saddle, to horse and away, 349 M
Booth led boldly with his big bass drum, 186 C
Boris Godunov, 256 C
Böse Farbe, Die, 318 B
Botschaft, 57 E
Boulangère a des écus, La, 264 H
Bow, bow, ye lower middle classes, 364 K
Boys are up in the woods, The, 185 F
Boys, be jolly, grief is folly, 79 B
Bracelet, Le, 44 F
Braconniers, Les, 264 I
Brahma, Dieu de croyants, 40 K
Braid the raven hair, 366 C
Brandenburgers in Bohemia, The, 346 L
Brauner Bursche führt zum Tanze, 55 C
Brauns Maidelein, 266 D
Brausen von den rauhen Winden, Das, 15 C
Brave Jonathan his bow ne'er drew, 165 B
Bravo, bravo, Don Pasquale, 94 L
Break the coconut, 145 O
Bredon Hill, 68 O, 389 H
Breit' über mein Haupt, 356 P
Brezairola, 72 R
Brezza aleggia intorno, La, 404 I
Brich dem Hungrigen dein Brod, 10 R
Brich entzwei, mein armes Herze, 28 J
Bridal chorus, 309 M
Bridal Chorus, Lohengrin, 410 C
Brigg Fair, 139 I
Bright April comes, 41 A
Bright as a ray, 353 C
Bright Cynthia, 290 G
Bright is the ring of words, 389 O
Bright Phoebus, 180 J
Bright Phoebus has mounted the chariot, 180 J
Bright stars fade, The, 168 G
Bright sunshine, 201 C
Brighter scenes I seek above, 160 I
Brightly dawns our wedding day, 366 F
Brilla sulla mia fronte, 127 A
Brillant auter de la lumière, 129 O
Brillar mi sento il core, 81 E
Brindisi, 220 D
Bring us in no brown bread, 420 H
Bring ye the cornet, 419 G
Bringet dem Herrn Ehre seines Namens, 18 B
Bringet des treu'sten, Herzens Grüsse, 228 N
Bringt her dem Herren, 339 S
Brise est douce et parfumée, La, 135 S

British Light Dragoons, 36 G
Brother, come and dance with me, 182 R
Brown Bird Singing, A, 440 C
Brown October Ale, 197 O
Brown Maid, The, 349 P
Brüderlein, Brüderlein und Schwesterlein, 351 R
Bruna gondoletta, La, 41 C
Brunete, 84 F
Brünnhilde's Immolation, Götterdämmerung, 416 B
Brünstiges Verlangen, 2 Q
Buch der hängenden Gärten, Das, 316 M
Buona sera, Signore, 308 E
Buona Zaza, 206 M
Bushes and briars, 388 F
Buss und Reu, 26 S
Busslied, 36 D
But as for his people, 159 R
But can I leave my pretty hussies, 273 G
But ere we this perform, 288 J
But lately in dance I embraced her, 6 D
But, Oh! sad virgin, 150 B
But oh! What art can teach, 150 M
But thanks be to God, 164 D
But the Lord is mindful of His own, 227 O
But the sheriff sold him, 196 S
But they dance in the city, 200 I
But Thou didst not leave his soul in Hell, 163 K
But who may abide the day, 162 M
Butterflies at Haga, 40 C
Buzzard, keep on flyin' over, 124 C
Buzzard Song, 124 C
By a lonely forest pathway, 145 C
By an' by, 67 K
By Celia's arbour, 231 E
By Killarney's lakes and fells, 30 G
By the bend of the river, 103 O
By the croaking of the toad, 289 J
By the Don a garden fair, 257 M
By the forest shady, 103 E
By the hatchet wounded, 140 I
By the old Moulmein Pagoda, 348 H
By the Rio Grande they dance, 200 H
By the River Don, 257 M
By the storm they breasted, 79 O
By the water, 259 Q
By the waters of Babylon, 102 D, 419 B
By the waters of Minnetonka, 207 H
By thee with bliss, 170 D
By yon bonny banks, 390 H
By-bye, by-bye sleep, 259 A

C

C., 280 B
Ca fait peur aux oiseux, 43 S
Ca n'a pas mordu, 298 C
Ca' the yowes, 390 D
Cachés dans cet asile, 132 G
Cäcilie, 357 F
Cadet Rousselle, 184 Q
Cadmus et Hermione, 212 F
Caid, Le, 379 R

Caille, La, 72 N
Calchas, d'un trait mortel blessé, 130 G
Calesera, La, 441 F
Calhé, Lo, 72 N
Caligaverunt oculi mei, 407 G
Call forth thy pow'rs, 161 J
Call of the Walküre, 413 R
Called to serve, 195 I
Callejeo, 139 L
Calm sea and mist, 41 F
Calmes dans le demi jour, 88 O, 109 O, 147 I, 375 O
Calumnia, La, 307 P
Calvaire, Le, 138 O
Came a bird a-flying, 195 A
Campanas del Amanecer, Las, 106 F
Camptown races, 115 F
Can anyone feel anyone moving, 382 I
Can love be controlled by advice?, 271 J
Can nothing warm me?, 291 I
Canards, les cygnes, les oies, Les, 361 J
Cançao de folha mortra, 406 K
Cançao de Saudade, 406 E
Cançao do carreiro, 406 O
Canción, 106 N
Canción del amor dolido, 106 B
Canción del fuego fatuo, 106 C
Canción gallega, 263 G
Cangio d'aspetto, 150 J
Can't help lovin' dat man, 191 I
Canta ó gala ven ó dia Erguete, 263 H
Canta pe' me, 85 M
Cantabile de Rysor, 266 M
Cantando, 390 O
Cantar, 262 R
Cantares, 387 E
Cantiga de Ninar, 235 L
Cantiguo do viuvo, 406 N
Cantilena, 387 K
Cantique de la bataille, 178 D
Cantique de la victoire, 178 G
Cantique des Prophètes, 178 R
Cantique des Vierges, 178 F
Cantique funèbre, 178 B
Cantique pour Noël, 1 J
Canto andaluz, 263 M
Canto baixinho uma vella cancao de ninar, 235 L
Canto de los pajaros, El, 263 K
Canto del lavoro, Il, 221 D
Canto di primavera, 80 O
Canto funebre, 301 P
Canzone di re Enzo, 302 C
Canzonetta, 210 E
Capinera, La, 41 A
Capriccio, 355 C
Capro e la capretta, Il, 248 S
Captain Stratton's Fancy, 376 D, 420 C
Captive, The, 140 O
Captive et peut-être oubliée je songe, 200 F
Cara sposa, 155 D
Cara sposa amato bene, 154 P
Caractacus, 104 G
Carattaco, 8 I
Caravane, La, 77 I, 294 G
Card Song, 47 D
Care for thy soul, 276 J

Care pupille, 48 G
Care selve, 151 R
Carefully on tiptoe stealing, 364 B
Cargoes, 92 Q
Carmen, 46 C
Carmena, 428 B
Carnations, 387 Q
Carnaval! joyeux Carnaval! 117 C
Carnevale di Venezia, 41 B
Carnival chorus, 305 C
Carnival of Venice, 41 B
Caro Amor, 152 I
Caro cibus, sanguis portus, 230 J
Caro laccio, dolce nodo, 122 P
Caro mio bin, 125 R
Caro voi siete all' alma, 156 N
Carol of bells, A, 349 I
Carpe, Le, 279 S
Carry me back to old Virginny, 48 E
Casta diva, 38 L
Castellana, 262 K
Castor et Pollux, 296 O
Cat and the bird cage, The, 258 O
Catalana, 262 N
Catalogue song, 250 A
Catarì, catarì, 73 M
Cattle in herds, The 169 R
Cavalier songs, 349 K
Cavaliero illustre, 50 A
Cavalleria rusticana, 219 E
Cavallo scalpita, Il, 219 I
Cavatine, 134 L
Ce Dieu que votre voix implore, 312 K
Ce que j'appelle beau, 224 K
Ce que je veux, 222 L
Ce moys de may, 187 D
Ce n'est la rosée, 236 F
Ce n'est pas ça que nous voulons, 281 J
Ce n'est plus le poids, 296 C
Ce n'était pas la même chose, 146 O
Ce que je suis sans toi, 137 Q
Ce qu'est le lierre sans l'ormeau, 137 Q
Ce sont gallons, 187 E
Cease, O my sad soul, 290 K
Cease your funning, 272 O
Celeste Aïda, 391 B
Celia has a thousand charms, 287 P
Celle que j'aime a de beauté, 109 M
Cenerentola, La, 308 H
Centenniel summer, 191 F
Cependant les soirs étaient doux, 87 K
Céphale et Procris, 141 D
C'era una volta un principe, 133 G
Cercherò lontana terra, 94 F
Certes, si nous avions vécu, 280 M
Certova sténa, 345 F
C'est ainsi que tu es, 281 F
C'est en vain, que l'enfer, 129 F
C'est ici même en cette place, 224 K
C'est la bossue de ma cour, 298 D
C'est là qu'après un jour, 137 J
C'est là que je voudrais vivre, 380 Q
C'est le Dieu de la jeunesse, 91 B
C'est le joli printemps, 280 H

C'est le printemps qui m'a surprise, 146 P
C'est l'extase langoureuse, 87 N, 109 Q
C'est l'heure discrète et tranquille, 350 D
C'est l'heure où l'amant nous conte, 76 J
C'est l'heure où las d'errer, 298 A
C'est l'histoire amoureuse, 7 P
C'est moi, 44 B
C'est mon ami, 85 G
C'est permis de fumer, 236 N
C'est sa banlieue, 147 B
C'est une chanson d'amour, 265 A
C'est une croixe qui de l'enfer, 134 O
Cet étang qui s'étend dans la plaine, 423 R
C'était dans la nuit brune, 199 P
C'était vers le vingt-cinq d'Aout, 184 M
Cette fleurette passe en peu de temps, 423 O
Chacun le sait, 96 E
Chaine d'Hymen m'étonne, La, 129 G
Chalet, Le, 1 K
Champs paternels, Hébron, 226 L
Chandos Anthem, 149 K
Chanson à boire, 280 E, 299 I
Chanson au bord la fontaine, 146 N
Chanson bien douce, La, 77 J
Chanson Bohème, 46 L
Chanson d'adieu, Une, 225 S
Chanson d'amour, 77K, 176 I
Chanson d'Avril, 47 S
Chanson de Chemin, La 76 K
Chanson de Clown, 77 L
Chanson de Florian, 132 K
Chanson de fol, 180 H
Chanson de Fortunio, 232 N, 264 J
Chanson de la fille frivole, 280 J
Chanson de la mariée, 297 G
Chanson de la nuit durable, 341 Q
Chanson de la puce, 42 M
Chanson de l'ours, 361 K
Chanson de magli, 135 S
Chanson de Marie Antoinette, 186 J
Chanson de Shylock, 109 L
Chanson d'Ophélie, 77 M
Chanson d'Orkenise, 279 I
Chanson du Pêcheur, 107 J
Chanson épique, 299 H
Chanson espagnole, 298 I
Chanson hebraique, 298 L, 305 J
Chanson Norvégienne, 117 D
Chanson perpetuelle, 77 N
Chanson poitevine, 384 H
Chanson pour le petit cheval, 341 R
Chanson provençale, 1 G
Chanson romantique, 299 G
Chanson slave, 76 C
Chanson triste, 100 F
Chansons de Basse-Bretagne, 52 I
Chansons de Bilitis, 88 D
Chansons des cueilleuses de lentisques, 297 J
Chansons du clair tamis, 280 F
Chansons française, 298 J
Chansons françaises, 201 I
Chansons gaillardes, 280 C

Chanson italienne, 298 K
Chansons madécasses, 299 C
Chansons villageoises, 280 F
Chant d'amour, 236 J
Chant d'automne, 107 L
Chant de forgeron, 236 K
Chant de la pitié, 236 H
Chant de Nourrice, 236 E
Chant de resignation, 236 I
Chant de Sion, 236 F
Chant des Oiseaux, Le, 187F
Chant du depart, 226 J
Chant du laboureur, 236 G
Chant Hassidique, 235 S
Chant Hindou, 40 K
Chant provençal, 225 M
Chant Vénitien, 40 M
Chantez, chantez, magnanarelles, 135 P
Chantons, célébrons notre Reine, 130 B
Chantons les amours de Jean, 423 K
Chants d' Auvergne, 72 H
Chants populaires hébraiques, 235 R
Chapelier, Le, 314 P
Chaque chose a son temps, 423 L
Charge is prepared, The, 273 D
Charité, 111 E
Charlie is my darling, 37 K
Charlie Rutlage, 186 A
Charmant oiseau qui sous l'ombrage, 86 Q
Charmant papillon, 72 F
Charmante promenade, La, 223 N
Charme, Le, 77 O
Charming Chloe, 123 F
Chasseur perdu en forêt, Le, 180 F
Chassons de nos plaisirs, 296 N
Château du Bartas, Le, 179 G
Che bella cosa 'na iurnata' e sole, 73 J
Che ciecamente crede, 254 H
Che faro senza Euridice, 131 O
Che fiero costume, 203 B
Che fiero momento, 131 M
Che gelida manina, 283 I
Che interminabile, 94 I
Che puro ciel!, 131 J
Che tua madre, 285 I
Che vuol dir cio, 113 M
Ch'ella mi creda libero, 284 I
Chemins de l'amour, Les, 280 L
Chemins de mon amour, 280 L
Cher anneau d' argent, Le, 76 B
Chère enfant!, 265 C
Chère nuit, 29 M
Cherry, The, 30 S
Cherry ripe, 181 E
Chers Tyriens, 43 A
Cherubim song, 52 D, 128 F
Chester, 44 J
Chevaux de bois, Les, 76 M, 87 Q
Chevelure, La, 88 E
Chèvre de Tibet, Le, 279 O
Chez la mariée, 360 D
Chez le marié, 360 H
Chi all' esca ha morso, 398 M
Chi bel sogno Doretta, 286 A
Chi del gitano, 403 B
Chi dise ca la femmena, 361 A
Chi la gagliarda, 93 D
Chi mai dell' Erebo, 131 C
Chi mai fra gl'inni, 391 J

Chi mi dirà, 113 P
Chi mi frena in tal momento, 97 N
Che mi giova cantar, 302 M
Chi mi toglie il regio scettro, 398 F
Chi ne consola ahi, 240 F
Chi può mirare, 152 S
Chi t'ha fatto quelle, 343 B
Chi vive amante, 154 M
Chi vuol comprar, 188 L
Chi vuole innamorarsi, 315 E
Chiamo il mio ben cosi, 130 R
Chien perdu, Le, 281 L
Child Jesus in his garden fair, 378 P
Children, keep step while you're marching, 86 F
Children of Don, The, 176 F
Children, see the wonder wrought, 183 S
Children's choruses, 281 K
Child's song, A, 257 N
Chinita mia ven por aqui, 441 D
Ch'io mi scordi di te, 249 F
Ch'io mai vi possa, 157 C
Ch'io t'ami, 238 I
Chiome d'oro, 238 H
Chloe proves false, 5 K
Chocolate soldier, The, 350 N
Chop Cherry, 420 D
"Choral" Symphony No. 9 (Finale), 38 E
Christ is risen, 295 H
Christ lag in Todesbunden, 8 M
Christ unser Herr zum Jordan kam, 8 S
Christ went up into the hills, 146 E
Christbaum, 83 I
Christe, 267 F, 267 R
Christe eleison, 22 N, 33 M
Christmas carol, A, 32 E
Christmas oratorio, 24 S, 313 B
Christmas song, 1 J
Christopher Robin is saying his prayers, 120 P
Christum wir sollen loben schon, 16 S
Christus, der ist mein Leben, 15 G
Christus, der uns selig macht, 26 E
Christus Oratorio, 207 N
Christus vincit, 207 N
Ciboulette, 146 O
Cid, Le, 221 P
Ciel a visité la terre, La, 137 R
Ciel est, par-dessus le toit, Le, 110 J, 147 G, 341 S
Ciel, qui du monde, 309 M
Cielo e mar, 278 F
Cielo pietroso, redila, 401 L
Cieux resplendissants, Les, 147 J
Cigány nóta, 194 Q
Cimetière de Campagne, 147 D
Cinderella, 308 H
Cinq ballades françaises, 73 B
Cinq chansons de Paul Vildrac, 235 T
Cinq mélodies populaires grecques, 297 G
Cinq poëmes de Baudelaire, 88 G
Cinque canti all' antica, 301 Q
Cinque, dieci, 247 O
Cinque tori in un sol giorno, 402 J
Ciribiribin, 275 H
Ciž pozbyla jsi ve mne viry, 345 G

Clair de lune, 88 Q, 108 Q, 375 M
Clang! Clang! Clang! Then huzzah for the anvil, 197 Q
Clärchen's Lied, 311 L
Clärchen's song, 35 O
Clari, or the Maid of Milan, 45 N
Classiques espagnoles du chant, 262 D
Claudine von Villa Bella, 326 M, 328 H
Clavelitos, 387 Q
Clear midnight, A, 389 R
Clemenza di Tito, La, 254 G
Climbing over rocky mountain, 368 G
Cloche, La, 313 L
Cloche du soir, 180 G
Cloche sonne l'angélus, La, 52 I
Cloches, Les, 88 N, 177 R
Cloches chrétiennes pour les matines, 87 M
Cloches du Soir, Les, 117 R
Clochettes des muguets, Les, 181 L
Clock scene, from Boris Godunov, 256 M
Cloris Hermosa, 262 G
Closely let me hold thy hand, 104 O
Cloths of heaven, The, 99 S
Clotilde, 177 N
Cloud and the mountain, The, 305 F
Clouds and darkness are round about Him, 101 Q
Cloudy heights of Tatra, 102 O
Clun, 389 I
Co chvíla, 186 N
Co to, holka, 347 K
Coelos ascendit hodie, 349 N
Coeur de ma mie, Le, 186 L
Coeur en peril, 310 Q
Coeur langoreulx, 189 G
Coeur que tu m'avais donné, Le, 114 J
Coffee cantata, 20 N
Col raggio placido, 151 B
Col ritornar, 41 A
Cold and raw, 271 F
Colibri, Le, 77 P
Colline's song, 294 B
Colloque sentimental, 89 A
Colombes, Les, 106 G
Colombetta, 69 I
Colonnes du temple, Les, 48 M
Colpa è vostra o Dei, 244 J
Columbine, 277 H
Com' è bello quale incanto, 98 E
Com' è gentil, 94 J
Combien j'ai douce souvenance, 118 I
Come again! Sweet love, 98 P
Come alla tortorella, 151 S
Come and trip it as you go, 150 C
Come away, 288 O
Come away, Death, 6 J, 53 I, 293 F, 342 P
Come back to Erin, 81 I
Come back to Sorrento, 85 N
Come col capo, 221 E
Come! Come! I love you only, 350 N
Come, come, thou goddess, 150 D
Come dal ciel precipita, 397 N

Come down to Kew, 90 C
Come due tizzi accesi, 80 I
Come, ever smiling liberty, 161 O
Come, fair Rosina, 180 Q
Come, friends, who plow the sea, 369 I
Come, gentle Spring, 170 F
Come, heavy sleep, 98 Q
Come home quickly, mother dearest, 194 M
Come in quest' ora bruna, 401 G
Come into the garden, Maud, 30 E
Come, little mousey, 183 N
Come live with me, 420 K
Come, love, and rest a while now, 40 H
Come mighty Must!, 370 E
Come, my Celia, 111 M
Come my darling Annie Miller, 195 N
Come notte a sol fulgento, 398 A
Come out! Come out! Listen on the air, 64 C
Come Paride, 95 B
Come per me serena, 39 I
Come raggio di sol, 71 D
Come rugiada al cospite, 394 H
Come scoglio immoto resta, 252 F
Come, sleep, and with thy sweet deceiving, 420 P
Come sweet lass, 273 A
Come to the fair, 217 P
Come un bel dì di maggio, 126 K
Come un sogno d'or, 384 P
Come unto these yellow sands, 199 K, 289 P
Come vinti da stanchezza, 97 E
Come where my love lies dreaming, 115 G
Come with native lustre shine, 150 E
Come, ye maidens all, and dance, 376 P
Come ye sons of Art, 292 E
Come you back to Mandalay, 348 I
Come you not from Newcastle, 64 K
Comes the broken flower, 373 G
Comfort, 103 J
Comfort ye, my people, 162 J
Coming of spring, 342 Q
Comm' la vie vous semble, 146 S
Comme autrefois, 47 M
Comme elle avait dormi cent ans, 117 B
Comme frère et soeur, 146 R
Comme le jour d'été, 178 F
Comme tout meurt vite, 108 G
Comme un rideau, 225 N
Comme une pâle fleur, 380 K
Commendador and Alquacil are there, The, 200 J
Comment, disaient-ils, 199 Q, 207 O
Como aves precur soras, 266 G
Compagne de l'éther, 147 L
Compagni, sostiamo, 396 L
Compère Guillery, 146 S
Complainte des Arches de Noé, 275 Q
Composer's song, 354 P
Comus, 6 K
Con lagrime e sospir, 427 R

Con queste paroline, 360 R
Con rauco mormorio, 155 J
Con substantialem patri, 34 A
Condotta ell'era in ceppi, 403 C
Conduisez-moi vers ce navire, 233 L
Confiteor, 23 N
Confusa si miri l'infida consorte, 155 I
Confutatis, 255 H
Connaissant, seigneur, 310 O
Connaissez-vous la blanche tombe, 100 J
Connais-tu le pays, 380 P
Consolati e spera, 315 Q
Console toi, 360 F
Consul, The, 231 O
Consume them all, 227 N
Contenta quest' alma, 308 Q
Contento forse vivere, 360 Q
Contento tu sarai, 274 E
Contes d'Hoffmann, 264 K
Contrabandiste, Der, 330 I
Conversation piece, 84 P
Convey me to some peaceful shore, 158 O
Cophtisches Lied, 429 P
Coq d'Or, Le, 304 G
Coqs chantent depuis l'aurore, Les, 305 C
Cor, Le, 113 F
Cor di padre, 157 N
Cor mio mentre vi miro, 238 J
Cor nel contento, Il, 439 K
Corazón que en prisión, 262 F
Core 'ngrato, 73 M
Core vi dono, Il, 252 L
Coronach, 322 R
Coronation Mass, 244 C
Coronation ode, 105 A
Coronation scene, from Boris Godunov, 256 D
Corpus Christi, 420 E
Correa nel peno amato, 315 H
Correa secura, 385 D
Cortigiani, vil razza dannata, 400 L
Cosa c'era nel fior, 385 I
Cosa sento!, 248 C
Cosi chiaro è come il sole, 94 R
Cosi dunque tradisci, K.432, 247 G
Cosi fan tutte, 251 S
Cottage maid, The, 38 B
Cotillon, 272 C
Couchant est si beau, Le, 310 I
Could I, 386 G
Could they grow and tell it so, 382 F
Could this ild world have been contriv'd, 37 Q
Count of Luxemburg, The, 204 F
Country feast, The, 257 O
Country lass, The, 73 P
Couple amoureux, 280 S
Couplets de l'aveu, 265 O
Couplets de sabre, 265 E
Couplets des fariniers, 264 H
Cour se fleurit de souci, La, 77 C
Cours, mon aiguille, 221 J
Courtiers, think it no harm, 272 F
Což ta voda s vyse stráni, 347 A
Crabe sort sur ces pointes, Le, 179 Q
Cradle hymn, 213 B
Cradle Song, 32 F, 57 L, 91 P, 140 K, 260 K, 345 O, 377 S

Cradle song of the poor, 257 P
Creation, The, 44 O, 169 J
Credo, 23 F, 33 S, 69 R, 134 D, 169 B, 208 I, 243 K, 247 D, 263 R, 268 B, 388 R, 398 Q
Credo du Paysan, Le, 133 M
Credo in unum Deum, 66 C
Crépuscule, 225 N
Cri, Un, 44 C
Criminal cried as he dropp'd him down, The, 366 K
Crois mon conseil, chère Climène, 89 F
Croisée est ouverte, La, 310 H
Crosspatch away, 182 Q
Crucifix, 111 G
Crucifixus, 23 K, 211 K
Cruda, funesta smania, 97 D
Cruda mia nemica, La, 267 C
Cruda sorte, amor tiranno, 308 R
Crudel! perchè finora, 248 K
Cruelle, non jamais, 129 S
Crusader's Song, 418 S
Crux fidelis, 188 J
Cry of Rachel, The, 314 E
Crying of water, The, 71 L
Crystal streams in murmurs flowing, 165 R
Cualquiera que el teja, 106 J
Cuando recuerdes los dias pasados, 140 A
Cuando sali de la Habana, 441 G
Cuando salí de Marbella, 263 B
Cuckoo, The, 204 P, 378 Q
Cuckoo sat in the old pear tree, The, 204 P
Cuerpo bueno, 263 Q
Cuffietta a pizza, Una, 283 O
Cujus anima gementem contristantem, 408 A
Cujus animam, 274 H, 309 R
Cum sancto spiritu, 23 E, 243 J, 247 A
Cuor mio, cuor mio non vedi, 93 H
Cupid in a bed of roses, 32 B
Cupid only throws the dart, 288 G
Currutacas modestas, Las, 139 M
Curse attends that woman's love, A, 272 S
Cycle of life, A, 306 J
Cygne, Le, 298 B
Cygne sur l'eau, 110 N
Cygnes, Les, 147 E
Cypress curtain of the night, The, 71 P
Czar's bride, The, 304 B

D

Da bleib ich, 19 R
Da die Heimath, o Vater, 338 A
Da die Welt zur Ruh gegangen, 56 E
Da droben auf jenem Berge, 329 G
Da geht er hin, 355 J
Da hast du die Stücken, 414 K
Da ich nun entsagen, 331 R
Da im weichen Sammt, 329 P
Da liegt der Feinde gestreckte Schaar, 339 F
Da quel dì, 96 Q
Da quel dì che t'ho veduta, 394 L
Da quel suon soavemente, 205 K

Da sah er eine blonde Frau, 210 D
Da schlägt die Abschieds-stunde, 247 L
Da streiten sich die Leut' herum, 199 B
Da tempeste, 153 G
Da unten im Tale läufts Wasser so trüb, 62 E
Da zu dir der Heiland kam, 410 I
Dagl' immortali vertici, 392 L
Dai campi, dai prati, 49 P
Daigne, daigne, très aimable mère, 360 E
Dainty fine bird, 125 E
Dainty fine sweet nymph, 241 C
Daisies, The, 30 L 295 N
Dal fulgor di questa spada, 153 H
Dal labbro il canto estasiato, 395 L
Dal mio permesso amato, 239 M
Dal più remoto esiglio, 394 B
Dal tuo stellato soglio, 309 E
Daland's Aria, 408 R
Dalibor, 345 D
Dalla cetra tua, 130 S
Dalla gaiba fuggito, 441 M
Dalle stanze, ove Lucia, 97 R
Dame blanche, La, 49 H
Dame d'André, La, 280 O
Dame du ciel, regente terrienne, 89 M
Dame noble et sage, Une, 234 D
Dämmern Wolken über Nacht und Thal, 41 O
Dammi ch'io baci, 284 S
Dämm'rung senkte sich von oben, 58 C
Dämm'rung will die Flügel spreiten, 333 Q
Damnation de Faust, La, 42 M
Damoiselle Elue, La, 86 S
D'amor sull' ali rosee, 403 Q
D'amour l'ardente flamme, 42 R
Dance a cachucha, 362 O
Dance and song màke glad the night, 428 B
Danger presse et le temps vole, Le, 234 I
Daniel was his father's name, 383 F
Dank, König dir, 409 O
Dank sei Dir, Herr, 149 J
Danksagung an den Bach, 317 G
Dann lachte ich saugend, 324 R
Dann schmeckte mir Trinken und Essen, 254 D
D'Anne jouant de l'espinette, 297 L
D'Anne qui me jecta de la neige, 297 M
Danny Deever, 85 S
Dans Arle, où sont les Aliscams, 44 D
Dans la forêt chauve et rouillée, 77 R
Dans la forêt de septembre, 110 L
Dans la forêt du charme et de l'enchantement, 77 Q
Dans la forêt les menuisiers, 275 Q
Dans la forêt près de nous, 91 H
Dans la plaine les baladins, 177 P
Dans la prairie fraiche, 174 G
Dans l'air nous suivons des yeus, 46 E

Dans l'air s'en vont les ailes, 146 L
Dans le broiullard s'en vont un paysan, 177 O
Dans le golfe aux jardins ombreux, 75 L
Dans le jardin d'Anna, 280 M
Dans le jardin fleuri, 294 I
Dans le royaume, 310 L
Dans le sang brûle, 127 H
Dans le sein d'un ami fidèle, 349 B
Dans le sommeil l'amour, 1 M
Dans le verger paisable, 48 K
Dans le vieux parc solitaire et glacé, 89 A
Dans l'ennui si désolément, 89 J
Dans les bois l'amoureux, 48 C
Dans les champs de Bethleem, 236 H
Dans les langes blancs fraîchement cousus, 118 K
Dans les ruines d'une abbaye, 107 G
Dans l'herbe, 280 P
Dans mon beau pays, 76 C
Dans son potager ma gran mère, 236 D
Dans son regard plus sombre, 380 F
Dans ton coeur dort un clair de lune, 100 F
Dans un baiser l'onde, 107 H, 148 M
Dans un bois solitaire, K.308, 244 A
Dans un de nos sites, 304 O
Dans un jardin, je ne sais où, 3 L
Dans un piège fatal, 211 Q
Dans un sommeil que charmait ton image, 107 P
Dans une charrette, 146 P
Dans Venise la rouge, 138 S
Dans vos viviers, 279 S
Danse avec nous dans le bel ocean, 177 S
Danse macabre, 313 M
Danse n'est pas ce que j'aime, La, 141 G
Danseuse, Une, 110 Q, 179 Q
Dansons, la gigue, 50 R, 277 I
Dante, 132 F
Danza, La, 307 G
Danza, The, 75 Q
Danza, danza, fanciulla gentile, 101 D
Danza del juego de amor, 106 D
Daphénéo, 314 Q
Daphne, 355 F
Darà la notte il sol, 238 P
Darf des Falken Schwinge, 102 O
Dark eyed sailor, The, 390 E
Darum, 300 G
Darum sollt ihr nich sorgen, 19 G
Das also, das ist der enge Schrein, 324 Q
Das ist der Herzallerliebste dein, 215 A
Das ist der Tag des Herrn, 199 A, 230 L
Das ist des Frühlings traurige Lust!, 359 H

Das ist ein Flöten und Geigen, 335 C
Das ist ein schlechtes Wetter, 359 M
Das ist galant, 21 D
Das ist im Leben hässlich ein gerichtet, 260 O
Das klinget so herrlich, 253 M
Das macht, es hat die Nachtigall, 41 Q
Das war der junge König, 139 F
Das war der Tag, 41 R
Das war ein Tag' voll Maienwind, '112 I
Das wahr sehr gut Mandryka, 354 N
Dashing white sergeant, The, 45 K
Dass der Ostwind Düfte, 323 F
Dass doch gemalt all' deine Reize wären, 429 R
Dass du so krank geworden, 332 O
Dass ich dich verloren habe, 320 Q
Dass sie hier gewesen, 323 F
Dass sie ruhen von ihrer Arbeit, 54 H
Daughter of the regiment, 96 D
Dauphin, Le, 279 Q
Dauphins, vous jouez dans la mer, 279 Q
Day in the cornfield, A, 190 M
Day's grown old, The, 64 S
Dazu ist erchienen der Sohn Gottes, 10 S
De aquel majo amante, 139 Q
De brouillards moroses, 378 R
De Camptown ladies sing this song, 115 F
De cet aveu si tendre, 96 H
De fleurs, 89 J
De grève, 89 I
De la Patria los ultimos ecos, 4 L
De la sangre de tus nobles, 255 R
De l'art splendeur immortelle, 92 M
De l'enfer qui vient émousser, 134 N
De loin, tu paraissais, 184 K
De mes plus doux regards, 129 K
De miei bollenti spiriti, 401 R
De mon amie, 47 N
De mon coeur jaillit un cantique, 179 A
De' nemici tuoi lo sdegno, 95 M
De plus en plus, 45 D
De profundis clamavi ad te, 242 J
De rêve, 89 H
De sadent soudaine et vorace, 100 K
De soir, 89 K
De son coeur j'ai calmé la fièvre, 381 H
De tout sui si confortée, 213 N
Dead City, The, 197 D
Dear friends, it is so beautiful, 383 P
Dear friends, take pity on my lot, 372 S
Dear Miss Constance Fletcher, 383 J
Dear Mother, 195 E
Dearest, 177 J

Dearest, our day is over, 385 S
Death, 140 R
Death and the peasant, 259 E
Death in life, 388 L
Death of Liù, 287 J
Death of Nelson, The, 53 B
Death of Valentine, 135 M
Death, the commander, 259 J
Death's lullaby, 259 G
Death's serenade, 259 H
Deborah, 159 E
Debout, mon gars!, 305 I
Decid que dami, 139 M
Decidi il mio destin, 206 D
Déclin, Le, 48 K
Deep is my bondage, 176 F
Deep river, 67 L
Deeper and deeper still thy goodness, 160 F
Deeps have music soft and low, The, 104 Q
Defend her, Heaven, 166 F
Deggio morire, o stelle, 157 D
D'Egitto là sui lidi, 397 S
Deh, contentatevi, 74 A
Deh! Lasciatemi il nemico, 157 O
Deh! non m'abbandonar, 396 A
Deh non parlare al misero, 400 B
Deh! non turbare, 278 G
Deh, non varcar quell' onda, 243 R
Deh! non volerli vittime, 38 S
Deh par questo istante solo, 254 O
Deh più a me non v'ascondete, 67 F
Deh placatevi con me, 131 D
Deh, se piacer mi vuoi, 254 G
Deh! ti rammenta, 74 Q
Deh torno mio bene, 282 Q
Deh! tu reggi in tal momento, 308 O
Deh vieni alla finestra, 250 N
Deh vieni non tardar, 249 C
Deidamia, 152 J
Dein Angesicht, 339 J
Dein Bildniss wunderselig, 333 I
Dein blaues Auge, 38 I
Dein Blut, 14 A
Dein Geburtstag ist erchienen, 17 P
Dein gedenk' ich, Margaretha, 235 I
Dein ist mein ganzes Herz!, 203 S
Dein Liebesfeuer, ach Herr, 435 E
Dein Lied erklang!, 359 J
Dein Lied von Lieb und Treue, 352 K
Dein Rat ist wohl gut, 142 J
Dein Schwert wie ist's von Blut so rot?, 208 R
Dein Tag ist aus, 338 C
Dein Wachstum sei feste, 21 L
Dein Wetter zog sich auf von Weitem, 11 H
Dein Will' gescheh', 25 R
Deine Güte, dein Erbarmen, 19 L
Deiner ew'gen Gattin, 414 C
Déjà la nuit plus sombre, 49 I
Del futuro, 398 H
Del minacciar del vento, 154 D
Del mio caro baco amabile, 156 O
Del mondo i disinganni, 397 A
Del più sublime soglio, 254 I

Del vostro Erebo, 155 E
Dell' antro magico, 75 E
Dell' aura tua profetica, 38 J
Delphinium, Le, 180 D
Dem Helden, 338 C
Dem Schnee, dem Regen, dem Wind entgegen, 320 M
Dem Unendlichen, 229 M
Dem Vogel, der heut' sang, 411 B
Dem wir das Heilig itzt, 17 E
Demande au prisonnier, 220 O
Den Báu, 145 H
Den Fischer fechten Sorgen, 324 K
Den kedsom Vinter gik sin Gang, 167 K
Den Tag hindurch nur einmal mag, 320 P
"Den Tag seh' ich erscheinen," 411 F
Den Theuren zu versöhnen, 113 S
Den Tod niemand zwinget kunnt, 8 N
Den vilde Gutten mit Sind, 144 G
Dengang jeg var Kun saa, 172 L
Denk es, O Seele!, 429 S
Denk' nicht an den alten Douglasneid, 210 A
Denn alles Fleisch es ist wie Gras, 53 N
Denn das Gesetz des Geistes, 24 K
Denn es gehet dem Menschen, 61 Q
Denn es wird die Posaune schallen, 54 E
Denn seh' ich mich, 19 J
Denn wir haben hie keine bleibende Statt, 54 D
Départ, Le, 179 I
Depols da chuvarada, 406 P
Deposuit, 22 G
Depuis le jour où je me suis donnée, 76 Q
Depuis l'instant, 96 G
Depuis longtemps j'habitais cette chambre, 76 O
Depuis lors, quand la nuit gagne, 233 N
Depuis neuf ans et plus, 148 G
Depuis ton départ, 148 A
Depuis un mois, chère exilée, 147 R
Der aber die Herzen forschet, 24 G
Der du den Tempel Gottes zerbrichst, 28 D
Der du so lustig rauschtest, 319 G
Der du von dem Himmel bist, 320 L, 436 L
Der er et Land, 303 S
Der Jäger, 317 R
Der so oft dem roten Hahn, 430 K
Dereinst, dereinst, Gedanke mein, 430 A
Dernière feuille, La, 77 R
Dernière Valse, La, 147 F
Derrière Murcie en fleurs, 178 K
Derweil ich schlafend lag, 435 O
Des Antonius von Padua Fischpredigt, 124 N
Des Baches Wiegenlied, 318 E
Des cris joyeux d'enfants, 225 J
Des Dichters Abendgang, 358 M

Des ersten Sehens Wonne, 142 I
Des Fischers Liebesglück, 327 C
Des fremden Kindes heil'ger
  Christ, 209 G
Des Glockentürmers Töchterlein,
  209 O
Des Grieux's dream, 223 M
Des Heines Tiere, 412 D
Des Jahres letzte Stunde, 330 E
Des jardins de la nuit, 108 L
Des Kindes Gebet, 300 P
Des Knaben Wunderhorn, 214 N
Des larmes ont coulé, 310 M
Des Liebsten Schwur, 58 P
Des Mädchens Klage, 323 D
Des Mondes Zauberblume lacht,
  324 N
Des Morgens zwischen drei'n und
  vieren, 215 Q
Des Müllers Blumen, 317 M
Des reinen Arm gieb
  Heldenkraft, 409 M
Des Schäfers sein Haus, 435 N
Des Sonntags in der
  Morgenstund', 332 Q
Des Souverains du rivage, 1 Q
Des trous à son pourpoint
  vermeil, 88 C
Des Waldes Sänger singen, 119 L
Des Wassermanns sein
  Töchterlein, 434 G
Descent of the Holy Ghost, The,
  5 B
Desejo, 406 Q
Desengañémonos ya, 262 H
Deserted, 212 S
Déserteur, Le, 237 R
Deserto in terra, 94 N
Deserto sulla terra, 402 Q
Déserts écartés, 266 I
Dessus le marché d'Arras, 201 L
Destruction's our delight, 288 R
Det Stiger, 172 M
Dettingen Te Deum, 149 Q
Deutlich liegt vor mir, 304 E
Deutsche Volkslieder, 62 C
Deutsches Requiem, Ein, 53 M
Deutschland über Alles, 171 H
Deux Avares, Les, 141 E
Deux bourrées, 72 M
Deux coeurs, Les, 114 J
Deux Grenadiers, Les, 418 B
Deux heures après diner, 180 C
Deux journées, Les, 78 N
Deux melodies hebraiques, 297 N
Deux robinets coulent, 299 N
Devant la maison de celui qui
  t'adore, 42 Q
Devil a monk would be, A, 175 I
Devil and Kate, The, 101 G
Devil's wall, The, 345 F
Devin du village, Le, 310 F
Devo talor da un lato, 395 D
Dew in the meadow, 79 K
Di ad Irene, 152 A
Di all'azzurro spazio, Un, 126 C
Di Cupido impiego, 149 L
Dì (ero piccina), Un, 220 M
Di felice eterea, Un, 401 N
Di geloso amor, 402 R
Di m'era di gioio, Un, 126 H
Di pasta simile son tutti quanti,
  252 E
Di pescatore ignobile, 98 F

Di piacer mi balza il cor, 308 L
Di Provenza il mar, 402 E
Di quella pira, 403 L
Di, se ben rammentomi, Un,
  400 S
Di sposo di padre le gioje
  serene, 133 I
Di tale amor, 402 P
Di tanti palpiti, 308 K
Di' tu se fedele, flutto, 392 S
Di tue pene sparve il sogno,
  97 C
Di vederlo ah, 113 O
Diamants chez nous, Les, 304 N
Diane et Acteon, 296 B
Diane, Séléné, 111 A, 276 K
Diaphenia, 237 I
Dicem que mi majo es feo, 139 N
Dicen que no nos queremos, 106 L
Dich frage ich, 408 J
Dich meiden, 120 O
Dich, teure Halle, 416 K
Dichterliebe, 334 N
Dichters Genesung, 333 A
D'ici je vois la vie, 138 Q
Did ever maiden wake from
  dream, 368 M
Did you ever hear of a gallant
  sailor, 273 G
Dido and Aeneas, 288 D
Dids't thou not hear, 376 L
Die du so gern in heil'gen
  Nächten, 35 M
Die ich mir aus erkoren, 411 K
Die ihr einem neuen Grade, 247 I
Die ihr schwebet, 432 I
Die ihr schwebet um diese
  Palmen, 60 F
Dies Bildniss ist bezauberd schön,
  253 F
Dies Engelsgesicht, 353 M
Dies Irae, 43 G, 255 D, 404 N
Diese ausdrucksvollen Züge,
  211 E
Diese Püppchen, 168 N
Diese Rose pflück' ich hier, 230 G
Diese Rosen von heimlichen
  Küssen, 192 I
Diese Wolken in den Höhen, 35 I
Dieses Saitenspiel der Brust, 348 B
Dieu de grâce, 4 D
Dieu, que ma voix tremblante,
  149 C
Dieu! qu'il la fait bon regarder,
  87 I
Dieu le dit: un jour viendra,
  179 E
Dieu s'avance à travers les
  champs!, 118 E
Dieux qui me poursuivez, 130 K
Diffusa est gratia, 260 I
Diga usted señor platero, 263 I
Diggi, daggi, schurry, murry,
  242 C
Dimanche à l'aube, 52 J
Dimanche sur les villes, 89 K
Dimitry, 101 H
Dimmi amor, 92 E
Dimmi, cara, 156 F
Din, don, suona vespera, 205 S
Ding, ding, ding, ding, 299 J
Dinorah, 233 N
Dio, che nell' alma infondere,
  393 E
Dio di Giuda!, 398 I

Dio di giustizia, 126 S
Dio, fulgor della bufera, 398 J
Dio Pietosa, 4 D
Dio ti giocondi, 399 F
Dioclesian, 289 C
Dios te salve, macarena, 387 I
Dioskuren, Zwillingssterne, 323 N
Dir, dir, Jehovah, will ich singen,
  28 K
Dir, hohe Liebe, 417 E
Dir töne Lob!, 416 F
Dirà che amor per me, 156 P
Dirge, 65 C
Dirigori armato, 355 I
Dis un seul mot soudain ta cour,
  1 R
Disappointment, 379 F
Dis-moi, Daphénéo, 314 Q
Dis-moi que je suis belle, 224 P
Dite alla giovine, 402 C
Dite voi, se in tanto affanno, 35 D
Ditelo, o fiumi e voi che udiste,
  238 O
Ditemi che il Signor, 385 O
Dites la jeune belle, 138 I
Dites-lui qu'on l'a remarqué,
  265 G
Dithyrambe, 323 I
Divination by water, 257 H
Divinité des grandes âmes, 130 O
Divinités du Styx, 128 Q
Dnieper, ho, 258 P
Do come Susan B. Anthony, 383 C
Do not go, my love, 146 G
Do you remember an Inn, 146 H,
  386 N
Doch eh' ich in des Todes Thal,
  133 B
Doch Jesu will, 11 I
Doch kann dem bleichen Manne,
  408 O
Doch meine Saiten tönen, 322 Q
Doch schön war der Knabe, 197 J
Doch uns ist gegeben, 54 L
Doch weichet ihr tollen, 9 A
Doch wie schnell schwand meine
  Freude, 245 M
Doe, The, 175 R
Dolce foco mio, Il, 156 E
Dolce pensiero, 309 J
Dolcissima effigie, La, 80 C
Dolcissima mia vita, 124 J
Dolly, 109 K
Dolly bye-bye, 258 K
Dolly's cradle song, 258 K
Dolores, La, 63 R
Dôme épais le jasmin, 90 N
Domine Deus, 23 A, 246 Q
Domine ego credidi, 313 C
Domine Jesu, 255 I, 405 D
Domine non sum dignus, 407 H
Domino noir, Le, 7 J
Don Carlos, 393 J
Don Giovanni, 249 E
Don Giovanni a cenar teco, 251 F
Don Juan, 249 R
Don Juan's serenade, 378 F
Don Pasquale, 93 R
Don Quichotte, 222 A
Don Quichotte à Dulcinée, 299 G
Don Quixote, 287 Q
Don Sebastiano, 94 N
Dona nobis, 169 I

Dona nobis pacem, 24 A, 34 I, 243 O
Donc, ce sera par un clair jour d'été, 110 E
Donde lieta usci, 283 Q
Donkey, The, 146 F
Donna a quindici anni, Una, 252 I
Donna è mobile, La, 400 R
Donna non vidi mai, 285 K
Donna russa, La, 126 R
Donne Curiose, Le, 439 J
Donne mie, la fate a tanti, 252 O
Donneurs de sérénades, Les, 89 B, 101 B, 109 N, 147 K, 277 K, 375 P
Donnez, donnez, pour une pauvre âme, 234 R
Don't throw against the prophets stones, 347 M
Donzelle, fuggite, 75 F
Dopo!, 385 D
Doppelgänger, Der, 318 R
D'Oreste, d'Ajace!, 245 A
Dorf, Das, 301 B
Dormi Jesu!, 213 B
Dormi pur, ma il mio risposo, 113 L
Dormi pure, 341 E
Dormirò sol nel manto mio regal, 393 N
Dormons tous, 212 H
Dors, dors, dors, ton papa ira, 235 R
Dors, ma douce créature, 304 J
Dors, ma fleur, mon fils cheri, 236 E
Dort blinket durch Weiden, 327 C
Dort, gen Mitternacht liegt ein wüstes land, 127 S
Dort in den Weiden steht ein Haus, 61 D
Dort ist ihr Grab, 327 N
Dort oben am Berg, 214 R
Dort wo der Morgenstern, 358 L
Dos horas ha que callejeo, 139 L
Dost thou see the stars shining yonder, 103 C
D'où viens tu?, 91 A
D'où vient, Seigneur, 133 R
Doubt, 128 G
Douce haleine des zéphirs, 44 H
"Douce Memoire" Mass, 202 H
Douceur de tes yeux, La, 178 J
Doute de la lumière, 380 A
Doux charme de la vie, 141 B
Doux lien, Un, 90 G
Doux liens de mon coeur, 84 E
Doux printemps parait, Le, 127 N
Dove, The, 441 G
Dove guardi, 398 S
Dove, misero, mai, 297 B
Dove sei amato bene?, 155 K
Dove sono, 248 N
Dovrò dunque morire, 70 J
Dovunque al mondo, 284 N
Down a down, 276 L
Down by the Sally gardens, 64 R, 185 K
Down here, 53 F
Down in the forest, 306 J
Down in yon forest, 390 F
Down on de Mississippi, 116 A
Down through the winter sunshine, 71 N

Down yonder green valley, 64 H
Dragons de Villars, Les, 216 F
Drauf schliess' ich mich in deine Hände, 24 R
Draw on, sweet night, 427 K
Dream, A, 31 F, 143 K
Dream, The, 399 C
Dream duet, from La Belle Hélène, 264 G
Dream of Gerontius, The, 104 C
Dreams, 295 O
Dreamy Lake, The, 145 D
Drei Kön'ge, 83 K
Drei Sonnen sah ich am Himmel stehn, 320 D
Drei Tage Regen fort und fort, 432 N
Drei Volkslieder, 231 F
Drei Wandrer, 174 D
Drei Zigeuner, Die, 207 P
Dreigroschenoper, Die, 426 G
Driftwood, 342 H
Drink to me only with thine eyes, 5 F
Dromadaire, Le, 279 N
Druben hinterm Dorfe, 320 E
Drunken scene, from Boris Godunov, 256 H
Dry those eyes, 289 R
Du Armste kannst wohl nie ermessen, 410 B
Du bist das traumsüsse Leben, 203 Q
Du bist die Ruh, 323 G
Du bist die Ruh', du bist der Frieden, 330 Q
Du bist der Lenz nach, 413 O
Du bist ein Kind, 426 C
Du bist mein Auge!, 358 E
Du bist meine Sonne, 203 H
Du bist Orplid, mein Land, 431 F
Du bist vom Schlaf erstanden, 332 N
Du bist wie eine Blume, 207 R, 311 B, 331 M
Du brachst sie nun, 326 D
Du denkst mit einem Fädchen, 430 P
Du er min mor, 143 N
Du frägst mich, 356 M
Du heilige Brunst, 24 H
Du Herr, du krönst allein, 19 F
Du herrlich Glas, 332 J
Du Hirte Israel, höre, 16 A
Du holde Kunst, 324 E
Du holdes Vöglein, 414 S
Du junges Grün, 332 I
Du kundest nun dein wahr Gericht, 409 L
Du lieber heilger Christ, 209 H
Du liebes Auge, 119 Q
Du liebes Kind, komm, geh mit mir, 326 S
Du liebicher Stern, 336 P
Du liebst mich nicht, 323 E
Du machst, o Tod, 16 N
Du mein Gedanke, du mein Sein, 142 A
Du Meine Seele, du mein Herz, 330 P
Du meines Herzens Krönelein, 357 A
Du milchjunger Knabe, 59 R, 430 C

Du mit deiner Fiedel, 174 R
Du moment qu'on aime, 141 O
Du pauvre seul ami fidèle, 7 S
Du Ring an meinem Finger, 334 G
Du rislende Boek, 144 J
Du sagst, mein liebes Mütterlein, 300 J
Du sagst mir, dass ich Keine Fürstin sei, 430 D
Du sagtest mir es, Mutter, 328 N
Du schläfst und sachte neig' ich mich, 358 D
Du schönes Fischermädchen, 318 O
Du, som har Sorg i Sinde, 167 M
Du Spiegelbild, 355 E
Du temps de nos pères, 299 E
Du Trotz des Glaubens!, 192 S
Du Ubermuth wohin, bist du entschwunden, 304 D
Du verstörst uns nicht, o Nacht!, 328 P
Du Wald, der sich heruber biegt, 143 G
Du wirst nicht weinen, 358 F
Du wirst sie zu befreien gehen, 253 H
Du wunderliche Tove!, 316 Q
Due bell' alme, 152 J
Due Forscari, I, 394 B
Duérmete, niño, duerme, 106 M
Duet from Faust, 135 D
Duets for alto and baritone, 56 E
Duettino des époux, 264 I
Duetto delle ciliege, 218 Q
Dulcissimum convivium, 243 P
D'un arbre séculaire, 282 L
D'un pensiero, 39 P
D'un Prison, 147 G
Duna, 226 N
D'une image hélas! trop chérie, 130 M
Dunkel ist das Leben, 215 G
Dunkel, wie dunkel in wald und in Feld!, 57 B
Dunkeler Schacht ist Liebe, Ein, 63 N
Dunklen Wolken hingen, Die, 337 R
Dunno a heap about the what an' why, 185 N
Dunque amate reliquie, 238 S
Dunque io son?, 307 Q
Duo d'Alsace, 265 H
Durandarte, 235 N
Durch alte Marmorhallen, 192 R
Durch den Wald, den dunkeln, 229 C
Durch dich musst' ich verlieren, 409 P
Durch die Lande auf und ab schreitet, 192 O
Durch die Reihen hin zu fliegen!, 344 G
Durch die Wälder, 421 O
Durch die Wälder streif ich munter, 65 S
Durch Feld und Wald zu schweifen, 324 F
Durch hohe Tannen, 192 Q
"Durch Mitleid wissend, der reine Tor," 412 C
Durch Sturm un bösen Wind verschlagen, 408 K

Durch Zärtlichkeit, 245 N
Dvě vdovy, 347 B
Dying Christian's last farewell, The, 44 K
Dylan, 176 G

E

E allor perche, 206 F
E amore un ladroncello, 252 R
E deggio e posso crederlo, 403 H
E, dio mè tu, lo calhé 72 N
E il sol dell' anima, 400 D
E ingrato, lo veggio, 122 G
E la virtute raggio, 240 M
E luceran le stelle, 286 Q
E lui è lui ne' palpiti, 392 R
E passerà la viva, 220 R
E Piquillo un bel gagliardo, 402 I
E prezzo leggiero, 154 N
E quest' asilo, 131 I
E scherzo od è follia, 393 A
E sdruscito il navil, 302 F
E se fia che ad altro oggetto, 94 G
E se un giorno tornasse, 302 D
E sempre il vecchio andazzo, 220 H
E sogno? o realtà, 395 H
E stamattina all' alba, 219 O
E troppo oribile, 278 O
E tu come sei pallida, 399 N
E tu m'amavi per le mie sventure, 398 P
E un di sul mio sorriso, 399 K
E verro che in casa, 81 C
E voi, piuttosto, 205 P
Early one morning, 386 Q
Earth is nowhere so real, The, 176 D
Easter cantata, 8 M
Easter day was a holiday, 64 N
Easter oratorio, 25 K
Eat, drink and be gay, 372 P
Eau de source, L', 72 I
Eaux du Nil toutes pâles, Les, 206 R
Ebben? ne andrò lontana, 74 S
Ebrezza, delirio, 279 A
Ecce quomodo moritur justus, 166 L
Ecce quomodo moritur justus, 269 L
Ecco il magico, 50 K
Ecco mormora l'onde, 238 K
Ecco Orfeo, 239 R
Ecco pur ch'a voi ritorno, 239 S
Ecco quel fioro istante, 37 G
Ecco ridenti, 307 J
Echelonnement des haies, L', 90 A
Echo, Das, 325 I
Echo song, 45 L
Eclat de Rire, L', 7 P
Ecoute-moi bien, 135 M
Ecoutez la chanson bien douce, 77 J
Ecoutez tous gentils gallois, 187 C
Ecrevisse, L', 279 R
Edward, 208 R
Efteraar, 201 B
Egész falut öszszejartam, 194 Q
Egli è salvo!, 396 K
Egmont, 35 O
Egy kicsi madarka, 195 A
Egy nagyórú bóha, 194 S

Eh' Du in der stillen Kammer, 351 F
Eh via, buffone, 250 M
Eh' wir uns trennen konnten, 438 L
Ehre Gottes aus der Natur, Die, 36 B
Ehrt eure deutschen Meister, 412 B
Ei, mi par che già pian, 274 B
Ei nun, mein Gott, 12 N
Ei, schmollte mein Vater, 58 P
Ei, wie mein Triangel, 102 J
Ei! wie schmeckt der Coffee, 29 O
Eia Mater fons amoris, 190 B, 274 M
Eichwald braust, Der, 323 D, 427 A
Eifersucht und Stolz, 317 S
Eile mich, Gott, zu erretten, 340 A
Eileen, 173 S
Eilt, eilt, 26 J
Eily Mavourneen, 40 R
Ein kleiner, hübscher Vogel, Ein, 63 D
Ein Meistersinger muss es sein, 410 Q
Ein nervöser Mensch auf einer wiese, 139 B
Ein Ton, 83 G
Ein Wolf der Sündenangst bewog, 175 I
Eine gute, gute Nacht, 58 G
Einen Brief soll ich schreiben, 300 L
Einer wind kommen, 204 I
Einerlei, 359 L
Eines gibt's darauf ich mich fruen darf, 192 P
Eingeschlafen auf der Lauer, 333 N
Einsam in trüben Tagen, 409 G
Einsam wachend in der Nacht, 417 P
Einsam wandelt dein Freund, 35 B
Einsame, Der, 275 L, 322 K, 359 C
Einsame im Herbst, Der, 215 H
Einsamkeit, 319 L, 337 Q
Einst glaubte ich, 425 J
Einst träumte meiner sel'gen Base, 422 G
Einstmal in einem tiefen Thal, 214 P
Eixa nit es nit, 262 M
Eja, Mater fons amoris, 408 C
Eleänore, 82 I
Elégie, 100 G, 225 O
Elegy, 65 B, 259 O
Elenden sollen essen, Die, 13 M
Elfenlied, 430 E
Elijah, 226 O
Eliland, 112 H
Elindultam szép hazámbul, 31 K
Elisir d'amore, 94 O
Elixir of love, The, 94 O
Elkráltom magamat, 194 R
Elle a fui, la tourterelle, 264 R
Elle a passé dans le vent d'automne, 48 J
Elle avait trois couronnes d'or, 111 R
Elle est aimée, 381 E
Elle est venue vers le palais, 111 S

Elle ne croyait pas, 381 I
Ellen's erster gesang, (from Scott's Lady of the Lake), 322 N
Ellen's Zweiter Gesang (from Scott's Lady of the Lake), 322 O
Elohim! Why hast thou thus forsaken me?, 48 N
Elsa's Dream, 409 G
Elsk, 144 G
Elverskud, 122 B
Embarquez-vous!, 132 L
Emperor Jones, 145 L
Empio, per farti guerra, 157 P
Empio rigor del fato, L', 155 L
Emporte ma folie, 108 M
Empty-handed traveler, The, 231 O
En allant se coucher le soleil, 280 Q
En Arles, 44 D
En barque, 275 R
En dépit de cette inhumaine, 299 P
En entrant en ung jardin, 341 M
En fermant les yeux, 223 M
En même temps que tous les bourgeons la rose, 236 J
En menant paitre mon troupeau, 423 P
En nymphas en pastores!, 292 H
En passant par la Lorraine, 184 N
En Prière, 111 C
En rentrant de l'école, 281 M
En silence pourquoi souffrir?, 200 A
En son temple sacré, 226 E
En sourdine, 80 O, 109 O, 147 I, 375 O
En stille Söndag sider hun i Li, 144 F
En un dernier naufrage, 43 D
En vain pour éviter, 47 D
Enamourée, L', 147 H
Endless pleasure, 165 G
Endlich, endlich wird mein Joch, 12 B
Enemy said, The, 160 C
Enfance du Christ, L' 42 G
Enfant court autours des marbres, Un, 298 M
Enfant et les sortilèges, L', 299 J
Enfant prodigue, L', 87 C
Enfant serait sage, L', 77 B
Engel, Der, 311 J, 418 D
Engel Gottes weinen, Die, 249 N
Englein haben's Bett gemacht, Die, 300 K
English Rose, The, 123 J
Enigme éternelle, L', 297 P
Enrico, 122 I
Entfernten, Der, 326 Q
Entflieh' mit mir, 336 D
Entführung aus dem Seraglio, Die K.384, 245 H
Entreat me not to leave thee, 137 S
Entweihte Götter, 409 R
Entzücket dich ein Wunderhauch, 438 P
Envoi de Fleurs, 138 A
Epiphanias, 430 G
Epis sont à Cérès. Les, 281 P
Epouse quelque brave fille, 224 C

Er, der herrlichste von allen, 334 E
Er ist gekommen, 118 S, 333 D
Er ist uns geschieden, 322 R
Er ist's, 337 F, 430 H
Er liebte mich so sehr, 378 C
Er liegt und schläft, 324 L
Er rufet seinem Schafen mit Namen, 18 S
Er soll dein Herr sein!, 237 F
Er und sie, 336 M
Er war mir sonst treu und ergeben, 242 E
Er zählet uns're Thränen in der Zeit der Noth, 229 I
Era la notte, 399 C
Erbarme dich, 11 S, 27 P
Erda! Erda!, 415 D
Erda's Warning, Das Rheingold, 413 H
Ere daylight awaketh, 144 B
Erforsche mich, erfahr mein Herz, 29 I
Erfreue dich, Seele, 9 Q
Erfreut euch, ihr Herzen, 12 O
Ergebung, 112 Q
Ergehst du dich im Abendlicht, 358 M
Erhebung, 316 F
Erhöre mich, 340 B
Eri tu, 393 G
Erik's Dream, 408 Q
Erinnerung, 58 J
Eriskay Love Lilt, An, 190 I, 305 Q
Erkenne mich, mein Hüter, 27 E
Erkennen, Das, 210 F
Erlafsee, 320 S
Erlaube mir, feins Mädchen, 62 C
Erleucht' auch meine finstre Sinnen, 25 H
Erl-king's daughter, The, 122 B
Erlkönig, 209 B, 326 R
Erlöseten des.Herrn, Die, 53 P
Ernani, 394 H
Ernani! involami, 394 J
Erndtelied, 228 F
Erntelied, 228 F
Eros, 144 L
Erschallet, ihr Lieder, 18 K
Erstarrung, 319 D
Erste Kuss, Der, 171 I
Erste Veilchen, Das, 228 K
Erster Verlust, 327 A
Erstes Begegnen, 142 I
Erstes Grün, 332 I
Erstes Liebeslied eines Mädchens, 430 I
Ertödt' uns durch dein' Güte, 10 B
Evviva! beviam!, 394 I
Erwäge, erwäge, 26 G
Erzeugt von heisser Phantasie, 249 O
Es bebet das Gesträuche, 63 P
Es bellen die Hunde, 319 Q
Es blinkt der Thau, 311 M
Es blüht ein Blümlein rosenrot, 300 O
Es brechen im schallenden Reigen, 228 P
Es brennt mir unter, 319 H
Es dämmert, all das Licht, 377 J
Es en balde majo, 140 D
Es fiel ein Reif, 336 E
Es flüstern und rauschen, 335 P
Es fürchte die Götter, 54 P

Es geht bei gedämpfter Trommeln, 334 C
Es glänzt der Mond nieder, 53 L, 57 H
Es grünet ein Nussbaum, 330 S
Es hat die Rose sich beklagt, 120 M, 311 H
Es hing der Reif, 61 K
Es ist bestimmt in Gottes Rath, 229 D
Es ist der alte Bund, 16 G
Es ist dir gesagt, Mensch, was gut ist, 11 G
Es ist ein halbes Himmelreich, 326 P
Es ist ein Ross entsprungen, 282 L
Es ist ein Schnitter, 228 F
Es ist gewiss ein frommer Mann, 175 G
Es ist in den Wald gesungen, 229 L
Es ist Nacht, 192 G
Es ist nun nichts, 24 J
Es ist schon spät, 187 Q, 333 J
Es ist so still, 330 B
Es ist so süss zu scherzen, 331 S
Es ist und bleibet der Christen Trost, 11 F
Es ist vollbracht, 18 L, 26 L, 28 L, 171 E
Es kam ein Pascha aus Türkenland, 168 M
Es kehret der Maien, 35 J
Es kehrt die dunkle Schwalbe, 59 I
Es läuft ein fremdes Kind, 209 G
Es leuchtet meine Liebe, 339 K
Es liebt sich so lieblich im Lenze, 59 D
Es lockte schöne Warme, 323 R
Es mahnt der Wald, 322 D
Es Muss ein Wunderbares sein, 207 S
Es muss gelingen!, 344 P
Es nehme zehntausend Ducaten, 21 G
Es ragt in's Meer der Runenstein, 120 J
Es rauschen die Wipfel, 333 M
Es rauschet das Wasser, 56 G
Es regt in den Lauben, 325 P
Es reifet euch ein schrecklich Ende, 15 A
Es rief in Versailles, 377 I
Es sangen die Vöglein, 414 M
Es schauen die Blumen, 60 S
Es schaukeln die Winde das Nest, 184 E
Es schlägt der Rache Stunde, 33 H
Es schwebte ein Engel, 311 J
Es schweige die Klage, 132 P
Es steht ein Lind in jenem Tal, 62 N
Es stürzen der Jugend, 192 E
Es taget vor dem Walde, 120 P
Es tanzen Mond und Sterne, 322 F, 327 J
Es tönt des Nöcken Harfenschall, 210 B
Es tönt ein voller Harfenklang, 53 H
Es träumte mir, 57 N
Es treibt mich hin, 330 K

Es war, als hätt' der Himmel, 333 L
Es war ein alter König, 311 D
Es war ein Kind, 209 F
Es war ein König in Thule, 320 O
Es war eine dämmernde Sommernacht, 142 C
Es war einmal ein König, 35 N
Es wartet Alles auf dich, 19 F
Es weiss und räth es doch keiner, 333 K
Es wenden die Herrscher, 54 Q
Es werde Licht, 438 F
Es wohnt am Seegestade, 210 L
Es zieht aus jener Wett, 198 Q
Es zog eine Hochzeit, 333 R
Es zog eine Hochzeit den Berg, 336 I
Es zogen drei Bursche, 209 A
Es zogen zwei rüst'ge Gesellen, 334 M
Esci, fuggi il furor, 97 Q
Esclave, L', 200 F
Esprits gardiens, 303 B
Esta tuimagen que admiro, 387 J
Esther, 159 I
Estrella do céo, 406 G
Estrella é lua nóva, 406 G
Estrellita, 277 M
Esurientes implevit bonis, 22 H
Et exultavit, 21 S
Et immisit in os, 359 S
Et in spiritum sanctum, 23 M, 242 I, 247 C
Et in terra pax hominibus, 22 Q, 66 B, 69 G, 69 Q, 388 Q
Et in unum Dominum, 23 I
Et incarnatus est, 23 J, 34 B, 66 D, 169 C, 247 B, 264 A
Et iterum venturus est, 43 H
Et maintenant parlez mes belles, 47 C
Et misericordia, 22 D
Et resurrexit, 23 L, 169 D
Et toi, Fréïa, 302 R
Et tu lui diras que sa mère songe, 46 I
Et vitam venturi saeculi, 34 C, 247 E
Et vous père et mère benissez votre enfant, 360 K
Etendue au seuil du bassin, 110 O
Eternel est ma lumière, L', 178 S
Eternel est mon berger, L', 178 N
Eterno! Immenso!, 309 O
Etienne Marcel, 312 H
Etoile dont la beauté luit, 100 N
Etoile du Nord, L', 233 R
Etoiles, Les, 147 J
Etre adoré, 147 S
Etre ou ne pas être, 380 J
Eu coa miña monteira, 263 G
Euch, Lüften, die mein Klagen, 409 Q
Euch macht ihr's leicht, 411 R
Euch werde Lohn in besser'n Welten, 33 G
Eugene Onegin, 376 L
Euridice, 70 K, 275 B
Euryanthe, 421 H
Eva, 203 M
Evangelimann, Der, 191 Q
Evènements Imprevues, Les, 141 F
Evening, 186 B
Evening hymn, 290 L, 374 M

Evening prayer, 183 G, 258 L
Evening songs, 347 L
Evocation, 235 E
Ev'ry valley shall be exalted, 162 K
Ewig war ich, 415 I
Ewigkeit, du machst mir bange, 9 K
Exaltabo te, Domine, 269 G
Exaudi orationem meam, 359 P
Excelsior, 30 F
Expectans expectavi Dominum, 359 R
Expressive glances shall be our lances, 369 S
Exsultate, jubilate, K.165, 242 P
Extase, 100 H
Exultate Deo, 269 M
Ex-voto, 179 P
Ezio, 152 M

F

Fa la nana, bambin, 312 E
Fac ut ardeat cor meum, 408 D
Fac ut ardeat cor meum, 274 N
Fac ut portem, 274 P, 310 C
Factus est, 3 B
Fäden, 438 G
Faery king's courtship, The, 167 Q
Faery song, 52 G
Fagnes de Wallonie, 279 K
Fahrt zum Hades, 327 B
Fain would I change that note, 293 K
Faintly the child signs, 259 G
Fair and true, 420 F
Fair at Sorochinsk, The, 257 B
Fair house of joy, 293 K
Fair is Rose as bright May day, 370 P
Fair moon to thee I sing, 363 O
Fair Phyllis I saw sitting all alone, 107 B
Fair springtide, 213 J
Fairest isle, 289 N
Fairy Pipers, The, 64 B
Fairy Queen, The, 289 E
Fairy's love song, A, 190 L
Fais rafraichir mon vin, 282 A
Faiseurs de religions, Les, 281 C
Faites-lui mes aveux, 134 R
Faithfu' Johnie, 37 S
Falling leaf, and fading tree, 385 E
Fall'n is the foe, 161 F
False destructive ways of pleasure, 166 H
Falstaff, 395 A
Familien-Gemälde, 332 E
Fanciulla del West, La, 284 D
Fanciulla, è sbocciato, 286 C
Fanciulla sui greppi, 98 J
Fann'd by Southern winds that chasten, 128 M
Fantaisie aux divins mensonges, 90 R
Fantoches, 88 P
Far across the desert sands, 440 J
Far across the village green, 194 R
Far away beyond three oceans, 305 N
Far croonin' is pullin' me away, A, 190 Q
Far from his fetters grim, 374 G

Far off I hear a lover's flute, 70 Q
Far out at sea, 295 A
Far the rugged misty isle, 191 A
Faramondo, 156 M
Farandole joyeuse et Folle, La, 135 R
Fare well, 349 R
Fare you well my dear, 390 J
Farewell, dear love, 188 N
Farewell, my own, 64 D
Farewell my son, 256 S
Farewell, ye limpid springs, 160 H
Farewell, ye rocks, 292 L
Farlaf's Rondo, 128 A
Fariniers, les charbonniers, Les, 264 H
Farmer's son so sweet, A, 388 G
Farruca, 387 J
Farvel, Lillie Grete, 122 D
Fate, 295 C
Father of Heav'n, 162 E
Father O'Flynn, 349 O
Father, swans flying, where do they go?, 201 B
Fatigues del querer, Las, 263 C
Faulheit, endlich muss ich, 171 N
Faulse beauté, qui tant me couste cher, 89 L
Faune, Le, 88 S
Faust, 134 H
Faust, Aus Goethe's, 35 N
Faut-il donc savoir tant de choses?, 224 J
Fauves las, 78 I
Fauvette avec ses petits, La, 141 P
Favorita, La, 95 G
Fear no danger to ensue, 288 F
Fear no more the heat o' the sun, 293 O
Fear ye not, O Israel, 66 L
Fearful deed is done, The, 373 B
Feast of Lanterns, A, 30 I, 144 S
Fecit potentiam, 22 E
Fedora, 126 N
Fée aux chansons, La, 108 K
Fein Rösslein, ich beschage dich, 337 M
Feinslieb, du hast mich g'fangen, 168 B
Feinsliebchen, 62 F
Feketeföd, 31 L
Feldeinsamkeit, 59 S
Fell rage and black despair, 165 C
Fels auf Felsen hingewälzet, 326 O
Felszántom a császár, 194 I
Femme sensible, entends tu le , ramage, 226 M
Fere selvagge, 70 L
Ferito prigionier, 117 C
Fermez-vous pour jamais, 212 A
Fermier du voisinage, Un, 236 C
Feste Burg, Eine, 234 B
Feste Burg ist unser Gott, Ein, 14 E, 21 L
Feste! Pane!, 277 O
Festgesang, 230 E
Fête de Bordeaux, 236 O
Fête de Montmartre, 236 P
Fêtes galantes, 88 O, 147 K, 280 N
Fêtes Vénitiennes, Les, 72 F
Feuer, Lebenslust, 351 O
Feuerreiter, Der, 430 J
Feuilles s'ouvraient, Les, 88 N
Feuilles tombent, Les, 147 F
Fia vero? lasciarti, 95 K

Fiançailles pour rire, 280 O
Fidèle Coeur, Le, 405 Q
Fidelio, 32 R
Field Marshall Death, 259 J
Field of the dead, 283 D
Fièvre brûlante, Une, 141 H
Fife and all the harmony, The, 292 C
Fifteen men on the dead man's chest, 125 P
Figlia a tal nome io palpito, 401 H
Figlia che reggi, 277 P
Figlia mia, non pianger. no, 157 Q
Figlia! Mio padre, 400 A
Figliol prodigo, Il, 279 B
Figure de force brûlante et farouche, 282 I
Files a marier, 45 E
Fileuse, La, 72 O
Fill ev'ry glass, 271 S
Fille des Rois, 233 G
Fille du Regiment, La, 96 D
Fille du Roi de Chine, La, 181 N
Filles de Cadix, Les, 90 K
Filli mia, 297 C
Filli non t'amo più, 74 B
Filli, tu vuoi partire, 297 D
Fin da sta notte, 49 S
Finch' han dal vino, 250 J
Finche lo strale, 153 D
Fine knacks for ladies, 98 S
Finken schlagen, Die, 174 Q
Finnish folk tune, 390 Q
Finnish lullaby, 269 S
Finta Giardiniera, La, K.196, 242 S
Fiocca la neve, 80 J
Fiolaire, Lo, 72 O
Fior di giagiolo gli angeli belli, 219 Q
Fire, fire, 241 D
Firefly, The, 121 G
Firenze è come un albero, 284 J
First book of ayres, 98 O
First kiss, The, 342 K
First Meeting, 142 I
First night I was married, The, 167 P
First time at the looking glass, The, 272 H
Fischermädchen, Das, 318 O
Fischerweise, 324 K
Fisher's Song, 144 B
Five Eyes, 125 J
Five songs on old texts, 175 G
Fjäriln vingad syns pa Haga, 40 C
Flambeau, Jeannette, Un, 384 D
Flamme vengeresse, 7 J
Flammen perdonnami, 221 C
Flavio, 152 Q
Flaxen headed cowboy, A, 64 P
Fledermaus, Die, 351 D
Fleur jetée, 108 M
Fleur promises, 281 A
Fleur que vous m'avais jetée, La, 46 R
Fleurissait une Rose, 223 C
Fleurs, 281 A
Fliegende Holländer, Der, 408 H
Fliegt der Schnee, 320 C
Fliegt nur aus, geliebte Tauben, 58 K
Flieh' wie du kannst und fürchte den Zigeuner, 353 I
Flocks are sporting, 73 O

Flokkendichte Winternacht, 192 N
Floods of spring, 295 B
Flora gave me fairest flowers, 427 L
Florentine song, 378 J
Florenz hat schöne Frauen, 375 F
Floridante, 153 B
Flos florum, 99 L
Flösst, mein Heiland, flösst, dein Namen, 25 F
Flot, miroir mouvant, Le, 306 P
Flow gently, sweet Afton, 182 N, 348 M
Flow, my tears, 99 A
Flower duet A, 295 C
Flower Maidens' Waltz, Parsifal, 412 J
Flower Song, 46 R, 134 R
Flowers of love, 51 P
Flowers that bloom in the spring, tra-la, The, 366 N
Flowing from the firmament, 176 S
Flügel! Flügel! um zu fliegen, 333 F
Flûte de Pan, La, 88 D
Flûte enchantée, Le, 298 Q
Fluten reicher Ebro, 339 N
Fly swift, ye hours, 290 M
Flying Dutchman, The, 408 H
Flyv, fugl, flyv, 167 D
Foglia di rosa, 386 F
Foggy, foggy dew, The, 64 L
Foi, de son flambeau divin, La, 136 I
Foin du bâtard, 299 I
Folgue, folgue minha gente, 145 O
Foiha cahiste ao meulado, lagrima, 406 K
Follow thy fair sun, 71 Q
Follow your saint, 71 R
Fond were the lovers, 79 I
For a month to dwell in a dungeon cell, 370 A
For he himself has said it, 364 C
For he is like a refiner's fire, 162 N
For he's going to marry Yum Yum, 366 A
For I am a Pirate King!, 268 F
For I'm falling in love with someone, 173 J
For it's always good weather, 67 A
For Jillian of Berry she dwells on a hill, 420 I
For the mountains shall depart, 227 I
For they're hangin' Danney Deever, 86 A
For today young Alexis Poindexter, 372 E
For unto us a child is born, 162 R
For You Alone, 123 B
Forelle, Die, 322 H
Forest flow'rs are faded all, The, 82 I
Forest song, 304 L
Forêt, La, 73 C
Forêt profonde, 180 E
Forgive, 350 R
Forgotten, 84 R
Forma ideal purissima, 50 G
Forsaken, 103 D
Forse, forse un giorno il cielo, 251 C

Första Kyssen, Den, 342 K
Fort denn eile nach Osten, 414 E
Forth went a comely lass, 103 K
Forto e lieto a morte andrei, 157 R
Fortune Teller, The, 173 C
Fortunio, 232 M
Forza del Destino, La, 395 N
Fo'ty days fo'ty nights, 68 C
Foudre et vent grondent en vain, 127 M
Fountains mingle with the river, The, 92 A, 293 E
Four American Indian Songs, 70 R
Four popular Spanish songs, 262 K
Four Russian peasant songs, 361 D
Four Saints in three acts, 382 B
Fourteen years I had seem'd just to be, 207 J
Fox, The, 420 G
Fox lay low 'neath the birchtree root, The, 193 D
Fox may steal your hens, sir, A, 271 M
Fra Diavolo, 7 L
Fra duri scogli senz' alcun governo, 270 D
Fra l'erbe, 98 J
Fra poco a me ricoverò, 98 C
Frage, 332 M
Frage und Antwort, 430 L
Fragment aus dem Aeschylus, 327 D
Fragst du mich, 430 L
Frägt die Velt, 297 P
Fraiche comme une rose, 179 N
Francesca da Rimini, 441 O
Franziskus einst, der Heil'ge, 209 L
Frasquita, 203 K
Frau Holde kam aus dem Berg, 416 H
Frau Sonne sendet lichte Strahlen, 415 Q
Frauenliebe und Leben 334 D, 334 G
Frauenwörth, 112 I
Frauenzimmer, Das, 379 K
Fredman's Epistel, 40 B
Fredman's farewell to Ulla, 40 H
Fredman's Song, 40 E
Free as the birds in the air, 198 D
Freer is the gypsy, 102 N
Freier kam zum Schwesterlein, 194 J
Freiheit Rom's sei dies Gesetz, Die 412 S
Freischütz, Der, 421 O
Freisinn, 330 R
Freiwilliges Versinken, 327 E
Frejas Stjerne, 167 E
Fremd bin ich eingezgen, 319 A
Frère Philippe, Le, 98 M
Frères, le froid, l'horreurs des bois profonds 127 P
Freschi luoghi, prati aulenti, 93 I
Freude schöner Götterfunken, 38 E
Freude, Tochter aus Elysium, 38 G
Freuden sonder Zahl, 329 H
Freudig begrüssen, 416 Q
Freudvoll und leidvoll, 35 P, 208 A, 311 L, 328 D
Freue dich, erlöste Schaar, 10 H
Freund, Der, 430 M

Freund ist dein, Der, 132 R
Freunde, das Leben ist lebenswert, 203 I
Freunde, Wasser machet stumm, 171 G
Freundliche Vision, 358 N
Freut euch des Lebens, 260 D
Friede, 300 Q, 438 H
Friede sei mit dir, Der, 19 P
Friede sei mit euch, Der, 329 D
Friedericus Rex, 209 J
Friederike, 203 D
Frisch auf, gut Gsell, 175 L
Frisch traube sonder Ruh' und Rast, 324 H
Frisch zum Kampfe!, 245 S
Frohe Botschaft, 430 N
Frohe Hirten, eilt, 25 C
Frohe Wandersmann, Der, 230 K
Frohsinn und Laune würzen das Leben, 261 L
From celestial seats descending, 159 N
From clouds of pretty woe, 237 A
From ev'ry kind of man Obedience I expect, 366 I
From far, from eve and morning, 389 E
From mighty kings he took, 161 R
From Monte Pincio, 143 I
From out the city thou has flown, 378 Q
From rosy bowers, 287 Q
From silent shades, 290 F
From the briny sea comes young Richard, 371 C
From the desert I come to thee, 276 Q
From the land of the sky-blue water, 70 R
From the North, 342 S
From the tree an apple fell, 194 P
Front comme un drapeau perdu, Le, 282 D
Früh wann die Hähne kräh'n, 336 C, 436 H
Frühhauch hat gefächelt, Der, 433 S
Frühling, Der, 143 E
Frühling lässt sein blaues Band, 337 F, 430 H
Frühling übers Jahr, 430 O
Frühling will kommen, Der, 325 H
Frühlings Ankunft, 337 D
Frühlingsfahrt, 334 M
Frühlingsfeier, 359 H
Frühlingsgedränge, 357 C
Frühlingsglaube, 321 P
Frühlingsgruss, 336 Q
Frühlingskinder im bunten Gedränge, 357 C
Frühlingslied, 112 S 228 G, 228 J, 228 P, 229 C, 311 C, 327 G
Frühlingslust, 339 G
Frühlingsnacht, 333 S
Frühlingssehnsucht, 318 H
Frühlingstraum, 319 K
Frühlingszeit, 32 P
Fu vile l'Editto, 220 S
Fuchsia tree, The, 294 A
Fugitif et tremblant, 380 M
Fugitive, The 102 R
Fühlt meine Seele, 430 P
Fühltest du mein Leiden, 377 H

Führ mich, Kind, 430 Q
Fuir à jamais, 266 N
Fuis mon âme fuis, 77 L
Fuisti a la siega y golviesti, 262 P
Full fathom five, 289 Q
Füllest wieder Busch und Tal, 326 G
Fumée, 147 L, 236 N
Fünftausend Thaler!, 210 S
Fünfzig Thaler baares Geld, 21 E
Funiculi, funicula, 92 G
Fuor del mar, 244 P
Für ewig vereint, 345 N
Für fünfzehn Pfennige, 357 S
Für Musik, 119 I
Furcht des Herren, Die, 340 C
Furibondo spira il vento, 154 J
Fürst des Lebens, starker Streiter, 10 I
Fürstenkind ein Wunder ist, Ein, 353 S
Furtiva lagrima, Una, 95 E
Fürwahr, fürwahr es ist ein Abenteuer, 198 P
Fussreise, 430 R

G

Gäbe Gott im hellen Himmel, 59 B
Gai papillon, papillon d'or, 117 E
Gaia canzone, La, 278 P
Gaily as I met thee, 103 B
Gaje comari di Vindsor!, 395 J
Galant jardinier, Le, 90 E
Gallega, 262 O
Game played in Erin-go-Bragh, The, 167 R
Gang zum Liebchen, Der, 53 L, 57 H
Ganymed, 321 N, 430 S
Ganz Erbarmen, Gnad und Liebe, 171 A
Ganze Nacht durchschwärmt, Die, 352 J
Gar viel und schön, 417 A
Gardez piti Milatte la, 261 I
Gars qui vont à la fête, Les, 280 G
Gärtner, Der, 53 J, 431 A
Gascon à mine fière, Un, 179 G
Gasparone, 237 D
Gathering mushrooms, 257 Q
Gaudent in coelis, 407 I
Gaudio, gaudio son al cuore queste pene, 131 R
Gavotte, 20 H
Gavotte des Mathurins, 205 H
Gavotte from Manon, 223 Q
Gay and gallant gondolieri, 362 E
Gazza ladra, La, 308 L
Gebet, 431 B
Gebet vor der Schlacht, 423 E
Gebet Während der Schlacht, 175 B, 327 H
Gebt euch du Hand!, 242 H
Gebt mir meinen Jesum wieder, 27 R
Geburt Christi, 175 P
Geburt Maria, 175 M
Gedenk an uns mit deiner Liebe, 10 G
Gedenke doch, mein Geist, zurücke, 28 M
Geduld, 356 D

Geduld, Geduld, 27 N
Gefrorne Tränen, 319 C
Gefrorne Tropfen fallen von meinen Wangen ab, 319 C
Gefunden, 359 D
Gegrüsset du gottesandter Held!, 409 H
Geh! Gehorche meinen Winken, 429 Q
Geh', Geliebter, geh' jetzt, 431 C
Geh' hin! dein Trotz soll mich nicht schrecken, 242 F
Geh schlafen, Tochter, schlafen!, 59 L
Geheimes, 321 K
Geheimnis, 35 Q, 59 F, 356 M
Geheimnisvoller Klang, 300 H
Gehorchen ist das Erste, 112 Q
Geist hilft uns'rer Schwachheit auf, Der, 24 F
Geist und Seele wird verwirret, 10 N
Geisternähe, 336 J
Geistliche Konzerte, 340 A
Geistliches Wiegenlied, 60 E
Gekommen wär' er, 344 F
Gelassen steig die Nacht ans Land, 436 C
Gelb rollt mir zu Füssen, 311 I
Gelido, in ogni vena, 157 E
Geliebter, komm!, 416 G
Gellert Lieder, 35 R
Gelobet sei der Herr, mein Gott, 17 D
Gelobet seist du, Jesus Christ, 15 B, 301 L
Geme la tortorella, 243 A
Gendarmes' duet, 265 D
General William Booth enters into heaven, 186 C
Generoso chi sol brama, 156 G
Genesene an die Hoffnung, Der, 431 D
Geneviève de Brabant, 265 D
Genialisch Treiben, 431 E
Gentil Coqu'licot, 184 P
Gentile di cuore, 133 D
Gentle airs, melodious strains, 158 R
Gentle Annie, 115 H
Gentle Zitella, whither away, 82 N
Georgine, Die, 356 C
Gepriesen sei die Stunde, 416 O
Gerechten Seelen sind in Gottes Hand, Der, 53 R
Gerechten werden weggerafft, Die, 199 F
German Flagellant's hymn, 5 C
German Requiem, A, 53 M
Germania, 117 J
Gern hab' ich die Frau'n geküsst, 204 D
Gern ja will ich dir vertrauen, 344 A
Gerne will ich mich bequemen, 27 G
Gesang aus Fungal, 43 K
Gesang der Parzen, 54 P
Gesang Weyla's, 431 F
Gesänge des Harfners, 321 D
Geschmückt mit König David's Bild, 411 S
Gesegnet, gesegnet, wer liebt und auch vertraut, 345 A

Gesegnet sei das Grün, 431 G
Gesegnet sei, durch den die Welt entstund, 431 H
Gesegnet soll sie schreiten, 410 A
Geselle, woll'n wir uns in Kutten hüllen, 431 J
Gesellenlied, 431 I
Gesellenreise, K.468, 247 I
Geständniss, 336 H
Gestern Abend in der stillen Ruh, 300 I
Gestillte Sehnsucht, 60 C
Getrost, getrost, 17 F
Geübtes Herz, 316 I
Geuss, lieber Mond, 323 C
Geuss nicht so laut, 57 D, 325 R
Gewaltige stösst Gott vom Stuhl, 9 C
Ghasel, 316 L, 431 K
Già che morir non posso, 154 Q
Già i sacerdodi adunansi, 392 G
Già il sole dal Gange, 315 F
Già la luna è in mezzo al mare, 307 G
Già la mensa e preparata, 251 D
Già l'empia ai tuoi, 74 H
Già! mi dicon venal, 286 L
Già mi sembra, 153 L
Già nella notte densa, 398 N
Già ti veggo, 278 M
Già torna, 217 F
Giacchè il sonno a lei dipinge, 149 M
Gianni Schicchi, 284 J
Giannina mia, 121 G
Giasone, 75 E
Gib Acht, es kracht, 354 B
Gieb dich zufrieden, 28 N
Gieb mir deine Hand, 316 F
Gieb, o Kriegsgott, mir ein Schwert, 128 B
Gieb, Schöne, viel Söhne, 21 H
Gin thou wert my ain thing, 271 R
Ging es, wie es uns gefällt, 344 H
Ging heut' Morgens über's Feld, 215 P
Gingerbread waltz, 183 P
Gioconda, La, 277 O
Gioielli della Madonna, I, 439 L
Gioite al canto mio, 275 B
Gioja, venite in sen, 151 M
Giori poveri vivea, 403 N
Giorno di pianto, 404 G
Giovani liete, fiori spargete, 248 E
Giovinette, 250 C
Gipsy fires are burning, The, 81 Q
Gipsy John, 81 Q
Girl of the Golden West, The, 284 D
Girometta, La, 343 B
Gitanjali, 74 J
Giuliano, 441 I
Giulietta e Romeo, 441 N
Giulietta! Son io, 441 N
Giulio Cesare, 153 G
Give a man a horse he can ride, 265 Q
Give a rouse, then, 66 S
Give me one hour, 121 I
Give to me the life I love, 389 N
Glaub' es mir jubelnde Kinderschar, 438 N
Glaube lebt, Der, 412 H

Gleich und gleich, 431 I
Gleich wie der Regen und Schnee von Himmel, 9 J
Gleichen hab' ich nie gesehn, Der, 428 F
Gleitender Mond du, 101 J
Gli aranci olezano, 219 F
Gli sguardi trattieni, 131 A
Gloire à Dagon, 313 A
Gloire au Dieu tout puissant, 178 H
Gloire au grand Dieu vengeur, 234 H
Gloria, 22 K, 22 P, 69 G, 69 Q, 168 Q, 168 R, 208 H, 243 G, 246 O, 267 S, 388 Q
Gloria al Egitto, 391 O
Gloria in altissimis Deo, 313 B
Gloria in excelsis, 33 N
Gloria in Excelsis Deo, 66 B
Gloria Patri, 269 N
Gloire immortelle de nos aieux, 135 K
Glorie, Lob, Ehr' und Herrlichkeit, 16 J
Glorificamus te, 33 O
Glory Road, De, 437 P
Glory to God, 162 S
Gloxinia, Le, 8 B
Glu, La, 138 B
Glück, 379 L
Glück, das mir verblieb, 197 D
Glück dir winkt, Ein, 203 L
Glücke kömmt selten, Das, 379 L
Glückes genug, 358 B
Glücklich ist, 351 I
Glücksbote mein, 142 P
Go away, Madam, I should say, 364 R
Go, crystal tears, 98 R
Go down, Moses, 67 M
Go down to de cottonfield, 116 E
Go down to Kew in lilac time, 90 C
Go, lovely Rose, 204 Q, 293 S
Go thou, and haste thee, 79 D
Go to bed, sweet muse, 188 O
Go ye heroes, go to glory, 369 A
Goat, The, 257 R
God is my shepherd, 102 A
God shall wipe away all tears, 374 L
Goin' home, 102 H
Going down the shady dell, 115 K
Golden Calf, The, 134 M
Golden legend, The, 374 M
Golden moonlight, The, 103 O
Golden sun was sinking, The 270 A
Gondelfahrer, Der, 322 F, 327 K
Gondolier du Rialto, 107 Q
Gondoliers, The, 362 B
Gone are the days, 116 G
Gonets, 305 I
Gönnt mir goldne Tages, 311 A
Good Ale, 420 H
Good morrow, good mother, 364 I
Good morrow, Gossip Joan, 272 P
Goodbye, 347 R, 385 E
Good-bye forever!, 385 F
Goodbye, sweetheart, goodbye, 168 G
Goodnight Quartet, 113 L
Gopak, 258 B

Gott, deine Güte reicht so weit, 29 G, 35 R
Gott, dem der Erdenkreis zu klein, 15 B
Gott, der Herr, ist Sonn' und Schild!, 14 D
Gott erhalte Franz den Kaiser, 171 H
Gott erhalte Gott be schütze, 171 H
Gott fähret auf mit Jauchzen, 11 D
Gott hat alles wohl gemacht, 10 P
Gott hat sich hoch gesetzet, 19 K
Gott in Frühlinge, 327 K
Gott ist mein Hirt, 325 J
Gott ist mein König, 13 F
Gott is mein Lied!, 36 C
Gott is unser Sonn' und Schild!, 14 D
Gott ist unsere Zuversicht, 19 M
Gott, man lobet dich in der Stille, 16 Q
Gott versorget alles Leben, 19 H
Götter! Bruder im hohen Olympos, 355 G
Götterdämmerung, 415 K
Göttergatte, Der, 204 G
Gottes Engel weichen nie, 18 C
Gottes ist der Orient!, 331 C
Gottes Macht und Vorsehung, 36 C
Gottes Zeit ist die allerbeste Zeit, 16 E
Gottestrost, 260 R
Gottlob! nun geht das Jahr zu Ende, 10 E
Goyescas, 139 S
Grâce à ce vilain ermite, 216 G
Grace, grace, pour toi même, 235 G
Graceful consort at thy side, 170 E
Graciosa moda, 262 G
Gram piant' agl' occhi, 200 Q
Granadina, 263 C
Grand sommeil noir tombe sur ma vie, Un, 178 L
Grande como el mismo sol, 63 R
Grande Duchesse de Gérolstein, La, 265 E
Grande spettacolo, Un, 205 Q
Grandes guerras se publican, 263 A
Grands Dieux! du destin, qui m'accable suspendez, 128 O
Grands vents venus d'outremer, Les, 297 Q
Grans regrets, Les, 124 R
Grateful am I for the happy time, 193 H
Gratias agimus, 22 S, 33 P
Grausame Frühlingssonne, 437 L
Grazie agli Dei rendete, 391 Q
Great God! who yet but darkly known, 159 B
Great minds, 288 S
Great White Host, The, 143 C
Greatest man, The, 186 D
Green, 87 R, 109 P
Green is on the grass again, The, 270 J
Greensleeves, 5 D
Greeting, 143 J
Greetings to all, 349 J
Greise Kopf, Der, 319 N
Grenouille du jeu, La, 315 A

Grenzen der Menschheit, 327 L, 431 M
Gretchen, 327 M
Gretchen am Spinnrade, 320 F
Gretchen lies in her gloomy bed, 343 K
Gretchen ligger i Kiste, 143 P
Gretchen, thränenvoll, 211 A
Gretel, 275 M
Grieve never, my beloved, 257 F
Grille ist ein armer Wicht, 196 E
Grillon, Le, 298 A
Grim King of the ghosts, 271 J
Grince, grince, grince patte en bouleau, 361 K
Grisélidis, 222 E
Gros dindons, à travers champs, Les, 75 K
Gross Glück und Heil lacht, 415 O
Gross ist Jehova, der Herr, 324 A
Grossen Dank dir abzustatten, 242 B
Grosser Herr und starker König, 25 B
Grossmächtige Prinzessin, 354 S
Grossvater und Grossmutter, 332 E
Grotte, La, 89 P
Grün ist der Jasminenstrauch, 331 Q
Grüne Hopfenranke, Die, 63 C
Gruppe aus dem Tartarus, 322 C
Gruss, 228 M, 230 B
Guarany, Il, 133 D
Guarda amor mio, 206 J
Guarda il mare com' è bello, 85 N
Guardate, pazzo son, 285 Q
Guardo una, "Ay!", 106 O
Gud skee tag og Lov!, 426 N
Guerir ma doleur, 201 M
Guerra è il mio stato, 238 M
Guerra, guerra, 38 R
Guerre, La, 187 C
Guerres sont terminées, Les, 199 S
Guglielmo Ratcliff, 220 H
Guide mes pas, 78 N
Guiditta, 203 H
Guillaume, Antoine, Pierre, 384 E
Guinta all' Albergo, 395 I
Guinto sol passo estremo, 50 I
Guitare, 199 Q
Guitares et mandolines, 313 O
Gurrelieder, 316 O
Gute Nacht, 25 O, 119 E, 319 A
Gute Nacht, du mein herziges Kind, 1 C
Gute Nacht, du Weltgetümmel, 10 D
Gute Ruh, 318 E
Guten Abend, Freund, 192 M
Guten Abend, gut Nacht, 57 L
Guten Abend, mein Schatz, 59 N
Guten Morgen, 317 L
Gwine to Hebb'n, 437 Q
Gyíytottam gyertyát, 194 E
Gypsy and the Bird, The, 41 D
Gypsy Baron, The, 353 D
Gypsy love, 204 N
Gypsy Love Song, 173 C
Gypsy roaming through the meadows, A, 41 D

Gypsy song, 194 Q
Gypsy Songs, 102 I
Gyulainé édes anyám, 195 E

H

H.M.S. Pinafore, 363 D
Ha l'inganno il sus diletto, 149 N
Ha seht es winkt, 353 N
Ha! welch' ein Augenblick, 33 B
Ha, welch ein Fest, 352 B
Hab' ein blause Himmelbett, 203 K
Hab' ich nur deine Liebe, 375 G
Hab' mir's gelobt, 355 R
Hab' nur dich allein, 204 L
Hab' Singen für mein Leben, 300 G
Habanera, 46 F
Had a horse, 196 R
Had I the heaven's embroidered cloths, 99 S
Had I the love of such as he, 371 A
Hagen's Call, Götterdämmerung, 415 N
Hagyj békét, viaskodó, 194 C
Hai ben ragione, 286 F
Haï luli, 82 Q
Hai tempo a ridirmelo, 206 C
Haide is braun, Die, 120 A
Haidenröslein, 426 F
Hail, Judea, happy land, 161 H
Hail the Bride of seventeen summers, 371 L
Hail to the chief, 314 H
Hakimegyek arr' a magas tetóre, 31 N
Halleluja Chorus, 163 S
Hallelujah, 161 N
Hallelujah, Stark' und Macht, 10 F
Halt!, 317 F
Halt' im Gedächtniss Jesum Christ, 12 R
Hamlet, 380 A
Han della porpora vivo, 218 R
Han gik til Ludlams Hule, 426 O
Hand of God, the awful judge is on me, The, 256 K
Handle nicht nach deinen Rechten, 15 Q
Hans Heiling, 217 K
Hans und die Grete tanzen herum, Der, 335 Q
Hansel spann deine sechs Schimmel an, 42 D
Hansel und Gretel, 182 P
Happily coupled are we, 371 P
Happy and blest are they, 227 M
Happy are we in our loving frivolity, 372 R
Happy Groves, 273 E
Hard by a crystal fountain, 241 E
Hard times, 115 I
Hard trials, 67 O
Harfenspieler, 431 N
Hark, all ye lovely saints, 424 O
Hark, hark the lark, 329 J
Hark, hark! 'tis the linnet, 160 P
Hark! Hark! What I tell to thee, 172 A
Hark, how my triangle, 102 J
Hark now the sailors cry, 83 R
Hark! the ech'ing air, 289 G

Hark the herald angels sing, 230 E
Hark, the hour of ten is sounding, 373 D
Hark ye, hark to the winding horn, 185 G
Harken! harken! music sounds afar, 92 H
Harmonie du soir, 88 H
Harmonie in der Ehe, Die, 171 J
Harm's our delight, 288 I
Harold, 260 K
Hary Janos, 193 L
Hassan, 91 Q
Hasse nur, hasse mich recht, 13 P
Hast du dir als Theil erkoren, 101 M
Hast Du dort oben vergessen auf mich, 204 K
Haste to town, 288 O
Hat dich die Liebe berührt, 218 C
Hat einen starken Geruch wie Rosen, 355 N
Hat gesagt, bleibt's nicht dabei, 358 A
Hat man nicht auch Geld, 33 A
Hat man nicht mit seinen Kindern, 20 N
Hätt' ich tausend Arme, 317 H
Hätten doch die Mädchen Flügel, 377 O
Hättest du der Einfalt nicht, 175 P
Hauts talons luttaient, Les, 88 R
Have I found her, 32 C
Have you heard of a frolicsome ditty, 272 M
Have you seen but a whyte Lillie grow, 5 G
He asked for a distant magpie, 382 M
He deceiv'd a girl confiding, 373 I
He digged a pit, 383 E
Hé garçons, le savez-vous?, 304 I
He met his death in foreign land, 257 L
He! réveille toi, 2 D
He shall feed his flock like a shepherd, 163 B
He trusted in God that He would deliver him, 163 I
He was despised, 163 E
He, watching over Israel, 227 G
He who shies at such a prize, 365 D
He, Zigeuner, greife in die Saiten ein, 54 R
Hear how the breakers angrily lash, 193 C
Hear my prayer, 5 Q, 231 I
Hear my prayer, O Lord, 101 S, 102 C, 102 S
Hear ye Amorea's daughters, 258 S
Hear ye, Israel, 227 B
Hearken unto me, Magyars, 195 S
Hears not my Phyllis, 291 F
Heart bowed down, The, 30 B
Heart worships, The, 176 R
Heartless Wife, The, 194 M
Heart's desire, The, 185 F
Heart's haven, 388 K

Heavens are telling the glory of God, The, 169 O
Heav'n, heav'n, 67 Q
Heav'n send it happy dew, 314 I
Heavy the sorrow that bows the head, 363 J
Heb' auf dein blondes Haupt, 431 Q
Hebraic song, 258 A
Hebrew melodies, 338 A
Hebt euer Haupt empor, 13 D
Hedgerow, 41 G
Hei! Siegfried gehört, 415 A
Heidenröslein, 320 H
Heigh ho, heigh, hi, 64 M
Heil dir, Sonne!, 415 G
Heil! Heil! Heil sei dem Tag, 33 I
Heil jenem Tag, 357 P
Heil sei dem Tag, 211 G
Heil und Segen, 16 R
Heil'ge Nacht, du sinkest nieder, 322 M
Heilige Franziskus, Der, 209 L
Heiligen drei König, 359 I, 430 G
Heiligste Dreieinigkeit, 18 Q
Heimkehr, 55 Q, 356 J
Heimkehr aus der Fremde, 230 R
Heimliche Aufforderung, 357 G
Heimliche Grüsse, 112 K
Heimweh, 431 R
Heinrich der Vogler, 209 I
Heiss mich nicht reden, 323 J, 338 J, 433 K
Heiterkeit und Fröhlichkeit, 211 B
Hej! A Mohi hegy borának, 195 B
Hej két tikom, 193 S
Hélas! enfant encore, 224 M
Hélas! mon âme est triste, 51 G
Hélas! mon coeur sensible et tendre, 129 R
Helas, quel jour, 201 N
Helas! si tu pouvais, 305 K
Helft mir, ihr Schwestern, 334 H
Helle Silberglücklein klingen, 339 H
Helle Sonne leuchtet, Die, 120 L
Helle Wehr!, 415 P
Hello! Hello?, 232 H
Hence, Care; thou art too cruel, 424 P
Hence Iris, hence away, 165 H
Hence! with your trifling deity, 287 S
Hennlein weiss, Ein, 315 C
Henry VIII, 312 I
Her die Hand, 353 Q
Heraus, beschlag' mir mein Ross, 209 Q
Herbe est molle au sommeil, L', 100 L
Herbe pauvre, Une, 282 G
Herbstlied, 65 S, 230 C
Herbstnebel wallen bläulich, 215 H
Herbstsonnenschein, 41 S
Herbststurm, 142 H
Herbstwind rüttelt die Bäume, Der, 228 S
Hercules, 159 N
Herdgirl's Sunday, 66 Q
Herdmaiden's song, The, 305 R
Here a sheer hulk, 92 O
Here amid the shady woods, 158 P
Here is a fix unprecedented, 363 C

Here stands the wand'rer now, 170 O

Here upon we're both agreed, 374 F

Here's a how-de-do!, 366 G

Here's the tale of what happened at Kazan, 256 G

Hérisson, Le, 281 O

Hérodiade, 222 I

Heroes, when with glory burning, 160 Q

Héros que j'attends, Le, 211 O

Herr Cavalier, 355 Q

Herr, deine Augen sehen nach den Glauben, 15 R

Herr, deine Güte reicht, 9 H

Herr, der du stark und mächtig bist, 9 B

Herr, du bist würdig zu nehmen Preis, 54 F

Herr erhör dich in der Not, Der, 340 H

Herr, gehe nicht in's Gericht, 16 C

Herr Heinrich sitzt, 209 I

Herr, ich glaube, 14 C

Herr ist König über all, Der, 340 J

Herr ist mein getreuer Heit, Der, 16 M

Herr Jesu Christ, wahr'r Mensch und Gott, 17 B

Herr, lehre doch mich, 53 Q

Herr Magnus han stirrer i Vinterhatten ud, 122 E

Herr Morold zog zu Meere her, 417 N

Herr! Schicke was du willt, 431 B

Herr, so du willt, 13 G

Herr, unser Herrscher, 25 O, 340 N

Herr, was du willst soll mir gefallen, 18 K

Herr, was trägt der Boden hier, 432 A

Herr, wie du willt, so schick's mit mir, 13 J

Herz, das seinen Jesum lebend weiss, Ein, 17 H

Herz, das so der Abschied, Ein, 247 M

Herz, mein Herz, 37 F

Herz und Mund und Tat und Leben, 18 A

Herz verzage nicht geschwind, 432 B

Herzentausch, 300 J

Herzliebe, gute Mutter, 325 I

Herzliebster Jesu, 26 R

Heure espagnole, L', 299 O

Heure exquise, L', 147 M, 277 J

Heure silencieuse, L', 350 D

Heures fortunées, 87 H

Heureux guerriers, 130 I

Heureux les coeurs, 117 P

Heureux petit berger, 136 F

Heureux qui meurt ici, 109 H

Heut' Nacht erhob ich mich um Mitternacht, 432 C

Heute noch, 20 Q

Hey, Hey, you young ones, 86 H

Hey, ho, the wind and the rain, 293 H

Hey, poor old man with a head so light, 259 F

Hey! The wine of Mohi, 195 B

Hey! what a joyful pleasure, 347 O

Hi my young and black-eyed lover, 257 G

Hiboux, Les, 342 A

Hidalgo, Der, 331 S, 332 A

Hide me from day's garish eye, 150 F

Hie un da ist an den Bäumen, 319 P

Hielt der Eine für sich, 207 Q

Hielt die allerschönste Herrin, 430 N

Hier, 281 B

Hier, c'est ce chapeau fané, 281 B

Hier dicht am Quell, 421 M

Hier im ird'schen Jammerthal, 421 Q

Hier in diesem Land Eure Wiege stand, 353 J

Hier in diesen erdbeklommnen Lüften, 331 O

Hier, in meines Vaters Stätte, 10 K

Hier, ist das rechte Osterlamm, 8 O, 19 S

Hier lieg' ich auf dem Frühlingshügel, 432 K

Hier sitz' ich zur Wacht, 415 L

Hier soir encore Fetis, 360 J

Hier soll ich dich denn sehen, 245 I

Hier unten steht ein Ritter, 328 I

Hier wo sich die Strassen scheiden, 61 M

High from the Ben a Hayich, 190 N

High in the branches, 183 I

High o'er earth in Heaven, 128 J

High on the giddy bending mast, 171 R

Hills, 199 L

Hills of home, The, 117 H

Himmel erzählen die Ehre Gottes, Die, 13 O

Himmel hat eine Thräne geweint, Der, 333 C

Himmel lacht, die Erde jubiliert, Der, 10 I

Himmel rühmen des Ewigen Ehre, Die, 8 E, 36 B

Himmel und Erde, 338 G

Himmel wölbt sich rein und blau, Der, 334 A

Himmel zahllos Heer, Der, 133 P

Himmelskönig, sei willkommen. 19 A

Hin und wieder fliegen die pfeile, 326 M

Hinter jenen dichten Wäldern weilst du, 57 K

Hirondelle, 44 C

Hirt auf dem Felsen, Der, 325 G

Hirten, Die, 83 J

Hirtenlied, 229 H

His sceptre is the rod, 164 H

His yoke is easy, 163 C

Histoire d'Ezechias, L', 74 C

Histoires naturelles, 297 R

Hither, dear husband, turn your eyes, 273 B

Hither, hither, Mary, 180 L

Hiver a cessé, L', 110 G

Ho, a song by the fire, 67 B

Ho! broder Teague, 291 L

Ho capito, 250 D

Ho dato moglie al padre, 80 L

Ho, jolly Jenkin, 374 Q

Ho perduto il caro sposo, 155 M

Ho sognato che stavi, 386 D

Hobby horse, The 258 M

Hobellied, 199 B

Hoch, hoch sind die Berge, 399 P

Hoch über stillen Höhen stand, 55 P

Hochgelobter Gottes Sohn, 8 R

Hochgetürmte Rimaflut, 54 S

Hochgewölbte Blätterkronen, 418 F

Hochländisches Wiegenlied, 331 G

Höchsten heiles Wunder!, 412 R

Höchster, Höchster, 11 N

Höchster Tröster, 19 D

Höchster, was ich habe, 10 R

Höchsterwünschtes Freudenfest, 20 A

Hochzeitslied, 209 E, 316 H

Hodie, Christus natus est, 375 H, 268 I

Hoffärtig seid Ihr, schönes Kind, 432 D

Hoffnung, 143 A, 301 H

Hogyan tudtál rózsám, 193 R

Höh'n und Wälder schon steigen, Die, 119 E

Hoi! for the gay Hopak, 258 B

Hoj! turdy Vyšehrad, 346 J

Hojotoho!, 413 R

Hol én elmények, Az, 194 N

Holde Schöne, hör' diese Töne, 375 D

Holden Lenzgeschmeide der Rose, Der, 337 N

Holder klingt der Vogelsang, 59 H, 228 E, 328 O

Hollah welch gutes Echo!, 202 N

Holle Netz hat dich umgarnt, Der, 421 S

Holle Rache, Der, 253 Q

Höllische Schlange, wird dir nicht bange, 10 S

Holly and the Ivy, The, 386 R

Holy City, The, 2 H

Home on the Range, 146 A

Home road, The, 74 L

Home sweet home, 45 N

Homeland mine, 140 J

Homing, 303 P

Homme a pour payer sa rancon, L', 107 S

Homme né de la femme, L', 178 R

Honest country girl, An, 170 P

Honey did you heah dat mockin-bird, 361 M

Honneur au Khan, 51 L

Honour and arms, 164 L

Hontoeller Dag og Stunde, 144 I

Hopak, 258 B

Hope, 185 A

Hope of my heart, 419 O

Hope the hornblower, 185 G

Hor ch'el ciel e la terra, 238 L

Hör' ich das Liedchen klingen, 335 D

Hör klokorna med ängsligt dan, 40 D

Hör uns, Allmächtiger!, 423 E

Horch der Abendglocke Ton!, 231 A
Horch, der Wind klagt in den Zweigen, 55 F
Horch, die Lerche, 261 N
Horch horch! die Lerch', 329 J
Horch, hörst du nicht, 438 I
Horch! Liebchen, horch, 114 B
Horch, wie˜ Murmeln des empörten Meeres, 322 C
Horch, wie schalt's dorten so lieblich, 38 C
Hörch, wie still es wird im dunkeln Hain, 119 J
Höre mit Sinn, 415 M
Horizon chimérique, L 110 R
Hörst du den Vogel singen?, 332 P
Hörst du nicht die Quellen gehen, 434 C
Hört doch! der sanften Flöten, 20 L
Hört, ihr Augen, auf zu weinen, 15 L
Hört, ihr Leut' und lasst euch sagen, 411 C
Hört, ihr Völker, 13 O
Hört mich, ihr fröstigen Herzen im Nord, 144 L
Hosanna, 134 F, 267 K, 267 N, 267 P
Hosanna! Gloire au Seigneur, 111 I
Hosanna in excelsis, 43 P
Hosanna to the son of David, 125 F
Hostias, 255 K
Hostias et preces tibi, 405 G
Hotel, 279 J
Hours I spent with thee, dear heart, The, 261 G
House I live in, The, 306 D
House of life, The, 388 H
How beautiful are the feet, 163 N
How beautiful they are, 52 G
How beautifully blue the sky, 368 L
How blest are shepherds, 289 L
How can I leave thee, 199 H
How can the tree but waste and wither away, 388 N
How can the tree but wither, 388 N
How could I dream a day would ever dawn, 341 A
How cruel are the traitors, 272 G
How delightful's the life, 290 N
How far ye seem behind me, 377 B
How happy are we, 272 I
How happy could I be, 272 M
How jolly are we beggars, 207 B
How lovely are the messengers, 228 A
How many a lonely caravan, 440 M
How many hired servants, 374 O
How many saints are there in it, 382 J
How merrily we live, 103 M
How my heart aches!, 295 G
How often at midnight, 295 I
How shall my soul, 290 J
How shall we sing the Lord's song, 419 D
How should I your true love know, 272 K

How sweet the moonlight sleeps, 389 L
How sweet the place, 295 F
How vain is man, 161 S
How willing my paternal love, 164 M
Huguenots, Les, 234 A
Hull Fisher's love song, The, 190 P
Hüll in die Mantille, 4 A
Humming chorus, 285 E
Hun er mager og mörk og myg, 144 D
Hungarian Folk Songs, 92 S, 194 J, 196 R
Hungarian folksong settings, 31 H
Hunting Chorus, Dei Freischütz, 422 I
Huntsmen's Chorus, 97 E
Hurrah die Schlacht, 354 C
Hurrah! Now sing the witch is dead, 183 P
Husar, Tra-ra!, Der, 339 E
Hush! Hush! with lovely eyes closed, 52 A
Hush, I hush, you hush. 383 H
Hush thee, dear one, 260 K
Hushed the song of the nightingale, 140 N
Husker Du i Höst, 172 O
Hvor Belgen heit mod, 142 G
Hy! Trot, trot, 258 M
Hyde Park, 281 C
Hymen, haste, thy torch prepare, 165 I
Hymn, 65 D
Hymn of praise, 229 H
Hymn of St. Adalbert, 4 P
Hymn to the sun, 304 G
Hymn to the Waters, 176 S
Hymne, 281 D
Hymne à la nuit, 138 C
Hytten, 142 G

I

I am a courtier grave and serious, 363 B
I am a maiden cold and stately, 370 F
I am a poor innocent clown, 5 J
I am he that comforteth, 226 C
I am never merry when I hear sweet music, 389 M
I am old now, 195 Q
I am seekin' for a city, 67 R
I am so proud, 365 P
I am the captain of the Pinafore, 363 G
I am the good shepherd, 104 K
I am the monarch of the sea, 363 K
I am the very pattern of a modern Major-General, 368 O
I am thy harp, 440 R
I am waiting here for you, 275 H
I arise from dreams of thee, 91 R
I attempt from love's sickness, 289 H
I believe in public school education, 383 I
I built upon a rock, 370 M
I cannot sing the old songs, 81 J

I cannot tell what this love may be, 367 A
I chant my lay, 102 I
I come from Alabama wid my banjo on my knee, 116 F
I don't feel no-ways tired, 67 R
I dream of Jeanie, 115 J
I dream too much, 191 G
I dreamt I dwelt in marble halls, 30 A
I envy not a monarch's fate, 290 O
I envy not the splendour fine, 38 B
I fain would be free, 290 P
I fancied once, 347 N
I fancy I heard a murm'ring, 183 J
I fear no foe, 276 S
I follow, lo, the footing, 241 F
I gave her cakes, 290 R
I gaze on the sun, it mounts in the sky, 66 Q
I give thee all, 193 F
I got a robe, 67 Q
I got plenty o' nuttin', 124 B
I hark to the voice of my dream, 48 L
I have a song to sing, O, 273 R
I have achieved the highest, 256 J
I have been there before thee, 270 L
I have desired to go where springs not fail, 30 N
I have golden hair, 101 O
I have heard the may is singing, 260 M
I have just converted Lillian Russell, 383 O
I Have twelve Oxen, 185 I
I hear an army, 30 M
I hear you calling me, 217 N
I heard a piper piping, 32 G
I heard you singing, 82 F
I know a lovely garden, 166 Q
I know a youth who loves a little maid, 371 B
I know my love, 182 C
I know not how lovely your face is, 378 H
I know that my redeemer liveth, 164 A
I know where I'm goin', 182 D
I, like a ship in storms was toss'd, 271 L
I love and I must, 291 A
I love him, I love him, with fervor unceasing, 373 K
I love life, 216 M
I love my love, 177 A
I love thee, 142 A
I love you truly, 50 N
I mean to rule the earth, 366 E
I must go down to the seas again, 185 L
I never sailed the Amazon, 123 K
I often think of home, Dee-oo-lee-ay, 198 C
I once loved a boy, 182 E
I once was a very abandoned person, 371 S
I Osten stiger Solen op., 426 P
I pass all my hours, 184 Q
I plays de banjo better now, 177 I
I praise Thee, O Lord my God, 227 R

I recall the mad delight, 173 F
I remember, 128 I
I rove, I look around, 194 N
I saw a ship a-sailing, 144 Q
I saw that you were grown so high, 291 C
I see she flies me, 291 D
I shall find for you shells and stars, 231 P
I shall go across the snow, 283 D
I shot an arrow into the air, 276 P
I shut the children's peepers, 183 D
I sing of a maiden that matchless is, 176 P
I sleep; my heart at break of day, 305 J
I stand in the dark, 313 E
I stole the Prince and brought him here, 362 G
I suffer, 86 C
I think that I shall never see, 296 R
I thought that love had been a boy, 69 L
I want my hills!, 199 L
I want to be ready, 68 A
I will go with my father a-plowing, 293 N
I will lift mine eyes up to the mountains, 102 F
I will make you brooches, 389 P
I will sing Jehovah's praises, 102 B
I will sing new songs of gladness, 102 B
I will sing of Thy great mercies, 228 B
I will walk with my love, 182 E
I wish, 378 I
Ich armer Mensch, ich Sündenknecht, 11 S
Ich armer Tamboursg'sell, 215 B
Ich atmet' einen linden Duft, 214 F
Ich auf der Erd, 324 B
Ich baue ganz auf deine Stärke, 246 C
Ich bin der Contrabandiste, 330 I
Ich bin der Schwanda, 425 Q
Ich bin der Welt abhanden gekommen, 214 G
Ich bin der wohlbekannte Sänger, 434 Q
Ich bin ein guter Hirt, 14 O
Ich bin ein vielgereister Mann, 230 R
Ich bin eine Harfe, 438 J
Ich bin schön wie der Lenz, 258 A
Ich bin vergnügt mit meinem Glücke, 14 M
Ich bin wie andre Mädchen nicht, 429 L
Ich bin's, 27 B
Ich blick' in mein Herz, 335 M
Ich blicke hinab in die Gasse, 58 A
Ich denke dein, 35 E, 320 N, 336 R, 428 N
Ich danke dem Herrn, 340 F
Ich elender Mensch, wer wird mich erlösen, 11 J
Ich esse mit Freuden, 14 N

Ich esse nun mein Brot nicht trocken mehr, 432 E
Ich fahr dahin wenn es muss sein, 62 P
Ich folge dir gleichfalls, 26 A
Ich frage keine Blume, 317 I
Ich freue mich auf meinen Tod, 14 L
Ich freue mich in dir, 17 F
Ich fürchte nicht, ich fürchte nicht des Grabes Finsternissen, 12 O
Ich fürchte zwar des Grabes Finsternissen, 12 P
Ich gebe Gastereien, 421 E
Ich geh' jetzt auf die Weide, 241 Q
Ich gehe, doch rathe ich dir, 245 O
Ich ging bei Nacht einst über Land, 436 V
Ich ging den Weg entlang, 357 O
Ich ging im Walde, 359 D
Ich ging unter Erlen, 29 H
Ich ging zu ihm, 197 I
Ich grolle nicht, 335 A
Ich hab ein glühend Messer, 215 Q
Ich hab' ein kleines Lied erdacht, 67 D
Ich hab eine Brieftaub, 318 S
Ich hab' es getragen sieben Jahr, 209 S
Ich hab' geschlagen meinen Geier tot, 208 S
Ich hab' im Traum geweinet, 335 G
Ich hab' in Gottes Herz und Sinn, 15 C
Ich hab' in Penna einen Liebsten wohnen, 432 F
Ich habe Daphnis gern, 377 M
Ich habe genug, 14 J
Ich habe mein Kindlein, 300 N
Ich habe wohl, 356 E
Ich halte dich in meinem Arm, 316 L
Ich halte treulich still, 28 O
Ich harrete des Herrn, 229 J
Ich hatte einst ein schönes Vaterland, 201 F
Ich hatte viel Bekümmerniss, 9 N
Ich heb mein Augen, 340 K
Ich hör die Bächlein rauschen, 333 O
Ich hör' meinen Schatz, 56 A, 188 A
Ich hört' ein Bächlein, 317 E
Ich kann wohl manchmal singen, 333 P
Ich kann's nicht fassen, nicht glauben, 334 F
Ich kenn ihn schon recht wohl, 355 O
Ich komme schon durch manches Land, 37 D
Ich komme vom Gebirge her, 320 J
Ich lade gern mir Gäste ein, 351 L
Ich liebe dich, 36 E, 142 A, 208 B, 358 C
Ich lieg' an meines Lagers End', 112 N
Ich liege und schlafe, 340 G
Ich liess mir sagen, 432 G

Ich möchte jubeln in alle winde, 143 A
Ich möchte ziehn in die Welt, 318 B
Ich nehme mein Leiden, 13 N
Ich nehme nicht, 327 F
Ich ruhe still im hohen grünen Gras, 59 S
Ich säe meine Zähren, 17 S
Ich sah das Kind, 412 M
Ich sah dem Wald sich färben, 282 O
Ich sah die Städte, 413 A
Ich sass zu deinen Füssen, 59 Q
Ich schau über Forth, 331 L
Ich scheue mich danach zu fragen, 377 G
Ich schnitt' es gern, 317 K
Ich schwebe wie auf Engels-schwingen, 358 O
Ich sehe dich in tausend Bildern, 218 D
Ich sehe schon im Geist, 11 E
Ich sende einen Gruss, 331 N
Ich sitz am Strande, 59 K
Ich stand gelehnet an den Mast, 231 H
Ich stand in dunkeln Träumen, 318 N
Ich stand in einer lauen Nacht, 61 I
Ich stehe in Waldesschatten, 275 N
Ich stehe mit einem Fuss im Grabe, 18 K
Ich such im Schnee, 319 D
Ich trage meine Minne vor Wonne stumm, 357 N
Ich trage, wo ich gehe, 209 R
Ich traue seiner Gnaden, 15 H
Ich träumte von bunten Blumen, 319 K
Ich trete ins Zimmer, 203 O
Ich unglückselger Atlas, 318 M
Ich wandelte unter den Bäumen, 330 L
Ich wand're über Berg und Thal, 324 G
Ich wandte mich, 61 R
Ich war bei Chloen ganz allein, 37 B
Ich war in meinen jungen Jahren, 210 O
Ich weiss dass mein Erlöser lebt, 8 K, 18 M
Ich weiss Euch einen lieben Schatz, 344 L
Ich weiss nicht was soll es bedeuten, 208 D, 343 I
Ich weiss nicht wie du bist, 354 I
Ich werde nicht sterben, 340 M
Ich werde sie nicht wiederehen, 197 G
Ich will bei meinem Jesu wachen, 27 F
Ich will den Kreuzstab gerne tragen, 12 A, 12 B
Ich will dich all mein Leben lang, 16 P
Ich will dir mein Herze schenken, 27 D
Ich will euch trösten, 54 C
Ich will leiden, 14 R
Ich will meine Seele tauchen, 334 R

Ich will nur dir zu Ehren leben, 25 G
Ich will von Atreus' Söhnen, 322 P
Ich wob dies Gewand, 65 N
Ich wollt' ich wär' ein Fisch, 328 F
Ich wollt' meine Lieb' ergösse sich, 229 S
Ich wünsche mir bei Gott, 10 O
Ich wünschte mir den Tod, 12 D
Ich würd' auf meinem Pfad, K.390, 246 G
Ici-bas! tous les lilas meurent, 108 A
I'd laugh my rank to scorn, 363 N
Ida was a twelve-month old, 369 N
Ideale, 385 G
Idol mio, mio dolce amore, 243 B
Idol mio, se ritroso, 244 Q
Idomeneo, K.366, 244 H
If any wench, 271 F
If God be for us, 164 E
If guiltless blood be your intent, 165 S
If he's made the best use of his time, 374 I
If I believe that I am right, 383 K
If I forget thee, 419 E
If I had a beau, 45 K
If I knew how to wipe out my fault, 345 R
If I should die, 185 M
If I were but like you, 287 K
If I were hang'd on the highest hill, 386 L
If in the great bazaars, 440 N
If in this world a kindly fortune, 376 Q
If love the virgin's heart invade, 271 G
If music be the food of love, 290 Q
If Saphir I chose to marry, 367 S
If she forsake me, 307 B
If somebody there chanced to be, 370 S
If that is so, sing derry down derry, 366 R
If the heart of a man, 272 B
If there were dreams to sell, 185 H
If to men, not to God, 231 N
If true her tale, thy knell is rung, 365 S
If we're weak enough to tarry, 365 E
If with all your hearts, 226 O
If you but knew, 379 B
If you can bring me calm after pain, 379 G
If you give me your attention, 369 Q
If you never have danced the Danza, 75 Q
If you want to know who we are, 365 F
If you wish in the world to advance, 371 D
If you're anxious for to shine, 367 E
Ignitum eloquium, 84 I
Igor, pour moi n'est qu'un guerrier, 51 J
Ihm hab' ich mich ergeben, 15 J
Ihr aber seid nicht fleischlich, sondern geistlich, 24 M
Ihr Bild, 318 N

Ihr Blümlein alle, 318 C
Ihr Gedanken, 105 D
Ihr Grab, 327 N
Ihr habt nun Traurigkeit, 54 B
Ihr jungen Leute, 432 H
Ihr kindeschen Buhlen, 412 L
Ihr Kleinglaübigen, 14 H
Ihr kommet, Winde, 56 C
Ihr lieben Mauern hold un traut, 324 P
Ihr Mädchen, flieht Damöten, 247 J
Ihr Menschen rühmet Gottes Liebe, 18 O
Ihr Mund ist stets derselbe, 359 L
Ihr seid die Allerschönste, 432 J
Ihr Sternlein, still in der Höhe, 328 G
Ihr wandelt droben im Licht, 54 K
Ihr wunderschönen Augenblicke, 58 J
Ihre Liebe schlägt mir entgegen, 355 D
Ihre Stimme, 338 F
Il a neigé des fleurs, 181 N
Il a quitté ce monde, 40 L
Il balen del suo sorriso, 403 F
Il bel giovanetto, 49 O
Il est des Musulmans, 294 F
Il est doux de se coucher, 299 F
Il est doux, il est bon, 222 I
Il est là, 96 F
Il est mort ayant bien souffert, 77 M
Il était un p'tit homme, 184 R
Il était un Roi de Thulé, 135 A
Il était une fois, 108 K
Il était une fois à la cour d'Eisenach!, 264 K
Il faut de mon destin, 130 E
Il faut nous séparer, 225 E
Il faut partir, 96 I
Il faut passer tôt ou tard, 211 P
Il faut que de tous mes esprits, 180 B, 375 J
Il faut que l'amour s'envole, 296 H
Il faut s'aimer toujours, 280 C
Il glisse sur le bassin, 298 B
Il m'a dit: "Cette nuit, j'ai rêvé," 88 E
Il M'aime, 135 F
Il mio bel foco, 217 C
Il mio Lionel perira, 114 A
Il ne revient pas, 135 G
Il partit au printemps, 222 G
Il pleure dans mon coeur, 87 O, 109 I
Il pleut des pétales de fleurs, 303 I
Il regardait mon bouquet, 237 S
Il rival salvar tu dei, 39 F
Il s'en est allé par la route, 276 C
Il s'en va loin de la terre, 42 H
Il tuo fu il mio pensiere, 307 E
Il va sûrement, 297 R
Il va venir, 149 D
Il vole, 280 Q
Il y avait une pomme, 236 B
Ile heureuse, L', 75 L
I'll follow my secret heart, 84 P
I'll hold my tongue, 256 H
I'll put the case, 237 C
I'll sail upon the Dog-star, 290 S
I'll see you again, 84 N

I'll sing thee songs of Araby, 81 S
I'll take you home again, Kathleen, 426 K
Ils étaient trois petits chats blancs, 275 S
Ils ne savent plus où se poser, 78 H
Ils se disent, ma colombe que tu rêves, 147 J
Ils vont, les petits canards, 75 M
Im Abendrot, 327 O
Im Arm der Liebe, 42 A, 218 G
I'm bubbled, 272 N
I'm called little Buttercup, 363 E
I'm coming, I'm coming, 116 H
Im Dorfe, 319 Q
Im Entschlafen, 438 K
I'm falling in love with someone, For, 173 J
Im Felde schleich' ich still, 320 I
Im Feuerstrom der Reben, 351 P
Im finstern geh ich suchen, 57 Q
Im Frühling, 327 P, 432 K
Im Frühlingsgarten, 329 F
I'm going out to clean the pasture spring, 260 F
Im Grünen, 228 I
Im grünen Tale dort, 301 D
Im Haine, 323 A
Im heimlichen Dämmer, 203 M
Im Herbst, 120 A
Im Kahn' 143 Q
Im kalten, rauhen Norden, 323 O
Im Kerker gefangen, 311 N
Im Lenz pflückt uns der Meister!, 412 K
Im Mohrenland, 246 D
Im Morgengrauen schritt ich fort, 316 K
I'm not crying for him, 231 O
Im Rheim, im heiligen Strome, 120 C, 334 S
Im Rhein, im schönen Strome, 208 C
Im Sommer wie war da so grün, 142 H
Im Spätboot, 359 F
I'm telling a terrible story, 368 Q
Im tiefen Keller, 113 D
I'm trampin', trampin', 186 H
Im Treibhaus, 418 F
Im trüben Licht verschwinden, 321 R
I'm up with early dawning, 183 H
Im Volkston, 174 P
Im Wald, 326 J
Im Walde, 140 Q, 324 G, 333 R, 336 I
Im walde wo Birken, 140 Q
Im wasser wogt die Lilie, 431 K
I'm wearing awa', 114 M
Im Wein ist Wahrheit, 210 O
Im Weinberg auf der Höhe, 432 R
Im Westen, 331 L
Im Winde, im Sturme, 321 Q
Im Winterboden schläft ein Blumenkeim, 429 C
Im wunderschönen Monat Mai, 120 F, 334 N
Im Zimmer, 41 S
Immensité, les cieux, L', 133 M
Immer ist Undank Loge's Lohn!, 413 E
Immer leiser wird mein Schlummer, 61 G
Immer nur lächeln, 203 O

Immer wieder, 438 L
Immortal hour, The, 52 G
Impatience, L', 296 C
Impious mortal, cease to brave us, 159 F
Impresario, The, K.486, 247 L
Improperium expectavit, 269 H
In a contemplative fashion, 362 R
In a doleful train two and two, 367 B
In a Myrtle Shade, 144 O
In a Persian garden, 204 R
In allen meiner Thaten, 15 H
In aller Früh, 433 D
In alto mare, 302 F
In Babylon Belshazzar the King, 419 F
In braccio alle dovizie, 404 E
In Cloris, all soft charms agree, 291 B
In days of old, when knights were bold, 2 M
In deine Hände, 16 H
In deine Hände', o Herr, 171 F
In dem Dornbusch blüht ein Röslein, 120 G
In dem Häuschen sitzen Freunde, 215 J
In dem Mondenschein im Walde, 228 L
In dem schatten meiner Locken, 55 L, 432 L
In dem Talen der Provence, 339 Q
In dem Walde süsse Töne, 228 J
In dem weiten, breiten, luft'gen Leinenkleide, 102 N
In den Garten wollen wir gehen, 57 I
In der Ferne, 318 K
In der Fremde, 55 K, 333 H, 333 O
In der Frühe, 432 M
In der Gasse, 58 A
In der Kindheit frühen Tagen, 418 D
In der Seele ein Wachsen und Keimen, 439 H
In des Lebens Frühlingstagen, 33 F
In des Seees Wogenspiele, 326 F
In des Todes Feierstunde, 325 B
In die tiefsten Felsen, 319 I
In diesem Wetter, 214 L
In diesen heil'gen Hallen, 253 S
In diesen Wintertagen, 358 Q
In dulci jubilo, 21 M, 271 B
In ein freundliches Städtchen, 429 D
In einem Bächlein helle, 322 H
In einer Zeit die jetzt vergangen ist, 425 L
In einsamen Stunden, 336 K
In enterprise of martial kind, 362 F
In fernem Land, 410 F
In gentle murmurs will I mourn, 160 J
In gloria Dei Patris, 33 R
In going to my naked bed, 103 S
In golden Abendschein getauchet, 60 C
In Grün will ich mich kleiden, 318 A
In grüner Landschaft Sommerflor, 429 A

In Han's old mill his three black cats, 125 J
In happy moments day by day, 418 O
In haven, 104 O
In heav'n the stars now are shining, 303 F
In Jesu Demuth kann ich Trost, 18 E
In Leid zu dem Wipfel lauscht, 416 A
In London one day, 167 R
In love she fell, 213 A
In mal punto son qui giunto, 248 D
In me you see poor Jonathan, 237 G
In meinen Adern, 34 P
In meiner Brust, da sitzt ein Weh, 335 R
In meines Herzens Grunde, 26 K
In mezo al mar, 312 F
In mezzo al campo, 219 H
In my attic, 259 K
In my blood the fire of desire burns, 128 H
In my gondola, love, let us glide, 121 G
In native worth, 170 A
In old Madrid, 387 C
In old New York, 173 R
In our deep vaulted cell, 288K
In our Russia great, 283 C
In our street it happened, 86 I
In paradisum, 109 F
In poetischer Epistel, 429 E
In prison, 341 S
In pure stille, 220 K
In quegli anni, 249 A
In quelle trine morbide, 285 L
In questa Reggia, 287 E
In questa tomba oscura, 36 F
In questo prato adorno, 240 A
In questo suolo, 95 O
In sailing o'er life's ocean wide, 371 F
In Scarlet town, where I was born, 386 P
In schwäbischer Mundart, 228 G
In seinem schimmernden Gewand, 327 K
In seiner Blüthe, 413 B
In seventy-six the sky was red, 306 B
In shadow black as night. 259 O
In shame and disgrace, 257 I
In si barbara, 309 K
In spring, 30 I, 78 S, 144 S
In Spring for sheer delight, 30 I, 144 S
In stiller Nacht, 62 O
In summertime on Bredon, 68 O 389 H
In testa la cappellina!, 284 M
In that case unprecedented, 368 A
In the battle fame pursuing, 159 G
In the beautiful isle of our dreams, 173 Q
In the Boat, 143 Q
In the brush the flames are leaping, 379 C
In the corner, 258 I
In the days of my youth, 272 R
In the forest, 196 I

In the gloaming, 167 B
In the gypsy's life, 29 S
In the Luxembourg Gardens, 216 Q
In the scented bud of the morning, 30 L
In the shadowy orchard, 48 K
In the silent night, 294 P
In the vale, oh! in the valley, 257 N
In thine arms enfold me, 173 S
In this hour of the night, 379 H
In tiefer Ruh, 318 G
In uomini, in soldati, 252 D
In vain to me the cowslips blow, 213 C
In valleys of springs of rivers, 389 I
In Waldeseinsamkeit, 59 Q
In Winter, 176 C
Inaffia l'ugola, 398 L
Inbrunst im Herzen, 417 K
Incantation, 178 C
Incassum, Lesbia, 292 G
Incenerite spoglie, 238 N
Incertitude, O!, 279 R
Incessament, 189 H
Incipit Oratio Jeremiae Prophetae, 269 O
Incoronazione di Poppea, L', 239 K
Incrédule, L', 147 N
Indes galantes, Les, 296 G
Indian Love Call, 121 J
Indian Love Lyrics, 440 F
Indian love song, 91 R, 207 H
Indian Queen, The, 289 H
Indifferent, L', 298 S
Infelice core, 401 C
Infelice! e tu credevi, 394 M
Infelice! Già del mio squardo, 230 S
Infidélité, 147 O
Inflammatus et accensus, 274 Q, 310 D
Ingannata una sol volta, 151 C
Ingemisco tamquam reus, 404 S
Ingénus, Les, 88 R
Ingrid's Song, 193 D
Ingrid's Vise, 193 D
Inn, The, 386 N
Innegiamo, il Signor non è morto, 219 L
Inno al sole, 220 I
Innsbruch, ich muss dich lassen, 185 Q
Ins Freie, 337 J
Ins Grüne, ins Grüne, 325 C
In's Joch beug' ich den Nakken demutvoll, 356 H
Insana parola, L', 391 E
Inspirez-moi, race divine, 136 S
Inter natos mulienem, 45 F
Intermezzo, 333 J
Into the night, 103 Q
Into the woods my Master went, 75 P
Intorno all' idol mio, 75 I
Introduxit me rex in cellam, 268 J
Intruse, L', 111 S
Inutiles regrets, 43 C
Invano!, 385 H
Invictus, 182 J
Invitation, 348 A
Invitation au voyage, L' 100 I
Invito alla danza, 302 E

Invocation, 42 S, 48 M, 310 J
Invocation à la Nature, 42 S
Invocation à Vénus, 264 F
Invocation aux parques, 280 D
Invocazione, 309 D
Io conosco un giardino, 276 F
Io di Roma il Giove sono, 151 D
Io la vidi e al suo sorriso, 393 J
Io morró, 393 R
Io non chiedo eterni Dei, 244 B
Io non ho amato ancor, 126 F
Io non ho che una povera
    stanzetta, 205 J
Io non son, 284 F
Io pingo, 220 L
Io seguo il mio destino, 284 Q
Io sento, che ancora, 252 Q
Io son' l'umile ancella, 80 B
Io son ricco e tu sei bella, 95 C
Io son sua per l'amor, 80 F
Io sono docile, 307 O
Io sono tanto stanca, 301 N
Io sperai trovar riposo, 154 F
Io tacerò, 124 K
Io ti seguii com' iride di pace,
    385 G
Iolanthe, 364 G, 377 E
Iphegénie en Tauride, 130 J
Iphigénie in Aulis, 129 O
Irdische Leben, Das, 214 O
Ireja vale un real, Una, 263 L
Iris, 2 O, 220 I
Iris, cette nuit en dormant, 2 O
Irish folk song, An, 114 N
Irish howl, 272 Q
Irish love song, 200 S
Irish songs, 36 G
Irish trot, 272 N
Irmeline Rose; 91 S, 262 B
Irons-nous garder, 72 J
Irrlicht, 319 I
Irto, El, 263 L
Is life a boon?, 373 Q
Is my team ploughing, 68 Q, 389 F
Is not His word, 226 R
Is then his fate decree'd, Sir!,
    272 J
Isabeau, 220 O
Island, The, 295 A
Islay reaper's song, 190 M
Isle of our dreams, 173 Q
Israel in Egypt, 159 R
Ist auch schmuck nicht mein
    Rösslein, 435 G
Ist auf deinem Psalter, 54 J
Ist der Himmel darum im Lenz
    so blau, 275 K
Ist ein Himmelslicht, 376 I
Ist ein Traum, 355 S
Ist mir's doch, 321 A
Ist nicht der Himmel so blau,
    56 H
Istar, Istar Deesse des batailles,
    178 C
Istenem, istenem, 31 O
It ain't necessarily so, 124 E
It all began on a Sunday, 232 J
It is a whisper, 390 A
It is enough, 227 E
It is not that I love you less, 48 R
It is not the wind blowing from
    the height, 305 L
It is sung to the moon. 373 S
It lies not on the sunlit hill, 32 I
It rises, 172 M

It sometimes comes into my head,
    64 F
It take a long pull to get there,
    123 S, 124 A
It was a comely young lady fair,
    390 E
It was a lovely summer eve, 142 R
It was a lover and his lass
    241 G, 293 P, 420 M
It was in days of early spring,
    378 G
It was on the fift' of August,
    139 I
It was the charming month of
    May, 123 F
It was the eve of Christmas, 2 L
Italian serenade, 355 I
Italian Street Song, 173 K
Italiana in Algeri, L', 308 P
Ite sul colle, 38 I
It's a-me, it's a-me, 145 L
It's pleasant in Holy Mary, 185 E
Ivan Sussanin, 127 M
Ivanhoe, 374 Q
I've been roaming, 181 F
I've just arrived, 195 P
I've often felt the passion, 237 B
I've wisdom from the East, 374 A

J

Ja da kann man sich doch nicht
    nur hinlegen, 425 K
Ja das alles auf Ehr, 353 E
Ja, das Schreiben und das Leben,
    353 F
Ja, du weisst es, 356 A
Ja, ich bins, den Ihr betrogen,
    352 H
Ja, ihr seid es, 410 P
Ja, ja, ich kann die Feinde
    schlagen, 12 E
Já nelekám se, smrti chladná,
    112 F
Ja, noch einmal könnt den
    Winter, 143 E
Ja nun hons pris, 303 L
Ja, o Herr! mein Heil, mein
    Leben, 422 L
Ja, tausendmal, 11 D
Jadis elles chantaient, 266 L
Jadis régnait en Normandie,
    235 A
Jaegersang, 167 F
Jagdlied, 230 N
Jäger, Der, 60 M, 432 N
Jäger Abschied, Der, 229 G
Jäger, ruhe von der Jagd!, 322 O
Jäger und sein Liebchen, Der,
    56 H
Jägerlied, 432 O
Jägers Abendlied, 320 I
Jahreszeiten, Die, 170 F
J'ai compris ta détresse, 314 R
J'ai cru rêver, 51 N
J'ai cueilli ce brin de bruyère,
    177 Q
J'ai des yeux, 264 M
J'ai gardé mon âme ingenue,
    303 A
J'ai le bonheur dans l'âme,
    265 B
J'ai longtemps habité, 100 R
J'ai perdu la beauté, 212 I
J'ai pleuré en rêve, 181 O

J'ai presque peur, en vérité, 110 C
J'ai renoncé à ce monde vain,
    3 N
J'ai revu le cimetière, 147 D
J'ai traversé les ponts de C,
    280 B
J'ai vu disparaître l'espoir, 78 M
J'ai vu passer l'hirondelle, 1 H
J'aimais la vieille maison, grise,
    232 M
J'aime le son du cor, 113 F
Jak jsi krásná, 112 I
Jako blahy ohlas doby zaslé, 112 C
J'allais dans la campagne,
    279 D
J'allais par des chemins, 110 B
Jamais dans ces beaux lieux, 129 M
Jamais ne cesserai de magnifier le
    Seigneur, 179 S
Jardin d'Amour, 408 F
Jardin Mouillé, Le, 310 H
Jardin nocturne, 110 P
Jardinier impatient, Le, 236 D
Jaro lásky, 348 B
Jasminenstrauch, 331 Q
J'au vu les Séraphims en songe,
    111 J
Jauchzet, frohlocket!, 24 S
Jauchzet, Gott in allen Landen,
    11 L
J'aurais sur ma poitrine, 225 G
J'ay bien cause de lamenter, 189 I
J'ay cherché la sçience, 201 O
Jazz dans la nuit, 310 P
Je connais, ma mère, 305 B
Je connais un berger discret,
    423 M
Je connais un pauvre enfant,
    381 A
Je crains de lui parler la nuit,
    141 I
Je crie à toi dans le bataille,
    178 E
Je crois en Dieu, 73 F
Je crois entendre encore, 47 K
Je descendis dans mon jardin,
    184 P
Je dirai la Rose, 109 J
Je dis que rien ne m'épouvante,
    47 E
Je hais l'ennui, 51 B
Je jure tant que je vivrai,
    280 D
Jé loe amours, 45 G
Je marche sur tous les chemins,
    223 P
Je me complains de mon amy,
    189 K
Je me metz en vostre mercy, 147 P
Je me suis embarqué, 110 S
Je n'ai envie que de t'aimer,
    282 H
Je n'ai jamais chéri la vie, 129 C
Je n'ai pas d'amie, 72 M
Je n'ai pas de regrets, 314 S
Je n'ai plus que les os, 281 S
Je ne crois pas que le Saveur soit
    né, 427 F
Je ne peux plus rien dire, 280 P
Je ne requier de ma dame, 140 F
Je ne t'envoie ni vase, 181 K
Je ne veux pas autre chose, 427 D
Je n'entends que le bruit, 148 P
Je porte l'épouvante, 212 J
Je puis trop bien, 213 O

Je réchauffe les bons, 299 L
Je sais attacher des rubans, 98 M
Je serai ta douceur profonde, 405 Q
Je suis alsacienne, 265 H
Je suis amour, 145 L
Je suis dans ma cage, 140 O
Je suis encore tout étourdie, 223 D
Je suis fou de la fille, 181 M
Je suis, hélas, je suis la pauvre femme, 234 S
Je suis jaloux, 266 O
Je suis l'oiseau, 222 H
Je suis prise d'une tristesse, 117 D
Je suis Titania, 381 G
Je suis triste je m'inquiète, 82 Q
Je t'aimerai Seigneur, 179 D
Je te veux, 314 R
Je t'implore et je tremble, 130 P
Je t'implore ô mon frère!, 380 I
Je tremble en voyant ton visage, 89 G
Je vais monter sur la montagne là, 90 E
Je vais revoir ma charmante maitresse, 310 F
Je veux que le matin, 108 J
Je veux vivre dans le rêve, 137 C
Je viens célébrer la victoire, 312 N
Je vois dans le grande île, 233 H
Je voudrais qu' à ma fenêtre, 8 B
Je vous salue, Marie, 73 E
Jean Martin prit sa besace, 280 I
Jeanie with the light brown hair, 115 J
Jeanne d'Arc, 376 K
Jeanneton où irons-nous garder, 298 J
J'écoute la voix de mon rêve, 48 L
J'écris à mon père, 223 J
Jeden Morgen, in der Frühe, 336 S
Jeder meint, das holde Kind, 171 K
Jeder meint, der Gegenstand, 171 L
Jeg synge skal en Vise, 167 G
Jehovah, to my words give ear, 164 I
Jemand, 331 A
Jen jediná, 345 I
Jenufa, 186 N
Jephtha, 160 F
Jerusalem, 270 M
Jerusalem, Jerusalem, lift up your gates and sing, 2 H
Jerusalem, thou that killest the prophets, 227 H
Jesu, bleibet meine Freude, 18 A
Jesu, der du meine Seele, 13 R
Jesu ist ein Schild der Seinen, 11 C
Jesu, joy of man's desiring, 18 A
Jesu, lass dich finden, 18 I
Jesu, lass durch Wohl und Weh, 19 C
Jesu, meine Freude, 24 I
Jesu nostra Redemptio, 267 M
Jesu, nun sei gepreiset, 11 A
Jesus in Gethsemane, 8 F
Jesus nahm zu sich die Zwölfe, 9 R
Jesus neigt sein Haupt und stirbt, 118 N
Jesus rufet, 171 D

Jesus schläft, was soll ich hoffen, 14 F
Jesus sweet, now I will sing, 176 N
Jesus, unser Trost und Leben, 28 P
Jet d'eau, Le, 88 I
J'étais loin sur la mer, 360 M
J'étais triste et pensif, 108 E
Jetzt giesst sich aus ein sanft'rer Glantz, 422 K
Jetzt ist die Geige mein, 198 K
Jetzt ist wohl ihr Fenster offen, 421 P
Jetzt kommt der Frühling, 228 G
Jetzt wird mein Eland, 175 Q
Jeu de Robin et Marion, Le, 2 C
Jeune fillette, 85 Q
Jeune fillette, profitez du temps, 423 N
Jeune homme de vingt ans, 280 A
Jeunes coeurs, 129 N
Jewel Song, 135 B
Jewels of the Madonna, The, 439 L
J'ignore son nom, 1 N
Jilguerito con pico de oro, El, 262 I
Jillian of Berry, 420 I
Jitro krásné, 347 R
Již plane slunce, 346 G
Joachim at Babylon, 40 E
Joachim of Babylon, 40 E
Joachim uti Babylon, 40 E
Jocelyn, 132 G
Johannes das Lämmlein auslasset, 216 C
Johannis freudenvolles springen, 16 S
Johannistag!, 410 R
Jo-ho-hoe!, 408 M
Jolie Fille de Perth, La, 47 H
Jongleur de Notre Dame, Le, 222 R
Jonny speilt auf, 198 J
Josef, lieber Josef mein, 60 E
Joseph, 160 M, 226 L
Joseph, lieber Joseph mein, 49 C
Joseph was an old man, 30 S
Joshua, 160 O
Josua Navîne, 258 S
Jota, 63 R, 106 L
Jota tortosina, 263 E
Jota volenciana, 263 F
Jour de printemps, Un, 48 B
Jour est levé, Le, 233 P
Jour et nuit, 264 S
Jour je m'en allai, Un, 426 I
Jour se lève, Le, 136 E
Jour s'endort, La, 99 M
Jour, sous le soleil béni, Le, 232 O
Jours de mon enfance, 174 K
Joy, shipmate, joy!, 389 S
Jsem voják, 346 S
Jsi krásná, jako letní noc, 112 D
Jubilate Deo, 2 S, 121 S, 269 P
Jubilate Domino, 69 B
Juchhe, 55 M
Juch-he! das Leben ist doch eine Freude, 265 I•
Judas Maccabeus, 161 B
Judea, 44 L
Judex, 134 G
Judith, 178 A

Jugement de Midas, 141 B
Jugement de Paris, Le, 264 E
Juive, La, 148 S
Julius Caesar, 153 G
Jung Volkers Lied, 339 I
Junge Mädchen pflukken Blumen, 215 K
Junge Nonne, die, 322 L
Junger Dichter denkt an die Geliebt, Ein, 218 B
Jungfrau, dein schöne G'stalt, 168 C
Jungfrau Maria, 114 G
Jüngling am Bache, Der, 327 Q
Jüngling an der Quelle, Der, 327 R
Jüngling auf dem Hügel, Der, 327 S
Jüngling liebt ein Mädchen, Ein, 335 E
Jüngling und der Tod, Der, 328 A
Jupiter, lance ta foudre, 130 V
Jupon serré sur le hanches, Un, 106 H
Just a song at twilight, 237 N
Just as the tide was flowing, 390 V
Just a-wearyin for you, 50 O
Just before the battle, mother, 306 L
Justitia tua, 84 J
Justorum animae, 70 D, 202 G
Jylland mellem tvende Have, 172 N

K

Kádár István, 195 H
Kádár Kata, 195 E
Kaddisch, 297 Q
Kam prchnout, 345 J
Kampfmüd und sonnverbrannt,, 429 M
Kann auch ein Mensch des andern, 434 E
Kann ich nur Jesum mir zum Freunde machen, 16 D
Kann mich auch an ein Mädel erinnern, 355 K
Kanonen-Song, 425 I
Kartenlegerin, Die, 332 B
Karwoche, 432 P
Kashmiri Song, 440 H
Kathleen Mavourneen, 85 I
Katona vagyok én, 195 I
Katy Bell, 115 K
Katze lässt das Mausen nicht, Die, 20 R
Kaunis Kirkas nyt on Aamu, 187 M
Kdy slysim jen tvého, 346 Q
Kdy zavitá máj, 347 F
Kein andres, 355 C
Kein Hälmlein wächst auf Erden, 29 K
Kein Haus, keine Heimat, 60 J
Kein Meister fällt vom Himmel, 431 I
Kein Schlaf noch Kült das Auge mir, 432 M
Kein Wort von dir, 378 D
Keng-ça-fou, Mah jong, 299 K
Kennst du das Land, 37 A, 208 F, 337 H, 433 N

Kennst du nur den alten Heeren, 139 E
Kentish Sir Byng stood for his king, 349 L
Kermesse, 134 K
Kerry dance, The, 237 L
Khovantchina, 257 H
Killarney, 30 G
Killingdans, 144 H
Kind Captain, I've important information, 364 A
Kind fortune smiles, 289 S
Kind, kind and gentle is she, 303 N
Kind sir, you cannot have the heart, 362 J
Kinder! Kinder! seht, nach sturm, 242 G
Kinderchen, sagt euch die Wahrheit, 425 S
Kinderspiel, Das, 253 A
Kinderstimmen, 112 M
Kindertotenlieder, 214 H
Kinderwacht, 337 E
Kindlein schlief ein, 91 P
King Arthur, 289 L
King Charles! and who'll do him right now!, 349 L
King of Thule, The, 135 A
King Olaf, 104 B
King Richard II, 288 C
King Saul, 258 C
Kingdom, The, 105 B
King's henchman, The, 376 E
Kishmul's Galley, 190 N
Kiss, The, 5 S, 345 N
Kiss in the dark, 173 F
Kiss me again, 173 H
Kit kéne elvenni, 195 J
Kitrákotty mese, 195 D
Klage I, 58 N
Klage II, 58 O
Klänge der Heimat, 351 N
Klare Bolger ruled, De, 426 M
Kleine Blumen, Kleine Blätter, 37 E
Kleine Fritz an seine jungen Freunde, Der, 423 A
Kleine Gäste, kleines Haus, 433 G
Kleine Spinnerin, Die, 251 M
Kleinzschocher müsse so zart, 21 F
Kling, Klang, 341 J
Kling! Meine Seele gibt reinen Ton, 358 P
Klinge, klinge, mein Pandero, 432 Q
Klinget, Glöckchen, klinget, 254 F
Knabe, Der, 328 B
Knabe und das Immlein, Der, 432 R
Knabe und Veilchen, 438 M
Knaben Wunderhorn, Des, 214 N
Knotting song, The, 291 F
Knud Lavard, 122 E
Kocsi szekér, 195 G
Köhlerweib ist trunken, Das, 432 S
Kom Kjyra, 384 B
Kom nu hit, död!, 342 P
Komm bald, 61 E
Komm, du süsse Todesstunde, 18 N

Komm herbei, Tod, 53 I, 342 P
Komm', Hoffnung, 33 C
Komm' in die Gondel, 352 O
Komm in mein Herzenshaus, 14 E
Komm, Jesu, komm, 24 Q
Komm Jesu, komm doch her zu mir, 2 Q
Komm, Jesu, komm zu deiner Kirche, 12 F
Komm'! Komm'!, Holder Knabe, 412 J
Komm leite mich, 18 S
Komm, liebe Zither, 244 G
Komm lieber Mai, 337 A, 252 S
Komm, mein Söhnchen, 344 M
Komm, o Tod, von Nacht umgeben, 433 A
Komm, süsser Tod, 28 Q
Komm, süsses Kreuz, 28 C
Kommen und Scheiden, 337 O
Kommen wir gerne, 345 B
Kommt dir manchmal in den Sinn, 55 E
Kommt, eilet und laufet, 25 K
Kommt ein schlanker Bursch, 422 C
Kommt er dann heim, 410 H
Kommt her, Leute all', 341 J
Kommt, ihr angefocht'nen Sünder, 10 H
Kommt ihr Töchter, 26 P
Kommt! Kommt! eilet, 13 K
Kommt, Seelen, dieser Tag, 28 R
Kön'ge aus Saba, Die, 12 L
König, Der, 139 F
König, in Thule, Das, 320 O
Königliche Morgensonne, 326 K
Königskinder, 184 A
Können nicht die Rothen wangen, 20 K
Können Thränen meiner Wangen, 28 B
Könnt' ich dich in Liedern preisen, 332 L
Köpfchen, Köpfchen, nicht gewimmert, 433 B
Körtéfa, 195 F
Kraft versagt dès Kampfels, Die, 132 O
Krähe, Die, 319 O
Krähe war mit mir, Eine, 319 O
Kranz, Der, 59 M
Kreuz und Krone sind verbunden, 9 E
Kreuzfahrlied, 418 S
Kreuzzug, Der, 328 C
Kriegers Ahnung, 318 C
Krönungs Messe, 244 C
Kuhreigen, Der, 191 S
Ku-ku-ku kus-kám, Szalli le hozzám, 193 Q
Kun een er Frejas Stjerne, 167 E
Kuss, Der, 37 B
Kvad, 142 K
Kyrie, 22 M, 22 O, 33 K, 66 A, 69 F, 69 P, 99 N, 108 S, 168 P, 189 L, 208 G, 213 P, 243 F, 246 N, 255 C, 263 Q, 267 E, 267 G, 267 Q, 388 P, 404 K, 404 M

L

Là ci darem la mano, 250 E
Là del patrizio, 278 L

La, la, la, air chéri, 233 T
La long du ciel grenat, 341 O
La rà, 400 K
Là tra foreste vergini, 392 E
Là turbini, 278 K
Labanc gúnydal a Kuruczra, 195 K
Là-bas dans la forêt plus sombre, 91 F
Là-bas dans le Limousin, 72 K
Là-bas, là-bas dans la montagne, 46 S
Là-bas, vers l'église, 297 H
Labbra di foco, 395 F
Laboravi, 296 L
Lacerato spirito, Il, 401 F
Laceri, miseri, 218 O
Lachen und Weinen, 323 H
Lacrimosa, 255 I
Lacrymosa dies illa, 43 L, 405 C
Lad down yonder, 190 K
Ladies fair, I bring you Lavender, 123 M
Lady fair, of lineage high, A, 370 H
Lady of the Lake, 322 N
Lady the birds right fairly, 424 Q
Lady, when I behold, 427 M
Lady's lament, 175 H
Laengsel, 193 E
Laer mig!, 167 H
Laggiù nel Soledad, 284 E
Laggiù nelle nebbie remote, 278 H
Lagrima d'amante al sepolcro dell' amata, 238 N
Lagunen-Walzer, 352 R
Laisse-moi, laisse-moi, 135 D
Laisse-moi cherir ton fantôme, 275 P
Lakmé, 90 L
Lakmé, ton doux regard se voile, 91 C
Läksin minä kesäyönä käymänn, 270 B
Lalla, Rookh, 86 O
Lament of Federico, 80 K
Lament of Jan the Proud, The, 145 A
Lamentation, 236 L, 258 S, 269 O
Lamento, 100 J
Lámento della Ninfa, 238 D
Land des Lächelns, Das, 203 O
Land of Heart's Desire, 190 O
Land of hope and glory, 105 A
Land of smiles, The, 203 O
Landkjending, 143 D
Landsighting, 143 D
L'Angélus, 52 I
Languir per una bella, 308 P
Largo al factotum, 307 L
Largo from New World Symphony, 102 H
Lark, The, 128 J, 311 P
Lark now leaves his wat'ry nest, The, 270 I
Lark Song, 346 C
Larmes, 109 G
Las! j'ay perdu mon espincel, 405 S
Las, povre coeur, 187 H
Lascia amor, 153 R
Lascia ch' io parta solo, 152 B
Lascia ch' io pianga, 155 F
Lasciar d'amarti, 122 Q

Lasciate i monti, 239 O
Lasciatemi morire, 239 A
Lass dein Lied erschallen, 346 C
Lass' der Spötter Zungen schmähen, 13 C
Lass dich mit gelinden Schlägen, 325 D
Lass mich ihm am Busen hangen, 331 F
Lass, o Welt, O lass mich sein, 436 G
Lass of Richmond Hill, The, 180 K
Lass' tief in dir mich lesen, 338 F
Lass uns, o höchster Gott, 11 A
Lass with a delicate air, The, 6 G
Lasset dem Höchster, 12 O
Lasset Gelehrte sich zanken und streiten, 429 P
Lassitude, 78 H
Lasst mich allein, 102 P
Lasst mich nur auf meinem Sattel gelten!, 330 R
Lassu in cielo, 401 E
Last hour, The, 197 S
Last judgment, The, 348 P
Last night I lay a-sleeping, 2 H
Last night I was dreaming of thee, 31 F
Last night the nightingale woke me, 193 E
Last rose of summer, The, 113 K
Last song, The, 386 E
Last time I went o'er the moon, The, 273 B
Lastu lainehilla, 342 H
L'Attente, 418 A
Lauda Sion, 230 J
Laudamus te, 22 R, 168 R, 246 P
Laudate dominum, 244 E, 269 I, 360 A
Laudate Eum in cymbalis, 360 C
Laudate eum in timpano et choro, 360 B
Laudate pueri Dominum, 268 K
Laude Sion, 267 O
Laue Lüfte, Blumendüfte, 321 G
Laura Lee, 115 L
Laut verkünde uns're Freude, 255 A
Law is the true embodiment, The, 364 M
Lawn as white as driven snow, 207 L
Lawyer's clerk, The, 86 D
Le long du bois couvert de givre, 88 F
Le long du Quai les grands vaisseaux, 108 H
Le minaccie, fieri accenti, 396 Q
Leandre le sot Pierrot, 277 H
Leave me alone, 102 P
Leave me, loathsome light, 165 J
Leaves in autumn fade and fall, 371 M
Leb' wohl, du kühnes, herrliches Kind, 414 H
Leb' wohl du warmes Sonnenlicht, 33 E
Lebantz mocking Kurutz, 195 K
Lebe wohl, 326 B, 433 C
Lebe wohl, mein flandrisch Mädchen, 211 F
Lebensfunke, vom Himmel, 329 Q

Leg' ich mich späte nieder, 15 I
Legend, 378 P
Légende de la sauge, 223 B
Légères hirondelles, 380 R
Leget euch dem Heiland unter, 19 B
Leggiero invisibile, 6 A
Lehn' deine Wang', 187 O, 343 Q
Leichte Segler in den Höhen, 35 H
Leiermann, Der, 320 E
Leis' rudern hier, 331 I
Leis' rudern hier, mein Gondolier, 188 D
Leise, aufgepasst ohne Ruh noch Rast, 345 Q
Leise fliehen meine Lieder, 318 I
Leise, leisee, fromme Weise, 422 D
Leise Lieder, 358 J
Leise nannt ich deinen Namen, 171 I
Leise, rieselnder Quell!, 327 R
Leise, um dich nicht zu wecken, 58 B
Leise wehet, 198 R
Leise zieht durch mein Gemüth, 228 M
Leiser, leiser, kleine Laute, 324 D
Leiser schwanken die Aste, 356 J
Lent Lily, The, 185 J
Lento la neve fiocca, 80 P
Lenz, Der, 174 Q
Lenz ist da, Der, 215 M
Lerche, Die, 311 P
Lerche steiget im Gesang, 311 P
Lerchengesang, 59 C
Les jets d'eau dansent, 310 N
Les voici, 47 F
Les voilà, ces meubles joyeux, 221 K
Less than the dust, 440 G
Let all your fears be banished hence, 44 R
Let each gallant heart, 291 G
Let hammer on anvil ring, 197 P
Let me wander not unseen, 150 G
Let my song fill your heart, 76 F
Let not the dreadful engines, 291 H
Let the bright Seraphim, 164 N
Let the merry cymbals sound, 367 H
Let tyrants shake their iron rod, 44 J
Let us break their bonds asunder, 163 Q
Let us dance, let us sing, 289 D
Let us gaily tread the measure, 368 H
Let us sing today, 103 G
Let us take the road, 272 A
Let us walk in the white snow, 381 R
Let us, who figure forth the Cherubim, 52 D
Let's go to the market in the moon. 421 C
Letter Duet, from Manon, 223 K
Lettera amorosa, 239 B
Letting pin in letting let in, 382 P
Lettre, La. 265 L
Letzte Hoffnung, 319 P
Leur vertu bizarre manque d'apparat, 90 Q
Lève-toi, 47 S

Leyer und Schwert, 423 B
L'ho perduta, 248 R
Libera animas. 405 E
Libera me, 109 E, 405 N
Libertine, The, 288 B
Libiamo ne lieti calici, 401 M
Libro de Villanelle (Madrigal), 202 N
Libusa, 346 D
Libusa's prophecy, 346 K
Licht tanzt freundlich, Ein, 319 S
Lichte Nacht, 144 M
Lichtlein schwimmen auf dem Strome, 435 M
Liden Karen, 172 O
Lieb' Liebchen, 330 M
Liebchen ist da!, 119 B
Liebchen, was zögerst Du? 332 R
Liebe des Nächsten, Die, 35 S
Liebe, Die, 328 D
Liebe, du Himmel auf Erden, 204 F
Liebe Farbe, Die, 318 A
Liebe hat gelogen, Die, 322 A
Liebe ist ein Rosenstrauch, Die, 332 C
Liebe kam fernen Landen, 56 M
Liebe kenn' ich die ist treu, Eine, 437 H
Liebe Mutter, heut Nacht heulte Regen, 209 C
Liebe schwärmt auf allen Wegen, 328 H
Liebe, seliger Traum, 203 G
Liebende schreibt, Die, 230 O
Lieber Gott, du weisst, 55 B
Lieber Schatz, sei wieder gut mir, 120 G
Lieber Spielman, 184 C
Liebes Mädchen hör' mir zu, 171 M
Liebesbotschaft, 318 F, 333 B
Liebesfeier, 426 D
Liebesgarten, 332 C
Liebeshymnus, 357 P
Liebeslauschen, 328 I
Liebeslieder (Waltzes), 62 R
Liebesode, 42 A
Liebestod, Tristan und Isolde, 417 S
Liebestraum (original version), 208 O
Liebestreu, 55 J
Liebhaber in allen Gestalten, 328 F
Liebliche Stern, Der, 328 G
Lieblingsplätzchen, 231 B
Liebst du um Schönheit, 251 E, 330 G
Liebster, deine Worte stehlen, 338 N
Liebster Gott, was werd' ich sterben?, 9 A
Liebster Herr Jesu, wo bleibst du so lange, 28 S
Liebster Jesu, mein Verlangen, 10 K
Liebt, ihr Christen in der That, 13 Q
Lied, 29 H, 117 S, 311 D
Lied an meinen Sohn, 358 G
Lied aus Ruy Blas, 230 M
Lied der Mignon, 323 J, 328 K
Lied der Suleika, 331 D
Lied der Trennung, Das, 249 N

Lied eines Schiffers an die Dioskuren, 323 N
Lied eines Schmiedes, 337 M
Lied eines Verliebten, 433 D
Lied im Grünen, Das, 325 C
Lied Maritime, 184 S
Lied von der Erde, Das, 215 F
Lied von der Unzulänglichkeit menschlichen Strebens, 425 M
Lied von Shakespeare, 53 I
Lied wom Winde, 433 E
Lieder der Braut, 331 E
Lieder der Liebe, 192 F
Lieder eines fahrenden Gesellen, 215 O
Lieder um den Tod, 192 K
Liederalbum für die Jugend, 336 P
Liederkreis, 333 H
Life and death, 82 J
Life for the Czar, A, 127 M
Life lesson, A, 261 B
Lift thine eyes, 132 S, 227 F
Lift up your heads, o ye gates, 163 L
Light, 310 M
Light and life in sadness languish, 170 N
Light of life, The, 104 H
Light of the world, The, 374 L
Like a choir of angels, 52 E
Like glad cherubim in heav'nly chorus, 128 F
Like watercress gather'd fresh, 190 J
Lilacs, 295 E
Lilliburlero, 291 L
Lily of Killarney, The, 40 R
Lincolnshire poacher, The, 386 S
Linda di Chamounix, 96 N
Linden Lea, 388 O
Linden Lüfte sind erwacht, Die, 321 P
Lindenbaum, Der, 319 E
Linger yet! 378 A
Lippen schweigen, 204 C
Lisch aus, lisch aus, mein Licht!, 37 H
Lischen et Fritzchen, 265 H
Lisette, 423 P
Lison dormait, 424 J
Lissen to yo 'daddy warn you, 123 P
List and learn, 362 B
List Reginald, while I confess, 367 J
Litanei auf das Fest "Aller Seelen," 328 L
Litanie de Venerabili Altaris Sacramento, K. 243, 243 P
Lithuanian song, 79 N
Little Belle Blair, 115 M
Little Boy Blue, 261 C
Little boy kneels at the foot of the bed, 120 R
Little Dustman, The, 55 I
Little fishing town, The, 40 G
Little Fish's song, The, 6 E
Little ring, The, 79 L
Little Sandman, The, 55 I
Little Sir William, 64 N
Little songs I'll sing thee. 269 S
Little star so bright, 258 D
Little tov dog is cover'd with dust, The, 261 C

Living echo, 45 R
Llega a mi reja, 140 B
Lo conosco, 273 S
Lo here the gentle lark, 45 O
Lo so che alsue, 285 H
Lo, the dove from her cot hath flown, 103 D
Lo vedremo, o veglio audace, 394 N
Lo vidi, e'l primo palpito, 397 I
Loathsome urns, disclose your treasure, 166 I
Lob der Faulheit, 171 N
Lob der Tränen, 321 G
Lob des hohen Verstandes, 214 P
Lobe den Herrn, meine Seele, 13 A
Lobet den Herrn, 21 N, 24 D, 282 N
Lobgesang, 229 H
Locas por amor, Las, 387 G
Loch Lomond, 390 H
Locutions, 179 N
Lodoletta, 221 B
Lohengrin, 409 G
Loin de moi, 77 K
Lola's ditty, 219 Q
Lolita, 69 J
Lombardi alla Prima Crociata, I, 397 B
Londonderry air, 5 H
Lonely and fetter'd, 259 I
Long ago, 213 F
Long day closes, The, 374 R
Long, long ago, 32 K
Long Nose comes a-calling, 194 S
Long years ago, 387 C
Longing, 193 E
Long-Nose Flea, 194 S
Longtemps captifs chez le Russe, 418 B
Lontan lontano il sol scompare, 85 B
Lontano, lontano, 50 E
Look down, harmonious Saint, 149 O
Look off dear love across the sallow sands, 66 N
Look out, Kurutz, run away now, 195 K
Lorché pifferie, 396 O
Lord God of Abraham, 226 Q
Lord God of Heav'n and earth, 348 P
Lord, I don't feel no ways tired, 67 S
Lord is a man of war, The, 160 D
Lord shall reign for ever, The, 160 A
Lord, thou art my refuge, 101 R
Lord, to thee, each night and day, 166 G
Lord worketh wonders, The, 162 A
Lord's prayer, The, 216 J
Lorelei, Die, 208 D, 343 I
Loreley, 74 O, 231 A, 335 P
Lorsq'autour de sa tête, 87 B
Lorsque au soleil couchant, 88 B
Lorsque je voy en ordre, 297 L
Lorsque l'enfant revient, 225 H
Los aux dames!, 314 A
Lost chord, The, 374 S
Lotario, 153 L
Lotosblume, Die, 331 B

Loué soit le Seigneur, plein de gloire, 178 O
Louez le Dieu caché, 118 F
Louise, 76 N
Lou'siana Belle, 115 N
Love, 142 D
Love Duet, Tristan und Isolde, 417 O
Love feeds on many kinds of food, 372 M
Love has eyes, 45 P
Love I gave you, troth I gave you, 93 A
Love in her eyes sits playing, 158 K
Love in May, 270 J
Love is a bable, 188 P, 270 N
Love is a plaintive song, 367 N
Love is just a game, 198 E
Love is meant to make us glad, 123 G
Love me or not, 341 G
Love sounds th' alarm, 158 L
Love that no wrong can cure, 367 O
Love the Magician, 106 B
Love to his singer, 388 M
Love went a-riding, 64 E
Loveliest of trees, 68 F
Lovely is the forest, 194 O
Lovely kind, and kindly loving, 420 F
Lovely lass of Inverness, The, 37 O
Lover in Damascus, A, 440 J
Love's blind they say, 45 P
Love's call, 180 L
Love's god is a boy, 188 Q
Love's last gift, 388 M
Love's like a summer rose, 75 R
Love's minstrels, 388 J
Love's old sweet song, 237 M
Love's philosophy, 92 A, 293 E
Love's ritornella, 82 N
Love-Sight, 388 H
Love-song of the idiot, 258 E
Lowlands of Holland, The, 167 P
Loy d'Honneur, La, 123 D
Luci care, 150 P
Lucia di Lammermoor, 97 D
Lucieta, è un bel nomme, 439 O
Lucrezia Borgia, 98 E
Ludlams Hule, 426 O
Luft ist blau, Die, 327 G
Luft ist kühl, Die, 208 E
Lug', Dursel, lug', 191 S
Luisa Miller, 397 I
Lullaby, 340 S
Lullaby, from The Consul, 231 P
Lullaby, my sweet little baby, 69 M
Lully, lullay, 420 E
Lumps of pudding, 273 J
Lune blanche, La, 77 H, 110 A, 147 M, 277 J, 375 N
Lune blanche luit dans les bois, La, 110 A
Lungi dal caro bene, 314 L, 341 H
Luoghi sereni e cari, 93 J
Lusinghe più care, 153 N
Lust der Sturmnacht, 332 F
Lustig im Leid, 415 B
Lustig oft unverhofft, 354 D
Lustige Kreig, Der, 352 S
Lustigen Weiber von Windsor, Die, 261 K
Lutzows wilde Jagd, 423 B

Lux aeterna, 405 K
Lydé, 147 Q
Lydia, 107 K
Lykken mellem to mennesker, 4 H
Lyre et les Amours, La, 44 F
Lysets Engel gaar med Glands, 426 Q

M

Ma belle amie est morte, 107 J
Ma bouche rit, 189 M
Ma chambre a la forme, 279 J
Ma che vi fece, o stelle, K.368, 245 C
Ma colombe, O ma tourterelle, 236 M
Ma come potrei 301 R
Ma dall' arido stelo divulsa, 393 B
Ma foi! pour venir de province, 232 R
Ma fu molto breve, 384 Q
Ma guitare, je te chante, 279 H
Ma maitresse, 266 B
Ma maitresse a quitté la tente, 86 O
Ma mère aux vignes, 265 J
Ma mère je la vois, 46 J
Ma n'atu sole, 73 K
Ma o pianto, o duol, 399 G
Ma pensée est un cygne, 110 N
Ma poupée chérie, 342 B
Ma se m'è forza perderti, 393 H
Ma te raccoglie, 238 Q
Ma traportar mi sento, 245 D
Ma tu re, tu signore, 391 R
Mab, la reine des mensonges, 137 B
Macbeth, 397 N
Macchia è qui tutt' ora, Una, 397 Q
Mach 'auf, mach' auf, doch liese, 356 L
Mache dich, mein Geist, bereit, 16 O
Mach dich, mein Herze, rein, 28 G
Macht dunkelgrüne Laub, Das, 120 E
Mad Bess, 290 F
Mad scene, from Lucia di Lammermoor, 98 A
Madama Butterfly, 284 N
Madame, 179 R
Madame Chrysanthème, 232 O
Madame Eustache a dix-sept filles, 281 I
Madame Favart, 265 J
Madamina! Il catalogo è questo, 250 A
Mädchen, Das 60 K, 328 M
Mädchen, die von harten Sinnen, 20 P
Mädchen ist's, Ein, 325 Q
Mädchen mit dem rothen Mündchen, 119 D
Mädchen oder Weibchen, Ein, 254 C
Mädchen spricht, Das, 61 N
Mädchenfluch, 59 A
Mädchenlied, 59 P, 60 O, 61 P, 316 J
Mlle. Modiste, 173 H

Madonna con sospiri, 439 L
Madonna, d'un braccio, 302 E
Madre al figlio lontano, La, 277 F
Madre, pietosa vergine, 395 R
Madrigal, 356 H, 387 L
Madrigal dans le style ancien, 184 J
Mag dir, du zartes Frühlingskind, 143 B
Magdaléenne à la croix, La, 224 H
Magdaléenne à la fontaine, La, 224 G
Magdalen at Michael's gate, 205 B
Magda's Aria from The Consul, 231 Q
Mägdlein sass am Meerestrand, Ein, 55 O
Mägdlein stund, Ein, 260 B
Mägdlein will ein' Freier habn, Das, 357 S
Magelone Romanzen, 56 L, 57 A
Magic flute, The, 253 E
Magische Töne, 133 A
Magnet hung in a hardware shop, A, 367 M
Magnificat in D, 21 R
Magpie, The, 258 F
Mah Lindy Lou, 361 M
Mai, 147 R, 313 P
Mai! les arbres du verger, 313 P
Maid and the sun, The, 305 N
Maid goin' to Comber, A, 182 F
Maid imprisoned, The, 103 I
Maid is like the golden ore, A, 271 H
Maid sings light, A, 213 H
Maiden, The, 270 O
Maiden and the Nightingale, The, 139 S
Maiden fair to see, A, 363 F
Maiden journeys forth a-mowing, 103 I
Maiden sang sweetly as a bird, A, 305 R
Maiden yonder sings, A, 342 M
Maidens fair of Mantua's city, 122 S
Maiden's wish, The 78 Q
Maienkätzchen, 61 O
Maienlied, 228 H
Mailied, 37 C, 337 A
Mainacht, Die, 57 C
Maison grise, La, 232 M
Maja de Goya, La, 139 R
Maja dolorosa, La, 139 P
Maja y el ruiseñor, El, 139 S
Majestät wird anerkannt, Die, 351 Q
Majo discreto, El, 139 N
Majo olvidado, El, 140 A
Majo timido, El, 140 B
Make believe, 191 J
Mal reggendo all' aspro assalto, 403 D
Malagueña, 263 B
Maledetto, Il, 398 D
Maledetto sia l'aspetto, 239 C
Maledizione, 396 C
Malheureux qui a une femme, 72 S
Malia, 385 I
M'allontano, 152 C
Malpropre, La, 236 C
Malurous qu'o uno fenno, 72 S

Maman, dites-moi, 423 Q
Mamma morta, La, 126 I
Mammy's little boy loves short'nin', 438 A
Man halte nur ein wenig stille, 15 E
Man may escape from rope and gun, 272 F
Man sagt mir, deine Mutter woll es nicht, 433 F
Man singet mit Freuden vom Sieg, 18 C
Man soll hören süsses Singen, 228 H
Mañana de Saint Juan, La, 255 S
Manche Trän' aus meinen Augen, 319 F
Mandoline, 89 B, 101 B, 109 N, 277 K, 375 P
Manège a vapeur regarde, Le, 236 O
Mann, der noch den Flitterwochen, Der, 8 G
Männer sind mechant, Die, 328 N
Manner Sippe sass hier im Saal, Der, 413 M
Manner suchen stets zu naschen, 247 H
Manoir de Rosamunde, Le, 100 K
Manon, 223 D
Manon Lescaut, 7 P, 285 J
Manteau de fleurs, 298 E
Manus tuae Domine, 268 L
M'appari tutt' amor, 113 Q
Már engem, mat kam, 194 F
March of the Smugglers, 47 A
Märchen, 438 N
Marco Aurelio, 350 F
M'ardea l'estro amatorio, 395 B
Marechiare, 385 J
Margaretlein, 143 O
Margot, labourez les vignes, 201 P
Margoton va-t-à l'eau, 424 K
Marguerite a fermé sa corolle, La, 48 A
Marguerite de Navarre, 179 J
Maria, du zarte, 438 P
Maria ging aus wandern, 62 G
Maria, Marì, 73 H
Maria sitzt am Rosenhag, 300 S
Maria und der Schiffer, 438 O
Maria Wiegenlied, 300 S
Maria wollt' zur Kirche gehn, 438 O
Mariage des Roses, Le, 118 A
Marianka, komm und tanz' me' hier, 352 A
Marie, 120 B
Marie am Fenster, 187 P
Marie-Magdeleine, 224 G
Marienkirche zu Danzig im Gerüst, 192 S
Marienleben, Das, 175 M
Marienlied, 218 D
Marienruf, 438 P
Marienwürmchen, 337 C
Marietta's lute song, 197 E
Marionettes, Les, 276 A
Marionettes de bois ont des robes, Les, 276 A
Maristella, 276 F
Maritana, 418 M
Marmotte, 37 D
Mârouf, 294 F

Marquez la dance, 40 P
Marriage of Figaro, The, K. 492, 247 O
Martern aller Arten, 245 Q
Martha, 113 I
Martin-Pecheur, Le, 298 C
Mary, 303 N
Mary of Allendale, 180 M
Mary of Argyle, 260 M
Mary, tremando l'ultima stella, 385 K
Märzveilchen, 334 A
Mas cerca de mite siento, 387 F
Mas, por otra parte, 106 R
Masked ball, The 392 N
Masonic cantata, 255 A
Masonic song, K. 468, 247 I
Mass, 69 P, 213 P, 267 E, 267 M, 267 O
Mass "Douce Memoire," 202 H
Mass in A Major, 29 C
Mass in B minor, 22 M
Mass in C, K. 317, 244 C
Mass in C minor, K. 427, 246 N
Mass in E minor, 66 A
Mass in F, 317 C
Mass in G, 317 B
Mass in G minor, 388 P
Mass in G, No. 12, K. anh. 232, 243 F
Mass No. 3 in C major, K. 66, 242 I
Mass No. 11, 168 P
Mass: "Se la face ay pale," 99 N
Massa's in de cold cold ground, 115 O
Master Portly, 361 G
Mastersingers of Nürnberg, The, 410 I
Mater Dolorosa, 117 Q
Mater ora filium, 32 H
Matin, dès que je te quitte, Le, 275 E
Matona mia cara, 202 L
Matrimonio segreto, Il, 81 B
Mattinata, 206 P, 302 G, 385 K
Maudite à jamais soit la race, 312 L
Mausfallan — Sprüchlein, 433 G
Maxwelton's braes are bonnie, 341 C
May her blest example, 291 M
May Morning, A, 92 I
May Night, 304 H
May no rash intruder, 165 M
May-Day carol, 376 G
Me Judah's daughters once caress'd, 290 I
Me l'ha fatte lo mio amore, 343 C
Me pellegrina ed orfana, 395 N
Me voici dans son boudoir, 381 C
Meco all' altar di venere, 38 K
Meco verrai su quella, 390 S
Medium, The, 232 A
Medjé, (Chanson Arabe), 138 D
Meer erglänzte, Das, 318 Q
Meere, Die, 56 D
Meeres Stille, 320 G
Meerfahrt, 61 A
Meerfee, Die, 339 H
Mefistofele, 49 M
Megégett rácország, 195 L
Meghalok, meghalok, 195 M
Mein!, 317 O

Mein Alles in Allem, mein ewiges Gut, 10 A
Mein Aug' bewacht bei Tag und Nacht, 353 L
Mein Aug' ist trüb', 331 P
Mein Auge, 358 E
Mein Elemer, 354 J
Mein Erlöser und Erhalter, 13 A
Mein Freund ist mein, 17 N
Mein gläubiges Herze, 12 S
Mein Gott, wie lang, 18 J
Mein Herr Marquis, 351 M
Mein Herr und Gott, 409 K
Mein Herr, was dächten Sie von mir, 351 J
Mein Herz ist betrübt, 331 A
Mein Herz ist im Hochland, 188 B
Mein Herz ist leer, 192 F
Mein Herz ist schwer, 331 H
Mein Herz ist stumm, 356 R
Mein Herz ist wie die dunkle Nacht, 230 P
Mein Herz ist zerrissen, 323 E
Mein Herz schmückt sich, 311 F
Mein Herz und mein Sinn, 343 E
Mein Herz voll treue, 408 P
Mein Herz war mit in des Lebens Streit, 143 F
Mein hochgebornes Schätzelein, 209 J
Mein Hund, du, 316 G
Mein Jesu, was für Seelenweh, 29 A
Mein Jesu, ziehe mich nach dir, 9 R
Mein Jesus ist erstanden, 12 R
Mein Jesus soll mein Alles sein, 13 M
Mein Jesus will es thun, 13 I
Mein Leben wagt ich drum, 3 S
Mein Lieb ist ein Jäger, 60 M
Mein Lieb' mit mir kriegen, 168 D
Mein Liebchen, wir sassen beisamen, 61 A
Mein lieber Schatz, nun aufgepasst, 344 S
Mein lieber Schwan!, 410 G
Mein Liebling ist ein Lindenbaum, 112 D
Mein liebster Freund hat mich verlassen, 241 P
Mein Liebster hat zu Tische mich geladen, 433 H
Mein Liebster ist so klein, 433 I
Mein liebster Jesus ist verloren, 18 H
Mein Liebster singt am Haus im Mondenscheine, 433 J
Mein Lied ertönt, 102 I
Mein Mädel hat einen Rosenmund, 62 J
Mein, mein gold'nes Haar ist mein, 101 O
Mein Muter mag mi net, 439 E
Mein Schatz der liegt auf der Todtenbahr, 105 L
Mein schöner Stern! ich bitte dich, 338 O
Mein schönes grosses Vogelhaus, 351 K
Mein Schwan, mein stiller, 142 O
Mein Seel' erhebt den Herrn, 9 B
Mein Seelenschatz ist Gottes Wort, 9 J
Mein Sehnen, mein Wähnen, 197 F

Mein Vater hat gesagt, 358 A
Mein Vater, Hochgesegneter, 412 P
Mein Verlangen, 18 N
Mein wundes Herz, 58 H
Meine Herrn heut sehn sie mich Gläser, 425 H
Meine Laute hab ich gehängt, 317 P
Meine Lebenszeit verstreicht, 36 A, 438 Q
Meine Liebe ist grün, 58 L
Meine Lieder, 61 L
Meine Lippen, sie küssen so heiss, 203 J
Meine Rose, 337 N
Meine Ruh ist hin, 320 F
Meine Seele ist erschüttert, 34 L
Meine Seele rühmt und preist, 19 I
Meine Seufzer, meine Thränen, 9 F
Meine wunderschöne Königin, 139 D
Meinem Hirten bleib' ich treu, 15 D
Meinem Kinde, 358 D
Meinen Jesum lass' ich nicht, 15 M
Meiner Liebsten schöne Wangen, 242 D
Meister Olus, 209 P
Meistersinger von Nürnberg, Die, 410 I
Mejerke, main Suhn, 298 L
Melancholie, 336 G
Melancholy, 79 K
Mélodies persanes, 313 Q
Melody, A, 79 G
Mêlons! Mêlons! Coupons, 47 B
Memnon, 320 P
Memory, A, 122 K
Men are so conservative, 383 B
Mon p'tit gars, si nous t'écrivons, 132 J
Men tiranne, 131 H
Mendiant, Le, 280 I
Menie, 213 C
Mensch lebt durch den Kopf, Der, 425 M
Mensch liegt in grösster Noth, Der, 215 S
Menschen glaubt doch dieser Gnade, 8 S
Mentre l'erbetta pasce l'aguella, 360 P
Mentre ti lascio, o figlia, 249 J
Menuet d'exaudet, 423 R
Mephistopheles' Serenade, 135 L
Mer, La, 306 P
Mer est infinie, La, 110 R
Mer est plus belle, La, 89 R
Mer hahn en neue Oberkeet, 20 S
Mercè, dilette amiche, 404 H
Merci, doux crépuscule, 42 P
Mère Bontemps, La, 423 S
Mère des souvenirs, 88 G
Merke, mein Herze, beständig nur dies, 17 R
Mermaid's Song, The, 171 O
Merrie England, 123 G
Mercy Mount, 166 N
Merry war, The, 352 S
Merry widow, The, 204 A
Merry wives of Windsor, The, 261 K

Mes amis, écoutez l'histoire, 1 L
Mes navires rapides, 304 K
Mes vers fuiraient doux, 148 N
Messe Solennelle, 118 D, 134 B
Messenger, The, 79 E
Messer notaio, 284 L
Messiah, 162 J
Métamorphoses, 281 E
Methinks I see an heav'nly host, 44 Q
Mets ta main sur mes yeux, 303 J
Meu amor meu amoriño, 262 O
M'ha preso alla sua ragna, 270 F
M'hai salvato, 75 B
M'han detto che domani, 386 E
Mi lagnerò tacendo, 157 F
Mi par d'esser colla, 308 B
Mi piaccion quelle cose, 283 L
Mi restano le lagrime, 151 H
Mi sento dal contento, 248 L
Mi tradi quell' alma ingrata, 250 S
Mia casetta e triste, La, 85 E
Mia Dorabella, La, 251 S
Mia gelosa! si, lo sento, 286 J
Mia letizia infondere, La, 397 C
Mia madre, 126 Q
Mia piccirella, 133 H
Mia speranza adorata, K. 416, 246 J
Michieu Banjo, 261 I
Mid pleasures and palaces, 45 N
Mid the thick liana, 221 N
Midnight Review, 128 K
Midshipmite, The, 2 J
Midwinter, 177 B
Miei signori, 400 M
Mighty fortress, A, 234 B
Mighty fortress is our God, A, 212 P
Mighty lak' a rose, 261 D
Mighty maiden with a mission, 370 C
Mignon, 37 A, 337 H, 380 K, 433 K
Mignonette, 424 L
Mignonne, allon voir si la Rose, 83 N, 418 I
Mignonne, sais-tu comment s'épousent les roses?, 118 A
Mignonne, voici l'Avril!, 226 A
Mignons Lied. 208 F
Mikado, The, 365 F
Mild un leise wie er lächelt, 417 S
Milenciny oci, 347 Q
Mille pene, 131 F
Miller, The, 86 E
Mimaamaquim, 178 I
Mime hiess ein mürrischer Zwerg, 415 R
Mimi's Farewell, 283 Q
Min sode Brud, 142 F
Mindnesang over de faldne, 167 I
Minha mae querida, 406 F
Minnelied, 59 H, 328 O
Minnelied in Mai, 228 E, 229 A
Minnie, dalla mia casa, 284 D
Minué cantado, 262 J
Minuit, Chrétiens, c'est l'heure solennelle, 1 J
Mio caro bene, 155 N
Mio piano è preparato, Il, 308 N
Mio sangue, la vita darei, Il, 397 K
Mio tesoro, Il, 250 Q
Mir hat die Welt, 27 M

Mir ist die Ehre, 355 M
Mir ist ein feins brauns Maidelein, 266 D
Mir ist so bang, 204 J
Mir ist so weh um's Herz, 57 S
Mir ist so wohl, 320 S
Mir ist so wunderbar, 32 S
Mir ist's so eng allüberall!, 337 J
Mir klingt ein Ton so wunderbar, 83 G
Mir träumte einst, 143 K
Mir ward gesagt, du reisest in die Ferne, 430 O
Mira, di acerbe lagrime, 403 S
Mira, o Norma, 38 O
Mirage, 184 K
Mirages, 110 N
Miranda, 146 H
Mirar de la Maja, El, 140 C
Mireille, 135 P
Mireille ne sait pas encore, 225 M
Miriams Siegesgesang, 325 M
Miroir, Le, 111 P
Mirth, admit me of thy crew, 150 I
Mirti, faggi, 71 E
Misera, dove son, K. 369, 245 E
Miserere (Il Trovatore), 403 P, 403 Q
Miserere mei, Deus, 189 N, 202 O
Miserere mei Domine, 202 P
Misero giovane, 131 E
Mismo que es fuego fatuo, Lo, 106 C
Miss Ellen, verrez-moi le thé, 196 M
Missa Brevis, 69 F
Missa Choralis, 208 G
Missa Hercules, 189 L
Missa Papae Marcelli, 267 Q
Missa sine Nomine, 263 Q
Missa Solemnis, 33 K
Missa super Maria Zart, 263 R
Mists are hanging low, The, 305 H
Mit Allem, was ich hab' und bin, 13 H
Mit deinen blauen Augen, 201 G, 359 G
Mit dem grünen Lautenbande, 317 Q
Mit der Freude zieht der Schmerz, 230 Q
Mit der Mutter sank zu Grabe, 344 B
Mit einer Primula Veris. 143 B
Mit einer Wasserlilie, 142 Q
Mit einem gemalten Band. 37 E
Mit Fried und Freud ich fahr dahin, 16 I
Mit Gewitter und Sturm, 408 H
Mit Hjerte of min Lyre, 193 F
Mit Ihren Augen, 355 P
Mit Lust thät ich ausreiten. 230 N
Mit Myrthen und Rosen, 330 O
Mit Regen und Sturmgebrause, 356 I
Mit Rosen bestreut, 300 N
Mit unsern Fischern, 112 M
Mit Verlangen, 20 C
Mit vierzig Jahren, 60 G
Mitrane, 307 D
Mitten im Schimmer des spiegelnden Wellen, 323 Q
Mitten in dem kleinen Teiche, 215 I

Mitternacht zog näher schon, Die, 336 A
Miya sama, miya sama, 366 H
Möchte wohl gerne ein Schmetterling sein, 3 P
Moderen Synger, 143 P, 343 K
Modest Maid, The, 103 F
M'odi, ah! m'odi, 98 I
Mögen alle bösen Zungen, 433 P
Mögst du, mein Kind, 408 R
Mohrenfürst auf der Messe, Der, 209 N
Moi du Sauveur — je suis la mère, 117 Q
Moi j'm'appelle Ciboulette, 146 Q
Molinara, La, 266 J
Moment I remember clearly, The, 128 I
Mon âme vers ton front, 300 B
Mon amour d'antan, 77 G
Mon beau tzigane mon amant, 177 R
Mon bras pressait, 427 E
Mon cadavre est doux comme un gant, 280 R
Mon coeur est mort, 275 F
Mon coeur ne peut changer, 136 B
Mon coeur se recommande à vous, 202 K
Mon coeur s'élance et palpite, 234 M
Mon coeur s'ouvre à ta voix, 312 Q
Mon Dieu, que les hommes sont bêtes, 265 N
Mon enfant, ma soeur, 100 I
Mon espérance n'est pas encore perdue, 236 Q
Mon odi là il martir, 127 E
Mónár Anna, 195 N
Monatsrose, 105 H
Mond, Der, 230 P
Mond hat eine schwere Klag' erhoben, Der, 433 Q
Mond ist schlafen gangen, Der, 119 S
Mond steht über dem Berge, Der, 61 J
Mond steigt aufwärts, Der, 218 B
Mondenschein, 59 O, 324 N
Mondnacht, 112 M, 333 L
Money O!, 172 G
Monica, Monica, dance the Waltz, 232 F
Monotone, The, 83 G
Montañesa, 262 S
Monte, écureuil, 313 I, 418 A
Montparnasse, 281 H
Moon drops low, The, 71 A
Moon has rais'd her lamp above, The, 40 S
Moon marketing, 421 C
Moon shines Bright, The, 376 G
Moon-Deer, how near your soul, 207 H
Moonlight shimmers thro' the vine, The, 71 B
Moonlight song, A, 71 B
Mor Danmark, 303 S
Morale è molto bella. La, 94 M
More love or more disdain I crave, 291 N
Morgen, 357 H
Morgengesang, 301 E
Morgengruss, 229 B, 317 L
Morgenlich leuchtend, 411 I

Morgennebel Lila, 357 R
Morgenrot, 358 L
Morgens steh' ich aur und frage, 330 J
Morgenstimmung, 433 R
Morgentau, 433 S
Morir! si pura e bella morir, 392 I
Moritat vom Mackie Messer, 425 G
Morn of life is past, The 116 I
Morning, 348 F
Morning a cruel turmoiler is, 36 H
Morning air plays on my face, The, 36 I
Morning Hymn, 172 R
Morning on the holy hills, 348 G
Morning skies are a-glow, 295 E
Moro lasso, 124 L
Morrai sì, 155 O
Morrò, ma prima in grazia, 393 F
Mors et vita, 134 F
Mort, La, 140 R
Mort de David, La, 179 E
Mort des amants, La, 88 K
Morte de Don Quichotte, 222 C
Moscow, 376 I
Mosè in Egitto, 309 D
Moses and the children of Israel, 159 S
Moses in Egypt, 309 D
Most beautiful appear, 169 Q
Most jöttem Erdélyböl, 195 P
Mot Kveld, 29 O
Mote, 144 F
Motets du Roy, 84 G
Mother and maiden, Mother of God, 4 P
Mother, mother, are you there?, 232 B
Mother o' mine, 386 L
Mother of us all, The, 382 S
Mother sings, The, 343 K
Mother, with unbowed head, 349 R
Moto di gioia, Un, 251 Q
Moulin, Le, 276 B
Mount of Olives, 34 L
Mourn, ye afflicted children, 161 B
Mouth of gladness! Music's laughter, 190 S
Möven, möven in weissen Flocken, 143 Q
Mower, The, 102 Q
Mozart (operetta), 147 S
Muette de Portici, La, 7 Q
Mühle seh ich blinken, Eine, 317 F
Mühvoll komm' ich 434 A
Müller und der Bach, Der, 318 D
Mund und Herze steht dir offen, 18 B
Münich steht in seiner Zell', Ein, 328 C
Murmelndes Lüftchen, 187 R
Murre nicht, lieber Christ, 17 Q
Musensohn, Der, 324 F
Musetta's waltz, 283 P
Musette, La, 296 F
Mushrooms brown and tall, 257 Q
Music for a while, 288 A
Music I heard with you, 146 I
Music in the air, 191 O
Musikant, Der, 434 B
Muss es eine Trennung geben, 56 R
Mut, 320 C
Mute and resign'd, 79 G

Mutter, ach Mutter, es hungert mich, 214 O
Mutter betet herzig, Die, 334 B
Mutter, hilf mir armen Tochter, 59 M
Mutter Jesu, die du trostlos, 171 B
Mutter, Mutter! glaube nicht, 331 E
Mutter, o sing' mich zur Ruh!, 119 K
Muttertändelei, 358 K
Muttertraum, 334 B
Muzio Scevola, 153 O
My blessing rest on ye, 378 L
My bonny lass she smileth, 241 H
My country, 140 J
My days have been so wondrous free, 180 R
My dear eyes, 347 Q
My dreams, 385 L
My eyes are fully open, 372 A
My father! ah, methinks I see, 159 O
My friends, I am going a long journey, 44 K
My gen'rous heart disdains, 180 S
My heart at thy sweet voice, 312 Q
My heart is like a singing bird, 440 Q
My heart, the bird of the wilderness, 181 H
My heart was frozen, 71 M
My heart was so free, 271 P
My heart, whenever you appear, 291 O
My heart, why weepest thou?, 257 B
My hero, 350 N
My joys, 79 J
My Lagan love, 167 O
My Leman is so true of love, 176 Q
My life is sweet, I hold it dear, 350 P
My love bound me with a kiss, 188 R
My lovely Celia, 237 P
My lover is a fisherman, 361 N
My man's gone now, 123 R
My moonlight madonna, 112 B
My mother bids me bind my hair, 171 P
My name is John Wellington Wells, 372 N
My Native Land, 140 J
My object all sublime, 366 J
My old Kentucky home, 115 P
My prairie home is beautiful, 117 G
My pretty Jane, 45 Q
My Redeemer and my Lord, 66 M
My soul has naught but fire and ice, 176 O
My soul is sad, 256 E
My sweetest Lesbia, 72 A
My sweetheart. 79 F
My teacher said us boys should write, 186 D
My young love said to me, 182 H
Myrthen. 330 P
Myself when young, 205 A

N

Na paz da outono, 406 M
Nabucodonosor, 397 S

Nac o tom dále bádat, 346 N
Nach dem Matteo, 354 K
Nach diesen trüben Tagen, 337 D
Nach Frankreich zogen zwei Grenadier', 335 K
Nach Rom gelangt' ich, 417 L
Nachen dröhnt, Der, 327 B
Nacht, Die, 41 O, 321 L, 328 P, 356 B
Nacht in Venedig, Eine, 352 K
Nacht ist heiter und ist rein, Die, 325 K
Nacht leigt auf den fremden Wegen, 59 O
Nacht und Träume, 322 M
Nachtgang, 357 K
Nachtgesang, 328 Q
Nachtgesang im Walde, 325 O
Nachthelle, 325 K
Nachtigall, Die, 41 Q 61 B, 229 R, 321 B
Nachtigall, o Nachtigall, 3 G
Nachtigall, sie singt so schön, 63 M
Nachtigallen schwingen, 55 N
Nachtlager in Granada, Das, 198 M
Nächtliche Heerschau, Die, 210 G
Nachtlied, 230 I, 338 D·
Nachts, 275 N
Nachts un die zwölfte Stunde, 210 G
Nachtstück, 322 I
Nachtviolen, 328 R
Nachtzauber, 434 C
Nacqui all' affano, 308 I
Nagya bonyban csak két torony, 194 B
Nah bei Temesvar, dem Städtchen, 102 Q
Nah is die Stunde, 128 A
Nahandove, 299 C
Nähe des Geliebten, 320 N
Naht euch dem Lande!, 416 E
N'aï pas iéu de mío, 72 M
Naissantes fleurs, 141 D
N'allez pas au bois d'Ormonde, 300 A
Nana, 106 M
Nancy Lee, 2 K
Nanette, 424 A
Nänie, 54 N, 339 B
Nanny, 77 S
Nanny, hark, Nanny, 258 J
Napolitana, 397 S
När jag blef sjutton ar, 207 J
Nasce al bosco, 152 M
Nature immense, 42 S
Nature loved she fair to see, 352 S
Naughty Marietta, 173 I
Nay, Maccus. lay him down, 376 F
Nazareth, 138 F
Ne bronchez pas, soyez gentil, 223 F
Né dans une crèche, 138 F
Ne jamais la voir ni l'entendre, 100 O
Nè mai dunque avrò pace, 75 A
Ne me refuse pas!, 222 K
Nè men con l'ombre, 156 Q
Ne parle pas, Rose, 216 F
Ne parlez pas tant, 43 S
Ne quier veoir la beauté. 214 B
Ne vous balancez pas si fort. 236 P
'Neath a marvelous roof, 128 L
'Neath the Southern moon, 173 M

Nebbie, 302 H
Nebensonnen, Die, 320 D
Necht' cokoliv mne, 347 J
Nègre, Le, 179 M
Nehmet hin meinen leib, 412 I
Nei cieli bigi, 283 H
Nei giardin del bello saracin, 393 L
Nei se, hvor det blaner her, 144 E
Neige, Il, 40 N
Nein, es ist nicht auszukommen mit den Leuten, 63 I
Nein, junger Herr, 434 D
Nein, nimmer liebte ich, 378 C
Nel cor più no mi sento, 266 J
Nel Dolce dell'oblio, 149 M
Nel mondo nell' abisso, 153 Q
Nel puro ardor, 275 C
Nel riposo e nel contento, 152 K
Nel sano a destarmi, 249 I
Nel suo amore, 127 C
Nel verde maggio, 74 O
Nell, 108 B
Nell and I, 115 Q
Nella bionda egli ha l'usanza, 250 B
Nella guerra è la follia, 396 E
Nelly Bly, 115 R
Nelly was a lady, 116 A
Nelson Mass, 168 P
Nem meszsze van ide kis Margitta, 31 Q
Nemea's Aria, 1 Q
Nemico della patria, 126 G
N'entrez pas, monsieur, 310 K
Neapolitan Love Song, 173 O
Nérac en fête, 179 K
Neri gli occhi ma non fulgide, 302 O
Nerone, 50 J
N'esse pas ung grant desplaisir, 189 O
Nessun dorma!, 287 H
N'est-ce pas?, 110 F
N'est-ce plus ma main, 224 E
Neue Liebe, 228 L, 434 E
Neue Liebe, neues Leben, 37 F
Neugebor'ne Kindelein, Das, 17 A
Neugierige, Der, 317 I
Neujahrslied, 230 Q
Never mind the why and wherefore, 363 S
Never star was in the sky, 348 F
Never weather-beaten sail, 72 C
Nevicata, 302 I
New Plymouth, 44 M
New World Symphony, Largo, 102 H
Next market day, The, 182 F
Next, winter comes slowly, 289 F
Nibble, nibble mousekin, 183 M
Nicht ein Lüftchen regt sich leise, 357 D
Nicht im schlafe hab ich das geträumt, 358 N
Nicht mehr zu dir zu gehen, 56 I
Nicht mit Engeln, 311 E
Nicht send' ich dich mehr aus Walhall, 414 F
Nicht so schnelle, 336 L
Nicht wandle, mein Licht, 63 O
Nichts kann mich erretten, 13 L
Nichts kann wir so genügen, 347 Q
Nicolette, 299 R
Nido di memorie in fondo, Un, 205 O

Nie werd' ich deine Huld verkennen, 246 F
Niemand hat's geseh'n, 209 D
Night, 140 M, 258 G
Night has spread her pall, 374 D
Night in Venice, A, 352 K
Night is calm, The, 374 N
Night that bounds my subject, The, 176 G
Nightingale, The, 3 G, 92 B, 378 S
Nightingale and the Rose, 305 E, 313 S
Nightingale has a lyre of gold, The, 293 M
Nightingale song, 442 A
Nightwatchman's Song, Die Meistersinger von Nürnberg, 411 C
Nil, Le, 206 R
Nile song, 391 S
Nimm einen Strahl der Sonne, 208 M
Nimm mich dir zu eigen hin, 12 M
Nimm sie hin denn, diese Lieder, 35 K
Nimm von uns, Herr, du treuer Gott, 15 Q
Nimm was dein ist, und gehe hin, 17 Q
Nimmer, das glaubt mir, 323 I
Nimmersatte Liebe, 434 F
Nina ninana, will ich dir singen, 218 J
Ninon, 385 M
Ninon, Ninon, que fais-tu de la vie, 118 B, 385 M
Nixe Binsefuss, 434 G
No, d'un imene il vincolo, 396 N
No, I cannot let you leave me, 439 R
No, I come not, reckless Martin, 195 O
No, la mia fronte, 80 H
No more dams I'll make for fish, 348 D
No, never any other, 376 O
No. 9 Letter scene, 376 N
No, no, che non sei capace, K.419, 246 K
No, no, il tuo sdegno mi placo, 157 S
No, no, mio core, 74 D
No, no, non si speri, 74 E
No, no, Turiddu, rimani, 219 R
No, no, unhallow'd desire, 161 P
No, non chiuder gli occhi vaghi, 117 K
No none è ver, 97 B
No, non udrai rimproveri, 402 F
No! Pagliacci non son, 206 K
No pow'r on earth, 272 Q
No rose in all the world. 314 J
No, soffrir non può, 152 H
No star is o'er the lake, 374 R
No watch, dear Celia, 291 Q
Nobles Seigneurs, salut!, 234 E
Nobody knows de trouble I've seen, 68 B
Nobody who was anybody believed it, 206 C
Noces, Les, 360 D
Noces de Jeanette, Les, 221 G
Noch bleibe denn unausgesprochen, 416 P
Noch ein Weilchen, 344 J

Noch glaub' ich dem, 355 A
Noch in meines Lebens Lenze war ich, 322 J
Noch seh ich die Wellen toben, 422 O
Nöck, Der, 210 B
Nocturne, 65 A, 78 A, 108 P, 118 C, 148 C, 218 E, 389 Q
Nocturne jardin, 110 P
Noden's song, 176 F
Noël, 108 O, 176 L
Noël des enfantes qui n'ont plus de maisons, 89 C
Noël des Jouets, Le, 298 F
Noël, Noëi! Sous le ciel étonné, 225 P
Noël Païen, 225 P
Noël Provençal, 384 D
Noi donne poverine, 242 S
Noi siamo figlie, 218 N
Noi siamo zingarelle, 402 G
Noisy streets are empty, The, 200 K
Non! ce n'est point en sacrifice!, 128 R
Non colombelle!, 220 P
Non contrastar, cogl' uomini, 378 J
Non credo, 427 F
Non cura il ciel tirano, 245 F
Non è ver, 8 I
Non fu sogno, 397 G
Non ho colpa, 244 I
Non imprecare, 396 S
Non, je ne crois pas, 424 B
Non, je n'irai plus au bois, 424 C
Non la sospiri, 286 H
Non lasciar, 153 E
Non lo dirò col labbro, 158 E
Non maledirmi, o prode, 394 E
Non me lo dite, 385 O
Non mi dir, 251 B
Non mi negate, ohimè, 121 B
Non mi resta che il pianto, 219 D
Non mi tentar!, 206 E
Non pianger, mia compagna, 393 M
Non piangere, Liù, 287 B
Non piango, e non sospiro, 70 K
Non più andrai, 248 F
Non più d'amore, 105 O
Non più di fiori, 254 S
Non più mesta accanto, 308 J
Non sai tu che se l'anima, 393 C
Non sapete quale affetto. 402 S
Non senti tu ne l'aria. 385 A
Non siate ritrosi, 252 G
Non so d'onde viene, 249 H
Non so più cosa son, 248 B
Non so qual io mi voglio, 302 A
Non so se sia la speme, 156 R
Non sono buffone, 439 P
Non t'amo più, 385 P
Non temer amato bene, 249 F
Non toccherò mai più arco, 441 I
Non v'è in China, 287 D
Non vi piacque, 157 G
Non vos relinquam orphanos, 70 E
None but the lonely heart, 377 R
None shall part us, 364 J
Nonne und der Ritter, Die, 56 F
Nonnes qui reposez sous cette froide pierre, 235 E
Norden, 342 S
Norma, 38 I

Norrona folket det vil fare, 142 K
North Star, The, 128 L
Norwegian echo song, 384 B
Nos qui sumus in hoc mundo, 202 M
Nos sentiers aimés, 78 D
Nos souvenirs, 78 B
Nostra morte è il trionfo della mor, La, 126 M
Not all my torments, 291 P
Not anymore, 383 G
Not that I'm fair, dear, 173 P
Note è bela, La, 146 M
Nothing I have ever heard, 236 S
Nothung! Nothung!, 414 P
Notre amour, 108 I
Notre amour est règlé, 279 M
Notre métier, 47 A
Notte, 302 J
Notte, al davanzale, Una, 302 L
Notte d'amore, 85 B
Notte e giorno faticar, 249 R
Nous allons partir, 132 F
Nous aurons des lits pleins d'odeurs, légères, 88 K
Nous avons en tête une affaire, 46 O
Nous avons fait la nuit, 282 J
Nous avons fait un beau voyage, 147 A
Nous bénissons la douce nuit, 196 K
Nous n'avons plus de maisons, 89 C
Nous venions de voir le taureau, 90 K
Nous vivrons à Paris, 223 H
Nova vobis gaudia, 140 G
Nous voulons une petite soeur, 281 I
Nóvérek, A. 194 J
Now ain't dem hard trials, 67 P
Now came still evening on, 186 B
Now cease, my wand'ring eyes, 99 B
Now hearken to my strict command, 369 M
Now heav'n in fullest glory, 169 S
Now here's a first rate opportunity, 368 N
Now I am all with fever shaken, 128 H
Now is the gentle season, 241 I
Now is the month of maying, 241 J
Now 'neath the silver moon, 83 Q
Now, o now I needs must part, 99 D
Now Phoebus sinketh in the West, 6 L
Now ponder well, ye parents dear, 271 N
Now sleeps the crimson petal, 294 C
Now tell us, we pray you, 367 I
Now that the sun hath veil'd his light, 290 L
Now the columns upholding the temple, 48 M
Now the dancing sunbeams play, 171 O
Now up and move again, 183 O
Nozani-nà, 406 H
Nozze di Figaro, Le, K. 492, 247 O
Nu brister i alle de klofter, 4 I

Nu ringer alle Klokker mod sky, 426 R
Nu vaagne alle Guds Fugle smaa, 426 S
Nuit, La, 196 K
Nuit a des douceurs de femme, La, 89 H
Nuit d'automne, 310 I
Nuit descend du haut des cieux, La, 108 O
Nuit d'espagne, 225 Q
Nuit d'étoiles, 89 D, 427 G
Nuit d'hyménée, 137 H
Nuit était pensive, 78 A
Nuit froide, La, 201 Q
Nuit, sur le grand mystère, 108 P
Nuits d'Eté, Les, 42 J
Nulla impresa per huom si tenta, 240 J
Nume, custode, 391 I
Numi, pietà del mio soffrir, 391 G
Nun die Schatten dunkeln, 119 I, 311 K
Nun, du wirst, mein Gewissen stillen, 14 B
Nun hast du mir ersten Schmerz gethan, 334 K
Nun heissen sie mich meiden, 175 H
Nun in Lust und Leide, 344 D
Nun ist die Heil und die Kraft, 11 K
Nun ist wohl Sanges Ende, 112 P
Nun komm, der Heiden Heiland, 12 F
Nun lass uns Frieden schliessen, 434 H
Nun merk ich erst, 319 J
Nun mögt ihr stolzen Feinde schrecken, 25 J
Nun seh' ich wohl, 214 I
Nun sei bedankt, mein lieber Schwann, 409 I
Nun stehen die Rosen in Blüthe, 339 G
Nun takes the veil, A, 30 N
Nun waltet Stille über Flur und Feld, 337 I
Nun wandre, Maria, 434 I
Nur wer die Sehnsucht kennt, 338 H
Nun will die Sonn' so hell aufgeh'n, 214 H
Nun, wohlan es muss ja sein, 347 R
Nun zag ich dir zum ersten Mal, 316 P
Nun ziehen Tage über die Welt, 42 B
Nunc dimittis, 268 M
Nur ein Wink von seinen Händen, 25 I
Nur eine Waffe taugt, 412 Q
Nur getrost, 105 E
Nur wer die Sehnsucht kennt, 323 M, 328 J, 377 R, 433 L
Nursery, The, 258 H
Nussbaum, Der, 330 S
Nymphes attentives, 136 P
Nymphs and shepherds, 288 B
Nymphs et Sylvains, 40 O

O

O admirabile commercium, 268 N
O anjo da guarda, 406 J

O amore, o bella luce, 219 C
O Bächlein meiner Liebe, 317 J
O banger Traum, was flatterst du, 119 F
O be gracious, ye immortals, 228 C
O beau pays de la Touraine, 234 F
O beauteous Queen, 159 J
O beaux rêves évanouis, 312 H
O bei nidi d'amore, 93 K
O bellissimi capelli, 105 P
O Bessie Bell, 272 S
O Bien, aimé, 224 H
O black swan, where, oh, where, 232 D
O blanche Tyndaris, 148 Q
O blanches colombe du soir, 146 N
O blicke, wenn den Sinn dir will die Welt, 339 D
O bone Jesu, 268 O
O Bože lásky, 345 M
O bricht nicht, Steg, 55 Q
O Care, thou wilt despatch me, 424 R
O cease thy singing maiden fair, 294 Q
O cessate di piagarmi, 315 G
O cet ennui bleu dans le coeur, 78 G
O Charlie is my darling, 37 K
O che bel mestiere, 219 J
O chiome d'or, 238 R
O ciel — quel supplice, quelle douleur, 129 B
O cieli azzurri, 392 A
O coeur ami! O coeur promis, 76 N
O Colombina il tenero, 206 I
O come, ev'ry one that thirsteth, 227 K
O come, let us worship, 149 K
O cruel case, 273 E
O crux ave, 266 S
O cuor, dono funesto, 278 B
O danke nicht für diese Lieder, 119 P
O dass ich dir vom stillen Auge, 35 L
O dass ich doch Räuber wäre, 237 D
O de Glory Road, 437 P
O death, where is thy sting?, 164 C
O del mio amato ben, 93 L
O del mio dolce arder, 132 A
O, der Alpen blanke Kette, 112 O
O die Frauen, O die Frauen, 63 A
O Dieu Brahma, 47 L
O Dieu de quelle ivresse, 264 Q
O Dieu, Dieu de nos pères, 149 A
O Dieu donne-moi deliverance, 180 A
O Divin Rédempteur, 138 K
O Divine Redeemer, 138 J
O dolci mani, 286 R
O Domine Jesu, 407 J
O Domine Jesu Christe, 109 A, 189 P
O don fatale, 393 O
O doux printemps d'autrefois, 225 Q
O dry those tears, 303 Q
O du Entrissne mir und meinem Küsse, 321 O
O du guter, armer Knabe, 344 C

O du mein holder Abendstern, 417 J

O euriges Feuer, o Ursprung der Liebe, 10 M

O Ewigkeit, du Donnerwort, 9 K

O eyes, O mortal stars, 111 N

O fänd ich Jubelweisen, 409 N

O Fatime, meine Traute, 421 F

O felix Roma, 267 A

O Felsen, lieber Felsen, 58 O

O fier jeune homme, 313 R

O figlio, 277 F

O Fledermaus, 352 I

O fleur fanée, 51 E

O for the wings of a dove, 231 J

O forêt d'Ephraim, 179 C

O forêt, toi qui vis passer bien des amants, 73 C

O forze recondite, 74 P

O fraiche nuit, nuit transparente, 118 C

O Freund, ich werde sie nicht mehr wiedersehen, 197 G

O Freund, mein Schirm, mein Schutz!, 338 P

O fröhlich Stunden, 69 C

O Frühlings Abend dämmerung, 59 F

O gieb vom weichen' Pfühle träumend, 328 O

O gladsome light, 374 M

O God, have mercy, 227 Q

O grandi occhi, 126 N

O great is the depth, 227 S

O grido di quest' anima, 277 S

O grosse Lieb', 25 Q

O Harp of Erin, 36 J

O Heil der Mutter, 415 H

O Heil euch, 34 N

O Heiland reiss die Himmel auf, 54 M

O Himmel! Lass' dich jetzt erflehen, 417 D

O Hoffnung holde!, 301 C

O holder Tag, 19 N

O, holdes Bild, 83 E

O, how can I be blithe and glad, 37 P

O ihr Herren, o ihr werthen, 333 J

O irmengard, 112 K

O Isis und Osiris, 253 N, 254 B

O jak blahá krásná tato chvile, 346 L

O jakou tisen, 347 D

O je, O je, wie rührt mich dies, 351 G

O Jenny, where hast thou been?, 271 K

O Jesu Christe, 41 M

O Jesulein süss, o Jesulein mild, 29 B

O joie de mon âme, 297 J

O jours heureux, 233 S

O Jugend, o schöne Rosenzeit, 229 O

O, kdyby on mé, 346 R

O kehr' zurück, 210 N

O king of glory, 217 G

O komme, holde Sommernacht, 57 R

O kühler Wald, 59 J

O Lamm Gottes unschuldig, 29 Q

O lass dich halten gold'ne Stunde, 188 F

O lass die Treue neimals wanken, 217 L

O légère hirondelle, 135 Q

O les passions en allées, 78 I

O Liberté, m'amie, 222 R

O lieb', 208 O

O lieber Herre Gott, 340 D

O liebliche Wangen, 57 G

O Lola, bianca, 219 E

O Lord our fathers oft have told, 44 M

O lovely moon, 101 J

O loving wisdom of our God, 104 E

O luce di quest' anima, 96 O

O Ludmilla!, 128 C

O ma belle rebelle, 138 H

O ma fille, 349 D

O ma lyre immortelle, 137 L

O ma tendre amie, 174 H

O ma tendre musette, 424 D

O Madame voilà ce qu'il faudrait comprendre, 179 R

O Mädchen, mein Mädchen, 203 E

O madre, dal cielo, 397 D

O magic castle, 183 K

O Magnum Mysterium. 407 K

O marchand si riche, 294 H

O' Marì! O Marì, 73 I

O Mary, at thy window be, 37 R

O Mary Mother Virgin mild, 5 C

O me beata Ritorna, 41 B

O Medjé, qui d'un sourire. 138 D

O, mein Heer, 258 C

O mein Leid ist unermessen, 421 I

O mein Ratmir, dich seh' ich wieder hier, 128 E

O, men from the fields, 32 F, 381 M

O Mensch, bewein' dein' Sünde' gross, 27 K

O Mensch errette deine Seele, 9 L

O Menscheit o Leben!, 329 L

O Menschen, die ihr täglich sündigt, 17 A

O mer, ouvre-toi, linceul du monde, 90 I

O Mère des amours, 201 S

O messager de Dieu. 224 R

O mhairead og, 190 P

O mia Regina, 393 P

O might I but my Patrick love, 36 K

O Mimi tu più non torni, 294 A

O mio Fernando, 95 Q

O mio piccolo tavolo, 206 N

O mio rimorso!, 401 S

O Miranda Dei Caritas, 4 S

O Mirtillo, 239 F

O misèr des Rois, 42 G

O mistress mine, 70 F. 293 G

O mon cher amant, 265 L

O mon maître, o mon Grand, 222 C

O monumento, 278 A

O mort! Venez finir mon destin, 212 K

O mort vieux capitaine, 140 R

O my Savishna, 258 E

O my warriors. 104 G

O Nachtigall, dein süsser Schall, 61 B

O Nadir, tendre ami, 47 P

O nature, plein de grâce, 225 C

O nevyslovné s těsti lásky, 345 E

O noble lame, étincelant, 221 P

O nuit d'amour, 135 E

O nume tutelar, 349 F

O occhi manza mia, 205 E

O palais radieux, 303 D

O pallida che un giorno, 219 B

O paradis, 233 K

O Pastorelle, 126 D

O peaceful England, 123 I

O petits enfants, 306 O

O pine-tree lonely standing, 314 F

O Polly, you might have toy'd and kiss'd, 271 K

O ponder well!, 271 N

O porte de l'hotel, 281 H

O premier rossignol, 148 L

O principi, 287 F

O printemps donne lui ta goutte, 381 J

O pure and gentle soul, 287 L

O qual funesto, 97 S

O quam gloriosum, 407 L

O quam tristis et afflicta, 274 I

O rendetemi il mio bene, 151 N

O rest in the Lord. 227 H

O rex gloria, 217 G

O riante nature, 136 N

O Richard, ô mon Roi, 141 J

O Rosalinde, il me faudrait gravir le Pinde, 223 O

O Rose, thou art sick, 65 B

O ruddier than the cherry, 158 M

O Sachs! mein Freund!, 411 L

O sacred oracles of truth, 159C

O säh' ich auf der Haide dort, 230 D

O salutaris hostia, 78 O

O Sancta Justitia, 211 D

O schöne Jugendtage, 191 Q

O Schwestern, klagt mit mir, 377 K

O Seelen Paradies, 18 R

O selige Träume, 261 P

O Seligkeit, dich fass'ich kaum, 421 K

O serre au milieu des forêts. 78 F

O signore, dal tetto natio, 397 H

O sink' hernieder, Nacht, 417 O

O slys to, předaleky svete, 346 M

O soave fanciulla, 283 M

O soft embalmer of the still midnight, 65 E

O sole mio, 73 J

O sole più ratto, 97 Q

O solitude my sweetest choice, 292 K

O sommo Carlo, 394 R

O song that from the sap art pouring, 176 B

O Sonnenschein, 332 S

O souverain, o juge, 221 S

O sprich wovon die Nachtigall, 378 S

O statua gentilissima, 251 A

O süsser Mai, 357 Q

O süsseste Wonne!, 413 P

O Sylvelin. 343 M

O Tanz, O Rausch, 197 E

O temps à jamais effacé, 87 G

O tentatrice!, 285 O

O terra addio, 392 K

O. Thäler weit o Höhen, 229 Q

O that it were so, 64 F

O the days of the Kerry dancing, 237 L
O the sad day, 184 H
O the time is long Mavourneen, 200 S
O thou billowy harvest field, 294 R
O thou doe, what vistas, 175 R
O, thou that tellest good tidings to Zion, 162 P
O Tod, wie bitter bist du, 61 S
O toi, de qui l'absence, 174 I
O toi, l'objet le plus aimable, 130 D
O toi qui berce un rêve, 107 I
O toi, qui m'abandonnes, 234 T
O toi, qui prolongeas mes jours, 130 J
O tu. che regoli, 96 S
O tu, Palermo, 404 D
O unbewölktes Leben!, 329 I
O vagabonda stella d'oriente, 80 D
O vecchio cor, 394 D
O versenk, o versenk dein Leid, 55 J
O vin de vigne, 202 A
O vin dissipe la tristesse, 380 G
O vos omnes, 240 R, 407 M
O vy lípy, 346 I
O war dein Haus durchsichtig wie ein Glas, 434 J
O wär' ich am Neckar, 1 B
O wär' ich schon mit dir vereint, 32 R
O was klag' ich um Ehe und Eid, 414 B
O was muss es die Engel gekostet haben, 175 M
O water, voice of my heart, 71 L
O welche Lust!, 33 D
O wert thou here, 342 N
O wert thou in the cauld blast, 230 D
O what comfort to the senses, 170 K
O what if the fowler, 293 A
O what num'rous charms, 170 I
O wie ängstlich, 245 K
O wie gerne blieb ich, 355 F
O wie lieblich ist das Mädchen, 339 M
O wie sanft die Quelle, 63 H
O wie schön die Worte, 211 H
O, wie schön ist deine Welt, 327 O
O. wie will ich triumphiren, 246 E
O Winter, schlimmer Winter, 229 M
O Woche, Zeugin heiliger Beschwerde, 432 P
O Wonne! Mein Hüton!, 422 Q
O wunderbare Harmonie, 171 J
O wüsst ich doch den Weg zurück, 58 M
Ob ich gehe, ob ich stehe, 140 S
Obal, din lou Limouzi, 72 K
Obéissons quand leur voix appelle, 223 Q
Oben in den Birnenbaum, 301 A
Oberon, 422 J
Obersteiger, Der, 441 Q
Obligato, ah! si, obligato, 94 S
Oblivion soave, 239 L
Obsecro, dómine. 74 C
Obstination. 114 K
Occasional Oratorio, 164 H

Occhi belli, 68 J
Occhi immortali, 70 M
Occhi sempre sereni, 297 E
Occhi soavi, 441 L
Occhietti amati, 105 Q
Ocean, thou mighty monster, 422 N
Och Mod'r ich well en Ding han, 62 K
Ode on St. Cecelia's Day, 291 R
Ode to Cynthia's walking on Richmond Hill, 292 D
Ode to Queen Mary, 292 E
Ode to St. Cecilia, 150 M
Odesli Jdi take!, 186 O
Odeur de vous flottait, L', 111 P
Odins Meeresritt, 209 P
Odysseus, 65 N
Oedipus, 288 A
O'er Nelson's tomb with silent grief, 53 B
O'er the hills, 181 A
O'er the tarn's unruffled mirror, 145 E
O'er yon mountainous height, 305 G
Ouvre ton coeur, 48 A
Of a noble race was Shenkin, 272 J
Of all the birds that I do know, 31 D
Of all the friends in time of grief, 273 F
Of all the girls, 273 F
Of all the girls that are so smart, 37 I, 73 R
Of all the simple things we do, 271 H
Of all the wives as e'er you know, 2 K
Of all the young ladies I know, 364 N
Of happiness the very pith, 362 M
Of Household Rule, 175 G
Of priests we can offer a charmin' variety, 349 O
Offertorium, 43 M, 109 A, 198 K, 243 D
Offne dich, mein ganzes Herze, 12 G
Offrande, 148 D
Oft am Rande stiller Fluten, 347 S
Oft denk ich, sie sind nur ausgegangen!, 214 K
Oft on a plot of rising ground, 150 K
Oft she visits, 288 N
Ofver drifvans iskristall, 342 Q
Og det war Olar Trygvason, 143 D
Og vad du den Dröm, 144 C
Ogni pena più spietata, 273 N
Ogni vento, 151 E
Oh! a private buffoon. 374 E
Oh, answer me a question, 361 R
Oh Bess, oh where's my Bess, 124 G
Oh Béthulie, Béthulie abandonnée, 178 N
Oh better far to live and die, 368 E
Oh, bitter joy! No words can tell, 373 A
Oh, boys, carry me 'long, 116 B
Oh breathe not his name, 349 P
Oh, but to hear thy voice, 378 I

Oh by an' by, 67 K
Oh, Caesar, great wert thou, 376 E
Oh! che muso, 308 S
Oh come to me!, 29 Q
Oh! Das wurde mir nun doch zu dumm!, 198 J
Oh de' verd' anni miei, 394 P
Oh! dear! what can the matter be?, 5 I
Oh, didn't it rain, 68 C
Oh! dolci baci, 286 Q
Oh, don't the days seem lank and long, 370 L
Oh, dry the glist'ning tear, 368 R
Oh excelso muro, 106 P
Oh fair enough are sky and plain, 68 N
Oh Father, whose almighty pow'r, 161 C
Oh, foolish fay, 365 B
Oh for you and me poor mother, 183 A
Oh, gentlemen, listen, 373 J
Oh, give me a home, 146 A
Oh, goddess wise that lovest light, 370 D
Oh, god-like youth, 165 D
Oh, had I Jubal's lyre, 160 R
Oh, happy the lily when kissed by the bee, 371 O
Oh, happy young heart, comes the young lad a-wooing, 372 I
Oh! have you seen the blushing rose, 180 M
Oh he cam' whistlin' up the glen, 30 J
Oh, here is love, and here is truth, 369 F
Oh I lived with my daddy, 64 M
Oh, if you could, 305 K
Oh ihr, der Eide ewige Hüter, 416 D
Oh I'm agoin' out to de Blackfish banks, 123 S
Oh, in the silent night, 294 P
Oh, is there not one maiden breast, 368 I
Oh! it's quiet down here, 53 F
Oh joy, oh rapture unforseen, 364 F
Oh, joy to be musing, 439 S
Oh, joy unbounded, with wealth surrounded. 373 L
Oh, la pitoyable aventure!, 299 Q
Oh Lawd, I'm on my way, 124 H
Oh Lemuel, 116 D
Oh! les filles, 109 L
Oh Liberty! thou choicest treasure, 161 L
Oh living I come, tell me why, 366 O
Oh London is a fine town, 271 I
Oh Lord, whom we adore, 158 S
Oh Lord, whose mercies numberless, 165 E
Oh! Lou'siana's de same old state, 115 N
Oh love, true love! unwordly, abiding, 372 Q
Oh, lovely peace, 162 I
Oh! ma petite princesse, 341 Q
Oh, Marie, 73 H
Oh! Mary go, 82 A
Oh, mely sok hal, 193 O

Oh meurte cruel, 139 O
Oh! mio babbino caro, 284 K
Oh, Mister, please be good, 258 R
Oh! moi quand je suis dans la rue, 76 P
Oh, my lover is a fisherman, 361 N
Oh! ne murmurez pas son nom!, 100 G
Oh! ne repousse pas mon âme, 138 J
Oh! ne t'éveille pas encore, 132 H
Oh, never shall I forget the cry, 366 L
Oh, oh, oh, oh, Mummy, 258 O
Oh patria mia, 391 S
Oh, Peter, go ring-a dem bells, 68 D
Oh, pretty maiden, 86 G
Oh, promise me, 197 M
Oh qual soave brivido, 393 D
Oh, quand je dors, 199 R, 208 N
Oh! quanta tenera gioia, 302 N
Oh! quanti occhi, 285 A
Oh! quanto io t'amerei, 385 R
Oh! qui me donnera, 302 Q
Oh Rose Marie, I love you, 121 K
Oh, se sapeste, 284 G
Oh sleep, why dost thou leave me, 165 K
Oh, some are fond of red wine, 376 D, 420 C
Oh stay, my love, 294 O
Oh, Susanna, 116 F
Oh! sweet were the hours, 37 M
Oh tell me, beloved, 439 Q
Oh! tell me, Harper, 36 N
Oh, that kiss in the dark, 123 G
Oh that now I held the scythe, 102 A
Oh, that we two were Maying, 138 G, 261 E
Oh, the happy days of doing!, 374 J
Oh, the old turf fire, 182 G
Oh! the pretty, pretty creature, 350 J
Oh, 'tis a glorious thing, 362 K
Oh, 'tis earth defiled, 166 N
Oh! Tsarevitch, 256 O
Oh, tu che in seno agli angeli, 396 H
Oh, what a beautiful city, 49 A
Oh! what pain it is to part, 271 R
Oh, when I was in love with you, 389 G
Oh, who, my dear Dermot, 36 L
Oh! why am I moody and sad?, 371 J
Oh would but Heav'n in pity, 378 I
Oh, you dearest, 351 B
Oh you little chocolate soldier man, 350 O
Ohimè ch'io cado, 239 D
Ohimè dor' è il mis ben, 239 E
O'seau qui pars, 222 F
Oiseaux de la charmille, Les, 264 N
Oiseaux quand sont ravis, Les, 187 G
Oiseaux, si tous les ans, K. 307, 243 S
Ojos Negros, Los, 4 K
Ol' man river, 191 K

Ola, O che bon echo, 202 N
Old black Joe, 116 G
Old Corporal, The, 86 F
Old dog Tray, 116 I
Old folks at home, 116 K
Old hundred, 52 M
Old refrain, The, 198 C
Old Simon the Cellarer, 168 H
Old Song Resung, An, 144 Q
Old turf fire, The, 182 G
Old witch within that wood, An, 183 C
Old woman, The, 305 S
Old woman clothed in gray, An, 271 D
Old Xeres we'll drink Manzanilla, 362 P
Oliver Cromwell lay buried and dead, 64 O
Oluf's Ballade, 122 B
Olympische Hymne, 359 N
Ombra cara, 154 R
Ombra mai fu, 156 S
Ombre des arbes, L', 87 P, 148 F
Ombre discrète, L', 304 H
Ombre est douce, L', 298 Q
Ombre légère, 233 O
Ombre opache, 315 H
Ombre, piante, 155 P
Omens, 103 H
Omnes, omnes generationes, 22 B
On a tree by a river, 366 P
On dit que le plus fier c'est moi, 186 J
On l'appelle Manon, 223 K
On me nomme Hélène la blonde, 264 F
On mighty pens uplifted, 169 P
On Richmond Hill there lives a lass, 180 K
On Saints' Day at Chigisakh, 361 D
On sunny days in our back yard, 186 F
On the banks of Allan Water, 181 D
On the brow of Richmond Hill, 292 D
On the day when I was wedded, 362 S
On the first day of May, 167 Q
On the Georgian hills, 305 H
On the massacre of Glencoe, 36 N
On the plains, 424 S
On the river, 259 Q
On the River Dnieper, 258 P
On the Road Home, 143 H
On the Road to Mandalay, 348 H
On tresse on tressera la tresse, 360 E
On voit des marquis, 280 N
On Wenlock Edge, 389 D
On wings of song, 228 O
Onaway! Awake, beloved, 82 K
Once a gnat, as all gnats should, 256 I
Once a pike swam out of Novgorod, 361 E
Once again, but how chang'd, 36 P
Once I went to market, 195 D
Once in a while and where, 382 O
Once more I hail thee, 36 M
Once Panonia lay in dire distress, 195 H

One flame-winged, 388 J
One morning in the month of May, 390 G
One sails away to the sea, 213 E
One small loaf is all my living, 195 R
One small word, 378 E
One spring morning, 261 F
One sweetly solemn thought, 4 N
Only a rose, 121 L
Only girl, The, 174 B
Onore! Ladri, L', 395 C
Onward, Christian soldiers, 375 A
Opal dream enchants the lake, An, 145 D
Open thy lattice, love, 116 L
Or che il cielo a me ti rende, 245 G
Or che tutti, o mio tesoro, 251 H
Or co dadi, ma fra poco giocherem, 403 I
Or damni il braccio tuo, 220 N
Or if more influencing, 287 R
Or la mia fede il desiderio, 385 Q
Or let the merry bells ring round, 150 H
Or musio tranquillo, 396 G
Or sai, che l'onore, 250 H
Or solo intorno, 220 Q
Or son sei mesi, 284 H
Or sus, or sus, vous dormez, 186 R
Or sus, serviteurs du Seigneur, 375 I
Ora e per sempre addio, 399 B
Ora in terra, 277 O
Ora pro nobis, 242 M
Ora si, ch'io son contenta, 247 P
Orage s'est calmé L', 47 P
Oraison, 78 J
Oraison domincale, 73 D
Orange Blossoms, 173 F
Oratorio de Noël, 313 B
Orchard, 176 D
Ore dolci e divine, 286 B
Oreg vagyok már én, 195 Q
Orfeo. 239 M
Orfeo ed Euridice. 130 Q
Oriental chant, 258 S
Orlando, 153 R
Ornen löfter med stoerke Slag, 172 K
Oro, o Tirsi, è vaga e bella, L', 285 M
Oro supplex et acclinis, 405 B
Orphan-girl, The, 258 R
Orpheus, 329 A
Orpheus with his lute, 6 N, 375 B, 389 J
Orride steppe! Torrida l'estate!, 127 D
Osana, 23 Q, 169 G. 268 E
Osana in excelsis, 255 N
Osana, osana in excelsis, 34 F
Osanna, 389 A
Ostende nobis domine, 84 G
Othello, 398 J
Ottone, 154 B
Où irons-nous garder? 72 K
Où le bedeau a passé, 280 F
Où va la jeune Indoue, 91 E
Où vas-tu souffle d'aurore, 379 E
Où voulez-vous aller, 138 I
Oublier que je t'ai vue, 91 A
Oui, c'est toi je t'aime, 135 O

Oui! c'est un rêve, 264 G
Oui, dans les bois et dans la plaine, 223 S
Oui, je veux par le monde, 380 N
Oui Marguerite an qui j'espère, 174 L
Ound' onorèn gorda, 72 J, 72 K
Our cockatoo was playing, 256 L
Our Father, which art in heaven, 216 J
Our God, heaven cannot hold him, 177 B
Our great Mikado, virtuous man, 365 H
Our next motion, 288 Q
Our Polly is a sad slut!, 271 I
Out from the vale, 419 P
Out of my lodge at eventide, 210 J
Out of my songs, 347 P
Out of the night that covers me, 182 J
Outward Bound, 142 C
Ouvre tes yeux bleus, 225 R
Ouvre-toi, forêt impénetrable!, 304 L
Ouvrez-vous sur mon front, 222 E
Over field and plain, 283 F
Over hill, over dale, 82 O
Over the Depths of the Sea, 127 K
Over the hills and far away, 271 Q
Over the meadow and homeward, 79 N
Over the mountains, 294 D
Over the Steppe, 140 L
Over yonder clouds are spreading, 194 K
Overhanging the fathomless ocean, 127 K
Ovinu malkenu, 216 N
Ovsen, 361 E
Oyez! Has any found a lad, 384 J
Ozean du Ungeheuer!, 422 N

P

Pace, pace, mio Dio, 396 R
Pace! pace! mio dolce tesoro!, 249 E
Pace, pace, o vita mia!, 250 L
Padraic sits in the garden, 125 K
Padraic the Fidiler, 125 K
Padre adorato, Il, 244 M
Padre! Germani, 244 H
Paganini, 204 D, 281 G
Page, Der, 331 B
Page, The, 311 D
Page sprach, Der, 139 D
Pagenlied, 231 K
Pagliacci, 205 M
Painted emblems of a race, 371 Q
Palästinalied, 418 S
Pale and purple rose, The, 293 A
Pâle aurore, tu viendras Baigner mes yeux, 127 R
Pâle et blonde dort sous l'eau, 380 J
Pale hands I loved, 440 H
Pale Moon, 210 J
Pale shines the moonlight, 259 Q
Palms, The, 111 H
Palmström, 139 C
Paloma, La, 441 G

Panis Angelicus, 118 D
Panis, piscis, crinis, 259 B
Paño moruno, El, 106 I
Pano Murciano, 263 I
Panurge, 225 B
Paolo, datemi pace, 441 O
Paon, Le, 297 R
Papagena! Weibchen, 254 E
Papillon, Le, 117 E
Papillon inconstant, 296 K
Papillons couleur de neige, Les, 78 C
Par che mi nasco in seno, 158·A
Par la crainte, 130 A
Par le rang et par l'opulence, 96 J
Par les nuits sans rivales, 1 G
Par les portes d'Orkenise, 279 I
Par Saint Gilles, 314 A
Par son charme divin, 222 S
Par son père cruel, 130 C
Par un matin Lisette se leva, 424 E
Par une grâce touchante, 141 C
Para jardines Granada, 4 K
Paradies und die Peri, Das, 335 L
Paradis, Le, 3 I
Paradis Retrouvé, Le, 3 L
Paradox, a paradox, A, 369 C
Parásha's revery and dance, 257 F
Pardon de Ploërmel, Le, 233 N
Pardon! mais j'étais là près de vous, 224 A
Pardonne: quand tu m'as aimé, 3 K
Parent bird in search of food, The, 166 A
Parents, quand on est bébé, Les, 146 R
Paresseuse fille, 134 I
Parez vos fronts, 128 P
Parfons regretz, 189 Q
Parfum impérissable, Le, 110 H
Pari siamo, 399 S
Parigi, o cara, noi lasceremo, 402 L
Paris et Helena, 132 A
Parla, 6 B
Parle moi de ma· mère, 46 H
Parmi les pleurs, 234 G
Parmi tant d'amoureux, 221 H
Parmi veder le lagrime, 400 H
Parsifal, 412 C
Parted, 385 S
Partenope, 154 J
Partenza, La, 37 G
Partida, La, 4 L
Parting, The, 30 J, 185 C
Parting without sorrow, 103 B
Partis d'une ménagerie un jour, 235 T
Partite? Crudele, 399 P
Parto, fuggo, 156 H
Parto, parto, ma tu, ben mio, 254 K
Partons en barque sur la mer, 78 E
Parysatis, 313 R
Pas d'armes du Roi Jean, Le, 314 A
Paséabase el Rey Moro, 121 P
Passing by, 293 C, 420 J
Passionate shepherd, The, 420 K
Passionslied, 29 I
Passo pel prat, 72 P
Pastor Fido, Il, 152 I

Pastoral, 64 S, 73 O, 390 S
Pastorale, 48 B, 361 H
Pastorella, La, 329 C
Pastorello d'un povero armento, 155 Q
Pastori, I, 277 D
Pastré, dè dèlaï l'aïo, 72 H
Pasture, The, 260 F
Patience, 366 S
Patrem omnipotentem, 23 H, 66 C, 69 R, 363 R, 388 R
Patria oppressa!, 397 O
Patrie, 266 L
Patron, das macht der Wind, 20 B
Paucitas dierum, 268 P
Paul et Virginie, 221 N
Pause, 317 P
Pauvre laboureur, Le, 384 G
Pauvre martyr obscur, 266 M
Pauvres gens, Les, 76 R
Pax vobiscum, 329 D
Paysage, 148 E
Paysage triste, 148 F
Paysages Belges, 87 Q
Peaceful hermit of simple mind, A, 256 Q
Pear tree, The, 195 F
Peasant cantata, 20 S
Peasant cradle song, 259 A
Peasant tastes the sweets of life, The, 160 M
Peccavimus, 269 C
Pêcheurs de Perles, Les, 47 J
Peer Gynt, 142 L
Pelajanella aberta, 406 Q
Pèlerins étant venus, Les, 42 I
Pellegrina rondinella, 352 L
Pena tiranna, 151 O
Penchée à ma fenêtre, 298 K
Pendant la nuit une rose avance, 179 O
Pendant un an je fus ta femme, 224 L
Pensa al la patria, 309 B
Pense que yo sabria ocultar, 139 K
Pensée d'automne, 225 S
Pensi a me, 171 Q
Penso, 386 A
Penso, oh bella, 156 I
People that walked in darkness, The, 162 Q
Per amor del Dio, 398 E
Per la gloria d'adorarvi, 67 G
Per lui che adoro, 309 A
Per me giunto, 393 Q
Per me ora fatale, 403 G
Per pietà ben mio, 252 N
Per pietà, non dirmi addio, 35 C
Per pietà, non ricercate, K.420, 246 L
Per questa bella mano, 253 B
Per queste tue manine, 250 R
Per salvarti, idolo mio, 153 M
Per sua madre andò una figlia, 96 P
Per te d'immenso giubile, 97 M
Per te ho io nel core, 274 D
Per valli, per boschi, 48 H
Per voi, ghiottoni, inutili, 218 P
Perche di pioggia, 217 H
Perchè tremar, 174 N
Perdida tengo la color, 235 O
Perdonate, Signor mio, 81 F
Peregrina, 434 K
Perfect day, A, 50 P

Perfido, di a quell' empio, 154 S
Peri gliarti ancor languente, 403 E
Périchole, La, 265 K
Perle du Bresil, La, 86 Q
Perle fulgenti cupole dorate, 385 B
Permettez, astre du jour, 296 I
Persée, 212 I
Persian Chorus, 128 D
Persian songs, 311 E
Pescator, affonda l'esca, 278 E
Petit cheval, 341 R
Petit garçon malade, Le, 281 N
Petit rentier, Le, 276 C
Petite dinde: Ah! quel outrage, 232 P
Petite fille sage, La, 281 K
Petite nymphe folastre, 187 I
Petites voix, 281 K
Petrus, der nicht denkt zurück, 26 D
Peut-être bien qu'en ce choc meurtrier, 418 C
Peuvent ils ordonner, 129 P
Phänomen, 434 M
Phidylé, 100 L
Philantropisch, 139 B
Philémon et Baucis, 136 J
Philémon m'aimerait encore, 136 M
Philine, 434 N
Philis, plus avare que tendre, 424 F
Phillis has such charming graces, 441 B
Phillis, I can ne'er forgive it, 292 F
Phoebus and Pan, 20 B
Phoebus eilt, 20 E
Phoenix, Der, 8 G
Phyllis, 148 G
Piaga c'ho nel core', La, 239 G
Pian, pianin!, 249 D
Piangea, 399 L
Piangerò la sorte mia, 153 I
Piangete ohimè, 74 F
Piangi, piangi, fanicuilla, 400 P
Piango su voi, 401 J
Piano, pianissimo, 307 I
Piccola tavola, La, 206 N
Piccolo Marat. Il, 220 G
Pie Jesu, 109 C
Piece en forme de Habanera, 298 G
Pierrot Song, 197 F
Pieta, 175 Q
Pietà, rispetto, amore, 397 R
Pietà, Signore, 350 L
Pietade in suo favore, La, 97 F
Pietoso al par del Numi, 96 B
Piff, paff, piff, paff, 234 C
Pigeons on the grass alas, 382 L
Piggesnie, 420 L
Pike, The, 361 F
Pilgers Morgenlied, 357 R
Pilgrim, Der, 322 J
Pilgrims' Chorus, Tannhäuser, 417 G
Pilgrim's song, 378 L
Pimen's monologue, 256 F
Pimen's tale, 256 Q
Pimpinella, 378 J
Pine-Tree, The. 314 F
Pintade, La, 298 D
Pioggia, 302 K

Pious orgies, pious airs, 161 E
Piovea per le finestra, 302 K
Piper, A, 172 F, 389 K
Piper in the streets today, A, 172 F, 389 K
Piper who sat on his low mossy seat, The, 36 S
Pipes of Pan, The, 104 L
Pique-Dame, 377 G
Pirate Song, 125 P
Pirates of Penzance, The, 368 C
Piros alma leesett a sárba, 193 N
Pity the poor persecutor, 383 D
Più nel dubbio non farmi penare, 6 B
Più non cerca liberta, 158 B
Più tempo, oh Dio, 94 P
Placet futile, 300 C
Plaine de dueil, 189 R
Plaisir d'amour, 217 R
Play to me beneath some summer moon, 84 O
Pleading, 104 M
Plebe! Patrizi, 401 I
Pledge of love, The, 103 C
Pleni sunt coeli et terra gloria tua, 34 E, 23 P
Pleurez! pleurez mes yeux, 221 R
Pleurons nos chagrins, 109 G
Plongeur, Le, 427 H
Plough boy, The, 64 P
Pluck root and branch, 159 K
Plus beau present, Le, 148 H
Plus blanche que la blanche hermine, 234 A
Plus d'amour, plus d'ivresse, 234 K
Plus de dépit, plus de tristesse, 141 E
Plus de tourments, 221 Q
Plus doux chemin, Le, 110 M
Plus grande, dans son obscurité, 137 A
Plus j'observe ces lieux, 129 H, 212 C
Pobre Céga, 406 I
Poèmes d'automne, 48 J
Poèmes de Ronsard, 281 P
Poèmes d'un jour, 108 E
Poèmes juifs, 236 E
Poet's Last Song, The, 142 E
Poichè in iscena, 205 N
Poils de cette chèvre, Les, 279 O
Pojd milko, 348 A
Poland's dirge, 79 O
Polish songs, 78 Q
Polo, 106 O, 263 O
Polonaise, 397 G
Polonaise, from Boris Godunov, 256 N
Polovetsian Dance with Chorus, Prince Igor, 51 K
Polyeucte, 136 O
Pomme et l'escargot, La, 236 B
Pomo d'Oro, Il, 75 H
Pomp and circumstance trio, 105 A
Poor Jonathan, 237 G
Poor soul sat sighing, The, 420 N
Poor wand'ring one, 368 J
Pope Marcellus Mass, 267 Q
Popoli di Tessaglia. K.316, 244 B
Popule meus, 407 O
Por darle gusto a tu gente, 263 N

Por traidores, tus ojos, 106 N
Por un alegre prado de flores, 387 E
Por ver si me consolaba, 106 K
Porgi amor, 248 G
Porgy and Bess, 123 O
Poro, 154 M
Porqué entre sombras, 139 S
Porque es en mis ojos, 140 C
Possente amor mi chiama, 400 J
Possente, possente, 391 H
Possente spirto, 240 G
Post, Die, 319 M
Postillon de Longjumeau, Le, 1 L
Poupette et Patata, 236 A
Pour Bertha moi je soupire, 234 N
Pour ce que plaisance est morte, 89 Q
Pour celle qui m'est chère, 233 E
Pour forth no more unheeded prayers, 160 K
Pour la Vièrge, 223 A
Pour le jour des Hyacinthies, 88 D
Pour me rapprocher de Marie, 96 M
Pour moi sa main cueillait des roses, 117 S
Pour mon pays, 380 B
Pour, O King, the pirate sherry, 368 C
Pour que le nuit, 310 J
Pour que le vént te les apporte, 100 P
Pour toujours, disait elle, 7 O
Pourquoi dans les grands bois, 90 S
Pourquoi leur envier, 296 D
Pourquoi me réveiller, 255 L
Pourquoi n'avez-vous pas surpris, 92 K
Pourquoi ne me bercez-vous plus, 181 P
Povera pellegrina, 315 I
Poveri fiori, 80 Q
Praise God from whom all blessings flow, 52 M
Praise of Harmony, 149 O
Praise to the holiest in the height, 104 D
Praise ye the god of silver, 419 H
P'raps if you address the lady most politely, 369 R
Pray, fair one be kind, 271 P
Prayer, 309 E, 399 M
Pré aux Clercs, Le, 174 F
Preach not me your musty rules, 6 K
Prega per chi adorando a te, 399 M
Preiset ihn, ihr Engelchöre, 34 S
Preist des Erlösers Güte, 34 M
Prenderò quel brunettino, 252 J
Prendi l'anel ti dono, 39 J
Prendi, per me sei libero, 95 F
Prendi quest' è l'immagine, 402 M
Prends cette ile qu'il est toujours, 222 D
Prends mon âme fais une lyre, 236 I
Prenes mon bras un moment, 135 C
Près des ramparts de Séville, 46 K
Près du Jourdain, 236 K
Presentation of the Rose, 355 M
Presto, presto, 113 N

Pretty creature, The, 350 J
Pretty maiden, 86 G
Pretty mocking bird, 45 R
Pretty Polly, say, 271 O
Pretty ring time, 420 M
Pria che spunti in ciel l'aurora, 81 D
Prières, Les, 73 D, 178 A
Prigioniera, abbandonata, 122 H
Prigioniera, ho l'alma in pena, 155 R
Prima di tutto, 395 G
Prince Igor, 51 A
Princesita, 266 F
Princess Ida, 369 L
Princess Pat, 173 O
Princess sat high in her lofty bow'r, The, 193 B
Princesse! à jalouser le destin, 300 C
Printemps, 8 C, 148 I
Printemps chasse les hivers, Le, 137 N
Printemps triste, 78 D
Printemps qui commence, 312 O
Prinz Eugen, 209 M
Prison, 110 J
Prisoner, The, 311 N
Prithee, pretty maiden, prithee, 367 G
Prize Song, Die Meistersinger von Nürnberg, 411 I
Pro peccatis, 310 A
Pro peccatis sue genti, 408 B
Procession, La, 118 E
Prodigal son, The, 374 O
Profitons bien de la jeunesse, 223 R
Promenade, La, 179 J
Promenoir des deux amants, Le, 89 E
Promesse de mon avenir, 224 I
Prometheus, 329 E, 434 O
Pronta io son pur ch'io, 94 D
Prophet, The, 305 M
Prophète, Le, 234 M
Prose lyriques, 89 H
Proserpine, 266 I
Proteger le repos, 265 D
Provenzalisches Lied, 339 Q
Psalm, 178 O
Psalm 19, 133 P
Psalm 20, 340 H
Psalm 22, 48 N
Psalm 23, 325 J
Psalm 25, 133 Q
Psalm 34, 179 S
Psalm 40, 340 A
Psalm 74, 340 I
Psalm 97, 340 J
Psalm 114, 48 O
Psalm 121, 340 K
Psalm 123, 133 R
Psalm 129, De profundis, K.93, 242 J
Psalm 130, 178 I
Psalm 137, 48 P
Psalm 138, 180 B, 375 J
Psalm 140 180 A
Psalm 150, 118 F, 226 E
Psalms and fuguing tunes, 44 N
Psyché, 266 O
Psyche wandelt durch Säulenhallen, 4 B
P'tit fi! P'tit mignon!, 388 D

Puce gentile, Une, 42 M
Puciné, 195 R
Puellare gremium, 5 A
Pueri Hebraeorum, 269 Q
Puisqu' ici bas toute âme, 148 K
Puisque l'aube grandit, 109 S
Puisque partout où nous entraîne, 117 O
Puisque rien ne t'arrête, 47 Q
Pulcinella, 360 P
Pulse of an Irishman, The, 36 O
Pupille nere, 67 H
Pupille sdegnose, 153 O
Pupillette fiammette, 361 C
Pur dicesti, 211 L
Pur to riveggo, 392 D
Pura siccome un angelo, 402 B
Puritani, I, 39 A
Pussy cat, 258 O
Put on de skillet, 437 R

Q

Quae maerebat et dolebat, 274 J
Quaerens me sedisti lassus, 43 K
Quaint name Ann-street, 185 S
Qual farfalletta, 154 L
Qual farfalletta amate, 315 R
Qual honor di te sia degno, 240 L
Qual nave smarrita, 155 A
Qual occhio al mondo, 286 I
Qual piacer!, 309 C
Qual piacere, qual dolcezza, 131 S
Qual volutà trascovere, 397 F
Qualunque via dischiuda, 133 F
Quam dilecta, 296 M
Quam olim Abrahae, 255 L, 405 F
Quam pulchra es, 100 C
Quand apparaissent les étoiles, 222 B
Quand ce beau printemps je voy, 8 C
Quand ero paggio, 395 K
Quand il s'agit de tromperie, 46 P
Quand j'ay esté, 187 J
Quand je boy, 187 K
Quand je fus pris au pavillon, 148 J
Quand je quittai la Normandie, 235 D
Quand je te vois souffrir, 3 M
Quand je vais au jardin, 408 F
Quand la femme a vingt ans, 222 A
Quand la flamme de l'amour, 47 H
Quand la fleur du soleil, 110 H
Quand le ciel et mon heure, 281 Q
Quand le marin revint, 384 H
Quand le silence et le mystère, 296 B
Quand le soleil s'enfuit, 133 N
Quand le son du cor s'endort, 180 F
Quand l'enfant s'endort, 303 H
Quand les cloches du soir, 117 R
Quand mon mary vient de dehors, 202 B
Quand nos jours s'éteindront, 222 Q
Quand papa trouve un hérisson, 281 O
Quand ta voix céleste, 137 O

Quand ton sourire me surprit, 77 Q
Quand tu chantes bercéle le soir, 138 M
Quand viendra la saison nouvelle, 42 J
Quando al mio sen, 404 F
Quando corpus morietur, 274 R
Quando da brisa, 407 B
Quando la patria, 221 D
Quando le sere al placido, 397 M
Quando le soglie paterne, 95 N
Quando mai spietata sorte, 155 B
Quando me'n vo', 283 P
Quando mi sei vicina, 308 D
Quando minha irma movreu, 406 J
Quando nascesti tu, 133 J
Quando navravi, 398 O
Quando repito, 97 H
Quando sorge la luna, 385 J
Quando to rivedrò, 93 M
Quando tu mi guardi e ridi, 216 S
Quann'a femmena vo', 85 C
Quant j'ai ouy le tabourin, 87 K
Quant Theseus, 214 A
Quanto dolci, 153 A
Quanto è bella! quanto è cara, 94 O
Quanto godrà, 150 S
Quanto mai felice siete, 152 N
Quarany, Il, 133 D
Quartet from Faust, 135 C
Quatre chansons pour voix grave, 178 J
Quatre chants populaires, 298 I
Quatre petits lions, Les, 235 T
Quatre versets d'un motet, 84 H
Quattro Rusteghi, I, 439 O
Qu' autour de moi tout sombre, 91 M
Que de fois seul, 113 G
Que fais-tu, blanche tourterelle, 137 G
Que j'aime tes yeux éveilles!, 264 I
Que le jour brille, 378 M
Que lentement passent les heures, 177 M
Que les songes heureux, 136 L
Que l'hymne nuptial, 137 I
Que m'importe que l'infante, 310 Q
Que ne suis-je la fougère, 424 G
Que rien ne trouble ici, 212 M
Que te dirai-Je, 235 S
Que ton âme si noble, 309 F
Que veulent dire ces colères, 265 M
Que vois-je? O spectacle effroyable, 212 E
Quebra O Côco, Menino, 145 P
Queen and huntress chaste and fair, 65 D
Queen of Lochlin, The, 190 H
Queen of Sheba, The, 132 R, 136 R
Queen of spades, 377 G
Queen of the Night aria, 253 Q
Queen's Epicedium, The, 292 G
Queen's lace handkerchief, The, 353 A
Quel bonheur je respire, 7 N
Quel galant m'est comparable, 297 I

Quel guardo il cavaliere, 94 B
Quel l'otre! quel tino!, 395 E
Quel ruscelletto, 270 G
Quel son, quelle preci solenni, 403 P
Quella che tutta fé, 157 A
Quella fiamma che m'accende, 217 C
Quelle douce clarté vient éclairer, 235 Q
Quelle prière de reconnaissance, 225 D
Questa dunque è l'iniqua mercede, 394 G
Questa è Mimi, 283 N
Questa è una ragna dove il tuo, 399 I
Questa o quella, 399 O
Questa vita cosi amara, 251 K
Qu'est-ce donc sur la garenne, 179 K
Qu'est-ce qui brille?, 76 K
Questi i campi di Tracia, 240 N
Questo è il fin, 251 I
Qui dat nivem, 84 K
Qui del padre ancor respira, 97 P
Qui dinanzi all' altare giuro, 276 H
Qui donc commande, 312 I
Qui est-tu inconnu, 281 L
Qui jamais fut de plus charmant visage, 184 J
Qui la voce sua soave, 39 D
Qui le Napee vezzose schiera, 240 B
Qui Mariam absolvisti, 405 A
Qui mi manca un mezzo foglio, 308 C
Qui miri il sole vostre carole, 239 P
Qui propter, 263 S
Qui propter nos, 213 Q
Qui sedes ad dextram Patris, 23 C
Qui sola vergin rosa, 113 K
Qui te fait si sévère, 224 O
Qui tollis, 33 Q, 168 S, 243 H, 246 R, 268 A
Qui tollis peccata, 29 C
Qui tollis peccata mundi, 23 B
Quia fecit mihi magna, 22 C
Quia quem meruisti portare, 242 L
Quia respexit humilitatem, 22 A
Quid sum miser, 43 I, 404 P
Quien amores ten afinque, 262 R
Quien lo habia de deci, 106 E
Qu'il est cruel d'aimer, 141 F
Qu'il eut la dernière pensée, 235 C
Quinquireme of Nineveh from distant Ophir, 92 Q
Quis est homo, 274 K, 309 S
Qu'on ne me dise, 84 D
Quoniam, 243 J, 246 S
Quoniam advena ego, 359 Q
Quoniam tu solus, 169 A
Quoniam tu solus sanctus, 23 D
Quond onorèn o lo fièïro, ié, 72 L
Quoy qu'on tient belles langagières, 89 N
Qu'un autre se marie, 221 G

R

Raccogli e calma, 279 B
Rachel, quand du Seigneur, 149 F

Rachem, 216 N
Radamisto, 154 P
Radiant Night, 144 M
Rain I thought it was, 92 S
Rákoczi kesergöje, 195 S
Rakoczi's lament, 195 S
Ralph's ramble to London, 5 J
Rameaux, Les, 111 H
Ramure aux rumeurs amollies, 110 L
Rançon, La, 107 S
Ranimez vos flambeaux, 296 G
Rankende Rose, 105 J
Rapide comme un rêve, 266 P
Rapture, rapture, when love's votary, 374 K
Rast, 319 J
Raste, Krieger! Krieg ist aus, 322 N
Rastlose Liebe, 320 M
Rat einer Alten, 434 P
Rataplan, 396 P
Rathswahlkantate, 10 F
Rattenfänger, Der, 434 Q
Rauschender Strom, 318 J
Rauschendes Bächlein, 318 F
Re, Il, 127 A
Re dell' abisso, 392 Q
Re pastore, Il, K.208, 243 E
Ready swain, The, 170 J
Realejo, 406 S
Recht wie ein Leichnam, 438 R
Reclined by the waters of Babel, 48 P
Recondita armonia, 286 G
Recordare, 255 C
Recordare, Jesu pie, 404 R
Recruiting, 196 G
Recueillement, 88 J
Red Mill, The, 173 P
Rede, Mädchen allzu liebes, 62 R
Redemption, The, 118 G
Redondilha, 406 R
Reflets dans l'eau, 110 O
Refrain, audacious tar, 363 M
Refuge, Le, 3 N
Regale you all, 376 R
Regard de ses yeux, Un, 1 O
Regardez-moi bien dans les yeux, 223 E
Regenlied, 58 E, 218 F
Regina coeli, K.108, 3 C, 219 K 242 K
Regina coeli laetare, 268 Q
Regnava nel silenzio, 97 G
Reif hat einen weissen Schein, Der, 319 N
Reigning in royal splendor, 259 D
Reimer Thomas lag am Bach, Der, 210 C
Rein gestimmt die Saiten, 102 M
Reina bella, 441 J
Reine de Saba, La, 136 R
Reine des mouettes, 281 E
Reiselied, 228 N, 228 S
Rejoice greatly, 163 A
Rejoice in the Lord alway, 292 I
Rejsen til Vinlandene, 167 J
Rencontre Imprévue, La, 132 C
Rendete a gli occhi mïei, 65 K
Rendez-vous, Le, 180 E
Rendezvous de noble compagnie, Le, 174 F
Rendi'l sereno al ciglio, 157 J
Repas de Noces, Le, 360 L

Repentir, 138 J
Réponse d'une épouse sage, 310 O
Repos, 299 F
Repos de la Sainte Famille, Le, 42 I
Repose-toi, mon âme, 138 R
Republique vous appelle, La, 226 K
Requiem, 43 E, 108 S, 177 H, 255 B, 337 S, 404 K
Requiem aeternam, 43 E
Requiem du coeur, 275 F
Resignation, 37 H, 259 N
Resolution, 186 E
Response, 269 L
Rest, sweet nymphs, 276 M, 420 N
Resta di darmi noia, 124 N
Resta, oh cara, 251 J
Reste, repose-toi, 77 A
Restons encor, Mignonne, 275 R
Resurrection, 4 D
Resveillez-moy, 122 M
Retir'd from any mortal's sight, 288 C
Retour du marin, Le, 384 H
Retour du sergent, Le, 280 K
Retrospect, 259 M
Return home, The, 79 M
Return, oh God of hosts, 164 O
Return to Ulster, The, 36 P
Revecy venir du printans, 205 F
Réveille-toi 297 G
Réveillez-vous coeurs endormis, 187 F
Revelge, 215 C
Revenez Amours, 212 L
Revenge, Timotheus cries, 150 A
Rêverie, 148 K
Revery of the young peasant, 257 B
Rêves, 298 M
Reviens, reviens, ma bien aimée, 42 L
Revolutionary chorus, from Boris Godunov, 256 P
Revue, Une, 147 F
Rex tremendae, 43 J, 255 P, 404 R
Rhapsody for Alto, Male Chorus and Orchestra, 54 I
Rheingold, Das, 413 D
Rheingold! Rheingold! Reines Gold, 413 K
Rheinlegendchen, 214 Q
Riccardo, 153 Q
Ricevete, o padroncina, 248 P
Richard Coeur de Lion, 141 G
Richard Cory, 260 G
Ricordati, oh bella, 158 C
Ricordi ancora il dì che c'incontrammo, 385 P
Riddiamo, 50 C
Ridente la calma, K.152, 242 O
Ridonami la calma, 386 B
Rien qu'au revoir murmuré tout bas, 92 J
Rienzi, 412 S
Righteous perisheth, The, 166 L
Rigoletto, 399 O
Rigour now is gone to bed, 6 M
Rills are brightly glitt'ring, 79 E
Rima, 387 H
Rimpianto, 384 P
Rinaldo, 155 D
Rinaldo, March from Handel's, 272 A

Ring, The, 103 G
Ring, Christmas bells of London, 349 I
Ring des Nibelungen, Der, 413 D
Ring forth, ye bells, with clarion sound, 372 D
Ring out, wild bells, 138 L
Ring, ring de banjo, 116 M
Ringel, Ringel, Rosenkrantz, 42 E
Rings ist der Wald so stumm und still, 102 K
Ringsum erschallt im Wald und Flur, 228 R
Rio Grande, The, 200 H
Riportai, gloriosa palma, 152 D
Rise! Up! Arise!, 227 P
Ritorna, oh caro, 155 S
Ritorna vincitor, 391 D
Rival sisters, The, 287 P
Rivedrai le foreste, 392 B
Rivendrà nell' estasi, La, 392 N
Rivolgete a lui lo sguardo, 251 R
Road to the Isles, The, 190 Q
Roadside fire, The, 389 P
Robert Bruce, 309 F
Robert le Diable, 235 A
Robert! Robert! toi que j'aime, 235 F
Roberta, 191 M
Robin Hood, 197 O
Robin m'aime, 2 C
Rock'd in the cradle of the deep, 193 J
Rodelinda, 155 J
Rodrigo, 156 C
Roi David, Le, 178 N
Roi de Lahore, Le, 224 I
Roi du ciel et des anges, 234 Q
Roi et le fermier, Le, 237 S
Roi s'en va t'en chasse, Le, 64 Q
Rois d'Egypte et de Syrie, Les, 280 K
Roitelet, Le, 266 P
Rolling Down to Rio, 123 K
Rolling in foaming billows, 169 J
Romance, 88 L, 127 G, 377 K, 381 I
Romance de Noureddin, 86 O
Romance du barde, 226 M
Romance of the young gypsy, 294 N
Romance Orientale, 127 H
Romany Life, 173 E
Romanza, 133 J
Romanze, 339 N
Romanze from "Rosamunde," 322 E
Romeo and Juliet, 441 N
Romeo et Juliette, 137 B
Ronde, La, 73 B, 300 A
Ronde des compagnons, La, 77 C
Ronde des vignes, 265 J
Rondel, 89 Q
Rondine, La, 286 A
Rondine al Nido, 85 D
Rondo of Antonida, 127 O
Ronsard à son âme, 298 N
Rosa del ciel vita del mondo, 239 Q
Rosalinda, 390 S
Rosamunde, 322 E
Rosary, The, 261 G
Rose, Die, 311 H, 323 R
Rose, die Lilie, die Taube, die Sonne, Die, 334 P

Rose, La, 109 J
Rose Bearer, The, 355 I
Rose chérie, aimable fleur, 141 Q
Rose et Colas, 237 T
Rose has charm'd the nightingale, The, 305 E
Rose lys, 214 C
Rose Marie, 121 J
Rose, softly blooming, 348 R
Rose stand im Thau, Die, 336 F
Rosebud, to the fields art going, 197 A
Röselein, Röselein, 337 K
Roselinde, 351 D
Rosen brach ich nachts mir am dunklen Hage, 60 I
Rosenband, Das, 329 F
Rosenkavalier, Der, 355 I
Rosenlieder, 105 H
Rosenzeit, wie schnell vorbei, 58 F
Rosenzweige, 112 J
Roses are blooming in Picardy, 440 D
Roses blossom as last year, The, 342 N
Roses d'Ispahan, Les, 108 N
Roses étaient toutes rouges, Les, 87 S
Roses of Picardy, 440 D
Röslein dreie in der Reihe blühn, 55 D
Rossignol des Lilas, Le, 148 L
Rossignol plaisant, Le, 202 C
Rossignols amoureux, 296 P
Rossz feleség, A, 194 M
Rostelbinder, 'Der, 204 H
Roulette couverte en tuiles, Une, 282 E
Round de meadows am a ringing, 115 O
Route est longue, La, 76 C
Roy d'Ys, Le, 199 S
Roy Loys, Le, 184 L
Rozenzeit! wie schnell vorbei, 428 I
Rozhodnuto, uzavreno, 347 G
Rückblick, 319 H
Ruddigore, 370 P
Rude vento, 301 P
Ruft die Mutter, ruft die Tochter, 59A
Rugiadose, odorose, 315 J
Ruh' von Schmerzensreichen Mühen, 337 S
Ruhe, meine Seele, 357 D
Ruhe, Süssliebchen, 56 P
Ruhet hie, matte Töne, 19 N
Ruh'n in Frieden alle Seelen, 328 L
Rührt die Cymbel, 325 M
Ruht wohl, 26 N
Ruine coquille vide, Une, 282 C
Ruisselet, bien clair, Un, 132 C
Rule Britannia 6 Q
Rusalka, 101 J
Russalka, 86 H
Russlan and Ludmilla, 127 S
Rustic chivalry, 219 E
Ruy Blas, 230 M

S

S bohem, 347 R
S' è tuo piacer ch'io mora, 152 E

Sa lunka vi sa smaningom, 40 F
Sabbath morning at sea, 104P
Sacerdotes domini, 70 G
Sacra la scelta è d'un consorte, 397 J
Sacri nomi di padre, I, 391 F
Sad and luckless was the season, 36 Q
Sad lies the Steppe, 140 L
Sad of heart, 103 E
Sadko, 304 K
Säeman, Der, 192 O
Saeta, 263 D
Saeta en forma de Salve a la Virgen de la Esperanza, 387 I
Saeterjendens Söndag, 66 Q
Säf, säf, susa, 342 J
Sag', welch' wunderbare Träume, 418 H
Sagesse est un trésor, La, 237 T
Saget mir, auf welchem Pfade, 316 M
Saget mir geschwinde, 25 N
Sagt, ihr weissen Rankröselein, 105 J
Sagte ein goldener Schmetterling, 3 P
Sah ein Knab' ein Röslein stehn, 203 D, 320 H, 426 F
Sai che gli ho dato, 80 M
Said the miller, home returning, 86 E
Said the thunder to the cloud, 305 D
Sailor's Song, The, 171 R, 408 H
St. Cecilia Mass, 134 B
St. John Passion, 25 O
St. John's Eve, 144 A
St. Matthew Passion, 26 P
Saint Michel en grève, 52 K
St. Nepomuks Vorabend, 435 M
St. Paul, 227 L
Sainte, 299 A
Sainte en son auréole, Une, 109 R
Sais-tu, 114 I
Salammbo, 302 Q
Sale ascende l'uman, 286 O
Saliam, Saliam, 240 O
Sally Gardens, The 64 R, 185 K
Sally in our alley, 37 I, 73 P
Salome, 58 S, 222 J
Saltimbanques, 177 P
S'altro che lacrime, 254 R
Saluste du Bartas, 179 G
Salut à la France, 96 K
Salut à toi, soleil de flamme, 304 G
Salut! demeure chaste et pure, 134 S
Salut nous est promis, Le, 200 B
Salut! ô mon dernier matin, 134 H
Salut! splendeur du jour, 303 C
Salutation angélique, 73 E
Salvator Rosa, 133 H
Salve, Regina, 3 D, 49 N
Samostatné vládnu já, 347 C
Samson, 164 K
Samson et Dalila, 312 J
S'ancor si piange, 394 A
Sancta Maria, 111 J
Sancta mater, istud agas, 274 O, 310 B
Sanctus, 23 O, 34 D, 43 O, 45 H, 66 E, 69 S, 109 B, 134 E, 169 E, 202 H, 208 I, 243 L, 255 M, 267 H, 268 C, 317 C, 388 S, 405 H

Sanctus fortis, sanctus Deus, 104 C
Sandman, Der, 337 B
Sandmännchen, 55 I
Sandman's Song, 183 D
Sands o' Dee, The, 82 A
Sanft ins Leben aufwärts schweben, 329 R
Sanfte soll mein Todeskummer, 25 M
Sanfter Schlummer, 83 D
Sanftes Clavier, 326 L
Sang das Vögelein, 311 Q
Sang wohl, sang das Vögelein, 311 Q
Sange af "Ambrosius," 167 K
Sänger klugen weisen, Der, 416 M
Sanglots, 279 M
Sank nicht die Sonne kaum erst zum meer, 144 M
Sankt Krispen, lobet ihn!, 411 P
Sans que nulle part je séjourne, 314 C
Sans toi, 166 R
Santa Lucia, 83 Q
Santo nome di Dio, Il, 396 B
Santuzza-Alfio duet, 220 A
Saper vorresti, 393 I
Sapphische Ode, 60 I
Sappho, 137 L, 224 J
Sarabande, 310 N
Sarka, 112 C
S'asseoir tous deux au bord du flot, 107 F
Saudadedo tempo, 406 L
Saudades da minha vida, 406 L
Saul, 165 B
Säuselnde Lüfte, 318 H
Sausendes, brausendes Rad der Zeit, 418 E
Sausewind, Brausewind, 433 E
Sauterelle, La, 279 F
Say dear, when will your frowning leave, 425 A
Say love, if thou didst ever find, 99 E
Say, whither art bound, 295 O
Scacciata dal suo nido, 156 A
Scaramouche et Pulcinella, 88 P
Scene and withers, A, 382 E
Scene in the Church, 135 J
Scenes that are brightest, 418 Q
Schad' um das schöne grüne Band, 317 Q
Schafe können sicher weiden, 20 M
Schäferin, ach, wie haben sie dich so süss begraben, 209 K
Schäfers Klagelied, 329 G
Schäfers Sonntagslied, 199 A
Schaffe in mir, Gott, 340 E
Schan', lieber Gott, wie meine Feind, 18 G
Schatz, ich bitt' dich, 203 K
Schatzgräber, Der, 334 L
Schau' hin dort in Gethsemane, 8 F
Schauet doch und sehet, ob irgend ein Schmerz sei, 11 H
Schäumenden Wellen, Die, 14 G
Schauspieldirektor, Der, K.486, 247 L
Schelmendiedchen, 300 R
Schemelli Gesangbuch, 28 J

Schenkt man sich Rosen in Tirol, 441 S
Scherzo, 80 Q, 302 L
Schiavo, Lo, 133 J
Schicksal der Liebe, 192 J
Schicksalslied, 54 K
Schiffer, Der, 321 Q
Schilflied, 41 P, 230 H
Schilfrohr, säusle, 342 J
Schlaf! du theuerster Knabe mein, 142 N
Schlaf' ein, 437 B
Schlaf, Herzenssöhnchen, 423 F
Schlafe, holder, süsser Knabe, 324 M
Schlaf', holdes Kind, 418 J
Schlaf', Kindlein, schlaf, 336 O
Schlaf' nun und ruhe, 335 L
Schlaf! süsser Schlaf!, 420 O
Schlaf wohl, du Himmelsknabe du, 301 J
Schlafe mein Kindlein, 345 O
Schlafe, mein Liebster, 25 D
Schlafe mein Prinzchen schlaf' ein, 244 P
Schlafe, schlaf' ein, 259 R
Schlafe, süsser kleiner Donald, 331 G
Schlafendes Jesuskind, 434 R
Schläfert aller Sorgen Kummer, 19 M
Schlaflied, 322 D
Schlafloser Sonne, 338 B
Schlage doch gewünschte Stunde, 11 P
Schlagende Herzen, 357 J
Schlechtes Wetter, 359 M
Schleicht, spielende Wellen, 20 L
Schlief am schattgen Bächelein, 337 L
Schlief die Mutter endlich ein, 332 B
Schliesse, mein Herze, dies selige Wunder, 25 E
Schlosser Auf!, 63 J
Schlummert ein, 14 K
Schlummre! Schlummre und träume, 229 F
Schmerzen, 418 G
Schmetterling, Der, 323 B
Schmied, Der, 56 A, 188 A
Schmiede, mein Hammer, 414 R
Schnee, der gestern noch in Flöckchen, Der, 337 G
Schneeglöckchen, 337 G, 338 E
Schnelle Füsse, 253 L
Schnur, die Perl an Perle, Die, 57 P
Scholar, Der, 434 S
Schon deckt die Felder dunkle nacht, 128 D
Schon die Abendglochen, 198 O
Schon streckt ich aus im Bett die müden Glieder, 435 A
Schön war, das ich dir weihte, 60 P
Schon winkt der Wein, 215 F
Schöne Fest, Johannistag, Das, 410 M
Schöne Fremde, 333 M
Schöne Helena, Die, 264 D
Schöne Liedle, 49 F
Schöne Müllerin, Die, 317 D
Schöne Sennin, 337 P

Schöne Wiege meiner Leiden, 330 N
Schönen von Sevilla, Die, 332 A
Schöner Augen schöne Strahlen, 62 M
Schönes war, Ein, 354 R
Schreckenberger, Der, 435 C
Schuhmacherei und Poeterei, 410 J
Schütz bin ich, Ein, 198 N
Schwaches Hertz, 105 F
Schwalbe, sing mir an, 61 N
Schwan, Ein, 142 O
Schwanda, 425 O
Schwanengesang, 318 F, 322 B
Schwarzes Vöglein, Ein, 192 K
Schweb' empor am Himmel, 338 Q
Schweig einmal still, 435 B
Schweig'! schweig'!, 421 R
Schweig! Schweig! aufgethürmtes Meer, 14 I
Schweigt gluh'nden Sehnens, 421 J
Schweigt stille, plaudert nicht, 20 N
Schwere Abend, Der, 337 R
Schwermut, 57 S
Schwert verhiess mir der Vater, Ein, 413 L
Schwesterlein, 62 H
Schwingend verschwiegen sie, 175 N
Schwingt freudig euch empor, 10 Q
Schwor ein junges Mädchen, 60 N
Scintille diamant, 264 P
Scipione, 156 F
Scorrendo uniti remota via, 400 I
Scotch songs, 37 J
Screw may twist and the rack may turn, The, 373 P
Scritto è in ciel il mio dolor, 95 R
Scuoti quella fronda, 285 Q
Se a caso madama, 247 Q
Se all' impero, amici Dei, 254 P
Se colà nè fati, 244 S
Se congie prens, 198 S
Se consultiam le stelle, 402 H
Se, der var en Gang, 262 B
Se dolce m'era già, 153 F
Se Florindo è fidele, 315 K
Se i languide miei sguardi, 239 B
Se il mio nome saper, 307 K
Se il padre perdei, 244 O
Se il tuo duol, 244 N
Se la face ay pale, 99 N
Se l'aura spira, 121 C
Se mormora rivo o fronda, 156 G
Se non vendicata, 81 G
Se penai amor tu solo, 152 L
Se pietà di me non senti, 153 J
Se tanto in ira, 97 A
Se tra l'erba, 93 N
Se tradirmi tu potrai, 97 L
Se tu della mia morte, 315 M
Se tu m'ami, 273 O
Se tu mi doni un' ora, 49 R
Se tu sapessi, 286 E
Se un bell' ardire, 152 O
Se vano è il pregare, 397 E
Se vedeste le piaghe, 217 A
Se vuol ballare, 247 L
Sea, The, 51 Q, 213 E
Sea fever, 185 L
Sea King's song, 176 G
Sea Queen, The, 51 R
Sea slumber-song, 104 N
Sea sorrow, 190 S

Sea tosses and raves, The, 51 Q
Seabirds are asleep, 104 N
Sea-pictures, 104 N
Seal man, The, 81 L
Search throughout the panorama, 369 L
Seasons, The, 170 F
Seated one day at the organ, 374 S
Second book of Ayres, 98 S
Secondate, aurette amiche, 252 K
Secret, Le, 108 J
Secret, The, 346 M
Secret of Suzanna, The, 439 Q
Sedenti in Throno et Agno, 134 G
See how beneath the distant sky, 294 N
See how the Fates their gifts allot, 366 M
See, see the heavens smile, 290 A
See, see, the shepherds' Queen, 384 K
See, the conqu'ring hero, 162 G
See the raging flames arise, 160 S
See the weeping willow's three and thirty branches, 196 C
Seele deine Specereien, 25 L
Seele ruht in Jesu Händen, Die, 17 B
Seeräuberjenny, 425 H
Seerose, 105 K
Segabo yo aquella tarde, 262 S
Segreto per esser felici, Il, 98 H
Segui, segui, dolente core, 105 R
Seguidilla, 106 H
Seguidilla Murciana, 106 J
Seguidille, 46 K
Seh' ich deine zarten Füsschen an, 311 G
Seh' ich in das stille Thal, 336 M
Sehet, 28 E
Sehet ihr am Fensterlein, 430 J
Sehet in Zufriedenheit, 20 H
Sehet, welch' eine Liebe hat uns der Vater erzeiget, 12 I
Sehet, wir geh'n hinauf gen Jerusalem, 18 L
Sehnsucht, 57 K, 311 A, 355 M, 357 O
Sehnsucht nach dem Frühlinge, 252 S
Seht am Strauch die Knospen springen!, 343 S
Seht mir doch mein schönes Kind, 358 K
Seht, was die Liebe thut, 14 O
Sei du mein Trost, K.391, 246 H
Sei euch vertraut, 411 J
Sei gegrüsset, lieber Judenkönig, 26 H
Sei mia gioja, 154 K
Sei mir gegrüsst!, 321 O, 352 N
Sei Lob und Ehr' dem höchsten Gut, 16 P
Sei Lob und Preis mit Ehren, 11 O
Sei nun wieder zufrieden, 149 H
Sei nur still, 118 O
Sei si caro, 350 F
Sei still, 295 K
Sei uns stets gegrüsst, O Nacht, 325 O
Seid meiner Wonne stille zeugen, 114 D
Seid umschlungen, millionen, 38 F

Seigneur, daignez permettre, 135 I
Seigneur Dieu de mes pères, 178 A
Seigneur, rempart et seul soutién, 234 B
Sein Same musste sich so sehr, 9 D
Sein wir wieder gut, 354 P
Seine fromme Liebesgabe, 198 M
Seit ich ihn gesehen, 334 D
Seitdem dein Aug' in meines schaute, 356 K
Sej, besoroztak, 194 A
Sej! verd meg Isten, 193 L
Sela fede regni miei, 254 Q
Self banished, The, 48 R
Selig ihr Blinden, 435 L
Selig ist der Mann, 12 C
Selig sind, die da Leid tragen, 53 M
Selig sind die Toten, 54 G, 340 L
Selig sind die Verfolgung, 191 R
Selig wie die Sonne, 411 Q
Selige Nacht, 218 G
Seligkeit, 329 H
Seligster Erquickungstag, 13 E
Seltsam Abenteuer ist gestern mir possiert, Ein, 352 G
Selve amiche, ombrose piante, 71 F
Semele, 165 G
Seminarist, 259 B
Semiramide, La, 132 D, 309 G
Semplicetto! a donna credi, 151 I
Sempre con fe sincera, 286 N
Sempre in contrasti, 273 Q
Sempre libera, 401 Q
Senkt die Nacht den sanften Fittig, 339 C
Sennin, Die, 337 P
Señor platero he pensado, 263 J
Señora, si te olvidare, 387 O
Senta's Ballad, 408 M
Senti come lieve, 85 O
Sentiers où l'herbe se balance, 107 M
Sento avvampar nell' anima, 401 K
Sento che un giusto sdegno, 156 M
Sento dire no' nce pace, 360 S
Sento nel core, 315 L
Sento un certo non so che che, 239 K
Sento una forza indomita, 133 E
Senza mamma, 286 D
Serenade, 58 B, 74 M, 94 J, 138 M, 276 D, 318 I, 356 L, 384 P
Sérénade à Watteau, 77 D
Sérénade de Méphistophélès, 42 Q
Sérénade du passant, 226 A
Sérénade Florentine, 100 N
Serenade for Tenor, Horn & Strings, 64 S
Sérénade italienne, 78 E
Serenade, L'Amant Jaloux, 141 L
Serenade to music, 389 L
Sérénade Toscane, 107 I
Serenata, La, 221 E, 307 K, 386 C
Serestas, 406 I
Sergeant's song, The, 177 C
Sergent s'en revient de guerre, Le 280 K
Serments ont des ailes, Les, 380 E
Serre d'ennui, 78 G

Serres chaudes, 78 F
Serse, 75 D, 156 N
Serva Padrona, La, 273 P
Settembre, andiamo, 277 D
Seufzer, 435 E
Seufzer, Thränen, Kummer, Noth, 9 O
Seule, 107 H, 148 M
Seule en ta sombre tour, 313 L
Seuls tous deux, 107 G
Seven last words of Christ, The, 170 S
Seven penitential psalms, 202 O
Seven popular Spanish songs, 106 I
Seven sonnets of Michelangelo, 65 F
Seven words of the savior on the cross, The, 170 S
Sextet from Lucia di Lammermoor, 97 N
Shades of eve, 196 D
Shades of night, The, 30 F
Shadrack, 213 L
Shake the cloud, 288 D
Shall I in Mamre's fertile plain, 161 A
Shall I sue, 99 C
Shall we roam, my love, 92 C
She can have no one, 382 D
She is far from the land, 200 N
She is gentle and also wise, 420 B
She is so proper and so pure, 420 L
She moved thro' the fair, 182 H
She never told her love, 171 S
She rested by the Broken Brook, 82 L
She went away on the wind of autumn, 48 J
Sheep and lambs, 177 K
Sheep may safely graze, 20 M
Shéhérazade, 298 O
Shepherd kept sheep, A, 272 R
Shepherd, see thy horse's foaming mane, 197 B
Shepherd, shepherd leave decoying, 289 M
Shepherd Song, Tannhäuser, 416 H
Shepherd's Carol, The, 44 Q
Shiloh, 44 Q
Shine bright and clear, 201 C
Ship went on with solemn face, The, 104 P
Shoot, false love, I care not, 241 K
Short'nin Bread, 437 R
Should auld acquaintance be forgot, 37 J
Should he upbraid, 46 A
Show Boat, 191 H
Shropshire lad, A, 68 L
Shut not so soon, 293 I
Shy one, 81 M
Si come nella pena e nell' inchiostro, 65 F
Si comm' a nu sciorillo, 385 C
Si de Amarilis, 262 J
Si de rama en rama, 262 E
Si dolce è 'l tormento, 239 H
Si d'une petite oeillade, 226 F
Si fine all'ore, 38 P
Si: fuggiam da queste mura, 392 F
Si fui soldato, 126 J
Si j'étais fleur des bois, 424 L
Si j'étais jardinier des cieux, 76 D
Si j'étais rayon, 405 P

Si j'étais Roi, 1 M
Si la rigueur et la vengeance, 148 S
Si, la starchezza m'opprime, 404 A
Si la voix d'un enfant peut monter, 111 C
Si l'amour sur ma route, 380 O
Si le bonheur à sourire, 135 H
Si les filles d'Arles sont reines, 136 D
Si l'on me trouvait bien digne, 51 C
Si l'on veut savoir qui m'envoie, 138 A
Si l'univers entier m'oublie, 141 K
Si mes vers avaient des ailes, 148 N
Si mi chiamano Mimi, 293 K
Si, pel ciel marmoreo giuro, 399 D
Si può? si può? Signore!, 205 M
Si. Quale vuoi, sarò, 441 J
Si ridesti il Leon di Castiglia, 394 Q
Si, si minaccia, e vinta, 157 K
Si ta marche attristée, 44 B
Si toutes les filles du monde, 73 B
Si, tra i ceppi, 152 Q
Si trahison ou perfidie, 149 B
Si tu le veux, 196 L
Si tu m'aimes, Carmen, 47 G
Si tu me quieres, 441 E
Si tu veux, Mignonne, 226 B
Si tu veux savoir, 107 O
Si, vendetta, 400 Q
Si vous croyez, 232 N
Si vous croyez que je vais dire, 264 J
Si vous l'aviez compris, 92 J
Si vous me disiez, 299 Q
Si vous ne savez plus charmer, 86 P
Siam giunti o giovinette, 113 J
Siàm nel fondo più profondo, 278 D
Siberia, 127 B
Sich üben im lieben, im Scherzen sich herzen, 20 G
Siciliana, 404 H
Siciliana: O Lola, 219 E
Sicut cervus desiderat, 268 R
Sicut locutus est ad patres nostros, 22 J
Sie blasen zum Abmarsch, 435 F
Sie lebt heir ganz allein, 354 Q
Sie wandelt im Blumengarten, 229 E
Sie werden aus Saba, 12 K
Sie werden euch in den Bann thun, 11 F, 19 D
Sieben frühe Lieder, 41 O
Sieben Lieder aus letzter Zeit, 215 B
Sieg, Der, 329 I
Siege of La Rochelle, The, 30 D
Siegfried, 414 J
Siegfried, Herrlicher!, 415 J
Siegmund heiss' ich, 413 Q
Siegmund! Sieh'auf mich!, 414 D
Sieh, Marie, was ich dir bringe, 142 Q
Sieh, welche Macht sie gebracht, 198 G
Sieh, wie ist die Welle klar, 63 L
Siehe, auch ich lebe, 192 D
Siehst du, was du für ein ungetreuer, Bursche, 425 R
Sieste, 180 C

Sigh no more, ladies, 350 H, 420 O
Signor, lo credi a me, 150 Q
Signor quel infelice che per queste di monte, 240 K
Signor una parola, 308 I
Signor, va ne, ho niente, 399 R
Signore, ascolta!, 287 A
Sigurd, 302 R
S'il est un charmant gazon, 118 H
S'il est vrai, Chloris, 146 K
Silbermond, mit bleichen Strahlen, 59 E
Silence in Heav'n, 176 R
Silent and lone the woods around, 102 K
Silent Night, holy Night, 145 J
Silent noon, 388 I
Silent the little room, 259 K
Silent town, The, 342 O
Silently floated a spirit, 259 C
Silently into the night I go, 103 Q
Silver Swan, The, 125 G
Silvered is the raven hair, 367 K
Silvestrik, 52 K
Silvia, now your scorn give over, 292 J
Simkin said that Sis was fair, 107 D
Simon Boccanegra, 401 F
Simon the Cellarer, 168 H
Simple sailor, lowly born, A, 363 R
Sin not, O King, 165 F
Since all is passing, 176 A
Since first I saw your face, 114 Q
Since my tears and lamenting, 241 L
Since the time when first I met my Brudeus, 257 E
Sind Blitze, sind Dunner, 27 J
Sind es Schmerzen, sind es Freuden, 56 L
Sing a song of Freedom, 74 L
Sing again, nightingale, 442 B
Sing hey, lack a day, 372 C
Sing hey to you good day to you, 367 Q
Sing, sing, Nachtigall Du, 92 B
Sing, sing, nightingale, sing, 193 G
Sing songs of praise, 159 L
Sing the Lord, ye voices all, 170 C
Sing unto God, 161 K
Sing us one of the songs of Zion, 419 C
Sing we and chant it, 241 M
Sing we at pleasure, 425 B
Sing ye a joyful song, 102 G
Sing ye to the Lord, 160 B
Singet dem Herrn, 24 B, 69 D
Singet nicht in Trauertönen, 434 N
Singt mein Schatz wie ein Fink, 58 S
Sinke, liebe Sonne, 325 E
Sinner, please doan let this harves' pass, 68 F
Sino da Aldeia, 407 A
S'intrecci il loto, 391 P
S'io dir potessi, 154 G
Sir Rupert Murgatroyd his leisure and his riches, 370 Q
Siralmas volt nékem, 196 A
Siroe, 157 C

Sirs, 'tis time we got to work, 256 P
Sister Angelica, 286 D
Sisters, The, 194 J
Sit and drink all Sunday, 196 F
Sitzt einem hier im Kopf, 168 K
Six poésies de Jean Cocteau, 179 M
Skin ud, du klare solskin, 201 C
Skogen sover, 4 F
Skreg en Fugl, Der, 143 R
Skreg un Fugl, Der, 343 L
Skye Fisher's song, 191 A
Sleale! Il segreto fu dunque violato, 396 M
Sleep, 420 P
Sleep! all nature now is sleeping, 270 Q
Sleep, deep in forest gloom, 51 S
Sleep, my darling, sleep, 140 K
Sleep, my Jesu sleep, my best, 66 O
Sleep now, 30 O
Sleep, O baby mine, 377 S
Sleep that flits on baby's eyes, The, 74 K
Sleeping Beauty, The, 51 S, 88 C, 117 B
Sleeping Princess, The, 52 A
Sleeps the noon in the deep blue sky, 191 B
Slighted heart, The, 103 A
Slighted swain, The, 5 K
Slow heave of the sleeping sea, The, 41 F
Slumber on, my little gypsy sweetheart, 173 D
Slumber song, 91 P, 304 J
Slumrer sodt i Slesvigs Jord, 167 I
Sly, 439 P
Sly peasant, The, 101 P
Small head drooping, 378 E
Small titles and orders for Mayors and Recorders, 363 A
Smanie implacabili, 252 C
Smiling dawn of happy days, The, 160 L
Smiling hours a joyful train, The, 159 P
Smoke gets in your eyes, 191 M
Smutek opuštěné, 347 S
Snart er Natten, 167 F
Snatched away by Jahveh, 48 Q
Sne, 207 F
Snégourotchka, 204 S
Snow, 207 F
Snowdrop, The, 140 Q
Snowdrops, 283 E
Snowfields in silence, 259 E
Snowflakes, 140 P, 283 F
Snow-maiden, 304 S
So aber Christus in euch ist, 24 N
So anch' io la virtù magica, 94 C
So anders sind die Leute, 304 B
So beautiful, 383 N
So ben che difforme, 206 B
So che se andiam, la notte, 395 A
So dip your fingers in the stew, 81 R
So du mit deinem Munde, 17 R
So elend und so treu, 353 H
So ell' encina encina, 262 L

So Freude, verhalte manch' himmlisches Lied, 321 C
So full of grief, so waste and worn?, 86 L
So go to him and say to him, 367 P
So hab ich doch die ganze Woche, 57 F
So hab' ich wirklich dich verloren?, 326 I
So hop, hop, hop, 183 L
So ist die Lieb', 434 F
So ist es denn aus mit den ewigen Göttern, 414 A
So ist mein Jesus nun gefangen, 27 I
So ist's recht, es freut uns alle, 345 C
So jemand spricht: Ich liebe Gott, 35 S
So lasst mich scheinen, 323 K, 338 L, 435 M
So, laugh, lads, and quaff lads, 197 O
So löschet im Eifer, 15 A
So mag kein and'res Wort erklingen, 83 F
So oft ich meine Tabakspfeige, 29 D
So oft sie kam, 337 O
So rapid thy course is, 161 Q
So rief der Lenz, 410 O
So ruhe denn mit ganzer Schwere, 34 O
So schweb' ich dir Geliebter zu, 261 O
So seh aufs neu ich jene Berg, 143 H
So sei gegrüsst viel tausendmal, 336 Q
So seid nun geduldig, 53 O
So shall the lute and harp awake, 162 F
So tanzen die Engel, 316 O
So voll Frölichkeit, 353 R
So voll und reich wand noch das Leben, 316 H
So wahr die Sonne scheinet, 333 G
So wälz ich ohne Unterlass, 431 E
So weit Leben und Weben, 413 F
So wie Sie sind, 354 L
So willst du des Armen, 56 N
So wird der Mann, 327 D
Sobald Damöstas Cloen sieht, 249 M
Soeur des soeurs, 110 Q
Soffri in pace, 152 F
Soffriva nel pianto, 97 K
Soffro, lontan lontano, 302 H
Soft complaining flute, The, 150 N
Soft day, A, 349 Q
Soft summer twilight is fading, The, 350 S
Softly and gently, 104 F
Softly each measure, gently each strain, 351 A
Softly purling, glides on, 169 K
Softly sighing to the river, 369 J
Sogno, 386 D
Sogno soave e casto, 94 A
Sohn der Jungfrau, Himmelskind, 434 R
Soir, 110 K

Soir, Le, 138 N, 381 K
Soir je chanterai, Le, 305 A
Soir qu'amour vous fit en la salle, Le, 281 R
Soir ramène le silence, Le, 138 N
Soir t'en souvient-il, Un, 261 S
Sois courageuse, O ma maîtresse, 148 B
Sois immobile, 309 P
Sois sage, ô ma douleur, 88 J
Sol tu nobile Dio, 240 H
Sola, perduta, abbandonata, 285 S
Solche hergelauf'ne Laffen, 245 J
Soldat, Der, 334 C, 435 G
Soldaten sind schöne Burschen, 42 C
Soldaten wohnen auf den Kanonen, 425 I
Soldatenart, 216 H
Soldatenbraut, Die, 336 B
Soldier, The, 36 R, 185 M
Soldier and a sailor, A, 271 M
Soldier in a foreign land, The, 36 S
Soldier's bride, The, 294 S
Soldier's Chorus, 135 K, 403 I, 403 J
Solenne in quest' ora, 396 F
Solingo, errante e misero, 394 S
Solitaire, La, 313 R
Solitude, 292 K
Soll ich denn sterben, 438 S
Soll sich der Mond nicht heller scheinen, 55 R
Solo per me l'infamia, 400 O
Solo, profugo, rejetto, 113 I
Solomon, 165 M
Solvejg's Slumber Song, 142 N
Solvejg's Song, 142 L
Sombre forêt, 309 N
Sombre nuit, 281 D
Some folks like to sigh, 116 O
Some one I hear prowling, 93 B
Some spirit seems to play, 45 L
Some think the world is made for fun and frolic, 92 G
Some time she would, 107 E
Somehow I feel that thou art near, 122 K
Something hath called me, 125 M
Sometimes between long shadows, 233 B
Sometimes she is a child, 388 K
Somewhere, I know, from the blue of the sky, 348 K
Sommerabend, 59 L
Sommertage, 42 B
Sommi Dei, 155 C
Son and stranger, 230 R
Son come i chicchi della melograna, 80 S
Son confusa pastorella, 154 O
Son du cor s'afflige, 89 S
Son geloso del Zefiro, 39 O
Son imbrogliato, 274 C
Son Io! Son Io la Vita!, 220 I
Son lo spirito che nega, 49 Q
Son nom est Jehovah, 178 G
Son pellegrino, 156 K
Son Pereda son ricco d'onore, 359 Q
Son pochi fiori, 218 M
Son quarant' anni, 238 B
Son sessant' anni, 126 B

Son troppo vezzose, 122 I
Son tutta duolo, 315 N
Son vergin vezzosa, 39 C
Soneto a Córdoba, 106 P
Sonett, Ein, 55 S
Song I sang you, The, 385 H
Song is you, The, 191 O
Song of destiny, 54 K
Song of Georges Brown, 49 K
Song of Hiawatha, 82 K
Song of India, 304 N
Song of Khivria, 257 D
Song of Momus to Mars, The, 52 O
Song of the blackbird, 293 M
Song of the clock, 299 J
Song of the cup, 299 K
Song of the dark forest, 52 B
Song of the earth, The, 215 F
Song of the fates, 54 P
Song of the fire, 299 L
Song of the flea, 259 D
Song of the gnat, 256 I
Song of the gypsy girl, 379 C
Song of the little old man, 299 N
Song of the open, 199 M
Song of the open road, 216 K
Song of the Parrot, 256 L
Song of the tiger, 221 N
Song of the Vagabonds, 121 M
Song of the Venetian Guest, 304 Q
Song of the Viking Guest, 304 M
Song to the Evening Star, Tannhäuser, 417 I
Songs and dances of death, 259 E
Songs for Women's Chorus, 2 Horns and Harp, 53 H
Songs for young people, 378 P
Songs my mother taught me, 102 L
Songs of a wayfarer, 215 O
Songs of Grusia, The, 294 Q
Songs of the Auvergne, 72 H
Songs of the Fleet, 349 R
Songs of the Hebrides, 190 H
Songs of travel, 389 N
Sonn' hat sich mit ihrem Glanz, Die, 21 O
Sonnambula, La, 39 I
Sonne entgegen in Liebesgluten, Der, 358 R
Sonne sah die Erde an, Die, 338 E
Sonne scheidet hinter dem Gebirge, Die, 215 N
Sonne scheint nicht mehr so schön, Die, 62 D
Sonne sinkt, Die, 328 A
Sonne sinkt in's tiefe Meer, Die, 324 C
Sonne taucht in Meeresfluthen, 235 I
Sonne, weinest jeden Abend, 418 G
Sonnenstrahlen durch die Tannen, 323 A
Sonnet, 65 E
Sonnet d'amour, 381 O
Sonnez les matines, 181 P
Sonntag, 57 F, 439 A
Sonntags am Rhein, 332 Q
Sonntagslied, 228 R
Sonntagsmorgen, 230 L
Sono andati, 294 C
Sonst spielt ich mit Scepter, 211 I
Soon night will pass, 172 R

Sorcerer, The, 372 D
Sorciers et les fées dansent, Les, 180 H
Sorge infausta una procella, 153 S
Sorrow, forsake thou me, 257 C
Sorrow in spring, 295 G
Sorrow of departure, 347 S
Sorrow of Mydath, 144 R
Sorry her lot who loves too well, 363 I
Sorte mia tiranna, La, 157 H
Sosarme, 157 J
Sospiraste, valdovinos, 262 Q
Sospiri miei, 45 A
Sospiro a me sol, Il, 39 S
Sotto la gronda de la torre, 85 D
Soulaud, vieux saloud, 360 N
Soulève ta paupière close, 42 K
Sound an alarm, 162 B
Sound the trumpet, 292 E
Soupir, 100 O, 300 B
Source délicieuse, 136 Q
Sous le ciel tout étoilé, 91 J
Sous le dome épais, 90 N
Sous le soleil, 381 O
Sous les ifs noir, 342 A
Sous les pieds d'une femme, 136 R
Sous vos sombres chevelures, 77 Q
Southern night, A, 305 G
Souvenance, 118 I
Souvenir d'avoir chante, Le, 148 O
Souvenirs d'enfance, 179 O
Souvenirs du jeune âge, 174 J
Souviens-toi du passé, 135 J
Sov min son, o slumre sodt, 142 B
Sovedrikken, 426 M
Sovra il sen la man mi posa, 39 K
Spähend nach dem Eisengitter, 335 O
Span, woher auf Wellenspuren?, 342 H
Spandono le campane, 302 G
Spanisches Lied, 55 L
Spanish serenade, 48 A
Spanish songs, 330 I
Spargi d'amaro pianto, 98 B
Spaziergang, 439 B
Speak not, O beloved, 377 P
Spectre de la Rose, Le, 42 K
Spectre infernal!, 380 C
Speed thee, birdie, 102 S
Spell is broke, The, 183 R
Spera, si, mio caro bene, 150 R
Sperai tanto il delirio, 206 L
Sperai vicino, 245 C
Speranza è giunta in porto, La, 154 H
Sperate, o figli, 397 S
Spiagge amate, 132 B
Spiegel dieser treuen braunen Augen, Der, 434 K
Spiel' ich die Unschuld vom Lande, 352 C
Spiel' ich 'ne Dame von Paris, 352 F
Spielman, Der, 174 R
Spietati, Io vi giurai, 156 B
Spinnerin, Die, 325 F, 339 A
Spinning Chorus, 408 L
Spira sul mare, 284 P
Spirate pur, spirate, 93 O
Spirit flower, A, 71 M
Spirito gentil, 96 A
Spirits of earth and air, 372 O
Spirits of nether worlds, 257 H

Spirit's Song, The, 172 A
Spirto ben nato, 65 G
Spleen, 87 S, 109 I
Splendon piu belle in ciel, 95 S
Splendour falls on castle walls, The, 65 A
Sprache der Liebe, 325 D
Spring, 170 F
Spring is fleeting, 342 F
Spring Showers, 143 M
Springtide, 143 E
Springtime, 176 B
Springtime of the year, The, 390 I
Spröde, Die, 435 I
Spunta l'aurora pallido, 50 F
Spurn not the nobly born, 364 O
Spute dich, Kronos!, 321 M
Squilli e cheggi la tromba guerriera, 403 J
Sta ben al nubile, 50 B
Stabat Mater, 190 A, 268 S, 274 F, 309 R, 407 S
Stadt, Die, 318 P
Stand das Mädchen, 60 K
Ständchen, 61 J, 119 S, 318 I, 325 L, 329 J, 332 R, 356 L
Ständchen, Das, 435 J
Ständchen euch zu bringen, Ein, 435 K
Standin' in de need of prayer, 145 L
Star, The, 306 H
Star of Bethlehem, The, 2 L
Star of me, 306 H
Star vicino al bell' Idol, 306 R
Stark ruft das Lied, 415 E
Starke Scheite schichtet, 416 B
Starkes Lieben, 19 A
Stastná vím on prijde dnes, 345 F
Statue at Czarskoe-Selo, 85 K
Statue de bronze, La, 315 A
Stay, Corydon thou swain, 427 N
Steh' auf Gesell, 411 N
Stehestill!, 418 E
Steht auf, ihr lieben Kinderlein, 301 E
Steig auf, geliebter Schatten, 60 H
Stein, der über' alle Schätze, 18 F
Stein Song, The, 66 S
Stell auf dem Tisch die duftenden Reseden, 201 E, 356 G
Stella del marinar, 278 I
Sterb' ich, so hüllt in Blumen meine Glieder, 435 L
Stern conviction's o'er him stealing, 363 Q
Sterne, Die, 324 I
Sterne mit den gold'nen Füsschen, 120 H
Steuermann! Lass die Wacht!, 409 E
Still beginnt's im Hain zu thauen, 325 S
Still I hear the changeful strain, 45 M
Still ist die Nacht, 318 R
Still sitz' ich an des Hügels Hang, 327 P
Still wie die Nacht, 49 E
Still you stand, O Pear tree, 195 F
Stille, Die, 333 K
Stille amare, 158 F
Stille Liebe, 332 L
Stille Nacht, heilige Nacht, 145 J
Stille Schlaf und nächtlich, 140 M

Stille Sicherheit, 119 J
Stille Stadt, Die, 342 O
Stille Thränen, 332 N
Stille Wasserrose, Die, 112 R
Stille Zelle, Eine, 112 H
Stiller Vorwurf, 336 K
Stilles Leid, 112 H
Stimmt an die Saiten, 169 M
Stirb, Lieb' und Freud!, 332 G
Stizzoso mio stizzoso, 273 R
Storchenbotschaft, 435 N
Store hvide Flok, Den, 143 C
Storm, The, 292 L
Stornellata marinara, 80 R
Stornellatrice, 302 M
Stornello, 80 S
Strange adventure!, 374 H
Strange vision, A, 101 K
Stranger in the storm swept forest, 79 M
Strano senso arcano, Uno, 276 G
Strauss, den ich gepflücket, Der, 429 O
Streamlet ioveth the sedges, 79 C
Streets of New York, The, 173 R
Streit zwischen Phoebus und Pan, Der, 20 B
Strephon's a Member of Parliament, 364 S
Striche des Todes, Die, 229 K
Stride la vampa, 403 A
Strider faceva, 217 I
Stridono, lassù, 205 T
Stript of their green our groves appear, 292 M
Studentersang, 167 L
Studenti! Udite, o voi, antichi e novi amici, 117 J
Studieren will nichts bringen, 436 K
Stündlein wohl vor Tag, Ein, 435 O
Sturm behorcht, Der, 358 G
Stürmische Morgen, Der, 319 R
Stürmt, nur stürmt, 18 G
Stuttering song, 344 K
Styrienne, 381 A
Su! del Nilo al sacro lido, 391 C
Su, dunque, 392 C
Sù e con me vieni, 131 L
Su su pastorelli vezzosi, 239 I
Su, venite a consiglio, 315 O
Sub tuum praesidium confugimus, 243 D
Subtle love, with fancy viewing, 158 Q
Such a space of silence, 200 L
Such dish by man not oft is seen, 353 A
Sui campi e su le strade, 302 I
Suicidio, 278 Q
Sul fil d'un soffio etesio, 395 M
Sul giardino fantastico, 302 J
Sul mare lucica, 83 Q
Suleika, 229 N, 321 I, 322 G, 331 D
Sull' aria!, 248 O
Sulla tomba che rinserra, 97 I
Sulle, Sulle labbra, 5 S
Sumer is icumen in, 188 H
Summ' und brumm', du gutes Rädchen, 408 L
Summer, 170 J
Summer evening, 270 A

Summer has flown, the leaves are falling, 125 B
Summer night, 270 B
Summertime, 123 O
Sun and the stars are all ringing, The, 342 D
S'un castro amor, 65 J
Sun goeth down, The, 105 B
Sun had loos'd his weary teams, The, 272 H
Sun has fallen, The, 232 C
Sun is a-shining, The, 217 P
Sun like visions of love, The, 142 D
Sun now mounts the eastern sky, The, 122 C
Sun shines bright, The, 115 P
Sun upon the Weirdlaw hill, The, 37 L
Sun, whose rays are all ablaze, The, 366 D
Sunday, 187 M
Sunless, 259 K
Sunnuntaina, 187 M
Sunset, 37 L, 66 N
Suoni la tromba, 39 G
Suor Angelica, 286 D
Super flumina Babylonis, 269 J
Supposed, beloved, that the gods should say, 197 S
Sur la mer les crépuscules tombent, 89 I
Sur la place chacun passe, 46 C
Sur la rive errait le rêve, 304 R
Sur la route, et gaiement, 176 K
Sur le coteau, 106 G
Sur l'eau, 148 P, 181 Q
Sur l'Herbe, 299 B
Sur mes genoux fils du soleil, 233 F
Sur nos chemins, 111 H
Sur ton sein pâle, 148 C
Sur un lys pâle, 100 H
Sure, by Tummel and Loch Rannoch, 190 R
Sure on this shining night, 30 P
Surely He hath born our grief, 163 F
Surgi de la croupe et du bond, 300 D
Surrexit pastor bonus, 202 Q
Susanna, 165 P
Susanne un jour, 202 E
Suscepit Israel puerum suum, 22 I
Süss duftende Lindenblüte, 218 E
Süss und sacht, 188 E
Süsse Lied verhallt, Das, 410 D
Süsse Schlaf, Der, 439 C
Süsse Stille, 149 P
Süsser Freund, du blickest, 334 I
Süsser Trost, mein Jesus kömmt, 18 D
Süsses Begräbnis, 209 K
Susy, little Susy, 182 P
Suzel, buon dì, 218 Q
Svarta rosor, 342 I
Swan, A, 142 O, 175 S
Swan bent low, The, 213 G
Swan is breasting the flow, A, 175 S
Swan o' the West, 191 C
Swanee River-Song, 198 J

Sweet and low, 31 B
Sweet, be no longer sad, 292 N
Sweet bird, 150 L
Sweet chance that led my steps abroad, 172 G
Sweet honey-sucking bees, 427 P
Sweet Nymph, 241 N
Sweet o' the year, The, 237 J
Sweet one, how my heart is yearning, 173 O
Sweet strains from fairy instruments, 143 M
Sweet summer breeze, 173 H
Sweet tyranness, 292 O
Sweet was the song, 7 H
Sweeter than the violet, 103 F
Sweetest flow'r that blows, The, 306 G
Sweetest li'l feller, 261 D
Sweetest story ever told, 361 R
Sweetheart, I ne'er may know, 340 R
Sweethearts, 174 A
Sweethearts make love their very own, 174 A
Sweetly she sleeps, 116 P
Sweet-scented breath of night, 259 H
Swift the springtime passes, 342 F
Swimmer, The, 104 R
Swing low sweet chariot, 68 F
Sylvelin, 343 M
Sylvia, 348 J
Sylvia's hair is like the night, 348 J
Sylvie, 107 O
Symboles des Apôtres, 73 F
Sympathy, 350 P
Symphonie de Psaumes, 359 P
Symphonie sacrae, 340 M
Symphony No 9 "Choral" (Finale), 38 E
Syng, Det, 144 C
Synnöve's Song, 193 H
Szegeny vagyok, szegénynek, 194 H
Szerettelek álnok lélek, 93 A
Szölöhegyen keresztül, 196 B
Szomoru füzfänak, 196 C

T

Ta chair, d'âme mêlée, 281 F
Ta duse ta touha, 345 D
Ta rose de pourpre a ton clair soleil, 108 B
Tabarro, Il, 286 E
Tableau Parlant, Le, 141 M
Tacea la notte, 402 Q
Tag ging regenschwer, Der, 61 H
Tag und Nacht, 13 F
Täglich ging die wunderschöne Sultanstochter, 311 O
Tajemství, 346 M
Tak vecne k tobe lnout, 345 H
Take a pair of sparkling eyes, 362 N
Take heart, no danger lowers, 368 K
Take heed, young heart, 125 L
Take, O take those lips away, 199 N, 293 Q, 420 Q
Take thou this rose, 123 B
Taken from the county jail, 365 L
Tal dispera, tal affanna, 131 Q

Tal gioco, credetemi, Un, 205 R
Tale of the clucking, 195 D
Tales of Hoffmann, 264 K
Talismane, 331 C
Talor dal mio forziere ruban, 283 J
Tambour, Der, 435 P
Tambour major, Le, 379 R
Tambourliedchen, 58 Q
Tamboursg'sell, Der, 215 B
Tamerlano, 157 L
Taming of the Shrew, The, 132 P
T'amo ben io, 74 R
Tancredi, 308 Q
Tandis que tout someille, 141 L
Tanke, hvars strider natten ser Toner, 343 O
Tannenbaum, Der, 418 K
Tannhäuser, 416 E
Tännlein grünet, Ein, 429 S
Tant de tristesses, 279 K
Tant pis, ma foi, 290 O
Tanto amore segreto, 287 I
Tantum ergo, 407 P
Tanzen und Springen, 168 E
Tarantella, 396 E
Tarantella Napoletana, 307 G
Tarde uma nuvem rosea, 406 D
Tardi s'avvede, 254 M
Täubchen, das entflattert ist, 351 D
Tauben von Gurre, 316 R
Taubenpost, Die, 318 S
Täuscht euch, ihr Augen, nicht, 439 D
Täuschung, 319 S
Te amare diosa Venus, 387 G
Te decet hymnus, 43 F, 404 L
Te Deum, 149 Q, 286 K
Te sol quest' anima, 392 M
Te souvenirs-il des marroniers fleuris, 176 I
Te souviens-tu, 132 M
Te souvient-il du lumineux voyage, 225 A
Te, vergin santa invoco, 397 B
Te voilà, rire du Printemps, 148 I
Tears, 379 G
Tears such as tender fathers shed, 159 H
Tecum principium, 313 E
Teklas sang, 427 A
Tel Jour, telle nuit, 282 B
Telephone, The, 232 H
Tell me angry flowing torrent, 79 A
Tell me, do you love me?, 361 S
Tell me lovely shepherd, 52 P
Tell me, Oh blue, blue sky, 125 B
Tell me, some pitying angel, 290 H
Tell me the tales that to me were so dear, 32 K
Tell me what grief overcomes you today, 342 I
Tell me where is fancy bred, 6 R, 82 G
Tell me why are the roses so pale, 377 Q
Tempest, The, 289 O
Temple bells are ringing, The, 440 F
Tempo è si mormori, 219 G
Temps a laissié son manteau de vent, Le, 89 O

Temps des lilas, Le, 78 K
Temps, l'étendue, Le, 196 N
Tender music, from my soul, 143 J
Tendre épouse bien aimée, 51 H
Tendresse, 303 J
Tenebrae factae sunt, 407 Q
Tenez moi en voz bras, 190 C
Termo! che fai T'arresta!, 287 C
Terre a tressaili, La, 118 G
Terre embrassée, La, 381 K
Terre les eaux va buvant, La, 178 M
Tes beaux yeux sont las, 88 I
Tes yeux, 294 L
Tes yeux sont doux, 298 S
Teseo, 158 B
Testa adorata, 205 I
Testament, 100 P
Testimon è il sol ch'io miro, 399 E
Tête de femme est légère, 181 R
Tetto Umil, Un, 172 B
Thah was three chillun frum nuh lan' uv Isriel, 213 L
Thaïs, 224 M
Thalatta!, 192 E
Thale dampfen die Höhen glühn, Die, 421 N
Thank you for your kindly proffer, 373 C
Thank you, gallant gondolieri, 362 D
Thanks be to God, 227 A
Thanks for the Rede, 142 J
Thanks to these lonesome vales, 288 M
That so long as the gorgeous ensign, 383 Q
Thé, Le, 196 M
Their eyes, their lips, their busses, 273 H
Their sound is gone out into all lands, 163 O
Thekla, 329 K
Then away they go to an island, 362 L
Then comes the great and glorious morn, 170 R
Then from the starry skies above, 183 E
Then give three cheers, 363 H
Then ho, jolly Jenkin, 374 Q
Then sing aloud to God our strength, 419 J
Then Soldier! come fill high the wine, 36 R
Then, then shall the righteous, 227 J
Then will I Jehovah's praise, 164 J
Then you'll remember me, 30 C
Theodora, 166 D
There are a great many persons, 382 C
There are as many saints as there are in it, 382 K
There are fairies at the bottom of our garden, 204 C
There are very sweetly, 382 N
There came an image, 388 L
There came once at vesper hour, 256 R
There can be no peace on earth, 382 G
There cried a bird, 343 L
There grew a little flower, 372 B

There is a flow'r that bloometh, 418 P
There is a green hill, 138 O
There is a lady sweet and kind, 114 R, 293 C, 420 J
There is a mill, 390 B
There is beauty in the bellow of the blast, 366 Q
There is naught on earth, 207 F
There is no death, 265 R
There is no rose of such virtue, 32 E
There, little girl, don't cry, 261 B
There lived a King, as I've been told, 362 Q
There once was a clerk to a lawyer, 86 D
There screamed a bird, 143 R
There stands a little man, 183 F
There stands the maiden of stone, 85 K
There was a king in days of old, 91 S
There was an old darkey, 116 Q
There was no other good enough, 138 P
There's a boat that's leavin' soon for New York, 124 F
Therese, 59 R
These children whom you see, 368 P
Thésée, 212 L
Theu-theu-theu-theurer Sohn, 344 K
They began to travel, 383 A
They had opened wide the mighty doors of oak, 257 O
They never knew about it green, 382 H
They wander'd a while, 295 D
Thine alone, 173 S
Thine eyes in the crowd, 259 L
Thine is my heart alone, 203 S
Things are seldom what they seem, 363 P
Think on me, 340 P
Thirteen Moravian duets, 102 R
This ae nighte, 65 C
This great world is a trouble, 207 D
This have I done for my true love, 177 D
This helmet, I suppose was meant, 370 O
This is thy hour, O Soul, 389 R
This poet sings, 290 D
This sport he much enjoy'd, 370 R
This sweet and merry month, 69 O
This the autumn of our life, 373 O
This was the charter, the charter of the land, 6 P
Tho' I should die for it, 376 N
Thomas, I cannot, 271 L
Thou art gone up on high, 163 M
Thou Giant Death, 142 E
Thou forest dear, farewell, 103 J
Thou only hast the words of life, 104 J
Thou shalt break them, 163 R
Thou shalt bring them in, 160 E
Thou turn'st this world, 291 S

Thou wilt come no more, gentle Annie, 115 H
Though Amarylis dance, 69 N
Though tear and long drawn sigh, 374 B
Threaten'd cloud has passed away, The, 365 Q
Three fishers went sailing, 182 L
Three Folksongs, 231 F
Three Irish folksongs, 167 P
Three little girls from school are we, 365 N
Three orphans, The, 195 C
Three-penny opera, 425 G
Three poems by Walt Whitman, 389 Q
Three Psalms, 179 S
Thrive and grow, 103 H
Thro' all the employments of life, 271 D
Thro' my garden wicket hopping, 258 F
Thro' the dewy valley, 78 S
Thro' the forest's moan, 52 B
Thro' the night a golden cloudlet, 305 F
Throng, The, 259 L
Through a field of flow'rs, 257 R
Through aisles of birchen forest, 172 P
Through bushes and through briars, 388 F
Through my book I seem to scan, 367 C
Through the old city's silence, 440 K
Through the vineyard, 196 B
Thus I stand like the Turk, 273 J
Thus saith the Lord to Cyrus, 159 D
Thus when the sun, 164 P
Thus when the swallow, 272 L
Thy beaming eyes, 203 D
Thy Dark Eyes to Mine, 145 B
Thy glorious deeds inspired my tongue, 164 Q
Thy gracious image spreads upon me, 258 G
Thy lips say, "I love thee, believe me," 51 O
Thy sword within the scabbard keep, 52 O
Thyrsis, sleepest thou, 41 K
Ti chiedo un sol momento, 249 K
Tief im Herzen trag' ich Pein, 339 L, 435 Q
Tief im Talgrund überm Bach, 300 Q
Tief im Walde, auf der Halde, 196 I
Tief in den Abruzzen, 114 E
Tiefe Stille herrscht im Wasser, 320 G
Tiefland, 3 Q
Tilimbom, 361 I
Till I wake, 440 I
Till the sun grows cold, 276 R
Time is nebber dreary, De, 116 M
Time was when I in anguish lay, 145 F
Time was, when love and I, 372 G
Timon of Athens, 287 S
T'incontrai per via!, 127 B
Ti-ra-la-la!, 350 Q

'Tis liberty, dear liberty alone, 161 M
'Tis Nature's voice, 291 R
'Tis spring, come out to ramble, 185 J
'Tis the last rose of summer, 113 K
Tis the song, the sigh of the weary, 115 I
'Tis Woman that seduces, 271 E
Tise kradme, 345 L
Tiszan innen Dunan túl, 193 P
Titus, 254 G
Tit-willow, 366 P
To a garden full of posies, 371 G
To a lovely myrtle bound, 144 O
To all you ladies now at land, 71 H
To Brune ojne, 141 S
To daisies, 293 I
To know, to know, to love her so, 382 B
To look for thee, cry for thee, 82 J
To my good wife I'm much indebted, 86 M
To my sorrow I fell in love with him, 294 S
To Norway, 143 N
To one who passed whistling through the night, 125 M
To shorten winter's sadness, 425 C
To the children, 295 I
To the hills and the vales, 288 H
To the Queen of heaven, 100 A
To the queen of my heart, 92 C
To thee and a lass, 292 P
To this we've come, 231 Q
To wander alone, 172 C
To you, 348 K
To your soul is it wine, 199 M
Tochter des Wald's, 429 B
Tochter Jephta's, Die, 338 A
Tod, das ist die kühle Nacht, Der, 60 Q
Tod, du Schrecken der Natur, 326 H
Tod und das Mädchen, Der, 320 R
Tod und der einsame Trinker, Der, 192 M
Today you are waiting, 258 Q
Todesmusik, 325 B
Todessehnen, 60 B
Tödlich grauter mir der Morgen, 431 D
Toh, Toh! Poffare il mondo!, 396 I
Toi, le coeur de la rose, 299 M
Toi que je laisse sur la terre, 349 G
Toi que j'implore, 349 E
Toi que l'oiseau, 309 O
Toi seul, 379 A
Tö!em a nap, 196 D
'Tollite hostias, 313 G
Tolomeo, 158 E
Töltik a nagy erdö útját, 31 R
Tom Bowling, 92 O
Tom der Reimer, 210 C
Tom Jones, 123 L
Tom lehnt harrend auf der Brücke, 330 A
Tom Tinker's my true love, 273 C
Tombeau, Le, 281 Q
Tombeau des Naïades, Le, 88 F

Tomorrow shall be my dancing day, 177 D
Tomsky's ballade, 377 I
Ton âme est un lac d'amour, 147 E
Ton qu'èrè pitchounèlo, 72 O
Tonada de valdovinos, 262 Q
Tonada del Conde Sol, 263 A
Toñerna, 343 O
Tonight the dew will kiss the rose, 197 L
Toreador, Le, 2 A
Toréador, en garde, 46 N
Toreador Song, 46 M
Torna a Surriento, 85 N
Torna di Tito a lato, 254 L
Torna la pace, 245 B
Tornami a dir, che m'ami, 94 K
Torrente cresciuto, 157 I
Tosca, 286 Q
Tosto che l'alba; caccia, 124 P
Tota pulchra amica mea, 269 A
Tota pulchra es Maria, 66 H
Total eclipse, 164 R
Tote Stadt, Die, 197 D
Toten Augen, Die, 4 B
Totengräbers Heimweh, 329 L
Toujours, 108 F
Toujours à toi, 378 M
Touraine est un pays, 225 B
Tourne, mon moulin, 276 B
Tournez, tournez, bons chevaux de bois, 76 M, 87 Q
Tournoiement, 314 C
Tourterelle, La, 236 M
Tous les trois réunis, 96 L
Tout gai!, 297 K
Tout là-haut dans le ciel, 199 D
Tout le long de la Baïse, 179 H
Toute pure comme le ciel, 180 D
Toutes les fleurs, 298 E
Toutes les nuitz, 202 F
Tove's Song, 316 P
Towards the empyrean heights of ev'ry kind of love, 370 B
Tower wanders, under orders, 373 N
Town lies in the valley, A, 342 O
Toyland, toyland, little girl and boyland, 173 B
Trá lá lá y el puntado, El, 140 D
Tra voi, belle, brune e bionde, 285 J
Tradito, schernito, 252 P
Traft ihr das Schiff im Meere an, 408 N
Tragödie, 336 D
Tramonto, Il, 302 N
Tramp, tramp, tramp along the highway, 173 N
Trampin', 186 H
Tränenregen, 317 N
Trau' nicht der Liebe, 435 R
Trauende, Der, 439 E
Traum, Der, 310 S
Traum durch die Dämmerung, 301 F, 357 I
Traum, Ein, 143 K
Traumbild, Das, 251 L
Träume, 418 O
Träume, traüme du, mein süsses Leben, 358 H
Traumerzählung, 3 R
Traumgekrönt, 41 R

Traure, mein Herz, 422 S
Traurigkeit ward mir zum Lose, 245 P
Traveller benighted, The, 181 B
Traviata, La, 401 M
Trav'llers all of ev'ry station, 30 D
Tre giorni son che Nina, 79 Q
Trees, 296 R
Treibe nur mit lieben Spott, 436 A
Tremin gl' insani, 398 B
Trenne nicht das Band der Liebe, 198 S
Trepak, 259 E
Trepp' hinuntergeschwungen, 209 D
Tresor du verger, Le, 279 G
Tresse, tresse, ma ma tresse, 360 D
Tretet ein, hoher Krieger, 435 S
Treu sein, das liegt mir nicht, 352 P
Treue Liebe, 55 O
Treue Liebe dauert lange, 57 A
Treulich geführt ziehet dahin, 410 C
Trial by jury, 373 D
Tribulationes civitatum, 269 B
Tricerbero humiliato, Il, 155 G
Tringles des sistres, Les, 46 L
Trinke, Liebchen, trinke schnell, 351 H
Trinket alle daraus, 27 C
Trinklied vom Jammer der Erde, Das, 215 P
Tripping hither, tripping thither, 364 G
Triptico, 387 J
Tristan musste ohne Dank, 175 J
Tristan und Isolde, 417 M
Triste estaba el Rey David, 256 A
Triste èt dans l'angoisse, 127 Q
Triste maggio, 85 E
Tristes apprêts, 296 O
Tristesse, 107 N
Tristis est anima mea, 202 R
Tritt auf, 56 F
Tritt auf die Glanbensbaum, 18 F
Trionfi Amore, 131 P
Triumph of time and truth, The, 166 H
Triumphlied, 198 K
Trockne Blumen, 318 C
Trocknet nicht, 38 D, 120 I
Trois anges sont venus, 176 L
Trois ballades de François Villon, 89 L
Trois beaux oiseaux du paradis, 299 S
Trois bourrées, 72 I
Trois chansons, 299 R
Trois chansons de Charles d'Orleans, 87 I
Trois chansons de France, 89 O
Trois histoires pour enfants, 361 I
Trois mélodies, 89 R
Trois poèmes de Claudel, 180 C
Trois Poèmes de Jean Cocteau, 236 N
Trois poèmes de Mallarmé, 300 B
Trois poèmes de Paul Fort, 180 F
Trois prières, Les, 266 Q
Trommel gerühret, Die, 35 O
Trompeten, 175 F
Trompeter von Sakkingen, Der, 260 O

Trooper before the battle, The, 79 H
Trooper's drinking song,. 175 K
Trop aimable Sylvie, 424 H
Tröste mir, Jesu mein Gemüthe, 17 I
Tröstung, 230 F
Trotz dem alten Drachen, 24 L
Troubador, The, 402 N
Troubled waters, 79 A
Troupeau verni des moutons, Le, 298 F
Trout, The, 322 H
Trovatore, Il, 402 N
Troyens, Les, 43 A
Trübe Augen, Liebchen taugen, 422 H
Trudged along the road three orphans, 195 C
True love, 175 J
Truffle song, 353 A
Trumpet shall sound, The, 164 B
Trunkene im Frühling, Der, 215 L
Try we life long, we can never, 362 H
Try'n a make Heav'n my home, 186 H
Tsaat een meskin, 264 B
Tu al cui sguardo, 394 C
Tu as tout seul, 375 K
Tu ch' hai le penne, amore, 70 N
Tu ch' odi lo mio grido, 220 O
Tu che a Dio, 98 D
Tu che di gel sei cinto, 287 J
Tu che le vanità, 393 S
Tu crois au marc de café, 147 N
Tu fosti traditor, 254 N
Tu l'as dit: oui tu m'aimes!, 234 J
Tu lo sai, 384 N
Tu m'as donné le plus doux rêve, 91 L
Tu m'as donné un coussin de soie, 148 H
Tu mia speranza, 151 P
Tu n'est pas beau, 265 O
Tu non sai, 39 M
Tu pauperum refugium, 190 D
Tu puniscemi o Signore, 397 L
Tu sa' ch' io so, 65 L
Tu sais, o gentile déesse, 201 S
Tu sè morta, 240 D
Tu sul labbro de'veggenti, 398 C
Tu te plais, 296 E
Tu tu, amore, 285 N
Tu? Tu? Piccolo Iddio, 285 G
Tu vas, m'a-t-elle dit, 46 H
Tu vedrai che amore in terra, 403 R
Tu virginum corona, 242 Q
Tua Santuzza piange, La, 219 S
Tuba mirum, 255 E
Tuba mirum spargens sonum, 404 Q
Tücsök lakodalon, 196 E
Tüeres aquel mal gitano, 106 D
Tuku, tuku, lampaitani, 390 Q
Tummel dich, guts Weinlein, 175 K
Tune thy strings, oh gypsy, 102 M
Tuoi occhi, I, 221 A
Tuol laulaa neitonen, 342 M
Turandot, 287 A
Turn, oh turn in this direction, 367 L

Turn back O Man, 177 E
Turn not, o Queen, thy face away, 159 M
Turiddu, mi tolse, 220 A
Turiddu's farewell, 220 F
Turiddu-Santuzza duet, 219 O, 219 R
Turn Thee to me, 102 E
Turn, turn then thine eyes, 292 Q
Turtle dove, The, 390 J
Tus ojillos negros, 106 Q
Tus ojos, ojos no son, 387 L
Tutta raccolta ancor, 156 L
Tutte le feste, 400 N
Tutte nel cor vi sento, 244 K
Tutti i fior?, 285 D
Tutto è festo, 399 Q
Tutto il prato d'un tappeto, 219 A
Tutto scordiam!, 206 G
Tutto sorridere, 308 M
Tutto sprezzo che d'Ernani, 394 K
Tutto tace, 218 S
'Twas a Marechal of France, 36 G
'Twas in fifty-five on a winter's night, 2 J
'Twas in Trafalgar's lovely bay, 53 C
Twas when the sea was roaring, 272 G
'Twas within a mile of Edinboro town, 180 N
T'was you alone, 379 A
Twenty lovesick maidens we, 366 S
Twenty popular Spanish songs, 262 Q
Twenty Spanish folk songs, 262 Q
Twilight musing, 193 B
Twilight of the Gods, 415 K
Twilight people, The, 390 A
Two Brown Eyes, 141 S
Two corpses, 79 I
Two Grenadiers, The, 335 K
Two little flowers, 186 F
Two widows, The, 347 B
Tyndaris, 148 Q
Tyrannic love, 287 O
Tyrolean, 309 O

U

Uber allen Gipfeln ist Ruh' 324 J, 338 D
Uber den Sternen ist Ruh, 1 D
Uber die Berge steigt schon die Sonne, 229 B
Uber die Heide, 60 A
Uber die See, 58 R
Uber meines Liebchens Augeln, 321 K
Uber Nacht, 436 B
Uber Stock und Stein, 413 G
Uber weite Wiesen schweif 439 B
Uber Wiesen und Felder ein Knabe ging, 357 J
Uber Wildemann, 325 A
Uber Wipfel und Saaten, 346 J
Uberläufer, Der, 57 I
Uber'm Garten durch die Lüfte, 333 S
Ubi est Abel, 3 F.
Udir talvolta, L', 301 Q
Udite, tutti, udite, 81 B
Udite! Udite! o rustici, 94 Q

Uhr, Die, 209 R
Ulla, my Ulla, 40 G
Ulla's Trip to the Deer park, 40 B
Ultima canzone, L', 386 E
Ultima prova dell' amor mio, L', 251 E
Um der fallenden Ruder, 356 N
Um frech den Ubermut zu fröhnen, 353 K
Um Mitternacht, 436 C
Um Mitternacht hab' ich gewacht, 216 D
Umsonst, 119 L
Un angeklopft ein Herr tritt, 428 E
Un bel di vedremo, 285 B
Un disprezzato affeto, 154 E
Un giorno la mano, 98 K
Un jour de printemps, 48 B
Una furtiva lagrima, 95 E
Una notte al davanzale ero, 80 Q
Una te falanz emprece, 361 B
Una voce poco fa, 307 N
Unbarmherziges Gerichte, Ein, 14 S
Uncle Ned, 116 Q
Und dass ihr's alle wisst, 21 J
Und der Engel sprach, 175 O
Und der Haifisch der hat Zähne, 425 G
Und die mich trug in Mutterarm, 339 I
Und diesen unberuhrten trunk, 354 O
Und du wirst mein Gebieter sein, 354 M
Und ein Duften zieht über die Erdenwelt, 112 S
Und gestern hat er mir Rosen gebracht, 218 H
Und mild sang die Nachtigall, 353 P
Und morgen wird die Sonne, 357 N
Und ob die Wolke sie verhülle, 422 F
Und steht ihr früh am Morgen auf, 436 D
Und wieder hatt' ich der Schönsten, 333 A
Und willst du deinen Liebsten sterben sehen, 436 E
Und. wüssten's die Blumen, 335 B
Under the greenwood tree, 6 S 270 P
Under the wide and starry sky, 177 H
Underneath a cypress shade, 276 N
Undine, 201 L
Une fois, terrassé par un puissant breuvage, 100 Q
Unfall, 436 F
Unforeseen, The, 341 A
Ungeduld, 317 K
Unglücksel'ge, Der, 416 N
Unis dès la plus tendre enfance, 130 M
United Nations, 342 D
Uns ist ein Kind geboren, 17 O
Unser Mund, sei voll Lachens, 16 K
Unser trefflicher lieber Kammerherr, 21 C
Unsere Leibe, 192 H

Unter blüh'nden Mandelbäumen, 421 H
Unter dem roten Blumen schlummere, 339 B
Unter die Soldaten ist ein Zigeunerbub' gegangen, 336 R
Unter verschnittenen Weiden, 175 F
Unter'm Fenster, 332 D
Until, 314 J
Unverliebare Gewähr, 192 P
Up in the sky someone is playing, 232 E
Upon a bank of roses, 419 Q
Urlicht, 215 S
Urna fatale del mio destino, 396 J

V

Va, charité, 111 F
Và godendo vezzoso e bello, 157 B
Va! laisse couler mes larmes, 225 K
Va nella tua stanzetta, 220 G
Va, pensiero, sull' ali dorate, 398 G
Va sur l'aîle des doux zéphirs, 51 K
Va! Va! Va! dit elle, 235 B
Vacant chair, The, 306 M
Vado a morir, 158 H
Vado ben spesso, 67 I, 306 S
Vado coro, 94 E
V'adoro, pupille, 153 K
Vagabond, 185 N, 389 N
Vagabond King, 121 L, 121 M
Vagabonde, La, 48 J
Vaghe pupille, 154 A
Vaghi fiori e l'amorose fronde, I, 267 D
Vaghissima sembianza, 93 P
Vague et la Cloche, La, 100 Q
Vagues en hurlant assiegent, Les, 304 M
Vainement ma bien aimée, 200 D
Vaisseaux! nous vous aurons aimés, 111 B
Valaki jár udvaromon, 93 B
Vallon, Le, 138 Q
Vallons de l'Helvétie, 1 K
Valse de Chopin, 218 I
Valse du Colibri, 388 D
Values, 388 B
Van, ven, ven!, 346 O
Vandring i skoven, 142 F
Vanne Orfeo felice a pieno, 240 P
Vanno laggiù verso, 206 A
Var det en dröm?, 342 L
Var förnimmelser, 342 Q
Varen flyktar hastigt, 342 F
Varlaam's song, 256 G
Vasárnap bort inni, 196 F
Vase brisé, Le, 118 J
Vase où meurt cette verveine, Le, 118 J
Vater, du führe mich!, 327 I
Vater! Hör' mich fleh'n zu dir, 422 M
Vater, ich rufe dich, 175 B, 327 H
Vater im Himmel, 170 S
Vater! Mutter! Hier will ich knien!, 184 A

Vater, Mutter, Schwestern, Brüder, 210 M
Vater unser im Himmelreich, 21 P
Vaterland, in deinen Gauen, 230 E
Ve' se di notte, 393 E
Veau d'or, Le, 134 M
Vecchia zimarra, 284 B
Vecchiotto cerca moglie, Il, 308 F
Vecerní Písné, 347 L
Ved Gjaetle—Bekken, 144 J
Ved Jaegerhuset, 167 M
Vedi? di morte l'angelo radiante, 392 J
Vedi io piango, 126 O
Vedi! le fosche notturne, 402 S
Vedi, vedi, son io che piango, 285 R
Vedrai, carino, 250 O
Vedrò mentr' io sospiro, 248 M
Vedrommi intorno, 244 L
Veggio co' vostri occhi, 65 H
Veglia o donna, 400 C
Veilchen, Die, K.476, 247 K
Veilchen auf der Wiese stand, Ein, 247 K
Veille sur eux toujours, 233 R
Veillez sur moi quand je m'éveille, 117 N
Velvet shoes, 381 R
Vendetta, La, 247 S
Venetian Night, 128 M
Venetianisches Gondellied, 229 P
Venetianisches Wiegenlied, 218 J
Venez agréable printemps, 424 I
Venez, secondez mes desirs, 129 I
Venez, venez, haine implacable, 129 L
Venezianisches Intermezzo, 192 R
Veni, o figlio, 154 I
Venise, 138 S
Venite al l'aggile, 83 R
Venite exultemus Domino, 84 L
Venite, inginocchiatevi, 248 I
Vent d'hiver souffle, Le, 313 N
Vent souffle et notre gondole, Le, 40 M
Venti scudi, 95 D
Verachtest du den Reichtum seiner Gnade, 15 S
Verachtet mir die Meister nicht, 412A
Verbirg dich, Sonne, 326 N
Verborgenheit, 436 G
Verbunk, 196 G
Verdankt sei es dem Glanz, K.392, 246 I
Verdi prati, 151 J
Verfliesset, viel geliebte, Lieder, 230 I
Verführer! warum stellt ihr so, 261 K
Vergangen is der lichte Tag, 230 I
Vergebliches Ständchen, 59 N
Vergessen, 119 F
Vergieb o Vater, 14 Q
Vergin, tutta amor, 101 E
Vergine bella, 99 O
Vergine degli angeli, La, 396 D
Vergine, un angiol, Una, 95 G
Vergissmeinnicht, 329 O
Vergnügte Ruh', beliebte Seelenlust, 18 P

Verirrt, 342 G
Verklärung, 329 Q
Verlassen, 316 K
Verlassen Mägdlein, Das, 336 C, 436 H
Véronique, 232 P
Verranno a te, 97 J
Verrat, 61 I
Versank ich jetzt, 409 D
Verschling' der Abgrund, 436 I
Verschweigung, Die, 249 M
Verschwender, Der, 199 B
Verschwiegene Liebe, 436 J
Verschwiegenen, Die, 356 E
Verspruch, 139 G
Verstumme, Höllenheer, 8 P
Vert colibri, Le, 77 P
Verwundete, Der, 143 F
Very warm for May, 191 E
Verzagen, 59 K
Verzeihe, wenn ich nicht weiss, 416 L
Verzweifelte Liebhaber, Der, 436 K
Veslemöy, 144 D
Vesperae solennes de confessore, K.339, 244 E
Vespers, 120 R
Vespri Siciliani, I, 404 D
Vestale, La, 349 B
Vesti la giubba, 206 H
Vévig mentem a tárkányi sej, haj, 31 S
Vezzosette e care, 105 S
V'ho ingannato, 401 D
Vi fida lo sposo, 152 P
Vi ravviso, 39 L
Vi ricorda o boschi ombrosi, 240 C
Via caro sposino, 94 H
Via resti servita, Madama brillante!, 248 A
Vibrez encor, sainte harmonie, 111 K
Vicenzella tesseva, 85 C
Vicino a te, 126 L
Victoire en chantant, La, 226 J
Victoria! Victoria!, 210 H
Vida Breve, La, 106 S
Vidĕl jsem ji Xenii jsem zrel, 101 I
Videt suum dulcem natum, 274 L
Vie Antérieure, La, 100 R
Vieille chanson, 48 C
Viel bin ich umhergewandert, 439 F
Viel Glück zur Reise, Schwalben!, 338 R
Viele Fäden gleiten, 438 G
Vien, diletto è in ciel, 39 E
Vien, Leonora, 95 L
Vieni a regni del riposo, 131 K
Vieni, ah vien, 96 C
Vieni, che poi sereno, 132 D
Vieni con me sui, 80 J
Vieni fra queste braccia, 39 H
Vieni Imeneo, 239 N
Vieni! la mia vendetta, 98 G
Vieni, l'aula è deserta, 399 H
Vieni meco, sol di rose, 394 O
Vieni: sul crin ti piovanno, 391 K
Vieni, torna, idolo mio, 158 D
Viens avec nous petit, 132 I
Viens, c'est le jour d'un Dieu, 147 Q
Viens dans ce bocage, 423 H

Viens, gentille dame, 49 J
Viens, lorsque dans l'azur, 138 C
Viens, ô mon épouse, 294 J
Viens par le pré, 72 P
Vier adlige Rosse voran, 358 C
Vier ernste Gesänge, 61 Q
Vier et lystigt, 167 L
Vierge à la Crèche, La, 118 K
Vieux faune de terre cuite, Un, 88'S
Vilia Song, 204 B
Villa vid denna Kalla, 40 H
Village bells are ringing, The, 116 R
Village maiden, The, 116 R
Villanelle, 1 H, 42 J, 196 N
Villanelle des petits canards, 75 M
Ville superbe, 304 Q
Villi, Le, 287 K
Vilse, 342 G
Vin ou bière, 134 K
Vingt chants populaires espagnols, 262 Q
Vingt-cinq d'Août, Le, 184 M
Viola quebrada, 407 B
Violetera, La, 266 G
Violon, Le, 280 S
Violon, hippocampe et sirène, 281 G
Virágos kenderem, 196 H
Virgin unspotted, A, 44 L
Virgin's Lullaby, 66 O
Virgin's slumber song, 300 S
Viri Galilaei, 84 V
Vision fugitive, 222 M
Vissi d'arte, 286 M
Vit encore ce faux dangier, 406 A
Vittoria mio core, 74 G
Viva il vino ch'è sincero, 220 E
Viva il vino spumeggiante, 220 D
Vivan los que rien, 106 S
Vivandiere, La, 132 I
Vivat Bacchus! 246 A
Vive David, vainqueur des Philistins, 178 P
Vivere in fretta, 126 E
Vivete in pace, 50 L
Vivra! Contende il giubilo, 404 C
Vladimir's Cavatina, Prince Igor, 51 F
Vo far guerra, 155 H
Vocalise, 295 M, 298 G
Voce di donna, 277 Q
Vogel, Die, 329 S
Vögelein durchrauscht die Luft, 63 K
Vögelein fliegt, Ein, 61 C
Vogelfänger bin ich, Der, 253 E
Vogelhändler, Der, 441 S
Vöglein Schwermut, 192 K
Vöglein singt im Wald, Ein, 300 F
Voi che sapete, 248 H
Voi dolci aurette al cor, 158 G
Voi lo sapete, 219 N
Voi partite mio Sole, 121 D
Voi siete un po' tordo, 251 O
Voici des fruits, 109 P, 148 D
Voici des roses, 42 N
Voici la fine sauterelle, 279 P
Voici la saison, mignonne, 135 A
Voici le printemps, 312 M
Voici le sabre, 265 E
Voici les fruits des fleurs des feuilles, 87 R

Voici l'hiver et son triste cortège, 111 E
Voici l'orme qui balance, 147 O
Voici que le printemps, 88 M
Voici que les jardins de la nuit, 110 K
Voici ton Jean, 341 P
Voici venir les temps, 88 H
Voi dovrete fare da madre, 220 F
Voilà donc la terrible cité, 224 N
Voir naître une enfant, 76 S
Vois ma misère, hélas, 312 S
Voix de l'amour, 138 E
Voix des chênes, La, 133 N
Voix légère chanson passagère, 221 M
Vola, o serenata, 386 C
Volate più dei venti, 153 P
Volgalied, 204 K
Volgi liete o fieri sguardi, 253 C
Völker! Seid des Volkes Gäste, 359 N
Volkskinderlieder, 55 I
Volkslied, 229 D, 300 F
Volksliedchen, 335 N
Vollmond strahlt auf Bergeshöh'n, 322 E
Volta la terre a fronte, 392 P
Vom Bade kehrt der König heim, 412 E
Vom Berg hinabgestiegen, 437 A
Vom Tode, 36 A
Von allen schönen Kindern auf der Welt, 229 O
Von Apfelblüten einen Kranz, 203 P
Von den Stricken meiner Sünden, 25 S
Von der Erde, 329 B
Von der Jugend, 215 I
Von der Schönheit, 215 K
Von der Strasse her ein Posthorn klingt, 319 M
Von der Welt verlang'ich nichts, 12 J
Von des Tayo Strand, 354 A
Von ewiger Liebe, 57 B
Von Himmel hoch, 212 Q
Von Jugend auf in dem Kampfgefild, 422 J
Von Melodien die mich umfliehen, 439 A
Von zwei Rosen, 192 C
Vond Dag, 144 I
Vor dem Fenster, 55 R
Vor der Tür, 56 F
Vor der Tür im Sonnenscheine, 275 M
Vor lauter hochadligen Zeugen, 429 I
Vor meiner Wiege, 324 Q
Vorfrühling, 192 Q
Vorrei, 386 G
Vorrei dir, 252 A
Vorrei morir, 386 I
Vorschneller Schwur, 60 N
Vort Dagwaerk er til Ende, 167 J
Vorüber, ach, vorüber!, 320 R
Vote, women have the vote, The, 383 R
Votre âme, est un paysage, 77 D, 88 Q, 108 Q, 375 M
Votre toast je peux vous le rendre, 46 M

Vouchsafe, O Lord, 149 Q
Vous aurez beau fair et beau dire!, 114 K
Vous avez dit vrai!, 225 F
Vous dansez, marquise, 205 H
Vous étiez ce que vous n'êtes plus, 141 M
Vous m'aimez dites-vous, 1 S
Vous me demandez de me taire, 108 F
Vous pouvez mépriser les yeux, 77 E
Vous qui du Dieu vivant, 149 E
Vous qui du haut des cieux, 136 G
Vous qui faites L'endormie, 135 L
Vous qui pleurez, 111 J
Vous savez, Seigneur, ma misère, 78 J
Voyage à Paris, 279 L
Voyageur, Le, 108 C
Voyez sur cette roche, 7 L
Voyons Manon, plus de chimères, 223 G
Vox dilecti mei, 269 D
Vrai, d'un coeur, Le, 305 M
Vsecko je tvoje, 346 P
Vug, o Vove, 143 L
Vuggesang, 142 B
Vulnerasti cor meum, 269 E
Vyzvání, 348 A

W

Wach' auf! 411 Q
Wach, auf mein Herzens schöne, 62 I
Wache, Wala!, 415 C
Wachet auf, ruft uns die Stimme, 17 K
Wacht auf, 9 M
Wacht auf ihr Adern und ihr Glieder, 16 L
Wachtel Schlag, Der, 38 C
Wachtelschlag, Der, 323 P
Waffenschmied, Der, 210 Q
Waft her, angels, through the skies, 160 G
Wagen musst du und flüchtig erbeuten, 435 H
Wahn! Wahn!, 411 H
Wahrlich, ich sage euch, 14 P
Waikiki, 144 P
Wald beginnt zu rauschen, Der, 359 A, 218 K
Waldeinsamkeit, 300 I
Waldemar's Song, 316 O, 316 Q
Waldesgespräch, 187 Q, 333 J
Waldmeister, 352 J
Waldschloss, Das, 231 L
Waldseligkeit, 359 A, 218 K
Waldtaube's Song, 316 R
Walking stronger under distant skies, 186 E
Walküre, Die, 413 L
Walle, Regen, walle nieder, 58 E
Wally, La, 74 R
Walpurgisnacht, 209 C
Waltz dream, 350 S, 351 A
Waltz, from Eugene Onegin, 376 R
Waltz, from The Count of Luxemburg, 204 F
Waltz Song, from Tom Jones, 123 L

Wälze dich hinweg, 329 A
Wandelnde Glocke, Die, 209 F
Wanderbursch, Ein, 210 F
Wanderer, Der, 320 J
Wanderer, The, 61 M, 172 C
Wanderer an den Mond, Der, 324 B
Wanderers Nachtlied, 311 R, 320 L 324 J, 436 L
Wanderlied, 332 H
Wandern, Das, 317 D
Wandern lieb' ich für mein Leben, 434 B
Wanderträume, 112 O
Wanderung, 332 K
Wandl' ich in dem Wald des Abends, 120 K
Wand'ring minstrel I, A, 365 G
Wann der silberne Mond, 57 C
Wann erscheint der Morgen, 336 G
Wann kommst du, 17 L
War es also gemeint, 317 G
Wär' es auch nichts als ein Augenblick, 203 N
War es ein Traum, 342 L
War es so schmählich, 414 G
War schöner als der schönste Tag, 210 E
Wäre dieser nicht ein Ubelthäter, 26 F
Warm perfumes like a breath, 144 P
Warnung, K.433, 247 H, 316 G
Warnung vor dem Rhein, 231 M
Warrior bold, A, 2 M
War 's das lachende Glück, 204 F
Wär's dunkel, ich läg im Walde, 275 L
War's Zauber, war es reine Macht, 416 J
Warst du nicht, heil'ger, Abendschein!, 332 M
Warum denn warten von Tag zu Tag, 61 E
Warum Geliebte, 434 L
Warum hast du mich mach geküsst, 203 F
Warum hast Du mich verlassen, 171 C
Warum hat jeder Frühling, 204 M
Warum kannte in früheren Tagen, 377 E
Warum so spät erst, 356 C
Was bedeutet die Bewengung?, 229 N, 321 I
Was des Höchsten Glanz erfüllt, 20 A
Was die Welt in sich hält, 12 I
Was doch heut' Nacht ein Sturm gewesen, 429 G
Was duftet doch der Flieder so mild, 410 S
Was frag' ich nach der Welt, 15 F
Was für ein Lied soll dir gesungen werden, 436 M
Was gehst du, armer bleicher Kopf, 192 L
Was glänzt dort vom Walde, 423 B
Was gleicht wohl auf Erden, 422 I
Was Gott thut, 15 K
Was i hab, 49 F

Was I not a blade of grass in meadow green, 378 N
Was ich längst erträumte, 204 G
Was im Netze?, 430 I
Was im Saal, in jedem Stübchen, 101 L
Was ist Silvia, 324 S
Was it a dream?, 342 L
Was leuchtet ihr Sterne, 174 P
Was lispeln die Winde, 60 D
Was mein Gott will, 27 H
Was mich auf dieser Welt betrübt, 69 E
Was mir behagt ist nur die munt're Jagd, 20 M
Was ruht dort schlummernd, 415 F
Was sind das helle Fensterlein?, 430 F
Was soll der milde Abend?, 323 S
Was soll der Zorn, mein Schatz, 436 N
Was soll ich aus dir machen, Ephraim, 14 S
Was soll ich sagen!, 331 P
Was spinnst Du?, 251 N
Was sucht denn der Jäger, 317 R
Was vermeid ich denn die Wege, 320 A
Was weht um meine Schläfe, 336 J
Was weilst du einsam an dem Himmel, 326 A
Was will die einsame Thräne?, 331 K
Wasp, The, 41 H
Wassail song, 177 F, 390 K, L
Wasserfahrt, 231 H
Wasserflut, 319 F
Water mill, The, 390 B
Water parted from the sea, 7 A
Way down on de old plantation, 115 C
Way down upon de Swanee Ribber, 116 K
We are dainty little fairies, 364 H
We are peers of highest station, 364 L
We are the chorus of the V.I.P., 383 L
We are warriors three, 369 O
We come, in bright array, 161 D
We do not heed their dismal sound, 366 B
We have a home 'neath the forest shade, 173 E
We have made a grave for little Belle Blair, 115 M
We parted in the springtime, 115 Q
We sail the ocean blue, 363 D
We shall meet but we shall miss him, 306 M
We shepherds sing, 425 E
We take the golden road to Samarkand, 91 Q
We the spirits of the air, 289 K
We triumph now for well we trow, 369 K
Weary the cry of the wind, 144 R
Wedding cantata, 19 N
Wedding of the cricket, 196 E
Weep and mourn, 257 A
Weep you no more, 293 J

Weep you no more, sad fountains, 99 F
Weeping willow, The, 196 C
Wegweiser, Der, 320 A
Weh! der Seele, 15 R
Weh, wie zornig ist das Mädchen, 339 O
Wehe dem fliehenden Welt hinaus ziehenden, 318 K
Wehe, Lüftchen, lind und lieblich, 57 E
Wehen mir Lüfte Ruh, 421 K
Wehet, weht ihr Flockensterne, 140 P
Wehmuth, 321 S, 333 P
Weht, Bäume des Lebens, 229 N
Wehvolles Erbe, 412 G
Weia! Waga! Woge, 413 D
Weiche, Wotan, weiche!, 413 H
Weichet nur, 20 D
Weicht all' ihr Ubelthäter, 17 J
Weigenlied, 188 E
Weihnachtslieder, 83 I
Weil auf mir, du dunkles Auge, 119 H
Wein' an den Felsen, 43 K
Weinen, Klagen, Sorgen, Zagen, 9 E
Weise nicht von dir mein schlichtes Herz, 316 I
Weiss, dass ein Trugbild du, 101 K
Weiss ich doch eine, 344 O
Weisse und rothe Rose, 105 L
Weisser Jasmin, 357 M
Weisst noch das grosse Nest, 184 B
Weit und breit schaut Niemand mich an, 55 G
Weite wiesen im Dämmergrau, 301 F, 357 I
Welch Ubermass der Güte schenkst du mir, 9 I
Welche Wonne, welche Lust, 245 R
Welcome, gentry, for your entry, 371 H
Welcome joy! adieu to sadness!, 372 K
Welcome sweet pleasure, 425 D
Welk sind die Blätter, 342 S
We'll to the woods no more, 185 O
Wellen blinken und fliessen dahin, Die, 59 D
Welsh lullaby, A, 270 Q
Welsh songs, 38 B
Welt, ade! ich bin denin müde, 19 Q
Welt kann ihre Lust und Freud', Die, 15 F
Welt verstummt, Die, 358 I
Welten singen, 34 R
Wem Gott will rechte Gunst erweisen, 230 K
Wenn alle Wälder schliefen, 334 L
Wenn auf dem höchsten Fels ich steh', 325 G
Wenn das Lieb' aus deinen blauen, 429 Q
Wenn dein ich denk', 235 J
Wenn dein Mütterlein, 214 J
Wenn der Frühling aug die Berge, 32 P

Wenn der uralte heilige Vater, 327 L, 431 M

Wenn die Frühlingslüfte Streichen, 20 F

Wenn die kleinen Kinder, 300 P

Wenn die Rosen blühen, 301 H

Wenn die Schwalben heimwärts ziehn, 1 E

Wenn die Sonne lieblich schiene, 231 K

Wenn die Sonne nieder sinket, 35 A

Wenn du es wüsstest was träumen heisst, 357 F

Wenn du, mein Liebster, steigst zum Himmel auf, 436 O

Wenn du mich mit den Augen streifst, 436 P

Wenn du nur zuweilen lächelst, 57 M

Wenn du zu den Blumen gehst, 436 Q

Wenn du zu mei'm Schatzl kommt, 199 J

Wenn durch Berg' und Thale, 332 F

Wenn durch die Piazzetta, 188 C, 229 P, 331 J

Wenn Filli ihre Liebesstrahl, 316 B

Wenn fromme Kindlein schlafen geh'n, 337 E

Wenn hell die liebe Sonne lacht, 300 R

Wenn ich auf dem Lager liege, 231 G

Wenn ich dich frage, 359 E

Wenn ich durch Wald und Fluren geh', 321 S

Wenn ich früh in den Garten geh, 335 N

Wenn ich, Herr, deinen Zorn, 377 F

Wenn ich im Kampfe für dich siege, 409 J

Wenn ich in deine Augen seh', 127 G, 334 Q

Wenn ich jenes Täubchen wär, 351 E

Wenn ich mit Menschen, 62 A

Wenn ich nur ein Vöglein wäre, 328 B

Wenn ich, von deinem Anschaun, 428 P

Wenn im sonnigen Herbste die Traube schwillt, 184 D

Wenn in braunen Hafen alle Schiffe schlafen, 438 D

Wenn kommt der Tag, 13 B

Wenn man beim Wein sitzt, 216 H

Wenn mein Bastien, 241 S

Wenn mein Herz beginnt zu klingen, 61 L

Wenn mein Schatz Hochzeit macht, 215 O

Wenn meine Grillen schwirren, 322 K

Wenn meine Mutter hexen, könnt', 435 P

Wenn nur ein Traum das Leben, 215 L

Wenn sanft du mir, 358 B

Wenn sich bei heilger Ruh, 316 N

Wenn sich zwei Herzen scheiden, 231 C

Wenn sich zwei lieben, 204 H

Wenn Sie das gesehn, 352 D

Wenn so lind dein Auge mir, 63 F

Wenn über Berge sich der Nebel, 322 I

Wenn zu der Regenwand Phöbus sich gattet, 434 M

Wer auf den Wogen schliefe, 430 M

Wer dank opfert, das preiset mich, 9 H

Wer ein holdes Weib errungen, 33 J

Wer ein Liebchen hat gefunden, 245 I

Wer Gott bekennt, 11 G

Wer hat dich, du schöner Wald, 229 G

Wer hat dich so geschlagen, 26 B, 27 O

Wer hat die Liebe uns ins Herz gesenkt, 203 R

Wer hat dies Liedlein erdacht?, 214 R

Wer hat's Lieben erdacht, 439 G

Wer hätt das ahnen können, 304 C

Wer in der Fremde will wandern, 431 S

Wer in Lieb' entbrannt, 344 N

Wer ist denn draussen, 214 S

Wer ist vor meiner Kammerthur?, 332 D

Wer kann's mit worten sagen auch, 101 P

Wer lieben will, muss leiden, 358 S

Wer macht dich so krank?, 332 O

Wer mich liebet, der wird mein Wort halten, 13 K

Wer nie sein Brot mit Tränen ass, 321 E, 338 I, 431 P

Wer nur den lieben Gott lässt walten, 21 Q, 260 R

Wer nur der lieben Gott lässt walten, 15 E

Wer reitet so spät durch Nacht und Wind?, 209 B, 326 R

Wer rief dich denn, 436 R

Wer sein holdes Lieb verloren, 436 S

Wer sich der Einsamkeit, 321 D, 338 K, 431 N

Wer Sünde thut, 11 R

Wer uns getraut, 353 O

Wer wagt's, 330 C

Wer weiss wie nahe mir mein Ende, 10 D

Werde heiter mein Gemüthe, 230 F

We're called gondolieri, 362 C

Were I a sun, 78 Q

Were I laid on Greenland's coast, 271 Q

Were I thy bride, 374 C

We're saved, we're freed, 183 Q

Were she but kind, 291 E

Were you not to Ko Ko plighted, 365 O

Were you there, 68 G

Werther, 225 C

Werther! Werther! Qui m'aurait dit, 225 I

Wesendock Songs, 418 D

Weste wünsch ich von Seide mir, Eine, 144 A

Westwärts schweift der Blick, 417 M

Wetterfahne, Die, 319 B

Weun der Freude Thränen fliessen, 246 B

We've been awhile a-wandering, 390 L

We've trod one road, 185 C

What a young maiden loves, 79 C

What are the bugles blowin' for, 85 S

What has the coming day in store, 377 C

What if a day, or a month, or a year, 72 D

What if I sped, 188 S

What in the world could be so sweet, 216 K

What is America to me, 306 D

What is our life?, 125 H

What is this crying, 145 A

What is your name? Magda Sorel, 231 S

What shall I do, 289 C

What shall we do with a drunken sailor, 146 B

What sounds are those, 52 R

What though I trace each herb, 165 N

What's sweeter than the new-blown rose, 160 N

Wheelcart, barrow, wheelcart, sleigh, 195 G

When a fellow's not engaged in his employment, 369 G

When a merry maiden marries, 362 I

When a woman love pretends, 291 K

When all the birds are gone to sleep, 64 B

When an eye like fire glowing, 79 F

When anger spreads his wing, 270 N

When as the rye reach to the chin, 420 D

When at night I go to sleep, 183 G

When Britain first at Heav'ns command, 6 O

When Britain really rul'd the waves, 365 A

When daffodils begin to peer, 237 J

When daisies pied, 7 C

When darkly looms the day, 364 Q

When David heard, 384 L

When do I see thee most, 388 H

When dull care, 207 D

When e'er I spoke sarcastic joke, 370 K

When first I laid siege to my Chloris, 272 E

When first I saw my lovely maid, 166 B

When first my old, old love I knew, 373 E

When fishes flew and forests walked, 146 F

When for a moment thou dost speak, 79 J
When Fred'ric was a little lad, 368 D
When he is here I sigh with pleasure, 372 F
When I a lover pale do see, 292 R
When I am dying, 440 I
When I am laid in earth, 289 A
When I bring to you colour'd toys, 74 J
When I first put this uniform on, 367 D
When I go out of door, 368 B
When I, good friends, was call'd to the bar, 373 F
When I had money O!, 172 E
When I have often heard, 289 E
When I have sung my songs, 76 G
When I no more behold thee, 340 P
When I think upon the maidens, 172 H
When I was a bachelor, 64 L
When I was a lad I serv'd a term, 363 L
When I was a little lad, 226 H
When I was bound apprentice, 386 S
When I was seventeen, 207 J
When I went to the bar, 364 P
When I with pleasing wonder stand, 44 O
When icicles hang by the wall, 7 B
When I'm a bad Bart, 371 N
When I'm calling you, 121 J
When I'm lonely dear, 305 Q
When Israel was in Egypt's lan', 67 M
When Jesus wept, 44 P
When lawyers strive to heal a breach, 177 C
When love is kind, 5 L
When maiden loves, she sits and sighs, 373 M
When midnight is striking the hour, 128 K
When my sire was twenty years, 442 A
When other lips and other hearts, 30 C
When shadows fall, 216 Q
When that I was and a little tiny boy, 293 R
When the cock begins to crow, 292 S
When the dawn flames in the sky, 70 P
When the foeman bears his steel, 368 S
When the king went forth to war, 196 P
When the lad for longing sighs, 68 M
When the night wind howls, 371 R
When the two sisters go, 146 D
When the woods are gay, 104 L
When thoroughly tired of being admired, 371 I
When thou tookest upon thee to deliver, 149 R

When to the lute Corinna sings, 72 B
When will you come again, 37 S
When yesterday we met, 295 K
When you censure the age, 272 I
When you come to the end of a perfect day, 50 P
When you had left our pirate fold, 369 B
When you're away, dear, 174 B
When you're lying awake with a dismal headache, 365 C
Whene'er I ride through the tender grove, 122 B
Whenever Richard Cory went down town, 260 G
Where are now, 291 J
Where are you, beautiful moonlight madonna, 112 B
Where blue the Danube flows, 102 R
Where corals lie, 104 Q
Where got ye that silver moon, 37 N
Where Lagan stream sings, 167 O
Where, oh where is my golden spindle, 232 A
Where tears of my passion have fallen, 51 P
Where the Abana flows, 440 K
Where the bee sucks, 7 D
Where the ripe pears droop heavily, 41 H
Where the wild rose, 353 B
Where will you take me, little boat, 419 S
Where'er you walk, 165 I
Wherefore, 86 L, 378 B
Whether day dawns, 378 K
Whether I live, 270 R
Which one should I marry, 195 J
Which way shall I turn me, 273 C
While the stormy winds do blow, 71 J
While the sun shines in wonted spendor, 379 F
While yet the fields are wrapp'd in snow, 295 B
Whispers of heavenly death, 389 Q
White dawn is stealing, The, 70 S
White Eagle, The, 121 I
White flowers along the way, 101 N
White peace, The, 32 I
White swan, The, 5 O
Who is Sylvia, 294 B, 324 S
Who was this that came, 270 O
Who would not love me, 257 D
Who'll buy my lavender? 123 M
Who's master of the golden strings, 347 L
Why, 377 Q
Why am I drawn to these unhappy shores, 86 J
Why are mine eyes still flowing, 273 H
Why did you come in dreams to me, 378 B
Why do the nations, 163 P
Why does the God of Israel sleep?, 164 S
Why has thy merry face gone from my side, 115 L
Why how now, Madam Flirt, 272 P

Why is your faithful slave disdained, 271 G
Why should I sit and sigh, 190 L
Why so pale and wan, 270 S
Why so restive, 79 H
Widerstehe doch die Sünde, 11 Q
Widmung, 119 P, 330 P
Wie aus der Ferne, 408 S
Wie bist du, meine Königin, 56 K
Wie blitzen die Sterne, 324 I
Wie braust durch die Wipfel, 322 L
Wie der Quell so lieblich klinget, 229 A
Wie des Abends schöne Röte, 63 B
Wie des Mondes Abbild, 119 G
Wie dünkt mich doch die Aue, 412 O
Wie ein blasser, Tropfen Blut's, 218 I
Wie eine trübe Wolke, 319 L
Wie erhebt sich das Herz, 329 M
Wie fremd und todt ist Alles umher, 344 R
Wie freundlich strahlt der Tag, 114 F
Wie froh und frisch mein Sinn sich hebt, 56 S
Wie furchtsam wankten meine Schritte, 10 L
Wie glänzt der helle Mond, 437 C
Wie hat der Sturm zerrissen, 319 X
Wie heimlicher Weise ein Engelein leise, 437 M
Wie hell am Himmel, 345 P
Wie herrlich leuchtet mir die Natur, 37 C
Wie im Morgenglanze, 321 N, 430 S
Wie in der Luft, 342 R
Wie ist die Nacht, 301 B
Wie ist doch die Erde so schön, 55 M
Wie kann ich denn vergessen, 426 A
Wie kann ich froh und lustig sein?, 231 F
Wie klag ich's aus, 322 B
Wie komm ich denn zur Tür herein, 62 L
Wie lang wet men ins sticken, 216 O
Wie lange schon war immer mein Verlangen, 437 D
Wie lieblich klingt es in den Ohren, 17 G
Wie lieblich sind deine Wohnungen, 53 S
Wie lieblich und fröhlich, 329 S
Wie Melodien zieht es mir, 61 F
Wie, mit innigstem Behagen, 331 D
Wie oft in Meeres tiefsten Schlund, 408 I
Wie Sankt Franciscus schweb, ich in der Luft, 175 D
Wie schäumet du in den Gläsern, 344 I
Wie schienen die Sternlein so hell, 119 M
Wie Schleier sch' ich's niederschweben, 168 O
Wie schnell verschwindet, 56 Q

Wie schön bist Du, freundliche Stille, 321 L
Wie schön geschmückt der festliche Raum, 83 I
Wie sehr lieblich und schöne, 340 I
Wie sich der Auglein kindlicher Himmel, 324 O
Wie sie schmeicheln, 352 R
Wie sie selig, hehr und milde, 417 R
Wie so innig, möcht' ich sagen, 328 M
Wie so schwül ist es heut', 379 D
Wie soll ich fröhlich sein, 437 E
Wie soll ich nicht tanzen? 323 B
Wie sollten wir geheim sie halten, 356 Q
Wie Sonne lauter, 416 C
Wie stark is nicht dein Zauberton, 253 K
Wie Todesahnung Dämm'rung, 417 I
Wie traurig ringsum, 101 G
Wie viele Zeit verlor ich, 437 F
Wie war so schön doch Wald und Feld!, 230 A
Wie will ich lustig lachen, 20 J
Wie wunderbarlich, 27 S
Wie wundersam, 316 D
Wie zittern und wanken, 16 C
Wieder Bäume kühne Wipfel, 338 G
Wieder möcht' ich dir begegnen, 208 P
Wiederschein, 330 A
Wiegenlied, 57 L, 184 E, 324 M, 324 O, 336 O, 358 H. 423 F
Wiegenlied der Hirten, 301 J
Wiegenlied (Im Sommer), 437 A
Wiegenlied (Im Winter), 437 B
Wiegenlied, K.350, 244 F
Wiegenliedchen, 359 B
Wien, du Stadt meiner Träume, 343 F
Wien, Wien, nur du allein, 343 F
Wild rose, The, 103 K
Wild swan, The, 191 C
Wild verwachsne dunkle Fichten, 337 Q
Wilde Rose, 105 I
Wildschütz, Der, 210 R
Will God, whose mercies ever flow, 159 A
Will they remember that it is true, 383 M
Will you come homeward, 104 M
William Tell, 309 L
Willkommen im Grünen!, 228 I
Willow song, 399 L
Willow, tit-willow, 366 P
Willow, Willow, 420 R
Willst du dass ich geh?, 59 G
Willst du dein Herz mir schenken, 29 E
Willst jenes Tag's du nicht, 409 F
Wilt thou leave us all unprotected, 256 C
Wind spiele mit mir, 355 H
Wind spielt mit mir der Wetterfahne, Der, 319 B
Winde sausen am Tannenhang, Die, 325 A
Wind's not blowing, The, 305 L
Winter, 170 N

Winter is gone, The, 390 C
Winter mag scheidem, Der. 142 L
Winter song, 67 B
Winterabend, Der, 330 B
Winterliebe, 358 R
Winternacht, 192 N, 356 I
Winterreise, Die, 319 A
Winter's tale, A, 207 L
Winterstürme wichen dem Wonnemond, 413 N
Winterweihe, 358 Q
Wintry winds are white, The, 41 G
Wir betan zu den Tempel an, 11 M
Wir danken dir, Gott wir danken dir, 10 F
Wir eilen mit schwachen, 13 S
Wir gehn nun wo der Tudelsack, 21 K
Wir geniessen die himmlischen Freuden, 216 B
Wir gingen durch die stille milde nacht, 357 K
Wir haben biede lange Zeit geschwiegen, 437 G
Wir haben ein Gesetz, 26 I
Wir Kinder, wir schmecken der Freuden recht viel, 253 A
Wir liefen wohl irre den andern voran, 342 G
Wir müssen durch viel Trübsal, 17 S
Wir müssen uns trennen, 56 O
Wir sassen so traulich, 317 N
Wir sehen jetzt durch einen Spiegel, 62 B
Wir setzen uns mit Thränen, 28 H
Wir sind einander, 139 G
Wir sind ja, Kind, im Maie, 338 S
Wir sind zwei Rosen, 192 J
Wir singen und sagen, 209 E
Wir sitzen im Dunkeln, 192 I
Wir suchen sie, wir finden sie, 346 A
Wir treten zum Beten, 198 H
Wir wandelten, 60 R
Wir wandelten, wir zwei zusammen, 60 R
Wir winden dir den Jungfernkranz, 422 B
Wirbel schlag ich gar so stark, Der. 58 O
Wird mir, Herr mein Gott, 376 J
Wird Philomele trauern, 421 G
Wirf, mein Herze, wirf dich noch, 18 J
Wirst du des Vaters Wahl nicht Schelten?, 409 B
Wirtin Töchterlein, Der, 209 A
Wirtshaus, Das, 320 B
Wise it were and timely even now to marry, 195 J
Wise men. flatt'ring, may deceive us, 162 D
Wisst ihr wann mein Kindchen, 55 A
Wisst ihr wo ich gerne weil in der Abendkühle?, 231 B
With a Primrose, 143 B
With a sense of deep emotion, 373 H
With a Water-Lily, 142 Q

With cat like tread upon our prey we steal, 369 H
With crash of battle, 259 J
With drooping wings, 289 B
With eagerness the husbandman, 170 G
With heart and with voice, 372 H, 372 J
With honour let desert be crown'd 162 H
With joyous shout, 365 R
With Nanny, 258 H
With pilgrim's staff, 295 C
With pious hearts, 162 C
With rue my heart is laden, 30 Q, 68 L
With short, sharp, violent lights, 104 R
With the Winter, Death, 176 C
With thee th' unsheltered moor I'd tread, 165 O
With verdure clad, 169 L
With wed led said, 382 Q
With your foot you tap, tap, tap, 182 S
Within a mile of Edinboro', 180 N
Within four walls, 259 K
Within the woodlands, 388 O
Wo bist du, Bild, 251 L
Wo bist Du, mein gelibtes Land, 320 K
Wo blüht das Blümchen, 35 Q
Wo die Berge so blau, 35 G
Wo die Rose hier blüht, 428 M
Wo die schönen Trompeten blasen, 214 S
Wo du hingehst, 174 S
Wo ein treues Herze, 318 D
Wo find' ich Trost, 437 H
Wo ich bin, 359 C
Wo ich ferne des Mikane, 218 F
Wo ich sei, und wo mich hingewendet, 329 K
Wo lange noch der Ruferschalle, 416 S
Wo Liebesgötter lachten, 168 L
Wo noch kein Wandrer gegangen, 231 L
Wo sie war die Müllerin, 441 Q
Wo soll ich fliehen hin, 8 P
Wo weht der Liebe hoher Geist 328 E
Wo zwei und drei versammlet sind, 11 B
Woe is me, 195 M
Woe, woe unto them, 226 S
Woglinde's Song, Das Rheingold, 413 O
Wohin?, 317 E
Wohin ich geh', 53 J, 230 B
Wohin nun Tristan scheidet, 417 Q
Wohin? o Helios!, 327 E
Wohin so schnell, 317 S
Wohl denk' ich allenthalben, 326 Q
Wohl denk' ich oft, 437 I
Wohl euch. ihr auserwählten Seelen, 10 M
Wohl hub auch ich voll Sehnsucht, 409 A
Wohl kenn' ich euren Stand, 437 J
Wohl manchen Rosenzweig, 112 J
Wohl schön bewandt war es, 63 B
Wohl wusst' ich, 417 F
Wohlauf. ihr lieben Gäste, 314 N
Wohlauf! noch getrunken, 332 H

Wohlauf und frisch gewandert, 332 K
Wolfserzählung, 3 S
Wolken die ihr nach Osten eilt, 333 B
Wolkenlos strahlt jetzt die Sonne, 422 P
Woman is a Sometime Thing, A, 123 P
Woman of the wisest wit, The, 370 I
Woman, woman, out of your bed!, 194 L
Wondrous machine, 292 A
Wonne der Wehmut, 38 D, 120 I
Woodland Stillness, 172 P
Woodman, spare that tree!, 312 B
World is but a broken toy, The, 370 G
World to soaring genius, The, 236 T
World when day's career is run, The, 159 Q
Worm, The, 86 M
Worthy is the lamb, 164 F
Would God I were the tender apple blossom, 5 H
Would I might be hang'd, 273 I
Would you gain the tender creature, 158 N
Would you have a young virgin, 272 B
Would you know the kind of maid, 370 J
Wounded Birch, The, 140 I
Wounded Heart, The, 143 F
Wozu der Vöglein Chöre, 230 M
Wozu noch, Mädchen, 356 O
Wozzeck, 42 C
Wren, The, 41 A
Wunder der Heliane, Das, 197 I
Würd ich auch wie manche Buhlerinnen, 242 A
Wüsst' ich nur, 439 H

X

Xango, 407 C
Xerxes, 75 D, 156 N

Y

Y' a des arbres, 147 B
Y avait un'fois un pauv' gas, 138 B
Ya deux fleurs sur la branche, 360 L
Ya está des puntando el día, 106 F
Ya suenan las campaniles, 441 F
Ye banks and braes o' bonnie Doon, 212 S
Ye Hielands and ye Lowlands, 64 J
Ye ladies fine and fair, 170 L
Ye Mariners of England, 71 J
Ye sons of Israel, now lament, 165 A
Ye twice ten hundred deities, 289 I
Ye verdant hills, 166 C

Ye who attend this charming ball, 377 A
Yearning, I wait now alone, 379 I
Year's at the Spring, The, 32 N
Yellow poplar leaves, The, 293 L
Yeoman of the guard, The, 373 M
Yeomen of England, The, 123 H
Yeremushka's cradle song, 259 R
Yes, I love you, yes, 376 M
Yes I was, said Susan, 382 S
Yes! let me like a soldier fall, 418 N
Yes, 'twas on the River Neva, 282 S
Yet a child wert thou, 79 L
Yet one more tale, 256 F
Yet this hero, 236 R
Yeux de Berthe, Les, 77 E
Yeux, la belle, hélas!, 76 I
Yithbera'kh weyischtaba'h, 297 O
Yithgadal weyith kadash, 297 N
Yo no alvidare en mi vida, 139 R
Yo no sé qué tienen, 106 Q
Yo soy ardente yo soy morena, 387 H
Yome iba madre a la romeria, 262 K
Yonder to the town I went, 183 B
Yorkshire feast song, The, 293 A
You are free, 198 D
You hold yourself like this, 367 R
You understand? Likewise the Bride, 371 K
You were glad tonight, 74 M
You'll think ere many days ensue, 272 K
You'll wander far and wide, 114 N
Young man despair, 365 I
Young Molly who lived at the foot of the hill, 6 G
Your Advice is Good, 142 J
Your hands lie open, 388 I
Your professed devotion, sir, 256 N
Youth's the season made for joys, 272 C
Youth's wonderhorn, 214 N
Yver, vous n'estes qu'un villain, 87 L

Z

Zahn, Der, 210 H
Zampa, 174 N
Zapoli tovani tě prosim, 346 F
Zar und Zimmermann, 211 C
Zarewitsch, Der, 204 I
Zauberer, Der, K.472, 247 J
Zauberflöte, Die, 253 E
Zauberlied, Das, 235 J
Zaza, 206 M
Zaza, piccola zingara, 206 O
Zdivoké hožití viru, 101 H
Zeffiretti lusinghieri, 244 R
Zefiro toma, 239 J
Zeisig, Der, 338 S
Zeit, die ist ein sonderbar Ding, Die, 355 L
Zeitlose, Die, 356 F
Zelte, Posten, Werdarufer!, 209 M

Zémir et Azor, 141 N
Zephire, modere en ces lieux, 84 F
Zéphoris est bon camarade, 1 P
Zerbinetta's Aria, 354 S, 355 A
Zerfliesse, mein Herze, 26 M
Zeugen sind da, Die, 411 M
Zierlich ist des Vogels Tritt, 432 O
Zig et zig et zig, 313 M
Zigeuner, 84 O
Zigeunerbaron, Der, 353 E
Zigeunerin, Die, 437 K
Zigeunerliebe, 204 N
Zigeunerliedchen, 336 R
Zigeunerlieder, 54 R
Zing, zing, zizzy, zizzy, zing, zing, Boom, boom, aye, 173 L
Zingara, La, 98 J
Zion hört die Wächter singen, 17 M
Zion now her head shall raise, 161 G
Zitronenfalter im April, 437 L
Zitti, zitti, 400 G
Zitti, zitti, piano, piano, 308 G
Zogernd leise, 325 L
Zöld erdöben, 196 I
Zorika, kehre zurück, 204 N
Zu Augsburg steht ein hohes Haus, 332 G
Zu meiner Zeit, 249 L
Zu neuen Thaten theurer Helde, 415 K
Zu Spreu nun schuf ich die scharfe Pracht, 414 Q
Zu Strassburg, 192 A
Zu sühnen meine grosse Schuld, 345 R
Zueignung, 356 A
Zufrudengestellte Aeolus, Der, 20 I
Zuhälterballade, 425 L
Zuleika, 228 Q
Zum Abendstern am Silberwolkenrande, 342 K
Zum Leiden bin ich auserkoren, 253 G
Zum letzen Liebesmahle, 412 F
Zum neuen Jahr, 437 M
Zum reinen Wasser, 16 M
Zum Schlafen, 301 A
Zum Schluss, 331 Q
Zum Sterben bin i verliebet in di, 439 G
Zur Burg führt die Brücke leicht, 413 I
Zur Johannisnacht, 144 A
Zur Ruh, zur Ruh, 437 N
Zürnende Barde, Der, 330 C
Zwangvolle Plage!, 414 J
Zwei blauen Augen, Die, 215 R
Zwei feine Stieflein hab' ich an, 337 B
Zwei Vaterunser bet' ich, 3 R
Zwei venetianische Lieder, 331 I
Zwei welke Rosen, 119 O
Zweier Augen Majestät, 158 I
Zweig' und Aeste, 20 I
Zweite Brautnacht!, 354 G
Zwerg, Der, 321 R
Zwielicht, 333 Q